PASSION

FOR

CREATION

The Earth-Honoring

Spirituality of

Meister Eckhart

MATTHEW FOX

INNER TRADITIONS
Rochester, Vermont

Inner Traditions International
One Park Street
Rochester, Vermont 05767
www.InnerTraditions.com

Library of Congress Cataloging-in-Publication Data

Eckhart, Meister, d. 1327.
    [Breakthrough]
    Passion for creation : the earth-honoring spirituality of Meister Eckhart /
[introduction and commentaries by] Matthew Fox.
        p.   cm.
    Originally published: Breakthrough. Garden City, N.Y. : Image Books,
1980.
    Includes bibliographical references and indexes.
    ISBN 0-89281-801-8 (alk. paper)
    1. Mysticism—Sermons. 2. Sermons, German—Translations into
English. 3. Sermons, Latin—Translations into English. 4. Sermons, English—
History and criticism. I. Fox, Matthew, 1940– II. Title.
BV5082.2 .E34 2000
230'.2—dc21   99-045739
                                                         CIP

Printed and bound in the United States

10 9 8 7 6 5 4 3 2 1

To my creation-centered brother, Meister Eckhart, exiled for six hundred and fifty years, welcome home! And thank you for your spirituality of passion and compassion, for your reminding us of our divine birthright and responsibility to create, for your humor and your capacity to let go, for your prophetic outrage and your imaginative outreach.

FOREWORD to the new edition
Meister Eckhart and the Spiritual Agenda
for the Nineties

Carl Jung once said that it is to the mystics that we owe what is best in humanity, and farmer/poet Wendell Berry says that it is necessary to "fight the worst with the best." If both these thinkers are correct, then it is clear that Meister Eckhart provides significant weaponry for the mystical and prophetic agenda that the human race faces in the nineties. Some may object to my using the military term "weaponry." However, I believe that one of the important items in the resuscitation of our species must be a spirituality which takes back the essentially *spiritual* archetype of the "warrior" from the militarism of our nation-state war departments. Meister Eckhart and indeed the whole spiritual tradition of the messiah as warrior (see page 306) need to be reseized by an awakened mystical tradition. "Into the heart of a doomed land the stern warrior leapt," we are told in Scripture (Wisdom 18:15). Notice that it is *into the heart* of the land that the messiah leaps—the mystic opens the heart. And Eckhart surely does that. The male liberation movement—so logical and so necessary an outgrowth of the feminist movement—will find a champion in Meister Eckhart, a truly liberated male. (Consider, for example, his discussion of fatherhood in pages 400f.)

In addition to taking back the warrior archetype we must also retrieve the archetype of eros. A pious and impotent religiosity has turned over the power of eros and passion to the pornography industry, fanned as it is by a thoroughly uncritical consumerist system—what Eckhart analyzes as the "merchant mentality" (see pp. 450ff.). Eros, which is essentially love of life and passion for living, belongs to the Godhead itself according to Eckhart (pages 76, 151) and, since "all the names which the soul gives God, it receives from the knowledge of itself" (page 175), it follows that by reunderstanding God's delight and passion for creation we allow ourselves permission for the same.

The issue of reexciting passion for creation, of rediscovering the mysticism of wonder and delight at creation, resists what philosopher

Josef Pieper calls the "essence of bourgeois mentality," namely that of *taking for granted*. And this refusal to take for granted lies, it seems to me, at the core of the ecological struggle and awakening in our time. How readily we have been taking for granted healthy rain forests, proper ozone protection, the wellness of soil and waters and air, and the immune systems of our bodies and of earth! Green activist Jonathan Porritt of England rightly speaks of the environmental crisis as being in fact "a spiritual crisis." And scientist Peter Russell writes of how it is the "spiritual aridity" of the West that must be addressed in the environmental era if the true "genius" of the human species is to shine in the world. Meister Eckhart's earth-based mysticism—his celebration of the "equality of being" among all creatures (see Sermon Five)—awakens us to the deep truth of animal liberation, of our need to recover reverence for being and thus to work our way out of our ecological malaise.

An era of "ecology" is necessarily a cosmological era since *oikos* means "home" in Greek and our home is the cosmos itself. Few mystics have celebrated the cosmos with the passion and awareness that Eckhart has (see Sermons Two and Three), and his love of the cosmos can help usher in an era like ours when a new creation story is unfolding. God is always "in the beginning," Eckhart insists (pages 111f.), and so as we learn more of the wonders of our shared beginnings as a species and as a planet, we teeter on the edge of an amazing God-awakening. This is why so many scientists today are publishing first-class mystical works. Mysticism—beauty and mystery—is returning to our stories of our cosmos.

Furthermore, an *environmental* consciousness is an "around" or rounded consciousness—one of panentheism, finding God "roundabout us completely enveloping us," as Eckhart puts it (see page 73). Eckhart becomes a master indeed in the issues of rediscovering cosmology and in carrying on an ecological and environmental awakening.

The pressing issue of addiction that overwhelms so-called "first world" cultures is also addressed by Eckhart's teaching of Letting Go and Letting Be (see Sermons Fourteen to Eighteen). His instruction that we are all on a spiritual journey and all can be mystics is something that AIDS patients and caregivers, among others dealing with ultimate journeys, can understand. Persons undergoing such journeys—including persons in prisons—deserve to be nourished with the teachings of mystics of the caliber of Eckhart. They will understand one another.

Finally, the struggle for justice that Eckhart so aligned himself with and the deeply felt trust in the creative powers of our species as representing the divinization experience challenge religion and culture alike to birth anew the Cosmic Christ, the Divine One imaged in every creature. Instead of referencing ourselves externally, Eckhart tells us to "become aware of what is in you" (page 70) and "announce it, pronounce it, produce it and give birth to it" (page 70). There is hope here. And there is challenge to the young, in particular, to find the mystic that they are—that "inward person" as distinct from the "outward person" (page 71)—and then to birth anew our lives and religions and to celebrate this birth unceasingly. There is a special invitation in Eckhart's work that reinvites the artist back to our midst in education, in worship, in all prayer, and in spirituality. No sentimentalism will do; the era of cynicism as well as of ego-based art is ended. The artist and the mystic are one, just as the mystic and the prophet are one. The spiritual agenda for the nineties is a rich one. Eckhart, among all our ancestors, is one of our finest guides.

The Good News goes on, namely that the path is "beautiful and pleasant and joyful and familiar" (page 165).

Matthew Fox
Institute in Culture.and Creation Spirituality
Holy Names College
Oakland, California

CONTENTS

INTRODUCTION   1

    Meister Eckhart's Influence
    The Purpose and Nature of This Book
    Eckhart's Times and Our Own
    Eckhart's Life
    Theological Influences on Eckhart's Spirituality
    Principal Themes in Eckhart's Spirituality
    How to Read This Book
    Acknowledgments

PATH ONE: CREATION

SERMON ONE: ALL CREATURES ARE WORDS OF
   GOD   57

COMMENTARY   60

    Eckhart's Theology of the Creative Word of God
    How All Creatures Are Words of God, Echoes of
      God, Gladly Doing Their Best to Express God
    Creation Is a Flowing Out and a Flowing Back
    The Creative Word as the Prophetic Word

SERMON TWO: CREATION: A FLOWING OUT BUT
REMAINING WITHIN   65

COMMENTARY   69

Eckhart's Panentheistic Theology of Inness
Words and Creatures Flow Out But Remain Within
The Highest Region of the Soul Is the Innermost Part
   of the Soul and It Is Here That God Creates
The Inner and Outer Person
God and Creation Are One So We Are to Love All
   Things Equally

SERMON THREE: HOW CREATURES ARE GOD
AND HOW GOD BECOMES WHERE CREATURES
EXPRESS HIM   75

COMMENTARY   78

How God and Godhead Differ
How God Melts Out from the Godhead When Creation
   Occurs
How God Enjoys Creatures and We Are to Do the
   Same
How We Love Creatures as God
Three Ways of Enjoying Creatures

SERMON FOUR: THE HOLINESS OF BEING   83

COMMENTARY   86

There Is No Need to Fear Death Because When Life
   Is Being That Is Eternal Life
Being Is God's Word and a Circle
The Nobility of Being
Being Is God

SERMON FIVE: HOW ALL CREATURES SHARE
AN EQUALITY OF BEING   91

COMMENTARY   94

Creation as Grace
The Equality of Being

Preaching the Gospel to
  All Creatures of the Cosmos
Soaring into the Primordial Source of Being
Cosmic Consciousness
Loving All Creatures Equally

SERMON SIX: THE GREATNESS OF THE HUMAN
  PERSON   102

COMMENTARY   105

  The Human Soul Is So Truly Made in God's Image
    That God Cannot Escape It
  Where We Are Totally in God—the Spark of the
    Soul
  How the Fullness of Time Is Experienced Now
  Where Eternity Is Newness and Nowness

SERMON SEVEN: THE BIGNESS OF THE HUMAN
  PERSON   114

COMMENTARY   117

  The Continual Growth of the Soul
  Spirituality Is About Growing Without Limit
  The Oneness of Soul and Body
  The Nearness of God and the Human Soul

SERMON EIGHT: THIS IS SPIRITUALITY:
  WAKING UP   126

COMMENTARY   129

  Spirituality—the Art of Wakefulness
  Thankfulness, the Ultimate Prayer
  Rising from the Dead Before We Die
  Why God Needs to Love Us

SERMON NINE: WAKING UP TO THE NEARNESS
  OF GOD'S KINGDOM   137

COMMENTARY   141

  The Time and Place of the Kingdom of God
  The Meaning of Jacob's Dream

The Kingdom of God as a Kingdom of Blessing
—the Blessing That Creation Is
We Are All Kings—If We Are Awake to It

SERMON TEN: A GOD WHO REJOICES AND
SUFFERS, BLESSES AND CONSOLES   151

COMMENTARY   154

God's Joy and Our Joy
Who Is God, Where Is God?
How the Consolation God Gives Is Born of God's
    Suffering
The Soul Is a Cornucopia of Blessing That Passes On
    the Blessing Called Creation
Eckhart's Theology as a Theology of Blessing

PATH TWO: LETTING GO AND LETTING BE

SERMON ELEVEN: DIVINITY'S DARK SIDE   166

COMMENTARY   170

Salvation as a Change in Consciousness
True Humility Is a Journeying into the Darkness of
    Oneself
The Tension Between Love and Sacrifice, Between
    the *Via Positiva* and the *Via Negativa*
Knowing the Unknown God
The Final Goal of Being is the Darkness of Divinity

SERMON TWELVE: SINKING ETERNALLY INTO
GOD   177

COMMENTARY   180

The Radical Insufficiency of Language About God
Three Occasions When God Is Not God
Letting Go—a Process of Subtraction That Allows Us
    to Love God Mindlessly
Reconciliation Within Oneself—the Sign of the New
    Creation

SERMON THIRTEEN: OUTSIDE GOD THERE IS
NOTHING BUT NOTHING   188

COMMENTARY   192

The Beauty and Blessedness of Being United with
  God
Purity Means Unity
God and the Soul: Two Experiences of Nothingness
Pure Knowledge Is Knowing Relationships
How a Dialectical Consciousness Is a Consciousness
  of Blessing

SERMON FOURTEEN: LETTING GOD BE GOD
IN YOU   199

COMMENTARY   202

Loving God Without a Why
Living Without a Why
Two Additional Meanings of Nothingness
Being Free of Nothingness
Distrusting Methods for Attaining God
Finding God as Much in the Stable as in Church

SERMON FIFTEEN: HOW A RADICAL LETTING
GO BECOMES A TRUE LETTING BE   213

COMMENTARY   218

How We Are to Become Free of All Things as God Is
Experiencing Our Preexistence in the Godhead by
  Entering into Nothingness
Why I Pray God to Rid Me of God
The Meaning of Letting Go and Letting Be
How Letting Go Becomes Letting Be and Reverencing
  All Things

SERMON SIXTEEN: LETTING THE WILL GO   226

COMMENTARY: 230

How to Free the Will
The Need to Let Suffering and Pain Go

Letting Differences Go So As to Experience the Communion of Saints and the Nobility of Humanity

SERMON SEVENTEEN: LETTING THE INTELLECT GO AND EXPERIENCING PURE IGNORANCE   238

COMMENTARY   245

The Via Negativa Explored
The Darkness and Ignorance That Is Knowledge
Solitude: A Way of Pure Nothingness and Emptiness
The Return to Creatures
How Love Is to Be Preferred to Mortifications

SERMON EIGHTEEN: LETTING GO OF INTELLECT CREATES A TRANSFORMATION OF KNOWLEDGE   251

COMMENTARY   257

Finding the Treasure That Ignorance Brings
How Knowledge Precedes True Ignorance and How True Ignorance Transforms Knowledge
The Need for Stillness and Silence
How the Soul, Alone of All Creatures, Is Generative Like God Is

SERMON NINETEEN: WISDOM AND FIERY LOVE—NOT REPRESSION—ARE THE RESULTS OF LETTING GO   266

COMMENTARY   267

All Deeds Are Accomplished in Passion
The Soul Needs to Be on Fire
Authentic Purity Means the Return to Our Divine Origins Where Wisdom Dwells

SERMON TWENTY: HOW LETTING GO AND LETTING BE ARE TO BEAR FRUIT   273

COMMENTARY   278

What a True Vine Really Does
How Bearing Fruit—Not Contemplation—Is the
    Fulfillment of Eckhart's Spirituality
How True Fruitfulness Takes Trust, Confidence, and
    Self-love
The Fruits of the Spirit That Come with Letting Go
    and Letting Be
How the Ultimate Letting Go Includes Letting Go of
    Letting Go

PATH THREE: BREAKTHROUGH AND GIVING
            BIRTH TO SELF AND GOD

SERMON TWENTY-ONE: THREE BIRTHS: OURS,
    GOD'S, AND OURSELVES AS GOD'S
    CHILDREN   293

COMMENTARY   302

The Meaning of Breakthrough
Three Kinds of Birth or Breakthrough
First, Our Birth into the Godhead
Second, God's Birth in Us
Third, Our Birth as Sons and Daughters of God

SERMON TWENTY-TWO: OUR DIVINITY AND
    GOD'S DIVINITY: TO BE GOD IS TO GIVE
    BIRTH   313

COMMENTARY   317

How Love Is God
How Love Is Between Equals
How the Essence of God Is to Give Birth
How God Gives His Whole Divinity to His Son and
    to Us Who Are God's Children, Receptors of Di-
    vinity

SERMON TWENTY-THREE: WE ARE CHILDREN
OF GOD AND MOTHERS OF GOD   325

    COMMENTARY   330

        Four Signs of Our Testing the Authenticity of Our
        Breakthrough and Rebirth
        What Does It Mean to Be a Child of God?
        Being in God and Being in the Son
        Eckhart's Mariology and Our Becoming Mothers of
        God

SERMON TWENTY-FOUR: WE ARE OTHER
CHRISTS   338

    COMMENTARY   345

        What It Means to Hear the Word of God and Keep
        It
        Who Is Jesus Christ?—Eckhart's Christology
        Christ as the Word of God
        Christ as the Model for Our Being Human and Di-
        vine
        How Christ Was Fruitful and We Are Fruitful

SERMON TWENTY-FIVE: OUR DIVINITY: THE
REASON GOD BECAME A HUMAN BEING   354

    COMMENTARY   358

        The Purpose of the Incarnation Explained
        Baptism into the Holy Spirit Whose Origins Are a
        Whirlpool
        In the Desert, God and We Become One Divine Per-
        son

SERMON TWENTY-SIX: THE HOLY SPIRIT, LIKE
A RAPID RIVER, DIVINIZES US   363

    COMMENTARY   369

        Who Is This Holy Spirit Who Divinizes Us?—
        Eckhart's Theology of the Holy Spirit

How Grace Shapes the Soul in God's Image
The Soul Should Stir and Be Stirred

SERMON TWENTY-SEVEN: HOW ALL CREATURES
EXPERIENCE THE DIVINE REPOSE   380

COMMENTARY   383

The Panentheistic Pleasure Called Repose
How the Creator Seeks Repose and the Trinity Seeks
Repose
How the Soul That Has Broken Through into God
Experiences Repose
How Repose Is the Law of Pleasure for All Creatures

SERMON TWENTY-EIGHT: WHERE THE SOUL
IS, THERE IS GOD   388

COMMENTARY   391

Our Inness with God Is a Oneness with God
How All Saintly Beings Who Share This Inness Cele-
brate Together
Where Action and Being Become One
The Union of Humanity and Divinity That Christ
Demonstrates to Us Who Are Other Christs

SERMON TWENTY-NINE: BE YOU CREATIVE
AS GOD IS CREATIVE   397

COMMENTARY   402

The Creator as Artist, the Son as Art
Eckhart's Theology of Creativity and the Artist
Because It Is God's Nature to Give Gifts, It Is Ours
Also
Our Best Gifts or Works of Art Come from Within
and Thus Praise God
Our Divine Destiny and Glory Is to Receive Beauty
and Birth Beauty—and This Is Salvation

PATH FOUR: THE NEW CREATION:
COMPASSION AND SOCIAL JUSTICE

"SERMON" THIRTY: BE COMPASSIONATE AS
YOUR CREATOR IN HEAVEN IS
COMPASSIONATE   417

COMMENTARY   428

Four Reasons Why Giving Birth to Compassion Is
the Finest Birthing We Can Do
Compassion Is a Divine Attribute and God Is Our
Model for Compassion
Compassion Is About Works and Deeds of Justice, as
Christ Teaches
Compassion Begins with Self—the Relationship of
Passion and Compassion
Compassion Is About Celebration and Glory

SERMON THIRTY-ONE: COMPASSION IS AN
OCEAN—THE MYSTICAL SIDE TO
COMPASSION   440

COMMENTARY   442

The Fullest of All God's Works Is Compassion
Compassion Is an Unfathomable Ocean Greater than
Knowledge and Love
We Are in Compassion When We Are in God
How This Inness of Panentheism Destroys All Oth-
erness and Creates Interdependence
The Need to Run into Peace

SERMON THIRTY-TWO: DRIVING MERCHANT
MENTALITIES FROM OUR SOULS: ECONOMICS
AND COMPASSION   450

COMMENTARY   455

We Are the Temple, Image, and House of God
Wonderful and Divine Events Happen in This Temple

How a Merchant Mentality Destroys a Consciousness
of Compassion and Ruins the Soul
How Dualism Is the Sin Behind All Sin

SERMON THIRTY-THREE: JUSTICE, THE WORK OF
COMPASSION   464

COMMENTARY   467

God Is Justice and to Be in God Is to Be in Justice
Birth and Breakthrough Are Resurrections into Justice
Toward a Spirituality of Work: Working Without a
Why or Wherefore
Our Work, Giving Birth to the New Creation

SERMON THIRTY-FOUR: WHEN OUR WORK
BECOMES A SPIRITUAL WORK WORKING
IN THE WORLD   478

COMMENTARY   486

How Work Is as Noble and Spiritual as the Desert It-
self
How Spiritual Maturity Is the Basis for a Spirituality
of Work and Where This Maturity Is Learned
Work Becomes Spiritual Work When We Are
Among Things but Not In Things
A Theology of Work Presumes an Appreciation of
Matter, the Senses, and Passion

"SERMON" THIRTY-FIVE: BREAD IS GIVEN US
FOR OTHERS, ON ACCOUNT OF OTHERS,
AND WITH OTHERS—ESPECIALLY THE
INDIGENT   495

COMMENTARY   503

We Are Children and Heirs of God's Parental Com-
passion
The Need for an Our—Not a My—Consciousness
Our Works of Compassion Inaugurate Heaven on
Earth

How All Are Our Brothers and Sisters—and Especially the Poor

"SERMON" THIRTY-SIX: EVERYONE AN
ARISTOCRAT, EVERYONE A ROYAL PERSON   510

COMMENTARY   518

The Nobility of Our Birth Makes Us All Kings
How All Are Called to Be Royal Persons
The Tradition of the Royal Person in Israel
Compassion: the Meaning of Being the Son or
    Daughter of God, a Royal Person
Eckhart's Democratic Political Philosophy

SERMON THIRTY-SEVEN: COMPASSION AS
CELEBRATION   531

COMMENTARY   537

The Meaning of Torah Is Compassion, Where Love
    of God and Love of Neighbor Are One
Holiness Means Wholeness
The Identity of Ourselves and Our Neighbor
The Mystical Body Rejoices Banquet-style Because
    All Things Love God
God Too Rejoices and Is Tickled Through and
    Through by Our Works of Compassion

NOTES   546

INDEX OF SCRIPTURAL REFERENCES   569

INDEX OF SPIRITUALITY THEMES   573

CROSS REFERENCES TO SERMONS
TRANSLATED IN THIS VOLUME   580

This, then, is salvation, when we marvel at the beauty of created things and praise the beautiful providence of their Creator or when we purchase heavenly goods by our compassion for the works of creation.

Meister Eckhart
("Sermon" Thirty)

INTRODUCTION: Meister Eckhart's Influence/The Purpose and Nature of This Book/Eckhart's Times and Our Own/ Eckhart's Life/Theological Influences on Eckhart's Spirituality/Principal Themes in Eckhart's Spirituality/How to Read This Book/Acknowledgments

Meister Eckhart of Hochheim (c. 1260–c. 1329) is a spiritual theologian whose time has come. Condemned posthumously by a papal decree issued on March 27, 1329, his profoundly this-worldly spirituality went underground where it fed many of the most significant movements of Western cultural and intellectual history.

Meister Eckhart's Influence
In Germany, his disciples and brother Dominicans Henry Suso and John Tauler drew extensively from his thinking even after his condemnation. Nicholas of Cusa in the fifteenth century commented on Meister Eckhart's works and Martin Luther in the sixteenth drew heavily from Eckhart by way of John Tauler, whom, as Hoffman points out,[1] Luther admired unwaveringly from his youth to his final days. Lutheran mystic Jakob Boehme (1575–1629) owed much to Eckhart, as did the radical mystic-politician Thomas Munzer, who was born in the same German province as both Eckhart and Luther. In England, the anonymous author of *The Cloud of Unknowing* as well as Walter Hilton and especially Julian of Norwich demonstrate a significant debt to Meister Eckhart. The work of seventeenth-century Polish mystic-poet Angelus Silesius has been called a "seventeenth-century edition of Eckhart" and the fourteenth-century Flemish mystic Jan van Ruysbroeck was influenced by him. "We can be sure," says scholar Jeanne Ancelet-Hustache, "that through the intermediary of the Flemish mystics, Eckhart's thought had anonymously found its way even to Teresa of Avila and Saint John of the Cross" since the Spanish dominated the Netherlands and the ex-

change of ideas was a regular one between the two countries. Ig-
natius of Loyola is recognized to have known Eckhart's theology[2]
and his brother Jesuit Peter Canisius, who edited John Tauler's
works in 1543, also was indebted to Eckhart. Saint Paul of the
Cross, founder of the Passionist Order in the eighteenth century,
owed much to Eckhart's spirituality. Modern philosophy, as represented by the nineteenth-century romantic idealist Friedrich
Schelling and the philosopher of evolving spirit, Hegel, admits an
indebtedness to Eckhart. Likewise Marxist scholars like Erich
Fromm and Ernst Bloch invoke Eckhart as a forerunner of the
spirit of Karl Marx.[3] Twentieth-century philosopher Martin Heidegger not only calls Eckhart a "master of letter and life" but
took one of the words Eckhart invented, *Gelassenheit* ("letting
be"), as a title for an address delivered in his homeland in 1955.
Asian scholars like Dr. D. T. Suzuki speak of the "closeness of
Meister Eckhart's way of thinking to that of Mahayana Buddhism, especially of Zen Buddhism" and Professor S. Ueda in
Kyoto, Japan, says that Eckhart breaks "the sound barrier of the
normal intellectual world of Christianity and thereby enters into
the world of Zen." Catholic monk Thomas Merton agrees, saying
that "whatever Zen may be, however you define it, it is somehow
there in Eckhart." Merton confesses to having been "entranced"
by Meister Eckhart, and it can be documented that his conversion from being a romantic, dualistic, and Augustinian-minded
monk in the fifties to being a prophetic Christian in the sixties
occurred while he was studying Zen and Meister Eckhart.[4] Hindu
scholar Ananda Coomaraswamy compares Eckhart to Vedantist
traditions. Quaker mystic Rufus Jones acknowledges a debt to
Eckhart as well he should, for Quaker founder George Fox is in
many ways Eckhartian-influenced (for example, his notion of the
"spark of the soul" seems more than coincidentally like Fox's
"inner light"). Josiah Royce and Rudolf Otto also revived Eckhartian studies outside of Christian theological circles. Psychologist C. G. Jung confessed that Eckhart offered him the "key" to
opening the way to grasp what liberation means in a psychological context. Wrote Jung:

> The art of letting things happen, action through non-
> action, letting go of oneself, as taught by Meister Eck-

hart, became for me the key opening the door to the
way. We must be able to let things happen in the psyche.
For us, this actually is an art of which few people know
anything. Consciousness is forever interfering . . .[5]

In twentieth-century American letters, writers Saul Bellow, John
Updike, and Annie Dillard, as well as spiritual seekers such as
Anne Morrow Lindbergh, Alan Watts, and Intensive Journal
guru Ira Progoff, have made extensive use of Meister Eckhart.

Who is this person who has attracted monks and Marxists, philosophers and psychologists, Zen thinkers and Hindu scholars,
Polish poets and American novelists? Why this universalist appeal in Meister Eckhart? Is Meister Eckhart's a spirituality that is
uniquely suited for an age of the global village and of ecumenism
of all world religions? I harbor my own answers to these questions, but the purpose of this book is to allow students of Meister
Eckhart to answer these questions for themselves.

Up to now this has not been possible for English-speaking persons since the publications of Eckhart's works have been either
unreliable or unavailable to most English-speaking readers. I
speak of course of the only American edition still in circulation,
that by Raymond Blakney (Harper Torchbooks) which was
translated from uncritical German editions in 1941 and which
contains three sermons that are not Eckhart's at all, along with
numerous non-Eckhartian sentences. Anyone who has tried to
teach a course on Eckhart would surely be frustrated, as I have
been, by having to work with this, the only edition of Eckhart's
writings available to English-speaking readers. Other translations
in English, those of Field, of Evans, of Clark, and of Clark and
Skinner, are out of print and have been for some time. Furthermore, the reliability of all but Clark and Clark/Skinner is
seriously in doubt as the German critical editions of Eckhart's
works were not available until recent years. The first critical text of Eckhart's German works appeared under the careful
editing of Franz Pfeiffer in 1857; his Latin works (which comprise half of Eckhart's writings and which were entirely ignored
by the papal court that tried Eckhart) were not published until
1886 by the Dominican scholar Henry Suso Denifle. In our times
the critical works of the Latin and German writings have been

steadily emerging, beginning in Rome in 1934 and continuing in Stuttgart in 1936. Four volumes in each language are now available, leaving only one volume to go in each language. The principal editors of this task have been Joseph Koch and Josef Quint, until their recent deaths.

Purpose and Nature of This Book

The purpose of this volume, then, is to bring to English readers a reliable and readable text of Eckhart's sermons and writings. It is by no means a complete collection—that would take several volumes. I have not picked sermons at random, however. For I, as a spiritual theologian, have another purpose in presenting this work to an English-speaking audience. It is to link Eckhart once again, *and ourselves* as well, to the mainstream of biblical spirituality. As brief as they are, my commentaries, I believe, offer a start along this important path. For I am absolutely convinced that the real victim in Eckhart's condemnation has not been Eckhart—he had lived a full, biblical, prophetic life and, in fact, died before his official condemnation—but the history of Christian spirituality. Creation-centered spirituality, the spiritual tradition that is the most Jewish, the most biblical, the most prophetic, and the most like the kind Jesus of Nazareth preached and lived, has been almost lost in the West since Eckhart's condemnation. In place of this spirituality of blessing and of passing on a blessing to others by way of justice and compassion, we have often been fed introverted, anti-artistic, anti-intellectual, apolitical, sentimental, dualistic, ascetic, and in many ways masochistic spirituality parading as Christian spirituality. As Professor Thomas F. O'Meara points out in his excellent article on the influence of Meister Eckhart, the very questions we have asked of spirituality and even of Eckhart have been strictly questions of a "post-Ignatian kind of spirituality of meditation." This is evident in P. Pourrat's history of spirituality and in the "outdated and unscholarly narrowness" of the article on Eckhart for English-speaking readers in the New Catholic Encyclopedia. The *devotio moderna* as represented, for example, by Thomas à Kempis, is profoundly sentimental and thus utterly unlike Eckhart, who is as different from the *devotio moderna* as justice is from righteousness, as true compassion is from sentimentalism, as passion is from repression, as dialectic is from dualism, as celebration and harmonious living are from ascetic dualisms, as creativity is from puny-minded control, as art is from religious entertainment. Yes, the condemnation of Eckhart left Christian spirituality so bereft of its sound rooting in Scripture that commentators on Eckhart, when there have been any at all, have in great measure missed the point of Eckhart's life and works. Many of them, being deprived of a theological grounding that included Scripture, have argued incessantly over whether Eckhart is an Aristotelian or a Platonist. He is neither. He is a biblical theologian, a biblical preacher, a biblical spiritual thinker. True, he is not narrow in his understanding of what biblical means—"every creature is a word of God" he declares—and so he is indeed steeped in the philosophical traditions of the West as we shall see. Primarily, however, he is a biblical theologian and this *fact* has been either missed or skirted over by even the best of commentators on Eckhart. Scholar Jeanne Ancelet-Hustache warns that Eckhart is "even more misunderstood than actually unknown" in the West[6] and she is correct. The main reason for this misunderstanding has been Christian spirituality's ignoring of its biblically rooted tradition of creation-centered spirituality. With this ignorance, much in Eckhart has been misunderstood or even forgotten; for example, his social consciousness and the prominent place he gives compassion in his understanding of the spiritual journey (see Path Four). In place of Eckhart's creation spirituality, the West has had at times an *anti*-creation spirituality, as, for example, in this statement by the immensely influential Thomas à Kempis: "If you look at creation the Creator withdraws from you."[7]

The second dimension and purpose to this book, then, in addition to laying out Eckhart's writings in a reliable translation, is found in the commentaries. These commentaries, though they represent only an introduction to Eckhart's spiritual theology, nevertheless represent an introduction that has been sorely absent in an appreciation of Eckhart. One reason for this lacuna has been the condemnation of Eckhart by church authorities, which in effect left Eckhart to be studied and kept alive either by the philosophical tradition of the West (thank you, philosophers!), or by the more radical spiritual movers who often found themselves ostracized from the mainstream of Christianity (thank you,

George Fox, Thomas Munzer, *et al.!*). Another reason for this lacuna has been the sorry state of theology and spiritual theology which has been called, believe it or not, "ascetic theology" from the seventeenth century to today in some circles—Eckhart would be outraged at such a term (see Path Two). A spiritual theology that divorces itself from Scripture will *never* understand Eckhart, will *never* grasp how it is that compassion is more important to his spiritual way than contemplation, will *never* appreciate his love of life, of nature, of animals, of the body, of music, of art, or of justice. There is no room for sentimentalism in true biblical thinking nor in Eckhart's theology; sentimentalists must leave their fears of intellect, of passion, of body, of art, of body politic, of the feminine side of God, of the earth, of this life, of death if they want to enter into Eckhart's spiritual vision—a vision so biblical that the Christian West barely understands it as spirituality. Thus the commentaries in this volume represent a link between Eckhart's sermons and the biblical and theological basis behind his thought. Probably eighty per cent of the commentaries is either Eckhart's words gathered from other sermons or writings or biblical texts that Eckhart himself points to as basic to his thinking. I genuinely believe that you will look long and hard in contemporary spirituality *and* in the past six centuries of Christian spirituality to find any writer who has so profoundly integrated biblical theology and spirituality, prophecy and mysticism, faith and reason, art and life. That is my opinion; I invite the reader to judge for herself or himself.

In this important matter of recovering the biblical in Eckhart's thought, I have my own tale to tell. For years I resisted reading Eckhart because numerous commentators on Eckhart had told me that he was basically a Neoplatonic mystic. From my own experience, coming of age in the sixties in the midst of the moral and spiritual decadence of Western civilization as represented, for example, by the Vietnam War, and from my studies at the Institut catholique in Paris where Thomas Merton urged me to go in my pursuit of an overview of the history of Western spirituality, I became absolutely convinced that more Neoplatonism was the last thing the West needed. More dualisms of soul vs body, of male vs. female, of intellect vs. creativity, of mysticism vs. politics, were the last categories with which to renew spirituality. It was the biblical tradition as represented by creation theology of the Hebrew Bible, by the prophets and by Jesus, that I was looking for and that I believed many in our times were looking for. This conviction underlay all the publishing I did and all the developing of my spiritual theology since, beginning with the publication of my doctoral thesis on culture and spirituality, *Religion U.S.A.* It found expression in my study of an adult and critical understanding of prayer, *On Becoming a Musical, Mystical Bear*; and then in my study on the everyday experience of mysticism in a prophetic context, *WHEE! We, wee All the Way Home.* It was after publishing that book that I discovered Eckhart for myself.

One winter evening during a break in semesters, I sat down with Coomaraswamy's book *Art and Spirituality* and started to read his chapter on Meister Eckhart. I was dumbfounded—in fact scared—when I read whole sentences in Eckhart that I had published in *WHEE!* and in an article on sacred space and sacred time that I had recently completed. So unnerved was I that I returned Coomaraswamy's book to the shelf unfinished. Three months later I returned to finish the Eckhart essay. On doing so I found still more lines in Eckhart that I had published myself over the years in my search for an authentic, biblical, and prophetic spirituality. Here, I realized, was not just one more Neoplatonist; here was a brother not only in the sense of a Dominican brother but in the wider sense of a companion for myself and as many others of our time who wanted to take a biblical spiritual journey. In my most recent book, *A Spirituality Named Compassion*, Eckhart plays a prominent and explicit part, for among all theologians the Christian West has produced, he is among the few for whom "compassion" is an operative, indeed crucial, category. This may be seen in Path Four of the present book.

And so, the second purpose of this volume is to introduce the Eckhartian scholar to Eckhart's biblical presuppositions. It is also to introduce students and livers of Christian spirituality to these same biblical roots in Eckhart and, hopefully, in one's own journey. One reason that Eckhart's biblical genius has been so easily glossed over is that biblical thinking *is so taken for granted by him.* He was a preacher, after all, and his sermons, both Latin and German, take biblical texts and comment on them. Furthermore, he integrates texts in a thoroughly nonproof-like manner into all of his talks and sermons. Above all, he has a theology—a creation-centered theology—as we shall see later, that is profoundly biblical and that constantly feeds him as he nourishes his listeners on it at the same time. I attempt an introduction to Eckhart's biblical theology in my commentaries which accompany each sermon. The result, I believe, offers to the reader a process of experiencing Eckhart in his sermon, analyzing his thought in the commentary, and, I hope, returning to the sermon to reexperience Eckhart at a deeper level. His spirituality took for granted a thorough rootedness in the Scriptures and biblical theology. This same presupposition, I am sorry to say, cannot be taken for granted by the majority of spiritual writers or commentators since Eckhart's time. We must make an explicit effort to regain the integration of Scripture and spirituality that Eckhart could take for granted. This is as much a demand on contemporary exegetes, who so often get lost in a forest of language studies and minutiae, never coming up for the light of day that surrounds the rest of us, as it is a demand on spiritual journeyers who imagine they can root themselves solely in their own private experiences, oblivious of the tradition that the Bible represents. Eckhart, being the artist he was and the theologian he was, could not have imagined the dualisms that so occupy church people today: dualisms between academic exegetes, for example, and the everyday believer; or between members of what Father William Callahan calls "the religious multi-nationals," who alone can afford such extravagances as thirty-day retreats or daily liturgies, and the lay believer. Eckhart, in contrast, insists that God and humans are already joined; they are already in intimate contact. The only obstacle is on the human side. Our consciousness and our language and our institutions remain too dualistic to realize this very Good News, however

I should emphasize the essential modesty of this book. Entire books, such as Reiner Schürmann's *Meister Eckhart: Mystic and Philosopher*, have been written as a commentary on only four of Eckhart's sermons. In this volume there are thirty-seven sermons with thirty-seven commentaries! Clearly, the commentaries presented are by no means the last word. It is comforting to this author, however, to realize that there will never be a last word spoken on Eckhart any more than there will be on Mozart. So

thoroughly an artist is Eckhart, so profound a poet as well as a
thinker, that we can only point to some directions and then urge
readers to make their own journeys. This I try to do in the commentaries, and for this reason I reemphasize that this book is a
process. I believe that at this stage of spiritual consciousness in
the West and at this stage of Eckhartian scholarship, a book that
offers a process approach to Eckhart represents an appropriate
methodology to pursue. Furthermore, I believe Eckhart, who was
himself primarily a *preacher*, would heartily approve of a process
approach to his very experientially based thinking and theology.
There is something unnerving about inhaling too much of academic approaches to a poet-preacher like Eckhart. Too much
analysis, too much dissecting, too much of the left side of the
brain can kill this holistic and experiential lover of life and depth,
who himself waged war all his life against bigness, imper-
sonalness, and structures, whether internal or external, which in-
terfered with the expansion of the person. Norman O. Brown has
commented that the only authentic way to criticize poetry is with
poetry; in an analogous way, the way to respond to a true mystic
is with mysticism. Since Eckhart is a poet and a mystic, I hope
that the reader of Eckhart will respond with art and mysticism—
dance, for example, or music—and I hope that my simple commentaries may in some way inspire such responses. I think
Eckhart would be eager to join such a dance.

   In order to facilitate the process that reading Eckhart must
necessarily be, I have structured this book and the sermons chosen for it in a very deliberate manner. The fourfold path of
Eckhart's spiritual journey forms the structure around which I
have chosen sermons and ordered them. As far as I know, this is
the first time that a structure has been followed in collecting
Eckhart's sermons. We will never know their chronological order-
ing but we can, I believe, by a careful analysis of his spiritual theology detect the path of spiritual journeying that is his. It is *not* a
journey up a ladder but a spiral of expanding consciousness that
has no limits. I have published in a recent article[8] the basis for
my coming to the naming of this fourfold path in Meister
Eckhart's journey and that article forms the structure for this
book. Briefly, the paths are as follows:

One: The experience of God in creation.

Two: The experience of God by letting go and letting be.

Three: The experience of God in breakthrough and giving birth to Self and God.

Four: The experience of God by way of compassion and social justice.

These four paths along Eckhart's spiritual way are taken from Eckhart's own language and theology. They comprise the divisions of this book. I have chosen from the wealth of Eckhart's sermons and commentaries and treatises those which most seemed to enunciate his insights about these ways. The arranging of the sequence of the sermons is also deliberate on my part. The titles I have given the sermons and the subtitles I have given the commentaries shed light on the gradual process of growth in Eckhartian language and experience that this book is about. There is a precedent in Blakney for my renaming Eckhart's sermons, although I feel he did a singularly bad job of it. My titles and subtitles are taken wherever possible directly from Eckhart's words themselves, and where this is not possible because of the evolution of language, they are taken directly from his spiritual theology. Since I am the first Christian spiritual theologian since the fifteenth century to comment on Eckhart, I do not apologize for the directions I invite the reader to take by way of my titling his sermons and commentaries. They are, as it were, signposts along the journey. For I honestly do believe that the person who has made this journey with Eckhart and myself will experience not only Eckhart but the creation spirituality tradition that he so richly represents. The indices—the Index of Scriptural References and the Index of Spirituality Themes—are meant to assist the serious student in making once again a biblically based and creation-centered spiritual journey.

Eckhart's Times and Ours

One of the most significant and telling dimensions to reading Meister Eckhart is appreciating the turbulent times in which he lived and from which he refused to escape Indeed, it was his throwing his lot in with the oppressed of his day—with lower-class women in the Beguine movement, with the peasants to whom he insisted on preaching in their own vernacular tongue, with the movements of church and social reform—that eventually got him condemned. The times in which Eckhart lived, times of institutional decadence and corruption of language and church and of a widening rift between haves and have-nots, have been described in a recent and best-selling study by Barbara Tuchman, entitled A *Distant Mirror: The Calamitous 14th Century*. Her thesis in that book is found in the title, A *Distant Mirror*, for Tuchman believes that the fourteenth century with its apocalyptic upheavals, its blatant social sins, and its potential for creativity does indeed mirror our own times. If Tuchman's analysis is correct, then the study of the finest mind and the most profound artist of that century may well shed light on the needs of our own time, for all spirituality is culturally influenced. Following are four aspects that marked the cultural setting of Eckhart's adult years. The reader can judge for himself or herself whether a certain "distant mirror" is set up apropos of the cultural revolution we know so well in our time.

1. A *population explosion*. Especially in the Rhineland area where Eckhart was established in Strassburg and then in Cologne, there was a population boom.[9] The economics of these areas had expanded in the twelfth and thirteenth centuries but were now contracting as the population expanded. Bad crops and a weather change caused the period to be known as the "Little Ice Age" (the Baltic Sea froze both in 1303 and in 1306-7) and forced a considerable reduction in the growing season. Notes Tuchman: "This meant disaster, for population increase in the last century had already reached a delicate balance with agricultural techniques . . . the clearing of productive land had already been pushed to its limits."[10] Floods from torrential rains in 1315 also forced crop failures and widespread famine. A consequence of an increase in population with a decrease in economic necessities and especially of food and shelter in a worsening climate was predictable: the few rich got richer and the many poor got poorer and increased in numbers. The nobles were driven to marrying

non-nobles and were often thrown into bankruptcy.[11] Tuchman
characterizes the situation as follows:

> Division of rich and poor became increasingly sharp.
> With control of the raw materials and tools of produc-
> tion, the owners were able to reduce wages in classic
> exploitation. The poor . . . felt a sense of injustice that,
> finding no remedy, grew into a spirit of revolt.

The "spirit of revolt" was aggravated by the need for more room
and more space that a burgeoning population began to feel. As
Tuchman puts it, the "size of population affects studies of everything else—taxes, life expectancy, commerce and agriculture, famine or plenty."[12] Some persons found the limits to physical expansion a matrix for spiritual or consciousness expansion so that the
most burgeoning area of population increase, the Rhineland area,
was itself the womb for the mystical movement that found so articulate a spokesman in Meister Eckhart.[13] This fact suggests a
tantalizing lesson: that physical limits can produce spiritual
unlimits. The reduction of physical frontiers and their contraction
can either give birth to the expansion of consciousness frontiers or
produce still more violence, or both.

   2. *Corruption in high places.* A second evident movement that
characterized these troubled times was the rapid demise of credibility of the institutions of the day. An example that Tuchman
develops is that of knighthood. Once considered the protectors of
the people, the defenders of the weak, knights were now part of
the problems and not the solutions of the time. "In practice, they
[the knights] were themselves the oppressors, and by the fourteenth century the violence and lawlessness of the sword had become a major agency of disorder. When the gap between the
ideal and real becomes too wide, the system breaks down." This
breakdown of the system was in evidence in every institution because, as Tuchman observes, "the presiding values of chivalry did
not change, but the system was in its decadence."[14] The church
was by no means exempt from this decadence. Institutional greed,
apathy, and corruption abounded there as elsewhere. Fourteenth-
century saints like Catherine of Siena and Birgitta are notorious
for their lamentations at ecclesial decadence. As Birgitta put it,

"fear of God is thrown away and in its place is a bottomless bag of money." The Ten Commandments were now reduced to one: "Bring hither the money." From 1309 to well beyond Eckhart's death the papacy settled in Avignon. Tuchman describes the central headquarters of Christendom at that time:

> Avignon became a virtual temporal state of sumptuous pomp, of great cultural attraction, and of unlimited simony—that is, the selling of offices. Diminished by its removal from the Holy See of Rome and by being generally regarded as a tool of France, the papacy sought to make up prestige and power in temporal terms . . . Everything the Church had or was, from cardinal's hat to pilgrim's relic, was for sale . . . To obtain a conferred benefice, a bishop or abbot greased the palms of the Curia for his nomination . . . Money could buy any kind of dispensation: to legitimize children, of which the majority were those of priests and prelates . . . Younger sons of noble families were repeatedly appointed to archbishoprics at eighteen, twenty, or twenty-two. Tenures were short because each preferment brought in another payment.[15]

Priests often could not read or write and made no effort to educate themselves; a Spanish Curia official reported seeing money brokers and clergy in the papal palace "engaged in reckoning money which lay in heaps before them." Pope John XXII, who was to condemn Eckhart, bought for his own use forty pieces of gold cloth from Damascus for 1,276 gold florins and had a personal wardrobe worth 7,500 florins annually, which included among other items his own ermine-trimmed pillow. The century was to end with there being not one but two and then three popes (1378–1409).

The secular government was not much healthier. For nineteen years—from 1254 to 1273—Germany's empire had no emperor. This interregnum period marked the beginning of the end of the imperial idea and the rise of particularism in Germany. In 1282, on Easter Monday, the "Sicilian Vespers" occurred in Sicily. French men, women, and children were massacred there and national passions were aroused by this event as never before all over

Europe. Church-State confrontations reached a new high in ferocity, a new low in morality during the reign of Philip IV. Philip IV of France, who reigned from 1285 to 1313 (this covers the years Eckhart was in Paris), challenged the papacy in rather direct terms: he had one pope killed, another poisoned, and a third completely cowed. He expelled Jews, destroyed the Knights Templar, confiscating their riches.[16] Clearly, society's governing institutions were a far cry from those of the saintly Louis IX of France (1214–1270), who was canonized in 1297. Less than ten years after Eckhart's death the One Hundred Years' War between England and France would break out. And in less than twenty years the Black Death would swipe its way through society, leveling a good thirty-five per cent of the population.

Academia was not in such good straits either, depending as it did on both papal support and government nonintervention. Scholasticism, which in its time had been an awakening and enlightening influence, a movement imported to Christian theology from Islamic tradition and a method for critical thinking about faith, was, like so much else in the culture, on the decline. Gone were the great minds of spirited thinkers of courage and daring such as Albert the Great (d. 1280), Thomas Aquinas (d. 1274), Bonaventure (d. 1274). Gone was much of the creative thinking that had made the age of Scholasticism an exciting time to live through. What was left was very often stark method, rehearsed answers to rehearsed questions, boredom and dullness and a rising anti-intellectualism. Even the language for thought, Latin, was on the decline and the newer images and creative ideas were being birthed in the new languages of Dante's Italian, Sister Mechtild of Magdeburg's German, and, in the latter half of the fourteenth century, Chaucer's English. There was a need, indeed a demand, for a new language that would be freer of the structural suppositions behind the decadent language of the schools that prevailed. Eckhart did not shirk this responsibility to contribute to a new language, as is clear from the fact that half of his extant works are in the German peasant vernacular of his day. Nor was he oblivious of the political ramifications of opting for the new language and the new social classes of poor who sought self-expression. Indeed, he could not be oblivious of this social dimension even if he tried, for he was three times accused, twice at his trial and once beforehand, of confusing the "simple people" by preaching in their own tongue in preference to the Latin tongue of entrenched academic privilege. Indeed, the fact that Eckhart gravitated more toward preaching and counseling than toward teaching might be taken as a subtle rebuke of academia in favor of new ways to educate. Henry Suso, a young disciple of Eckhart, observed that most students of theology entered academia in order to make more money. Eckhart was first and foremost a preacher—that is, an artist. Here lies the key to his language, his ambiguity, and his genius. He lived in a time of the end of a culture and, as Charles Fair has pointed out, at such a time language is lost and the very meaning of "soul" is lost. Eckhart sought all his life for new images, new names for "soul." At one time he says that the soul, like God, is "ineffable" and cannot be named. At another time he says that soul is the space where God works compassion (see Sermons Six, Seven, Ten, Thirteen, and Thirty-one).

Eckhart's thinking is dialectical and so, of course, his language is paradoxical, even shocking at times. As Norman O. Brown indicates, "dialectical language always includes paradox" and "paradox is shocking."[17] Eckhart's problem as an artist-teacher was this: How do you talk about eternal life having already begun? What language do you choose for the really Good News? How do you announce the end of the collective and individual quest for immortality and the beginning of resurrected life? He turned to the music of symbols and poetry to express his deeply felt experiences. His inquisitors, the literalists of yesterday as well as the rationalists of today, will not be able to hear his music, eager as they are to judge and not to listen. Did they have a better language? I doubt it, for such persons have not learned to be open enough (to "let go" in Eckhart's terminology) to experience the depths from which authentic language is born. Jesus the preacher spoke like Eckhart the preacher when he said: "Let those who have ears to hear, hear, and eyes to see, see" Like the artist that he was, and gifted with a sense of poetry, Eckhart sought in his German sermons to give birth to the God beyond God, the values beyond culture's forgotten values, thinking beyond academia, images beyond what the world had to give. It was not for nothing that he prayed, "I pray God to rid me of God."

3. *Radical movements.* In such a period of cultural upheaval and social disintegration many persons who cared became disillusioned with the structures that were failing so many and with institutional leaders who nevertheless clung to their own privilege and power. Some of the movements that emerged as groupings of these disillusioned yet caring persons were the Pastoureaux, the Beguines and Beghards, witches, mystical sects, and, toward the end of the century, the religious reformers John Wycliffe in England (d. 1384) and Jan Hus in Bohemia (d. 1415). The Pastoureaux rebellion began as a movement of rural persons and shepherds, as Tuchman explains:

> In 1320 the misery of the rural poor in the wake of the famines burst out in a strange hysterical mass movement called the Pastoureaux, for the shepherds who started it . . . The Pastoureaux spread the fear of insurrection that freezes the blood of the privileged in any era when the mob appears.[18]

These persons, like the Beguines and Beghards who were working-class women and men who sought a religious life in common while working for their living with their hands, were excommunicated by John XXII, who was also to condemn Eckhart. We will discuss the Beguines in greater detail below in considering the influences on Eckhart's thinking. John XXII equated sorcerers with heretics and ordered their books burned, but it was King Philip IV's use of the charge of black magic and black arts against the Knights Templar that raised the art of torturing accused witches to a new level of sadism. By the end of the century witchcraft would become one more refuge for the growing numbers of disenfranchised persons, especially elderly women. In spite of papal condemnations, mystical sects like the Spiritual Franciscans, inspired by Joachim of Floris, and the Brethren of the Free Spirit flourished from the end of the thirteenth century right up to the Black Death calamity in the middle of the fourteenth century. Indeed, the year 1260, the year of Eckhart's birth, saw the burgeoning of visionaries following the prophecy of Joachim, who preached penance all over southern France, and hordes of flagellants flowed through Italy, Southern Germany, and Bohemia, lacerating their bodies in a spirit of self-abuse and remorse.

4. *A spirit of despair, guilt, and the end times.* A sense of frustration grew into a sense of hopelessness and despair that began to take over much of the human spirit at this time of "eschatological heave" (to borrow Norman Mailer's expression for America in the late sixties). A world was indeed coming to an end—the world of papal and temporal power equitably balanced; a world of intellectual integrity and creativity; a world of economic solidarity and development; a world of institutional credibility; a world of common values mythologized in knighthood, religious life, or law; a world of a common, shared language. A certain death wish accompanied by guilt feelings was abroad. Barbara Tuchman says: "The sense of a vanishing future created a kind of dementia of despair." Granted, the Black Death two decades after Eckhart's death would add considerably to this guilt-ridden spirit and this feeling of hopelessness. But the seeds for this profound spiritual frustration were already sown during the events of Eckhart's own lifetime. Married people questioned whether they wanted to bring children into such a world at all, animals lay dead all around, the work force was decimated. "Only a profound materialism and cynicism could have permitted the placing of Robert of Geneva in the chair of Saint Peter" as the Antipope Clement VII, Tuchman comments, since Robert of Geneva, known as the "butcher of Cesena," had allowed his troops to slaughter between 2,500 and 5,000 citizens of that town over a period of three days and three nights.[19] Saint Catherine of Siena's response to this election was to cry out that "the poison of selfishness destroys the world." Apocalyptic plays abounded no less than apocalyptic movies in our own times, for they seemed to image the doom and emptiness that society and psychic instability were bent on foreseeing. At least one observer of these times blamed the guilt on the social conditions that spawned such destitution. Giovanni Villani of Florence lay the reasons for the Black Death at the feet of human inhumanity to humanity. These sins were "the sins of avarice and usury that oppressed the poor. Pity and anger about the condition of the poor, especially victimization of the peasantry in war, was often expressed by writers of the time and was certainly on the conscience of the century."[20]

These four movements were pillars of the ravaged period

through which Eckhart lived and which he tried to influence. No monk he, Eckhart lived in the midst of all this upheaval, a student in France, a preacher in Germany, a vicar general in Bohemia. Tuchman summarizes the spirit of those times. It was, she says, a "violent, tormented, bewildered, suffering and disintegrating age, a time, as many thought, of Satan triumphant." And she draws her own parallel with today: "If our last decade or two of collapsing assumptions has been a period of unusual discomfort, it is reassuring to know that the human species has lived through worse before." Reiner Schürmann has summarized Eckhart's vocation as preacher in the midst of societal upheaval. Preaching is:

> the literary form chosen by Meister Eckhart. It is not accidental that he was a preacher . . . His preaching urges our freedom to commit itself upon a path which, from the being of provenance or from the creatures' nothingness, leads to the being of imminence or to the Godhead's nothingness. Being as coming forth is encountered first of all in the preached word itself.[21]

Such were the times that formed Eckhart and that he influenced as he could. The readers can judge for themselves if, as Tuchman believes, there are some noteworthy parallels to our own day.

Eckhart's Life

How was Eckhart prepared for his destiny with socio-spiritual upheaval? The basic facts of Eckhart's life as we have come to ascertain them are as follows. He was born about 1260 in the province of Thuringia, the home province of Saint Elizabeth (1207–1231), who did so much for the poor there, and the Beguine mystic Mechtild of Magdeburg (1210–1297). It was also the home province of Martin Luther, who would follow two centuries later. As a young man, Eckhart joined the Dominican Order at Erfurt, near his native village of Hochheim. Today both Hochheim and Erfurt are in East Germany. Since Eckhart's family was one of knights, it is worthwhile to speculate if one of the important sources of Eckhart's radicalization was not the awareness of the corruption in this once-proud institution. From this awareness there grew within him a freedom and courage to question even the skeletons in his own background. He never lost this capacity for radical criticism, which means criticism of one's *own* institutions and not just others'. Indeed, he incorporates such an attitude as an integral dimension to the spiritual journey (see Path Two).

Eckhart went through the ordinary training for a Dominican preacher of the times, which included a year's novitiate, two years of studying the Divine Office and the Constitutions of the Order, five years of philosophy and three years of theology—the first year given over to biblical studies and the next two to Peter Lombard's *Sentences*. Showing more promise for intellectual aptitude than the average recruit, Eckhart was sent to the *studium generale* located in Cologne for his advanced studies. This school had been founded in 1248 by none other than the great master, Albert. His spirit must have been richly present when Eckhart arrived apparently just a few months before Master Albert's death in 1280. In 1293 Eckhart was sent to Paris for the first of three sojourns there. In a university sermon preached at Easter, 1294, he refers to Albert the Great in a manner that suggests he had studied directly under him for a brief period before his death. After returning to Germany in 1294 he was elected prior at Erfurt and appointed vicar of the province of Thuringia. Around the turn of the century he returned to Paris, where in 1302 he accepted the same chair of theology that Thomas Aquinas had occupied, namely, that reserved for a non-Frenchman. Professor at Saint Jacques and teacher at the University of Paris, he was henceforth to be known as "Master [German: *Meister*] Eckhart." What did Eckhart find in the University of Paris at the turn of the century?

Jeanne Ancelet-Hustache describes the meaning of Paris in Eckhart's day: "Rome had the Pope, Germany the empire; but in the heritage of Charlemagne, France was no less favored, having been accorded this other, intellectual sovereignty."[22] The Dominicans had planted themselves in Paris and at the hub of intellectual activity within a year of their official organization as an Order. Since September 1217, they had lived there, settling near the Porte Saint Jacques at the south end of the city. The priory where Eckhart lived had also been home to Thomas Aquinas and Albert the Great before him, and Saint Dominic, the founder of this movement of preachers in touch with the intellectual currents of their day, had stayed there in his Parisian visit of 1219. The principal conflict of Eckhart's time, like that of the preceding half century at the University of Paris, was that between the Augustinian spiritual philosophy and that of the Aristotelians. Augustine's Neoplatonism had dominated Christian theology in the West for centuries. Aristotle's more in-the-world, nature-based, moderate realism was considered avant-garde, an upstart, a dangerous incursion of reason into faith by many of the guardians of the status quo ever since Abélard introduced Aristotelian dialectical methodology in the twelfth century. Thomas Aquinas' last act in Paris had been to defend the use of Aristotle as a tool for faith against a secularist Aristotelian, Siger of Brabant. Those theologians who like Aquinas found the "modern" Aristotle insightful and useful even for theological issues were thus fighting a two-front battle: against a dualistically oriented Augustinianism on the one hand, and against secularists who wanted only Aristotle and no faith on the other. On March 7, 1277, the Bishop of Paris, Stephen Tempier, condemned two hundred and nineteen Aristotelian theses, several of which were critical to Thomas Aquinas' philosophical and theological thought. This was the first of three such condemnations of Aquinas' theology that were to be delivered in Paris or at Oxford during Eckhart's adult lifetime. This fact must never be lost sight of: that Eckhart's intellectual career was spent under a constant cloud of condemnations of his brother Aquinas and these condemnations gave impetus to Augustinianism at both universities—for example, to Henry of Ghent, who held a theological chair at Paris from 1276 to 1292, and to Duns Scotus, professor at the University of Oxford (1300–2 and 1303–4), and Paris (1302–3 and 1304).

After a brief sojourn in Paris, Eckhart was recalled to Germany once again to assume administrative responsibilities. This time he was elected the first provincial of the newly formed Province of Saxony, a territory that covered an area from the Netherlands in the north to Prague in the east and which contained fifty convents of friars and nine houses of nuns. Since the Netherlands was the birthplace of the Beguine movement (there is still a house extant in Holland today), there is every likelihood that Eckhart's association with this lay-oriented women's movement dates from this period. In 1307, Eckhart was nominated vicar general of Bohemia. Bohemia, which in sixty-five years would produce the church reformer Jan Hus, was also an area of profound social and spiritual conflict and creativity. Eckhart did not spend his years as administrator as a bureaucrat sitting behind a desk; not only did he have to hike the long distances from country to country but he was constantly being educated while on the road to the various responses then emerging to the ills of his time. Eckhart did not opt for a sheltered life-style or a sheltered, exclusively academic, education. Indeed, he himself declared that life is the best teacher there is (see Sermon Thirty-four).

After this decade of education in international movements and social-spiritual and feminist spiritualities, Eckhart returned to Paris for a third time in the academic years 1311–13. At this time Eckhart conceived of a major intellectual project, that of a *Work in Three Parts*, the *Opus Tripartitum*. Most likely he never completed it. We possess today only the General Prologue and the Prologue to the first part (*Opus Propositionum*) and the third part, the *Opus Expositionum*.

A turning point in Eckhart's career occurred upon his return to Germany in 1314. In that year he was made prior, professor, and preacher at Strassburg. That city, together with Cologne, was to occupy Eckhart's life and work until his death. Both cities were hotbeds of the spiritual renewal movement that we know as "Rhineland mysticism." It was here, in the midst of popular spiritual ferment, that Eckhart discovered his vocation as a preacher and a spiritual counselor. He became a popular, indeed a famous, preacher, the most renowned of his century in a century that turned to preachers more than to academicians or administrators for spiritual insight in a changing time. By 1323 Eckhart had moved to Cologne, the trade center for eastern and southern Europe and another hotbed of spiritual, economic, and political agitation. His duties included preaching and directing the Dominican *studium generale* where he had once studied. Within three years of Eckhart's arrival and of the canonization of Aquinas, the Franciscan Archbishop of Cologne succumbed to rumors and envies that surfaced in the form of heretical charges against Eckhart. Eckhart appealed in this trial of 1326 to his right to be tried by a papal court. He was granted this opportunity and went to

Avignon to defend himself there. As it turned out, Eckhart died
after that appearance and before the papal bull *In Argo Domi-
nico* of John XXII was delivered on March 27, 1329, which condemned seventeen of his propositions and labeled nine others capable of being construed as heretical. (Two articles of which he
was accused were dropped when Eckhart said he had never
preached them at all.) He died in good graces with the church
since before his death he put in writing that he submitted his
ideas to the faith of the church. The bull itself says that Eckhart

> at the end of his life, confessing the Catholic faith,
> recanted and rejected the twenty-six Articles . . . as well
> as anything he had written or taught in the schools as
> well as in his sermons, that could produce in the minds
> of the faithful an heretical or erroneous sense opposed
> to the true faith.[23]

We do not know the date of his death nor the place of it; nor do
we know where he is buried. It has been speculated that he died
on the way home from Avignon. Some have suggested that he
died of a broken heart, knowing he was to be condemned by a
church that he had served so generously for sixty-seven tumultu-
ous years in so many demanding tasks. But the transcripts of the
trial, recovered in our century by F. Pelster, suggest a different
scenario altogether. They suggest a person well aware of the political dimension to his trial—a person who twice reminds his accusers that they were the types who had three times condemned
Thomas Aquinas and then canonized him just three years previous. Eckhart also compared his troubles with those his fellow
Dominican Master Albert had undergone. Eckhart was angry and
he named envy as a key factor in his trial when he said: "I condemn and detest those errors which envious men neither can nor
should impute to me . . ." He also accused his accusers of ignorance: "They regard as error whatever they fail to understand and
also regard all error as heresy, whereas only obstinate addiction to
error constitutes both heresy and the heretic."[24] Thomas Merton
has written of Eckhart's trial:

> He was a great man who was pulled down by a lot of
> little men who thought they could destroy him: who

thought they could drag him to Avignon and have him utterly discredited. And indeed he was ruined, after his death in twenty-eight propositions which might doubtless be found somewhere in him, but which had none of his joy, his energy, his freedom . . . Eckhart did not have the kind of mind that wasted time being cautious about every comma: he trusted men to recognize that what he saw was worth seeing because it brought obvious fruits of life and joy. For him, that was what mattered.[25]

Eckhart's theology of letting go (see Path Two) included, in almost a psychic way, the need to let go even of one's own condemnation. In Sermon Twenty-four, he said: "Even if God should ordain one's condemnation so that one's existence would not be violated, even then the person should let God take over as if it did not matter, as if one did not exist." I wonder if Eckhart did not decide to let go of life, having lived so full a one. And whether he decided that they would—quite literally—condemn him over his own dead body. Since laughter is surely as profound an expression of letting go as there is, then Eckhart probably died laughing. We know for a fact that his sense of humor was very well developed and devoid of the sadism that most likely characterized any sense of humor his accusers possessed. For we know that Eckhart was free enough to be able to laugh at himself (see Sermon Three).

Today it is universally agreed among scholars that Eckhart was unjustly condemned. Says M. D. Knowles, "Of his radical traditionalism and orthodoxy there is no longer any doubt."[26] If his accusers had bothered to read his Latin works and if they had known the history of spirituality half as thoroughly as Eckhart, they would have known this and not allowed politics to take over their judgment of the greatest spiritual theologian the West had produced up to their time. For it was not Eckhart who was the loser in this condemnation; it was the Christian church, which to this day still seeks as holistic a spiritual vision as Eckhart once had.

Theological Influences on Meister Eckhart's Spirituality

Because Eckhart was condemned by church authorities, he has rarely been examined by spiritual theologians. Now that he is coming out of the heretical closet, however, we need to take a more critical theological look at Eckhart since by far the majority of studies on Eckhart have been undertaken by philosophers or philologists. Because Eckhart was first and foremost a theologian, it is very likely that we will never enter into his thought until we study his theology. And first this means considering the influences on his thinking, with special attention paid to the theological influences.

Eckhart was an extremely well-read person, a man hungry and passionate for ideas as his brother Dominican Thomas Aquinas had been and of whom it was said that when he was shown the Cathedral of Notre Dame for the first time by a proud and awed Parisian host, he responded simply: "I would give it all for one copy of Chrysostom's Manuscript." Eckhart knew what every true intellectual knows: the immense importance of ideas for peoples' freedom, integrity, courage, and ecstasy. Eckhart knew the traditions and schools of the past. He was ecumenical in his thought. His works are heavily annotated with references to Greek, Arab, and Jewish philosophers as well as the Greek and Latin Church Fathers. The three authors he cites most often are Augustine, Albert, and Thomas Aquinas. But not all these authors were of equal importance in forming Eckhart's spirituality. Eckhart was himself an original and creative thinker and not merely an eclectic browser in the history of ideas. He was too logical to believe that all ideas are compatible or of equal merit. I believe that the following list represents in descending order the most important influences on Eckhart's thought for understanding his spirituality.

1. *The Bible and Jewish thinking.* Eckhart is absolutely steeped in biblical modes of thinking and in biblical themes of spirituality. His is a theology of blessing, of the blessing that creation is. One reason that his inquisitors had so much difficulty in understanding his thought is that they were overly saturated in Scholasticism and Augustinianism and while Eckhart knew both well, he also knew their inherent weaknesses. This is one reason why he preferred to begin and end his theological thought with authentic biblical categories. An example would be his putting compassion (see Path Four) ahead of contemplation as the basic goal of spiritual journeying. Such biblical thinking has not been seen much

in Christian circles since Eckhart's time. Yet it is profoundly Jewish, profoundly biblical.[27]

Eckhart is the finest and surest witness to his own dependence on Scripture in his spirituality. He says: "I believe more in Scripture than I do in myself."[28] Again, he confesses that "the holy Scriptures make me wonder, they are so full." The Holy Scripture is like the sea, it is so deep, says Eckhart. "No one is so wise that if he wished to probe it, he would not find something more and deeper in it."[29] That Eckhart depends on the Scriptures is evident simply from reading his German sermons, which are based on scriptural texts or from studying his Latin works. One author counted over twenty scriptural texts taken from ten books of the Hebrew Bible and New Testament in just one brief exegesis of 2 Corinthians 13:11.[30] But Eckhart's dependence and indeed saturation with Scripture goes far deeper than numbers of texts cited. It goes to the themes he wrestles with in the name of spirituality. It goes to the questions he asks, the questions he doesn't ask, to the language he develops and the categories he employs. All this we will consider in the following section when we discuss the principal theological themes in Eckhart's writings. We shall see how before all else Eckhart's dependence on Scripture is evident in the theological themes that most occupy him—themes that form the basis of the biblical, creation-centered spiritual tradition. This tradition is light years away from that of Augustine or Thomas à Kempis. Eckhart states explicitly that his method in his preaching is to select scriptural passages and then consider them in detail and in their relation with one another (see Sermon Twenty-four). I am personally convinced that Eckhart's insight into Scripture is that of a genius so far ahead of his time that contemporary scriptural exegetes will find much in Eckhart that they have struggled long years to discover for themselves.[31] Indeed, Eckhart is more of a poet with the Scriptures, making connections that others have not seen, and more of a prophet with them, urging persons on to action and creativity, than a number of comfortably ensconced biblical academicians of our time.

What most influences Eckhart's spirituality from the Hebrew Bible is the writings in the wisdom literature, including Psalms,

Wisdom, Proverbs, Ecclesiasticus (Sirach), and the prophets, especially Isaiah, Jeremiah, and Amos. The "royal person" literature from the tenth century in ancient Israel also attracted his attention, including Genesis (12–26), 1 Kings, 2 Samuel. In the New Testament he is most indebted to Pauline doctrine of our graced sonship and divinization (cf. Rm. 8:14–29) and Johannine theology's emphasis on the creative Word, on our divinization and our rebirth as sons of God (cf. 1 Jn. 3:1f.). There is simply no grasping of Eckhart's message without a return to the scriptural sources and themes which nourished him so deeply. And this means a return to creation-centered spirituality, as we shall see in the following section of this introduction. Eckhart's affinity with Jewish thinking is not restricted to the Bible, however. He calls Christ the "Great Reminder," and it was the founder of the Jewish mystical movement of Hasidism, Baal Shem-Tov, who once said: "In remembrance resides the secret of redemption." There is much more to be learned by a critical study of Hasidic and other Jewish traditions in Eckhart's writings. For example, Eckhart's famous term "spark of the soul" has antecedents in, among other places, the medieval Jewish philosophers Isaac Ben Solomon Israeli (855–955) and Judah Halevi (1095–1145).[32]

2. *Thomas Aquinas and the Dominican spiritual movement.* Eckhart, who joined the Dominican Order between fifteen and seventeen years of age and remained a steadfast member of it through fifty-three years of hard work, able administration, and controversial times, was imbued with Dominican spirituality. What most characterized Dominican spirituality is that it was a way of life for friars actively involved in the world—the world of the universities, towns and cities, in particular. Like his contemporary Saint Francis of Assisi, Saint Dominic (1170–1221) saw the terrible spiritual malaise of his time. He attributed much of this spiritual malaise to a monastic system and spirituality that offered solace if you were a rural person and refuge from the world if you had a monastic vocation but which left the ever-increasing numbers of persons fleeing from countryside to the cities and towns, to the trade centers and to the universities, untouched. It was in this spirit of an in-the-world spirituality that the second-generation Dominican Thomas Aquinas developed a theological vision that was based not on Augustinian Neopla-

tonism with its suppositions about this world vs. another world and body at war with soul, but on Aristotle's nature-centered philosophy. In many ways this option of Aquinas' for joining the new kind of spiritual movement called the Order of Preachers was a political option—as he learned as a young man when he was put in prison by his family for choosing this upstart Order. Aquinas was a man of immense talent and of proper noble blood and his family had intended that one day he would be abbot of Monte Casino. For him to join the Dominican Order instead of the well-established Benedictines was tantamount to running away and marrying a gypsy, G. K. Chesterton has commented. When in his mature years Aquinas stood side by side with the learned Franciscan, Bonaventure, to do battle on behalf of the mendicant spiritual movement against strong and organized opposition in Paris, Aquinas surely knew once again the political implications of his choices.

In Germany the Dominican spirit was incarnated in the bigger-than-life figure of Albert the Great, who survived his most famous pupil, Thomas Aquinas, by six years and who, when Aquinas was under fire at the time of his first condemnation, hastened to Paris in a futile effort to fend off the condemnation of his brother Dominican. Albert was more partial to Platonist philosophy than was Aquinas, though in his methodology—he was an experimenter in botany and biology and in many ways a natural scientist by vocation—he was much closer to the naturalist Aristotle than the idealist Plato. Between Eckhart and Albert there stood Thomas Aquinas' classmate at Cologne, Ulrich of Strassburg. Interestingly enough, this latter Dominican spoke of an *"esse divinum per similitudinem"* ("a divine isness by way of likeness") in his *Liber de Summo Bono* (Book on the Highest Good). This phrase would seem to be a key one to Eckhart's philosophy and spirituality (see Sermon Four). The Platonist language of the school of Albert combined with the mystical tradition of the Rhineland (see point 3 below) challenged Eckhart's capacities toward mystical experience and poetic expression.

Eckhart did not use his poetic genius to pass on Neoplatonist flight-from-the-world spirituality, however. What it meant intellectually to be a Dominican in his day was to follow the in-the-world spirituality of his famous—indeed notorious—brother

Thomas Aquinas. And this Eckhart, who inherited Aquinas' chair
at Paris, did. On all the major issues in spirituality—the issue of
trust in human nature, of the equality and dignity of women, on
the harmony of soul and body, on the role of anger and moral
outrage, on injustice as a sin, on the basic goodness of creation,
on the potential of human nature to develop, on the holiness of
being, on the reconcilability of mysticism and prophecy—Eckhart
was not only loyal to his brother Aquinas in preference to Augustinian Neoplatonism, he actually surpassed him in boldness of expression and often in depth of insight. Eckhart is an Aquinas
with imagination, an Aquinas freed of too tightly woven Scholastic language, an Aquinas in poetry. Eckhart's loyalty to Aquinas is
all the more striking when one considers the constant cloud that
Aquinas was under during Eckhart's entire adulthood and life as
a Dominican right up to Aquinas' canonization three years before
Eckhart's own trial. Eckhart was fourteen years old when Aquinas
died, seventeen and a Dominican when he was condemned for
the first and second times, twenty-four years old when he was condemned for the third time. Yet this cloud of heavy suspicion over
Aquinas did not daunt Eckhart in the least from invoking him
often in his writings and talks and above all from incorporating
his ideas into his own spiritual vision. It was safe and expected
that one would invoke Augustine as an authority and this Eckhart does often. But it was suspect to invoke Aquinas as an authority and this Eckhart does even more convincingly. It must
never, never be forgotten that Eckhart invokes his brother
Aquinas in spite of the political-religious hegemony of Augustinian and Neoplatonist spirituality.

Areas in which Eckhart follows Aquinas would be the following. Being is radically relational. Aquinas expresses the internal
relationship of all being in terms of act and potency; Eckhart
does so in his spirituality by breakthrough and birth (see Path
Three). On the external relationship of all being, Aquinas speaks
of the unity of the cosmos, of *universitas* or the universal harmony of all things. Eckhart says that "all things are connected"
(see Sermon Thirty-one) and also urges a cosmic vision, a cosmic
trust. Eckhart follows or improves on Aquinas' creation-centered
spirituality on the subjects of the cosmos, women, nature, being,
justice, creation, ecstasy, joy, consubstantiality of soul and body,

ecumenism, extrovert meditation, creativity, compassion. Furthermore, a very strong case could be made for Eckhart's learning a deep element of his spiritual teaching from his meditations on the last year of Aquinas' life. During that year Aquinas was, as it were, struck dumb. He was unable to write, to work, and was barely able to speak. The year began with an experience in which he understood that all his work was as straw. It was a year of radical letting go for Aquinas that climaxed only with a letting go of this life, for he died on the way to the Council of Lyon never having recovered from this vision of nothingness. Surely Eckhart and his young Dominican confreres must have conversed often on this strange final year in the life of their most famous brother, only two to three years dead when Eckhart entered the Dominican Order. Did this spiritual experience of Aquinas play a large role in Eckhart's development of his Second Path, letting go and letting be (see Path Two)? Did Aquinas—whose voice was heard all over Christendom with such authority and daring—bequeath to Eckhart in his last year of enforced dumbness a never-to-be-forgotten lesson in the primacy of silence? I rather think so.

While Eckhart depended a lot on Aquinas, it should also be emphasized that he was himself an original thinker living in a very different time from his famous and somewhat notorious predecessor. Thus there are differences between the two thinkers as well, of which the major ones influencing spirituality appear to be as follows. Their primary vocations and style differed greatly. Aquinas was a teacher dedicated to precision and exactness that under the methodology of high Scholasticism reached a level of art. Eckhart, on the other hand, while he taught a lot (and Aquinas also preached), reached his stride and indeed the peak of his influence as a preacher, not a teacher. As a preacher he sought to move people, to motivate people, even to disturb people. For this purpose he found the Scholasticism of his day far too confining and he reached out to poetic and paradoxical expression and indeed became one of the creators of the German language, helping to shape and mold it from the variety of peasant dialects that it was in his day to a unified expression of soulful urgency. He was indeed an artist—he urged others to be—he practiced what he preached (see Sermons Eighteen, Twenty, Twenty-nine). We should also remember the vast differences between the cultural periods in which each man operated. Aquinas' period was basically one of optimism, of expansion economically, intellectually, politically, while Eckhart's time was ripe with pessimism, with the awareness of limits of all kinds, economic, political, and intellectual. What is all the more striking about Eckhart, however, is that in the midst of this mood of contraction he preached a spirituality of joyful expansionism and optimism that was as thoroughly non-Augustinian and as wholly that of Aquinas as anything Aquinas ever wrote or taught.

While Aquinas' spirituality is creation-centered and his trust and love of creation permeates his theology, Eckhart goes him one better. Eckhart calls creation a "grace" (see Sermon Five), something that Aquinas never did. Eckhart is more exclusively a spiritual theologian than is Aquinas, who, in his academic career, always sought balance and breadth in relating philosophy and theology. Eckhart probes more deeply themes that are present in Aquinas but in a less intense, less developed manner—themes such as panentheism, realized eschatology, the divinization of the human race, the marriage of being and consciousness resulting in compassion as the culmination of spiritual experience, dialectical consciousness, our multiple experiences of nothingness, creativity. In this respect Eckhart might be called in today's parlance more of a psychologist than Aquinas.

In underscoring Eckhart's relationship to Aquinas, I deliberately avoid using the term "Thomist." Very few Thomists I have ever met knew enough about biblical spirituality or the history of spirituality to know the creation-centered spirituality tradition which Aquinas himself knew well but which Eckhart knew even better. Eckhart is not a Thomist—he is a biblical theologian.

3. *The Celtic mystical tradition and Eastern Christianity.* A significant influence on Eckhart flows from his roots in the Celtic tradition of spirituality. It appears that the Celts in their European variety originated around 1900 B.C. in the very area where Eckhart was to preach and develop his spirituality the most—in southwestern Germany and the Strassburg area. From there the Celts fanned out into what we know as France, Spain, Italy, and the British Isles. It is likely that the earliest Celtic origins were in India, and Celtic scholars Alwyn and Brinley Rees make several interesting comparisons between the Bhagavad-Gita and Celtic

myths—a connection that might explain some of Hindu philosopher Coomaraswamy's interest in Eckhart. The Celtic people
were profoundly nature-oriented in their religion. "The Celts
found divinity in nature all around them, for they revered it in
the sky, mountains, stones, trees, lakes, rivers, springs, the sea, and
every kind of animal."[33] Mother goddesses and feminine deities as
well as feminine animals played a large role in their faith. Indeed,
there are hints in Eckhart—as when he talks of God as a "great
underground river"—of the chthonic and more matriarchal period
of consciousness when spiritual experiences were bound to the soil
and were localized there with "deities dwelling in the interior of
the earth."[34] Eckhart is not convinced that God dwells on high,
Olympian style, as Hellenism taught. Transcendence for him is
not necessarily up. The Celts in the British Isles were Chris-
tianized by the third century at the latest. The Celtic spiritual tradition of northern Europe was a bastard child in Christian spirituality in the West ever since Pelagius, who was a Celt and from
England, lost his fight with Saint Augustine, who was a devoted
son of the Roman Empire. It is useful to recall that two of
Augustine's and Jerome's most ferocious charges against Pelagius
were his circulating freely with women and his admitting that he
learned a lot from them. Jerome called the women with whom
Pelagius associated "Amazons." The Celts were far more at home
in their sexual identities than Augustine or Jerome. They had a
long tradition of male/female monasteries and in their tribal
decision-making women were on a par with men, and in religious
ritual often had privileges denied the men. They were close to the
earth and had to earn their livelihood there from an intimate relationship of harmony with earth and animals. They did not champion, as Mediterranean Gnosticism did, a dualism between the
human race and nature's other creations. Saint Patrick's creed was
not redemption-oriented, as was that of Nicaea, but was creation-
centered.[35] For Pelagius, as for Eckhart, creation is itself a grace
and asceticism is uncalled for. The Celts did not treat art dualistically—storytelling lay at the heart of the tribe's spiritual and
physical survival. Nor were art and politics separated—indeed,
that tradition linked the blessings of fertility and justice,[36] as Jewish, biblical spirituality does and as Meister Eckhart would do.
The chief lawgiver of the Celtic tradition was the poet of the

tribe, and it was taken for granted that all members could participate in common folk celebrations and creativity. This Celtic tradition, which strongly influenced Francis of Assisi and Abélard,
and which gave the West William Blake and W. B. Yeats,
identified salvation with being an artist, a healer, and whole-
maker. William Blake has said as much: "A Poet, a Painter, a
Musician, an Architect: The Man or Woman who is not one of
these is not a Christian."[37] And Meister Eckhart says the same
(see Sermon Twenty-nine). The Celtic tradition, it has been
pointed out, "is particularly rich in *coimperta* (tales of conception
and birth)."[38] So, too, is Eckhart's entire spirituality. His is a
spirituality of birth and fertility that borrows both from the biblical images of fertility as a blessing and of fruit-bearing vines and
from the Celtic insistence on birthing as a spirituality (see Path
Three). The Celtic tradition, unlike the Augustinian, does not
reduce the term *justitia* to a kind of personal "righteousness."[39]
Justice is the moral norm of Celtic society and it is presumed
among these people, as it was among the prophets of ancient
Israel, that people could only survive by doing justice to one
another. Justice as justice and not as personal righteousness is a
basic category in Eckhart's spirituality of birthing, as we will see
(Sermons Thirty, Thirty-three). Interestingly enough, the creator
and artist-leader of the Celtic people was to be, before all else, a
justice-maker. This is the lesson from Eckhart as well. Salvation
for Eckhart is creativity plus justice, or creativity at justice-
making. Celtic scholars Alwyn and Brinley Rees comment on the
role of the poet as prophet in the Celtic tradition:

> The poet's praises confirmed and sustained the king in
> his kingship, while his satire could blast both the king
> and his kingdom. There was a tradition that the learned
> poets (*filid*) of Ireland were once judges. They were
> certainly the experts on the prerogatives and duties of the
> kings, and a master-poet (*ollam*) was himself equal to a
> king before the law. Such priestly functions as divination
> and prophecy also came within the province of these
> early Irish poets who, it may be added, wore cloaks of
> bird-feathers as do the shamans of Siberia when, through
> ritual and trance, they conduct their audiences on jour-
> neys to another world.[40]

Over the centuries the hegemony of southern European theology has obliterated for many students of Christian history the fact that it was the Celtic and Irish traditions that evangelized much of northern Europe, even as far south as central Italy. Over two hundred and twenty parish churches and hundreds of smaller churches, chapels, and shrines in Italy are dedicated to Irish saints to this day.[41] The most important Irish monastic foundation outside of Ireland was founded in 1090 in Ratisbon (now Regensburg), in an area of Germany over which Eckhart was himself a vicar general. So Irish was the church of Eckhart's Germany that whole abbeys in Nuremberg and Vienna were exclusively Irish right up to 1418. Dominicans had important foundations in both Ratisbon and Nuremberg which Eckhart surely frequented. The Dominican presence in the Celtic atmosphere of Ratisbon was a very early one, as Albert the Great lived and lectured there as a young Dominican. Franciscan scholar Edward Armstrong has argued convincingly that Francis of Assisi was strongly influenced by Celtic currents of spirituality and has characterized the Celtic Christian tradition as being conspicuous for its "complete dedication to Christ, blithe acceptance of poverty, loose organization, adventurous missionary enterprise, and love of nature."[42] In addition, Celts were well known for their wandering spirit as Irish *peregrini*, along with their love of poetry, music, and song. Saint Columban composed songs and Francis sang them. The Celts loved animals as did Francis and Eckhart. And they held scholarship in high esteem. Armstrong's thesis is a new one, since the southern Mediterranean influence has been dominant, up to now, in looking at Christian history. Much research remains to be done.

As convincing as Armstrong's thesis is regarding Francis' link to the Celtic tradition, I believe that Eckhart's link is even more evident. Not only because the Celts imbued much of Eckhart's Germany with their Christianity, but also because they settled widely along the Rhine where Eckhart's most active years as poet/preacher were played out to their untimely end. It was a Celt, John Scotus Erigena, who was born in Ireland c. 810, who first translated Pseudo-Dionysius' works for Westerners. Although he was condemned in a strange trial held three centuries after his death, John the Scot left a heritage that Eckhart did not ignore: namely, an alternative to the domination of Western Christian spirituality by Augustine—"in almost every case he [John] sides with the Greeks" against the Latin theologians, Erigenan scholar Jean Potter comments.[43] John the Scot built his division of all of reality on the basis of a four-part understanding of creation and creativity. Creativity for John is the essence of being human; all of creation is a theophany. God is called Nonbeing or Nothing, as with Pseudo-Dionysius, and deification more than sinfulness is what holds John's attention, as it did Gregory of Nyssa. Celtic Christianity was far more dependent on Eastern than on Western spiritual theology, and in many respects—in his emphasis on creation and creativity, on divinization, on his downplaying of original sin, in his sense of cosmic grace, in his facility with the *via negativa*—Eckhart follows this same Eastern Christian spiritual tradition, as did his predecessors in creation spirituality in the West such as Irenaeus (who was born in the East but theologized in the West), Benedict, Cassian, and John the Scot. Indeed, the most substantial work published on Eckhart's theology until now has been that by a theologian of the Eastern church, Vladimir Lossky.

Because of his truthfulness to the creation-centered tradition of spirituality that is so biblical and so Celtic at once, Eckhart, in my opinion, qualifies as quite possibly the most *Franciscan* spiritual theologian of the church. Armstrong demonstrates that the second-generation Franciscan hagiographers of Francis, Thomas of Celano and Bonaventure, projected onto Francis' very nature-centered spirituality a lot of Platonic dualisms as regards body and soul, matter and spirit, women and men, imagination and prayer, politics and mysticism that Francis himself never succumbed to and that in the long run rendered a lot of so-called Franciscan spirituality dualistic.[44] Reading Francis and reading Eckhart is a very harmonious experience. They are, as Francis and Dominic were, brothers in spirituality. Eckhart can be read by any Franciscan eager to regain a critical understanding of Francis' compassionate spirituality and willing to let go of the sentimental lore that has more often than not reduced that great saint's hagiography to maudlin pietisms. While much research remains to be done about the linkage between Eckhart and the Celtic tradition, there can be no doubt that the connection is strong and constant. This bond between Eckhart and the Celtic tradition ought to be of particular significance to English-speaking readers of Eckhart. His creation-centered spirituality is an expression of their own deepest spiritual roots. Jansenism, a seventeenth-century latecomer to Irish spirituality, is a betrayal of those roots. Today's Irish church, then, in its search for its religious heritage, ought to consider the study of Eckhart as one valuable means to get back to its more holistic origins. And Dominicans might meditate on whether Dominic himself—that redheaded Spaniard —was not of Celtic stock.

4. *The Beguine movement.* Another movement that strongly influenced Eckhart and which he influenced in turn was that of the Beguines. Eckhart spent his most mature years circulating between Holland and Bohemia as administrator or preaching along the Rhineland from Strassburg to Cologne. This was the very area where the Beguines most flourished—indeed, they began in Holland. Alexian scholar Christopher J. Kauffman points out the similarities between Beguine theologian Hadewijch of Antwerp, who died around the late thirteenth century, and Meister Eckhart. He comments that: "Meister Eckhart preached to Beguines and apparently learned as much from them as they learned from him."[45] Eckhart admits, as we have seen, that life itself is the best teacher. This means that we must look to the influences in Eckhart's life, and not only to manuscripts that academic experts are so well trained in deciphering, to grasp the fullness of Eckhart's education. He reached his maturity not in academia but in his activity along the Rhine preaching in convents and churches and counseling and listening to lay women who were known as Beguines. If much of Eckhart's spiritual vision is profoundly feminist—and it is—that is because he listened and read what women had to say about the spiritual journey. And they listened to him as well, for it is from women—both Beguines and nuns—who took down his sermons that we have the German texts of his preaching. Eckhart was in many respects explicitly anticlerical, as is clear in Sermon Twenty-five, and sensitive to male chauvinism. "I am surprised at many priests who are very learned and would like to be important priests," he comments, "because they allow themselves to be so easily satisfied and made fools of."[46] Frequently he alludes to the ignorance of the clergy in his

sermons, and at his trial he was particularly caustic about those who held powerful positions but were ignorant people. His was a critical mind, critical of his culture, of his sex, and of his church. "The Lord's words have been wrongly understood," he states simply at one point.[47] He was a critic of the institutions of his day, as every prophet must be. It is inconceivable that strong and educated women, many of whom banded together as Beguines and who were also critical of the institutions of their society and church, would not influence this sensitive and honest preacher. Influence him they did.

The Beguines were one chapter in a distinguished history of women mystics in northern Europe. Eckhart is a son—not a father—of that history, as Ancelet points out: "German mysticism has earlier representatives [than Eckhart], the greatest of them being women."[48] The first mystic to write in German was the great Mechtild of Magdeburg. Magdeburg was a town only 140 miles from Eckhart's hometown and novitiate in Erfurt. For fifty-two years of her life she was a Beguine and her spiritual directors were Dominicans. Her book, *The Flowing Light of the Godhead*, is famous for its mystical bridal poetry after the style of the Song of Songs, but the language and theology of its title are particularly significant. Eckhart also made important use of the term "Godhead" in his spiritual theology (see Sermon Three). Mechtild employs many images in common with Eckhart. Among them are the images of sinking, of dancing, of God's delight, of growth, of awakening, of letting go, of compassion, of God as a flowing stream, of the dialectic between isness and nothingness. Her work deeply influenced German mysticism and Eckhart in particular. Eckhart and the Dominican Order were involved in counseling and preaching to many women's groups along the Rhine, both nuns and Beguines. There was a great influx of women into these alternative life-styles in the latter half of the thirteenth century, perhaps because there seems to have been a precipitous decline in the male population and perhaps, too, for economic reasons, for as the population grew and the economy declined neither marriage nor living singly was always so viable an option. In 1277 there were forty convents of Dominican nuns in Germany and ten years later there were seventy. By 1303 the city of Strassburg alone had seven houses of Dominican nuns.

Each of these houses might comprise eighty to a hundred women. They were often very well educated persons. By the year 1267 this new ministry of preaching to women in the convents was felt so strongly by church administrators that Clement IV officially charged the Dominicans to direct these nuns. By the time Eckhart appeared on the scene it was a foregone conclusion that interaction with religious women was an important dimension to Dominican ministry.

The Beguines were not nuns. They could not be. For to become a nun meant you had to be of noble class and pay a dowry. They were groups of women who banded together to live a life of dedication to spiritual development and to ministering to others but who were not recognized officially as "religious" or nuns. They did not take formal vows and thus were free of church authorities—a freedom that, one can imagine, was not always relished by those same authorities. They made their living by their own hands, working as artisans and craftspeople. In an important study on the *Beguines in Medieval Strassburg,* Dayton Phillips concludes that while some wealthy women distributed their money and joined the Beguines, "it is obvious . . . that the beguine condition found its greatest following among the lower classes."[49] He also observes that it was these women, who might be called the forerunners of the active Orders of religious women and who lived and worked and ministered in the world and not in cloistered convents, who "seem to have been almost a sister status of the friars. Living in the midst of the world, beguines, rather than nuns, were the true feminine parallel of the friars . . . The friars were the chief influence in the spread of the movement."[50] No wonder the Dominicans like Eckhart had so much in common with them and vice versa. Their life-styles were basically the same.

The first Beguines in Cologne appeared in 1223 in the person of two sisters, Elizabeth and Sophie, who sold properties they inherited on the banks of the Rhine. In 1260 there were eight Beguine houses in the city and by 1320 there were ninety-seven.[51] Dominicans were closely associated with the Beguines of Cologne and its environs. For example, the prior at Cologne, Henry de Sincere, visited the mystic Beguine Christine of Stommeln (1242–1312), Stommeln being a town northwest of Cologne. Her biography, drawn up by a Swedish Dominican friar, Peter of Dacia, gives evidence of how powerful the mystical current among women who were not nuns was at this time. She drew around her an entire house of Beguines in Cologne. These houses often served as something of a refuge for peasants who were moving to the city for the first time, guaranteeing them safety, companionship, shelter, and economic support. Very often, as is evident in Phillips' study, the houses the Beguines bought were leased to them at cheap rates by the Dominican or Franciscan friars. And very often they were in close physical proximity to Dominican priories. Over two thirds of the Beguine houses in Strassburg were located within a three-block radius of Dominican or Franciscan houses.

The relationship of the Beguines to church authority was a spotty affair. Pope Gregory IX extended official recognition and placed them under his protection in 1233, and in 1236 the Bishop of Cambrai was actively promoting them in his diocese. By 1311, however, the mystical movements all over Germany had multiplied to such an extent with Flagellants, Brethren of the Free Spirit, and numerous other groups of apocalyptic spirituals, that the Beguines were lumped together with them in a blanket condemnation promulgated by Pope John XXII, the same Pope who would condemn Meister Eckhart eighteen years later. In his Bull of Condemnation he said:

> There are certain women, commonly called Beguines who, although they promise no one obedience and neither renounce property nor live in accordance with an approved rule, and consequently can in no wise be considered regulars, nevertheless wear a so-called Beguine habit, and cling to certain religious to whom they are drawn by special preference. It has been repeatedly and reliably reported to us that some of them, as if possessed with madness, dispute and preach about the Highest Trinity and divine essence . . . Therefore . . . we must prohibit forever their status and abolish them completely from the church of God. We must forbid these and all other women, on pain of excommunication which we wish to impose forthwith on the recalcitrants, to retain in any way in future this status which they have long

assumed or to be allowed to accept it again in any form. Moreover, the aforesaid regulars who are said to promote these women in the status of the Beguinage or induce them to assume this status are strictly forbidden, on pain of like excommunication which they shall immediately incur if they oppose prescribed rules, to admit any women who long ago adopted the status in question or perhaps wish to adopt it . . .[52]

Such strong measures indicate a strong movement. So strong was it that this bull, promulgated by the Council of Vienna, was modified in a second bull that was issued later that same year. In this second bull, admission is made that there are faithful women who live lives of penance and service though they have not taken a vow of chastity and who are called Beguines. Such conflicting attitudes from church authorities confused bishops and clergy and revealed an ambivalence toward noncloistered women that has not entirely disappeared up to our own time. The Beguines continued to flourish. In 1317 Bishop Johannes Durbheim of Strassburg wrote that there were over two hundred thousand Beguines in Germany. In Strassburg, a city of twenty thousand in Eckhart's day, there were over three hundred Beguines. Phillips rightly comments that such a group would have represented a "considerable phenomenon in the spiritual life of the town." One effect of the decrees against the Beguines was to swell the ranks of Third Order Dominicans and Franciscans. By 1318 Rome made the distinction between heretical and orthodox Beguines on the basis of their being transients or being connected with a house. The transient Beguines were considered the heretical ones.[53]

Joan Evans has observed that "the women of the Middle Ages tended to be anonymous, but they were not soft or sheltered."[54] These strong and imaginative women known as Beguines, who sought a place in the world apart from the institution of marriage and a place in the church apart from the institution of the enclosed cloister, were a powerful force on Eckhart's own spiritual imagination. Furthermore, they and Eckhart have shared a similar fate in death as they did in life. Not only were they condemned by the same pope but the great majority of male historians—for example, Ronald Knox and Norman Cohn—have dismissed both the Beguines and Eckhart as rank kooks or heretics. In fact, they were persons seeking personal and collective renewal in a period of institutional decadence. Their common vision and courage challenges us to do the same.

5. *Neoplatonism via Augustine.* As I have hinted elsewhere in this introduction, the influence of Augustine on Eckhart's spirituality has been grossly exaggerated. And this exaggeration has in turn led to a distortion of Eckhart's spiritual theology by persons who have been ignorant of creation-centered theology and have projected onto Eckhart their own Augustinian biases. A glaring example of such distortion can be found in the work by the former Benedictine, C. F. Kelley, who ends his study on Eckhart with stage two of Eckhart's spiritual Path and who actually says that Eckhart "cannot be counted with those among the faithful who insist that they must before all else be agents for healing social injustice."[55] As is typical of Augustinian projections onto creation spirituality, Kelley talks at length of "contemplation" in Eckhart but does not even list the word "compassion" in his index. Thus he has utterly missed both the term and the meaning of the fullness of spiritual experience for Eckhart, and he and other would-be distorters of Eckhart ought to take a good, long look at Path Four in this book. For as Reiner Schürmann has rightly understood, Eckhart's is not a spirituality of contemplation but of compassion.[56] And compassion to Eckhart means both cosmic consciousness and social justice (see Sermons Thirty, Thirty-one, Thirty-three).

The fact is that on every important issue in spirituality—on humanity's deification, on women, on nature, on grace, on beauty, on creation, on creativity, on consubstantiality of soul and body, on justice and injustice, on realized eschatology, on dialectical consciousness, Eckhart, like his brother Thomas Aquinas, refuses to follow Augustine. It is true that he cites Augustine often—as did Aquinas—and knew him well. But like Aquinas his use of Augustine is extremely circumspect. It had to be, for Augustine was still the chief authority of Eckhart's day in Western theology and political-intellectual circumstances dictated that theologians invoke him. Especially is this the case considering how Aquinas and Aristotle were under the cloud of condemnations they were during Eckhart's lifetime. But Eckhart—in direct contradiction to Augustine—refuses to build a spirituality around dualisms and preoccupations with original sin that so characterized Augustine's Neoplatonic quest to leave the world, leave the earth and the body behind. Nor does Eckhart share Augustine's misogyny. In his commentary on the creation of Eve in Genesis, Augustine remarks that "man but not woman is made in the image and likeness of God"; in contrast, Eckhart says that the reason Eve was said to be created from Adam's side was to demonstrate the absolute equality of woman to man. Eckhart and Augustine are as unlike in their spiritual theologies as are the creation-centered spiritual tradition which Eckhart so heartily represents and the fall/redemption tradition of which Augustine is the chief spokesperson in the West.

One area where Eckhart does demonstrate an indebtedness to Neoplatonism is in the area of mystical and poetic language. Schürmann comments that Meister Eckhart

> turns toward Neoplatonism in his quest for a language that would suit his intuition of identity. From this shift in vocabulary he expects a language that would overcome the exteriority of man "before" God and would allow us to see man introduced "into" God. However, Eckhart by no means rejects Aristotle out of hand . . . The Neoplatonic vocabulary permits Eckhart to go further in his search for identity [with God].[57]

There can be no question that Neoplatonism lends itself more to mystical poetic expression than did Scholasticism of either Eckhart's or Aquinas' day. Nor can there be any question that Augustine himself was well endowed with artistic and rhetorical talent in his often poetic prose. Eckhart, like Augustine, chose a rhetorical mode—the art of preaching in the former's case, the art of autobiographical writing in the latter's—to express much of his spiritual theology. In that respect he is more like Augustine than Aquinas, who, as it were, wrote poetry as an avocation but whose principal theological contribution was made within the formalized strucutre of Scholastic methodology. This structure Eckhart, in his spiritual and ministerial maturity, found overly confining. Another interesting parallel between Augustine and Eckhart is to consider how both theologian-preachers were living in immensely pessimistic times from a cultural point of view.

Augustine wrote as the Roman Empire was literally collapsing all around him and Eckhart as the unity of Western Christendom was doing the same. Given this common cultural milieu, it is all the more striking that their spiritualities differ so utterly. Augustine's betrays the pessimism he felt toward human nature and the world that humanity makes, while Eckhart chose a far more hopeful and grace-centered response, emphasizing the divine potential humanity possesses for creativity, compassion, and deification itself. Eckhart, like his brother Aquinas, is an incurably joyful optimist, though he is without illusions about human potential for dualism or sin (see Sermon Thirty-two).

Anyone who continues to suggest that Eckhart is Augustinian in his spiritual theology has understood neither Eckhart, Augustine, nor the history of spirituality. The Platonically influenced theologian who has most penetrated Eckhart's theology is in fact Pseudo-Dionysius, as we have seen, and not Augustine.

Principal Theological Themes in Eckhart

It may assist the reader and student of Meister Eckhart to summarize very briefly the key theological categories which mark Eckhart's spirituality. This outline is especially needed, given the fact of the Augustinian projections onto Eckhart and other creation-centered spiritual theologians by so many Neoplatonically trained spiritualists over the centuries. It is also mandated by the hegemony of the southern Mediterranean spirituality over the northern, Celtic variety in Western Christianity ever since the condemnation of Pelagius in the fifth century. Eckhart—much more than Augustine—is a biblically rooted spiritual theologian. This means that his is a creation-centered and not a fall/redemption-centered spiritual theology. There are themes in this spiritual tradition that are basic to Eckhart's way of seeing the world and humanity and God and which are not emphasized in the fall/redemption tradition, whose basic categories might be understood as original sin, cleansing from original sin, sin (pride and lust in particular), heaven, hell, body vs. soul, asceticism, prayer as a lifting up of mind and heart to God, woman as temptress, action vs. contemplation, introvert meditation, climbing Jacob's ladder as a model for spiritual contemplation, and a basic unwillingness to leave a world of private mystical experience with God to criticize or create alternatives to economic, political, or religious systems of injustice and oppression. Professor O'Meara has described what I have called a one-sided theological projection onto Eckhart in the following manner: "Eckhart's fate in the earlier part of this century coincided with a prevailing narrow interpretation of theological expression joined to a rigid view of the role of the church in doctrinal discussion." I would add that no area of theology has been more narrowly interpreted for centuries than that area called "spirituality" and which some theology schools and seminaries still refer to exclusively as "ascetic theology"—a term that was never even invoked until the seventeenth century! How could such distorted language ever allow one to reexperience Meister Eckhart? O'Meara is hopeful, however. "Theological developments of recent decades, and especially since Vatican Council II, have freed Eckhart from that destiny of rejection."[58] We shall see.

The creation-centered spiritual tradition which has been so often condemned and for so long repressed and forgotten in the West in favor of ascetic and tactical exercises, is that tradition on which Eckhart fed so plentifully and which he in turn nourished by his own unique genius for spiritual experience and expression. There are certain themes in particular which play a prominent role in that spirituality and the reader is encouraged to look out for them in reading Eckhart. For Eckhart, unlike the vast majority of spiritual writers since his time, is primarily a spiritual theologian who knows his Scripture and the biblical roots of Christian faith. He is not an apologist for Jansenist dualisms, ascetic disciplines, Cartesian rationalisms, capitalist economic systems, male chauvinism, introverted journeys away from politics and conflicts in the world, academic ivory tower privileges or emotional sentimentalism. Indeed, his is one of the last antisentimental spiritualities in the West. What follows are the principal themes in Eckhart's spirituality. To list these themes is to make a veritable outline of what constitutes a creation-centered spiritual theology. These themes, played over and over throughout Eckhart's sermons, include the following:

1. *The creative word of God* (Dabhar). In many respects Eckhart's is an entire theology of the creative word of God—the word that gives birth to the blessing that creation is. (See Ser-

mons One and Two in particular.) Because of the goodness of God, God's word—which is creation—is also good (Sermon Three). Eckhart's theology of the goodness of creation, of God's word that "flows out but remains within," is representative of the *cataphatic* (yes) dimension to his spirituality.

2. *Blessing.* Eckhart's is a spirituality of blessing as so much of the spirituality of the Hebrew Bible is also. For example, we read in the prophet Jeremiah:

> They will come and shout for joy on Mount Sion,
> they will stream to the blessings of the Lord,
> to the flocks of sheep and the herbs.
> Their life will be like a watered garden.
> They will never be weary again. (Jr. 31:12)*

For Eckhart, all of creation is a divine blessing, the holy "isness" permeates all things (Sermon Four) and renders all things equal at the level of being (Sermon Five). And a new definition of humanity is suggested: a human being is a blessing destined to bless other beings in a conscious way by way of creativity and compassion. Other creatures on this earth bless the rest of us unconsciously (see Path One and Sermon Ten in particular). For Eckhart, as for the Yahwist theologian of the Hebrew Bible, "life is blessing and blessing is life."[59] The purpose of living is not to flee the earth or run from its pleasures but to return the blessings one has received by blessing other creatures and other human generations as well (cf. Gn. 1–4).

3. *Panentheism.* For Eckhart it is basically wrong to think of God as a Person "out there" or even of God as wholly Other "out there." God is in us and we are in God. This is the theology of inness and of panentheism which forms the basis of Eckhart's God talk and God consciousness (see especially Sermon Two). This theology emphasizes the *transparency* of God, who is omnipresent.

4. *Realized eschatology.* An equally false consciousness is established, Eckhart believes, by imagining that heaven is something that begins after this life. Eternal life is now for Eckhart, and if heaven has not already begun for us it is our dualistic way

* Translated by Dr. Helen Kenik.

of envisioning our lives that is the major obstacle. For if we are already in God, what prevents our experience of the full time in this present life time? (See especially Sermons Eight, Twenty-three, Twenty-seven.) The king/queendom of God is already among us (Sermon Nine).

5. *Celebration of all beings in God's blessing-filled cosmos.* If all of creation is a blessing, if it all flows out from God but remains within God in a panentheistic ocean of divine pleasure, then what would prevent these beings from rejoicing at this fullness of time already begun? Eckhart's spirituality is a cosmic one, not an introverted one. His search for soul takes him into the entire universe in which we are so fully immersed and which is in us and outside of us. The key words to this universe are rejoicing and celebration (see Sermons Four, Seven, Twenty-eight, Thirty-seven in particular).

6. *Letting go, and letting creation be the holy blessing that it is.* That which most prevents our rejoicing and celebrating with creation is our tendency to grab, to control, to dictate, to possess, to cling. Therefore Eckhart's advice on spiritual method is profoundly simple, though radical and by no means easy. Simply learn to let go and let be, he counsels. By letting go of clinging to things we learn what true reverence and appreciation can be. When we let go even of our fear of nothingness we can "sink" into the blessing and grace that all creation is about, and into its Creator and even more deeply into the God beyond the Creator God who is the Godhead (see Path Two in particular).

7. *The unknown, unnameable God who is a non-God.* Eckhart develops an *apophatic* (no) as well as a *cataphatic* (yes) spirituality, a *via negativa* as well as a *via positiva*. But his experience of nothingness is not accomplished by a putdown of self but by a letting go of self and of culture's images for self and even for God. This is why he "prays God to rid me of God," in order to sink deeply into the ineffable depths of the unfathomable ocean that is God (see especially Sermons Eleven, Twelve, Thirty-one).

8. *The divinization and deification of humanity.* Eckhart says that there are some mysteries that only faith and revelation can tell us about. Psychologists, philosophers, and philologists cannot bring us to these truths. Such knowledge requires a breakthrough in our consciousness, a resurrection, a second birth, an awakening

to a deeper truth (see Sermons Seventeen, Twenty-one). One such truth is the fact that we are sons and daughters of God and therefore have divine blood within us. We need to let go of our limiting perspectives and let this truth wash over us with its implications that we, like God, can create and be compassionate (see Sermons Twenty-two, Twenty-five, Twenty-nine, Thirty in particular).

9. *Spirituality is a growth process.* For Eckhart, spirituality is a constant expansion of the divine potential in us all. "If people lived a thousand years or even longer," he insists, "they might still gain in love."[60] There are no limits to the growth we can undergo, he is saying, no limits to our own divinity, for there are no limits to the divine. Spiritual growth is not a matter of climbing Jacob's ladder in a competitive and compulsive way but is spiral-like, an ever-expanding bigness that touches the ends of the cosmos itself and returns us to our primal origins refreshed. Expansion and contraction, in and out, form the basic dynamics for the spiritual journey as conceived by Eckhart. He rejects up/down as proper categories for such a journey (see Sermons Six, Seven, Eight, Seventeen).

10. *Creativity is the work of God in us.* If we are divine and subject to growth in our divinity, then we are also creators. God is the Creator and we, the images of God, follow in God's footsteps. Indeed, creative or artistic work is the only work worthy of the human person, it is the only work that satisfies, for it is the only work that works as God works. In such work a Trinity gives birth: the Trinity in us of being, knowing, and doing. Doing alone is activism; knowing alone is quietism and rationalism; but knowing and doing that are born from being and return to being—this is divine work, for it is what true creativity is all about (see Sermons Eighteen, Twenty, Twenty-nine, Thirty-three, Thirty-four in particular). Eckhart does not get trapped in the contemplation vs. action dualistic dilemma because his is truly a trinitarian theology. The prominence he gives creativity in his spirituality means that he also endorses extrovert meditation, which is centering by way of giving birth. It is the *flowing out* that all creative people must discipline themselves to do in order that beauty and blessing be shared. In this birthing we are born again and God is born in

human history again. We are to give birth to the Son of God in us and in our culture (see Path Three).

11. *Compassion, the fullness of spiritual maturity.* Only God is compassionate and so to touch our own divine roots is to make contact with compassion. Compassion for Eckhart entails two dimensions—one of consciousness of the interdependence of all beings that swim together in this divinely pantheistic sea called creation—and the other concerns justice. The first side to compassion is mystical; the second is prophetic. Creating justice or compassion constitutes the ultimate act of birthing and creativity since injustice is the ultimate act of violence and dualism. But to create justice one must have experienced oneness and mystical compassion. This oneness is the basis of the creation of all things, for all things were born in compassion and want to return there (see Path Four in particular).

12. *Everyone a royal person.* Eckhart draws heavily from the biblical tradition of the royal person, who is noble and dignified but also responsible for creating justice and compassion. Indeed, Eckhart insists that all persons are called to such nobility (see Sermons Four, Nine, Thirty-six).

13. *Jesus Christ as reminder of what it means to be God's child.* If we are all royal persons, then it helps considerably to be reminded that such a birth is possible. Jesus Christ is first and foremost such a reminder. He is the Word of God calling us to be words of God. He is the Son of God calling us to be children of God. He is a creative and compassionate person, in touch with his divine origins and his divine destiny (see Sermon Twenty-four). He is a royal person, a king, reminding all persons that we are to be as responsible as was he in returning blessing for blessing. And not only all persons but "all of creation" is to hear this Good News from us (see Sermon Five). Jesus on leaving this earth sent his Spirit to vivify us and render us other Christs (see Sermon Twenty-six). Psychologist C. G. Jung utilizes Eckhart's redemption as reminding motif. He writes:

> Despite the word "be transformed" in the Greek text [of Romans 12:2] the "renewal" of the mind is not meant as an actual alteration of consciousness, but

rather as the restoration of an original condition, an apocatastasis. This is in exact agreement with the empirical findings of psychology, that there is an ever-present archetype of wholeness which may easily disappear from the purview of consciousness or may never be perceived at all until a consciousness illuminated by conversion recognizes it in the figure of Christ. As a result of this "anamnesis" the original state of oneness with the God-image is restored.[61]

14. *Laughter, newness, and joy.* For Eckhart, God is the eternally new, the eternally young. To receive the Spirit of God sent when Jesus left the earth is to open ourselves up to the gifts of newness and youthfulness. Letting go means letting joy be—the divine joy that creates the universe continually and that calls it back to its joyful, ever-new origins (Sermon Eighteen) where true repose lies (Sermon Twenty-seven). Compassion also constitutes our first and primary origins—all things were born in compassion and proceed from compassion (Sermon Thirty-one). Pleasure is an integral part of spiritual experience. Rather than fleeing pleasure, we are to penetrate it to find God there and we are to struggle to share it. (See Sermons Three, Ten, Nineteen, Twenty-seven, Twenty-eight, Thirty.) Laughter may well be the ultimate act of letting go and letting be: the music of the divine cosmos. For in the core of the Trinity laughing and birthing go on all day long. Eckhart warns us, therefore, never to trust a so-called spiritual person for whom laughter does not lie at the center of his or her spirituality. (See Sermons Three, Six, Nine, Ten, Twenty-seven, Thirty-seven.)

From this brief summary of Eckhartian themes it is evident how central to all his thought the theme of creation is. "To give birth is the very root of God's divinity," he asserts, and he urges us to be birthers as well: "What help is it to me that the Father gives birth to his Son unless I too give birth to him?" (see Sermons Twenty-two and Twenty-three). Eckhart begins and completes his theology with the theme of creation—for we are born of the creative Word of God and we are to birth the new creation which is the compassion of God. In naming the spiritual journey as a journey from creation to new creation, Eckhart remains true to the creation-centered spiritual tradition of both the Celtic and the biblical heritage. About the latter, biblical scholar Claude Tresmontant has written: "The Hebrews showed a passionate attention to the process of fecundity, the maturing process."[62] So does Eckhart. One of the synonyms Eckhart invokes for birthing is a word he invented, namely, "breakthrough," or *Durchbruch* in his language. Eckhart's spirituality itself represents a new birth or a "breakthrough," which constitutes a fitting title for this book because Eckhart's spirituality does indeed represent a breakthrough for us Westerners. While the fourteen themes I have listed constitute an outline of Eckhart's spirituality, they also constitute an outline of creation spirituality in general. Eckhart assists us to break through and to break out of and to break beyond the one-sided spirituality of fall/redemption that has occupied the West overly much in the past centuries. To break through into a more biblically based, creation-centered, and more blessedly and joyfully and justice-oriented spiritual vision. But as Eckhart warns us, it takes courage to break through. "Only those who have dared to let go can dare to reenter." To reenter God we need to let go of dualism and all dualistic spiritualities. Then we can break through and break beyond the hegemony of fall/redemption spiritualities that have hung like an albatross around the neck of the mystical body of Christ in the West for centuries. For something was lost in Western spirituality when Eckhart was condemned. Something ceased. What was it? It was prophecy *with* mysticism, that is, a compassionately oriented spirituality that included social justice along with deep growth in consciousness; it was a deep reverence for the artist in us and among us in our midst; it was laughter and joy as core elements of spirituality; it was simplicity instead of fanciful spiritual methods; it was the conviction that lay persons can be mystics and not just professional religious. In short, what had been lost was creation-centered spirituality. Eckhart invites us back to this rich and wholesome, indeed holistic, tradition.

How to Read This Book

This book is meant to be a process, a process that is designed to take the reader on a spiritual journey of ever greater expansion into spiritual experience. This is the way a presentation of Eckhart ought to be, for Eckhart was before all else a preacher bent on inviting his hearers from their experience to new experiences and ever deeper ones. As Schürmann rightly puts it, Eckhart's is "not a theoretical doctrine but a practical guide."[63] So too with this book—it too is a practical guide. I believe that reading Eckhart is more than a process—it is also a trip in the sense in which that word has become common today. One can—and indeed ought—to get high on a line from Eckhart, an idea from Eckhart, or a passage from Eckhart. It does not hurt to rest with that thought, mull it over, let it envelop you, and thus to utilize this book as a meditation book. For this is a meditation book that is meant for savoring. Like a book of poetry, it requires a disciplining of that much-neglected right side of the brain: the intuitive, mystical, and communion-making side. I can guarantee —for I have seen it happen so often—that the language in which Eckhart expresses his faith, when savored to the full, will create energy and creativity for the reader's spiritual life. That is why Eckhart moved so many persons six and a half centuries ago and why he possesses still a unique power to move. Eckhart deserves to be read with the heart as well as with the head, for he himself, like any authentic mystic, experienced life that way and thinks on his experience in that way. I especially encourage readers to read Eckhart's sermons out loud with a friend or friends. They are oral works, spoken verbally by Eckhart and destined for ears and not only eyes. Indeed, there is a considerable degree of oral rhetoric in them, as one gets in any good preacher in our day. One reader of these sermons has commented how they are often similar in rhetorical style to that mode of preaching developed in black religion in America. There are repetitions, music-like refrains, and there is clearly rapport with the audience. At times Eckhart apparently had his listeners howling with laughter, as he is forced to tell them to be quiet and pay attention to what he is about to say. Humor is absolutely essential for reading and grasping Meister Eckhart, a requirement no doubt that his inquisitors lacked. No wonder they misunderstood so much of his thought.

I believe that there are three steps to reading Eckhart or indeed any mystic. They are as follows:

1. Enjoy—savor
2. Analyze
3. Enjoy—savor

Pleasure is the goal of reading Meister Eckhart and this book. He said so himself: "People do all their deeds for the sake of these two things: repose and pleasure. I have also said that people can never feel joy or pleasure in any creature if God's likeness is not within it" (Sermon Twenty-seven). The analysis that is sandwiched between our two stages of enjoying Eckhart is meant, of course, to enhance the pleasure, to deepen the making of connections within Eckhart and to our lives and those elements in spirituality that have influenced Eckhart's own theology. The first step in reading Eckhart, then, should be letting go and letting Eckhart speak to us from his vantage point of six hundred and fifty years ago. If we find a line or a paragraph that doesn't immediately strike us or that has a certain opaqueness to it, let go of that and do not let it hinder what has gone before or what is coming up. Eckhart is indeed capable of what Schürmann calls a "malleability of expression"[64]—even that can delight us and add to our pleasure. The commentaries, brief as they are, are meant to be an integral part of the process of deepening one's journey with Eckhart. Words from Eckhart's sermon are italicized within the Commentary on that sermon. As the title of this book indicates, these commentaries will center around his creation spirituality and are not intended in any way to bog down the reader with esoteric jargon. The great percentage of the commentary is either from scriptural allusions Eckhart makes in the sermon or a bringing together of his thought from other works of Eckhart to form some sort of cohesive unity.

A chart is presented on pages vi and vii that cross-references the thirty-seven sermons of this volume with the critical German and Latin works plus the four best-known English translations of Eckhart's works. This chart should assist the reader and scholar alike who has met Eckhart in other versions or translations. The Index of Scriptural References and the Index of Spirituality Themes are meant to assist the student seriously bent on deepening his or her grasp of the theology behind Eckhart's thinking. Titles and subtitles have been drawn as much as possible from the very words of Eckhart himself. If the commentaries allow the reader to enjoy Eckhart more fully, then they have accomplished their purpose. And if this book as a whole allows us to enjoy life more fully and to struggle more imaginatively and courageously to share its gifts by way of compassion, celebration, and justice, then its purpose has been accomplished. And Eckhart, who spoke often of how the entire communion of saints and beings rejoices when we rejoice, will rejoice with us at our accomplishment.

Acknowledgments

I am indebted to many persons for assisting me with the germination and completion of this work. My thanks to three Eckhartian scholars whose scholarship has assisted me in this study, namely, Thomas Aquinas O'Meara, Reiner Schürmann, and John D. Caputo. A special thanks to Thomas Aquinas O'Meara for his encouragement and advice on the sermons I have chosen to reproduce and to the translators of these sermons: Ron Miller, for his translations of Sermons 1, 4, 6, 11, 22, 30, 35; Robert Cunningham, for his translations of Sermons 3, 5, 8, 9, 10, 13, 15, 16, 17, 18, 20, 21, 23, 25, 26, 27, 28, 29, 32, 36; Sister Elizabeth Heptner, SAC, for her translations of Sermons 7 and 24; and to Thomas O'Meara for Sermon 2. Remaining sermons I have translated myself. All translations are from the critical German or Latin texts (abbreviated DW or LW respectively on the opening page of each sermon) or, in the case of Sermons 3, 17, 18, 20, from Quint (abbreviated Q), because these sermons are not yet published in the DW edition. Fuller references to these editions are given on page 546. What I call for neatness' sake "Sermons" in numbers 30, 35, and 36 are not that, strictly speaking. Numbers 30 and 35 were originally scriptural commentaries and number 36 was a treatise. Thanks for the insights about Eckhart and Scripture to Dr. Helen Kenik of the Jesuit School of Theology, Chicago, and to Sister Mary Anne Shea, whose brilliant study on the royal person in Meister Eckhart demonstrated Eckhart's immersion in biblical thinking. Also to Marv Anderson for his excellent study on "The Ethic of Being in Meister Eckhart" and who, being a farmer, grasped so intuitively the earthiness of Eckhart's language and imagery and who has put together the indices for this volume. Thanks to the typists of this manuscript, Mary Cunningham, Mary Hunt, Judy and Tim Rowan. Finally, thanks to Brendan Doyle whose musical way of conceiving reality comes so close to Eckhart's own symphonic sermons; and to Tristan who has been a constant companion during my long hours of work

with Meister Eckhart and who has demonstrated the wisdom of
Eckhart's advice that those who write big books ought to have a dog
with them with which to share the equality of being (see Sermon Five,
page 99).

December 1979, the six hundred and
fiftieth anniversary of Meister Eckhart's
death and condemnation

PATH ONE: CREATION

The first path that we are to travel in our deepening journey into spirituality and into God is the pathway of creation. For Eckhart, creation is a revelation of God, a home for God and a temple for God. It is a grace, an overflow of the goodness and beauty that God is. For Eckhart, "being is God," and our spiritual depth depends on our ability to grasp this truth. For while all beings are equal and are words and revelations of God, humans have a unique capacity, due to their having been created in the image and likeness of God, to relate to all of being and to return to their primordial origins, which are in God. This journey of return and renewal is a return to the truth of creation: namely, that creatures, like fish in an ocean, swim in an ocean of divine grace. Our spiritual journey is waking up to the divine sea in which we swim. The return is not a narcissistic return but a refreshing and energizing one which is meant to renew us to ourselves, carry on the holy work of creation and birthing (Path Three below) and even of the new creation which will be known as compassion (Path Four below). For one reason we should return to creation is to learn what human history has done to destroy its goodness and to detract from its divinity.

Creation for Eckhart is a blessing. Like the Yahwist theologian of the Hebrew Bible, Eckhart is firmly convinced that "life is blessing and blessing is life" and that the purpose of spiritual journeying is to reenter the blessing that all creation is about on the one hand, and to bless creation and others of the human community on the other.[1] Eckhart could make his own the prom-

ise made to Abram, the father of faith, when he was invited on a
spiritual journey:

> Go forth from the land of your kinsfolk and from your
> father's house to a land that I will show you.
>
> I will make of you a great nation, and I will bless you;
> I will make your name great, so that you will be a bless-
> ing.
>
> I will bless those who bless you and curse those who
> curse you. All the communities of the earth shall find
> blessing in you.
>
> Abram went as the Lord directed him. (Gn. 12:1–4)*

* *The New American Bible.*

Sermon One: ALL CREATURES ARE WORDS OF GOD

"The Lord has stretched his hand out and has touched my mouth and has spoken to me." (Jr. 1:9)*

When I preach, I try to speak of letting go and that human beings should become unwed from themselves and from all things. Second, I try to say that they should be conceived again in that simple good which is God. Third, I stress that people should reflect on that great nobility which God has put in their souls so that they might come to God in a wonderful manner. Fourth, I talk of the purity of the divine nature—that brightness of the divine nature which is ineffable. God is a Word but an unexpressed Word.

Augustine says: "The entire Scripture is vain. If you say that God is a Word, then it is thereby spoken; but if you say that God is unspoken, then God is also unspeakable." But God is clearly something, so who can speak this Word? No one can except for one who is this Word. God is a Word which speaks itself. Wherever God is, there he speaks this Word; wherever he is not, there he does not speak. God is spoken and unspoken. The Father is a speaking action and the Son is an active speech. What is in me goes out from me; if I am only thinking it, then my word reveals it and yet remains inside me. It is in this way that the Father speaks the unspoken Son and yet the Son remains in the Father. I have often said that God's exit is his entrance. As much as I am near God, to that extent God speaks himself in me. To the extent that all creatures who are gifted with reason go out from themselves in all that they do, to that same extent they go into themselves. With merely material creatures this is not the case; the more they do, the more they go out from themselves. All crea-

* "Misit dominus manu suam et tetigit os meum et dixit mihi . . . Ecce constitui te super gentes et regna." (DW II, ℀53)

tures want to express God in all their works; let them all speak, coming as close as they can, they still cannot speak him. Whether they want to or not, whether it is pleasing or painful to them, they all want to speak God and he still remains unspoken.

David says: "The Lord is his Name" (Ps. 68:4). "Lord" signifies the higher rank in authority; "servant" refers to the lower rank. Certain names belong properly to God and are disconnected with all other things—as, for example, the word *God*. This name *God* is the most proper name of God, as *human being* is the name of a human being. A human person is always human, whether he be foolish or wise. Seneca says: "It is a pitiable human being who does not come out more than a human being." Certain names indicate relationships in God, as, for example, Fatherhood and Sonship. When you speak of a father, you think simultaneously of a son. You cannot first have a father who only later has a son nor a son who later has a father. But both carry in themselves an eternal being transcending time. There is a third category of divine names which suggests a relation to God but at the same time a reference to time. One also finds many names for God in the Bible. Yet despite all of this I maintain that whenever someone recognizes something in God and puts a name on it, then it is not God. God is higher than names or nature. We read about a good man who in his prayer pleaded to God and wanted to give him a name. Then a brother said: "Be still, you blaspheme God." We can find no name which we dare to give God. Nevertheless, we are allowed those names with which the saints have named him and which God has dedicated in their hearts and which God has permeated with divine light. And this is where we first learn how we are to pray to God. We should say: "Lord, with that same Name which you have dedicated in the hearts of your saints and permeated with your light, we beseech you and praise you." We should also learn that there is no name we can give to God such that we would seem to be implying that by means of it we had sufficiently praised and honored God, for God is elevated over all names and remains inexpressible.

The Father speaks the Son from his entire power and he speaks him in all things. All creatures are words of God. My mouth expresses and reveals God but the existence of a stone does the same and people often recognize more from actions than from words. That work which the highest nature does from its highest potential, that is something which the nature which is beneath that cannot grasp. If the latter were able to do the same thing as the former, it would not be beneath the former but equal to it. All creatures may echo God in all their activities. It is, of course, just a small bit which they can reveal.

Even someone who ascends beyond the highest angel and touches God is as unlike God by any comparison to that which God is as white compared to black. Even all creatures together, in all they have received, are totally unequal in any comparison to that which is in God, even though all creatures are gladly doing the best they can to express him. The prophet says: "Lord, you say one and I understand two" (Ps. 62:11). When God speaks in the soul, then the soul and God are one; as soon as this unity is decreased (by going outward from the inner center of the soul in the powers of the soul and from there through the senses outward to creatures), it is divided. And the more we climb inward with our knowing faculty, the more we are one in the Son. And so the Father speaks the Son eternally in oneness and pours out in the Son all creatures. They all cry out to come back there where they have flowed out. Their whole life and being is a crying and a hurrying to be back again whence they came out.

The prophet says: "The Lord has stretched forth his hand" (Jr. 1:9). And he means by that the Holy Spirit. Now he goes on to say: "He has touched my mouth" and means by this that "he has spoken to me" (Jr. 1:9). The mouth of the soul is the highest part of the soul and this is meant by saying "He has put his word in my mouth" (Jr. 1:9). That is the kiss of the soul: there mouth comes to mouth; there the Father gives birth to the Son in the soul, and there is where the soul is addressed. Now God speaks: "It is true that I have chosen you today and placed you over all peoples and over kingdoms" (Jr. 1:10). God has chosen us in a "today"—there where nothing is, there will now be for an eternity a "today." "And I have placed you over people"—that is, over the whole world; and you must be unmarried from all things, for "over kingdoms" means: everything which is more than one and is therefore too much for you who must die to all things in order to have them all restored to you again in the heights where we live in the Holy Spirit.

May God the Holy Spirit help us to this end. Amen.

COMMENTARY: Eckhart's Theology of the Creative Word of God/ How All Creatures Are Words of God, Echoes of God, Gladly Doing Their Best to Express God/Creation Is a Flowing Out and a Flowing Back/The Creative Word as the Prophetic Word

All of Meister Eckhart's theology can be understood as an exegesis of or development of the biblical concept of *Dabhar* or Word. This is the Word with which Genesis begins the Scriptures—it is the dynamic, active word that, when spoken, creates. God said, "Let there be light" and there was light, we are told. God's Word gets things done. Thus Eckhart can say that the Father or Creator *is a speaking action*—who truly creates and does not merely cogitate about truth or about creating. So full of mystery and power is this creative Word who is God that we humans are left dumb and speechless by the beauty of creation. Creation is almost too holy for us, surely too holy for mere human words. "The entire created order is sacred," says Eckhart.[1] The only Word that comes close to saying the divine word is the Son of God who is God's own "active speech." Like all truthful and authentic words, this Word of God both left God *and* remained within God: *God's exit is his entrance*, we are told. We must be on our guard, as the ancient Israelis were when they forbade the pronouncing of the divine name, against the blasphemy that is intrinsic to our imagining we can name God. We cannot name God who *is higher than names or nature* and when we try to put a name on God, *then it is not God*. God is bigger than we think, bigger than we speak. God is the God beyond God.

And yet God has spoken a divine word in creation itself. There is revelation in creation and natural things—*the existence of a stone reveals God*—and all creatures may indeed echo God. Creatures are an echo of the divine, they are a communication of the divine.

> The perfection of God could not refrain from allowing creatures to flow out of himself, to whom he was able to communicate himself. They were able to receive equality with him

—indeed, as much equality as if he had emptied himself. And the creatures flowed out so boundlessly that there are more angels than there are grains of sand or grass or leaves. Through all of them light and grace and gifts flow down to us.[2]

All creation is good and gift-giving. It is itself a blessing from God. Creatures—*all* of them—are a divine blessing and a word from God. It is in their activities and in expressing their fullest potential that creatures echo God most loudly. Moreover, the most successful of all God's words, the word that is God's Son, is intimate to creatures and the continual act of creation. As Eckhart puts it, *The Father speaks the Son from his entire (creative) power and he speaks him in all things.* Elsewhere Eckhart says: "God pours out in the Son all creatures."[3]

Eckhart has said that *all creatures are words of God* and elsewhere he explains that "the purpose of a word is to reveal."[4] Thus again, all creation itself is forever going on. It is a process we can experience daily. "God created the world in such a way that he is still continually creating it."[5] The word is always being spoken and wanting to be spoken—which is also to say that it is never fully spoken and never satisfactorily expressed. *God is spoken and unspoken* at the same time: already *today*—and not yet—the kingdom to come.

Eckhart hints in this sermon at the powerful connection between the word and work, between creation and the new creation. Creatures reveal God best, he says, in their actions and in their richest activities. In their striving to bring about the not yet, creatures are bringing God to birth—yet the whole work is that of the Holy Spirit that made cosmos of chaos and gave birth from a state of hovering over the waters.

There are tensions in the word and the work of creation and new creation. First, there is tension between in and out. A true word goes out but remains within—*God's exit is his entrance.* This in/out tension or dialectic is a crucial one in all of Eckhart's imaginings of the way God works and humans work spiritually. In/out and not up/down represents the basic dynamic of true living and true creating for Eckhart. Unlike Thomas à Kempis, who said that every time he went out of the monastery he came back less a man, Eckhart says that *to the extent that all creatures who are gifted with reason go out from themselves in all they do, to that same extent they go into themselves.* Inness is not in opposition to going out. In and out are related and interrelated. In fact, so eager are all creatures, these echoes of God, to *flow back* as well as to *flow out*, that *they all cry out to come back there where they have flowed out.* Eckhart trusts creation to return to its source and origins. For the *whole life and being* of creatures is nothing but *a crying and hurrying to be back again whence they came out.*

Another tension in creation is that between expressing God and failing to express God.

> All creatures want to express God in all their works; let them all speak, coming as close as they can, they still cannot speak him. Whether they want to or not, whether it is pleasing or painful to them, they all want to speak God and he still remains unspoken.

As much as creatures strive to reveal God, they are not in the long run up to that task, for *the brightness of the divine nature is ineffable. God is a Word but an unexpressed Word.* The Word retains something of the divine silence, the divine mystery. This silence can be painful to creatures and can be pleasant but it is always present, even in the fullest of revelations. But creation does not get discouraged and does not give up, nor does it operate in vain. In fact, creation is joyful in its efforts to express the divine: *All creatures are gladly doing the best they can to express God.* But in doing so the creatures do not lose touch with their origins or their innermost ground with the Creator. Instead, while they go out and flow out from God, they also seek to return. They seek the homeyness and warmth of their divine origins. They seek the wellspring of their creation which is the Spirit of creation.

> God in creating all creatures instructs and enjoins, advises and commands them, by the very fact that he creates them, to follow him and conform themselves to him, to turn and hasten back to him as the first cause of their entire being, in accordance with the passage in Ecclesiastes (1:7): "Unto the place from whence the rivers come, thither they return again." This is why the creature has a natural tendency to love God and loves him more even than he loves himself . . . Just as every created thing follows and pursues its end, so likewise it follows its beginning.[6]

The flowing out that creation is about is also a flowing back, a return. The exit is a return; the return an exit. Only in God are end and beginning identical, just as in God only word and work, speaking and creating, creation and new creation are identical. For us creatures the dialectical journey must be made and remade—and that journey constitutes our journey of living in the Holy Spirit.

The flowing out and the hurrying back that all creatures are involved in comes about because, in fact, "all things love God."[7] Loving God, they seek God and they seek to be like God so that it can be said that all nature seeks God.

> Know that all creatures are driven and take action by their nature for one end: to be like God. Heaven would never revolve if it did not search for God or a likeness of God. If God were not in all things, nature would not accomplish or yearn for anything in all kinds of things. For whether you wish it or not, and whether you know it or don't know it, within its very self nature seeks and strives for God.[8]

The most dynamic of the words that nature speaks is that of the human person, the prophetic word of Jeremiah, for example, that tells of the nearness, the mouth-to-mouth nearness, of God and which challenges persons to make unity of the whole world and to begin eternity now. It is the human person or "soul" that is especially required to stand up and be heard.

> But in the first outpouring, when the truth pours out and springs forth, in the gate of the house of God, the soul should stand and should express and bring forth the Word. Everything that is in the soul should speak and praise . . .[9]

In spite of the tensions, whether in season or out of season, we are to praise the creative Word that has no name but is the power behind every word.

The text for this sermon by Eckhart is taken from the prophet Jeremiah, the first chapter. There we read about the word of Yahweh and the word of the prophet:

The word of Yahweh was addressed to me, saying,
  "Before I formed you in the womb I knew you;
  before you came to birth I consecrated you;
  I have appointed you as prophet to the nations."

I said, "Ah, Lord Yahweh; look, I do not know how to speak: I am a
    child!"
    But Yahweh replied,
    "Do not say 'I am a child.'
    Go now to those to whom I send you
    and say whatever I command you . . ."
Then Yahweh put out his hand and touched my mouth and said to me:
    "There! I am putting my words into your mouth.
    Look, today I am setting you
    over nations and over kingdoms
    to tear up and to knock down,
    to destroy and to overthrow,
    to build and to plant." (Jr. 1:4–7, 9–10)

The prophet in this passage has been invited to share in the Creator's
efficacious word—the word that when spoken makes things happen. The
creative word becomes the prophetic word. But Jeremiah is reluctant to
accept such a godly vocation and responsibility. The prophetic word will
include a tearing up as well as a building up kind of message and commitment. "Because the word of a prophet is the word of Yahweh, it is
more deadly than a sword, or it is like a consuming fire" (Jr. 5:14;
23:29).[10] Word and deed go together in the biblical theology of the
Word. It is noteworthy too that the concept of the preexistence of the
prophet—as later the concept of the preexistence of wisdom—is found in
this passage of Jeremiah since this notion of preexistence caught
Eckhart's imagination and too many commentators have jumped to the
conclusion that he got the idea from Plato or Neoplatonism. In this sermon, then, Eckhart has brought together the efficacious and creative
word of God with the demanding and disturbing word of the prophet.
For we have been placed over the whole world to see that God's word
returns fulfilled and renewed to its source.

Sermon Two: CREATION: A FLOWING OUT BUT REMAINING WITHIN

"Preach the Word." (2 Tm. 4:2)*

The phrase which we read today and tomorrow for the feast of our master, Saint Dominic, comes from Saint Paul's Letter. In the vernacular, it runs this way: Announce the word, pronounce it, produce it, give birth to the word (2 Tm. 4:2).

It is an amazing thing that something flows forth and nonetheless remains within. Words flow forth and yet remain within— that is certainly amazing! All creatures flow outward and nonetheless remain within—that is extremely amazing. What God has given and what God promises to give—that is amazing, inconceivable, and unbelievable. And that is as it should be, for if it were comprehensible and believable things would not be right. God is in all things. The more he is in things, the more he is outside of things. The more he is within, all the more he is without. I have often said God is creating this entire world full and entire in this present now. Everything God created six thousand years ago—and even more—as he made the world, God creates now all at once. God is in everything, but to the extent that God is godly and to the extent that he is intelligible, God is nowhere as much as he is in the soul and also, if you wish, in the angels. He dwells in the innermost dimension of the soul and in the highest aspect of the soul. And when I say "the innermost," I mean the highest. When I say "the highest" I mean the innermost region of the soul. The innermost and the highest realms of the soul—these two are one. There where time never penetrates, where no image shines in, in the innermost and highest aspect of the soul God creates the entire cosmos. Everything which God created six thousand years ago and everything which will be created by God after thousands of years—if the world lasts that long—God is creating

* "Praedica verbum." (DW II, #30)

all of that in the innermost and highest realms of the soul. Everything which is past and everything which is present and everything which is future God creates in the innermost realms of the
soul. Everything which God works in all of his saints, that God
works in the innermost realms of the soul. The Father gives birth
to his Son in the innermost part of the soul and gives birth to you
with his only begotten Son as no less. If I am to be a son then I
must be a son in the same being in which the Son exists and in
no other being. If I am to be a human being, I cannot have the
being of an animal and also be a human being. I must, rather, be
a human being in the being of a human person. If I am to be this
particular human person then I have to have the existence of this
particular human person. Saint John says, "You are children of
God" (Jn. 4:4).

"Announce the word, pronounce it, bring it forth, give birth to
the word." "Pronounce the word!" What is spoken forth externally and penetrates into you, that is something ordinary. But
that word which is spoken inwardly is what we have been discussing. "Pronounce the word"—that means that you should become
inwardly one with what is in you. The prophet says: "God spoke
one and I heard two" (Ps. 62:11). That is true. God is constantly
speaking only one thing. His speaking is one thing. In this one utterance he speaks his Son and at the same time the Holy Spirit
and all creatures. And yet there is only one speech in God. The
prophet says, "I heard two." That means I heard God and the
creature. There where God speaks the creatures, there God is.
Here in space and time the creature is. People think God has only
become a human being *there*—in his historical incarnation—but
that is not so; for God is *here*—in this very place—just as much
incarnate as in a human being long ago. And this is why he has
become a human being: that he might give birth to you as his
only begotten Son, and as no less.

Yesterday I was at a particular place and I spoke a phrase
which is in the Our Father: "Let your will be done." It would be
better to express this in this way: "Become your will." My will
would become your will. I would become your will—that is what
the Our Father means. This phrase has two meanings. First, "Be
asleep to all things": that means ignore time, creatures, images.
The masters say that if a person who is sleeping soundly would

sleep for a hundred years, she would forget all creatures, time, and images. And then you could perceive what God works in you. That is why the soul says in the Song of Songs, "I sleep but my heart watches" (Sg. 5:2). Therefore, if all creatures are asleep in you, you can perceive what God works in you.

Second, this phrase means: "Concern yourself with all things." And this has three meanings. It means, "Take advantage of all things." That means, first, seize God in all things, for God is in all things. Saint Augustine says God has created all things not that he would let them come into existence and then go their own way, but rather he remains in them. People think that they have an advantage if they bring things to God as if God didn't have anything. That is incorrect, for all things added to God are no more than God alone. And if someone who has the Father and the Son with the Father says that he now has more than when he only had the Son without the Father, that would be incorrect. For the Father with the Son is no more than the Son alone. And again the Son with the Father is no more than the Father alone. Therefore, lay hold of God in all things and this will be a sign of your birth, a sign that God has given birth in you himself as his only begotten Son, and nothing less.

The second meaning of "take advantage of all things" is this: "Love God more than all things and your neighbor as yourself" (Lk. 10:27). This is the commandment of God, but, I tell you, it is not only a commandment. Rather, God has made us a gift here and has promised to make us a gift. If you prefer to keep a hundred dollars for yourself rather than giving it to another, that is wrong. If you love one human being more than another, that is wrong. If you love your father and mother and yourself more than another human being, that is wrong. And if you love your own happiness more than another's, that is also wrong. "Good heavens! This can't be right. Should I not love external happiness for myself more than for another?" There are many learned people who do not understand this and who find it too difficult. On the contrary, it is quite easy. I want to show you that it is not difficult. In each member of the human body with its particular function, nature perceives a double goal. The first goal which that member pursues in its operation is to serve the body in its totality. And second, each individual member serves itself and no less than itself. Within its operations, it doesn't pay any more attention to itself than to another member. How much more must this be true in the realm of grace. God ought to be a rule and foundation for your love. The first intention of your love must be oriented purely toward God, and next toward one's neighbor as toward oneself, and no less than toward oneself. If you love beatitude for yourself more than for another you are simply loving yourself. And when you love yourself God is not your pure love, and that is wrong. In effect, if you love the beatitude which is in Saint Peter or in Saint Paul as your own, you possess then the same beatitude which they have for themselves. If you love the happiness of angels as in yourself and if you love the beatitude of our Lady equally with yourself you would enjoy then the same happiness as she does. It belongs to you properly as to her. That is what it says in a book of wisdom: "He has made him equal to his saints" (Si. 45:2).

The third meaning of finding your advantage in all things is this: Love God in all things equally, that is to say, love God as freely in poverty as in riches and look for him in illness as well as in health. Look for him outside of temptation as well as in temptation, in suffering as well as without suffering. The more suffering is great, the more suffering is little, and the more it is like carrying two buckets. The heavier the one, the lighter is the other. The more a person abandons, the easier it will be to abandon. A person who loves God can renounce the entire earth as easily as renouncing an egg. The more one gives, the easier it is to give—as with the Apostles. The heavier their suffering, the easier they were able to support it.

"Apply yourself in all things" means finally that when you find yourself occupied with various things more than with the pure One, test your application. That means "occupy yourself in all things" in view of bringing fulfillment to your service. All of this refers also to the phrase "Lift up your head," and this phrase has two meanings. The first is: Empty yourself of all that is yours and give yourself over to God. Make God to be your own as he is for himself his own, and he will be God for you as he is God for himself, and nothing less. What is truly mine I have received from no one. If I have it from someone else it is not mine, it is hers or his from whom I have it. The second sense of "Lift up your head" is: Direct all your works to God.

There are many people who do not understand this, and this astonishes me. Yet the person who is to understand this must be very detached and elevated above all worldly things. That we should come to this perfection—may God help us.

COMMENTARY: Eckhart's Panentheistic Theology of Inness/Words and Creatures Flow Out But Remain Within/The Highest Region of the Soul Is the Innermost Part of the Soul and It Is Here That God Creates/The Inner and Outer Person/God and Creation Are One So We Are to Love All Things Equally

In this sermon Meister Eckhart continues his own *amazement* based on his observation of creation's relation to the Creator. He develops the same simile he used in Sermon One of the word that flows out but remains within, comparing again all things that exist with the existence of a word. He is *quite amazed* that creatures and words both flow outside their origin and yet remain within that origin. He invites us to explore more in depth the mystery that amazes and which concerns the inness of things. For in the inness of things is God—*God is in all things* he repeats three times in this discourse, as if we had not up to now spent enough effort on communing with this truth of creation and Creator's oneness. He urges us to alter our consciousness and way of seeing things in order to enter into this mystery, telling us to *seize God in all things, for God is in all things.* Elsewhere Eckhart urges us to alter our consciousness so as to "bring God down" to where God truly resides, which is within the inness of things.

> I reflected tonight that God should be brought down, not absolutely, but only within, and so this means a God who is brought down. This pleased me so well that I wrote it in my book. It runs thus: A God who is brought down, not completely, but only within, that we may be raised up. That which was above came to be within. You shall be united and by yourself in yourself, so that He may be within you. Not that we take away anything from Him, who is above us. We should

take into ourselves and should take from ourselves into ourselves.[1]

Notice that for Eckhart "bringing God down" means taking God in. God is not up for Eckhart and we down. Rather, God is—and wants to be—in the *innermost* part of us and fully among us. Divinity dwells on the inside: *When I say the "innermost," I mean the highest*—the innermost becomes the sublime, *and these two are one.* The in/out dynamic that we saw in Sermon One as integral to the motion of creation also holds for the deepest levels of our spiritual experience. We can keep God outside by being too little in touch with our inside and for this reason Eckhart repeats as a constant refrain, and like a good preacher would, this forgotten but sacred place: *the innermost part of the soul.* Almost drugging us with this chant to the *innermost part of the soul,* Eckhart is insisting that we remember it. For it is here that God creates and that the new creation will be either born or aborted.

But if God is in, we need to get to know the within. Indeed, if we understood how deeply within us God dwells, our lives would change. That is why Eckhart urges us in this sermon to *become aware of what is in you*—then we will be ready to *announce* it, *pronounce* it, *produce* it and *give birth to* it. Then our consciousness will change from thinking two words—God and creatures—to thinking one word: God. For the Creative Word has, in the act of creation, only uttered one word still one more time: *God is constantly speaking only one thing.* What is that one word? It is God and creation: *In this one utterance he speaks his Son and at the same time the Holy Spirit and all creatures.* The word of God appears as things created here below and so we imagine that we hear two distinct words—*God and the creature.* But we need to improve our hearing. We are to hear just one, we are to hear creation and listen to the Creator in one act. For God and creation are one utterance. Creation is an expression of divinity, indeed a kind of divinity, as we shall see in Sermons Three and Four. Were we more aware of the divinity of our own creation and of what is in us we would know the truth being spoken of. It would be less a surprise and more an experience of Good News.

This theology of inness and this God of the innermost requires a person who is not "out for a walk," as Eckhart puts it. He distinguishes between the outward and the inward person.

> The outward person is the old person, the earthly person, the
> person of this world, who grows old "from day to day." His
> end is death . . . The inward man, on the other hand, is the
> new person, the heavenly person, in whom God shines.[2]

The deep word of God can only be spoken to a person with an inner
self. And when it is spoken, unity takes place, for barriers of ego and
time, competition and dualism, only exist at the level of superficiality or
the outer person's consciousness. *There Time never penetrates and no
image shines* into the inner person; there God is free to play, to interplay, and to create. Or, as Freud put it, "in the id there is nothing
corresponding to the idea of time."[3] Here all creation takes place—God
creates the entire cosmos and time is suspended so that the eternal is
now. And there too the Father begets both the perfect Word and ourselves as the children or words of God. The new creation also takes
place at this level of innermost sublimity, where all time stops.

> The inward person is not at all in time or place but is purely
> and simply in eternity. it is there that God arises, there He is
> heard, there He is; there God, and God alone, speaks.
> "Blessed are they that hear the word of God" (Lk. 11:28)
> there.

Since place as well as time is suspended in this inner depth, the person
experiences spacefulness and his or her own greatness.

> There the inward person attains his full amplitude (*spatiosis-
> simus est*) because he is great without magnitude. This is the
> person the apostle commends to us in Colossians (3:10f.):
> "Putting on the new person which is renewed in the knowl-
> edge of God after the image of him that created him; where
> there is neither male nor female, Gentile nor Jew . . . barbar-
> ian, Scythian, bond or free: but Christ is all and in all."[4]

The word Eckhart uses, *spatiosissimus*, means literally: the most spacious.
At this level of inner depth we are most spacious, more without limit,
most spacy one might say. We are also most together—at one with the
Creator and in the process of becoming a truer and truer image of God
and at one with our neighbor irregardless of sex, race, or nation.

Eckhart has not only observed that God is in all things but also that, because of the amazing nature of all creativity, all things are also in their Creator. *All creatures flow outward, and nonetheless remain within.* He elaborates on this understanding of creation and creativity elsewhere:

> When the Father begat all creatures, he begat me also, and I flowed out with all creatures and yet remained in the Father. In the same way, the words that I am now speaking first spring up in me, then secondly I reflect on the idea, and thirdly I express it and you all receive it; yet it really remains in me. In the same way, I have remained in the Father.[5]

Our "remaining in the Father" is an expression of the authentic and altogether orthodox doctrine of panentheism, which means, literally, that all is in God and God is in all. Such a doctrine differs from heterodox pantheism, which means literally "all is God and God is all" and thus disregards the beyondness of God. Indeed, Eckhart takes special pains in this sermon to demonstrate that he is not trafficking in pantheism (a charge that contributed most to his condemnation) when he indicates that creatures do not add to God. God is greater than the sum of creation's parts: *All things added to God are no more than God alone.* Eckhart's panentheistic theology, which refuses to see God as a Subject or as an Object outside ourselves or outside creation, is developed time and time again. He invokes scriptural evidence for his doctrine: "All things are in God. 'Having all things in thee alone' (Tb. 10:5); 'from him and through him and in him are all things' (Rm. 11:36)."[6] "In him we live, move, and have our being" (Ac. 17:28).

> God created all things, not that they might stand outside of himself or alongside of himself or beyond himself, the way other artifacts [made by humans] do, but he calls them from nothing, that is from nonbeing, so that they may come into and receive and dwell in himself. For he is being.[7]

We do not need to ascend to God but to open our hearts and persons to the truth of how "God is everywhere and always equally omnipresent."[8] We ought not to climb up to God, since God is all around and not up. "As long as we are still in the ascent we do not attain into him."[9] God, Eckhart declares, is "round-about us completely enveloping us,"[10] we are indeed bathed in God as fish who swim in the ocean are bathed in the ocean no less than the ocean bathes in them. "The light embraces all the powers of the soul. Accordingly he [a master] says: 'The light of heaven bathed him.' "[11] For God "is a being that has in itself all being."[12] Elsewhere, Eckhart describes creation as a panentheistic creation, namely as a divine birth within God:

> He created all things in such a way that they are not outside himself, as ignorant people falsely imagine. Everything that God creates or does he does or creates in himself, sees or knows in himself, loves in himself. Outside himself he does nothing, knows or loves nothing; and this is peculiar to God himself.[13]

To be unaware of panentheism, of how all beings are in God, is to be "ignorant," Eckhart insists. For things are in God and God is in things. For God this being in and out is no more difficult than it is for the sea that passes through the gills of a fish. God is in all things. The more he is in things, the more he is outside of things; the more he is within, all the more he is without. Inside and outside are not opposed for God. We can be inside God and God can be inside us at the same time.

Eckhart warns us not to underestimate what being in God implies. It is a far richer existence than merely being with God and in this sense being in God is deeper than mere friendship wherein friends are *with* one another. For there is implied in being with, a separation and a distance. But being in erases those differences, being in is union and unity. That is why Eckhart, following the Synod of the Council of Reims and Thomas Aquinas as well,[14] can say that "to be in God is to be God." The Word of God came to demonstrate to us how fully in God we were, so fully in God that we too are God's *only begotten Son and no less*. Our becoming God is the very purpose of the Incarnation, which happened in order that *he might give birth to you as his only begotten Son, and as no less*. So like God are we that we become God's will. *I would become your will—that is what the Our Father means*. Our goal is to become as God is—to "be all in all, as God is all in all," as Eckhart puts it elsewhere.[15] Thus we too are to become transparent and panentheistic, bathers and bathed, as God is. And in doing so we experience the same God that God experiences. *God is for himself his own, and he will be God for you as he is God for himself, and nothing less.*

How does this panentheism happen in the everyday world of our lives? It happens in the Mystical Body and in our working to breathe life into new creation. *Direct all your works to God.* It happens by the marriage of word and work: *Announce the word, pronounce it, produce it, give birth to the word!* In the scriptural passage that Eckhart is preaching from we read the following admonition to the builders-up of the mystical body:

> Proclaim the message and, welcome or unwelcome, insist on it. Refute falsehood, correct error, call to obedience—but do all with patience and with the intention of teaching . . . Be careful always to choose the right course; be brave under trials; make the preaching of the Good News your life's work, in thoroughgoing service. (2 Tm. 4:2, 5)

Thus Eckhart addresses himself to the charism of teaching and service of one's lifework, which is preaching the Good News. It is here that he cannot remain silent, even in the moment of his deepest mystical utterances of union of God and creatures, to admonish us to love our neighbor as ourself. Lest the mystically inclined get too carried away with Eckhart's unitive vision and imagine that he is talking of a singular life privately passed with God, he includes the great commandment in this sermon and applies it to a way of living that vivifies the entire mystical body. For if all that is in God is God and if all of creation is in God, then surely we are to *love God in all things equally.* Christ's admonition to love our neighbor as ourself is more than an ethic—it is a way of life that is *not only a commandment* but a *gift* and a way in which we see the world. If we still see self and others as objects or as subjects we still live by commandments only. But if we see the world and its inhabitants as they are—namely in the unity of panentheism—then our actions are ways of *serving the body in its totality.* We have a holistic way of viewing and responding to our neighbor's pain and joy. We begin to act out the truth of what we have grasped: that we are one body, one sole word of God. Furthermore, in loving God we are loving neighbor and vice versa, for our neighbor is in God and God is in neighbor. *Love God more than all things and your neighbor as yourself* (Lk. 10:27). Truly, all creatures do flow outside their origin and yet remain within and this *is certainly amazing.*

Sermon Three: HOW CREATURES ARE GOD AND
HOW GOD BECOMES WHERE CREATURES
EXPRESS HIM

"Do not fear those who kill the body but cannot kill the soul." (Mt. 10:28)*

"Do not fear those who wish to kill you according to the body," for a spirit does not kill a spirit (Mt. 10:28). A spirit gives life to the spirit. Blood and flesh are what wish to kill you. However, what flesh and blood are dies together. The most noble thing about a person is the blood when it is well disposed. At the same time, the worst thing about a person is the blood when it is ill-disposed. If blood triumphs over the flesh, a person is humble, patient, and chaste, and has all the virtues. If, however, flesh triumphs over the blood, a person becomes arrogant, angry, and unchaste, and has all the vices. In this respect Saint John is praised. I cannot praise him more than God has.

Now pay attention! I will now say something that I have never said before. When God created heaven, earth, and all the creatures, he was not accomplishing anything. He had nothing to accomplish, and there was no action *within* him. Then God said: "We wish to make an image like to ourselves" (Gn. 1:27). Creating is something easy; we do it when and as we wish. But whatever I *make*, I make myself and with and in myself, and press my image completely into it. "We wish to make an image like to ourselves." This means not you the Father, or you the Son, or you the Holy Spirit, but rather we in the deliberation of the Holy Trinity—we wish to make an image like to ourselves! When God made human beings, he accomplished a deed like to himself in the soul—his masterful deed and his everlasting deed. This deed was so great that it was nothing other than the soul, and the soul,

---

* "No lite timere eos, qui corpus occidunt, animam autem acccidere non possunt." (Quint, ⚹26)

in turn, was nothing other than God's deed. God's nature, his being, and his Godhead depend on the fact that he *must* be efficacious in the soul. May God be twice blessed! When God is efficacious in the soul, he loves his deed. Now wherever the soul is in which God accomplishes his deed, the deed is so great that this deed is nothing other than love. Again, love is nothing other than God. God loves himself and his nature, his being, and his divinity. In the same love, however, in which God loves himself, he also loves all creatures, not as creatures but he loves the creatures as God. In the same love in which God loves himself, he loves all things.

Now I shall say something I have never said before. God enjoys himself. In the same enjoyment in which God enjoys himself, he enjoys all creatures. With the same enjoyment with which God enjoys himself, he enjoys all creatures, not as creatures, but he enjoys the creatures as God. In the same enjoyment in which God enjoys himself, he enjoys all things.

Now pay attention! All creatures set their course on their highest perfection. Please now perceive what I am about to say, which I swear by my soul is the everlasting truth: I shall repeat what I have never said before: God and his Godhead are as different as heaven and earth. I will go still further: The inner and the outer person are as different as heaven and earth. But God's distance from the Godhead is many thousand miles greater still. God becomes and ceases to become, God waxes and wanes.

Now I shall return to my statement that God enjoys himself in all things. The sun casts its bright light upon all creatures. Whatever the sun casts its light upon draws the sun up into itself; yet as a result the sun does not lose any of its power of illumination.

All creatures want to divest themselves of their *lives* for the sake of their *being*. All creatures are brought into my understanding in that they are spiritually within me. I alone bring all creatures back to God. Look to see how all of you are doing!

Now I shall return to my inner and outer person. I look at the lilies of the field—their bright splendor and their color and all their petals. But I do not see their fragrance. Why is this so? Because the fragrance is in myself. On the other hand, what I say is in myself, and I utter it from within myself. To my outer person all creatures taste like creatures only—like wine and bread and meat. My inner person does not taste things as a creature but rather as a gift of God. My innermost person, however, does not taste a creature as God's gift but rather as something eternal.

I take a basin of water, place a mirror in it, and set it under the sun's orb. The sun then casts its brightness out of its disk and out of its core, and still is not diminished. The reflection of the mirror in the sun is like a sun within the sun, and yet the mirror is what it is. This is the way it is with God. God is in the soul with his nature, his being, and his Godhead, and yet he is not the soul. The reflection of the soul is God in God, and yet the soul is what it is.

God becomes God where all creatures express God: There he becomes "God." When I was still in the core, the soil, the stream, and the source of the Godhead, no one asked me where I wanted to go or what I was doing. There was no one there who might have put such a question to me. But when I flowed out from there, all creatures called out: "God!" I was asked, "Brother Eckhart, when did you go out of the house?" For I had been inside. In this way all creatures speak about "God." And why don't they speak about the Godhead? Everything within the Godhead is unity, and we cannot speak about it. God accomplishes, but the Godhead does not do so and there is no deed within the Godhead. The Godhead never goes searching for a deed. God and the Godhead are distinguished through deeds and a lack of deeds. When I return to "God" and then do not remain there, my breakthrough is more noble than my flowing out. I alone bring all creatures out of their spiritual being into my understanding so that they are one within myself. When I come into the core, the soil, the stream, and the source of the Godhead, no one asks me where I'm coming from or where I've been. No one has missed me in the place where "God" ceases to become.

If anyone has understood this sermon, I wish him well. If no one had been here, I would have had to preach it to this offering box. There are some poor people who will return to their homes and say: "I shall sit down somewhere, eat my loaf of bread, and serve God!" I swear, however, that these people will have to remain in their errors, for they can never attain what these others attain who follow God in poverty and in exile.

COMMENTARY: How God and Godhead Differ/How God Melts Out
from the Godhead When Creation Occurs/How God
Enjoys Creatures and We Are to Do the Same/How
We Love Creatures as God/Three Ways of Enjoying
Creatures

Meister Eckhart sets about exploring more deeply the creative word or
the act of creation by God. First, he asks the question: What changes
take place in the Creator in the act of creation? And his response calls
upon a theological distinction in understanding the Deity that numerous
theologians, including Pseudo-Dionysius, Thomas Aquinas, Gilbert of
Porreta, and others, made before Eckhart. That is the distinction between
God and the Godhead. From our perspective they are *as different as the
earth and the heavens,* for one operates on earth and the other remains
still in the heavens. The Godhead does not act—there *are no deeds
there.* While God does act—this is God the Creator who *becomes God
where all creatures (who are the words of God) express him.* God is relative to creation; the Godhead is not. God the Creator is busy in creating things but God the Godhead—who is end as well as beginning—is
not busy. "God Himself does not rest where He is the beginning of all
being. He rests where He is the end and the beginning of all being."[1]

The distinction between God and Godhead is an effort at the *via
negativa,* the God beyond God. The Godhead tradition is an effort to
restore the transcendence of the name God to an ineffable Deity. It is
also noteworthy that the "Godhead" is feminine gender in both languages in which Eckhart thought. In German it is *Gottheit* and in Latin,
Deitas. At the same time, the word for "God" is masculine in both languages (*Gott* and *Deus,* respectively). Thus "Godhead" is also an effort
to undo an overly masculine gender that a culture and its language have
projected onto God—an effort to go beyond the all-male God.

In striving for images of this God beyond God who is the Godhead,
Eckhart talks of the deep "ground" out of which the Trinity with its Persons flows. But it is a "hidden" ground, an "abyss," a divine "waste-
land." The Godhead is the "divine God" which is the "naked being" of
God.[2] Eckhart is urging his listeners not to settle for what one's culture—
including one's religious culture—takes for granted by the often overly
familiar name of "God." By letting go of this overly used name for
"God" we let God be God and let the Godhead emerge. We also
allow ourselves to experience the deep experience of the Godhead.

One might think that human creation would be capable only of God the Creator. Not so, says Eckhart. The human person is so much like God—Eckhart takes so literally the image of God theme within the human person—that even the Godhead finds a home there. The human person is capable of both God and Godhead. Like the mirror in water that the sun shines upon, *God is in the soul with his nature, his being, and his Godhead.* And yet Eckhart resists all temptations to confuse his teaching with pantheism, for he declares that *Yet God is not the soul. The reflection of the soul is God in God, and yet the soul is what it is.* The soul is a mirror of God's beauty and light but it is no more God than is the mirror the sun. These images further delineate Eckhart's panentheism and theology of inness.

Eckhart applies his theme of flowing out and remaining within and of exiting and entering to the human experience of the God and Godhead and also to the Creator's experience. Of his own experience in exiting from his divine origins in the Godhead, Eckhart confesses that only silence preceded his birth. The Godhead is utterly ineffable and there is no talking, no words, in the Godhead: *Everything within the Godhead is unity, and we cannot speak about it.* But in leaving the Godhead and being born, or as Eckhart puts it, when he *flowed out from there,* all the creatures of the world could stand up and shout: "God!" Why? Because creatures, on seeing creatures, see God. In another sermon Eckhart repeats this same theme. "When I flowed out from God," he says, "all things spoke: God is."[3] *In this way all creatures speak about "God."* God, after all, is the Creator of creatures. And creatures know, however dimly it can be remembered, that they speak for God. Indeed, they are Bibles and revelations about God. "He who knew nothing other than creatures would have no need for thinking of sermons, for each creature is full of God and is a book" about God.[4] Humans, too, actually need the world in order to know God. "If they could know God without the world, the world would never have been created for the soul's sake."[5]

But Eckhart also observes that we are destined to return not only to God but to the Godhead. And when we do, no one will ask any questions, for no one will have missed us. No one is missed in the Godhead, for everyone is there. This return will be even more wondrous, more noble, and more divine than his original flowing out or creation. The return will constitute a genuine breakthrough and we will explore this in greater detail in Sermon Twenty.

What about God's exit and return? Does God suffer a diminution by

becoming a Creator who creates and continually creates and who becomes and not only rests? Eckhart applies the principle of the word that
remains within but flows out to God's relationship to the Godhead. God
remains "entirely within himself, not at all outside himself. But when he
melts, he melts outwards. His melting out is his goodness."[6] Thus Eckhart
uses the image of melting to suggest how things can both go out but
remain within and he explains that God's exiting from the Godhead
was a thousand-mile journey. God's leave-taking is a melting. Creation
is a melting of God's goodness. "Goodness is present when God melts
out and unites with all creatures."[7] The melting and molting that creation
is about is thoroughly good. "All creatures have flowed out of God's
will . . . All good flows from the superabundance of God's goodness."[8]
The key to a worthy love of creatures is never to lose sight of the source
of their beauty and goodness—which source is God. "All the good that
can exist in creatures—all their honey—is gathered together in God."[9]
Eckhart's is not a repressive spiritual psychology but a pleasure-oriented
one. He urges us to imbibe in the goodness and "honey-sweetness" of
creation instead of standing back to judge it. However, he urges us to
enter so fully into creation's beauty, to dive so deep into it, that we get
to the source of this goodness who is God. "Creation, and every work
of God," he declares, "is perfect as soon as it begins. As Deuteronomy
32 says, 'The works of God are perfect.' "[10] We have nothing to fear
from creation. Only from our own shallowness or unwillingness to dive
deep into creation where the Creator creates and is always creating.
Eckhart's is a spirituality of natural or creation ecstasies: God is truly
present in the goodness and honey-sweetness of things and in the experiences of ecstasy we have in communion with such gifts.[11] For if God
loves his own melting and therefore savors it in creation and creation in
it, then we who are images of God are not forbidden such pleasure either.

Eckhart derives his trust in creation from the Scriptures. The text for the
present sermon is as follows:

> Do not be afraid of those who kill the body but cannot kill the
> soul; fear him rather who can destroy both body and soul in
> hell. Can you not buy two sparrows for a penny? And yet not
> one falls to the ground without your Father knowing. Why,
> every hair on your head has been counted. So there is no
> need to be afraid; you are worth more than hundreds of spar-
> rows. (Mt. 10:28–31)

The Father or Creator watches over the little things of creation as well as ourselves and there is a trust, a cosmic trust, between Creator and creature. Thus Eckhart reminds us that *a spirit does not kill a spirit. A spirit gives life to the spirit.* What is life-giving—and surely God's Word called creation is such—is not to be feared but trusted, entered into and listened to.

Creation is more than good. Because it is in God, it is God in the sense that we have seen this expression in the previous sermon. The divine relationship between creatures and their Creator is one of intense love on the part of the Creator—love and joy. *In the same love in which God loves himself he also loves all creatures, not as creatures but as God.* God also enjoys all creatures *not as creatures but as God.* Creatures, the words of God, are not only good but divine.

But whether we experience the creatures as they are divine depends on us. We can be puny-minded and timid in our vision like those Eckhart says will return to their house, *sit down somewhere, eat their loaf of bread, and serve God.* Such persons are pitiful, for they settle for so little. They imagine their physical house to be their home whereas in fact God is their home—and not only God but even the Godhead. Why is it that some people settle for so little when there is so much divinity everywhere? It is because they live lives of entertainment of the outer person alone and never bother to explore the inner and then the innermost person. The outer person enjoys the loaf of bread, a glass of wine, and a slice of meat merely as bread, wine, and meat. This way lies boredom and, one might imagine, obesity. The inner person also enjoys bread, wine, and meat but in that enjoyment does not taste merely the food but also the gift that the food is. Thus the inner person nourishes a sense of gratitude and even wonder at the gift that the ecstacies of creation bless us with. But there is still a third way to experience the gifts of creation. That is the way of *something eternal.* In this tasting, the finiteness of human pleasure is overcome and the grace-filled satisfaction of divine beauty is imbibed. This beauty, the taster knows, will never die. It lasts forever and always tastes delicious.

This analysis of the three levels of consciousness that humans are capable of vis-à-vis creation reveals how for Eckhart the problem with our lives is not our lives but the way we respond to them. We need to pass from mere problem (eating the foods at hand for survival's sake alone) to appreciation and to mystery. As Schürmann puts it, Eckhart "aims at an education of seeing."[12] People who live superficial lives of the outer self alone will never taste eternity in this life—never know what it is to love or to live and thus will always kick at the coming of death, for they will have no firsthand experience that beauty does not die.

So powerful is the consciousness of a person in touch with his or her deepest self that such a person *alone prepares all creatures again for God.* Such a person is capable of a divine act—unifying creation, making cosmos of chaos. *I alone bring all creatures out of their spiritual being into my reason so that they are one within myself.* Such a person knows what God knows: that in God all is one and ought to be one.

Eckhart confesses that, were no one present, he would have been compelled to preach this sermon to the poor box that always stays in church. And, Eckhart confesses, there may be very few who have understood it. Eckhart's humor and capacity to enjoy himself and his work and to laugh at his word, his creation, and his preaching, testify to how free a person he is. He seems to taste of some of the joy and rejoicing that he attributes to God at his creation. If it is true that God enjoys *himself in all things* then Eckhart is trying to practice what he—and God—preach. It is as if Eckhart is not overly attached even to his own work—he lets it flow without, while remaining within—and so, in the last analysis, humor best bespeaks God.

Sermon Four: THE HOLINESS OF BEING

"They died under the sword." (Heb. 11:37)*

We read about the martyrs and how "they died under the sword" (Heb. 11:37). Our Lord said to his disciples: "Happy are you when you suffer something because of my name" (Mt. 5:11; 10:22).

Now the Scripture reads that "they are dead." The expression "they are dead" means first of all that everything we ever suffer in this world and in our lives has an ending. Saint Augustine says that all suffering and every deed of distress have an ending, but the reward that God gives for them is eternal.

Second, we must help one another; our whole life is mortal; and we should not fear all the pain and all the distress that may afflict us because all of it has an ending.

Third, we should regard ourselves as if we were dead so that neither love nor sorrow can disturb us. A master of the spiritual life says: "Nothing can disturb heaven, and this means that an individual is a heavenly person. All things should not mean so much to a person that they can disturb him or her." A master of the spiritual life asks this question: "Since all creatures are void, how is it that they can so easily turn a person from God? Is not the soul in its smallest particle of greater worth than heaven and all creatures?" He answers: "It is due to the fact that people esteem God so little. If people esteemed God as they should, it would be almost impossible for them ever to fall from grace." And it is a good teaching that people should conduct themselves in this world just as if they were dead. Saint Gregory says: "No one can possess God in such rich measure as one who is thoroughly dead to the world."

The fourth lesson, however, is the best of all. It is written of the martyrs that "they are dead." Death, however, gives being to

* "In occasione gladii mortui sunt." (DW I, ☙8)

them. A master of the spiritual life says: "Nature destroys nothing without replacing it with something better." If air becomes fire, this is something better. If, however, air becomes water, this is a destruction and an aberration. If nature can do this, God can do it all the more. He never destroys without giving something better in its place. The martyrs are dead and have lost *life*, but they have received *being*. A master of the spiritual life says that the most noble conditions are being, living, and knowing. Knowing is higher than living or being in this respect that it means knowing, and at the same time it has life and being. On the other hand, living is more noble than being or knowing. An example of this is a tree that has *life* while a stone only has being. If we conceive of being, however, in its pure and unadulterated state, as it is within itself, then being is more noble than knowing or living in this respect, that it has being and at the same time it has knowing and living.

The martyrs have lost life and found being. A master of the spiritual life says that God is like nothing so much as being. To the extent that anything has being it resembles God. A master of the spiritual life says that being is so pure and lofty that everything that God is is being. God is aware of nothing but being; he knows nothing but being; and being is a circle for him. God loves nothing but his being, and he thinks nothing but his being. I say that all creatures are a form of being. A master of the spiritual life says that certain creatures are so close to God, and possess so much of the divine light compressed within them, that they can bestow being on other creatures. But this is not true, since being is so high and pure and closely related to God that no one can bestow it except God alone and in himself. God's most unique existence is being. A master of the spiritual life says that a creature can indeed give *life* to others. This is because everything that *is* is based only on *being*. Being is its first name or appellation. Everything that is defective is a falling off from being. Our whole life should be a form of being. To the extent that our life is being, it is in God. To the extent that our life is enclosed in being, it is related to God. Our life may be very small. But if we grasp it to the extent that it is being, then it is more noble than anything that ever attained life. I am certain that if a soul only knew the smallest object that has being, that soul would never turn away from it, not even for a moment. If we were to know the smallest object as it is in God—say, if we were to know only a flower that has being in God—this object would be more noble than the whole world. To know the smallest object in God—to the extent that it is *being*—is better than it would be for someone to know an angel.

If an angel were to be concerned with knowing creatures, night would fall. Saint Augustine says that if the angels know creatures *without* God, it is twilight. On the other hand, if they know creatures *in* God, it is dawn. When again they know how pure a being God is in himself, it is bright daylight. Human beings should know and understand how noble being is. No creature is so small that it does not long for being. When caterpillars fall from trees, they crawl high on a wall in order to preserve their being. So noble is being. We esteem dying in God so that he may remove us to a being better than life—a form of being in which our life goes on living to the extent that our life becomes being. People should go willingly toward death so that a better form of being will be theirs.

Moreover, I say that wood is better than gold, which is a remarkable statement. A stone is more noble insofar as it has being than God and his Godhead would be without being, that is, insofar as being could be removed from God. This must be an extremely powerful form of life in which dead things become alive and in which death itself becomes life. To God nothing dies, for all things live in him. "They are dead," says the Scripture about the martyrs who have been removed to eternal life—to that life in which life is being. We should be dead right down to our very foundation so that neither love nor sorrow can disturb us. We should know what we must know in its first cause. We can never know a thing correctly in itself if we do not know it in its first cause. No knowledge can be a true knowledge unless it knows something in its first cause. In like manner life can never be complete unless it is brought to its manifest first cause in which life is a form of being that the soul receives when the soul dies to its very foundation. And this foundation is what we live on in that life in which life is a form of being.

A master of the spiritual life points out what prevents us from constantly being in this form of life. He says that we are concerned about time. Whatever is concerned with time is mortal. A master of the spiritual life says that the course of heaven is eternal. Of course, it is true that time comes from heaven, but this happens as a kind of falling away from grace. In its course, on the other hand, heaven is eternal; it knows nothing about time. This is an indication that the soul should be fixed in a pure form of being. The second thing that acts as a hindrance for us is when anything has an opposition within itself. What is meant by opposition? Love and sorrow, white and black—these are in opposition to one another, and opposition has no permanency in *being*.

A master of the spiritual life says that the soul is given to the body so that the soul might be purified. If the soul is separated from the body, it has neither reason nor will. The soul is one; it cannot find the strength to be able to turn to God. The soul finds reason and will, indeed, in its foundation as well as in its roots, but not in its deeds. The soul is purified in the body in that it gathers what was scattered and carried away. When the things that our five senses have carried away return into the soul, the soul has a form of strength in which all becomes one. In addition, the soul is purified by the exercise of the virtues, that is, when it soars into a form of unified life. The purity of the soul lies in the fact that it is purified by a shared form of life. Everything in the lower object that is separate will be united when the soul soars into a form of life in which there is no opposition. When the soul comes into the light of reason, then it knows nothing of opposition. Whatever falls away from *this* kind of light falls down into mortality and dies. A third result of the purity of the soul is that it is not inclined to anything. Whatever is inclined toward another object dies and has no permanency.

We pray to God, dear gentlemen, that he will help us away from a love that is divided to one that is unified. May God help us to this end. Amen.

COMMENTARY: There Is No Need to Fear Death Because When Life Is Being That Is Eternal Life/Being Is God's Word and a Circle/The Nobility of Being/Being Is God

It is typical of Eckhart's recognition of the paradox of all life that he treats the holiness and indeed divinity of being in a sermon about death.

Indeed, being for him transcends death and for people to enter into the fullness of being is to find eternal life, which he says is *that life in which life is being.* Eternal life and death happen simultaneously, but the death that interests Eckhart the most are the deaths we undergo before our departing this earth. "Being dead to the world" is not so simplistic a matter with Eckhart as fleeing the world or as leaving it by hating life or by dying a literal death. Rather, being dead to the world means being open to *that life in which life is being.* Life for Eckhart is meant to be a *form of being,* which means it is a deeply lived experience of the mystery that unites all mystery and does not separate. Life is not a form of grabbing or safeguarding or conquering or boasting, but a *form of being.*

The scriptural context for Eckhart's discussion of the holiness of being and how it transcends death is the scriptural readings used in the liturgy for feasts of the martyrs. Eckhart is preaching from the following biblical texts that warn of the deaths that prophets undergo:

> Happy are you when people abuse you and persecute you and speak all kinds of calumny against you on my account. Rejoice and be glad, for your reward will be great in heaven; this is how they persecuted the prophets before you. (Mt. 5:11–12)

> You will be hated by all men on account of my name; but the person who stands firm to the end will be saved. (Mt. 10:22)

> There is not time for me to give an account of Gideon, Barak, Samson, Jephthah, or of David, Samuel and the prophets. These were men who through faith conquered kingdoms, did what is right and earned the promises . . . They were weak people who were given strength, to be brave in war and drive back foreign invaders. Some came back to their wives from the dead, by resurrection; and others submitted to torture, refusing release so that they would rise again to a better life. Some had to bear being pilloried and flogged, or even chained up in prison. They were stoned, or sawn in half, or beheaded; they were homeless, and dressed in the skins of sheep and goats; they were penniless and were given nothing but ill-treatment. They were too good for the world . . . With so many witnesses in a great cloud on every side of us, we too, then, should throw off everything that hinders us, especially the sin that clings so easily, and keep running steadily in the race we have started . . . In the fight against sin, you have not yet

had to keep fighting to the point of death. (Heb. 11:32–33, 34–38; 12:1, 4)

Eckhart does not succumb to idealizing the saints and heroes of old nor of conjuring up visions of the magnificence of life after death in commenting on these biblical texts. Rather, he takes up the themes of resurrection and of eschatology in which these passages are immersed and he asks: What is eternal life and when is it?

For Eckhart eternal life is now. This is why he is so impatient with the sinful consciousness of time. Time, he says, can separate us from eternal life now, for everyday consciousness of time does not admit that eternity has begun. It is time that *prevents us from constantly being in the form of* (eternal) *life. Whatever is concerned with time is mortal.* Time consciousness amounts to a sinful consciousness for Eckhart, because to cling to time is to refuse to be vulnerable to timelessness, to depth, to awe, to the suspension of time in ecstasy of being, which is where we learn that eternal life has begun. To experience being is to go deeper than time and to transcend time.

Why is this so? Because "being is the word whereby God speaks and addresses all things."[1] Being is God's Word, the word of creation, the word of glory and goodness, the word that flows out but remains within, the word of our inness with God. Being is the Creator's word to creation, for "creation is the giving of being."[2] Being is what Creator and creature have in common, for in their panentheistic bathing all beings swim in God, who encircles them like an ocean. *Being is a circle for God.* Thus, *to the extent that our life is enclosed in being, it is related to God.* It is our responsibility, however, to develop our consciousness and ways of living so as to grasp the depth of being and therefore of God and ourselves. Even if *our life may be very small, if we grasp it to the extent that it is being, then it is more noble than anything that ever attained life.* Being is our entrance to God and to inness, for Eckhart explains elsewhere that "being is that which keeps to itself and does not melt out; indeed it melts inward."[8] Melting inward, it takes us inward to the God within and to the origin out of which we have flowed. Being is our life in God. That is why Eckhart can say that *to know only a flower that has being in God would be more noble than the whole world. To know the smallest object in God—to the extent that it is being—is better than to know an angel.*

Being is bigger than life; it is the substratum for living and for knowing;

it is what carries on after this life. *The martyrs are dead and have lost life, but they have received being.* It is true that *our whole life is mortal,* but our being is not. Why is this? Because being is so close to God, who is a God of the living. "God is life"[4] says Eckhart, for *to God, nothing dies, for all things live in him.* Our life goes on living precisely *to the extent that our life becomes being.* Eckhart says that *God's most unique existence is being,* for being is peculiar to the Creator to give. Creatures pass on life but not being. Only God can do that.

But Eckhart perceives even more to the mystery, indeed the divine mystery, of being. As Schürmann has put it, the "superabundance of the divine being . . . becomes visible in the objects all around" us.[5] Being is indeed all around us but for Eckhart being is more than being. It is the presence of the divine. *God is like nothing so much as being. To the extent that anything has being it resembles God.* Every creature is a lover of his or her own being and knows that the divine is present in this being that it seeks at all costs to preserve. Even caterpillars know this! *When caterpillars fall from trees, they crawl high on a wall in order to preserve their being. So noble is being.* There is no creature that is not noble precisely because it has being and is in God who is being. Even suffering people still can love being.

> All things are pure and noble in God . . . All things beget themselves. Each one begets its own nature . . . so dearly does a creature love its own being, which it has received from God. If someone were to pour forth on a soul in all the tortures of hell, it would still not wish not to be, so dearly does a creature love its own being, which it has received directly from God.[6]

Eckhart's brother Dominican, Thomas Aquinas, had declared that God is being (*Deus est esse*) but Eckhart, inebriated by the experience of being that is "being in God" that he finds all around him, goes much further than Aquinas. He declares that "being is God." All being is "rooted" or made radical in God[7] and God is the fullness of being and the purity of being who includes all being.[8] Eckhart devotes a considerable portion of his philosophical treatise of the Prologues to the Opus Tripartitum to his proposition that "Existence (or being) is God."[9] From a theological point of view, which is Eckhart's approach in this and his other sermons, there is no need for intricate philosophical apologetics.

"What is in God is God" and all being is in God. It has all flowed out
in creation while remaining in the Creator. Indeed, its tendency is to melt
back into its origins in the Creator, as we have seen. Eckhart is inviting
all people to wake up to the nearness of the divine. It is as close as existence or being is.

> God's isness is my life. If my life is God's isness, then God's
> isness is my isness and God's mode is my mode, neither more
> nor less . . . In the book of wisdom we read that "the just
> live eternally, and their reward is in God"—identically so![10]

The only obstacle that can prevent our experiencing and indeed tasting the truth of how being is God is ourselves. Our attitude toward time
can so prevent us, as we have seen. But even more deadly is our attitude of dualism. Dualistic consciousness is the ultimate sinful attitude that
prevents our experiencing the union with being and with God. For *opposition has no permanency in being.*

> The second thing that acts as a hindrance for us is when any-
> thing has an opposition within itself. What is meant by opposi-
> tion? Love and sorrow, white and black—these are in opposi-
> tion to one another, and opposition has no permanency in
> being.

This is why, to experience being and God and being in God, we need
to soar *into a form of unified life.* "He who sees duality or distinction
does not see God," Eckhart declares elsewhere.[11] Dualism blinds us to
the divinity of being that even a flower boasts of. All dualism or opposition gives way to the light of wisdom wherein all is known in a unitive
state of consciousness. Thus it is that Eckhart ends his sermon with a
prayer that we move away *from a love that is divided to one that is
unified.* That way the intuition of our own finitude and mortality with
which he began this discourse on the martyred prophets does not make
us afraid. For the unity he speaks of is a unity of life and death, of this
life and another, of God and us. It is the unity of being, the wholeness
and holiness of being. It is the union of God and his Word. *While all
suffering has an end in this life,* being does not come to an end. It is too
intimate to the never-ending God. It is too holy, too much like God. Thus
nothing can separate us from God—except our own refusal to fall in
love with being.

Sermon Five: HOW ALL CREATURES SHARE AN
EQUALITY OF BEING

"A new commandment I give to you, that you love one
another as I have loved you . . ." (Jn. 13:34)*

In the Holy Gospel written by John, we read that the Lord said
to his disciples: "I am giving you a new commandment, that you
love one another as I have loved you, and this is how people shall
know that you are my disciples, that you have love for one another."

We find here a threefold love which our Lord has and which
we must imitate. The first is natural; the second, graced; the
third, divine. There is, of course, nothing in God which is not
identical with God, but it is from our perception that this love is
threefold, for we have to advance from something good (natural
love) to something better (graced love) and from something better to something even more perfect (divine love). But in God
there is no smaller and greater; he is only the one, simple, pure essential Truth.

The first kind of love which God has and which we should
learn is that which compelled his natural goodness to form all of
creation, for in the images contained in his foreknowledge, God
was pregnant with every creature from all eternity so that all creatures might enjoy with him his goodness. And among all these
creatures he does not love any one more than any other. For insofar as creatures are open to receive him, to that extent God pours
himself out into them. If my soul were as open and expansive as
one of the seraphim, who have nothing in themselves because
they are completely empty and receptive, then God would pour
himself out as fully in me as in that seraphic soul. It is just like
when one draws a circle with many points on the circumference

* "Mandatum novum do vobis, ut diligatis invicem, sicut dilexi vos . . ."
(DW III, #75)

and one point in the center. The central point is equally near and far from all the other points. If one of the little points is to come closer, it must leave its own position on the circumference, for the point in the middle remains where it is. It is the same with the divine being; it seeks nothing outside of itself, remaining constant in itself. If it is to be that a creature receive from this divine being, then it is necessary that the creature be moved from its own self-centeredness. Though we talk about human beings, we are speaking at the same time of all creatures, for Christ himself said to his disciples: "Go forth and preach the gospel to all creatures." God poured his being in equal measure to all creatures, to each as much as it can receive. This is a good lesson for us that we should love all creatures equally with everything which we have received from God. If some are naturally closer to us through relationship or friendship, we should nonetheless respond from divine love with equal friendliness to all because we see all in relationship to that ultimate good which is God. Sometimes I seem to love one person more than another; but I promise, nevertheless, the other person, whom I have never seen, the same friendliness. The only difference is that some people ask for and call forth from me this friendliness more often and therefore I am more likely to give myself more to them. So God loves all creatures equally and fills them with his being. And we should lovingly meet all creatures in the same way. We find this attitude among the pagans, people who came to this sense of love-filled equanimity through the knowing faculties given them by their basic human nature. It is a pagan teacher who tells us that a human being is an animal which is naturally gentle.

The second kind of love is graced or spiritual and it is the love by which God flows into a human or angelic soul in such a way that this creature gifted with reason might be moved out of its own self-centeredness by the brightness of a light outshining all the lights of creation. If my eye, for example, were a light so strong that it could receive the light of the sun in its full strength and thereby be one with it, then my eye would be seeing not only with its own strength but with the light of the sun and the strength which belongs to it. Now it is the same with my reason. If I turn my reason—which is, after all, a light—away from all created things and focus it on God, then my reason, into which God uninterruptedly pours his grace, is enlightened and united with this divinely given love and thereby knows and loves God as he is in himself. Thus we are taught how God is poured out in creatures gifted with reason and how we with our reason draw close to his graced light and can ascend to that light which is God.

The third kind of love is divine and through it we come to know how God from all eternity has given birth to his only begotten Son and continues to give him birth now and into all future eternities—so teaches a master—and so God lies in the maternity bed, like a woman who has given birth, in every good soul which has abandoned its self-centeredness and received the indwelling God. This birth is God's self-knowledge, which from all eternity has sprung from his fatherly heart, wherein lies all his joy. And everything which God desires to bring forth is consumed in his self-knowledge, which is its birth, and he seeks nothing outside of himself. He has all his pleasure in his Son and he loves nothing but his Son and everything which he finds in his Son. For the Son is a light which has burned from all eternity in God's fatherly heart. If we want to come there, we must rise from natural light to the light of grace and thereby grow to that light which is the Son himself. There we will be loved in the Son by the Father with that love which is the Holy Spirit. For the Holy Spirit is the love which has sprung up from eternity and blossomed in an eternal birth. This is the Trinity's third Person, blossoming from the Son to the Father as their mutual love.

A master says that he thinks now and then on the words the angel spoke to Mary: "Hail, full of grace" (Lk. 8:21). What help is it to me that Mary is full of grace, if I am not also full of grace? And what help is it to me that the Father gives birth to his Son unless I too give birth to him? It is for this reason that God gives birth to his Son in a perfect soul and lies in the maternity bed so that he can give birth to him again in all his works. Thus a pagan girl says of Joseph, the son of the patriarch Jacob, "I don't regard him as a human being but as a god, for God shines from his works" (cf. Gn. 39:23).

And so it is that we should be united with the love of the Holy

Spirit in the Son, and with the Son we should know the Father and we should love ourselves in him and him in us with the love with which the Father and Son love each other.

Whoever will be perfect in this threefold love must of necessity have four things. First, a real ability to let go of everything created. Second, a true Lea's life, which means an active life which is stirred in the very depth of the soul by the movement of the Holy Spirit. Third, a true Rachel's life—that is, an inward, meditative disposition. Fourth, an upward-soaring spirit. A student once asked his teacher about the status of an angel. He instructed him, saying: "Go away and sink deeply into yourself until you understand the angel and give yourself up to that with all your being and realize that you consist of nothing else than what you find in that angel. Then you will realize that you are one with the angels. And when you give yourself to this realization with all your being, then it will dawn on you that you are all angel and with all the angels." The student went away and lived deeply and inwardly in himself until he found the truth of all of this. Then he went again to his teacher and thanked him and said: "Everything happened just as you said. As I gave myself over to the essence of the angel and soared into its being, I realized that I was all angel with all the angels." Then the teacher said: "And now, if you would advance even further into the primordial source of being, then miracle upon miracle will be performed in your soul." For as long as souls soar and still receive everything through creatures, they have not yet come to rest. But when souls soar to God, then they receive in the Son and with the Son from the Father everything which God desires to offer. May God help us to soar from one love to the other and finally to be united with him and remain so for all eternity. Amen.

COMMENTARY: Creation as Grace/The Equality of Being/Preaching the Gospel to *All* Creatures of the Cosmos/Soaring into the Primordial Source of Being/Cosmic Consciousness/Loving All Creatures Equally

Meister Eckhart has confessed that he finds the world "amazing." He is amazed by the grace-filledness of creation. Indeed, he calls creation "the first grace," "the grace of creation," "the gift of creation," and even "gratia gratis data" or grace gratuitously given.[1] He is amazed by the beauty and fullness of creation and above all by the ever-present law of creation, that what flows out remains within. Eckhart does not counsel those seeking a deeper spiritual consciousness to put down creation or to separate themselves violently from it, for he is aware that human beings are very much a part of the *circle* that being and all creation is. Rather, he advises us to alter our way of seeing creation, to alter our consciousness. Previously, in Sermon Three, he spoke of the person who tastes food and wine merely as food and wine; and the person who tastes food and wine as a gift of God; and of the person who tastes food and wine as intimations of eternity. Here too he speaks of a threefold path of consciousness. Only here he compares our love of creatures to that of God. God, he says, loves creatures first in a natural way. We cannot afford to skip over this path of spirituality as so many ascetic and fundamentalist spiritualists would have us do. *The first kind of love which God has and which we should learn is that which compelled his natural goodness to form all creation.* We need, as Eckhart insists, to *learn* this love of nature and creatures for our own stodginess or cynicism or our culture's ill-treatment of creation or even our bad theologies all may have contributed to our being tainted in our love of what is. Creation, after all, flows very much from the goodness that God is, for God created so *that all creatures might enjoy with him his goodness.*

The second kind of love with which God loves creation and with which we can learn to love creation is graced love. This is a new dimension of union between Creator and creature that takes place with those beings who have the fullest potential for consciousness, namely humans and angels. This kind of love goes beyond "self-centeredness" and receives enlightenment from a divinely given love. In such an experience we *know and love God as he is in himself.*

The third kind of love is *divine* and is less our going out to know God than it is God's indwelling being accepted by us. Here God gives birth within us. Through this kind of love we *come to know how God from all eternity has given birth to his only begotten Son and continues to give him birth now and into all future eternities . . . in every good soul which has abandoned its self-centeredness and received the indwelling God.* It is a divine love because it is creative and birth-oriented and because it is *God's self-knowledge.* It alone gives God full joy and it is shareable with us. This is the way God loves, namely, all creatures within the circle

of being of which the Creator is the center point. For beings to participate more fully in the divine love and energy, they must, like points on a
circumference, *be moved from their own self-centeredness.* Creatures
are invited to travel deeper and deeper toward the center or vortex of
this circle where the divine love radiates. This traveling, however, is not
a climbing but a *sinking. Go away and sink deeply into yourself,* we are
urged. Where does the journey of sinking stop? Not short of the *primordial source of being,* says Eckhart. Our sinking into the center is a sinking
into the divine source of all being. It is a panentheistic plunge.

Eckhart reminds us of another characteristic of God's love for creatures that ought to be ours as well. That is the equality of love that God
shares with each and every being. *Among all these creatures God does
not love any one more than any other.* Elsewhere he declares that "in
God no creature is more noble than another."[2] Why is it that God is so
scrupulously egalitarian in the love for creatures? It is because God is
truly *in* all creatures on an equal basis with the differences being attrib-
utable solely to the creature's capacity to receive. *God poured his being
in equal measure to all creatures, to each as much as it can receive.* Divine love is a cosmic love that extends to all creatures equally. This law
of equality of love Eckhart applies to ourselves when he urges that *this is
a good lesson for us that we should love all creatures equally with everything which we have received from God.* True love demands equality,
Eckhart points out elsewhere. "There can be no love, however, where
love does not find equality or does not create equality."[3] Coercion is
the relationship between unequals but love is the relationship among
equals.

> Love will never be anything else than there where equality and
> unity are. Between a master and a servant he has there is no
> peace because there is no real equality. A wife and a hus-
> band are not alike but in love they are equal. This is why the
> Scripture is quite right in saying that God has taken the
> woman from the rib and side of the man—neither therefore
> from the head nor from the feet for where there are two, there
> we find deficiency. Why? Because the one is not the other, for
> this "not" that makes the difference is nothing other than bit-
> terness, precisely because there no peace is available.[4]

It is because all things are equal in God that our love, like God's, is to
open to such friendship with all. When we talk about loving some peo-

ple in our lives more than we do others, what we are really saying, says
Eckhart, is that love is a twofold energy of both receiving and giving
and that, in extending our love energy outward, some persons return it
to us more readily than others. If some are naturally closer to us through
relationship or friendship, we should nonetheless respond from divine
love with equal friendliness to all because we see all in relationship to
that ultimate good which is God.

> Sometimes I seem to love one person more than another; but I
> promise, nevertheless, the other person, whom I have never
> seen, the same friendliness. The only difference is that some
> people ask for and call forth from me this friendliness more
> often and therefore I am more likely to give myself more to them.

It is the *calling forth of friendliness* that varies among people but not the
equality with which we extend our friendship.

Eckhart does not rest content in urging us to a consciousness of
equality with all people. He insists that our equality is not with humans
alone but with all animals and indeed all beings of the cosmos. He urges
us to a cosmic consciousness and a cosmic love. This outward orienta-
tion of Eckhart's toward all of creation bathed in God's grace is especially noteworthy since it is set in the context of a scriptural passage that
many Christian mystics would reduce merely to a kind of divine tête-à-
tête with the individual human soul. Ekhart will have none of such sentimentalism, however, and interprets the following passage in light of his
cosmically reaching, creation-centered spirituality. Following is the scriptural passage which Eckhart was using for this sermon:

> "My little children,
>   I shall not be with you much longer.
>   You will look for me,
>   and, as I told the Jews,
>   where I am going,
>   you cannot come.
>   I give you a new commandment:
>   love one another;
>   just as I have loved you,
>   you also must love one another.

By this love you have for one another,
everyone will know that you are my disciples." (Jn. 13:33–35)

It is in preaching from this text that Eckhart examines this mode of love with which Jesus loved ("just as I have loved you") and concludes that Jesus' love is a cosmic one that extends equally to all creatures. Eckhart says: *Though we talk about human beings, we are speaking at the same time of all creatures, for Christ himself said to his disciples: "Go forth and preach the gospel to all creatures."* For Eckhart, then, true love of creation means love of all creation equally, the way God loves all creation. "A flea, to the extent that it is in God, is nobler than the highest angel is himself. Now in God all things are equal and are God himself."[5] To be in God is to be God in an equal manner. "The highest angel, the mind, and the gnat have an equal model in God."[6] Only a consciousness of our equality with all things results in authentic *gentleness* and *peace*. "The greatest blessing in heaven and on earth is based on equality," Eckhart tells us.[7]

It is because of this equality of being that we share with all creatures that we can learn from all creatures instead of lording it over them. Eckhart tells us, for example, to learn the following lesson from a dog. A dog can instruct humans how to love one another.

When I came to this convent yesterday, I saw sage and other plants on a tomb, and I thought to myself: here lies someone's dear friend, that is why this parcel of ground is so dear to him. If someone has a friend whom he truly loves, he will also love everything that belongs to him; likewise, what is repugnant to his friend, he will not love. Take for example a dog, which is only an animal without intelligence. He is so faithful to his master that he hates everything that can harm his master, while to his master's friends he extends friendliness without regard for wealth or poverty. Much more, if there were a poor blind man with great affection for the dog's master, the dog would love him more than a king or an emperor who would dislike his master. The truth is that, if the dog could be unfaithful to his master with one half of his being, he would hate himself with the other half.[8]

Animals, Eckhart observes, do not love half-heartedly. Elsewhere he presents another example of learning from a dog and from a child but in this case the learning is at the deep level of shared energies and shared being.

> If I was alone in a desert and feeling afraid, I would like to have a child with me, for then my fear would disappear and I would be strengthened—so noble, so full of pleasure, and so powerful is life itself. If I could not have a child with me, and if I had at least a live animal with me, I would be comforted. Therefore, let those who bring about great wonders in big, black books take an animal—perhaps a dog—to help them. The life within the animal will give them strength. For equality gives strength in all things.[9]

This excellent testimony to the "power of life in itself" and to the equality that "gives strength in all things" is Eckhart's memorable way of underlining the importance of the equality of all creatures that derives from their all being in God and in the divine circle of being. I once shared this story of Eckhart's with a young minister, who told me this story in return. He said that he and his wife bought a house very cheaply, since there had been a murder in it during its previous occupancy. Their first night in the house they could not sleep because of fear and bad vibes in the room. Finally, they went and got their little baby, placed it down between them in the bed, and slept soundly that night and thereafter. The baby blessed them and their new home—*so noble, so full of pleasure, and so powerful is life in itself.*

One reason we have so much in common with other creatures is that our origins are the same. "When the Father engendered all creatures, he brought me forth. I emanated together with all creatures and yet I remain within, in the Father."[10] To return to our roots or origins is to make contact with our common ancestry, thus with the sisterhood and brotherhood of all beings. "I have sensory perception in common with all creatures."[11] In the circle that being is, *the central point is equally near and far from all the other points.* This is the *primordial source of being* into which we are invited to plunge. Eckhart resists all temptation to human chauvinism and even animate chauvinism. For him, all of creation partakes of divine equality. "Creatures were able to receive equality with God—indeed, as much equality as if he had emptied himself."[12] Eckhart's consciousness extends to the cosmos itself: "I, for my part, say that the heavens in their movement strive for the same end as matter . . .

the end sought by the heavens in their movement is the existence of the
universe, or the conservation of the universe."[13] For Eckhart, there are
lessons in spirituality to be learned from the planets and stars:

> There are various things we should know about the heavens
> above: that they are firm, pure, all-embracing, and fruitful.
> These same qualities should be found in human beings, for
> each of us should be a heaven in which God dwells. Thus if
> the heavens are firm, we should be firm. What happens to us
> should not change us.

The heavens teach us the vastness of our love and the creativity of our
love.

> The heavens . . . surround everything and contain everything
> in themselves. This too is something human beings can obtain
> in love, that they are able to contain everything in themselves
> —friends and foes alike. Friends are loved in God; enemies
> for the sake of God; and everything created is loved with ref-
> erence to God, our Lord, insofar as it furthers our progress to
> him.
>   The heavens are fruitful for they are helpful to every en-
> deavor. The heavens work more than a carpenter when he
> builds a house.[14]

As was typical of the medieval's interest in the interrelationship of
microcosm and macrocosm, Eckhart looks at the cosmic direction of nature. "Nature, looking after the good of the universe, intends the generation of everything and destruction in order to assist generation. Its first
intention is the preservation of the universe."[15] Given this cosmic dimension to Eckhart's spiritual consciousness, it is no wonder that Schürmann
can declare that "Eckhart actually abolishes the methodological distinction between theology, anthropology, and cosmology."[16] Eckhart's is not
a piecemeal vision but a holistic one. This is because he believed that
we are to love as God loves, and God loves holistically. So *God loves
all creatures equally and fills them with his being. And we should lovingly meet all creatures in the same way. Meet all creatures*, he is urging
us. Open up and wake up. Learn what it means to be in God with all
other beings that are in God. In so doing we are exposed not only to
what has been—our common origins—or to what is—our common isness

—but also to what is to be. For the cosmos contains a future thrust to it as well for Eckhart. What is this future? It is an assimilation of all things to God. "Each being . . . of the created universe strives, in as much as it is, to cooperate in the assimilation of all things to God."[17] This assimilation of all things to God is similar to Teilhard de Chardin's vision, and it means that we "become all things as God is."[18] We are destined to become what we already are. Truly, our flowing out is a remaining within.

This sermon is deeply feminist and might very likely have been preached to the Beguines and from ideas Eckhart derived from the Beguines and other women he listened to. In it he calls God a pregnant woman on three occasions, recalling the same image from the Scriptures (see Is. 42:14). God *lies in the maternity bed, like a woman who has given birth,* Eckhart observes. Because God wants to keep giving birth, God remains *in the maternity bed so that he can give birth to him again in all his works.* God is a mother as well as a father. Parent of all that is, birther of all being. God's work is to give birth to being. He tells us to imitate Mary, Lea, and Rachel but he avoids all pedestal pieties and Mariolatry when it comes to invoking Mary's example. He enlists Mary as the first of God's creatures to demonstrate how literally we can all give birth to God. *What help is it to me that Mary is full of grace, if I am not also full of grace?* He drives the lesson of religious models or saints home to his listeners: Don't pine after others who had God's favor; find God's favor yourself. How does one do this? By *letting go* and *sinking deeply into yourself* where awareness of the equality of all being will make itself known to you. *Then it will dawn on you that you are all angel and with all the angels.*

This marks the way in which we love one another as we have been loved. That is, we learn to love as God loves. And we move *from one love to another* because our perception demands it. However, in God there is only the one love that is natural, graced, and divine altogether. For *in God there is no smaller and greater. There is only the best.* There is only the one commandment, "that you love one another as I have loved you."

Sermon Six: THE GREATNESS OF THE HUMAN
PERSON

"Saint Paul says . . ."*

Saint Paul says: "Take Christ inside yourselves"—that is to say,
grasp him interiorly (cf. Rm. 13:14). As we are emptied of ourselves, we take within us Christ, God, bliss and holiness. When
people come along telling unusual stories, you tend to believe
them, but Paul makes great promises and you believe him with
difficulty. He promises you (when you are stripped of your ego)
God, bliss and holiness. This is astonishing—we strip away our
egos, empty ourselves of our very selves, and then take in Christ,
holiness and bliss—and we become greater than ever. Now the
prophet is astonished over two things. First, he marvels over
God's activities with the stars, the moon and the sun. But,
second, he marvels at something concerning the soul—namely,
that God has done so many great things with it and on its behalf
and still continues to do them, for God does what he wants for
the soul's sake. He does countless great things for the soul's sake
and is fully occupied with it and this because of the greatness in
which the soul is made (see Ps. 8:2ff.). Note that the concern is
with how great the soul is. I form a letter according to the image
of that letter in me, in my soul, but not according to my soul itself. It is very much the same with God. God made everything according to the image that he had of all things, but not according
to himself. He made some things in a very special way according
to what flows from himself—like goodness, wisdom, and whatever
qualities we attribute to God. But the soul is what God made,
not only according to the image which is in him or even according to what flows from himself and what we humans can express
of him. The soul is what is truly made in God's own image, in
the image of all that he is according to his nature, according to

* "Sankt Paulus spricht . . ." (DW I, ⅺ24)

his Being, and according to his outflowing, yet remaining within works, and according to the ground where he remains himself, where he gives birth to his only begotten Son and from which the Holy Spirit blossoms. It is according to this outflowing, yet remaining within works, that God has made the soul.

It is the rule of nature for everything that the higher always flows into the lower, so long as the lower is turned to the higher. For the higher never receives from the lower; it is always the other way around. Now since God is above the soul, God is always flowing into the soul and can never escape the soul. But the soul can easily escape God. As long, however, as a person remains under God, that person receives the unmediated divine influx purely from God and stands under nothing else, neither under fear nor love nor suffering nor under anything other than God. So cast yourself totally and completely under God and you will receive the divine influence in its total purity. How does the soul receive this from God? The soul receives from God not as a stranger, as, for example, the air receives light from the sun. The air receives as a stranger. But the soul does not receive God in the condition of a stranger still under God, for whatever is under something else has some strangeness with reference to it and some distance, too. But the masters say that the soul receives as a light from light, for in this way there is neither strangeness nor distance.

There is something in the soul which is only God and the masters say it is nameless, having no proper name of its own. It is and has no existence of its own since it is neither this nor that, neither here nor there. For it is what it is in another and that in this. For what it is, that is in that, and that in this, because that flows into this and this into that and herein (in this something in the soul) lies the meaning of Paul in saying that you should unite yourself to God in bliss. For herein the soul takes its whole life and being and from this source it draws its life and being, for this is totally in God. That other part of the soul, however, is here on the outside and therefore the soul is always in God according to this inner part, lest it carry it outward or quench it.

A master says that this is so present to God that it can never turn from God and God is always present and inward to it. I say that God was eternally in this without interruption and that the human person is one with God in this. Nor is this a matter of grace, for grace is a creature, but here there is no creature to make, for in the ground of the divine Being where the three Persons are one Being, there is the soul one with God, according to this ground. So you might say that all things and God too are yours. That is to say—empty yourself of your ego and of all things and of all that you are in yourself and consider yourself as what you are in God.

The masters say that human nature has nothing to do with time and is completely unmovable and much more inward and present to a person than the person is to himself or herself. And this is why God took on a human nature and united it with his Person. Thus the human nature became God, for God assumed the pure human nature and not a human person. So if you want to be this same Christ and God, empty yourself of everything which the eternal Word did not assume. The eternal Word did not assume a human being, so empty yourself of everything which is purely personal and peculiarly you and assume human nature purely, then you will be the same in the eternal Word as human nature is in him. For your human nature and that of the divine Word are no different—it's one and the same. What it is in Christ, it is in you. Therefore, I said to my audience in Paris that in the just person there is fulfilled what the Holy Spirit and the prophets said about Christ. For if you are just, then everything which is in the Old and New Testaments will be fulfilled in you.

How can righteousness be yours? There are two ways of understanding that, according to the prophet's word, which says: "In the fullness of time was the Son sent" (Ga. 4:4). There are two meanings to this "fullness of time." For a thing is full when it is at its end, as each day is full in its evening. Therefore, the time is full when all time falls from you. The second meaning of fullness of time is when time comes to its end—that is, in eternity. For in eternity all time has its end and there is neither before nor after. There everything is present and new, everything which is there. And there you have in a present vision everything which ever happened or ever will happen. There is no before or after, there in eternity: everything is present and in this ever-present vision I possess everything. That is the "fullness of time" and that means that I am just and so I am truly the proper Son and Christ. God help us that we come to this "fullness of time." Amen.

COMMENTARY: The Human Soul Is So Truly Made in God's Image That God Cannot Escape It/Where We Are Totally in God—the Spark of the Soul/How the Fullness of Time Is Experienced Now Where Eternity Is Newness and Nowness

Eckhart has marveled at the greatness of creation, at its grace-filledness, at the equality of all being in God, at the fact that all beings are words —indeed books—about God. In this sermon he turns more specifically to the human creation. He marvels at *the greatness in which the soul is made* by God, as does the psalmist, who sang this hymn to the God of creation:

> I look up at your heavens, made by your fingers,
> at the moon and stars you set in place—
> ah, what is man that you should spare a thought for him,
> the son of man that you should care for him?
>
> Yet you have made him little less than a god,
> you have crowned him with glory and splendor,
> made him lord over the work of your hands,
> set all things under his feet,
>
> sheep and oxen, all these;
> yes, wild animals too,
> birds in the air, fish in the sea
> traveling the paths of the ocean.
>
> Yahweh, our Lord,
> how great your name throughout the earth! (Ps. 8:3–9)

While all creation has flowed out from God according to the image that God held of things in the creative mind and while wisdom and goodness have been created *in a very special way according to what flows from himself,* still the soul is yet greater and more God-like. For it alone is *what is truly made in God's own image, in the image of all that he is according to his nature, according to his Being and according to his outflowing yet remaining within works, and according to the ground where he remains in himself.* Eckhart is nearly beside himself with the implications of our having been made in the image of God and not only according to the image God had. Why is the soul so God-like? Because it is *truly made in God's own image,* it shares the divine *nature according to his Being, to his works, to the ground where he remains himself and where he gives birth and where the Holy Spirit blossoms.* This theme of the Godliness of human creation in particular—"you have made him little less than a god"—is returned to time and again in Eckhart's sermons:

> From the very moment of its creation God has endowed the soul, out of the kindness and love he feels for it, with a divine light inasmuch as he could accomplish things with pleasure in the likeness of himself.[1]

> When God made creatures, they were so small and narrow that he could not operate in any of them. He made the soul, however, so like and similar in appearance to himself that he could give himself to the soul.[2]

> Our Lord teaches us . . . how noble people have been created in their nature, how divine is the state to which they can rise through grace and, in addition, how people are to reach that point. A large part of the Holy Scripture touches upon these words.[3]

> People are created in the image of God . . . they are of God's lineage and God's family.[4]

People are the new temple:

> This temple, which God wished to rule over powerfully according to his own will, is the soul of a person. God has formed and created the soul very like himself, for we read that our Lord said: "Let us make human beings in our own image" (Gn. 1:26). And this is what he did. So like to himself did he make the soul of a person that neither in the kingdom of heaven nor on earth among all the splendid creatures that God created in such a wonderful way is there any creature

that resembles God as much as does the soul of a human
being alone.[5]

Humanity, then, is the Creator's masterpiece, a likeness of the divinity
that has no parallel.

> The soul is destined for such a great and noble good . . . The
> soul must always hurry to this goal, that it can by every avail-
> able means come to the eternal good that is God—for it is for
> that the soul was created.[6]

Rather than concentrating on original sin, Eckhart, in true creation theology tradition, waxes ecstatic about the divine likeness that the human
person bears, as he said above, "from the very moment of its creation."
He explains that an image is recognizable by four elements.

> An image is not of itself, nor is it for itself. It rather springs
> from the thing whose reflection it is and belongs to it with all
> its being. It owes nothing to a thing other than that whose
> image it is; nothing else is at its origin. An image takes its
> being immediately from that of which it is the image and has
> one sole being with it, and it is that same being.[7]

This would mean that in the case of human beings, we are made not of
ourselves but for God, of whom we are the image, and that we belong
to God "with all our being"; that only God is at our origin; that our
being comes immediately from God; and that we are "one sole being"
with God. Thus Eckhart further elaborates in this sermon on how, between the soul and God, *there is neither strangeness nor distance.* Furthermore, though *the soul can easily escape God, God is always flowing
into the soul and can never escape the soul.* We are to remain *under
God* as in standing under a waterfall to receive the *unmediated divine
influx purely from God.* For this reason, in the long run, "the person who
hopes to escape God . . . cannot escape him. All hiding places reveal
God; the person hoping to escape runs into his lap."[8] Our nearness to
God is the nearness of light to light. To flee God is to kill God, who so
loves the divine image in us.

> Know now that God loves the soul so dearly that, if we took
> away from God his love for the soul, we would take away his

life and his being. We would kill God insofar as we could say such a thing. For the love with which God loves the soul is the same love in which the Holy Spirit blows, and this same love *is* the Holy Spirit. Since God loves the soul so dearly, the soul must be also something just as great.[9]

Eckhart admits that the soul, like God, is ineffable. No one can name what the soul is. "God who is without name—he has no name—is ineffable; and the soul in its ground is likewise ineffable: just as ineffable as he is."[10] We ought to experience the soul "in its transparency" like we do God instead of trying to name it. "He who wants to name the soul such as it is in itself, in its simplicity, in its clarity, and in its nakedness, will find no name to fit."[11] The soul, being divine, is unnameable. "When we speak of divine things, we have to stammer, because we have to express them in words."[12]

And yet Eckhart finds two ways of identifying elements of the soul, if you will. The first is the power of the soul to reason. "Reason is the temple of God," he declares. "God dwells nowhere more authentically than in his temple, in reason."[13] Human beings, Eckhart contends, have a "little spark" of this reason in the ground of their soul so that God can truly be at home in the temple which is human beings. "Here God's ground is my ground and my ground is God's ground."[14] Eckhart often calls this "spark of the soul" a "something," as in the sermon we are considering:

> There is something in the soul which is only God and the masters say it is nameless, having no proper name of its own. It is and has no existence of its own since it is neither this nor that, neither here nor there. For it is what it is in another and that in this.

Thus, this spark of the soul exists in God. It overlaps the divine soul and the divine reason. It is where human spirit and divine spirit become one, for here is the union of the point in the circle of being and the circle's center. *Herein the soul takes its whole life and being and from this source it draws its life and being, for this is totally in God.*

Here lies the inness of our being in God. It is here that we are most God-like and God is most imaged in us: "In this spark, as the higher part of the spirit, is located the image of God that the mind is."[15] In the soul, Eckhart maintains, there is "something like a spark of divine nature, a divine light, a ray, an imprinted picture of the divine nature."[16]

It is important to point out that Eckhart was not a Cartesian or a rationalist. Reason as the temple of God does not mean one side of the brain that is analytical or the domain of academic footnotes and scholarship. As Schürmann puts it, what is meant by the Thomist concept of *mens* is "a fundamental disposition to know and to love, and the spiritual vestige of the divine life in man."[17] That is why a better word than reason, suggests Schürmann, might be "spirit." The reason being spoken of here is an "interior knowledge by intuition." It is intuitive reason, not discursive reason. Caputo puts it this way: "When Eckhart speaks of the 'little spark' of reason, he does not refer to the faculty of discursive reasoning, the power that moves from premises to conclusions and which uses concepts and representations."[18] Rather, Eckhart speaks of a "power that has nothing at all in common with anything else," one that "is so high and noble that it grasps God in his own naked being."[19] This power is the "ground of freedom"[20] which "apprehends God naked, as he is, divested of goodness and being. Goodness is a garment under which God is hidden,"[21] but intuitive reason needs no such intermediaries. It is in this ground of the mind that, at their root, people are divine. But we have to make contact with this divine spark by emptying ourselves or letting go. And then we will know the unity that already exists.

> Then you will be the same in the eternal Word as human nature is in him. For your human nature and that of the divine Word are no different—it's one and the same . . . So if you want to be this same Christ and God, empty yourself . . .

If we fail to empty ourselves and thus sink into the truth of the divine image and its spark in us, then in this way too we can "kill God" insofar as we put the spark itself to death, quenching the divine flame.

> There is in the soul a something in which the soul dwells in God. However, if the soul turns outward to other objects, it will die, and God will die for the soul. Of course, God does not die to himself, but he rather continues to live in himself.[22]

God is a fire and we have within us, in our core, sparks of that fire. "This spark is so closely related to God that it is a unique indivisible unity, and bears within itself the images of all creatures, image without

image, and image above image."[23] Thus, at our core, we are as free as
God is, free even of images or free to become all possible images, since
"God is in the ground of the soul with all his divinity."[24]

Just as Schürmann has recommended the term *spirit* as preferable to
intellect or reason for translating Eckhart's term *mens*, I would suggest
that imagination might be the best translation. First, because the term
imaginatio did not mean in medieval psychology anything like its meaning today and so Eckhart could not use it then; and second, because in
trying the impossible task of naming what is most God-like in humans,
Eckhart does make clear that creativity and birthing are the essence of
God. Thus, if imagination is the term we use today to name the womb of
creativity where images are born and where images are let go of, then
that term may come the closest to what Eckhart is trying to say. It is our
capacity to give birth to images that parallels God's capacity to create;
this image-birthing is a source of our freedom, for in birthing images we
must choose some and reject others; and the images we choose enkindle
a kind of fire that enlightens self and society.

To be in touch with our own ground, then, is to be in touch with God.
To touch the spark is to touch the fire. What does this kindling between
the divine fire and our divine spark bring about? One of its fruits is a
new sense of time. It is eternity, for "God is eternity." It is, in theological
terms, the new times, the Messianic times, the end times, the last times. It
is realized eschatology. It is the sense of time that the Scriptures speak of
in the two citations around which Eckhart has constructed his sermon.

> Besides, you know "the time" has come: you must wake up
> now: our salvation is even nearer than it was when we were
> converted. The night is almost over, it will be daylight soon—
> let us give up all the things we prefer to do under cover of the
> dark; let us arm ourselves and appear in the light . . . Let your
> armor be the Lord Jesus Christ. (Rm. 13:11–12, 14)

This Pauline exhortation constitutes the text from which Eckhart first wrote
this sermon. But he adds another:

> When the appointed time came, God sent his Son, born of a
> woman, born a subject of the Law, to redeem the subjects of
> the Law and to enable us to be adopted as sons. The proof
> that you are sons is that God has sent the Spirit of his Son into

our hearts: the Spirit that cries, "Abba, Father," and it is this
that makes you a son, you are not a slave any more. (Ga.
4:4–7)

It is evident that Eckhart gets his theme that traces our likeness to God,
our likeness to Christ, from these scriptural passages—*what it is in Christ
it is in you*—and the new sense of time based on the *fullness of time.*

Eckhart calls this "fullness of time" *eternity.* What most characterizes
this eternity that we can now experience is newness and the presence of
newness now.

> There everything is present and new, everything which is there.
> And there you have in a present vision everything which ever
> happened or ever will happen. There is no before or after,
> there in eternity; everything is present and in this ever-present
> vision I possess everything.

This same theme of realized eschatology, of the fullness of time now,
is developed at length by Eckhart elsewhere. To begin with, he defines
what he means by eternity. "What is eternity? Pay attention. Eternity is
the peculiarity that being and being young are one. For eternity would
not be eternity if it could become new and were not continually the
same."[25] Eternity to Eckhart is the unending state of youthfulness,
freshness, newness, and vitality. It belongs uniquely to God, though by
God's gratuitous gift-giving we too can share in eternity in this life.
"Whatever God gives is always prepared. Its preparation is now new
and fresh, and proceeds fully in an eternal now."[26] For "both newness
and life are proper to God."[27] One reason why there is an eternal now
is that such is God's conception of time and creation.

> God so created all things that he nevertheless always creates
> in the present. The act of creation does not fade into the past
> but is always in the beginning and in process and new.[28]

To return to our source and our origins is to return to this beginning that
is eternally young, eternally now. "New means inexperienced, close to
some beginning. God is the beginning and if we are united with him, we
become 'new' again . . . God's works have to be understood as timeless, as being created without effort."[29] Everything God does is new.

The Book of Wisdom says: "He created, so that all things might have being" (1:14). Now existence is the beginning, the first, and the source of all things. From this it is clear that every work of God is new. Wisdom says: "remaining in himself, he makes all things new" (2:27). Revelations says: "Behold, I make all things new" (21:5). So it is said in Isaiah: "I am the first and the last" (44:6). He so created, therefore, that he nevertheless always creates: for what is in the beginning, and whose end is the beginning, always arises, always is being born, always has been born.[30]

Newness is integral to our creation and our re-creation. "All things . . . are timelessly new in God. Of this Saint John speaks in the Apocalypse: 'The one who sat upon the throne said: "I shall make all things new"' " (Rv. 21:5). All things are new with the Son, for "he is born today from the Father just as if he had never been born."[31] God's creation with its newness never stops. "Here the end is the beginning, the completed is always starting and the born is always being born. This is how God created all things: he does not stop creating, but he forever creates and begins to create."[32] God is new and all God does is new and we too in our godliness are new. "Every action of God is new and 'he makes all things new' (Ws. 7:27)."[33] Our contact with God renews us.

> Existence . . . does not grow old, nor is it changed . . . The psalmist says: "Your youth will be renewed like an eagle's" . . . Thus God, who always operates and always is new. Therefore every being is new insofar as it is from God and has newness from no other thing. By ascending to God, by drawing near to God, by running back to God, by returning to God—all things are made new, all things become good, are purged, cleansed, made holy. On the other hand, by receding from God they grow old, they perish, they sin as Paul says: "The wages of sin are death" (Rm. 6:23).[34]

God is "novissimus," or the "most new thing there is," Eckhart declares, since God is the Alpha and Omega, the origin of all being and therefore of all newness. "Everything is made new when it receives being—through being itself and in being itself all things are made new." When God bestows being, God bestows newness. To be renewed is to return to our Godly origins, which are resplendent in newness.[35]

God is essentially young or eternal. But the soul, made so perfectly in God's image, is of the same ilk.

> The soul is as young as it was when it was created. Old age concerns only the soul's use of the bodily senses . . . My soul is as young as it was when it was created. Yes, and much younger! I tell you, it would not surprise me if it were younger tomorrow than it is today![86]

Indeed, for Eckhart, one is worthy of shame if one is not younger every day. How does one grow in youthfulness? By letting go of everyday time and entering into the eternal now. "To follow and imitate God is eternity," he advises.[87] God is always wanting to share the divine newness with us. "God gives himself ever new to the soul in a constant becoming. He does not say: 'It has become' or 'It will become,' but: it is always new and fresh in incessant becoming."[88] Everyday time is shattered when the human soul, capable of the eternal now, meets God, who dwells in the eternal now.

> God is in this power as in the eternal now. Were the spirit at every moment united with God in this power, people could never grow old . . . People dwell in the light of God; therefore there is in them neither suffering nor the sequence of time but an eternity which remains the same.[39]

Thus Eckhart can indeed identify the Messianic times with the fullness of time that occurs when all time falls from you. Such a new time gives us new visions of the end time already begun. For those who are ready, all has been prepared.

> There everything is present and new, everything which is there. And there you have in a present vision everything which ever happened or ever will happen . . . everything is present and in this ever-present vision I possess everything.

Possessing everything—there lies the magnificence and God-likeness of the human person. An amazing creation indeed, this word that flows out but remains within.

Sermon Seven: THE BIGNESS OF THE HUMAN PERSON

"The Spirit of the Lord fills the whole world." (Ws. 1:7)*

One scholar says: All creatures bear the imprint of God's nature, from which they emanate, so that they might act according to it. Creatures flow out in two different ways. The first manner of emanation has to do with rootedness, as roots bring forth a tree. The second manner of emanation is created through a bond; it is a twofold emanation, as God's is. First there is the emanation of the Son from the Father through birth. The second occurs through a bond with the Holy Spirit; it is a bond of love, and proceeds from Father and Son who love themselves in the Holy Spirit. All creatures manifest their flowing out from God's nature through their actions. A Greek scholar remarks that God surrounds all of his creatures as with a fence, so that they might act according to his own image. That is why all of nature aspires continuously to that which is highest. Creation wishes not only to reflect the Son, but if it were possible, it would want to reflect the Father as well. And that is why, if all creatures were to act outside of time, without limit, creation would be without imperfections. A Greek scholar says: Because creation is immersed in time and place, creatures differ from the Father and the Son. Another scholar expresses it thus: Any builder of a house must build that house first in his mind, and if the building material were so in accord with the plan of the builder and wholly subject to the will of its maker, that house would exist as soon as the builder conceived it in his mind, because the internal and external plan would be distinct only as giving birth and being born are distinct. Thus it is with God: in him there is neither time nor space, and that is why Father and Son are one God, and they are not distinct except for the mode of emanation and being emanated.

* "Spiritus domini replevit orbem terrarum." (DW II, ⚡47)

"The Spirit of the Lord." Why is his name "Lord"? So that he might impregnate us. Why is his name "Spirit"? That he may be united to us. "Power" is recognized in three ways. First, the Lord is *rich:* rich means to possess everything, not to suffer want. But no matter how rich a man is, he remains but one person. And if one could encompass all human beings, that would not make one an angel. And if one could be an angel and human being at the same time, one would only be *one* angel, not all angels. That is why in the true sense God alone is rich, because he alone contains all in himself. And that is the reason why he can give always; that is the second aspect of his wealth. A certain scholar said that God offers himself to all his creatures and it is up to them to accept as many of God's gifts as they want. I say that God offers himself to me as to the highest angel, and if I were ready to receive as much as the angel accepts, I would receive as much as he from God's plenty. I have said on many occasions that God from all eternity has acted thus: God acts as if he was occupied with how he could become pleasing to the soul. The third aspect of being rich is that one gives without expectation of any return, for if someone gives in order to get something in return, such a one is not rich in the true sense. The proof that God is truly rich lies in the fact that he gives disinterestedly. That is why the prophet remarks: "I said to my Lord, you are my Lord because you have no need of me" (Ps. 16:2). Only such a one is "Lord" and "Spirit" and our blessedness consists in his uniting himself to us. The most noble thing God works in his creature is existence. Though my earthly father passes on his nature, he does not give me existence; existence I receive solely from God. That is why all that exists rejoices in its existence. As I have said on different occasions—and frequently been misunderstood in the process—Judas does not want to be someone else, whether in heaven or in hell. Why? Because if he had to become another, he would have to abandon his existence, he would come to nothing. But that is impossible, because existence does not negate itself. The existence of the soul is sensitized to the influence of God's radiance. However, since the soul is not wholly pure or transparent, it is not able to receive God's light in its fullness; God's light must enter the soul veiled. Though the sun's rays are reflected on a tree and other objects, the sun itself cannot be seen by us—directly. So it is with God's gifts: they have to be measured according to him who is to *receive* them and not according to the one who gives them.

One scholar says: God is the measure of all that exists, and to the degree that one person embraces God's gifts more fully than another, to that degree he is wiser, nobler, and better than the other. To possess more of God than others means nothing else than to resemble God to a higher degree; the more we are an image of God, the more spiritual we are. One scholar observes: At that point where the lowest spiritual aspects end, the highest corporal things begin. That means: Since God is a spirit, that which is spirit in the lowest order is nobler than that which is corporal in the highest. Therefore, the soul is nobler than all things corporal, noble though they might be. The soul, as it were, was created at that point which divides time from eternity; it touches both of these points. With its highest faculties the soul touches eternity, with its lowest, however, it is in touch with time. That is why the soul acts in time, not according to time, but in accordance with eternity. That quality it has in common with the angels. One scholar says: The soul can be compared to a sleigh that can travel anywhere—the soul likewise "travels" into all parts of the body, and thus establishes a unity. Though the intellect is gifted with understanding, and though it directs and accomplishes all that finds expression in the body, one should not conclude, therefore, that the soul does this or that; rather, one should say: *I* do this or recognize that, because body and soul are one. If a stone could absorb fire into itself, it would act like fire. And though the air absorbs the light of the sun, it does not thereby take on the qualities of the sun. Because air is diffusive, light can shine through it. Thus it is that in a stretch of one mile more light is absorbed than in half a mile. If there exists an intimate unity between body and soul, the unity that binds two spirits must be more intimate still. The "Lord" and "Spirit" is in union with us so that we might reach blessedness.

A question that is difficult to answer is this: How can the soul endure to absorb God into itself without being annihilated? I respond: Every gift that God bestows on the soul is he himself. If God were to bestow upon the soul a gift that were outside himself, the soul would reject it. Because God gives himself, the soul is immersed in him, it lives in him. Because the soul proceeds from God, all that "belongs" to the soul is really his, and that is the reason why the soul is not crushed when God unites himself to it. This is "the spirit of the Lord, who fills the whole world."

Why the soul is called "world" and how the soul reaches blessedness, I did not discuss. But remember this: As he is "Lord" and "Spirit," in the same way are we to be spiritual "soil" and a "domain" that can be penetrated with the breath of life, which is "Lord" and "Spirit." Amen.

COMMENTARY: The Continual Growth of the Soul/Spirituality Is About Growing Without Limit/The Oneness of Soul and Body/The Nearness of God and the Human Soul

In the previous sermon Eckhart brought to our attention how rooted in divinity we are. Our souls, he insists, contain God's very image in them. In this sermon Eckhart develops this theme of the beauty of human creation in greater depth, for he discusses how spirituality is a growth into our truest nature. Our truest nature is like God's.

> God has formed and created the soul very like himself, for we read that our Lord said: "Let us make human beings in our own image" (Gn. 1:26). And this is what he did. So like to himself did he make the soul of a person that neither in the kingdom of heaven nor on earth among all the splendid creatures that God created in such a wonderful way is there any creature that resembles him as much as does the soul of a human being alone.[1]

There are degrees to getting in touch with our divine depths. We can possess more and less of God. *To possess more of God than others means nothing else than to resemble God to a higher degree; the more we are an image of God, the more spiritual we are.* This, then, is what it means to be spiritual: to develop the image of God in us. But this development is a process, a growth process. *We are to be spiritual "soil"* where the seed of God can grow to life and which *the breath of life* can *penetrate.* After all, we all receive this *breath of life* at creation—but is it allowed to grow in us? Eckhart develops this theme of soil, of seeds, and of roots on several occasions. In us

> God has sowed his image and his likeness, and . . . he sows the good seed, the roots of all wisdom, all knowledge, all virtues, all goodness—the seed of the divine nature. The seed of divine nature is the Son of God, the Word of God.[2]

The divine seed is in us but it must maturate and grow, as does any seed.

> The seed of God is in us. If the seed had a good, wise, and industrious cultivator, it would thrive all the more and grow up to God whose seed it is, and the fruit would be equal to the nature of God. Now the seed of a pear tree grows into a pear tree, a hazel seed into a hazel tree, the seed of God into God.[3]

This seed, a spark of God, burns like an unquenchable fire even when we try to ignore it or cover it up. Eckhart borrows the following image from Origen:

> God himself has sown this seed, and inserted it and borne it. Thus while this seed may be crowded, hidden away, and never cultivated, it will still never be obliterated. It glows and shines, gives off light, burns, and is unceasingly inclined toward God.[4]

"The seed," Eckhart repeats elsewhere, "is the Word of God."[5] It cannot be covered up, silenced, or forgotten for long. It will burn wherever it finds material to ignite. Seeds grow and need to grow. So do we; so does the divine seed in us.

There are no limits to this growth. God is the limit. The ambition of the soul to expand into its divine dimensions is a starting point for spiritual growth. Our discontent ought to be recognized.

> You should never be content with what you have of God, for you can never have enough of God. The more you have of God, the more you want of him. If you, in fact, could have

enough of God, so that there came about a satiety of God in you, then God would not be God.[6]

The soul will not rest content with anything smaller than God. "Everything God has a mind to give is still too little for the soul unless God gives himself among his gifts."[7] Our souls are boundless in their eagerness and capacity for the gifts of God.

> Every divine gift increases our receptivity and longing to receive what is higher and greater. For this reason many masters of the spiritual life say that in this the soul is equal in birth to God. For to the extent that God is boundless in his giving, the soul is equally boundless in taking and receiving. Just as God is omnipotent in his deeds, the soul is just as profound in its capacity to receive. For this reason it is transformed—with and in God.[8]

Eckhart is touching on a theme here of the divinization of the human person that we will develop more fully in Sermons Twenty-five and Twenty-six. The only rest that the human person can know is a rest in its own divine origins, roots or seed. "Because the soul has the capacity to know everything, it is never at rest until it comes to the original image, where all things are one. And there it comes to its rest which is in God."[9] This capacity of the soul to know everything is a cosmic capacity that the human has in common with the Creator of the cosmos. As Schürmann puts it:

> The intellect is capable of receiving the universe; this is why and how it is naturally like God. Man's similarity with God consists in his openness to the totality of what is; tradition attaches the label of intellect to this capacity of total openness . . . the intellect is naturally connected with the universe.[10]

This boundless openness to all that is invites us to ever greater expansion of soul and consciousness. It is God who does the expanding: "If God so changes little things, what do you think he will do with the soul, which he has already fashioned so gloriously in his own image?"[11] Once again, we are admonished not to flee from dissatisfaction but to recognize it as the proper starting point for a divine adventure. The human spirit does not allow itself to be satisfied with that light (which is come down from heaven). It storms the firmament, and scales the heavens until it reaches the spirit that drives the heavens. As a result of heaven's revolution, everything in the world flourishes and bursts into leaf. The spirit, however, is never satisfied; it presses on ever further into the vortex (or whirlpool) and primary source in which the spirit has its origin.[12]

By calling the source a vortex, Eckhart conjures up his previous images of sinking into God. He is suggesting that the inside of the inside, the core of the seed as well as the core of our origins, which means the core of the Godhead, may well be understood as a vortex. This falling into the vortex and sinking into our divine origin knows no limit. So deep is God that we could fall—and grow—forever. "If people lived a thousand years or even longer, they might still grow in love."[13] Neither God nor we have any limits, so great is our likeness to God. To test and fill these limits we must be on the move, "running to heavenly peace," as Eckhart puts it. "We should not rest satisfied with anything, and never remain standing still. In this world there can be no standing still in any way of life, and there never was for any man, however far he traveled."[14] This development of the soul includes a development of our talents and gifts. "We should not destroy any good, however small, in ourselves, nor any small way for the sake of a greater one, but we should perfect them all in the highest possible manner."[15] Another way to *run* to our divine capacities is to be receptive and to develop our receptive capacities. *God offers himself to me as to the highest angel, and if I were ready to receive as much as the angel accepts, I would receive as much as he from God's plenty.* To receive we must be alert, awake and prepared to receive. "Above all, persons should at all times be prepared for the gifts of God and always prepare themselves anew." For God "is a thousand times more eager to give than we are to receive. But we do him violence and wrong if we impede him in his natural activity by our unpreparedness."[16] Growth is intrinsic to spiritual experience because, after all, "the 'being' is only found in the 'becoming.' "[17] This becoming knows no boundaries.

A person should in all things become a God-seeking and a God-finding person at all times and among all kinds of persons and in all ways. In this quest one can grow and increase without intermission, and never come to an end of the increasing.[18]

One should never expect an end to such expansion in this life for "spiritually, one never reaches satisfaction, because the more one feeds on spiritual food, the more one longs for it."[19]

Having considered the theme of spiritual growth and limitlessness of the human potential for the divine, we can more readily grasp Eckhart's exegesis of wisdom literature with which he began this sermon. His text was as follows:

> The spirit of the Lord, indeed, fills the whole world,
> and that which holds all things together knows every word that is
>   said . . .
> Death was not God's doing,
> he takes no pleasure in the extinction of the living.
> To be—for this he created all;
> the world's created things have health in them,
> in them no fatal poison can be found,
> and Hades holds no power on earth;
> for virtue is undying. (Ws. 1:7, 13–15)

Eckhart calls the soul that is filled with the Spirit who is *the breath of life*, the world. In so doing he urges humans to consider their beauty and divinity. He also takes delight in Wisdom's declaration: "To be—for this God created all," and he calls on Psalm 16, a psalm of trust, in his exhilaration at the gift of existence: *All that exists rejoices in its existence.*

> To Yahweh you say, "My Lord,
> you are my fortune, nothing else but you" . . .
> So my heart exults, my very soul rejoices,
> my body, too, will rest securely,
> for you will not abandon my soul to Sheol,
> nor allow the one you love to see the Pit;
> you will reveal the path of life to me,
> give me unbounded joy in your presence,
> and at your right hand everlasting pleasures. (Ps. 16:2, 9–11)

Another issue is at stake in our becoming like God and growing in spiritual consciousness. In Sermon Two, Eckhart introduced the subject of dualistic consciousness, saying that dualism can never touch God. In this present sermon he applies that principle to the subject so easily made dualistic by fundamentalists and spiritualists: the soul and the body's relationship. Eckhart rejects the dualism of Neoplatonism in favor of a Jewish holism: "My heart exults, my very soul rejoices, my body, too, will rest securely," the psalmist has sung. Augustine said that what is spiritual is "whatever is not a body" and that body and soul are related as slave and master.[20] Eckhart says that the soul *travels into all parts of the body, and thus establishes a unity.* The soul's work is to heal and make whole, to make a harmonious unity of us. We are not divided, body against soul, but are one entity. *One should not conclude that the soul does this or that; rather, one should say: I do this or recognize that, because body and soul are one.* Not only are *body and soul one* for Eckhart, but they form *an intimate unity.* He takes the unity of body and soul and, using it as an analogy, suggests that two spirits will be bound in a similar though even greater unity. We have seen in this and the previous sermon how noble and divine the soul of the human person is, but the body too is noble. *All things corporal are noble,* he declares. After all, they all share in the grace of existence. Eckhart conceives of the relationship of soul and body as a relation of friends, not of objects at war. He says: "The soul loves the body."[21] This attitude of mutual interdependence between soul and body is much like Aquinas' theory on the consubstantiality of soul and body and very much unlike Platonic theories about conflict that the Augustinian tradition presumes. The living body forms one substantial unity according to both Eckhart and Aquinas.[22] The senses are not put down by Eckhart. Rather, he calls them the "ins and outs" of the world. They profit the soul. Senses

> are the "ins and outs" through which the soul goes out into the world, and through these ins and outs the world, in turn, goes to the soul. A master of the spiritual life says that the powers of the soul are to run back to the soul to its good profit. When they emerge, they always bring something back again . . . I am certain that whatever *good* people see will improve them. If they see bad things, they will thank God for guarding them from such things and ask God to convert peo-

ple in whom there is evil. If they see goodness, however, they
will long to have it accomplished in themselves.[23]

Thus the senses are vehicles for good persons who see, feel, taste, hear
to their profit whether the objects of such senses be good or bad. A
good person bears good fruit and has learned to trust his or her senses
with the goodness that comes from one's inside. For outside things can
make one neither good nor bad. That is why he can say elsewhere that
"we experience all things according to our own goodness."[24] Knowledge of the world that comes through the senses "strengthens the soul so
that the soul can endure the divine light."[25] One reason people are
dualists in thinking about body and soul is that they think in object terms
instead of in energy terms. Eckhart turns any object thinking about body
and soul inside out when he says that "my body is more in my soul than
my soul is in my body."[26] Thus, as we saw above, "soul" for Eckhart is
not a private little motor that sits inside our body making it run until
death. Rather, it is an energy that gives form and unity to our person and
that far excels our physical place by its infinite capacity to grow.

More evidence that Eckhart abolished dualistic thinking about soul
and body is the care he took to distinguish soul from spirit. Like the Jewish thinkers who wrote the Bible, Eckhart distinguishes soul, spirit, and
body and does not overly identify soul and spirit. Nor does he overly
exaggerate a competition between soul and body. For all dualistic thinking about body and soul ultimately rests on the supposition that soul is
spirit and body is not spirit.[27] Eckhart thinks otherwise. He distinguishes
between spiritual being and soul being. "Saint Paul was drawn up and
yet remained with his soul in his body. He was drawn up in his spiritual
being; he remained with his soul being."[28] The soul points in two directions: toward body and toward spirit. But these are not mutually exclu-
sive directions by any means.

> The word soul is used with reference to the fact that it gives
> life to the body and is the form of the body. Renewal pertains
> to the soul also insofar as it is called spirit. And the soul is
> called spirit because it is separated from the here and now
> and from everything natural. But in that respect in which the
> soul is an image of God and is, like God, nameless, there the
> soul knows no renewal but only eternity, like God.[29]

Eckhart speaks of our need to grow into being "more truly human"[30] just as he spoke above, as we saw, about our growing into our divinity. Our divinity is not won at the price of sacrificing our humanity. Rather, it pertains to the very soul of a person to be human and divine. For no dualism reigns either between body and soul or between humanity and divinity. The intimacy of the union of the first pair presages the even *more intimate union* of the second.

How intimate is this intimate union of two spirits, the human and the divine? Eckhart elaborates: "God leads this [human] spirit into the desert and solitude of himself, where he is pure unity and gushes up only within himself . . . Here the spirit remains in unity and freedom."[31] The union is comparable to that of a seal on wax:

> If the seal is pressed completely through the wax so that no wax remains without being impressed by the seal, then it becomes undistinguishably one with the seal. Similarly the soul becomes completely united with God in his image and likeness, if the soul touches him in proper knowledge.[32]

This experience of God is a "simple knowing" that "is so pure in itself that it knows without mediation the pure, bare divine being. And in this influx of the divine being, it receives the divine nature just like the angels who take such joy in that."[33] Here our divine origins are met up with at last.

> If I am to know God in such an unmediated way, then I must simply become God and God must become me. I would express it more exactly by saying that God must simply become me and I must become God, so completely one that this "he" and this "I" share one "is" and in this "isness" do our work eternally. For this "he" and this "I", that is, God and the soul, are very fruitful as we eternally do one work.[34]

Thus our isness is reunited to God and so too is our work. The word that is ourselves returns to its origins but continues to flow out while, of course, remaining within. The youthfulness, newness, or eternity of God sets the time for this union. And in this union God rediscovers God. "Only the infinite God who is in the soul, only he himself understands God, who is infinite. There in the soul God understands God and begets God himself in the soul and 'shapes' it after himself."[35] Then it can indeed be said that "where the soul is, there is God . . . where I am, there is God" (see Sermon Twenty-eight). And in this way, through human transformation and expression of this transformation in work, the spirit of the Lord will indeed *fill the whole world* and establish unity there. When Eckhart says that *the soul is called "world,"* he is revealing what a cosmic and non-introverted kind of spirituality he is espousing—one where the "out" and the "in" so interpenetrate that their differences melt. So big is the potential of the soul that it is to become the world, take it in, and give a new birth to it. Indeed, it should not stop there. It should become a place big enough for God—heaven itself. "Each of us should be a heaven in which God dwells."[36]

Sermon Eight: THIS IS SPIRITUALITY: WAKING UP

"Young man, I tell you to get up." (Lk. 7:14)*

We read in the Gospel that Saint Luke writes about a young man who was dead. Then our Lord came by and appeared at the right time, took compassion on him, touched him, and said: "Young man, I tell you to get up!" (Lk. 7:12ff.).

Understand now that God is entirely in every good person. There is in the soul a something in which God dwells, and there is in the soul a something in which the soul dwells in God. However, if the soul turns outward to other objects, it will die, and God also will die for the soul. Of course, God does not die to himself, but he rather continues to live in himself. If the soul separates from the body, the body is dead, but the soul continues to live in itself. In the same way, God is dead for that soul, even though he continues to live in himself. Understand now that there is a power in the soul that is wider than the widest heaven, which is so unbelievably wide that we cannot correctly express it. Yet that power is even wider still.

Come now and pay careful attention! In that noble power the heavenly Father now says to his only begotten Son: "Young man, get up!" The union of God with the soul is so great that it is scarcely believable, and God is so lofty in himself that no perception or longing can attain him. Longing extends beyond everything we can attain through perception. It is wider than all the heavens; indeed, it is wider than all the angels. And at the same time all that is on earth lives merely from a tiny spark of an angel. Longing is wide, immeasurably wide. But all that perception can grasp and all that longing can long for—that is not God. Where understanding and longing end, it is dark but God *shines* there.

* "Adolescens, tibi dico: surge." (DW II, ₩42)

Our Lord now says: "Young man, I tell you to get up!" If I am to perceive God's word within myself, I have to be alienated from all that is mine, especially from the realm of the temporal, just as whatever is beyond the sea is alien to me. The soul is as young as it was when it was created. Old age, which falls to the soul's lot, has effect with respect to the body only to the extent that the soul is active in the senses. A master of the spiritual life says: "If an old person had the eyes of a young person, he or she would see just as well as the young person." Yesterday I sat in a dwelling place and made a statement that sounded quite unbelievable. I said that Jerusalem is as close to my soul as the place in which I am now. Yes, quite truly, an object a thousand miles farther away than Jerusalem is as near to my soul as is my own body—and I am as certain of this as I am of the fact that I am a human being. And it is easy for learned priests to comprehend what I am saying. Understand that my soul is as young as it was when it was created. Indeed, it is even younger! And understand that it would not surprise me if it were younger tomorrow than it is today!

The soul has two powers that have nothing to do with the body—reason and will, which operate beyond time. Would that the eyes of the soul were opened so that perception could gaze clearly at the truth! Understand that for such a person it would be easy to abandon all things as if they were but a pea or a bean. Yes, by my soul, all that would be to such a person like nothing! Now there are certain people who abandon things out of love, yet still are concerned about the things they have abandoned as if they were important. People, however, who truly know that, even if they give up themselves and everything else, all this is just nothing—ah, people who live *in this way* truly possess all things.

In the soul there is a power for which all things are equally delightful. Indeed, for this power the least important and the best of things are totally one and the same. This power grasps all things beyond "here" and "now." "Now" means time, and "here" means place, that is, the place in which I am at present. If, however, I had completely left myself and become quite empty of myself, oh, then the Father would indeed have produced his only begotten Son in my spirit so completely that my spirit would produce him again. Yes, in all truth, if my soul were just as prepared as the soul of our Lord Jesus Christ, the Father would have had the same pure effect in me as in his only begotten Son; the effect would have been no less. For the Father loves me with the same love as the one with which he loves himself.

Saint John said: "In the beginning was the Word: and the Word was with God and the Word was God" (Jn. 1:1). Now then, whoever should hear this Word in the Father—where it is completely still—must be quite still and cut off from all images and forms. Indeed, such people must conduct themselves so faithfully toward God that all things can cause them neither delight nor dismay. Such people should rather accept all things in God, just as they are.

Now Jesus says: "Young man, I tell you to get up!" He wishes to accomplish the deed himself. If anyone were to order me to carry a stone, he might just as well order me to carry a thousand stones as only one, to the extent that that person wishes to execute by himself or herself the act of carrying. Or if someone were to order another to carry a hundred weight, then the person might just as well order that a thousand weight be carried if the person giving the order is willing to carry the weight by himself or herself. Now then, God wishes to carry out this deed by himself. The individual needs only to follow and not resist him in anything. Ah, if the soul would dwell only *inwardly*, it would then have all things present.

There is a power in the soul, and not only a power but much more—there is a form of being and not only a form of being but rather something that detaches a person from being. This is so complete and high and noble in itself that no creature can enter it except God, who dwells within it. Indeed, in all truth, God himself cannot enter it to the extent that he has modes for himself or even to the extent that God himself is a mode or is good or is abundant. Quite truly, God cannot enter with any mode whatsoever. Rather, only with his purely divine nature can God enter it.

Now then, pay attention to what Jesus says: "Young man, I tell you . . ." What now is God's "declaration"? It is God's *deed*, and this deed is so noble and elevated that God *alone* accomplishes it. Know then that all our perfection and all our bliss depend on the fact that the individual goes through and beyond all creation and all temporality and all being, and enters the foundation that is without foundation.

We ask of God, our dear Lord, that we should become *one* and *indwelling*. May God help us to this end. Amen.

COMMENTARY: Spirituality—the Art of Wakefulness/Thankfulness, the Ultimate Prayer/Rising from the Dead Before We Die/Why God Needs to Love Us

Spanish poet Antonio Machado has written that God sent his Word in the person of Jesus Christ to announce just one word. That word is: "Wake up!" This theme of waking up, of getting up, of rising up may well signify the meaning of spirituality the world over. Spirituality is our waking up—in our consciousness and our work lives and our ways of living—waking up to the divine presence everywhere. The Kabir spiritual tradition from fifteenth-century India spoke similarly of the need for waking up. Says the Kabir:

Friend, wake up! Why do you go on sleeping?
   The night is over—do you want to lose the day the same way?
Other women who managed to get up early have
   already found an elephant or a jewel . . .
So much was lost already while you slept . . .
and that was so unnecessary!

My inside, listen to me, the greatest spirit,
   the Teacher, is near,
wake up, wake up!

Run to his feet—
he is standing close to your head right now.
You have slept for millions and millions of years.
Why not wake up this morning? . . .

Oh friend, I love you, think this over
   carefully! If you are in love,
then why are you asleep?

In Sermon Six we saw Eckhart invoking this same theme of waking up by citing Paul's treatment of that theme in Romans and also Jesus' referring to it in the Gospels. In this sermon, we see Eckhart reiterating this theme but with a new dimension to it. Here, it is not just a matter of our sleeping away our lives and sleeping away our divine potential. Here we are actually dead to the divine and dead to our own potential. And so Jesus not only says "Wake up" but "Get up."

Following is the fuller scriptural reading of Jesus' waking the young man from the dead. It is a story about Jesus' compassion and about Jesus' being called "Lord" for the first time in Luke's Gospel. The reason for this new appellation is twofold: In the Jewish mind, only God is capable of compassion and in the Jewish mind only God can give life and thus wake one from the dead.

> Jesus went to a town called Nain, accompanied by his disciples and a great number of people. When he was near the gate of the town it happened that a dead man was being carried out for burial, the only son of his mother, and she was a widow. And a considerable number of the townspeople were with her. When the Lord saw her he felt compassion for her. "Do not cry," he said. Then he went up and put his hand on the bier and the bearers stood still, and he said, "Young man, I tell you to get up." And the dead man sat up and began to talk, and Jesus gave him to his mother. Everyone was filled with awe and praised God. (Lk. 7:11–16)

Since this scriptural passage invokes the divine name of Jesus, that of Lord for the first time, Eckhart feels justified in introducing what he considers a parallel passage from the Gospel of John that announces the nearness of the Word to God and especially how the gift of life comes to humans through this Word. Following is the fuller passage from that which Eckhart cites in this sermon:

> In the beginning was the Word:
> the Word was with God
> and the Word was God.
> He was with God in the beginning.
> Through him all things came to be,
> not one thing had its being but through him.
> All that came to be had life in him
> and that life was the light of men,
> a light that shines in the dark,
> a light that darkness could not overpower. (Jn. 1:1–5)

Eckhart paraphrases this last line in his sermon by saying that *where understanding and longing end, it is dark, but God shines there.*

Eckhart distinguishes between enlightened and unenlightened persons as between those who are awake or aware and those who are not. It is a question of experience and of tasting or not tasting. Eckhart's attitude toward those who do not taste is a certain exasperation at a great waste. Such persons are wasting their lives just as a person who keeps a good wine cellar but never tastes the wine is wasting his wine.

> People who know all that God knows are a God-knowing people. People apprehend God in his own selfhood and in his own unity and in his own presence and in his own truth. With such people all is well. But the person who is not accustomed to inward things does not know what God is. Like a man who has wine in his cellar, but has not drunk it or tasted it, such a person does not know that it is good. Thus it is with people who live in ignorance. They do not know what God is, and yet they think and believe that they are alive.[1]

Such people only imagine they are alive—they are not yet alive, not yet risen from the dead. Notice that the waking up and getting up is related by Eckhart to consciousness or knowledge of God, which is a tasting knowledge. We need to wake up and get up from our mortal slumber by an adventurous exploration of the mysteries that lie behind mysteries and of the core behind the core of things.

> The shell must be cracked apart and then what is in it must come out; for if you want the kernel, you must break the shell. And therefore, if you want to discover nature unconcealed, you must destroy all likenesses and the farther you get in, the nearer you come to its being.[2]

Getting up also means entering in—you must break the shell if you want the kernel. Or, as Eckhart puts it in the present sermon, *we should become one and indwelling.* In fact, so deep and so deeply divine is our inner kernel that only God can enter there. And even God has to take his shoes off to enter. *Only with his purely divine nature can God enter there.*

So important is the theme of getting up and waking up to Eckhart's spirituality that he devoted another sermon to a similar scriptural passage from the following chapter of Luke's Gospel. Indeed, he may well have had this Gospel story in mind in his present sermon. In this case, Jesus raises a young woman from the dead, the daughter of a synagogue official. Her parents and others

> were all weeping and mourning for her, but Jesus said, "Stop crying; she is not dead, but asleep." But they laughed at him, knowing she was dead. But taking her by the hand he called to her, "Child, get up." And her spirit returned and she got up at once. (Lk. 8:52–55)

In this passage we hear Jesus pronouncing the subtle difference between being asleep and being dead and we have, together with the passage from Luke 7 that forms the basis of the current sermon, testimony that Jesus gets people up, both from sleep and from death. In his sermon based on raising this young woman from her sleep that is a death, Eckhart outlines four reasons for "getting up":

> The soul advances to God in four steps. The first step is the one that fear and hope and longing cause to grow in the soul. A second time the soul makes an advance is when fear and hope and longing are completely broken off. A third time the soul falls into a forgetfulness of all temporal things. A fourth time the soul advances into God, where it will remain forever with God reigning in eternity. Then the soul will think no longer of temporary things or of itself. The soul has rather dissolved into God and God into the soul. And whatever the soul then does, it does in God.[8]

Eckhart talks of similar truths we wake up to in the present sermon. He elaborates, for example, on the first step of longing that grows in the soul. Longing is *wider than all the angels . . . immeasurably wide. It extends beyond everything we can attain through perception.* Rather than flee from longing, or control it, or keep it in check, we are to enter fully into it. And when we do, we discover what he has called the second stage, "when fear and hope and longing are completely broken off." Or, as he puts it in this sermon: *All that perception can grasp and all that longing can long for—that is not God. Where understanding and long-*

ing end, it is dark but God shines there. The third soulful experience, Eckhart has said, occurs when we "fall into a forgetfulness of all temporal things." Thus he talks in the present sermon of our experience of the youthfulness and newness of eternity. *Understand that my soul is as young as it was when it was created. Indeed, it is even younger! And understand that it would not surprise me if it were younger tomorrow than it is today!* In his sermon on Luke 8 he has spoken of the "timelessly new" experience of all things in God and of the extraordinary joy that accompanies the new time-consciousness that comes when we wake up to realized eschatology. "Just as one can die of anxiety before the blow, that is, before a murder is carried out, in the same way one can die of joy or of its anticipation. And so the soul dies within itself in joyful expectation of eternal bliss before it passes over to God."[4] So great is the joy that it can kill us—but it is a joy in eternal life that is tasted previous to earthly death.

It is not only time that the soul forgets in its journey into God—it is also place. Our place consciousness as well as our time consciousness is broken through and we wake up to a new sense of space as well as of time. For deep within the soul *a power grasps all things beyond "here" and "now." "Now" means time, and "here" means place, that is, the place in which I am at present.* It is in this context of breaking through place awareness that Eckhart can talk about Jerusalem being

> *as close to my soul as the place in which I am now. Yes, quite truly, an object a thousand miles farther away than Jerusalem is as near to my soul as is my own body—and I am as certain of this as I am of the fact that I am a human being.*

Our waking up, then, is a waking up to a new space (instead of place) consciousness.

The fourth stage of waking up concerns our entering into God where we reign for eternity and are dissolved, us in God and God in us. It is, in other words, our waking up to inness: ours and God's. It is our waking up to the fullness of God's love for us and what this means. *The Father loves me with the same love as the one with which he loves himself.*

Elsewhere, Eckhart repeats this theme of the thoroughness of God's love for us, a theme so basic to his entire spirituality and to our waking up.

"God loves." What mystery! What is God's love? His nature and his being: that is his love. Whoever would take away God's love for us would take away his essence, because his being is dependent upon his love for us . . . What a mystery that is! God loves me with his whole being—his being depends on it—God loves me as if his being and his becoming depend on it. God knows only one kind of love, and with exactly that same love with which the Father loves his only-begotten Son, with the same love he loves us.[5]

God is dependent on us for his essence, which is to love. Eckhart develops this theme elsewhere as well:

"God is love." O my beloved, listen to me! This I ask of you! God loves my soul so much that his life and his being depend on it, and he *must* love me whether happily or unhappily for himself. Whoever should rob God of this, namely, that he love my soul, would be taking his divinity from him. For God is as truly love as he is truth.[6]

We rob God of divinity to the extent that we fail to wake up to his love for us. We are loved with the divine love—have we waked up to this truth yet? Furthermore, *God is entirely in every good person*—have we waked up to this truth yet? Furthermore, *the union of God with the soul is so great that it is scarcely believable*—have we waked up to this truth yet? The nearness to God that is ours to experience is experienced not by manufacturing it but by accepting it, for it already is. *Accept all things in God, just as they are.* Our waking up is a waking up to the truth of the panentheistic world we live in. As in the case of the dead young man or the dead young woman, we do not do the work of waking ourselves up. God does it, it is a divine deed of divine compassion. *Jesus wishes to accomplish the deed himself.*

Now then, God wishes to carry out this deed by himself. The individual needs only to follow and not resist him in anything. Ah, if the soul would dwell only inwardly, it would then have all things present.

Eckhart properly insists that only God can raise from the dead, only God can give life. *It is God's deed, and this deed is so noble and elevated that God alone accomplishes it.* What is our role? We can recognize the steps of the journey into God which is a journey of waking up. And we can let ourselves be waked up. The journey is summarized by Eckhart:

> Know then that all our perfection and all our bliss depend on the fact that the individual goes through and beyond all creation and all temporality and all being, and enters the foundation that is without foundation.

Our getting up and waking up is also an opening up. When we open up we accept and receive. Spirituality then becomes the art of wakefulness, the art of being awake, of being aware, conscious and alive. It is the art of living the truth of our inness with God and God's with us. One might say it is the art of swimming in the divine ocean all day long. Such an art should not take a lot of conscious effort but should become second nature to us, as all art must be to the artist.

> Human beings should turn their will to God in all their activities and keep their eyes on God alone, marching along without fear and without hesitancy about being right or not doing anything wrong. For if a painter wanted to consider every stroke of his brush when he made his first stroke, no picture would ever result. If someone is supposed to go to a city and wanted to consider beforehand how he was to take the first step, nothing would come of the enterprise. This is why we should follow the first suggestion and move forward. This is how we move forward and arrive where we are supposed to be and that is as it should be.[7]

Move right along, we are told—flow, like the art flows from the artist. Do not fear making mistakes or counting every step. Trust. Let go. Elsewhere Eckhart compares the art of spirituality to that of a writer who, by much practice, can get beyond the skills and techniques needed to write. "He will then write fluently and freely."

> The same would apply to fiddling or any kind of art which was to result from his skill. It is quite enough for him to know that he is going to practice his art. Even if he is not concen-

trating on it the whole time, whatever he may be thinking about, his art will nevertheless proceed from his skill.

In the same way, a person should be so penetrated with the divine Presence and transformed into the form of his beloved God and be essential in him that his Presence may shine in him without any effort on his part, and he should acquire freedom from bondage and be entirely untrammeled by things.[8]

The art of spirituality is truly an art of waking up.

People should be as our Lord said: "You should be like unto people who at all times watch and wait for their lord" (Lk. 12:36). Now those persons who wait are awake and on the lookout for their lord, whom they are expecting. And they are expectant whenever anything comes, however strange it may be, and look to see whether perchance it is he who comes. In the same way, we should be on the lookout for our Lord in all things.[9]

What is the end result of all our getting up and our waking up? In the scriptural passages pertinent to this sermon we read that "everyone was filled with awe and praised God" (Lk. 7:16) and "her parents were astonished" (Lk. 8:56). Awe, astonishment, and praise are the fruits of our wakefulness, our resurrections from dead consciousness. There follows, at the root of our being, a sense of gratitude and thankfulness. All we can say for this gift of a divine universe, divinely infused and divinely present, is thank you. We are overcome with a sense of the gift that being, life, and creation are. And the gift that the Creator is. "With all these other gifts he wishes to prepare us for the gift that is himself."[10] The only prayer we can utter is a prayer of thank you. But that suffices. "If people had no other communication with God than that of being thankful to him, that would suffice."[11] The end of all waking up and all getting up, the end of all the art of wakefulness that spirituality is, is a simple thank you. An act of praise for the gift of life extended even to the dead.

Sermon Nine: WAKING UP TO THE NEARNESS OF
GOD'S KINGDOM

"Know that the kingdom of God is near." (Lk. 21:31)*

Our Lord says: "Know that the kingdom of God is near" (Lk. 21:31). Yes, the kingdom of God is within us, and Saint Paul says that our salvation is nearer to us than we believe (Rm. 13:11).

"We should know" first of all how "near" the kingdom of God is, and next when the kingdom of God is near us. Therefore we must think carefully about the meaning of this passage. For if I were a king and did not know it, then I would be no king. If, however, I firmly believed that I was a king, and if everyone supposed this to be the case, and if I knew for certain that everyone supposed it, then I really would be a king. And thus the whole wealth of a king would be mine, and nothing of a king's wealth would be lacking to me. These three conditions must occur of a necessity if I am to be a king. If one of the three conditions is lacking, I could not be a king. A master of the spiritual life—as well as our best masters—says that happiness lies in the fact that we perceive and "know" and this consists in a necessary urgency for truth. I have within my soul a strength that is totally sensitive to God.

I am as certain as I am that I am a man that nothing is so "near" to me as God. God is nearer to me than myself. My being depends on the fact that God is "near" to me and present for me. He is also near and present for a stone or piece of wood, but they know nothing about this fact. If a piece of wood knew about God and perceived how "near" he is to it, as the highest angel perceives this fact, then the piece of wood would be just as happy as the highest angel. And for this reason people are happier than a

* "Scitote, quia prope est regnum dei." (DW III, ⅙68)

stone or piece of wood because they are aware of God and *know*
how "near" God is. And I am all the happier to the extent that I
am aware of this fact. I am all the less happy to the extent that I
am unaware of it. I am not happy because God is within me or
"near" me or because I possess him, but rather because I am
aware of how "near" God is and because I *know* about God. In
the Psalms the prophet says: "You should not be unknowing like
a mule or a horse." The patriarch Jacob makes another statement: "Truly, God is in this place, and I never knew it!"
(Gn. 28:16). We should "know" about God, and perceive that
"the kingdom of God is near."

When I reflect on the "kingdom of God," I am often left mute
by its greatness. For the "kingdom of God" is God himself with
all his wealth. The "kingdom of God" is no small thing. If we
could imagine all the worlds that God might create, they would
not be the kingdom of God! From time to time I am accustomed
to state that it is not necessary to preach or give lessons to a soul
in which the kingdom of God is visible or which knows that the
kingdom of God is near. For that very reason the soul is instructed in and assured of eternal life. Whoever *knows* and is
aware *how near* the kingdom of God is can say with Jacob: "God
is in this place, and I never knew it!" (Gn. 28:16). Now, however, I do not know it.

God is equally near to all creatures. The wise man says in Ecclesiasticus: God has his net, his hunter's ploy, spread out over all
creatures (cf. Ho. 7:12; Ezk. 12:13). Thus all people can find him
in everything, so long as they can penetrate this net filled with
creatures and keep God in mind and recognize God in everything. Thus we find a teacher saying that the person who knows
God most truly is the one who can find him equally in all things.
I also said on one occasion that it is good to serve God in fear,
better to serve him in love, but best of all to be able to find love
in the very fear itself. It is good that a person has a peaceful life;
it is better that a person bear a troublesome life with patience.
But best of all is that a person can have peace even in the very
midst of trouble. A person can be walking across a field, saying his
prayers, and perceive God, or he might be in a chapel and perceive God. If the situation is such that he can better perceive

God when he is in peaceful circumstances where he is comfortable, this is due to his own insufficiency and not to anything on God's part. For God is equally in all things and in all places and he is ready to give himself in the same way and to the same degree in every circumstance. The one who knows God best is the one who recognizes him equally everywhere.

Saint Bernard asks: "Why is my *eye* aware of heaven and not my feet? This is due to the fact that my eye resembles heaven more than my feet. If my soul is to know God, it must be of a heavenly nature." What causes the soul to become aware of God and to "know" how "near" God is? The master says: Heaven cannot receive any strange impression. No painful need that would seek to bring heaven out of its course can have any effect. Thus the soul that is to know God must be so established and fixed in God that nothing can make an impression on it—neither joy nor suffering nor love nor sorrow nor anything else could take the soul from its own course. Heaven in all places is equally distant from the earth. Similarly the soul should be equally distant from all earthly matters so that it is not nearer to one than another.

The sky is equally far from any point on the earth's surface. So too should the soul be equally far from all earthly things so that it is no closer to one thing than to another. Wherever there is a noble soul, it should be equally far from all earthly things, from hope, from joy and misery—no matter what it is, the soul should keep itself fully removed from it. When seen from the moon, our sky looks pure and clear and without blemish. The teachers call the moon, that heavenly body closest to the earth, the midwife of the heavens. Neither space nor time touch the heavens. There is no corporeal thing which has a place there; and whoever knows the Scripture well knows that heaven has no appointed place. Neither does heaven stand within time, for its course is unbelievably swift. The teachers say that its course is timeless, though time itself stems from its course. Nothing so much hinders the soul's understanding of God as time and space. Time and space are parts of the whole but God is one. So if the soul is to recognize God, it must do so beyond space and time. For God is neither this nor that in the way of the manifold things of earth, since God is one. If the soul wants to know God, it cannot do so in time. For so long as the soul is conscious of time or space or any other earthly representation, it cannot know God. If the eye is to recognize color, then it must be free from having any color of its own beforehand. A teacher tells us that if the soul is to know God, it must have nothing in common with anything else. Whoever knows God knows that all creatures are nothing. When you rank one creature against another, then the first might seem beautiful or having some other quality. But when anything is placed over against God, then it is nothing.

I must sometimes point out that the soul wanting to perceive God must forget itself and lose itself. For if it perceives itself, then it does not perceive God. But in God the soul finds itself again. Insofar as it knows God, the soul knows itself and in God knows all things from which the soul has separated itself. In the degree to which the soul has separated itself from itself and from all things, to the same degree the soul knows itself fully. If I am truly to recognize goodness, then I must know goodness where it exists in itself and not where it exists in a divided form. And if I am truly to know being, then I must likewise know being where it is in itself—that is, in God. There one can know the fullness of being. As I have said earlier, all humanity does not exist in one human being, for one human being is not all human beings. But in God the soul knows all of humanity and all things in their highest form, for the soul knows them according to their being. If a person lives in a beautifully painted house, other people who have never been inside may indeed have opinions about it; but the one whose house it is *knows*. In the same way I am certain that I live and that God lives. If the soul would know God, it must know God beyond time and space. The soul who gets this far, and has knowledge of the five things we spoke of earlier, perceives God and knows how close God's kingdom is—that is, God with his whole kingdom.

The teachers throw out meaningful questions in their lectures about how it is possible for the soul to know God. It is not because of God's righteousness or strength that he asks a lot of human beings. It is because of his great joy in giving when he wants a soul to be enlarged. God enables the soul to receive much so that God himself has the opportunity to give much.

No one should think that it is a burdensome thing to come to this point, even though it sounds serious and significant. It is true enough that it is somewhat difficult at the beginning when one is separating oneself from himself and from all things. But when one has made some spiritual progress, he discovers that there has never been a lighter, more delightful, or more joyful life; and God is very concerned always to be present to such a person and teach him or her, so that he can bring the soul to that point where God wants it to follow. Never has a person longed after anything so intensely as God longs to bring a person to the point of knowing him. God is always ready but we are very unready. God is near to us but we are very far from him. God is within but we are outside. God is at home in us but we are abroad. The prophet says: "God leads the righteous through the narrow way into the broad path" (Ws. 10:10). This is so that they come to the fullest life.

God help us that we all follow him so that he can bring us to the point where we truly know him. Amen.

COMMENTARY: The Time and Place of the Kingdom of God/The Meaning of Jacob's Dream/The Kingdom of God as a Kingdom of Blessing—the Blessing That Creation Is/We Are All Kings—If We Are Awake to It

It is generally agreed upon among theologians that if Jesus' message can be summarized in one sentence that would be that the reign of God has begun. The preaching of the kingdom of God and its arrival lies very much at the center of the message of Jesus.[1] This can also be said of Eckhart's preaching. All the themes we have seen treated thus far in his sermons—the goodness of creation, the reality of inness and panentheism, the presence of the creative Word, the equality of all beings, the nobility of being and the special nobility of the human person, realized eschatology, the theme of waking up to all this—all these themes can be summarized by saying that *the kingdom of God is near.* Eckhart's numerous scriptural references in this sermon reveal the context out of which he was preaching, a context bathed in the tradition of the kingdom of God literature. Thus, the text for his sermon is found in Luke's Gospel as follows, and the fig tree referred to is a symbol in Israel for the people of God.

And he told them a parable, "Think of the fig tree and indeed every tree. As soon as you see them bud, you know that summer is now near. So with you when you see these things happening: know that the kingdom of God is near." (Lk. 21:29–31)

It would seem that Eckhart's sermon is responding to this same issue—looking for the "buds" in our lives that indicate the presence of the kingdom. Eckhart most assuredly has in mind the reference to the kingdom from just a few chapters earlier in Luke's Gospel, for Eckhart declares: We should know first of all how near the kingdom of God is, and next when the kingdom of God is near us. How near? Where? and When? appear to be the identical questions that were put to Jesus.

Asked by the Pharisees when the kingdom of God was to come, he gave them this answer, "The coming of the kingdom of God does not admit of observation and there will be no one to say, 'Look here! Look there!' For, you must know, the kingdom of God is among you." (Lk. 17:20–21)

Jesus says, in answer to the question When, that the kingdom of God is among you. So does Meister Eckhart—the kingdom is here when we are awake enough to see it. For Eckhart the coming of the kingdom depends upon our consciousness. A person is not a king unless or until one truly believes and is believed to be a king—then I would be a king. The timing of the coming of the kingdom is relative to our preparedness and readiness: God is always ready; but we are very unready. Eckhart associates the kingdom of God with eternal life, which, as we have seen in previous sermons, has already begun. Contemporary exegetes like C. H. Dodd also associate Jesus' preaching of the kingdom of God with eternal life and realized eschatology. Says Dodd:

The expression "the kingdom of God" is used in Mark 9:43–47, 10:17, 24, 25, alternately with "life" or "eternal life." The latter expression is an equivalent for the rabbinic term "the life of the Age to Come," which is in our Jewish sources a far more usual expression than "the kingdom of God" for the great object of hope, the eschaton.[2]

It is not only Mark who interprets the kingdom as eternal life but also John and, according to Dodd, Jesus himself:

When the Fourth Evangelist presents the works of healing as "signs" of the coming of "eternal life" to men, he is rightly interpreting these sayings in our earliest sources. For eternal life is the ultimate issue of the coming of the kingdom of God . . . Here then is the fixed point from which our interpretation of the teaching regarding the kingdom of God must start. It represents the ministry of Jesus as "realized eschatology" . . .[8]

Since Eckhart interprets this kingdom as realized eschatology, he too is being true to what we now know to be our "earliest sources" and to that "fixed point" from which interpretation of Jesus' message must flow. Like Eckhart, Dodd would agree that the long-awaited hope of humankind called "eternal life" has begun here and now. "The *eschaton*, the divinely ordained climax of history, is here."[4]

Eckhart also answers the question of When? from Paul's letter to the Romans in a passage we have considered earlier. It too relates to our waking up. "Besides, you know 'the time' has come: you must wake up now: our salvation is even nearer than it was when we were converted" (Rm. 13:11). The time of eternal life is already upon us and with it our salvation, which is God's kingdom.

But the second question Jesus answered was a question of place: Where is the kingdom? Jesus says that it cannot be objectified in a place, it is neither "here nor there." Eckhart follows suit. He calls for a new sense of space consciousness to replace our overly developed place consciousness. *Heaven in all places is equally distant from the earth. Similarly the soul should be equally distant from all earthly matters so that it is not nearer to one than another.* One might say that the place of the kingdom is relative to our letting go of place, as the time is relative to our letting go of time. *Nothing so much hinders the soul's understanding of God as time and space. God is neither this nor that in the way of the manifold things of earth, for God is one. It is by letting go of objects in time that we begin to experience God. God is where there is no place.* This is why Eckhart addresses himself to the subject of sacred places in this sermon. If the kingdom is not identifiable with a particular place but rather with human consciousness, then it would seem that churches are superfluous and even misleading. This can indeed be the case, Eckhart points out. He compares a person's crossing a field and being aware of God to being aware of God in church. The reason it is easier for some people to find God in church is due to *their own insuf-*

ficiency *and not from anything on God's part. It is not that God is
more in church than in the field but that some people are too closed to
find God except in church.* Such people are in a sorry state of spiritual
development, for *God is equally in all things and in all places, and he is
ready to give himself in the same way and to the same degree in every
circumstance. The one who knows God best is the one who recognizes
him equally everywhere.* People need churches out of the weakness of
the human condition; it is not God who needs churches.

There is a further implication to what Eckhart is saying in bringing up
the subject of churches in the context of the kingdom of God. He is bla-
tantly and even tantalizingly refusing to confuse kingdom with institutional church. He is making as clear as he can the distinction between
the coming of the kingdom of God and any pretensions to ecclesial
triumphalism. This position has important political and social ramifications,
as we shall see below.[5]

Eckhart also speaks out on the timing and the placing of the kingdom
of God when he introduces on two occasions the exclamation from
Jacob that followed on his famous ladder dream. Since the theme of
Jacob's ladder has been the most dominant symbol in Christian mysticism,
it is extremely significant how Eckhart does and does not interpret it.[6]
Eckhart refuses to make a ladder of ascent to God out of the symbols of
the dream, as so many male Christian mystics before him and after him
have done. Instead, he interprets the dream very much as Jewish exegetes do. The setting for Eckhart's scriptural citation is as follows:

> Jacob had a dream: a ladder was there, standing on the
> ground with its top reaching to heaven; and there were angels
> of God going up it and coming down. And Yahweh was
> there, standing over him, saying, "I am Yahweh, the God of
> Abraham your father, and the God of Isaac. I will give to you
> and your descendants the land on which you are lying. Your
> descendants shall be like the specks of dust on the ground;
> you shall spread to the west and the east, to the north and the
> south, and all the tribes of the earth shall bless themselves by
> you and your descendants. Be sure that I am with you; I will
> keep you safe wherever you go, and bring you back to this
> land, for I will not desert you before I have done all that I
> have promised you." Then Jacob awoke from his sleep and
> said, "Truly, Yahweh is in this place and I never knew it!" He
> was afraid and said, "How awe-inspiring this place is! This is

nothing less than a house of God; this is the gate of heaven!"
(Gn. 28:12–17)

Eckhart wants us to be other Jacobs who can shout: "How awe-inspiring
this place is! This is nothing less than a house of God, a gate of
heaven!" But when can we say such a thing and where? When we wake
up, says Eckhart. *Whoever knows and is aware of how near the kingdom of God is can say with Jacob: "God is in this place, and I never
knew it!"* Eckhart interprets Jacob's dream to mean that the kingdom of
God is here and now, among us and within us. He makes no effort
whatsoever to develop a ladder-like journey from the symbol taken from
the dream. The issue is our consciousness—Do we know it? Are we
awake?

Eckhart invokes another scriptural passage concerning Jacob and the
coming of the kingdom of God. In the Book of Wisdom which Eckhart
refers to we read:

> The virtuous man, fleeing from the anger of his brother,
> was led by Wisdom along straight paths.
> She showed him the kingdom of God
> and taught him the knowledge of holy things.
> She brought him success in his toil
> and gave him full return for all his efforts;
> she stood by him against grasping and oppressive men
> and she made him rich. (Ws. 10:10–11)

Today's exegetes agree that "the virtuous man" spoken of here is
Jacob.[7] Thus Jacob is one who has seen the kingdom of God and, says
Eckhart, we are to follow in his way. By so doing, we will *come to the
true freedom of the Spirit, which has become one Spirit with God.* The
riches promised by Wisdom are nothing less than God. *For the "kingdom
of God" is God himself with all his wealth.* God is the kingdom of God.
This means that the kingdom of God is immense like God is. *The "kingdom of God" is no small thing. If we could imagine all the worlds that
God might create, they would not be the kingdom of God!* The kingdom
of God is greater than the cosmos itself.

Where is this great treasure, this pearl of great wealth? We are told it
is now, but where is it? It is as near in place as it is in time. It is not only
now, it is also here. But where is here? Near as God. Near as my being

and closer than my being. *I am as certain as I am of my own life that nothing is so "near" to me as God. God is nearer to me than myself. My being depends on the fact that God is "near" to me and present for me!* But where is this nearness of God? It is, quite literally, everywhere. If we are truly bathed in a divine sea because we live in God panentheistically and God lives in us, then the kingdom is everywhere and in everything and everything is in it. *God has his net, his hunter's ploy, spread out over all creatures,* says Eckhart, borrowing an image from Ezekiel (12:13) and Hosea (7:12) that pictures the panentheistic world-view beautifully. God is the net; we are the creatures within the net. *The person who knows God most truly is the one who can find him equally in all things.* We need to see the net to see creatures—and God—properly. But Eckhart insists that for humans it is not enough that we *be* in the net —we must become conscious of our being in the net, ever awakening to this awareness. We need to expand constantly, filling the net with our awareness of the divinity enclosed therein. *God wants a soul to be enlarged. God enables the soul to receive much so that God himself has the opportunity to give much.* This enlargement or expansion is characteristic of human consciousness and human will. It alone makes us happy. *We can find him and know him in everyone if only we wish to perceive this fact.* In arriving at this awareness, *there has never been a lighter, more delightful, or more joyful life.*

What distinguishes us from a stone or tree or mule or horse is not that God is more distant from them, for God is intimate to all that has being. What distinguishes us is that *they know nothing about this fact.* We can be happier than a stone or piece of wood because we are conscious of God and know how near God is.

> I am all the happier to the extent that I am aware of this fact.
> I am all the less happy to the extent that I am unaware of it.
> I am not happy because God is within me or "near" me or because I possess him; but rather because I am aware of how "near" God is and because I *know* about God.

This is what it means to know that the kingdom of God is near. And to be alive and conscious and spiritually awake. *God is equally "near" in all creatures.* The question of God's nearness, then, is not a question at all. The only question is our own awareness, our nearness to what is and the way things are. *God is near to us, but we are very far from him.*

God is within, but we are outside. God is at home in us, but we are abroad. We are capable—but God is not—of putting distance between us and God, but even then the distance is ours, not God's.

> A person should never in any way think of himself or herself as far from God, either because of some sin or weakness, or for any other reason. If at any time your great sins drive you away, so that you cannot feel to be near God, you should nevertheless feel that God is near you. For it does great harm if a person removes God far away from himself. For, although a person wanders far away or near, God never goes far; he always remains standing near and if he cannot remain within, he still does not go farther away than just outside the door.[8]

We have seen Eckhart identify the kingdom of God with the kingdom of heaven, with eternal life, with God. He also links the kingdom of God to the blessings of God. He does this, for example, by invoking Jacob's dream, as he does twice in this sermon, for in the Genesis account of the dream of Jacob, God promises that "all the tribes of the earth shall bless themselves by you and your descendants." Blessing is the motif of Jacob's dream, and the blessing is here and now. *"Truly, Yahweh is in this place and I never knew it!"* Eckhart's entire creation theology is a blessing theology, as we have seen in the previous eight sermons. All of life is a gift and blessing from the Creator, including being, life, equality of being, and shared divinity. Such blessings God is a "thousand times more eager to give than we are to receive."[9] The kingdom of God demands our receptivity. Eckhart and Jesus insist on this. "Whoever does not receive the kingdom as a little child will never enter into it" (Mk. 10:15).[10] While the Gospels link the coming of the kingdom to repentance and metanoia or change of heart, Eckhart's parallel idea is: Wake up! Repentance and metanoia for Eckhart mean: Wake up to the truth of our fishnet existence in the graced blessings of the Creator. The kingdom is prepared and ready, if we are.

Contemporary biblical scholars like Kenik and Westermann are criticizing what has been called a one-dimensional understanding of salvation, one that ignores the praise-blessing motif of the Scriptures and concentrates solely on salvation as deliverance. This results in a "serious distortion of the biblical data" notes Westermann. It spiritualizes and privatizes the saving event. "From the beginning to the end of the biblical story, God's two ways of dealing with mankind—deliverance and blessing—are found together . . . Here lies the error that led Western theology to a number of further misinterpretations of and deviations from the message of the Bible."[11] Eckhart, being true to a creation-centered spiritual tradition, does not ignore the blessing tradition of biblical spirituality. In the creation theology tradition, creation itself is the first of all God's blessings. "In the primeval history (Gn. 1–11) blessing is found in the context of creation and extends to all living creatures," notes Westermann (p. 29). In his study on the Psalms, Professor Mowinckel relates blessing to creation. "First and foremost, blessing is life, health, and fertility for the people, their cattle, their fields . . . Blessing is the basic power of life itself." Blessing is so holy because it is the Creator's work.

> Life, the power of life, and blessing came to be regarded as holy because they have their origin in the Holy, in the Deity. God is the creator and preserver of life . . . Each Israelite encounters Yahweh as the one who creates and bestows life and blessing and by so doing upholds the world.[12]

This tradition of blessing and creation is Meister Eckhart's tradition.

One experience that is common to the blessing/creation tradition is the blessing that eating is. Eckhart links the heavenly kingdom to the heavenly feast, which is a celebration of the kingdom. Eckhart says:

> Our Lord said to one of his disciples: "Those who follow me will sit at my table in my Father's kingdom and will eat my food and drink my drink—the table which my Father has prepared for me and which I have prepared for you" (Mt. 19:28; Lk. 20:29). Happy is the person who has come to that point that he or she draws with the Son from the same source out of which the Son draws. It is there that even we will receive our happiness and there where his happiness lies, wherein he has his being; in this same ground all of God's friends will receive their blessedness and create from it. That is the "table in the kingdom of God." May God help us that we may come to this table.[13]

Here Eckhart links the table of the kingdom of God with the blessings of a divine meal. Elsewhere we saw that Eckhart identified the kingdom with the following of Jesus and we see from the scriptural citation in this sermon where he got this idea. Eckhart links happiness and blessedness with the celebration of the kingdom. The very table of the kingdom of heaven, then, is to be identified with the community celebration that all being engages in around the table of the ground of being. All beings rejoice at their own being and gather around this table. It should be noted, too, that Eckhart emphasizes how "all of God's friends" will be blessed at this table, just as in the present sermon he begins with the statement that the kingdom of God is nearer to us than we believe. This emphasis on the plural, "us," rather than the singular, "me," is welcome and refreshing, for many spiritualist theologians since Eckhart's day have overly privatized the translation of Luke's Gospel as "within me." Eckhart, as we have seen, abolishes the I/you and in/out dualisms in favor of a celebrative feast of "all of God's friends." Further development of this theme of the heavenly feast of Eckhart will be found in the Commentary to Sermon Thirty-seven.

Eckhart links the kingdom of God to the blessedness and happiness of persons in still another way. In one sermon he says that the kingdom of God consists of five things, and in another he says blessedness consists of four things. They are as follows:

The Kingdom of God

1. God is the first cause and pours himself out in all things.
2. God is the inwardness of all things.
3. God pours forth and therefore shares himself with everything that is.
4. God is unchangeable and therefore the most everlasting.
5. God is perfect and therefore the most desirable.[14]

Blessedness Lies in Four Things

1. That people have everything which has being and is desirous and brings pleasure;
2. That people have this completely undivided with their whole soul;
3. That people have this in God and in its clearest and highest form, pure, uncovered in its first outbreak and in the ground of being;
4. That people have it always taken there where God himself takes it.[15]

In this parallel schema we can see how Eckhart identifies the kingdom of God with blessedness—"All people desire blessedness," he declares.[16] But the elements of both the kingdom of God and of blessedness overlap, and, since the elements of the kingdom are all blessings, so too is our blessedness. Both the kingdom and blessedness are a blessing. It should be noticed also that the kingdom of God is identified not with institution nor with privatized feelings toward him but with the cosmic presence of God found "in *all* things" insofar as they exist and insofar as they desire. The kingdom of God is a kingdom of panentheism, or, in Eckhart's image borrowed from Ezekiel, a kingdom of a fishnet encompassing all being. The happiness or blessedness which Eckhart referred to in Sermon Nine is a blessedness of knowing how near God's blessing is. *Such people will know that the kingdom of God is near.* An awareness of the proximity of the blessing makes human consciousness so divinely happy and blessed. Such an awakened—or repentant—individual is also aware that he or she is of royal blood . . . *then I really would be asking. And thus the whole wealth of a king would be mine, and nothing of a king's wealth would be lacking to me.* We shall explore later (Sermon Thirty-six) Eckhart's development of the royal tradition in the Hebrew Bible. But here, in the context of this sermon on God's kingdom, it suffices to point out that those who belong to the kingdom of God and know it are indeed kings. All creation is of royal lineage, but the human species are kings because they can know they are. *For if I were a king and did not know it, then I would be no king.* Long live this royal race!

Sermon Ten: A GOD WHO REJOICES AND SUFFERS, BLESSES AND CONSOLES

"Rejoice, ye heavens, and let the earth exult." (Is. 49:13)
"I am the light of the world." (Jn. 8:12)*

I have made two brief statements in Latin. The first is written in the Lesson, and is by the prophet Isaiah: "Rejoice, heaven and earth, God has consoled his people and will take pity on his poor" (Is. 49:13). The second is in the Gospel, and in it our Lord says: "I am the light of the world, and whoever follows me will not walk in the dark, and he will find and have the light of life" (Jn. 8:12).

Now pay attention to the first statement that the prophet makes: "Rejoice, heaven and earth!" Truly, truly! By God, by God! Be as certain of this as that God lives. All the saints in heaven and on earth as well as all the angels rejoice with such joy over the smallest good deed or the smallest goodwill or the smallest good desire that this whole world could not offer a joy like it! And the higher each saint is, the greater is his joy. And all this joy together is quite as small as an eye's lens in comparison with the joy God has in this deed. For God has sheer delight and laughter over a good deed. For all other deeds that do not take place in praise of God are quite like ashes in God's sight. On this account the prophet says: "Rejoice, heaven and earth! God has consoled his people."

Note now how he says: "God has consoled his people and will take pity on his poor." He says: "*His* poor." The poor are indeed left to God, for no one else takes an interest in them. If a person has a friend who is poor, he or she does not acknowledge the friend. If the friend, however, **has** possessions and is wise, this person says, "You are my relative," and quickly acknowledges the

* "Laudate coeli et exultet terra; et ego sum lux mundi." (DW III, ℵ79)

friend. But to a poor person he or she will say, "May God look after you!" The poor are left to God; for wherever they are, they find God and have God everywhere. God takes an interest in them because they are handed over to him. For this reason the Gospel says: "Blessed are the poor" (Mt. 5:3).

Note now the brief statement our Lord makes: "I am the light of the world" (Jn. 8:12). "I am"—with this he touches on being. The masters of the spiritual life say: "All creatures can indeed say 'I'; this word is current. However, no one can utter the word *sum* ('I am') in its correct meaning except God alone." The word *sum* means more or less "something that bears God within itself." It is, however, denied to all creatures that any of them could have everything that might *completely* console human beings. If I had everything I could desire and only my finger hurt me, I would not have complete consolation as long as my finger hurt. Bread is quite consoling for a person so long as he or she is hungry. If, however, that person is thirsty, he or she would have as little consolation from it as from a stone. It is exactly the same way with clothing, which is quite comforting to someone who is freezing. But when a person is too hot, he or she has no comfort in clothing. This is exactly the way it is with all creatures. For this reason, it is true that all creatures bear bitterness within themselves. On the other hand, it is quite true that all creatures bear within themselves a form of consolation, like skimmed honey. All the good that can exist in creatures—all their honey—is gathered together in God. Thus it is written in the Book of Wisdom: "With you [Wisdom] all good things come to my soul" (Ws. 7:11). This consolation comes from God. The consolation of creatures is not perfect, however, because it brings a mixture with it. But God's consolation is pure and unadulterated; it is complete and perfect. And it is so necessary for him to give to you that he cannot wait to give *himself* as the first gift to you. God has been made so foolish by his love of us that it is as if he had forgotten the kingdom of heaven and the kingdom of earth and all his happiness and all his Godhead. It is as if he had nothing to do except what he does with me, so that he gives me everything that might console me. He gives this to me totally and he gives it to me perfectly. He gives it in its purest state and at all times and to all creatures.

Now he says: "Whoever follows me will not walk in the darkness" (Jn. 8:12). Note how he says: "Whoever follows me." The masters of the spiritual life say that the soul has three powers. The first power always seeks what is sweetest. The second always seeks what is highest. And the third power always seeks what is best. For the soul is so noble that it can rest nowhere but in the source from which trickles forth whatever goodness accomplishes. Behold how sweet God's consolation is so that all creatures seek it and pursue it. And I shall say something further, namely, that the being and life of all creatures depend on their seeking and pursuing God.

Now you can ask: "Where is this God whom all creatures pursue, and from whom they have their being and their life?" I shall speak gladly about the Godhead, because all our happiness flows from it.

The Father says: "My Son, I generate you today in the reflected glory of the saints" (Ps. 110:3). Where is this God? "In the fullness of the saints I am embraced" (Si. 24:16). Where is this God? "In the Father." Where is this God? "In eternity." No one could ever discover God, as the wise man said: "Lord, you are a hidden God" (Is. 45:15). Where is this God? God has acted exactly like people who hide themselves and then clear their throats, thus giving themselves away. No one could ever have discovered God, but he has now given himself away. A saint says: "I receive now and then such happiness with you that I forget myself and all creatures, and fly completely to you. If I wish to embrace this happiness completely, Lord, you remove it from me. Lord, what do you mean by this? If you entice me, why do you not then take me? If you love me, why do you flee from me? Alas, Lord, you are doing this so that I can receive much from you!" The prophet says: "My God!" "Who tells you that I am your God?" "Lord, I can never rest except in you, and I am only happy in you" (Ps. 16:2).

May the Father and the Son and the Holy Spirit help us to seek and find God in this way! Amen.

COMMENTARY: God's Joy and Our Joy/Who Is God, Where Is
           God?/How the Consolation God Gives Is Born of
           God's Suffering/The Soul Is a Cornucopia of Blessing
           That Passes On the Blessing Called Creation/Eckhart's
           Theology as a Theology of Blessing

Eckhart preaches this sermon with two biblical texts in front of him. One
represents the first reading in the liturgy, which is from Isaiah, and the
second is the Gospel and is from John. The fuller Isaian text from
which Eckhart preaches is as follows:

> Thus says Yahweh:
> At the favorable time I will answer you,
> on the day of salvation I will help you.
> (I have formed you and have appointed you
> as covenant of the people.)
> I will restore the land
> and assign you the estates that lie waste . . .
> They will never hunger or thirst,
> scorching wind and sun shall never plague them;
> for he who pities them will lead them
> and guide them to springs of water . . .
> Shout for joy, you heavens; exult, you earth!
> You mountains, break into happy cries!
> For Yahweh consoles his people
> and takes pity on those who are afflicted.
>
> For Zion was saying, "Yahweh has abandoned me,
> the Lord has forgotten me."
> Does a woman forget her baby at the breast,
> or fail to cherish the son of her womb?
> Yet even if these forget,
> I will never forget you. (Is. 49:8, 10, 13–15)

It is in commenting on these scriptural texts that Eckhart discusses the
deeds that save and create rejoicing for creature and Creator alike, the
different kinds of consolation that creatures are offered by a compassionate God, and the radical unforgetting or remembering that God undergoes toward creation.

First Eckhart, like the Scriptures, calls for exulting. We need to exult at the exultation of all of creation. *Be as certain of this as that God lives. All the saints in heaven and on earth as well as all the angels rejoice with such joy . . . and the higher each saint is, the greater is his joy.* Joy is the end result of all saintly living, whether on earth or in heaven. Schürmann has called Eckhart's spirituality one of a "wandering joy." For joy is the fruit of love and our existence is bathed in such love for those who are awake and aware. But as great as the joy of creatures is, the joy of God is even greater—*all this joy together is quite as small as an eye's lens in comparison with the joy God has.* Eckhart's God is a God who rejoices—a pleasurable, joyful, feeling, laughing God. *For God has sheer delight and laughter over a good deed.* Eckhart speaks elsewhere of God's good humor forming the very core of the Godhead.

> When God laughs at the soul and the soul laughs back at God, the persons of the Trinity are begotten. To speak in hyperbole, when the Father laughs to the Son and the Son laughs back to the Father, that laughter gives pleasure, that pleasure gives joy, that joy gives love, and love gives the persons [of the Trinity] of which the Holy Spirit is one.[1]

God rejoices over deeds that bring justice.

> God rejoices at every work of the just person, however small it is. When this work is done through justice and results in justice, God will rejoice at it. Indeed, God will rejoice so thoroughly that nothing will remain in his ground which does not tickle him through and through out of joy. Ignorant people have to believe this, but enlightened ones must know it.[2]

Elsewhere Eckhart talks of God's rapture at creation. "God finds joy and rapture to the full and the person who dwells within God's knowing and God's love becomes nothing other than what God himself is."[3] The inness of all creation dwelling in God gives God immense pleasure.

> God is so joyful in this equality that in it he completely pours out his nature and his being through himself. This is a joy to him. In the same way, if one were to let a horse run about in a green meadow, which was quite flat and level, it would be the horse's nature to pour forth its whole strength in leaping about

in the meadow. This would be a joy to it and would be in accordance with its nature. In the same way, it is a joy to God and a satisfaction to him when he finds equality. It is a joy to him to pour out his nature and his being completely into his likeness, since he is the likeness himself.[4]

Eckhart says that in the soul's core "God is fully verdant and flowering, in all the joy and all the honor that he is in himself. There reigns such a dear joy, so incomprehensibly great a joy, that no one can ever fully speak of it."[5] Thus the divine joy is as ineffable as the divinity itself. "In God there is neither wrath nor grief, but only love and joy."[6] Elsewhere, Eckhart talks in a similar vein. God "wishes himself to be only and absolutely our own . . . His greatest bliss and joy depend upon this. The greater and more comprehensively he can be this, the greater is his bliss and joy."[7]

This very real joy on God's part is a joy of giving, for God enjoys giving the divine gifts. "God gives away nothing so happily as big gifts . . . This is quite the way it is with grace and gifts and virtues: the bigger they are, the more happily does God give them. For it is his nature to give big gifts. Therefore, the more valuable the gifts are, the more does he bestow them."[8] In fact, so much does God enjoy giving the best gift—which is himself—that he "forgets" *the kingdom of heaven and the kingdom of earth and all his happiness and all his Godhead and is made foolish* by his eagerness to give.

> It is so necessary for him to give to you that he cannot wait to give himself as the first gift to you . . . It is as if he had nothing to do except what he does with me . . . He gives it to me perfectly; he gives it in its purest state and at all times and to all creatures.

God's giving is not only a giving of self but also a giving of consolation, as Isaiah had said: "Yahweh consoles his peoples and takes pity on those who are afflicted" (49:10). However, the consolation the biblical God gives is not a condescending kind of consolation. It is a consolation of authentic compassion which means that before God gives consolation out of compassion, God has first to suffer. Eckhart's God is one who rejoices and one who suffers.

> However great suffering is, if it comes through God, God
> suffers from it first. Indeed, by the truth which is God, however
> slight the suffering that befalls a person may be, let us say
> some discomfort or trial, provided that one places it in God, it
> would affect God immeasurably more than the person and it
> would be more obnoxious to him, insofar as it is obnoxious to
> the person . . . God suffers for the sake of some benefit that
> he has destined for you by this means . . .[9]

The suffering that God suffers is in turn meant to turn our sufferings to
joy. "If it is the case that God has suffered previously, before I suffer,
and if I suffer for the sake of God, then indeed all my sufferings will easily become comfort and joy to me, however great and varied they are."
God not only rejoices with and more than us, God also suffers with and
more than us.

> God suffers with man, indeed he suffers in his way before and
> incomparably more than the person who suffers for his sake
> . . . God suffers so gladly with us and for our sakes that, if
> we suffer for the sake of God alone, he suffers without suffer-
> ing. Suffering is so blissful to him that for him suffering is not
> suffering . . . God suffers with me, and suffers for my sake
> through the love which he has for me.[10]

This capacity of Eckhart's God to suffer and to rejoice with humanity is
what distinguished the biblical God from many Gods of the philosophers,
as Rabbi Heschel points out.[11] Eckhart's God, like Heschel's God, is a
caring, passionate God.

God's suffering is especially oriented toward the poor. The poor in
Isaiah, as Eckhart notes, are called "his poor." The poor are God's in a
special way. The poor are indeed left to God, for no one else takes an
interest in them. We acknowledge the better-off as our friends, but not
the poor of whom we feel ashamed. The first of the Beatitudes reads:
"Blessed are the poor" (Mt. 5:3) and this is so because wherever they
(the poor) are, they find God and have God everywhere. Eckhart seems
to have in mind Matthew 25:31–46 when he comments that we console
one another with bread only if the issue is starvation; with clothing, only
if one is cold. He also seems to be suggesting a link with Jesus' story on
persons who ask for bread but receive a stone (Mt. 7:7–11). Thus there

exist two kinds of consolation to creatures: that which comes from creatures themselves and that which comes from God. Creatures fall short in
their giving of consolation; they often give bread when a person is
thirsty or clothing when a person is too hot. *The consolation of creatures
is not perfect . . . But God's consolation is pure and unadulterated; it is
complete and perfect.*

What makes God's consolation so complete and perfect? Only God
has that which *might completely console human beings.* This is, first of
all, the kingdom of heaven known as being. God alone can say: "I am."
To be means *more or less something that bears God within itself. The
being and life of all creatures depends on the* being and life of God,
who alone consoles fully. What consoles is being, what is. Thus what
consoles fully is God, who is alone fully being. *No one can utter the
word sum ("I am") in its correct meaning except God alone.* Only God,
being fully being, is fully capable of consolation. Eckhart, commenting on
John 8:12, "I am the light of the world," first concentrates on the "I am"
(or eimi) statement. Like contemporary scholars such as Raymond Brown,
Eckhart sees the connection between Jesus' "I am" statement and that
name with which Yahweh named himself in Exodus 3:14. Brown calls this
the "all-important text for the meaning of 'Yahweh.'"

> If we understand "Yahweh" as derived from a causative form,
> the Hebrew reads, "I am who cause to be," or perhaps more
> originally in the third person, "I am 'He who cause to be.'"
> But LXX reads, "I am the Existing One," using a participle of
> the verb "to be," and thus stressing divine existence.[12]

In his commentary on Exodus, Eckhart elaborates on the name of God as
"I am":

> When God says, "I am," "am" is here the predicate of the
> sentence and the second element in the sentence. Whenever
> this is the case, it signifies pure and naked existence in the
> subject and regarding the subject, and that it is the subject, in
> other words the essence of the subject, thus expressing the
> identity of essence and existence—which is proper to God
> alone, whose quiddity is in *anitas* . . . and who has no quid-
> dity except *anitas* alone, which is expressed by existence.[18]

Applying Eckhart's principles to Jesus' saying, then, we would have to say that Jesus is declaring himself related to "pure and naked existence" by his "I am" declaration.

But Eckhart sees still more in the divine affirmation of "I am." And that more is what is *not* being said, and what is being denied by this affirmation. All negation is being denied of God.

> The repetition of "am" in the statement "I am who am" points out the purity of the affirmation, which excludes every negation from God. It also indicates a certain reversion and turning back of his being into and upon itself, and its abiding or remaining in itself: also a sort of boiling up or giving birth to itself: an inward glowing, melting and boiling in itself and into itself, light in light and into light wholly penetrating its whole self, totally and from every side turned and reflected upon itself.[14]

Here Eckhart connects "I am" and light, making a subtle connection between Exodus and John's Gospel statement, "I am the light of the world." Light was the first of the creatures made by the Creator (Gn. 1:3), light reveals the hidden God, light is the symbol of the Feast of Tabernacles at which Jesus spoke these words, light is a symbol for Wisdom and in the next chapter of John's Gospel, Jesus will restore sight (that is, light) to the blind man (Jn. 9). His deed will follow on his declaration of who he is.[15] Thus, in walking after this light, one does *not walk in the darkness*. For God is the light of existence and of being, "an inward glowing, melting and boiling in itself and into itself, light in light and into light." Nor does one any longer need to walk in sadness. Light is also a symbol for the Messianic age and the life and joy that this age ushers in with it. God is a light of passion and feeling who laughs, rejoices, suffers, and ultimately comforts. Such comfort is not condescending, for it is born of the divine suffering wherein passion truly precedes compassion. Only this divine light gives the light of authentic consolation to the world.

> Behold how sweet God's consolation is so that all creatures seek it and pursue it. And I shall say something further, namely, that the being and life of all creatures depend on their seeking and pursuing God.

The being that God is and the light that God is exclude all negation from God. God consoles so fully because he despises negation so totally, with all God's being and all God's light. God even negates negation. "The negation of negation is the quintessence, purity, and doubling of affirmed being" (Ex. 3:14: "I am who am."). Hence it is aptly said: "Show us the Father"—that is, the One—"and it is enough for us."[16] The unity of God excludes all negation.

> Unity is a negation of negation and a denial of denial. What does unity mean? It means oneness, to which nothing is added as an attribute . . . God is one. He is the negation of negation.[17]

Only this thorough oneness with all suffering and all wholeness and healing can truly console. God's consolation is pure and unadulterated; it is complete and perfect. Creaturely consolation will always fall short of total healing because "all creatures have a negation in themselves; one denies that it is the other."[18] Creatures are subject to separation and division. Only God is panentheistically one and therefore capable of ultimate holism.

If God is the "negation of negation," then God is the negation of darkness—God is light; God is the negation of separateness—God is unity; God is the negation of superficiality—God is depth; God is the negation of control—God is freedom; God is the negation of ugliness—God is beauty; God is the negation of sadness—God is consolation; God is the negation of names—God is silent namelessness. Thus Eckhart passes in this sermon from the cataphatic treatment of who God is—God as amness, God as light—to where God is.

> Now you can ask: "Where is this God whom all creatures pursue, and from whom they have their being and their life?" I shall speak gladly about the Godhead, because all our happiness flows from it.

Already Eckhart has begun to answer his question of the where of God. God is beyond God to the Godhead, from which all happiness flows. Citing Scripture wherever he meets the Godhead, he declares that God may be found in the fullness of the saints, in the Father, in eternity. These three meeting places for God can be understood as the communion of saints, the Creator of the world, and youthfulness or newness of spirit. But they are not enough. For God remains a hidden God. *Lord, you are a hidden God and no one could ever discover God.* And yet, an amazing revelation has happened. God, while remaining hidden, has also revealed himself like a person in hiding who clears his throat. *No one could ever have discovered God, but he has now given himself away.* God has revealed himself and so our seeking after our origins is not in vain.

The ultimate giveaway of the hiding place of God, the place where God may be found for certain, is where there is rejoicing over the blessings of God's creation. Where there is rejoicing, there plays God. Creation itself—being and life—are the first of the divine blessings. *All the good that can exist in creatures—all their honey—is gathered together in God.* No one rejoices over the blessing that creation is more than God. *All the saints in heaven and on earth as well as all angels rejoice with such joy . . . yet all this joy together is quite as small as an eye's lens in comparison with the joy God has.* But the joy of conscious creation, namely of angels and of humans, must be a joy taken at becoming blessings by way of their deeds. Conscious creation is destined to become blessings to creation. These deeds concern the poor in particular who are God's own. For all persons are not equally blessed. The poor are more blessed than others. *God takes an interest in them because they are handed over to him. For this reason the Gospel says: "Blessed are the poor"* (Mt. 5:3) . . . *God has sheer delight and laughter over a good deed. For all other deeds that do not take place in praise of God are quite like ashes in God's sight.*

The *praise of God* that creation returns to God is the return of blessing for blessing. Blessing is the work of the human soul, the masterpiece of creation. As Westermann puts it, talking of Jewish theology of blessing:

> "Soul" is seen as expressing the person's total state of being alive. The soul is a totality, filled with power. This power lets the soul grow and prosper so that it can maintain itself and do its work in the world. This vital power, without which no living being can exist, the Israelites called *berakhah*, "blessing."[19]

Westermann's explanation of the Jewish understanding of soul corresponds with Eckhart's emphasis on spirituality as soul growth, which we have considered in the previous two sermons. If there exists an "identity" between us and God, then our growing into this likeness and our developing the image of God the Creator in us also means our developing our powers to bless. As Mowinckel puts it, "blessing is a capability of the soul, a power that lives in the clan and its members . . . The power that brings blessing in the 'name of Yahweh.' "[20] The human person, being a part of creation that is conscious of creation, is also responsible for creation and for blessing. That which is blest, blesses. To bless is to praise. What it means to be "submerged" in the grace of creation is that one passes on the blessing to others. "God is one; there is the soul blessed."[21] Blessing is the name given the power of the soul that so resembles God because it is God's image. "Blessing is the center of life; it is life itself and it includes all phases of life. It is the positive vital power, which for the people of Israel is manifest above all in fertility."[22] Eckhart will develop this blessing theme of fertility at great length in Path Three, where he elaborates on our calling to give birth. The power that the soul is has no intrinsic limits, says Westermann, echoing what Eckhart said in Sermon Seven.

> The total "soul" of a person embraces everything within the circle of his life, everything around him. If his soul is strong, it must leave an impression on all his undertakings . . . Blessing is the soul's power that produces all progress (salah). This means it is related to wisdom . . . The act of blessing, berekh, means imparting vital power to another person. The one who blesses gives the other person something of his own soul.[23]

The picture that Westermann paints of the soul that embraces everything within the circle of its life parallels the picture we have seen described by Eckhart in the past ten sermons, and the last three in particular. Both theologians insist that the one who possesses blessing and is therefore "blessed" is one from whom power of praise and consoling deeds flows out in every direction. Nothing is unholy, nothing unsacred, nothing hostile to this flow of creation's energy. The senses too participate in this flowing out and flowing in. The blessing, like the Word of creation which it is, flows out but remains within. The innermost core, the ancilla animae, the divine spark, may well be conceived as a bonfire of blessing that burns its way into all of creation. "God loves all things in all his works. The soul is in 'all things.' "[24] Eckhart, who, we have seen, describes the human spirit as a "vortex" or "whirlpool," thus suggests that the depth of our psyches is a cornucopia of blessings! From the world, which is also the soul, to the innermost spark of the soul, all is blessed. Our spiritual journey is a sinking into the innermost depths of the whirlpool or vortex, which is a cornucopia, for that is where God is most at home. "It is proper to God and to everything divine, insofar as they are divine, to be within, to be innermost."[25]

For all is divinely bestowed, divinely poured out. This is why all of Eckhart's theology—and especially this phase of the First Path called Creation—is a theology of blessing. For creation, and human creation in particular, is a cornucopia of blessings.

PATH TWO: LETTING GO AND
LETTING BE

Eckhart says that the way to God is not a burden but a blessing. "The path is beautiful and pleasant and joyful and familiar."[1] And so, from our experience in Path One with the blessing that creation is as it flows out but remains within the Creator, that is the case. As an act of faith purely made, this is the case: all creation praises God. However, Eckhart is not naïve about the brokenness of the way we perceive creation and interact with it. "Every angel is with his whole joy and his whole bliss inside me and God himself with his whole bliss. Yet I do not perceive this."[2]

In Path Two, then, Eckhart deals with how we heal our broken ways of seeing and loving the world. "We love everything according to our own goodness," he declares.[3] If we could heal our own goodness we would begin to heal the beings we love. In the first path, that of creation, we have traveled the *via positiva* toward the cataphatic God or the God of light, of being, of life, of creation. In this path we will travel the *via negativa* toward an apophatic God, the unnameable, hidden, dark God of nothingness. Neither way to God is a way of fear, however. For this path too is a path that is "beautiful and pleasant and joyful and familiar."

Sermon Eleven: DIVINITY'S DARK SIDE

"This Word is written in the Gospel."*

We find in the Gospel the verse: "There was a noble man who went out into a strange land" far from himself "and came home again richer" (Lk. 19:12). Now we read in another gospel passage that Christ said: "No one can be my disciple unless he follow me" (Lk. 14:27) and has emptied himself of his ego, keeping nothing back for himself. Such a person has everything, for to have nothing is to have everything. This means to throw oneself completely under the will of God and always to put one's own will in God's, casting not even a glance at anything created. Those who thus go out from themselves will indeed be given back their true selves.

Goodness in itself, good things, these do not give rest to the soul. If God gave me anything *without* his will, I would pay no attention to it. But the least thing which God gives me *with* this will makes me happy.

All creatures have flowed out from God's will. If I could desire only God's goodness, then this will of mine would be so noble that the Holy Spirit would immediately flow out from it. All good things flow from the overflow of God's goodness. But the will of God tastes good to me only in that unity where the peace of God is for the goodness of all creatures, wherein this goodness and everything that has being and life rest as in their final goal. There is where you should love the Holy Spirit, as he is there in unity, not in himself, but there where he tastes with the goodness of God alone in unity, where all goodness flows out from the overflow of the goodness of God. Such a person "comes home richer" than when he went out. Those who go out from themselves in this way will be given themselves again in a more real sense. And every-

* "Dieses Wort steht geschrieben im Evangelium." (DW I, ℀15)

thing which such persons leave in multiplicity will always be returned to them in simplicity, for they find both themselves and everything else in the present now of unity. And those who go out in this way come home much nobler than they went out. Such persons live now in bare freedom and complete emptiness, having no need to possess or acquire anything, whether little or much. For everything belonging to God belongs to them.

The sun is like God: the highest part of its unfathomable depths answers the lowest depth of humility. Yes, the humble need not beg God so much as bid him, for the heights of divinity can disregard everything else but the depths of humility, for the humble person and God are one and not two. Such humble people are powerful with God because they are so powerful with themselves. They possess all goodness in all the angels and saints, just as God does. God and such a humble person are totally one and not two. Whatever God does, the humble person does; whatever God wants, the humble person wants; and whatever God is, that the humble person is as well—one life and one being. Yes, by God, if such a person were in hell, God would be constrained to join that person there and hell itself would be for such a person like heaven.

God must do this of necessity; he would be constrained to do it. For this humble person is the divine being and the divine being is this person. For there takes place in the unity of God and in the humble person a kiss. For the virtue which is called humility is a root in the ground of divinity where it is planted so that it has its existence only in the eternal One and nowhere else. I said to those at the University of Paris that all things come to perfection in the truly humble person. And therefore I say that the truly humble can neither come to harm nor wander astray. For there is nothing which does not run away from whatever would destroy it. The humble run away from all created things because they are nothing in themselves. And thus the humble run away from everything which can make them wander from God in the same way that I flee hot coals because they could destroy me and rob me of my being.

And Christ said: "A man went out." Aristotle began a book and wanted to talk about everything. Now pay attention to what

Aristotle says about human beings. *Homo* is the same thing here as a human being to whom a substantial form is proper. This form gives a human person an existence and life in common with all creatures, both those with the faculty of reason and those without it—the former including all material creatures and the latter including the angels. And Aristotle says that all creatures with their ideas and forms are grasped intellectually by the angels. The angels intellectually understand each thing in itself. This affords great joy to the angels and it would be a miracle for them *not* to have received and enjoyed this intellectual vision. And Aristotle goes on to say that it is just in this way that human beings with their reasons know the ideas and forms of all creatures in their distinctions. Aristotle ascribes this to human beings as precisely that which makes them human. For Aristotle this is the highest meaning by which he can specify human existence.

Now I will give you my opinion about what it means to be human. *Homo* is the same thing here as a human being to whom a substance has been given, and this gives a human being existence and life, and it is an existence endowed with reason. The truly reasonable human beings are those who understand themselves with their reason and then free themselves from all material things as well as forms. The more people are free of all things and turn to themselves, the more they will know in themselves all things clearly with their reason, without any hindrance from outside. And the more they do this, the more they are truly human.

Now I ask how that can be, this freeing of our knowing from all form and images and yet knowing things in themselves without hindrance from outside or change in oneself? I answer that it comes from the simplicity which is ours as human beings. For the more purely human beings are free from themselves and in themselves, the more simply they know all diversity in themselves and remain unchangeable in themselves. Boethius says that God is an unmovable good, remaining in himself, undisturbed and unmoved and yet moving all things. A simple knowing is so pure in itself that it knows without mediation the pure, bare divine being. And in this influx of the divine being, it receives the divine nature just like the angels who take such great joy in that. People might be willing to spend a thousand years in hell to be able to see an angel. This knowing is so simple and clear in itself that an angel would spring from everything seen in this light.

Now pay careful attention to the fact that Aristotle speaks of pure spirits in the book called *Metaphysics*. The chief among the teachers who have ever discussed the natural sciences talks about these pure spirits and says that they are not the form of anything but receive their existence as it flows out immediately from God. And so they also flow back in and receive the outflow from God without mediation, higher than the angels as they gaze at the pure existence of God without differentiation. This simple pure existence is called by Aristotle a something. That is the highest teaching Aristotle ever spoke about the natural sciences, and no teacher has ever cared to express anything higher unless he were speaking in the Holy Spirit. Now I say that the "noble man" in our gospel story was not satisfied with the being which the angels grasp without form and on which they hang without mediation. For the "noble man" of our gospel story nothing was enough but the only One.

I have spoken in other places of the first beginning and the last end. The Father is the beginning of the Godhead because he understands himself in himself. It is from the Father that the eternal Word, though always remaining within, nevertheless goes out, and the Father does not give birth to him, for he remains within and is the goal of the Godhead and all creatures, the One in whom there is pure peace and rest for everything which ever received being. The beginning is for the sake of the final goal, for in that final end everything rests which ever received existence endowed with reason. The final goal of being is the darkness or the unknowability of the hidden divinity, which is that light that shines "but the darkness has not comprehended it" (cf. Jn. 1:5). Therefore Moses said: "He who is there has sent me" (Ex. 3:14), he who is without name and is the denial of all names and who has never been given a name. And therefore the prophet said: "You are truly a hidden God" (Is. 45:15) in the ground of the soul where the ground of God and the ground of the soul are one ground. The more we seek you, the less we find you. You should seek him in such a way that you never find him. For it is when you do not seek him that you find him. May God help us to seek him in such a way that we may remain with him forever. Amen.

COMMENTARY: Salvation as a Change in Consciousness/True Humility
                Is a Journeying into the Darkness of Oneself/The Ten-
                sion Between Love and Sacrifice, Between the *Via
                Positiva* and the *Via Negativa*/Knowing the Unknown
                God/The Final Goal of Being Is the Darkness of Divin-
                ity

The reasons for Path Two, the way of letting go and letting be, are
outlined in this sermon. For the reasons concern our way of seeing reality, which is very often obstructive of the truth of the wholeness and holiness of all things, and also the immense darkness that God is and the
unknowability of God. Both of these journeys coincide, however, for we
will know God as we know ourselves. We will journey into God as we
journey into ourselves. If we can face the darkness within, we can face
the darkness that is God.

Eckhart perceives a tension in our everyday experience of God that
he wants all of us to share in. Creation is good—divinely good—but are
we? "If we had divine love, God and all the works that God ever performed would delight us."[1] Creatures are good but so often they *do not
give rest to the soul*. Why not? Because we do not see with the divine
goodness.

> If I could desire only God's goodness, then this will of mine
> would be so noble that the Holy Spirit would immediately flow
> out from it. All good things flow from the overflow of God's
> goodness. But the will of God tastes good to me only in that
> unity where the peace of God is for the goodness of all crea-
> tures, wherein this goodness and everything that has being and
> life rest as in their final goal.

The problem is the way we relate to creation. "You yourself are the very
thing which hinders you. For you are related to things in a perverted
way."[2]

Some spiritual traditions emphasize the fall at the expense of the
blessings of creation. Eckhart, being a creation-centered theologian, will
have none of that rejection of creation or the labeling of creation as
sinful. Spiritualities constructed on a fall-oriented theology will leap immediately into ascetic practices to mortify the human person and control
impulse and emotional élan. Eckhart is not so simplistic. He knows how to

live with the tension of the positive and the negative ways rather than merely controlling passions and calling such control sanctity. He derives his nuanced way of spiritual practice from the two Gospel stories he employs in the present sermon. The first of these represents the *via positiva* and the responsibility to develop one's talents. It comes from the Gospel of Luke (19:11–26). This parable of the pounds in Luke is "in substance the same story" as that of the parable of the talents in Matthew's Gospel (25:14–30), C. H. Dodd points out. It is a story of the need to develop the gifts that creation gives.

> At an early stage the parable of the money in trust was used to illustrate the maxim that a person who possesses spiritual capacity will enlarge that capacity by experience, while a person who has none will decline into a worse condition as time goes on . . .[8]

The individual in the parable is chastised for his lack of vision, of opportunism, and of self-assertiveness and his overly cautious attitude.

Eckhart consciously contrasts this *via positiva* kind of biblical parable with another saying of Jesus from Luke's Gospel:

> Great crowds accompanied him on his way and he turned and spoke to them. "If any man comes to me without hating his father, mother, wife, children, brothers, sisters, yes and his own life too, he cannot be my disciple. Anyone who does not carry his cross and come after me cannot be my disciple." (Lk. 14:25–27)

Eckhart comments immediately on this passage that it means that a person *empty himself of his ego, keeping nothing back for himself.* But the tension still remains between the *via positiva* and the *via negativa* and Eckhart makes no effort to relieve the tension. Rather, he invites us to explore the tension in greater depth. For, on the one hand, God is love whom all creatures seek to love.

> If anyone asked me what God is, I would say now that God is love. Indeed, God is so completely worthy of love that all creatures seek to love his amiability, regardless of whether they do so wittingly or unwittingly, whether they do so happily

or unhappily. Thus God is love, and he is so worthy of love that everything that can love must love him, whether happily or unhappily.[4]

While we have seen in Path One that "being is God," we read in Path Two that "nothing that has been created is God."[5] On the one hand, we can say that isness is God's proper name.

> Among all names of God, there is none more apt than "he who exists" . . . Fully detached and pared down and stripped so bare that nothing remains but a simple "is"—that is the proper nature of God's name. That is why God said to Moses: "Tell the people that 'he who is' has sent you."[6]

On the other hand, commenting on the very same passage from Exodus 3:14 in the present sermon, Eckhart declares: *He who is without name and is the denial of all names and who has never been given a name.* On the one hand we have called God being; but on the other, God is beyond being.

> Before there was being, God acted. He accomplished being when there was as yet no being. Coarse-minded masters of the spiritual life say that God is a pure being. But he is as high above being as the highest angel is above a gnat. I would say something just as incorrect if I were to call God a being as if I were to call the sun light or dark. God is neither this nor the other.[7]

This tension between developing talents and carrying the cross, between naming God and not naming God, is also found in nature itself. That is why Eckhart does not overreact or want us to overreact to the tension. When we overreact, then "we are the cause of all our difficulties,"[8] for we have misperceived and misconstrued what living is about. The parallel in nature is found in the seed that dies in order to give birth. The paradox of the spiritual life is the paradox of all life. "Life can never be complete unless it is brought to its manifest first cause in which life is a form of being that the soul receives when the soul dies to its very foundation. And this foundation is what we live on in that life in which life is a form of being."[9] Dying is part of nature and nature and grace go hand in hand. So does the development of talents and the shadow of the cross.

> God is not a destroyer of any good thing, but he is a per-
> fecter. God is not a destroyer of nature, but he is a perfecter.
> Moreover, grace does not destroy nature but rather perfects it.
> If God destroyed nature in this way at the outset, it would
> suffer violence and injustice. He does not do that. Man has a
> free will, with which he can choose or decide between good
> and evil . . . There is nothing in God that would destroy any-
> thing that has any kind of being, but he is a perfecter of all
> things. In the same way, we should not destroy any good,
> however small, in ourselves, nor any small way for the sake of
> a greater one, but we should perfect them all in the highest
> possible manner.[10]

Eckhart advises that we accept all that comes our way, nature included, as grace. "Strive to accept everything equally from God's hand as grace, gift, whatever it may be, whether inside or outside us."[11]

How do we do this? How do we live the holistic life of tension, being true to the nameable and unnameable God at once? By humility, Eckhart says. "The impediments are in" us and so self-knowledge is the way to freeing self of impediments.[12]

> It is always you yourself that hinder yourself, because your at-
> titude toward things is wrong. Therefore begin first with your-
> self and let yourself go. Truly, if you will not flee first from
> yourself, wherever else you may flee, there you will find im-
> pediments and restlessness, wherever it may be.[13]

This truthful self-knowledge which is humility is "the root of all good, and follows the good."[14] In true humility, God who is truth becomes one with the truth of ourselves. The humble person and God are one and not two. There is no distance between God and us when we truly know our own depths. This humble person is the divine being and the divine being is this person . . . For the virtue which is called humility is a root in the ground of divinity, where it is planted so that it has its existence only in the eternal One and nowhere else. Humility is like a vacuum that sucks God into oneself. "The All-highest in his unfathomable Godhead yields to the very lowest in the depths of humility . . . If a person were truly humble, then God must either destroy all his Godhead and renounce it entirely, or he must pour himself out and must flow entirely into this person."[15] While one can say that "the heights of the Godhead are nothing else but the depths of humility," still we should not conceive of humility as a putting down of self or anyone else. Indeed, a truly humble person would "despise being despised."[16] God does not come down to the humble person but rather within. The purpose of humility is to bring God in, not down. "That which was above came to be within. You shall be united and by yourself in yourself, so that he may be within you."[17] What is within, where we take God? Darkness is within. "The ground of the soul is dark," says Eckhart.[18] Eckhart urges us not to be afraid of the dark, not to flee from the truth of ourselves, which is that deep down we are dark and even in the dark. To admit this and to explore the darkness is the deepest kind of humility.

It is also the deepest kind of exploration into God. For God too is dark in the divine depths. *The prophet said: "You are truly a hidden God"* (Is. 45:15) *in the ground of the soul where the ground of God and the ground of the soul are one ground.* It is significant that this section of Isaiah is also ambivalent about the hidden vs. the clear God. The God who saves is hidden, but not the God who creates.

> Truly, you are a hidden God,
> the God of Israel, the saviour . . .
>
> Yes, thus says Yahweh,
> creator of the heavens,
> who is God,
> who formed the earth and made it,
> who set it firm,
> created it no chaos,
> but a place to be lived in:
>
> "I am Yahweh, unrivaled,
> I have not spoken in secret
> in some corner of a darkened land.
> I have not said to Jacob's descendants,
> 'Seek me in chaos.'
> I, Yahweh, speak with directness
> I express myself with clarity." (Is. 45:15, 18–19)

Thus the way to finding God is similarly paradoxical and two-sided. *You should seek him in such a way that you never find him. For it is when you do not seek him that you find him.* Humility, or the seeking after the truth of oneself, is necessary for us to seek anything as it is, and especially God as God is. We will project onto God as onto others whatever names we harbor within ourselves. "All the names which the soul gives God, it receives from the knowledge of itself."[19]

By knowing our own darkness we can get to know God's darkness. By knowing that our own soul is nameless, we can get to know the nameless side of God. Moreover, our truest rest will be in this darkness. *The final goal of being is the darkness or the unknowability of the hidden divinity, which is that light that shines "but the darkness had not comprehended it"* (Jn. 1:5). God's light is a light that does not break the darkness. One might say that it is warm but not illuminating. *There lies pure peace and rest for everything which ever received being.* God's darkness is a light: one more paradox at the root of all life, divine and creaturely.

What more can be said of the dark side of God? First, that God is utterly dark—the darkness behind darkness, the "superessential darkness" as Pseudo-Dionysius calls God.[20] The darkness of God is the darkness of mystery. "What is the final end? It is the mystery of the darkness of the eternal Godhead and it is unknown and was never known and never will be known." So deep is this mystery of the Godhead that there God remains unknown to God. "God dwells therein, unknown to himself, and the light of the eternal Father has forever shone in there and the darkness does not comprehend the light."[21]

Because God's depths are so shrouded in mystery, God cannot be named. "No one can really say what God is . . . The ineffable One has no name."[22] God is "the Unnameable."[23] While being revealed on the one hand as "being"—I am who am—God also remains hidden (*esse absconditum*).[24] Following the apophatic tradition of Pseudo-Dionysius that his brother Thomas Aquinas called "the peak of the human knowledge of God," Eckhart emphasizes what we do not know of God. "Whatever one says that God is, he is not; he is what one does not say of him, rather than what one says he is."[25] This God is *he who is without name and is the denial of all names and who has never been given a name . . . a truly hidden God.* In this way, by reverencing the hiddenness of God, we respect God's transcendence. In this way of the *via negativa* we come to a union with the "naked

God." And in this kind of union, *everything belonging to God belongs to us. And we come home much nobler than we went out. In this way our love of creation is enhanced—not forgotten—for there everything that has being and life rests as in its final goal and we with them.*

Sermon Twelve: SINKING ETERNALLY INTO GOD

"You should be renewed in spirit and mind." (Ep. 4:23)*

"You should be renewed in your spirit"—the Latin word *mens* means *mind* [or *spirit*]. This is what Saint Paul is saying in Ephesians 4:23.

Now Saint Augustine says that God has made a certain power together with the existence of the soul in that highest part of the soul which is called *mens* or *mind*. The teachers call this power a container or shrine of spiritual forms or formlike images (ideas). This power is the foundation of the likeness between the soul and the Father. On the one hand, the Father pours out his divinity in such a way that he gives the entire possession of his divine being to the Son and to the Holy Spirit, with the only distinction being that between the three persons. On the other hand, the memory of the soul pours out the treasure of images into the other powers of the soul. Whenever the soul views something with this power —whether it be the image of an angel or its own image—there is a sense of insufficiency. Even if it were to see God insofar as he is God (as opposed to the Godhead) or insofar as he can be imagined or insofar as he is a threeness, this same insufficiency would be there. But when all images of the soul are taken away and the soul can see only the single One, then the pure being of the soul finds passively resting in itself the pure, form-free being of divine unity, when the being of the soul can bear nothing else than the pure unity of God.

Now Saint Paul says: "You should be renewed in spirit." Renewal pertains to all creatures under God. God himself, however, needs no renewal but only eternity. What is eternity? Pay attention. Eternity is the peculiarity that being and being young are one. For eternity would not be eternity if it could become new and were not continually the same. I maintain that newness does

* "Renovamini spiritu *mentis vestrae*." (DW III, ✠83)

pertain to the angel and precisely with regard to the angel's information about future things, for the angel knows about future things only so much as God reveals. The soul too experiences renewal insofar as it is called *soul*, for the word *soul* is used with reference to the fact that it gives life to the body and is the form of the body. Renewal pertains to the soul also insofar as it is called *spirit*. And the soul is called *spirit* because it is separated from the here and now and from everything natural. But in that respect in which the soul is an image of God and is, like God, nameless, there the soul knows no renewal but only eternity, like God.

Now notice this. God is nameless, for no one can know or articulate anything about God. A pagan teacher speaks to this point in saying that what we can know or express about the First Cause is more than anything else what we are than anything that the First Cause is or might be, for it is beyond all expression and understanding. If I were to say that God is good, I would be wrong; it is more correct to say that I am good and God is not good. The point I am making is that I end up saying that I am better than God, because whatever is good can become better and what is better can become best. But God is not good and therefore cannot become better. And because God cannot become better he cannot become best, for all three of these terms—good, better, and best—are far from God's reality, for he is exalted above everything. If I go on to say that God is wise, it is not true—I am wiser than God. If I further say that God is a being, that is not true. God is a being beyond being and a nothingness beyond being. This is why Saint Augustine says that the most beautiful thing which a person can say about God consists in that person's being silent from the wisdom of an inner wealth. So be silent and do not flap your gums about God, for to the extent that you flap your gums about God, you lie and you commit sin. If you want to be without sin and perfect, then do not flap your gums about God. Nor should you want to know anything about God, for God is above all knowledge. A teacher says: "If I had a god whom I was able to know, I would never be able to regard him as God." But if you know something about him, he is nothing of that which you think you know. With this business of knowing about God you run into complete lack of knowledge, and through this you fall into a beastlike state of existence, for that part of a creature which is without knowledge is beastlike. So if you do not want to be a beast, know nothing about that God who is inexpressible in words. And if you ask: "How can I keep myself from doing this?" then I advise you to let your own "being you" sink into and flow away into God's "being God." Then your "you" and God's, "his," will become so completely one "my" that you will eternally know with him his changeless existence and his nameless nothingness.

Now Saint Paul says, "You should be renewed in spirit." If we want to be renewed in spirit, the six powers of the soul, the highest and the lowest, must each have a golden finger ring, gilded with the gold of divine love. Now pay attention. There are three lower powers of the soul. The first is called the power of making distinctions, *rationalis*; on this power there should be a golden ring, namely, enlightenment. This enlightenment consists in the rational faculty always being enlightened by divine light. The second power is called anger, *irascibilis*; on this power there should be the golden ring called peace. Why? Insofar as one is in peace, one is in God; insofar as one is outside peace, one is outside God. The third power is called desire, *concupiscibilis*. On this power you should wear a ring called self-content, so that you can be content with all creatures under God. But you should never be content with what you have of God, for you can never have enough of God. The more you have of God, the more you want of him. If you, in fact, could have enough of God, so that there came about a satiety of God in you, then God would not be God.

You must also have golden rings on the higher powers of the soul. There are also three of these. The first is called the power of retention, *memoria*. This faculty makes one like the Father in the Trinity. On this power you should have a golden ring called preservation, so that you can preserve in yourself all the eternal things, that is, the eternal ideas of things. The second power is called intellect, *intellectus*. This power makes one like the Son. On this faculty you should wear the ring which is called knowledge, so that you can always know God. How should you do this? Without image, without mediation, and without likeness. If I am to know God in such an unmediated way, then I must simply become God and God must become me. I would express it more exactly by saying that God must simply become me and I must become God—so completely one that this "he" and this "I" share one "is" and in this "isness" do one work eternally. For this "he" and this "I"—that is, God and the soul—are very fruitful as they eternally do one work together. But as soon as a single here and now come into the picture—that is, when we are not talking about an eternally timeless and spaceless doing—then already this "I" and this "he" could never do anything together or be one. The third power is called will, *voluntas*. This faculty makes one like the Holy Spirit. On this faculty you should wear the golden ring which is called love, so that you might love God. You should love God with no regard to his being lovable, that is, not because he is lovable. For God is really not lovable, since he is above all love and lovableness. How then should one love God? You should love God mindlessly, that is, so that your soul is without mind and free from all mental activities, for as long as your soul is operating like a mind, so long does it have images and representations. But as long as it has images, it has intermediaries, and as long as it has intermediaries, it has neither oneness nor simplicity. And therefore your soul should be bare of all mind and should stay there without mind. For if you love God as he is God or mind or person or picture, all that must be dropped. How then shall you love him? You should love him as he is, a not-God, not-mind, not-person, not-image—even more, as he is a pure, clear One, separate from all twoness. And we should sink eternally from something to nothing into this One. May God help us to do this. Amen.

COMMENTARY: The Radical Insufficiency of Language About God/Three Occasions When God Is Not God/Letting Go—a Process of Subtraction That Allows Us to Love God Mindlessly/Reconciliation Within Oneself—the Sign of the New Creation

In the previous sermon Eckhart explored the darkness of the hidden God or the apophatic God. In this sermon he elaborates on the implications of God's unknown or dark side—namely the apophatic side of God—

for our own spiritual journey. In this sermon, therefore, Eckhart explores the *via negativa* as a way to know God. Indeed, he ends this sermon with a classic statement on what is meant by the *via negativa* or negative way into God, saying: *You should love him as he is, a not-God, not-mind, not-person, not-image—even more, as he is a pure, clear One, separate from all twoness.*

The setting for this sermon is the Epistle to the Ephesians, wherein the author talks about the new creature and what will constitute the new man and new woman remade after God's image. In a previous section of his letter, the writer wrote of "putting on the new person" (2:15) in order to be re-created in Christ, a theme Paul had developed in Galatians: "you have all clothed yourselves in Christ, and there are no more distinctions between Jew and Greek, slave and free, male and female, but all of you are one in Christ Jesus" (Ga. 3:28). For Paul as for Eckhart, oneness—a "separation from all twoness"—characterizes God and the children of God. Unity will be a sign of the new creation. So will renewal be such a sign, and renewal as the author of Ephesians saw it forms the textual basis for Eckhart's present sermon:

> I want to urge you in the name of the Lord, not to go on living the aimless kind of life that pagans live. Intellectually they are in the dark, and they are estranged from the life of God, without knowledge because they have shut their hearts to it. Their sense of right and wrong once dulled, they have abandoned themselves to sexuality and eagerly pursue a career of indecency of every kind. Now that is hardly the way you have learnt from Christ, unless you failed to hear him properly when you were taught what the truth is in Jesus. You must give up your old way of life; you must put aside your old self, which gets corrupted by following illusory desires. Your mind must be renewed by a spiritual revolution so that you can put on the new self that has been created in God's way, in the goodness and holiness of the truth. (Ep. 4:17–24)

Eckhart's sermon is an elaboration on how he interprets the "spiritual revolution" that renews the mind and puts on a "new self" fashioned after God's way.

The first point that Eckhart makes is that to take on God's mind we must stop projecting onto God our notions of who God is. In doing so, we destroy God. Or, as he puts it, there are three situations in which

God would not be God. Each of these situations is of our own choosing —it is we who slay God. The first of these occasions when we destroy God is when we try to name God. We need to reverence the "hidden God" that Eckhart preached about in the previous sermon, for *God is nameless and no one can know or articulate anything about God.* When we talk about God we are in fact talking about ourselves, for *God is beyond all expression and understanding.* Language is radically insufficient for naming God. Eckhart demonstrates this with an elaboration of our words, "good," "better," "best" and "wise," "wiser," "wisest." In this sense too, God can be said to be *not lovable, since he is above all love and lovableness.*

> If I were to say that God is good, I would be wrong; it is more correct to say that I am good and God is not good. The point I am making is that I end up saying that I am better than God, because whatever is good can become better and what is better can become best. But God is not good and therefore cannot become better. And because God cannot become better he cannot become best, for all three of these terms— good, better, and best—are far from God's reality, for he is exalted above everything. If I go on to say that God is wise, it is not true—I am wiser than God. If I further say that God is a being, that is not true. God is a being beyond being and a nothingness beyond being.

It is in this sense—namely, that our God talk falls so short of God—and *not* as a putdown of creation or as a denial of the previous ten sermons we have studied in Path One, that Eckhart says: "All the creatures cannot express God, for they are not receptive of that which he is."[1] Eckhart swings between the cataphatic (beings are the Word of God) and the apophatic traditions (no being can express God). If "the unfathomable God is without a name,"[2] what are we to do? Eckhart advises silence.

> The most beautiful thing which a person can say about God consists in that person's being silent from the wisdom of an inner wealth. So be silent and do not flap your gums about God, for to the extent that you flap your gums about God, you lie and you commit sin. If you want to be without sin and perfect, then do not flap your gums about God.

God's bigness and our language's puniness demand silence on our part about God. Interestingly enough, this is the first time in twelve sermons that Eckhart has used the word *sin*. He calls our putting talk about God ahead of silence with God a *sin*. For such relationships to God are a kind of control over God that all projection is about. To project onto others, especially the divine Other, is to operate from a sinful consciousness, one that lacks reverence for the other. Those who *flap their gums about God* are sinful.

A second way in which we turn God into a God *who would not be God* is by imagining that we can know God. To imagine this is to reduce God to our size. Such a God is not worthy to worship. *If I had a god whom I was able to know, I would never be able to regard him as God.* God is beyond our knowledge of God and bigger than all our knowledge. This is why God remains a "hidden God."

But how does one know and love such an unnameable and unknowable God? By letting go or detaching oneself (*Abgeschiedenheit*) from all images. "God is not found in the soul by adding anything, but by a process of subtraction."[8] This "process of subtraction" allows us to make contact with the *oneness and simplicity* that is our knowledge of God, a God already deeply present in us. In this way we make contact with the non-God who is a *not-mind, not-person, not-image*.

> You should love God mindlessly, that is, so that your soul is without mind and free from all mental activities, for as long as your soul is operating like a mind, so long does it have images and representations. But as long as it has images, it has intermediaries, and as long as it has intermediaries, it has neither oneness nor simplicity. And therefore your soul should be bare of all mind and should stay there without mind.

Loving God mindlessly means loving God without images or intermediaries. It is our unitive act with God, an act of pure intuition and union, not of analysis or of names or knowledge derived from analysis. It is an act of *sinking* rather than of striving, for the spirit is a vortex or whirlpool, as we have seen in Path One, and to get in touch with the divine depth of the vortex is to sink. *We should sink eternally from something to nothing into this One.* The oneness of God is the inness of the panentheistic God who sinks into us and into whom we sink. Just as we have seen Eckhart say previously that to "rise up" means to "enter within" ("by sublime I mean innermost"), so here he equates "rising up" with "sinking." "The spirit should rise up with its whole strength and sink unfettered into its God."[4] True letting go of something to pass to nothing —in other words, true sinking—results in the most indescribable union between God and ourselves.

> I advise you to let your own "being you" sink into and flow away into God's "being God." Then your "you" and God's, "his," will become so completely one "my" that you will eternally know with him his changeless existence and his nameless nothingness.

Another reason why we are called to *sink* into God is that sinking is what God does, and we who are God's images are to imitate God.

> God is being and all being is derived immediately from him. Therefore he alone sinks into the essences of things. All that is not being itself, stands outside, is alien and distinct from the essence of each thing. Moreover, being is more inward to each thing than the essence of the thing itself.[5]

Eckhart is suggesting that the way we get to the essence of anything is by sinking. Those who love each other sink into each other, as in the case of God and us. God and we become one I, one us in such an act of sinking. And from this union, a shared work takes place. We share a common isness and a common fruitfulness.

> If I am to know God in such an unmediated way, then I must simply become God and God must become me. I would express it more exactly by saying that God must simply become me and I must become God—so completely one that this "he" and this "I" share one "is" and in this "isness" do one work eternally. For this "he" and this "I"—that is, God and the soul —are very fruitful as they eternally do one work together.

Eckhart explains why, from the point of view of psychology, an act of letting go and sinking and loving God mindlessly effects so total a union with God. He considers *the highest part of the soul to be a container of spiritual forms or formlike images* (ideas). And this dynamic power forms the very *foundation of the likeness between the soul and the Father.* In other words, the *imago Dei* or true likeness between people and the Creator is the very capacity to make images. Eckhart talks of the *treasure of images* that flow *out* from this most divine aspect of our psyches but does not use the word "imagination," because in medieval Scholasticism *imagination* did not mean what it means to us today.[8] Eckhart's word is *mens*, which we usually translate in a literal sense as *mind* but which in this sermon has every right to be translated as creative imagination. Eckhart goes on and comments that, as great as imagination is with its divine capacity for birthing images, nevertheless, even in being creative we experience an *insufficiency*. In other words, there are times for letting go even of our images. Such times constitute the *via negativa* and they allow the soul to be true to its deepest self, which, like God, is both nameless and eternally youthful.

> When all the images of the soul are taken away and the soul can see only the single One, then the pure being of the soul finds passively resting in itself the pure, form-free being of divine unity, when the being of the soul can bear nothing else than the pure unity of God.

Notice that the soul "finds God passively resting" therein. Thus, the need to let go and sink mindlessly rather than to strive. The knowledge that we are capable of at this level of intuition is possible because of the power called intellect. It affords a direct knowledge of God, *without image, without mediation, and without likeness.* It is at this level of depth that *we become as God is and God as us.*

The third way in which we can reduce God to not being God is by imagining that we ever have enough of God. God is too infinite for our desire for God ever to be sated.

> You should never be content with what you have of God, for you can never have enough of God. The more you have of God, the more you want of him. If you, in fact, could have enough of God, so that there came about a satiety of God in you, then God would not be God.

Eckhart makes a conscious and deliberate effort to avoid dualisms regarding body, soul, and spirit in this sermon in the *via negativa.* This is all the more striking since the letter to the Ephesians on which he based this talk is, as we have seen, quite conscious of the sexual license of pagan living, their "pursuing a career of indecency of every kind." Eckhart resists any temptations to preach on sexual immorality that a lesser preacher might have picked up on. In fact, he does just the opposite. He points out once again that body and soul are not in opposition and that soul and spirit are not synonymous. The renewal of what Ephesians calls the "spiritual revolution" of the new person needs to take place in the soul as it pertains to both body and spirit. One would think that Eckhart, like so many spiritual theologians, would fall into dualism when discussing the so-called "lower powers" of our psyches. But that is not the case. In fact, he invents a gentle image, an image of reconciliation, namely that of a "golden ring" to describe how we are to live in harmony with these energies and not be putting them down in the name of ascetic practices. In talking of concupiscible desires, he says simply: *Wear a ring called self-content so that you can be content with all creatures under God.* We see in this statement a consistency with Path One of Eckhart's spiritual journey wherein all creatures are in God and we also see that Eckhart's perspective on concupiscence is from the point of view of contentment and discontent. He does not want us to be discontent, but he refuses to endorse dualistic methods of controlling desire. He prefers reconciliation, the harmony symbolized by a ring on the finger (cf. p. 221). In this regard he may very well have had at hand a text from Paul that parallels the one he is preaching from. In it Paul elaborates on what attitudes will characterize the new person.

> For anyone who is in Christ, there is a new creation; the old creation has gone, and now the new one is here. It is all God's work. It was God who reconciled us to himself through Christ and gave us the work of handing on this reconciliation. In other words, God in Christ was reconciling the world to himself, not holding men's faults against them, and he has entrusted to us the news that they are reconciled. (2 Co. 5:17–19)

Eckhart sets himself the task of "handing on this reconciliation." It is a reconciliation of creation that begins with a reconciliation in oneself. For the power of reason to make distinctions becomes, by reconciliation, an experience of enlightenment; the power of anger, an experience in peace; the power of desire, an experience in contentment; the power of memory, an experience of the Creator or Father and the goodness of creation; the power of intellect, an experience of knowing God without intermediaries; and the power of will, an experience of love of God. These are the signs of the new creation for Eckhart. They are the way of God that has become our way. They are the fruits of the spirit of letting go and knowing and loving God mindlessly. In this way we enter into a oneness that is a *separation from all twoness.* Here God can be God once again. And so can we.

Sermon Thirteen: OUTSIDE GOD THERE IS NOTHING
BUT NOTHING

"One God and Father of all." (Ep. 4–10)*

I have cited a text in Latin written by Saint Paul in his Epistle:
"One God and Father of all, who is blessed above all and
through all and in us all" (Ep. 4:6). I take another text, this one
from the Gospel. In it our Lord says: "Friend, go higher up,
move up higher" (Lk. 14:10).

In the first, spoken by Saint Paul, "one God and Father of all,"
he omits a word that implies a change. When he says "one God,"
he means that God is one in himself and separated from everything else. God belongs to no one, and no one belongs to God.
God is one. Boethius says: "God is one and does not change."
Everything that God ever created, he created in change. All
things when they are created are branded with the marks of
change.

Therefore we ought to be one in ourselves and separated from
everything and steadfastly unmoved and one with God. Outside
God there is absolutely nothing but nothing. Therefore it is impossible that any change or transformation would be able to
affect God. Whatever seeks another place outside him suffers
change. God has all things in himself in abundance. Hence he
does not seek anything outside himself except in the same abundance as it is in God. How God carries such an abundance himself no creature can understand.

There is a second teaching in the words "Father of all, blessed
are you." Now the first word implies a change. When he says,
"Father," we are at once included. He is our Father, so we are his
children, and the honor or dishonor that is shown him goes to
our hearts. When a child realizes how dear it is to its father, it

* "Unus Deus et Pater omnium." (DW I, ※21)

knows why it is duty bound to live a pure and innocent life. For that reason we should also live a life in purity, for God himself says: "Blessed are the pure in heart, for they shall see God" (Mt. 5:8). What is purity of heart? Purity of heart means to be separated and cut off from all physical things, to be gathered and enclosed in oneself. Then one hurls oneself out of the purity into God and becomes united with him. David says: "Those works are pure and innocent which run and are accomplished in the light of the soul, and those are still more innocent that remain inward and in the spirit and do not come out." "One God and Father of all."

The second text is: "Friend, come up higher, rise higher up." I will combine both. When he says, "Friend, come up higher, rise higher up," that is a conversation of the soul with God, and the answer is given: "One God and Father of all." A master says: "Friendship lies in the will." Insofar as friendship lies in the will, it does not unite. I have already said elsewhere that love does not unite. It is certainly true that it unites in activity, but not in being. Therefore love alone says: "One God . . . Go up higher." Nothing can enter the ground of the soul but the pure Godhead. Not even the highest angel, as near and as similar as it is to God, however much of God it may have in itself. Its works are constant in God. It is united with God in being but not in work, and boasts an indwelling in God and a steadfast remaining within. As noble as the angel is, it is truly a surprising thing that, for all this, it cannot enter the soul. A master says: "All creatures that have distinctions are unworthy that God himself should work in them." The soul in itself, when it is above the body, is so pure and delicate that it knows nothing but the pure Godhead. Yet God cannot enter unless everything is taken away that is added to the soul. Therefore, the answer is: "One God."

Saint Paul says: "One God." Unity is something purer than goodness and truth. Goodness and truth add something; they add a thought. When the thought is conceived, it adds. Unity does not add when God is in himself, before it flows out into the Son and the Holy Spirit. Hence, he said: "Friend, move up higher." A master says: "Unity is the negation of negation." If I say, "God is good," I am attributing something to God. Unity is a negation of negation and a denial of denial. What does unity mean? Unity means that nothing has been added. The soul knows the God-head when it is purified in it, where nothing is added and where nothing is thought. Unity is a negation of negation. All creatures carry a negation in themselves; one denies that it is the other. One angel denies that it is another. But God has the negation of negation; he is one and denies every other, for outside God there is nothing. All creatures are in God and are his own Godhead, and that means abundance, as I have said already. He is the Father of the whole Godhead. I speak therefore of a Godhead from which as yet nothing emanates and nothing moves or is thought about. When I deny God something—for instance, if I deny God goodness (of course I cannot really deny God anything)—when I deny God something, I understand something of him, namely, what he is not. Now even this must be done away with. God is one. He is the negation of negation.

A master says: "The nature of angels has no power and no works. It knows nothing except simply and solely God alone. They know nothing of anything else." Therefore, he said: "One God, the Father of all." "Friend, go up higher." Some of the powers of the soul receive impressions from outside; for example, the eye. As purely as it draws things into itself, and leaves the roughest things out, it still receives something from outside, something that is related to "here" and "now." But the understanding and reason peel everything off and understand where there is no "here" and "now." In this capacity for abstraction, reason touches the angelic nature. Yet it receives from the senses; what the senses bring in from outside, the reason receives. The will does not do this. In this respect the will is nobler than reason. The will receives nowhere but in pure knowledge, where there is neither "here" nor "now." God is saying that however high, however pure the will is, it must go up higher. This is God's answer: "Friend, go up higher, then honor will be given to you" (Lk. 14:10).

The will desires blessedness. I was once asked what was the difference between grace and blessedness. Grace, as long as we experience it here in this life, and blessedness, which we are to enjoy later on in eternal life, are related like the flower and the fruit. If the soul is completely full of grace, so that no part of it is unaffected, grace does not complete anything that the soul accomplishes. Grace does not enter at all into the works. When it is in the soul, whatever the soul is to do is done by the soul. I have also stated previously that grace does no work; rather it infuses all beauty into the soul. This is abundance in the kingdom of the soul. I say, grace does not unite the soul with God; rather, it is a conveyor of fullness. This is its work, to bring the soul back to God. There the fruit of the flowers is given to it. The will, when it desires blessedness, and when it desires to be with God, and as it is thus drawn up in purity—God slips into a will so pure as this and thus reason knows God purely. God slips into the intellect as the truth that he is. But when he descends into the will, it must rise up higher. Therefore he says: "One God . . . friend, go up higher."

"One God." Since God is one, the Godhead of God is perfect. I say that God could never beget his only begotten Son unless he were one. Inasmuch as God is one, he knows everything that he works in the creatures and in the Godhead. I will say more: God alone has unity. Unity is peculiar to God. From this fact it follows that God is God. Otherwise, he would not be God. Everything that has number depends on unity, and unity depends on nothing. God's riches and wisdom and truth are entirely one in God. He is not only one, he is unity. God has everything that he possesses in unity; it is one in him. The masters say: "The sky runs around in order to unify all things in one; that is the reason why it moves so swiftly." God has all abundance as one, and God's nature depends on this, and it is the blessedness of the soul that God is one. It is its beauty and its honor. He said: "Friend, come up higher, then honor will be done to you." It is the honor and beauty of the soul that God is one. God acts as though he were one just in order to please the soul and adorn himself so that he may convince the soul to love him alone. Hence people desire first one thing and then another; at one time they practice wisdom, at another time they practice skill. Since it has nothing of the One, the soul will never rest until it becomes completely one in God. God is one: that is the blessedness of the soul and its beauty and its repose. A master says: "God loves all things in all his works." The soul is "all things." God pours into the soul whatever is the noblest, the purest, the highest among all things which are under the soul. God is all and is one.

May "one God, the Father of all" help us thus to be united with God. Amen.

COMMENTARY: The Beauty and Blessedness of Being United with God/ Purity Means Unity/God and the Soul: Two Experiences of Nothingness/Pure Knowledge Is Knowing Relationships/How a Dialectical Consciousness Is a Consciousness of Blessing

In this sermon Eckhart combines two scriptural texts, an Epistle and a Gospel. The Epistle is a classical locus for a panentheistic understanding of God and the Gospel describes the exaltation that results from humility. Eckhart weaves the two texts together throughout this sermon because he believes that the true expression of exaltation is a unitive experience with the panentheistic God, whose characteristic is unity. *Unity is peculiar to God. From this fact it follows that God is God; otherwise he would not be God. God is not one, he is unity.* The Gospel text, urging our exaltation, reads as follows in its fuller form:

> He then told the guests a parable, because he had noticed how they picked the places of honor. He said this, "When someone invites you to a wedding feast, do not take your seat in the place of honor. A more distinguished person than you may have been invited, and the person who invited you both may come and say, 'Give up your place to this man.' And then, to your embarrassment, you would have to go and take the lowest place. No; when you are a guest, make your way to the lowest place and sit there, so that, when your host comes, he may say, 'My friend, move up higher.' In that way, everyone with you at the table will see you honored. For everyone who exalts himself will be humbled, and the person who humbles himself will be exalted." (Lk. 14:7–11)

Eckhart devotes this sermon to interpreting what "being exalted" or "moving up higher" might possibly mean. He understands the invitation of the host to be an invitation from God to each person and the "moving up higher" means entering more fully into God. For, as we have seen previously, "higher" in Eckhart's thinking denotes deeper or more fully inward. Upness is inness. Going up higher means entering more fully within the Godhead. *When he says, "Friend, come up higher, rise higher up," that is a conversation of the soul with God.*

If moving up higher and being exalted mean entering more fully into God, then Eckhart wants to analyze more fully what the inwardness of God is like. It is here that he turns to his second scriptural text, that of Ephesians. It reads as follows:

> I, the prisoner in the Lord, implore you therefore to lead a life worthy of your vocation. Bear with one another charitably, in complete selflessness, gentleness and patience. Do all you can to preserve the unity of the Spirit by the peace that binds you together. There is one Body, one Spirit, just as you were all called into one and the same hope when you were called. There is one Lord, one faith, one baptism, and one God who is Father of all, over all, through all and within all. (Ep. 4:1–6)

The text is clearly devoted to the unity that binds the members of Christ's body together and to the unity that God is. One present-day exegete, commenting on this passage, says: "Unity is the hallmark of the church and of all creation."[1] Unity is God's special gift. This experience of God's unity with God and with all of creation is what Eckhart considers the innermost experience that we can have of God. Thus he sets about analyzing the meaning of unity. He begins negatively. For if panentheism is the way things are, and we are in God and God in us, which is to say that God is "over all, through all, and within all," then what is there that exists outside of God? Absolutely nothing. *Outside God there is absolutely nothing but nothing.* Nothing can exist outside of God; therefore everything is already united to God.

What then does unity mean? *Unity is a negation of negation and a denial of denial.* It is the removal of all separation, the melting down of opposites and of distinctions. This is why creatures do not know unity as such, for they are busy making themselves separate from one another. *All creatures carry a negation in themselves; one denies that it is the other.* But God is not active in such negations or in such denials. *God is one. He is the negation of negation.* And yet, because *all creatures are in God,* such creatures are called to wake up and see the unity of which they are capable, a unity within the Godhead. The ultimate names for God are names of negation, since we can more profoundly know what God is not than what God is. For talking about God, the highest affirmation is a negation. "No negation, nothing negative, befits God except the negation of negation, which is what the one, taken negatively, signifies. God is one. But a negation of a negation is the most pure and full affirmation."[2] Above all, God is not separations but unity, not negation but the negation of negation, not denial but the denial of denial.

As we let ourselves go and sink into this unity that is God, we too begin to taste this unity that is ours by grace. Thus Eckhart is urging us not to be afraid of nothingness, but to enter it so fully that we learn the meaning of God as nothingness and of what it means to negate negation. For those who enter more fully into God, there is nothing to fear and especially not nothingness. "There is nothing in God that is to be feared. Everything that is in God is only to be loved."[3]

Our first experience of nothingness, then, is an experience of God. For "God is nothing. It is not, however, as if he were without being. He is rather neither this thing nor that thing that we might express. He is a being above all being. He is a beingless being."[4] Thus God is a nothing. A non-object. For such a no-thing, the highest affirmation is a negation. Commenting on Paul's blindness at his conversion, as reported in the Book of Acts (9:8), Eckhart says that when Paul rose from the ground he

> saw nothing, and this nothingness was God. Indeed, he saw God, and that is what he calls a nothingness . . . I cannot see what is One. He saw nothing, that is to say, God. God is nothingness, and yet God is something.[5]

Unity is not visible; it is transparent. To see God is to see nothing, and to be able to be blinded and not see objects is to be able to see nothing, or God. In the previous sermon, developing the concept of the *via negativa*, Eckhart had called God "nameless nothingness." The person who cannot see nothing cannot see the nameless nothingness who is God. Objects obscure our vision of God who is a no-thing.

But it is not only God who is a nameless nothingness. The human soul, made in the image and likeness of God, is also nameless; and human consciousness, the "temple of God," is also nothingness. For Eckhart, "intellect is the opposite of being and a form of nonbeing,"[6] for it is not bound by the conditions of being. It can see interconnections and not merely objects. It can produce universals and they do not exist as such. Thus the product of the intellect is a "nonbeing." As he puts it in his philosophical work on the *Parisian Questions*, "those things which belong to the intellect are as such nonbeing."[7] If the intellect were bound too closely to being, it would not be able to reflect on being. "The intellect is nothing," he declares.[8] "It is a sheer, open-ended capacity for knowing being," comments Caputo.[9] The intellect is pure potentiality: it can know any-thing because it is a no-thing. That, to Eckhart, is what makes humans the *imago Dei*; we are so Godly because we are so full of potential. Like his brother Aquinas, Eckhart would declare that one human mind is potentially capable of knowing all things. That is because we have a part of us which, like God, is no-thing. Another way of conceiving the nothingness of both God and the human intellect is in terms of freedom. If there is a part of us that is no-thing, then there is a part of us that can choose any-thing. "The intellect is free from the conditions of being . . . it is free to negate being as it is, to envisage other possibilities, to make a disposition of things which does not or even cannot exist."[10] In other words, the intellect can know not only being but nonbeing. It can imagine what is not yet. Like God can and did in creating the world.

It is because the intellect is a form of nothingness that it can negate. Negation is a form of transcending. It is to deny this or that of something; for example, of God. The *via negativa* is itself testimony of the nothingness that the intellect is and of its capacity to negate. We too are capable, as images of God, of a certain "negation of negation and denial of denial." This ecstatic activity is what knowing is all about. "Knowledge is an ecstatic relationship toward what is 'without' (*extra*), toward being."[11] It is what goes on as we sink deeper into the inwardness of the Godhead, *in pure knowledge where there is neither "here" nor "now."* Notice that "pure knowledge" for Eckhart includes the will. There, in our ecstatic unity of mind and will in God, *grace pours all beauty directly into . . . the kingdom of the soul.* The kingdom of God is the soul of the person where "pure knowledge" happens. There true "blessedness" takes place, the blessedness promised in the Beatitudes, "they shall see God" (Mt. 5:8). What is seen is unity and unity is a blessing. *It is the blessedness of the soul that God is one. It is its beauty and its honor.*

But who sees God? The blessed see God. But who are the blessed?

The pure in heart. "Blessed are the pure in heart; they shall see God" (Mt. 5:8). What does it mean to be pure in heart? To Eckhart, it means to be able to see unity. Oneness. To be rid of dualism and separateness. To negate and deny separation in favor of the deeper truth of things, which is oneness.

> What is purity of heart? Purity of heart means to be separated and cut off from all physical things, to be gathered and enclosed in oneself. Then one hurls oneself out of the purity into God and becomes united with him . . . "one God and Father of all."

Purity, like unity, is a process of negation. *God cannot enter unless everything is taken away that is added to it.* A process of subtraction is how Eckhart described it in the previous sermon. Unity and purity are so alike that *unity is something purer than goodness and truth. Goodness and truth add something*—but unity and purity subtract.

The purity of which Eckhart speaks means unity, and this "pure knowledge" is a purity that takes place in our consciousness when it beholds the unity of creation and of God and of their mutual relation. For the *God who is blessed above all and through all and in us all . . . is all.* What Eckhart has emphasized in this sermon, and what this commentary has been demonstrating, is that the experiences of nothingness in our lives are unexpected blessings of God toward us. The first of these nothingness experiences pertains to God, who is nothing and capable of denying all nothingness. Next is ourselves. We too, like God, have a nameless nothingness to our depths and thus to explore the depths is to enter into nothingness. Both these journeys, though journeys of negation and of the *via negativa*, are blessings.

But if unity is Godly, how about diversity? Is Eckhart asking us to develop our unitive consciousness to such a degree that we shut our eyes to how separate and diverse things truly can be? Eckhart would answer that our problems lie in us, not in beings. "All creatures are interdependent," he declares.[12] All beings are interrelated in the panentheistic God. But it is true that when we know beings we need to separate them. But the separation itself is not definitive; it is not a last word. It is not, when we know correctly, an either/or. True knowing is a both/and knowing. In other words, dualism is not knowing, but dialectical consciousness is true knowing. It is the way we know things and respect their differences, but all within the truth of the panentheistic interrelatedness of all that is.

Eckhart returns to this theme of dialectical consciousness as distinct from dualistic consciousness on numerous occasions. Indeed, it is taken for granted in his own often paradoxical ways of expressing himself. For example, Sermon Ten was devoted to how God undergoes change and suffering and rejoicing, whereas in the present sermon he says that *it is impossible that any change or transformation should affect God.* Such theologizing demands both/and thinking on our part. There exists a dialectic between Path One, which is a *via affirmativa,* and Path Two, the *via negativa.* There is required a dialectical consciousness to grasp the cataphatic God on the one hand and the apophatic God on the other. Dialectical consciousness is presumed when Eckhart says that "height and depth are the same thing."[13] And when he says that "God is in all creatures insofar as they have being, and yet he is above them."[14] Thus God's inness is in dialectical tension with the divine beyondness. Grace and nature work dialectically in God's plans for us. "Do not consider anxiously whether God works with nature or above nature. Both nature and grace are his."[15] He draws lessons of everyday living from a dialectical model when he says that people ought to "eat with perfect propriety who would be just as ready to fast."[16] Thus fasting and eating are not dualistically opposed, but dialectically related. Hatred and love are related dialectically, Eckhart observes. "The very hatred of evil is itself the love of good or of God. It is one habit, one act."[17] This is why all evil also praises God: "Darkness, privations, defects, and evil praise God and bless God."[18] Eckhart explains as well that the reason the *via negativa* is useful at all for knowing God is that knowledge is dialectical.

> It is necessary that the senses be without every sensible object if it [the mind] is to receive every sensible object. Thus the intellect too is nothing of those things which it understands, as the philosopher says, in order that it might understand all things. Thus too, someone who wants to follow God, in whom all things exist, ought to leave behind all things.[19]

Thus the reason for letting go or a *via negativa* is not the putting down of creation or the control of it—it is *not* a form of asceticism. The reason for letting go is to know more fully. The reason for emptiness is fullness. Emptiness and fullness are also dialectically related. The interrelatedness of all beings itself reveals the ultimate unity of things and so demands of us a dialectical and not a dualistic consciousness. Relation does not seek out differences.

> Relation accordingly is present in the essence of a thing, receives its being in the essence, but does not confer distinctions on the essence itself, because relation as such, that is to say in being, discards its natural qualities of relation and distinction . . .[20]

Thus relationship and not distinction lies at the very core of things. To know is to know relationships. Thus it is to know dialectically. And this is to know unity or to know purely. This is "pure knowledge."

The blessed person, then, knows and loves things as they truly are—which is in God and interrelated among themselves. This dialectical way of knowing is integral to the *blessedness which we are to receive later in life eternal.* It is the fruit of a life in God. It is heaven. "Heaven is in the middle of things. It is equally close to all the extremities."[21] Dialectical consciousness too is in the middle of things and equally close to all the extremities, that is, it is both/and thinking and relating. Dialectical consciousness constitutes a reconciliation of differences that was alluded to in the previous sermon. It is a sign of the new person, the heavenly person. Indeed, a dialectical consciousness is a consciousness of blessing, a consciousness of the blessed person. For if a blessed person is a pure person, and if purity means no twoness, then blessing means the end of dualism. It means all beings swimming together in one ocean of divine grace. Since being is "a circle of being," Eckhart talks of heaven as "being round" and our hearts too are "active constantly in a circular manner."[22] The blessing that comes with eternal life is the end of twoness and the beginning of unity. "Two as duality does not produce love; two as one naturally gives willing, fervent love."[23] This is the fervor of those who have known true humility and been blessed by a Father who is through all and in us all. Only a blessed consciousness that knows nothingness and that operates dialectically can receive such a guest. For *nothing can enter the ground of the soul but the pure Godhead.* For in a panentheistic theology, grace is not only what dwells in us, it is also what we dwell in. "Grace is the indwelling of the soul in God."[24] *Grace does no work; rather, it infuses all beauty into the soul.* The beauty it infuses is an *abundance,* a divine abundance.

Sermon Fourteen: LETTING GOD BE GOD IN YOU

"In this God's love was revealed in us." (1 Jn. 4:9)*

"God's love was revealed and made visible in that he sent his
only begotten Son into the world so that we live with the Son
and in the Son and through the Son" (1 Jn. 4:9). For all who do
not live here through the Son are not really living as they should.

If there were somewhere a rich king with a beautiful daughter,
and if he gave her as a wife to the son of a poor man, all who belong to that family would as a result be raised up and ennobled.
Now a master of the spiritual life says: "God became man, and
as a result the whole human family has been raised up and
ennobled. We can indeed rejoice because Christ, our brother, has
ascended of his own power beyond all the choirs of the angels and
is seated at the right hand of the Father." This master has spoken
correctly. But in truth I would not make too much of it. How
would it avail me if I had a brother who was a rich man and I
were a poor man? How would it avail me if I had a brother who
was a wise man and I were a fool?

I make another, more penetrating statement: "God has not
only become man, but even more, he has taken on human nature." The masters of the spiritual life commonly state that all
people are equally noble with respect to their nature. All the
blessings possessed by all the saints, by Mary, the mother of God,
and by Christ according to his humanity—all these blessings are
my very own in my nature. Now you may ask me: "Since I have
in my nature everything Christ can offer according to his humanity, why do we raise up Christ and revere him as our Lord and
our God?" This is because he has been God's messenger to us and
has brought us our blessedness. The blessedness he brought us
was our own. In the place where the Father generated his Son

* "In hoc apparuit caritas dei in nobis." (DW I, ⚔5b)

within his most spiritual foundation, this same human nature is suspended. This nature is one and onefold. Of course, something might peep out of it and adhere to it, but that has nothing to do with this unity.

I make a further, more difficult statement: People who wish to remain in the nakedness of this nature must have avoided all that is personal so that they can wish well to a person beyond the sea whom they have never seen with their own eyes just as much as they do to one who is near them and is a trusted friend. So long as you wish better things for the one near you than to the person you have never seen, you are not all right and you have not yet peeped even for a moment into that onefold foundation of God's nature. Of course, you may have seen the truth in an abstract image as in a comparison. However, it was not the best you might have hoped for.

Second, you must be pure of heart, for *that* heart alone is pure that has put an end to all worldly things. Third, you must be free of nothingness. The question is asked as to whether hell burns. The masters of the spiritual life commonly say that willfulness is the cause of this. I say, however, quite truthfully that nothingness burns in hell. Understand this comparison. Let a burning coal be taken and placed on my hand. If I wished to say that the piece of coal was burning my hand, I would not be correct. If I were to state accurately, however, what is burning me, I would say that "nothingness" is doing it. For the piece of coal has something in it that my hand does *not* have. Beyond, this "nothingness" is burning me. If my hand, however, had in itself all that the coal is and can endure, it would have quite completely the nature of fire. If someone should take all the fire that ever burned and shake it out on my hand, it could not give me pain. Similarly I say: "Since God and all who are in God's contemplation in happiness have something in themselves that those separated from God do *not* have, this 'nothingness' gives pain to the souls in hell more than willfulness or some kind of fire." I say quite truly that, to the degree that you are grasped by "nothingness," you are imperfect. Therefore, if you wish to be perfect, you must be free of "nothingness."

In this connection the passage I proposed for you states: "God sent his only begotten Son into the world." You ought not to understand this in connection with the external world, as, for example, that he ate and drank with us. You must understand it with respect to the spiritual world. As truly as the Father naturally in his onefold nature generates his Son, he generates him in the most spiritual part of his spirit, and this is the spiritual world. Here God's foundation is my foundation, and my foundation is God's. Here I am living from my very own, just as God is living from his very own. Whoever has peeped into this foundation for a moment regards a thousand gold marks as if they were only a false penny. From this most spiritual foundation you ought to accomplish all your deeds without a reason. I emphatically state that, so long as you accomplish your deeds for heaven's sake or God's sake or your eternal happiness from the outside, you are not doing things properly for yourself. You may be accepted, but this is not the best arrangement. If someone thinks of obtaining more by spirituality, devotion, sweet rapture, and the special grace of God, than in the fire of the hearth or in the stable, you are behaving no differently than if you took God, wrapped a coat around his head, and shoved him under a bench. For whoever seeks God in a definite mode accepts the mode and misses God, who is hidden in that mode. Whoever seeks God without a mode, however, grasps him as he is in himself. If anyone were to ask life over a thousand years, "Why are you alive?" the only reply could be: "I live so that I may live." This happens because life lives from its own foundation and rises out of itself. Therefore it lives without a reason so that it lives for itself. Whoever asked a truthful person who accomplishes deeds from his or her own foundation, "Why do you accomplish your deeds?" that person, if he or she were to reply correctly, would say only: "I accomplish so that I can accomplish."

God begins where the creature comes to an end. Now God longs for nothing from you more than that you should emerge from yourself in accord with your being as a creature, and that you should admit God within yourself. The smallest image of a creature that is formed in you is as big as God. Why? Because it prevents you from forming a whole God. For just where this image is formed in you, God and his whole Godhood must yield. Wherever this image emerges, however, God can go in. God longs as much for you to emerge from yourself in accord with your being as a creature as if his whole happiness depended on it. Now then, my fellow human being, what harm does it do you if you let God be God within you? If you emerge completely from yourself, for God's sake, God will emerge completely from himself for your sake. If both of these beings emerge, what is left behind is a onefold unity. In this unity the Father generates his Son in his most spiritual source. The Holy Spirit comes to flower there, and a will that belongs to the soul originates there in God. As long as this will remains undisturbed by all creatures and all creation, it is free. Christ says: "No one goes up to heaven except the one who comes down from heaven" (Jn. 3:13). All things are created from nothing. For this reason their true source is nothing, and to the extent that this noble will is inclined to creatures, it flows with the creatures into nothing.

Now the question is raised whether this noble will flows so far away that it can never return. The masters of the spiritual life commonly say that it never returns to the extent that it has flowed with time. I say, however, that if this will returns to its original source from itself and from all creation even for a moment, this will is again in its true nature and is free. And in this moment all the lost time will be regained.

People often say to me: "Pray for me!" Then I think: "Why do you go out of yourselves? Why don't you stay within yourselves and grasp your own blessings? After all, you bear essentially all truth within yourselves."

May God help us to be able to remain truly within ourselves in this way, and may he help us to possess all truth immediately and without any distinction! Amen.

COMMENTARY: Loving God Without a Why/Living Without a Why/ Two Additional Meanings of Nothingness/Being Free of Nothingness/Distrusting Methods for Attaining God/ Finding God as Much in the Stable as in Church

In this sermon Eckhart is commenting on the First Epistle of John, which reads as follows:

My dear people,
let us love one another
since love comes from God
and everyone who loves is begotten by God and knows God.
Anyone who fails to love can never have known God,
because God is love.
God's love for us was revealed
when God sent into the world his only Son
so that we could have life through him;
this is the love I mean:
not our love for God,
but God's love for us when he sent his Son . . . (1 Jn. 4:7–10)

Eckhart develops the theme of what it means not only to be in God, but also in God's love. *Here God's foundation is my foundation, and my foundation is God's.* What does it mean to share a foundation with God? It means, among other things, that we experience our original freedom once again. *If this will returns to its original source from itself and all creation even for a moment, this will is again in its truly free nature and is free.* Part and parcel of the freedom enjoyed in a return to our original source, the wellspring of the Creator's love that gave us existence, is that we learn to live and to love as God lives and loves. How is that? Without a why. Without goals, without needs for self-justification; without everything a means to an end. We must learn to live a life of ends and not just means. Living without a why relates to our having experienced God as nothing. Elsewhere Eckhart relates a story to illustrate this point:

> I shall tell you a little story. A cardinal asked Saint Bernard, "Why should I love God, and how?" Saint Bernard said, "This I shall tell you, that God himself is the reason we should love him. The way of this love is *without a way.*" For God is nothing . . . Therefore the way in which we must love him has to be *without a way.*[1]

This wayless way is also without a why, a wherefore, or a reason. *From this spiritual foundation you ought to accomplish all your deeds without a reason.* This doing away with goals for loving God extends to religious goals such as heaven or eternal happiness, however well intentioned, because to operate from such goals *from outside* oneself is to act out of dualism. It is to forget that heaven and eternal life are already here. It is to forget that we are already living the divine life. What kind of life is this divine life? How does God live? It is a life without a why. The life of God is "without a why."[2]

> If anyone were to ask life over a thousand years, "Why are you alive?" the only reply could be: "I live so that I may live." This happens because life lives from its own foundation and rises out of itself. Therefore it lives without a reason so that it lives for itself.

Eckhart repeats his explanation of living without a why on another occasion. He imagines a dialogue dedicated to the subject:

"Why do you love God?" "I do not know . . . because of God."
"Why do you love the truth?" "Because of the truth" . . .
"Why do you love goodness?" "Because of goodness."
"Why do you live?" "My word, I do not know! But I am happy to be alive."[3]

Eckhart elaborates on what this life is that lives for life's sake. "Life means a sort of overflow by which a thing, welling up within itself, completely floods itself, each part of it interpenetrating every other part, until at last it pours itself out and boils over into something external."[4] Thus creation is God's life that has welled up in God and then boiled over into creatures. One returns to the source of this welling up and boiling over for its own sake and not for any why or wherefore. Our work is to be like God's work of creation: without a why or wherefore. *Whoever asked a truthful person who accomplishes deeds from his or her own foundation, "Why do you accomplish these deeds?" that person, if he or she were to reply correctly, would say only: "I accomplish so that I can accomplish."* We are to let go of all whys in our working and living. Good works—including those with one's eye on an eternal reward—are no substitute for letting go and living without a why.

> Our Lord says: "Whoever gives up something for my sake and for my name will be repaid a hundred times over and will re-

ceive in addition eternal life" (Mt. 19:29). If you give it up, however, for the hundred times over and eternal life, you have given up nothing. Indeed, if you give up something for a reward a thousand times over and for eternal life, you have given up nothing. You must abandon yourself, and do so completely. Then you've abandoned rightly.

Once a man came to me—it is not too long ago—and said that he had given away much landed property and many goods for his own sake so that he might save his soul. Then I thought: "How little and how insignificant is what you have let go of! It is blindness and foolishness for you to continue looking at all you've let go of. If, however, you've let go of yourself, then you've really let go."[5]

For Eckhart, all deeds that are authentic imitate the original deed of creation and well out of life and love. Thus they are without why or wherefore. For what Eckhart interprets John's phrase "God is love" to mean is that God loves without a why or wherefore.

God does not look for any "why" outside himself, but only for what is for his own sake. He loves and works all things for his own sake. Therefore, when people love him himself and all things and do all their works not for reward, for honor or happiness, but only for the sake of God and his glory, that is a sign that they are sons of God.

Furthermore, God loves for his own sake and does all things for his own sake, that is, he loves for the sake of love and he acts for the sake of action . . . Therefore, whoever is born of God as a son of God loves God for his sake, that is to say, he loves God for the sake of loving God and does all his work for the sake of working.[6]

To be called "children of God," as John has called us in the scriptural text Eckhart is commenting on, means that we are to follow God's way of living, loving, and working. They are wayless ways without a why or wherefore. Only this kind of living and working is powerful enough to be called prayer and it is powerful because it is so free.

The most powerful prayer and ultimately the most powerful to obtain all things, and the worthiest work of all, is what pro-

ceeds from a free mind . . . A free mind has power to perform all things. What is a free mind? A free mind is one that is
not confused by anything or bound to anything. It has not attached its advantage to any way of life . . . However mean a
work, man can never do it without its deriving from this source
its strength and power.[7]

Living without a why means enjoying gifts but going beyond them and
not clinging to them. *God begins where the creature comes to an end.*

People should learn to carry themselves out of themselves in
all their gifts and not to retain anything whatever that is their
own, nor to seek anything, either gain or pleasure, or devotion
or sweetness, or reward or heaven or self-will. God never
gave himself, nor does he ever give himself except in his own
will.[8]

Creatures must go, not because creatures are bad, but because we have
to learn to be empty if we are to be filled. This emptiness extends even
to being empty of purposes, goals, and whys and wherefores. In this
way we can learn to live our deep lives as an artist paints, without goals
but as a flow and an overflow.

When one performs works of virtue without the preparation of
the will, and without a special purpose of one's own toward a
just or great cause, and it works more for its own sake and
from the love of virtue and has no "why," then one possesses
virtue perfectly and not before.[9]

Learning to love without a why means learning what love between
friends is all about. Such a love "has no why."

Whoever dwells in the goodness of his [God's] nature dwells
in God's love. Love, however, has no why. If I had a friend
and loved him because all the good I wished came to me
through him, I would not love my friend but myself. I ought to
love my friend for his own goodness and for his own virtue
and for everything that he is in himself . . . This is exactly the
way it is with people who are in God's love and who do not
seek their own interest either in God or in themselves or in

things of any kind. They must love God alone for his goodness
and for the goodness of his nature and all the things he has in
himself. *This* is the right kind of love.[10]

Eckhart elaborates on the way we make a means of God by not loving
without a why. Some people

> want to love God in the same way as they love a cow. You
> love it for the milk and the cheese and for your own profit. So
> do all people who love God for the sake of outward riches or
> inward consolation. But they do not love God correctly, for
> they merely love their own advantage.[11]

When we let go of this kind of living and loving and working, we
emerge from the depth of the vortex that our spirits form and at the same
time we allow God to emerge. *If you emerge completely from yourself,
for God's sake, God will emerge completely from himself for your sake.
If both of these emerge, what is left behind is a onefold unity.* This
"onefold unity" is the love that we and God give birth to; *the Holy Spirit
comes to flower there.* Living itself, so long as it is so deep that it is without a why or wherefore, becomes the ultimate prayer, the ultimate act of
experiencing and giving birth to God.[12] Under these circumstances we
are truly letting God be and thus *letting God be God in us.* We are refusing to manipulate God and allowing God to "boil over" as God the
Creator once did and as even now God *longs to do . . . as if his
whole happiness depended on it.*

Eckhart does not hesitate to apply this way without a way and this
way without a why or a wherefore to the question of religious devotion
and exercises. These can very easily reduce God to the mode in which
we perceive them, forcing God into a kind of ascetical and willful
procrustean bed.

> If someone thinks of obtaining more by spirituality, devotion,
> sweet rapture, and the special grace of God, than in the fire
> of the hearth or in the stable, you are behaving no differently
> than if you took God, wrapped a coat around his head, and
> shoved him under a bench. For whoever seeks God in a
> definite mode accepts the mode and misses God, who is hid-
> den in that mode.

To shove God under a bench is really to dismiss God for the sake of our own self-made godly spectacles. We say we come to watch God perform, but in fact we wrap God up and put him under the bench, out of our way, so we can get on with *our* show. Eckhart abhors our using God, even for religious purposes.

> You are looking for something along with God, and you are behaving exactly as if you were making of God a candle so that you could look for something. When we find the things we are looking for, we throw the candle away. Whatever you are seeking along with God is *nothing*. It does not matter what it is—be it an advantage or a reward or a kind of spirituality or whatever else—you are seeking a nothingness, and for this reason you find a nothingness.[18]

Commenting on the lines from the Song of Songs that read, "I passed by a little, and I found him whom my soul loves," Eckhart remarks: "No matter how transparent, how subtle, a means may be by which I know God, it must go . . . One must take God as the mode without mode, and as being without being, for he has no mode. This is why Saint Bernard says: 'Whoever, God, wishes to know you, must measure you without measure.' "[14] Eckhart elaborates on this theme of not overassociating our experience with God with any particular place:

> If someone is well disposed, he or she is right in all places and in society. But if one has a wrong attitude, one is in the wrong place in all places and in society. If one is rightly disposed, one has God with one in actual fact, and if one really has God with one, one has him in all places, in the street and in the presence of everyone, just as well as in the church, or the desert, or in the cell.[15]

Eckhart is urging that we become the temple of God and not rely excessively on outside places or supports. "If God is not really within someone, but such a person must always receive God from outside in this and that . . . whether it be in works or people or places, such a person does not possess God."[16] The God we are called to union with is a God who "does not disappear" and therefore far outlasts any particular methods of piety.[17]

Just as we cannot expect external places to allow God to be God for us, so, too, external works or what has been called tactical ecstacies are not to be relied on excessively. Asceticism is "of no great importance," he counsels.[18]

> A person should not judge his participation in a really good life by how much he fasts or performs certain external works. A much better criterion is whether he cherishes more love for what is eternal and more disdain for whatever is only transient.[19]

We should be wary of tying our spiritual consciousness down to any one kind of method or exercise.

> You should not restrict yourself to any method, for God is not in any one kind of devotion, neither in this nor in that. Those who receive God thus, do him wrong. They receive the method and not God . . . Those who wish to have many kinds of devotion thrust God under a bench. Whether it be weeping or sighing, however much there is of it, it is not God at all.[20]

Eckhart calls people who confuse tactical ecstacies with the experience of God "asses."

> Those people who in penitential exercise and external practice, of which they make a great deal, hold fast to their selfish I. The Lord have pity upon such people who know so little of the divine truth. Such people are called holy on account of their external appearance, but internally they are asses, for they do not grasp the actual meaning of divine truth . . . They are highly considered only in the eyes of those who know no better. I, however, say that they are asses, understanding nothing of divine truth.[21]

What is this "divine truth" that such persons are so abysmally ignorant of and whose ignorance drives them to too much ascetic exercising? Eckhart names it in the present sermon: *After all, you bear essentially all truth within yourselves.* It is the truth that the kingdom of God is already among us, the truth that "first God has loved us."

Eckhart introduces a third meaning of nothingness in this sermon when he says that *all things are created from nothing. For this reason their true source is nothing, and to the extent that this noble will is inclined to creatures, it flows with the creatures into nothing.* For Eckhart, this third use of nothingness applies to all creatures not because creatures are bad or inferior (this would contradict his position in Path One wherein "being is God") but because creatures have received all that they are one hundred per cent. Being is either all or nothing; creatures have being, but before they had being they were nothing. If you are thirty-five years old, Eckhart would suggest you meditate on thirty-six years ago. That would put one in touch with one's *true source which is nothing.* Eckhart develops this experience of nothing on several occasions.

> All creatures are a pure nothing; neither angels nor creatures are something. They defile, because they are made from nothing. They are and were nothing. What is disliked by all creatures and gives them trouble is the nothing. If I placed a burning coal on my hand it would give me pain. This is due only to the "nothing," for if we were free from "nothing" we should not be impure.[22]

In this example, Eckhart is saying two things. First, that we are born of nothing; and second, that the nothing we are born of is not like God's nothingness or our intellect's nothingness which makes us capable of receiving all things (such as a burning coal), but that we have a nothingness in us that separates us from other things and is thus able to be burned and wounded. Eckhart elaborates on the nothingness of our creaturely origins. Eckhart defines nothing in the following manner: "Nothing is that which can receive something from nothing; something, on the other hand, receives something from something."[23] Eckhart invites us in this sermon to be *free of nothingness* by letting go of all things.

> All creatures are a pure nothingness. I do not say that they are of little value or that they are something at all—they are a pure nothingness. Whatever has not being is nothing. All creatures lack being, for their being depends on the presence of God. If God were to turn away from all creatures even for a moment, they would come to nothing.[24]

Thus our nothingness exists in relationship to God's everythingness. Only God is being and has being; creatures all receive being and are therefore independently nothing. "As soon as creatures flow out of God into the nearest creature, however, they become as different as something and nothing. For in God is light and being, and in creatures there is darkness and nothing.[25] It is because we are in God that we are something. Outside of God "there is nothing but nothing." "All creatures are in themselves a nothing, but when they are in that light in which they receive their existence, then they are a something."[26] We are light and darkness, everything and nothing. "Every created thing is tainted with the shadow of nothingness."[27] Commenting on Paul's conversion in falling from his horse and being blinded, Eckhart says, "When he saw God, he saw all things as nothingness." For it is in relation to God's fullness that we are nothing. "He saw all creatures as a nothingness, for God has all creatures' being in himself. He is a being that has in itself all being."[28] Thus, outside of God, creatures have no being and are nothing. Eckhart gives an analogy for this radical dependence intrinsic to all creatures:

> The color on the wall is preserved on the wall. Similarly, all creatures are preserved in their being through love, which is God. If we were to take away the color from the wall, it would then lose its being. In the same way all creatures would lose their being if we should remove them from love, which is God.[29]

Eckhart draws an important conclusion from this insight about our metaphysical nothingness (he never tells persons to consider themselves psychologically nothing or to put themselves down or to deny their gifts). If we are, at a radical level of the source of our being, nothing, then a person immersed in "divine knowledge and love" would need to develop a way of seeing things transparently—of seeing through things to their divine source and origin. This is why he emphasized that we "see all things as nothingness"—because we see "God where we see all creatures are nothing." Becoming "bathed in the light, we see nothing else."[30] God's light is so to flood us that we are washed in the truth of creatures' origins of nothingness and that we can see through them to God, their origin. In this way, nothing stands in our way of seeing God. "If we are to know God, it must be without mediation . . . Only then do we have immediate knowledge of the eternal life."[31] In this experience of the transparency of things and the immediateness of the Creator, *all the lost time will be regained*. Eternal life is tasted. There the oneness of humanity shines, *it is one and onefold*. There too we *remain in the na-*

kedness of this nature and are able to love people beyond the sea as much as those next to us. Why? Because place, like time, is suspended in favor of a new experience of the communion of all saintly beings, those living and those dead. "If I ask for nothing, then I am asking rightly. If I am united in this, where all things are present—the past, the present, and the things to come—all of them are equally near and equally one."[32] All time is cut through in such a communion wherein *all these blessings* [of *the saints before us*] *are my very own in my nature.* There we dwell in the *onefold foundation* of God, who very truly is love. And in this dwelling place to which we have returned, we can shout with all being. Here "God's love is revealed in us." Just as John said (1 Jn. 4:9).

Sermon Fifteen: HOW A RADICAL LETTING GO
BECOMES A TRUE LETTING BE

"Blessed are the poor in spirit, for theirs is the kingdom of
heaven." (Mt. 5:3)*

Blessedness opened its mouth of wisdom and spoke: "Blessed are
the poor in spirit, for theirs is the kingdom of heaven." Every
angel and every saint and everything that was ever born must
remain silent when the wisdom of the Father speaks; for all the
wisdom of the angels and of all creatures is sheer nothingness before the groundless wisdom of God. And this wisdom has declared that the poor are blessed.

Now there exist two kinds of poverty: an *external* poverty,
which is good and is praiseworthy in a person willing to take it
upon himself or herself through the love of our Lord Jesus
Christ, because he was himself poor on earth. Of this poverty I
do not want to speak any further. For there is still another kind
of poverty, an *inner* poverty, by which our Lord's word is to be
understood when he says: "Blessed are the poor in spirit."

Now I beg you to be just so poor as to understand this speech.
For I tell you by the eternal truth, if you are not equal to this
truth of which we now want to speak, then you cannot understand me.

Various people have questioned me about what poverty is in itself and what a poor person is. That is what we want to answer.

Bishop Albrecht says that a poor person is one who takes no
satisfaction in any of the things that God ever created—and that
is well said. But we say it better still and take poverty in a yet
higher understanding: he is a poor person who wills nothing and
knows nothing and has nothing. Of these three points we are

* "Beati pauperes spiritu, quia ipsorum est regnum coelorum." (DW II,
⚹52)

going to speak and I beseech you for the love of God that you understand this truth if you can. But if you do not understand it, do not worry yourselves because of it, for the truth I want to talk about is of such a kind that only a few good people will understand it.

First, we say that one is a poor person who wills nothing. What this means, many people do not correctly understand. These are the people who in penitential exercise and external practices, of which they make a great deal, cling to their selfish I. The Lord have pity upon such people who know so little of the divine truth! Such people are called holy on account of external appearance, but inwardly they are asses, for they do not grasp the real meaning of divine truth. Indeed, these individuals too say that one is a poor person who wills nothing. However, they interpret this to mean that one should so live as to never fulfill one's own will in any way, but rather strive to fulfill the ever-beloved will of God. These people are right in their way, for their intention is good and for that we want to praise them. May God in his mercy grant them the kingdom of heaven. But in all divine truth, I say that these people are not poor people, nor do they resemble poor people. They are highly considered only in the eyes of those who know no better. I, however, say that they are asses who understand nothing of divine truth. Because of their good intentions, they may receive the kingdom of heaven. But of that poverty of which I now want to speak, they know nothing.

These days, if someone asks me what a poor person is who wills nothing, I answer and say: So long as a person has his own wish in him to fulfill even the ever-beloved will of God, if that is still a matter of his will, then this person does not yet possess the poverty of which we want to speak. Indeed, this person then still has a will with which he or she wants to satisfy God's will, and that is not the right poverty. For a human being to possess true poverty, he or she must be as free of his or her created will as they were when they did not yet exist. Thus I say to you in the name of divine truth, as long as you have the will, even the will to fulfill God's will, and as long as you have the desire for eternity and for God, to this very extent you are not properly poor, for the only one who is a poor person is one who wills nothing and desires nothing.

When I still stood in my first cause, there I had no God and was cause of myself. There I willed nothing, I desired nothing, for I was a pure being and a knower of myself in delight of the truth. There I willed myself and nothing else. What I willed, that I was; and what I was, that I willed. There I stood, free of God and of all things. But when I took leave from this state of free will and received my created being, then I had a God. Indeed, before creatures were, God was not yet "God"; rather, he was what he was. But when creatures came to be and when they received their created being, then God was no longer "God" in himself; rather, he was "God" in the creatures.

Now we say that God, insofar as he is "God," is not a perfect goal for creatures. Indeed, even the lowliest creature *in* God possesses as high a rank. And if a fly possessed reason and could consciously seek the eternal abyss of divine being out of which it has come, then we would say that God, with all he is as God, would still be incapable of fulfilling and satisfying this fly. Therefore we pray God to rid us of "God" so that we may grasp and eternally enjoy the truth where the highest angel and the fly and the soul are equal. There is where I stood and willed what I was, and I was what I willed. So then we say, if people are to be poor in will, they must will and desire as little as they willed and desired when they were not yet. And in this way is a person poor who wills nothing.

Second, a poor person is one who knows nothing. We have said on other occasions that a person should live a life neither for himself, nor for the truth, nor for God. But now we say it differently and want to go further and say: Whoever achieves this poverty must so live that they not even know themselves to live, either for oneself or for truth or for God. One must be so free of all knowledge that he or she does not know or recognize or perceive that God lives in him or her; even more, one should be free of all knowledge that lives in him or her. For, when people still stood in God's eternal being, nothing else lived in them. What lived there was themselves. Hence we say that people should be as free of their own knowledge as when they were not yet, letting God accomplish whatever God wills. People should stand empty.

Everything that ever came out of God once stood in pure activity. But the activity proper to people is to love and to know. It is a moot question, though, in which of these happiness primarily consists. Some authorities have said that it lies in knowing, some say it lies in loving, still others say that it lies in knowing and in loving. These are closer to the truth. We say, however, that it lies neither in knowing nor in loving. Rather, there is a something in the soul from which knowing and loving flow. It does not itself know and love as do the forces of the soul. Whoever comes to know this something knows what happiness consists in. It has neither before nor after, and it is in need of nothing additional, for it can neither gain nor lose. For this very reason it is deprived of understanding that God is acting within it. Moreover, it is that identical self which enjoys itself just as God does. Thus we say that people shall keep themselves free and void so that they neither understand nor know that God works in them. Only thus can people possess poverty. The masters say that God is a being, an intelligent being, and that he knows all things. We say, however: God is neither being nor intelligent nor does he know this or that. Thus God is free of all things, and therefore he is all things. Whoever is to be poor in spirit, then, must be poor of all his own understanding so that he knows nothing about God or creatures or himself. Therefore it is necessary that people desire not to understand or know anything at all of the works of God. In this way is a person able to be poor of one's own understanding.

Third, one is a poor person who has nothing. Many people have said that perfection consists in people possessing none of the material things of the earth. And indeed, that is certainly true in one sense: when one holds to it intentionally. But this is not the sense that I mean.

I have said before that one is a poor person who does not even will to fulfill God's will, that is, who so lives that he or she is empty both of his own will and of God's will, just as they were when they were not yet. About this poverty we say that it is the highest poverty. Second, we have said one is a poor person who himself understands nothing of God's activity in him or her. When one stands as free of understanding and knowing [as God stands void of all things], then that is the purest poverty. But the third kind of poverty of which we are now going to speak is the most difficult: that people have nothing.

Now give me your undivided attention. I have often said, and great masters say this too: People must be so empty of all things and all works, whether inward or outward, that they can become a proper home for God, wherein God may operate. But now we say it differently. If people stand free of all things, of all creatures, of God and of themselves, but if it still happens that God can find a place for acting in them, then we say: So long as that is so, these persons are not poor in the strictest poverty. For God does not desire that people reserve a place for him to work in. Rather, true poverty of spirit consists in keeping oneself so free of God and of all one's works that if God wants to act in the soul, God himself becomes the place wherein he wants to act—and this God likes to do. For when God finds a person as poor as this, God operates his own work and a person sustains God in him, and God is himself the place of his operation, since God is an agent who acts within himself. Here, in this poverty, people attain the eternal being that they once were, now are, and will eternally remain.

There is a saying of Saint Paul's which reads: "But by the grace of God I am what I am" (1 Co. 15:10). My own saying, in contrast, seems to hold itself above grace and above being and above knowing and above willing and above desiring. How then can Saint Paul's word be true? To this one must respond that Saint Paul's words are true. God's grace was necessarily in him, and the grace of God accomplished in him the growth from accidental into essential being. When grace finished and had completed its work, Paul remained what he was [that is, what he had been before he was].

Thus we say that a person must be so poor that he or she is no place and has no place wherein God could act. Where people still preserve some place in themselves, they preserve distinction. This is why I pray God to rid me of God; for my essential being is above God insofar as we consider God as the origin of creatures. Indeed, in God's own being, where God is raised above all being and all distinctions, there I was myself, there I willed myself, and I knew myself to create this person that I am. Therefore I am cause of myself according to my being, which is eternal, but not according to my becoming, which is temporal. Therefore also I am unborn, and following the way of my unborn being I can never die. Following the way of my unborn being I have always been, I am now, and shall remain eternally. What I am by my [temporal] birth is destined to die and be annihilated, for it is mortal; therefore it must with time pass away. In my [eternal] birth all things were born, and I was cause of myself and of all things. If I had willed it, neither I nor any things would have come to be. And if I myself were not, God would not be either. That God is "God," of this I am the cause. If I were not, God would not be "God." It is not necessary, however, to understand this.

A great master says that his breakthrough is nobler than his flowing out, and this is true. When I flowed out from God, all things spoke: God is. But this cannot make me happy, for it makes me understand that I am a creature. In the breakthrough, on the other hand, where I stand free of my own will and of the will of God and of all his works and of God himself, there I am above all creatures and am neither God nor creature. Rather, I am what I was and what I shall remain now and forever. Then I receive an impulse which shall bring me above all the angels. In this impulse I receive wealth so vast that God cannot be enough for me in all that makes him God, and with all his divine works. For in this breakthrough I discover that I and God are one. There I am what I was, and I grow neither smaller nor bigger, for there I am an immovable cause that moves all things. Here, then, God finds no place in people, for people achieve with this poverty what they were in eternity and will remain forever. Here God is one with the spirit, and that is the strictest poverty one can find.

If anyone cannot understand this discourse, let them not trouble their hearts about it. For, as long as people do not equal this truth, they will not understand this speech. For this is an unveiled truth that has come immediately from the heart of God.

That we may so live as to experience it eternally, so help us God. Amen.

COMMENTARY: How We Are to Become Free of All Things as God Is/Experiencing Our Preexistence in the Godhead by Entering into Nothingness/Why I Pray God to Rid Me of God/The Meaning of Letting Go and Letting Be/How Letting Go Becomes Letting Be and Reverencing All Things

This sermon is more than a sermon based on Jesus' Beatitudes from the Sermon on the Mount. One might even say that it represents Eckhart's

Sermon on the Mount. For he deliberately and consciously copies the style of Jesus' sayings, as, for example, when Jesus says, "You *have learned* how it was said to our ancestors: You must not kill; and if anyone does kill he must answer for it before the court. *But I say this to you* . . ." This refrain of "You have learned . . . But I say to you" is repeated several times in this, Eckhart's imitation of the Sermon on the Mount. It was clearly an important sermon in his own estimation since he claims that the truth of it *has come immediately from the heart of God* and that to grasp it one must have experienced it.

In this sermon Eckhart carries forward on his ideas of nothingness that we have considered in the last two sermons. He recalls to our minds what he has said elsewhere, that our origins are *an eternal abyss of divine being* and that God *stands empty of all things* and that *God is free of all things, and therefore he is all things.* Eckhart desires that people too would become so God-like as to touch these states of nothingness that are God's and ours because we are God's images. We too should *stand empty* and should *will nothing, desire nothing, and have nothing.* He wants us to arrive at a point where *God is one with the spirit* and where it happens that *I and God are one.* For it is only this oneness that can give the human person full joy. *Whoever comes to know this something knows what happiness consists in.*

How does one arrive at such oneness and such happiness? It is not enough to travel the cataphatic road to God exclusively. Path One cannot stand by itself because even awareness of our own divinity does not make one happy to one's roots. *When I flowed out from God, all things spoke: God is. But this cannot make me happy, for it makes me understand that I am a creature.* Eckhart seeks to experience our precreaturely state, a time when God was the Godhead and not yet God the Creator, a time before time, a space before place, an eternal youthfulness before aging, a wholeness before brokenness. Eckhart's reflections on this mystical return to the womb before our womb, to our home before home and our God before God are borrowed from wisdom literature, where we read:

> "Yahweh created me when his purpose first unfolded,
>   before the oldest of his works.
> From everlasting I was firmly set,
>   from the beginning, before earth came into being.
> The deep water was not, when I was born,
>   there were no springs to gush with water.

Before the mountains were settled,
    before the hills, I came to birth . . .
I was by his side, a master craftsman,
    delighting him day after day,
    ever at play in his presence,
at play everywhere in the world,
    delighting to be with the sons of men." (Pr. 8:22–25, 30–31).

Eckhart applies these words to Jesus in this sermon, for he says, *Blessedness opened its mouth of wisdom and spoke . . . And this wisdom has declared that the poor are blessed.* Blessedness, as we have seen earlier, means a return to our origins and Eckhart takes the person of Jesus Christ, who was *himself poor on earth,* as a model of what our preexistence must have been back in the Godhead. If it is true, as Eckhart says often, that "Christ is our humanity," and if Christ is an expression of preexisting wisdom, then we too who are called to be other Christs and sons and daughters of God also share in some way in an expression of preexisting wisdom. Indeed, we have seen this theme of humanity's preexistence discussed in Sermon One, in the context of the prophet Jeremiah's vocation. Back in the Godhead from which we came, *when the wisdom of the Father speaks,* all is silence. We are not then flowing out but only remaining within. It is the exquisite unity with Godhead—this remaining within—that Eckhart invites us to in this sermon. He answers the question: How do we, who are "other Christs" and therefore other wisdoms, set about to be "ever at play in God's presence"? How is the interplay between God and people to happen?

His answer is in terms of poverty. It is poverty that renders us blessed as Jesus, who is *Blessedness* itself, and that renders the kingdom of heaven to happen in our time and where we live. *"Blessed are the poor in spirit, for theirs is the kingdom of heaven."* But Eckhart has a very definite understanding of what he means by poverty. It is an *inner poverty* and a *radical* poverty. A poverty so radical and so in touch with our ground where Godhead and we are one, that such a poor person *wills nothing, knows nothing, and has nothing.* This kind of blessedness and poverty is in touch with nothingness. Previously we have seen Eckhart use nothingness in four ways: as God who is no-thing; as our intellects which, like God, are no-thing; as creatures insofar as they depend absolutely on God for being and without God are nonbeing or nothing; and as the transparent way in which we see through creatures who are nothing into God. All four of these experiences of nothingness are alluded to in this sermon and are integral to the truly poor, that is the truly blessed and happy person.

But how does this happen? Not by a lot of ascetic practices, not by penitences and external practices which *cling to the selfish I*. Rather, it happens by our learning to let go. Eckhart invented the words for letting go and letting be. The two words are *Abgeschiedenheit* and *Gelassenheit* respectively and while some people translate the former as "detachment," that word has borne too heavy a burden from dualistic and ascetic spiritualists since Eckhart's day to do justice to his meaning. Letting go is what Eckhart means. As Schürmann puts it, speaking of *Abgeschiedenheit:* This evokes "a mind that is on the way to dispossession from all exteriority which might spoil its serenity."[1] The letting go of all things is the act by which we enter into nothingness. "If a person wants to become like God, insofar as a creature can have any likeness to God, then this can only happen through letting go."[2] Letting go allows us to touch nothingness. "Letting go is so near to nothingness, that nothing but God is subtle and rare enough to be contained in letting go."[3] As Caputo puts it, "the object of detachment is 'nothing,' the nothing; indeed, he [Eckhart] says, 'it aims at a pure nothingness.' "[4] Letting go is the virtue behind virtue, the purity behind purity. "Letting go is the best of all, for it purifies the soul and cleans the conscience and inflames the heart and awakens the spirit and enlivens the desires and lets God be known."[5] It is this radical letting go of willing, of knowing, and of having that allows God to enter. "To be empty of all creatures is to be full of God; and to be full of creatures is to be empty of God."[6] The person who has learned to let go is one without objects in his or her life, even life itself is no longer an object. There is true living without why or wherefore. Such a person *must so live that they not even know themselves to live, either for oneself or for truth or for God.*

Furthermore, there are no limits to this kind of poverty, no depths, one might say, to the vortex that is our spirit and our potential for letting go and for nothingness. One might say that nothing is the limit to letting go or, if you will, God is the limit. For so radical is Eckhart's invitation to let go that he confesses twice in this sermon that he prays to God to *rid us of God.* Why does he do this? *This is why I pray God to rid me of God; for my essential being is above God insofar as we comprehend God as the origin of creatures.* In other words, believing he is capable of the Godhead and not only of God, he prays to let go of our images for

God—even for the Creator God. And of our will for God. To experience the true Godhead where all creation exists now as earlier and now
as in the future, it is necessary to be rid of all—including our names for
God. We need to let go of all our works as well in order that God
might work. We are to keep ourselves so *free of God and of all one's
works that if God wants to act in the soul, God himself becomes the
place wherein he wants to act—and this God likes to do.* Full emptiness
is required, or true poverty. He alludes to this same letting go of God on
other occasions:

> The highest and loftiest thing that a person can let go of is to
> let go of God for the sake of God. When Saint Paul let God
> go for the sake of God, he let everything go that he could get
> from God, and he let everything go that God could give him
> and he let everything go that he could receive from God.
> When he let go of all this, he let God go for the sake of God
> and then God remained with him where God is most truly in
> himself . . . He did not give anything to God, nor did he re-
> ceive anything from God, for he and God were one unity and
> one pure union.[7]

The allusion to Saint Paul is from Romans, where we read:

> What I want to say now is no pretense; I say it in union with
> Christ—it is the truth—my conscience in union with the Holy
> Spirit assures me of it too. What I want to say is this: my sor-
> row is so great, my mental anguish so endless, I would
> willingly be condemned and be cut off from Christ if it could
> help my brothers of Israel, my own flesh and blood. (Rm.
> 9:1–4)

It is here—in Paul's willingness to be "cut off from Christ"—that Eckhart
derived his concept of *Abgeschiedenheit* (from the word "to cut off")
and letting go even of God. He explains this elsewhere: "Saint Paul says
that he would like to renounce God for the sake of God, in order that
the glory of God might be extended."[8] It is significant that Eckhart invokes Paul in the present sermon as an example of someone whom God
favored. *Paul's words are true. God's grace was necessarily in him, and
the grace of God accomplished in him the growth from accidental
into essential being.* In Eckhart's scriptural text for this verse from

Romans, the word Paul uses that expresses his being cut off even from Christ is *geschieden*. This, then, is a major biblical text for Eckhart's teaching of a path of letting go.

The purpose of letting go is not to renounce things as bad or immoral or even to forget things. If that were the case, then Eckhart's admonition to let go of God would be tantamount to repressing God. The purpose of the *via negativa* and the experience of the apophatic God or God of nothingness is not to put down or to forget the God of creation. In Eckhart's journey, Path Two does not stand by itself. Nor does it substitute for Path One. The purpose of letting go is to experience the divinity in all creation to an even greater depth. "He who has God essentially apprehends God in a godly manner, and to such a person God shines in all things, for all things have a divine savor for him, and God becomes visible for him in all things." In fact, letting go lets us see the divinity behind the divinity of things. "This person is highly praised before God because he perceives all things in a godly manner and values them more than the things are worth in themselves."[9]

Thus the ultimate experience of letting go is an experience of letting be. Letting God be God and letting the Godhead be the Godhead. Letting oneself be oneself and letting others be themselves. Letting things be things and letting God be God in things and things be God in God. Letting inness be and letting panentheism be and letting the circle of being that God surrounds be. Schürmann puts it this way: "As existence moves ahead on this road [of *Abgeschiedenheit*], all ascetic imperatives vanish. Thus detachment turns progressively into releasement, *Gelassenheit*, which, as has been said, is a broader concept."[10] Letting be or *Gelassenheit* comes from the word *lassen*, to let go, to relinquish or abandon. It also means to allow or permit. Thus, says Caputo, "it suggests openness and receptivity."[11] It is a state of being open and sensitive. It means, says Eckhart, to be "receptive of all spirit."

> Our Lord speaks very clearly: "Blessed are the poor in spirit." He who has nothing is poor. "Poor in spirit" means that, as the eye is poor and bare of color and yet receptive of all colors, in the same way the person who is poor in spirit is receptive of all spirit, and the spirit of all spirits is God.[12]

Thus what letting go does is to develop sensitivity and openness to the spirit and this receptivity results in letting be. Schürmann describes letting be as an act of respecting the autonomy of things. "It designates the attitude of a human who no longer regards objects and events according to their usefulness, but who accepts them in their autonomy."[13] Thus a good synonym for letting be might be reverence. Letting be is an attitude of reverence for all things that allows them to be themselves and God's selves. This represents one more reason why the path of letting go and letting be is not one of putting down anything or any event. It is rather to enter so fully into events and things that we reverence all that is there. This reverence is a gentle letting be. "What is being spoken of here is to meet with gentleness, in true humility and selflessness, everything which comes your way."[14] Such an attitude of reverence and letting be actually forbids our running away from things and requires our return to them to see them newly. As Caputo puts it:

> the detached man in Meister Eckhart is not simply to be understood as one who has divested himself of all self-love, but also as one who, like Martha, is at home in the world of things, who has a new relationship to creatures, who understands them for what they are, who lets them be.[15]

Thus Meister Eckhart can say:

> One cannot learn this [to perceive God in all things] by flight, by fleeing from things, and from externality to solitude, but one must learn to cultivate an inward solitude, wherever or with whomsoever one may be. One must learn to break through things and to grasp one's God in them and to be able to picture him powerfully to oneself in an essential manner.[16]

Thus letting go and letting be are about a *return* to creation, not a flight from it. They are our way of seeing creation newly, which actually means the way it is and originally was and was always intended to be, namely, in God.

In this blessed and new creation, where letting go and letting be result in reverence even for nothingness in all its forms, the *groundless wisdom of God* is allowed to speak once again. It will speak with the word that no one has heard since before they were born. It will utter a word of silence and unity that only silence can shout of. It will not be an abstract or a distant silence, however, but one that accompanies all of our activities. This attitude of utter reverence and gentle receptivity we are to bring to all we do, advises Eckhart, even to the sermon that he speaks. *If you are not equal to this truth of which we now want to speak, then you cannot understand me.* This is the *gentle and receptive silence that precedes all understanding.* By traveling this path we shall return to the God before God, to the space and time where *God was not yet "God,"* that is, to the Godhead who was God before creation. And there we shall be free—as free as God is—to play "by his side . . . delighting him day after day, ever at play in his presence, at play everywhere in the world." There we will come to know the *something in the soul,* the spark of our souls and our touch of divinity *from which knowing and loving flow.* And there, in the unity of our origins with God, joy will not cease. *Whoever comes to know this something knows what happiness consists in.* There all barriers will break down; we will no longer be a people who *preserve distinctions.* We will be one in God and God in us so that, like Paul, we will remain what we are and what we have been from all eternity. For when the distinction between God and us is let go of and allowed to break down, then too the distinction between existence and preexistence gives way. Time no longer holds power over us. We become, in the Godhead's presence, eternally at play. *Here God is one with the spirit.*

Sermon Sixteen: LETTING THE WILL GO

"Moses pleaded with the Lord his God." (Ex. 32:11)*

I have made a brief statement in Latin that is written in today's Epistle. In German it means: "Moses pleaded with God his Lord: 'Why should your wrath blaze out against your people?'" (Ex. 32:11). Then God made answer and said to him: "Moses, let me blaze forth; grant this to me; allow it to me; permit me to blaze with anger and avenge myself on the people." And God made a promise to Moses and said: "I will raise you up and make you great and I will increase your descendants and make you lord over a great people" (Ex. 32:10). But Moses said: "Lord, blot me out of the book of the living or spare the people!" (Ex. 32:32).

What does it mean when it is written: "Moses pleaded with God his Lord"? Truly, if God is your Lord, then you must be his servant. If you accomplish your deeds for your own use or your own pleasure or your own happiness, truly you are not his servant. For you are not seeking God's honor alone, but you are seeking your own advantage. Why does he say: "God his *Lord*"? If God wants you to be sick while you wish to be well, if God wants your friend to die while you want him to live, contrary to God's wish, then truly God is not *your* God. If, however, you love God and *then* are sick, let it be in God's name! If your friend dies, let it be in God's name! If you lose an eye, let it be in God's name! With such a person, may it be all right. If you are sick, however, and ask God for health, your health is dearer to you than God, and he is thus not your God. He is the God of the kingdom of heaven and of the kingdom of the earth, but he is not *your* God.

Now notice how God says: "Moses, let me blaze forth!" You can say to this: "Why is God blazing forth?" Over nothing less than the loss of our happiness, for he is not seeking his own inter-

* "Moyses orabat dominum deum suum." (DW II, ✳25)

est. So sorry is God that we are behaving in a way contrary to our happiness. Nothing more sorrowful could happen to God than the martyrdom and death of our Lord Jesus Christ, his only begotten Son. This death Christ suffered for *our happiness*. Now notice once again that God says: "Moses, let me blaze forth!" See now what a good person can do with God. It is a certain and necessary truth that whoever always surrenders his will completely to God captures and binds God so that God wishes nothing but what that person wishes. Whoever always gives up his will completely, receives in return from God so completely and so truly God's will that it becomes that person's own will. And God has sworn to himself that he wishes nothing other than what that person wishes. For God will never belong to anyone who has not first become God's own.

Saint Augustine says: "Lord, you will belong to no one until that person has first become yours." We deafen God day and night and cry out: "Lord, your will be done!" (Mt. 6:10). And yet when God's will takes place, we blaze forth, which is quite improper. If our will is God's will, it is good. But if God's will becomes our will, it is far better. If your will becomes God's will, and you then get sick, you would not wish to become well against God's wish, but you would wish that it might be God's will for you to become well. And if you are ill, you would wish that it might be God's will for you to be well. On the other hand, if God's will is your will and you are *then* sick, let it be in God's name! If your friend dies, let it be in God's name! This is a more certain and more necessary truth: if it were true that all the pain of hell and all the pain of purgatory and all the pain of the whole earth depended on it, our will would wish to endure it with God's will in the pain of hell eternally and continuously. And our will would regard this forever as its happiness and would add to God's will the happiness and all the perfection of our Lady and all the saints; in eternal pain and bitter suffering our will would also wish to persevere and not to turn away from all this for a moment. Indeed, our will could not wish to raise a thought of wishing to change anything in this situation. If our will thus becomes so one with God's will that a single unity is formed as a result, then the Father from the kingdom of heaven will produce his only born Son in himself together with me. Why do I say "in himself together with me"? Because I am one with him and he *cannot* exclude me. And in this deed the Holy Spirit receives his being and his deed and his becoming from me as much as from God! That is because I am after all in God. If the Holy Spirit does not receive these things from *me*, then he also does not receive them from God. He *cannot* exclude me in any way. So completely had Moses' will become *God's* will that God's honor toward the people was dearer to him than his own happiness.

God gave to Moses a promise, but Moses did not pay attention to it. Indeed, even if God had promised him his entire Godhead, Moses would not have allowed him to blaze forth. Moses, rather, pleaded with God and said: "Lord, blot me out of the book of the living" (Ex. 32:32). The masters of the spiritual life raise this question: "Did Moses love the people more than himself?" And they say no, for Moses knew very well that, if he sought God's honor before the people, he was thus nearer to God than if he had abandoned God's honor before the people and had sought his own happiness. It is characteristic of good people that in all their deeds they seek not their own interests but God's honor alone. So long as you are somehow more attentive in your action to yourself, or more attentive to one person than another, God's will has not properly become your will.

Our Lord says in the Gospel: "My teaching is not my own teaching, but it is of the one who sent me" (Jn. 7:16). In the same way a good person must consider: "My deeds are not *my* deeds; my life is not *my* life." And this is the way I conduct myself so that all the perfection and all the happiness of Saint Peter, and all the happiness of Saint Paul as a result of sticking out his head, and all the happiness they received from their deeds—all this gives me joy as much as it does them. Moreover, I shall participate in these deeds as if I myself had accomplished them. In addition, I shall receive eternal joy through all the deeds of all the saints and all the angels, and even through the deeds of Mary, the Mother of God, as if I had accomplished them myself.

I now state that "humanity" and "human being" are twofold. Humanity is so noble in itself that the highest of humanity has equality with the angels and kinship with the Godhead. It is possible for me to obtain the greatest unity that Christ possessed with the Father if only I could put aside what is from this individual or that individual, and could conceive of myself as "humanity." Then God would give to me what he gave to his only begotten Son. He would give it to me as completely as to the Son, and no less. Indeed, he would give it to me in a higher measure. For he would be giving to my humanity in Christ more than he gave to Christ himself, for the Father *gave* him nothing since Christ possessed it already from eternity in the Father.

If I strike you, I am first of all striking a Tom or a Dick, and then I am striking a "human being." Who is a human being? Whoever has his own name after Jesus Christ. For this reason our Lord says in the Scriptures: "Whoever disturbs one of these here touches me in the eye" (Zc. 2:8).

Now I repeat myself: "Moses pleaded with God his Lord." Many people plead with God for everything that *he* can do for them. They do not wish, however, to give God all *they* are capable of giving. They want to share with God, and they would like to give him the less valuable part, and only a little at that. The first thing that God gives, however, is himself. And if you have God, you have all things along with God. I have at times said that whoever has God and all things in addition, that person has no less than one who has God alone. I add to this that a thousand angels are in eternity not more numerous than two or a single one, for in eternity there is no number. Eternity is beyond numbering.

"Moses pleaded with God his Lord." "Moses" means something like "one who has been raised from the water." Now I shall speak again about the human will. If someone were to give a hundred gold marks for God's sake, that would be a good deed and would seem something significant. But I say that if I have such a *wish*—provided that I possess a hundred marks so that I can give them away—and if it is my complete wish, then I have in this way really made a payment to God, and he must reward me, just as if I had paid him a hundred marks. In addition, I say that, if I had a wish—to the extent that I possessed a whole world—to give it to God, I *have* paid God a whole world. He must reward me for it, just as if I had counted out a whole world for him. Yes, I say that if the Pope were struck dead by my hand, quite against my wish, I would all the same go up to the altar and say Mass! I say that "humanity" in the poorest and most despised human being is just as complete as in the Pope or the Emperor. For "humanity" in itself is dearer to me than the human being I carry about in myself.

May the truth of which I have spoken help us to be united in the same way with God! Amen.

COMMENTARY: How to Free the Will/The Need to Let Suffering and
            Pain Go/Letting Differences Go So as to Experience
            the Communion of Saints and the Nobility of Humanity

In the previous sermon Eckhart urged us to a radical letting go in order to let be. In this sermon, drawing on readings from the Lenten liturgy, Eckhart develops this way of letting go as it applies to the will and especially as it applies to suffering and pain in our lives. The Gospel Eckhart read for the day comments on our doing the will of God. Jesus is speaking:

> "My teaching is not from myself:
> it comes from the one who sent me;
> and if anyone is prepared to do his will,
> he will know whether my teaching is from God
> or whether my doctrine is my own.
> When a person's doctrine is his own
> he is hoping to get honor for himself;
> but when he is working for the honor of one who sent him,
> then he is sincere
> and by no means an impostor.
> Did not Moses give you the Law?
> And yet not one of you keeps the Law!" (Jn. 7:16–19)

Eckhart repeats these very lines in his sermon when he warns that *we are not seeking God's honor alone, but you are seeking your own advantage* and he relates the cause for this self-seeking to the distance between God's will and ours. *Whoever always gives up his will completely, receives in return from God so completely and so truly God's will that it becomes that person's own will.* Eckhart seeks nothing less than an exchange of wills between God and us. *If our will is God's will, it is good.*

But if God's will becomes our will, it is far better. How does it happen that we exchange wills with God? By letting God's will be God's will and by letting go of our will in order for God's will to emerge. Eckhart draws on Moses' encounter with an angry God and listens attentively to God's prayer to Moses: *"Moses, let me blaze forth; grant this to me; allow it to me; permit me to blaze with anger and avenge myself on the people."* These words are, in fact, an elucidation of the biblical text by Eckhart that reveals how taken Eckhart was by the simpler biblical text which reads: "Leave me, now, my wrath shall blaze out against them and devour them" (Ex. 32:10). Eckhart, pursuing his theme in the previous sermon of letting go of God, asks his listeners to listen to God's desire to let the divine anger be anger and to let God be God.

Eckhart's advice as to how we are to let God be God is that we need to let our wills go. In doing so we touch the nothingness that we share in common with God.

> A human being should seek nothing—neither discernment nor knowledge nor inwardness nor devotion nor rest—but only the will of God . . . Knowledge of God with the exclusion of God's will is nothing. In God's will all things are and are something, are pleasing to God and perfect; outside of the will of God, on the other hand, all things are nothing, are displeasing to God and imperfect. A human being should never pray for something, pray for God's will and nothing else . . . then everything else will be given.[1]

When we let our will go we are transformed into God's will.

> Now you might ask: When is the will right? The will is unimpaired and right when it is entirely free from self-seeking, and when it has forsaken itself and is formed and transformed into the will of God, indeed, the more it is so, the more the will is right and true.[2]

The God of the kingdom of heaven and of earth is not your God until that same God exchanges wills with us. *Whoever always gives up his will completely, receives in return from God so completely and so truly God's will that it becomes that person's own will.* How does this happen? By our letting go of our will.

> This is why a person should give up everything he has for the kingdom of heaven, especially his own self-will. As long as he still holds on to some part of his own self-will, he has not earned the kingdom of heaven. But whoever can let go of himself and his own self-will will find it easy to relinquish all material things.[3]

The transformation from our will to God's will is a matter of abandoning oneself or letting oneself go. "Hence our Lord said: 'Blessed are the poor in spirit,' that is, poor in will . . . Consider yourself and where you find yourself, abandon yourself: That is the very best course."[4] Our letting go of our will is a way of entrapping God. *See now what a good person can do with God . . . whoever always surrenders his will completely to God captures and binds God so that God wishes nothing but what that person wishes. And this wishing is always for our happiness.*

One reason why letting go of will and sinking into the freedom that is God's will is a way to be trusted is that the goodness of the Creator is to be trusted. Evil is not as radical to creation as goodness is.

> Evil is accidental in its nature: it stands outside, draws and directs things outward, distracts from inner things, draws to what is other, smacks of otherness, of division, withdrawal, or falling away. Evil, therefore, is nothing but a defect or shortcoming.

Evil does not have the last word. "What is evil for one person is good for another or for the universe; and he who takes harm from it now and in the present instance will benefit from it later in other circumstances."[5] Thus evil is profoundly relative and ought not to be clung to as if it were something absolute. Thus no suffering is pure suffering, no pain is total, for the good Creator of the good earth would not tolerate pure evil. "God and nature do not allow pure evil or pain to exist."[6] The biblical text for this sermon from Exodus 32:1–35 is a text dedicated to the subject of evil. "You yourself know how prone this people is to evil," Aaron warns Moses (v. 23). Thus Eckhart is fully justified from a biblical point of view in discoursing on the meaning of divine anger and human suffering in this context. But what most occupies Eckhart's attention, like Moses', is not the evil but how to turn the evil to good, the suffering to joy, the sin to blessing. "*I will raise you up and make you great and I will increase your descendants and make you lord over a great people.*" Eckhart turns his attention to what a great people would be. Eckhart does not carry on with an abstract discourse on the nature of the free will or even whether the human will is free. He is interested in freeing the will and setting it free so that it can bless and be blessed once again. We free the will by letting it go.

But if God wishes our happiness and we wish our happiness, why are we not happier? Why is there so much suffering and so much pain? Eckhart would reply that it is because we have not let go of our wills radically enough. "The restlessness of all our storms comes entirely from self-will, whether we notice it or not."[7] Eckhart urges us, within the context of discussing our need to let go of will, to let go of suffering as well. Too often we cling to our suffering and become attached to it.

> This is the meaning, in a good sense, of our Lord's words, "If any one will come to me, let him deny himself and take up his cross," that is, he should lay down everything and get rid of everything that is a cross and a shadow.[8]

It is suffering with attachment which is "hard for you to bear," but suffering "for the love of God . . . does not hurt and is not hard to bear."[9] Eckhart tells the story of a man who had one hundred marks and lost forty. When he concentrates only on the lost forty, he

> remains in despair and grief. How could he be comforted and free from sorrow if he turns to his loss and his pain and pictures it to himself and himself in it, and looks at it, and it looks at him again and talks to him. He speaks to his loss and the loss talks to him again, and they see each other face to face.

This is no way to let go of suffering, Eckhart is cautioning. Pain compulsively clung to is pain that is doubled. "Turn your back" on the lost forty marks, Eckhart advises, and concentrate

> on the sixty and look at them face to face and talk to them . . . That which is good has the power to comfort, but what is nothing and is not good, what is not mine and is lost to me, must necessarily give despair and pain and distress. Hence Solomon says: "In the days of pain forget not the days of goodness" (cf. Si. 11:27). That means, when you are in pain and suffering, remember the good and the comfort that you still have and retain.[10]

We suffer to the extent that we are shallow in our letting go of things and to the extent that we cling to things instead of experiencing their transparency.

> All suffering comes from love and affection. Therefore, if I suffer because of transient things, I still have, and my heart still has, love and affection for transient things, and I do not love God with all my heart . . .[11]

Caputo points out how similar this diagnosis of suffering and of its cure —letting go—is to Buddha's problem with suffering or *dukkha*. Buddha's solution to suffering was to overcome it by releasing oneself from self-will and craving. "Like Buddha, Eckhart prescribes a comparable remedy: abandon yourself, let go of yourself (*lass dich!*)."[12] Eckhart paints a picture of what this abandonment of self-will does for a person.

> A true and perfect will means to tread absolutely in the will of God and to be without self-will. The more one has of this, the more and more truly one is placed in God. Indeed, it is more profitable to say one Ave Maria if one has forsaken oneself than to read a thousand psalters without this. One step would be better with self-surrender than making a pilgrimage overseas without it.

> The person who has thus let go of all that is his would therefore be so completely enveloped in God that when one wanted to touch him one would first have to touch God. For such a person is absolutely in God, and God is round about him, just as my hood is round my head. If anyone wanted to seize me he would first have to touch my garment.[13]

In the sermon we are reading, Eckhart has also spoken of his being *in* God. Our being "absolutely in God" is the fruit of our letting our will go.

Another experience of letting suffering go is letting God take it. Give the burden to God, Eckhart is saying. God is not a mere consoler: God is the one who is to bear the pain and the suffering provided we let him. "*Moses, let me blaze forth; grant this to me; allow it to me; permit me to blaze with anger and avenge myself on the people,*" Eckhart has pictured Yahweh as saying.

> It is God who carries the burden . . . If there were a person
> who liked to suffer for God and purely for God alone, and if
> this person felt in a single blow all the suffering that all people
> have ever suffered, and all the suffering the entire world
> bears, it would not hurt him and would not weigh him down,
> for it is God who would carry the burden.[14]

But there is no way to let God bear the burden except by relinquishing it
ourselves and thus letting God be the bearer of the suffering. Our God
is a God who can and does bear suffering.

> However great suffering is, if it comes through God, God
> suffers from it first. Indeed, by the truth which is God, how-
> ever slight the suffering that befalls a person may be, let us say
> some discomfort or trial, provided that one places it in God, it
> would affect God immeasurably more than the person . . .[15]

Schürmann comments on Eckhart's teaching on suffering that "it is not
enough to receive suffering passively as a 'virgin,' free of all attachment,
but suffering must in turn be borne back into God. God is not only a
consoler; he is no longer the 'why' of suffering, but its subject."[16]

When we return the suffering to God we experience the joy and the
equanimity that the spirit brings. "What constitutes man as Son most of
all is equanimity. Is he sick? May he be as gladly sick as well, as gladly
well as sick."[17] "So long as God is satisfied," Eckhart counsels, "be content."[18]

> If anyone had forsaken himself and had denied himslf alto-
> gether, nothing could be a cross or sorrow or suffering to him.
> It would all be happiness, joy, and gladness, and he would
> come and truly follow God. For, as God cannot make anyone
> sad or sorrowful, in the same way, nothing could make such a
> person unhappy or sad.[19]

To be in God is to experience an equanimity of joy regardless of pain
and suffering.

> Your joy reaches to the greatest evenness; it never alters.
> Therefore Christ says: "No one can take your joy away from
> you." And when I am correctly translated into the divine

being, God becomes mine as well as everything he has. This is
why he says: "I am God, your Lord." I have rightful joy only
when neither sufferings nor torments can ravish it from me.
Then I am translated into the divine being where no suffering
has a place. We see indeed that in God there is neither wrath
nor grief, but only love and joy.[20]

Our being in God is a source of equanimity and balance. There every
tear is wiped away, "so that suffering is not suffering for you and that all
things are sheer joy for you."[21]

The joy that is experienced in the *kinship with the Godhead* is not restricted to my personal joy alone. Rather, the entire communion of saints
dances to this same deep joy—Saints Peter and Paul and Mary too. *All
the happiness they received . . . gives me joy as much as it does them.*
And this sharing of *eternal joy* applies to *all the deeds of all the saints
and all the angels.* By letting go of that which separates us from God,
we also let go of that which separates us from others in the communion
of saints and even from what separates us from our deepest self. For
deep within us we are not ruggedly individualistic and separatist—*my
life is not my life*—but we are, in God, a unity so that the happiness of
one is the happiness of all. We bathe in one life; God is round about
us all.

If you love the angel's happiness as much as your own, and if
you love our Lady's happiness equally as your own, then you
enjoy the same happiness quite properly as she does; it is your
own as it is her own. Therefore it is said in the book of
wisdom: "He has made him equal to the saints" (Si. 45:2).[22]

Likewise, when I offend another I not only offend this particular person
named *Tom* or *Dick* but I offend humanity. And where we offend humanity we offend Christ, who is a representative of humanity and not just a
single human being. The mystical body rejoices when one member
rejoices and suffers when a single member suffers.

But the key to realizing the oneness in joy and in suffering of all people is letting go of willfulness. This Moses was willing to do, namely, to let
go of his will for the sake of the honor of his people. But first he had to
let go of his will before God. *So noble is humanity in itself that the
highest of humanity has equality with the angels and kinship with the
Godhead.* We attain the unity with humanity that Christ had to the ex-

tent that we *put aside what is from this individual or that individual and could conceive of ourselves as "humanity."* Humanity as such is not a respecter of persons. *I say that "humanity" in the poorest and most despised human being is just as complete as in the Pope or the Emperor. It is also a more worthy object of our love than we are as individuals. Humanity in itself is dearer to me than the human being I carry about in myself.* The letting go Eckhart advocates, then, is a letting go of our splendid isolationisms and rugged individualisms. It is a letting go of the I in order to let the We happen. It is a letting go of subject/object relations in order to let panentheistic relations happen. It is a letting go of My to let Our happen.

When we let go in such a radical way, then anything can happen. For our will, when united to God's, is a source of action so thoroughly that it needs no action to justify its activity or its nonactivity. Such a will chooses without a why or wherefore. If it is my complete wish [to pay God a hundred marks], then I have in this way really made a payment to God, and he must reward me, just as if I had paid him a hundred marks. And if evil was done by my hand but *quite against my wish*, it would not be a sin that was laid on my responsibility.

> In this will you can achieve all things, whether it is love or whatever else you like . . . The place of love is in the will alone; those who have more will have also more love. But no one knows whether someone else has more of it. It lies hidden in the soul as long as God lies buried in the ground of the soul.[23]

It is from this freed will that our work takes on the character of being the work of God. Then, one "is working for the honor of one who sent him" and is "by no means an impostor" (Jn. 7:18). When the will is set free, we are free and God is free and our work is free.

Sermon Seventeen: LETTING THE INTELLECT GO AND
EXPERIENCING PURE IGNORANCE

"And when Jesus was twelve years old . . ." (Lk. 2:42)*

We read in the Bible: "When our Lord Jesus Christ was twelve
years old, he went with Mary and Joseph to Jerusalem to the temple, and when they returned, Jesus remained in the temple, but
they did not know this. And as they returned home and found
him missing, they sought him among their acquaintances and relatives and in the throng, but did not find him. They had lost him
in the throng. And for this reason they had to turn back to the
place they had come from. And when they returned to their departure point at the temple, they found him" (Lk. 2:42-46).
    In the same way, if you wish to discover this noble birth, you
must truly leave the throng and return to your origin, to the foundation from which you have emerged. All powers of the soul and
all its deeds—all these things are the "throng." Memory, reason,
and will—they all diversify you. For this reason you must leave
them—the activities of the senses and imagination and especially
all that you have in mind or in view. Only then will you be able
to discover this birth—otherwise, not at all. He will never be
found among friends or "among relatives or at the home of acquaintances." Instead, we shall lose him there completely.
    On this account the following question is raised for us. Can
people really find this birth by means of certain things that, although divine, are still conveyed to us through the senses? An example of this is the concept that God is good, wise, merciful, or
whatever other concept the reason is able to create within itself
that is truly divine. Can we really find this birth by means of all
this? Of course not! For even though all this may be good and divine, it is still conveyed from outside us through the senses. In-

* "Et cum factus esset Jesus annorum duodecim . . ." (Quint, ⅋59)

stead, it should rise up out of God *from within us,* unique and alone, if this birth is to send out its light in a characteristically pure way. At the same time, your whole action has to reach submission, and all your powers have to serve *his* interest and not *your* interest. If this action is to be completed, God alone has to accomplish it, and you have only to endure it. Wherever you truly emerge from your will and your knowledge, God truly and willingly goes in and emits his radiant light. Whenever God is to know himself in this way, *your* knowledge can neither stand up nor be of service. You are not allowed to imagine that your reason can grow to the point that you could know God. In addition, if God is to shine divinely within you, *your natural light* will not help you in any way, but it must become a pure nothing and divest itself completely of itself. For God can *then* enter with *his* light, and he will bring inside with him whatever you have given up a thousand times over—and in addition he will bring a new form that contains everything within itself.

We have a comparable situation in the Gospel when our Lord spoke in a friendly way with the pagan woman at the well (Jn. 4:5ff.). She left her pitcher and ran into the city and told the people that the true Messiah had come. The people did not believe her words but went out with her and saw him themselves. Then they said to her: We do not believe your words; rather, we believe only because we have seen him *ourselves* (Jn. 4:42). In a similar way, neither knowledge of all creatures nor *your own wisdom* nor *all your* knowledge can bring you so far as to know God in a *divine* way. If you wish to know God in a *divine* way, your knowledge has to become pure ignorance and forgetfulness of yourself and all creatures.

You might say next: "Now, sir, what is my reason to do if it is to remain wholly unencumbered and without all its activity? Is this the best way for me—to raise my mind up to a knowledge that is unknowing—something that cannot exist? For if I know something, that would still not be ignorance, and it would not mean being unencumbered and bare. Am I to stay completely in the darkness? "Certainly, this is so! You can never be better off than when you are completely in the darkness and ignorance." "Alas, sir, does it all have to go? Can there be no turning back?" "No, indeed, there can be no real turning back." "But what is this darkness? What is it called? What is its name?" "Its name means nothing other than an aptitude for sensitivity that is not at all lacking in or devoid of being. It is rather a rich sensitivity in which you will be made whole. For this reason, there is positively no turning back. If you were still to turn back, you would do so not out of any kind of truth but rather on account of something else, say, the senses, the world, or the devil. If you give yourself up to this turning back, you would of necessity fall into sin, and you might go so far astray that you would bring about your eternal downfall. Therefore, no turning back is possible but only a constant pushing forward, an attainment, and a fulfillment of the aptitude. There is no rest short of being filled with total being. This is fitting; matter also is never at rest, and reason never rests until it is filled with everything that is within *its* potential."

In this connection a pagan master says: "Nature has nothing swifter than heaven, which overtakes all things in its course." All the same, the mind of a person outflies heaven in its course, provided the mind remains active in its powers and keeps itself free from degradation and mutilation by lowly and coarse things. In this case, it will overtake the highest heaven and will never rest until it comes to the highest of all places, where it will be fed and nourished by the best of all good.

Do you ask how *useful* it is to realize this potential, to keep yourself unencumbered and bare, to give yourself up solely to this darkness and ignorance, and to search them out and not turn back from them? In this aptitude lies the possibility of gaining *the One* who is all things! The more self-abandoning and ignorant of all things you are, the nearer do you come to him. Of this desert it is written: "I shall lead my beloved into the desert and I shall speak into her heart" (Ho. 2:16). The true Word of eternity will be spoken only in solitude, where people are made desolate and estranged from themselves and all multiplicity. The prophet longed for this desolate self-alienation when he said: "Oh, who would give me the wings of a dove so that I could fly away and find rest?" (Ps. 55:6). Where can we find rest and repose? Truly only in abject desolation, and estrangement from all creatures. In this connection David says: "I prefer to be abject and despised in the house of my God to dwelling with great honor and riches in a den of sinners" (cf. Ps. 84:10).

You might say: "Oh, Lord, if it is necessary for us to be so deprived and desolate of all things, both without and within, of our powers as well as of their deeds—if all this must be put aside, it is a difficult situation if God leaves people without his support. As the prophet says: 'Woe is me! My misery has been extended' (cf. Ps. 119). It is difficult if God extends my abandonment *without* illuminating me, speaking to me or being effective in me, just as you here teach and give us to understand."

If people find themselves in *this* way in pure nothingness, is it not better for them to do something to drive away the darkness and the abandonment? Should such people not somehow pray, read, listen to a sermon, or carry out other works that are virtuous so as to help themselves? No! Understand this truly that remaining quite still and for as long at a time as possible is the best thing you can do! It is certain that you cannot turn your attention to things of any kind without harm. You would gladly be prepared *partly* through *yourself* and *partly* through *him*, but this cannot be. You can never think so quickly or so long of preparing yourself that God has not already been there to prepare you. Now let us assume that this *may be* shared: preparation is *your* task, and influencing or infusing is *his* task. All the same you should know that God *must* be effective and infuse himself as soon as he finds you ready. You are not permitted to believe that God is like an earthly carpenter who works or does not work according to his own wish, and who has it within his willpower to do something or not according to his own pleasure. *This* is *not* the way it is with God. Wherever and whenever God finds you ready, he *must* act and infuse himself into you. In the same way, whenever the air is clear and pure, the sun *must* infuse itself into the air and *cannot* keep from doing so! Of course, it would be a great deficiency in God if he did not accomplish great deeds in you and infuse a great blessing into you, provided he finds you unencumbered and bare.

Thus the masters of the spiritual life inform us in writing that at the same moment as the substance of a child is ready within the womb, God infuses a living spirit into the child's body, namely, the soul, which is the body's form. It is a *single* moment: readiness and the infusion. If *nature* attains its highest point, God will give *grace*. At the same moment that a spirit is ready,

God enters into it without delay and hesitation. In the Book of Revelation it is written that our Lord announced to the people: "I stand in front of the door, knocking and waiting for someone to let me in. I shall share an evening meal with that person" (Rv. 3:20). You don't need to seek him here or there. He is not farther off than the door of your heart; there he stands and tarries and waits to find someone ready to open up to him and let him in. You don't need to call him from afar; he can scarcely wait for you to open to him. He is a thousand times more eager for you than you for him. Opening up and entering in are but a *single* moment.

You might ask how can this be? I cannot notice him at all. Pay attention now! It is not within *your* power to notice him but in *his*. If it suits him, he *will show* himself. Still, he can also conceal himself if he wishes. This is what Christ meant when he said to Nicodemus: "The wind blows where it will; you hear its voice but do not know from where it is coming or where it is blowing" (Jn. 3:8). He spoke and at the same time contradicted himself: "You hear and yet *do not know*." After all, we become knowledgeable by listening! Christ meant that by listening we absorb him or bring him into ourselves as if he had wished to say: "You *receive* the spirit and yet do not know about it." Understand now that God cannot leave anything empty and unfilled. God and nature cannot permit anything to be unfilled or empty. Therefore, if it seems to you that you are not aware of him and that you are completely empty of him, this is not the case with him. For if something empty existed under heaven, no matter what you wish and no matter whether it be large or small, he would either have to carry it up to himself in heaven or have to come down and fill it with himself. In no way does God, the ruler of nature, allow anything to be empty. Therefore, be still and do not flinch from this emptiness. For you can indeed turn away from this moment, but you will never again return to it.

You might say: "Yes, Lord, you constantly mean that it must come to this, that this birth should take place *within me*, namely, that your Son should be born within me. Fine then! Could I have a sign whereby I might become aware that it had really taken place?" Yes, indeed, there will be three reliable signs! I shall now give only one of them. I am often asked if people can reach the point where time no longer hinders them and where neither diversity nor material goods hinder them any longer. Indeed this is so! If this birth has really taken place, all creatures can no longer hinder you. Rather, they all point you toward God and toward this birth for which we find a similarity in lightning. It turns into itself whatever it strikes—be it a tree or an animal or a person. If a person has turned his or her back to the lightning, it turns the person's face around in a second. If a tree has a thousand leaves, all of them turn their right side to the lightning bolt. Behold, this is what happens to all who are affected by this birth. They are quickly turned toward this birth in whatever is actual to them, no matter how coarse it might be. Yes, what formerly was a hindrance for you now is a benefit to you. Your countenance will be completely turned toward this birth. Truly, in whatever you see or hear, no matter what it is, you can absorb in all things nothing but this birth. Indeed, all things become for you nothing but God, for in all things you have your eye only on God. It is like a person who looks at the sun for a long time; afterward, no matter what he or she might look at, the image of the sun appears there. If you fail to seek God and have your eye on him in each and every thing, you will miss this birth.

Now you might ask this question: "Are people who have gotten on so well still to accomplish works of penance, or are they neglecting something if they do not practice them?" Listen to this! Every form of penance—be it fasting, keeping vigils, praying, kneeling, mortification, wearing hair shirts, lying on a hard bed, or whatever similar kind of thing there is that's ever been discovered—was thought up because our body and flesh are constantly in opposition to the spirit. The body is often too strong for the spirit, and thus a battle constantly goes on between them, an eternal quarrel. The body is bold and strong here below because it is here in its own country. The world helps it; this earth is its fatherland, and all its relatives, such as food, drink, and good living, are helpful. All these things are against the spirit. The spirit is in a foreign land here. All its relatives and its whole family are in heaven. There *it* is well befriended if it turns in that direction and makes itself at home there. We place the restraint of penitential practices on the flesh in order to come to the spirit's aid in a foreign land, and in order to weaken the flesh somewhat in this battle. This is so that the flesh will not conquer the spirit and that the spirit can defend itself. If you do this to the body in order to imprison it, and if you wish to burden the flesh and make it a thousand times more subject, then place on it the bridle of love. Through love you will overcome it most quickly, and through love you will burden it most heavily. That is why God lies in wait for us with nothing so much as love. For love is very like a fishhook. A fisher cannot catch a fish unless the fish picks up the hook. If the fish has swallowed the hook, the fisher is certain of the fish. No matter how much the fish twists this way or that way, the fisher is quite certain of it. I speak in the same way about love. Whoever is captured by love bears the strongest bonds and yet a sweet burden. Whoever has accepted this sweet burden will attain more and thereby come further than through all the penitential practices and mortification that all the people together could carry out. They will even be able to bear and endure happily whatever befalls them and whatever God inflicts upon them. They will be able to forgive in a kindly way all the evil that is done to them. Nothing brings you nearer to God and unites you so to him as this sweet bond of love. Let whoever has found this way seek no other. Whoever takes up this hook is caught in such a way that foot and hand, mouth, eyes, heart, and all that is in that person must always belong *to* God. Therefore you can never overcome this enemy in a better way so that the enemy cannot hurt you than through love. For this reason it is written: "Love is as strong as death, as harsh as hell" (Sg. 8:6). Death separates the soul from the body, but love separates all things from the soul. It will not endure at all whatever is not God or divine. Those who are caught in this noose or who wander along this way will find whatever deeds they accomplish or fail to accomplish of no importance. Whatever such people do or do not do matters not at all. Yet the slightest deed or practice of such people is more useful and fruitful for themselves and all others and God is better disposed toward it than toward the practices of others who, while without mortal sin, have less love. The leisure of such people is more useful than the *deeds* of others. Therefore, look only for this fishhook, and you will be happily caught. The more you are caught, the more you will be liberated.

May he who himself is love help us to be caught and liberated in this way! Amen.

COMMENTARY: The *Via Negativa* Explored/The Darkness and Ignorance That Is Knowledge/Solitude: a Way of Pure
Nothingness and Emptiness/The Return to Crea-
tures/How Love Is to Be Preferred to Mortifications

In this sermon Eckhart continues his exploration of the process of *return to our origins*, the process known as the *via negativa*. As in the previous sermon, he elaborated on what a radical letting go of the will entails, so here he develops the implications to a radical letting go of the intellect. It is a letting go that God *alone* will *accomplish* but we must *prepare* for it by keeping ourselves *unencumbered and bare* and by not *turning back* and by *remaining quite still*. We are advised to leave behind the "throng" of memory, reason, and will plus the senses and imagination. We are to leave them because they distract us by diversifying us and separating us from a deeper unity that is within and among us. Eckhart underscores the need for the *via negativa* by arguing that the fact that God *is good, wise, merciful* and the concepts used to describe God's activity are not adequate for all we need to know about ourselves and about God. *Even though all this may be good and divine, it is still conveyed from outside us through the senses.* Eckhart seeks an inner journey in this sermon. He wants to explore solitude, which is what is left in the person who has learned to let go and let be. What is going on there?

To name what is going on in the person who has learned to let go and let be, Eckhart rains down graphic phrase after graphic phrase. He speaks of *becoming a pure nothing*, of experiencing *pure ignorance*, of an *unknowing knowledge* that is *unencumbered and bare*. This *way into pure nothingness* is a way into *darkness*. There is *emptiness* and *solitude* and a *desert* where we are to *remain still* for what God has prepared for us. We do not prepare so much as God does. Provided we are found *unencumbered and bare*, God will *infuse a great blessing into us*. God is driven to do this, much as God infuses a soul into the fetus of a new child. The union is mutually effected: We do the opening up and

God does the entering in. The action is a single action, *opening up and entering in are but a single moment.*

Eckhart draws many of his images for this process of the *via negativa* from the Scriptures. The image of the desert and of solitude, for example, are images found in Hosea and in the psalm which Eckhart cites:

> . . . I am going to lure her
> and lead her out into the wilderness
> and speak to her heart. (Ho. 2:16)

> And I say,
> "Oh for the wings of a dove
>   to fly away and find rest."
> How far I would take my flight,
>   and make a new home in the desert!

> There I should soon find shelter
>   from the raging wind,
> and from the tempest, Lord, that destroys
>   and from their malicious tongues. (Ps. 55:6–9)

The preparation for these wilderness and desert experiences we have discussed in the previous three sermons. It is letting go. Once we have been so emptied, God is driven to fill the vacuum, for nature and God both abhor a vacuum. Both reason and will are radically deficient and must be let go of for this filling to happen.

> Wherever you truly emerge from your will and your knowl-
> edge, God truly and willingly goes in and emits his radiant
> light. Whenever God is to know himself in this way, your
> knowledge can neither stand up nor be of service.

Our natural reason is to become a *pure nothing* and then divine light will take over. We are to let go of creatures in this *via negativa* not because they are evil but because a different kind of knowledge is called for. *If you wish to know God in a divine way, your knowledge has to become pure ignorance and forgetfulness of yourself and all creatures.* Eckhart sets up an imaginary dialogue with a listener which allows him to develop more fully what this *divine way* of *pure ignorance* is about and why it is so valuable a pathway to travel. We cannot turn back

from this darkness, we must not run from it or allow ourselves to be distracted from it. Pushed to identify it more fully, Eckhart comes up with a
name: It is our *aptitude*, or potential, for *sensitivity*. It is a rich sensitivity
that has the power to perfect us and heal us and make us whole. It truly
exists—we are all capable of it—but it needs to develop by a *constant
pushing forward, an attainment, and a fulfillment.* This potential is a potential for *being filled with total being*—one might even call it a potential
for potential, it is so rich. The total being of which we are capable does
not stop short of that Being that encircles all being—there is included in
the depths of our potential for sensitivity a sensitivity for God. *In this aptitude lies the possibility of gaining the One who is all things!* By putting
aside our reasoning and imagining powers for a time, as well as our accomplishments, we enter on the way of *pure nothingness.* We will be
tempted to keep busy and need to resist compulsions that would invite us
even to *pray, read, listen to a sermon.* But Eckhart counsels us to leave
such activities, for the period when we are experiencing the *via negativa.* Let them go too. If we can let them go, then God, who stands at the
door knocking and waiting, can come in. He is so close and so eager to
enter.

> You don't need to seek him here or there. He is not further off
> than the door of your heart; there he stands and tarries and
> waits to find someone ready to open up to him and let him in.
> You don't need to call him from afar; he can scarcely wait for
> you to open to him. He is a thousand times more eager for
> you than you for him.

Letting go and letting be allow letting in to occur. Elsewhere, Eckhart
elaborates on this theme of emptying:

> No cask can have two kinds of wine in it. If it is to contain
> wine, one must necessarily pour out the water; the cask must
> be bare and empty. Therefore, if you would receive divine joy
> and God, it is necessary for you to pour out the creatures.[1]

We pour out the creatures not because creatures are bad but because
we are not empty enough to enjoy both God and creatures. The limits
are inside of us. He goes on: "Everything that is to receive and to be
receptive must and should be empty." The eye can rejoice at all colors,

Eckhart says, because it is empty of them all. So too with us and creatures. The letting go is necessary for our fuller enjoyment of them. And of God in them and them in God.

Eckhart equates the entering in of God with the birth of a divine Son that *should be born within me*. He does this in the context of the story of Nicodemus in John's Gospel (3:1–21). This story of birth is the story of being reborn "through water and the Spirit" and there are traces of a baptismal motif in this elaborate story. In addition, another story that Eckhart invokes in the present sermon, that of the woman at the well, develops the theme of "living water" that signified the coming of the spirit (Jn. 4:1–42). Since Eckhart himself draws an analogy between God's infusing a fetus with a soul and God's infusing us with himself, it can be said that Eckhart is at the least associating his theme of the birth of the Son in us and the Spirit of that Son with the rebirth motifs of baptism and of the sending of the Spirit. Like the author of John's Gospel, Eckhart is subtle in his analogies and does not talk a lot about sacrament, not even the sacrament of baptism. However, he is suggesting by the very texts he uses that such is the context in which he speaks. *You receive the Spirit and yet do not know about it*, he cites Christ as admonishing his listeners, as, no doubt, Eckhart is admonishing his.

Another influence in this sermon is Pseudo-Dionysius, who so described knowing as an unknowing. Indeed, this could be called the most Dionysian of any of Eckhart's sermons, but still there are differences. Pseudo-Dionysius does not stress the return to creation that Eckhart insists on at such length toward the end of this sermon. Nor does he stress the panentheism of all beings in God to the extent that Eckhart does.[2]

Eckhart is never satisfied in talking exclusively of the *via negativa*. As we saw in Path One, Eckhart's whole spirituality is creation-centered and not ascetic. Thus he returns to creation in this sermon, first when he provides the very test of whether the journey of the *via negativa* is authentic or not. What is that test? *If this birth has really taken place, all creatures can no longer hinder you. Rather they all point you toward God and toward this birth.* All creatures are returned to and seen in a new light, as focusing on God and the potential between God and us. Mortification of the senses is not what follows from this experience; rather, a sensitizing of the senses results from having made contact with our *rich potential for sensitivity*. We come away from the *via negativa* more sensitized and more ecstatic vis-à-vis creation than ever before.

> Yes, what formerly was a hindrance for you now is a benefit
> to you. Your countenance will be completely turned toward
> this birth. Truly, in whatever you see or hear, no matter what it
> is, you can absorb in all things nothing but this birth. Indeed,
> all things become for you nothing but God, for in all things
> you have your eye only on God.

All things become nothing but God—there is the first principle of
Eckhart's spirituality of blessing, that being is God. Truly we have returned to our origins and can now go out from there. For we have seen
the truth of the divinity of all being in ever greater depth and insight in
our journey into the *purity of nothingness.* Clearly, the *via negativa* is
dialectically related to the *via affirmativa* for Eckhart. Path Two leads
from and back to Path One.

Another creation issue that Eckhart addresses in this sermon is that of
ascetic practices. How important are fastings, vigils, kneelings, prayers,
wearing hair shirts? How useful are they for entering into this unknowing
knowledge? They are far less useful than the restraint called love.

> If you wish to burden the flesh and make it a thousand times
> more subject, then place on it the bridle of love. Through love
> you will overcome it most quickly, and through love you will
> burden it most heavily.

Eckhart resists the dualism that is inherent in mortification practices and
we are reminded of his statement in another sermon, "the soul loves the
body." Like his brother Thomas Aquinas, Eckhart insists that any tension in
the relationship between flesh and spirit is to be resolved amicably and
not by coercion or force. Why? Ultimately, because that is God's way.
God lies in wait for us with nothing so much as love. Love is like a
fishhook and we are to be hooked on love, not on ascetic practices.
*Whoever has accepted this sweet burden will attain more and thereby
come further than through all the penitential practices and mortification
that all the people together could carry out.* This is a more gentle way
of God experience. From it one learns to *endure happily whatever
befalls* one and to *forgive in a kindly way all the evil that is done to*
one. Compassion is learned by this route and not by the route of
mortifications. It suffices. *Let whoever has found this way seek no other.*
With love, our whole body and all our senses belong to God and there

is no need to mortify them. Whoever takes up this hook is caught in such a way that *foot and hand, mouth, eyes, heart, and all that is in that person must always belong to God.* This is the way of liberation and joyful spiritual journeying. *Look only for this fishhook and you will be happily caught. The more you are caught, the more you will be liberated.* Love unites the dialectic of being caught and being liberated. Such a love is the love that God is and that God employs to catch us by.

Sermon Eighteen: LETTING GO OF INTELLECT
CREATES A TRANSFORMATION OF KNOWLEDGE

"Where is he who has been born as king of the Jews?"
(Mt. 2:2)*

"Where is he who has been born as king of the Jews?" (Mt. 2:2).
Pay attention now to *where* this birth has taken place. "*Where*
has he been born?" I state, however, as I have often stated, that
this eternal birth takes place in the soul totally in the way it takes
place in eternity, neither less nor more. For it is only *one* birth,
and this birth takes place in the *being* and *foundation* of the soul.

Behold how questions are now raised. First, since God is spiritually in all things and dwells within them more inwardly and naturally than things do within themselves, and since God, wherever
he is, must have effect, know himself, and declare his Word, the
question is raised: What special characteristics does the soul have
for this accomplishment of God more than other creatures endowed with reason in which God is also present? Heed the following explanation!

God is present, effective, and powerful in all things. He is only
generative, however, in the soul. For *all* creatures are a footprint
of God, but the soul is formed like God, according to its nature.
This form must be adorned and completed through this birth.
For this accomplishment and this birth no creature is more receptive than the soul. Truly, whatever perfection is to enter the soul,
be it divine, unique light or grace or happiness, all of it must
come into the soul of a necessity *through this birth* and in no
other way. Wait only for this birth within yourself, and you will
discover all blessing and all consolation, all bliss, all being, and all
truth. If you neglect *this*, you will neglect *all* blessing and all happiness. Whatever enters you *in this* brings to you pure being and

* "Ubi est, qui natus est rex Judaeorum?" (Quint, ℀58)

constancy. Whatever you seek or love beyond this, however, will spoil, take it as you will and where you will. All of it will spoil. On the other hand, this thing alone gives being; everything else will spoil. In this birth, however, you will participate in the divine influence and all his gifts. *Creatures* in whom God's image does not exist do *not* become receptive to it, for the soul's image belongs especially to this eternal birth, which quite uniquely especially takes place within the soul, and is accomplished by the Father in the soul's foundation and its most spiritual place. This is the place where no image has ever shed its light and into which no power has ever stolen a glance.

The second question is as follows. Since the effect of this birth takes place in the being and foundation of the soul, it takes place just as much in a sinner as in a good person. What grace or advantage is there in it *for me?* Does this mean that the foundation of nature is in both of them the same, and is the nobility of nature preserved even in those who are in hell?

Pay heed to this explanation. It is a characteristic of this birth always to take the lead with new light. It always brings a bright light into the soul, for it is a characteristic of goodness that it must be poured out wherever it is. In this birth God infuses himself into the soul with light in such a way that the light becomes so abounding in the soul's being and foundation that it pushes out and overflows into the powers as well as into the external person. This is what happened to Paul when God touched him on the road with his light and spoke to him. A reflection of the light was externally visible so that all his fellow travelers saw it, and it surrounded Paul as light surrounds the saints (Ac. 9:3). Now the excess of light that is in the soul's foundation overflows into the body, which as a result becomes full of brightness. *Sinners*, however, cannot receive any of this, nor are they worthy of it because they are filled with sin and evil, which is called "darkness." For this reason it is said: "The darkness receives and does not understand the light" (Jn. 1:5). The blame for this is that the ways along which this light is to enter are burdened and blocked with falseness and darkness. Light and darkness cannot be together, nor can God and a creature. If God enters, the creature must at the same time go out. People become aware, of course, of this light. Every time they turn to God, a light at once shines and gleams within them and causes them to know what they are to do and give up, as well as many other good instructions concerning which they had previously known and understood nothing.

"Whence and how do you know this?" Look and pay attention! Your heart is often touched and turned away from the world. How could this take place unless through that illumination? It takes place so gently and pleasantly that everything that is not God or divine grieves you. You are attracted to God, and you become aware of many good admonitions and still do not know from where they come to you. In no case does this inner inclination come from either creatures or any kind of an indication from them, for what a creature indicates or accomplishes always comes from outside itself. But the *foundation* alone is touched by *this* deed, and the more unencumbered you keep yourself, the more light and clarity of vision you will discover. Therefore, people have only gone astray because they have right at the beginning gone out of this foundation and have wanted to cling too much to externals. Saint Augustine says: "There are many who have sought light and truth, but always only outside, where they did not exist." On this account they end up so far outside that they never come home again or inside again. Thus they have not found the truth. For truth is inside in the foundation and not outside. Let those who wish to find light and insight into all truth look out and pay attention to this birth within themselves and within their foundation. Then all the powers as well as the inner person will be illuminated. For as soon as God touches the inner *foundation* with the truth, light is cast into the powers, and people can at times accomplish more than anyone else can teach them.

Thus says the prophet: "I have gained knowledge over all who have ever taught me" (cf. Pr. 1:16). Understand also that *because* this light cannot shine and give light within *sinners*, this birth could not possibly take place within *them*. This birth cannot exist along with the darkness of sin, even though it does not occur in the powers but rather in the soul's being and foundation.

Now an additional question is raised. What difference does it make that God the Father only generates in the soul's being and foundation, not in the powers themselves? What has their service to do with the fact that they are to remain idle and take a rest?

Why is it necessary that the act of generation should not take place at all in the *powers*? This is a good question. Now pay attention to the following explanation:

Every creature carries on its activity for the purpose of a goal. The goal is always the first in intention and the last in execution. In the same way, God aims at a quite blissful goal, which is himself, so that he can bring the soul with all its powers to this goal, namely, himself. *For this reason* God accomplishes all his deeds; *for this reason* the Father generates his Son in the soul so that all the powers of the soul will come to this goal. He traces everything that is in the soul and invites all of it to this hospitality and to this celebration. The soul, however, has extended and scattered itself through its powers outside itself, each power through its own activity: the power of seeing into the eye, the power of hearing into the ear, the power of taste into the tongue. As a result, the soul's inner powers for effective deeds are all the weaker, for every divided power is incomplete. If the soul wishes to be effective inside itself, it must recall all its powers and gather them together from all the scattered things to an internal activity.

Saint Augustine says: "The soul is more in the place where it loves than in the place where it gives life to the body." Let's make a comparison. A pagan scholar who was devoted to the science of arithmetic concentrated all his powers on it. He sat at his hearth, making calculations and exploring this science. Then someone came by and brandished a sword, not knowing who the scholar was, and exclaimed: "Tell me right away what your name is, or I'll kill you!" The scholar was so engrossed with himself that he neither saw nor heard his enemy. He was unable to pay attention to what the other wanted or to realize that he had only to open his mouth just far enough to say: "My name is so and so." After the enemy screamed loudly and fiercely at him, and he still did not answer, his enemy cut his head off. This took place in pursuit of one of the natural sciences. How much more should we remove ourselves from all things and gather all our powers in order to look at and know the unique, immeasurable, uncreated truth! For this purpose, gather up all your senses, all your powers, your whole reason, and your whole memory. Direct all these things to that foundation where this treasure lies hidden. If this takes place, you should understand that you must divest yourself

of all other accomplishments and arrive at ignorance if you wish
to find this treasure.

Here another question is raised. Would it not be more worthwhile if each power kept its *own* deed, and if one power did not
hamper the other in its deeds, and also if it did not hamper God
in *his* deeds? Can there not be in me some kind of natural knowledge that does *not* have a hindering effect, just as God knows all
things without hindrance, and just as the saints also know them?
This is a useful question. Pay attention now to the following explanation!

The saints see in God only a *single* image, and in this image
they know *all* things. Indeed, God himself looks thus into himself, and knows himself thus in all things. He has no need to turn
from one thing to another, as we must do. If it could be so in this
earthly life that we at all times might have a mirror before us in
which we in a *single* moment could see all things, and could
know them in a *single* image, neither deed nor knowledge would
be a hindrance for us. Since *we* have to turn, however, from one
thing to another, there can be *for us* no departure from the one
without a hindrance of the other. For the soul is so closely tied to
the powers that it must flow where they are flowing. This is because in all deeds that the powers accomplish, the soul has to be a
part—and, indeed, with dedication. Otherwise, the powers could
not have any effect *at all*. If the soul flows off, then, with its dedication into external deeds, it must of necessity be all the weaker
spiritually in its inner effect. For God wishes to have, and has to
have, an unencumbered, untroubled, and free soul for this birth, a
soul in which there is nothing but him alone, a soul that looks
out for nothing and no one but for him alone. Christ spoke in
this sense when he said: "Whoever loves something other than
me and tenderly loves father or mother and many other things is
not worthy of me. I have not come on earth to bring peace but a
sword in that I cut off all things and separate sister, brother,
mother, child, and the friend who truly is your enemy. For the
one who is close to you is your enemy" (Mt. 10:34–36). If your
eye wishes to see all things and your ear to hear all things and
your heart to ponder all things, your soul *must* truly be dispersed
in all these things.

Therefore a master of the spiritual life says: "If people are to accomplish a spiritual deed, they must collect all their powers, as if into a corner of their souls, and conceal themselves from all images and forms." Then they can accomplish their deed. In this connection they must arrive at forgetfulness and unself-consciousness. Wherever this Word is to be heard, it must occur in stillness and in silence. We cannot be of greater service to this Word than through stillness and silence. *There* we can hear it and understand it correctly, in that state of unknowing. Where we know nothing, it becomes apparent and reveals itself.

Now another question is raised. You might say, "Sir, you are placing all our salvation in ignorance." This sounds wrong. God created human beings so that they could *have knowledge.* As the prophet says: "Lord, make them knowledgeable!" (cf. Tb. 13:4). Where there is ignorance, there is a defect and emptiness. This is the way an animal-like person is, an ape or a fool! This is true as long as the person *persists* in this ignorance. Meanwhile, we must come here to a transformed knowledge. At the same time, this ignorance should not come *from* ignorance; instead, *from* knowledge we must come to a state of ignorance. Then we shall become knowledgeable with the divine knowledge, and then our ignorance will be ennobled and adorned by supernatural knowledge. And in this situation where we are suffering, we are more perfect than if we were accomplishing deeds. Therefore, a master of the spiritual life says that the power of hearing is much more noble than the power of sight. For we learn more wisdom through our sense of hearing than our sense of sight, and we live more in wisdom through our hearing. Let's consider the following incident involving a pagan scholar. As he lay on his deathbed, his disciple spoke in his presence of a higher science. He raised up his head, even though he was dying, listened to him, and said: "Oh, let me learn only about this science, and I shall have eternal joy in it." Listening brings more inside us, while seeing directs us more to external things; at least this is the case for the activity of seeing itself. On this account, we shall be much happier in the eternal life thanks to our hearing than to our sight. For the event of hearing the eternal Word is *within* me while the act of seeing departs from me. I *undergo* hearing, but I *accomplish* seeing.

Our happiness, however, does not lie in our accomplishments but rather in the fact that we undergo God. For to the same extent that God is more noble than a creature, God's accomplishment is more noble than mine. Indeed, God in his immeasurable love has placed our happiness in our capacity to undergo. For we undergo more than we accomplish, and we receive a good deal more than we give. Every gift, however, benefits our receptivity for a new gift and, indeed, for a greater gift. Every divine gift increases our receptivity and longing to receive what is higher and greater. For this reason, many masters of the spiritual life say that *in this* the soul is equal in birth to God. For to the extent that God is boundless in his giving, the soul is equally boundless in taking and receiving. Just as God is omnipotent in his deeds, the soul is just as profound in its capacity to receive. For this reason it is transformed, with and in God. God has to accomplish deeds while the soul has to receive. He has to know and love himself in the soul, while the soul has to know with *his* knowledge and love with *his* love. For this reason, it is much happier through God's interests than through its own. Similarly, its happiness is placed more in *his* accomplishment than in its own.

The disciples of Saint Dionysius asked him why Timotheus surpassed all of them in perfection. Dionysius replied: "Timotheus is a man who undergoes God." Whoever has a clear understanding of this point would surpass all others.

Thus your ignorance is not a defect but your highest perfection, and your undergoing is *thus* your highest accomplishment. In this way you have to divest yourself of all your activities and bring all your powers to silence if you really wish to experience this birth within yourself. If you wish to find the newborn King, you must outrun and cast behind you everything else you may find.

May he who became a human child so that we could become God's children help us to outrun and put aside everything that does not please this newborn King! Amen.

COMMENTARY: Finding the Treasure That Ignorance Brings/How Knowledge Precedes True Ignorance and How True Ignorance Transforms Knowledge/The Need for Stillness and Silence/How the Soul, Alone of All Creatures, Is Generative Like God Is

In the previous sermon Eckhart asked *when* the union of God and people takes place and his response was that it takes place in a "single moment" of time or of what might be called timeless time or ecstasy. Like a flash of lightning, enlightenment takes place. In this sermon Eckhart develops the same basic theme of the kind of knowing that takes place when we let go of all things. This knowing he calls in this sermon an arrival *at forgetfulness and ignorance*, a *knowing nothing*, an *internal activity* that *gathers together all the soul's powers* that have been scattered about outside. Letting go allows nothingness to be, as he says elsewhere. "Letting go borders so closely on nothing that between perfect letting go and nothingness there can be nothing."[1]

In commenting on a previous sermon (number Fifteen), we traced Eckhart's use of the term *Abgeschiedenheit* to an expression of Paul's in his letter to the Romans. In the present sermon Eckhart reveals another biblical source for his use of that term. He interpolates Jesus' words in Matthew's Gospel. In the Gospel we read: "I have not come on earth to bring peace but a sword. For I have come to set a man against his father . . ." But Eckhart interjects his interpretation when he says in the present sermon: "*I have not come on earth to bring peace but a sword in that I cut off all things and separate sister, brother . . .*" The words he interjects are *abschneiden* and *abscheiden*, root words of *Abgeschiedenheit*, letting go. Thus Eckhart looks on letting go as a sort of sword that cuts us off from other creatures. And he derives his concept of letting go from Paul and from Jesus' sayings as reported in Romans and the Gospel of Matthew. The aim of letting go of knowledge is, in fact, nothingness. "What is the object of pure letting go? I answer that neither this nor that is the object of pure letting go. It aims at a mere nothing and I will tell you why: pure letting go aims at the highest goal in which God can work entirely according to his will."[2] Only emptiness allows God's fullness to take place. "When the heart that has let go takes the highest aim, it has to be toward the nothing, because in this there is the greatest receptivity."[3]

In the present sermon, speaking from the text in Matthew's Gospel where the Wise Men are in search of the infant King of the Jews, Eckhart asks: *Where* does this union of God and people take place? The text reads:

> After Jesus had been born at Bethlehem in Judaea during the
> reign of King Herod, some wise men came to Jerusalem from

the east. "Where is this infant King of the Jews?" they asked. "We saw his star as it rose and have come to do him homage." (Mt. 2:1–2)

Eckhart responds: *Pay attention now to where this birth has taken place . . . this eternal birth takes place in the soul totally in the way it takes place in eternity, neither less nor more.* And, as in the previous sermon he said the union was one single moment and not two, so here he declares that the place is not two places, but one sacred place or space. *It is only one birth, and this birth takes place in the being and foundation of the soul.* Now he names this place that is more than a place and has become the most sacred of spaces. It is *the being and foundation of the soul.* It is there, just as much as in Bethlehem, that the King of the Jews is born. The person is truly the kingdom of God, as we saw in Sermon Nine, and Bethlehem, the place for the birth of the new creation, where God's birth is taking place. Do not look to institutions for the real incarnations of God, Eckhart is subtly declaring, but look to the *being and foundation of the soul.* We are the new Bethlehem. Wise men and wise women search here for the divinity in our midst.

How is this possible? It is because the soul is a *boundless soul,* as oblivious of time and place and as without boundaries as God is. The soul is as *omnipotent* in its capacity to receive as God is to give. In our letting go we experience this bigness and we create a void that God must enter into. God has to accomplish deeds while the soul has to endure. "Letting go forces God to love me."[4] *For, wherever God is . . . he must declare his Word.* In our sinking into unknowing, we are known by God and we begin to know all things. To do this we need to *collect all our powers and conceal ourselves from all images and forms.* It is not that seeing things or acting on things is bad—God sees all things, and saints do, but they see them in the unity that they are or *in a single image.* We, however, see things piecemeal and in a fragmented way and so we need to let go of such piecemeal consciousness in order to see things in the whole in which they truly are: in their inness in God and God's inness in them, for God is *spiritually in all things and dwells with them more inwardly and naturally than things do within themselves.* As Schürmann comments: Eckhart's "doctrine must not be reduced to a bewildered discrediting of the things that envelop our existence. Rather, it aims at an education of seeing."[5] *The goal is to look at and know the unique, immeasurable, uncreated truth! This is a treasure that lies hidden.*

To arrive there we need to pass through the *via negativa*, wherein we *gather up all our senses, all our powers, our whole reason, and our whole memory. Then we direct all these things to that foundation of being where the treasure lies.* What is needed is utter concentration such as the scholar had whose head was cut off. Concentration on one thing, for example, God, is an ignorance of all other things. *Arrive at ignorance if you wish to find this treasure.* The foundation of the soul and the foundation of being do not yield their secrets to the noisy, busy, and superficially compulsive goings-on of the world. They are laid open to those who know *silence* and *stillness, ignorance and nothing.*

> Wherever this Word is to be heard, it must occur in stillness and in silence. We cannot be of greater service to this Word than through stillness and silence. *There* we can hear it and understand it correctly, in that state of unknowing. Where we know nothing, it becomes apparent and reveals itself.

To explore our deepest depths, the unknown unconscious of the vortex that is our spirit, we need to listen. "Faith comes through hearing," says Paul, and Eckhart insists that we *learn more wisdom through our sense of hearing than our sense of sight, and we live more in wisdom through our hearing.* Biblical scholar Thorleif Boman points out how the Jewish way to experience reality is primarily through hearing, while the Greek way is primarily through sight.[6] In another sermon Eckhart elaborates on the need for silence at our depths:

> The Word lies hidden in the soul in such a way that one does not know it or hear it. Unless room is made in the ground of hearing, it cannot be heard; indeed, all voices and sounds must go out, and there must be absolute silence there and stillness.[7]

The ground of the soul needs to meet the ground of hearing in the stillness that encompasses all grounding. I listen to what is deepest within me, but I see what is outside me. *The event of hearing the eternal Word is within me, while the act of seeing departs from me. I undergo hearing, but I accomplish seeing.*

Eckhart is intent on contrasting inner and outer knowledge, which corresponds to what we saw in Sermons Two and Three as the difference between the inner and outer person. The *via negativa* is a journey to inner stillness and ignorance and in Eckhart's theology it is parallel to Jesus' story of the seed dying. For in speaking of the need of the soul to be *unencumbered, untroubled, and free* so that God can be born there, he invokes the following text from Matthew's Gospel, included in its fuller pericope:

> Do not suppose that I have come to bring peace to the earth: it is not peace I have come to bring, but a sword. For I have come to set a man against his father, a daughter against her mother, a daughter-in-law against her mother-in-law. A man's enemies will be those of his own household.
> "Anyone who prefers father or mother to me is not worthy of me. Anyone who prefers son or daughter to me is not worthy of me. Anyone who does not take his cross and follow in my footsteps is not worthy of me. Anyone who finds his life will lose it; anyone who loses his life for my sake will find it. (Mt. 10:37–39)

This dialectical and paradoxical way of finding life from losing it is the way Eckhart is thinking of the *via negativa*. Elsewhere, Eckhart distinguishes two kinds of knowledge, "evening knowledge" and "morning knowledge." The former is "when we know a creature in its own essence." In this way of seeing creatures we see "in images of multiple difference." In other words, such outer knowledge is fragmented. Morning knowledge, however, is a unifying and synthetic knowledge that "knows a creature in God." By such knowledge "we see a creature without all differences, deprived of all images and stripped of all similarity in the one who is God himself."[8] Eckhart's goal in the way of ignorance is that we might see creatures *in* God, which is how, in fact, they are, as we saw in Path One.

Thus Eckhart takes great pains in this sermon, as he does on numerous occasions, that he not be misunderstood when he says ignorance is a good thing. Knowledge is a good thing in Eckhart's estimation; "even the knowledge of evil things is good," he declares.[9] He was most likely the finest intellect with the best education of any philosopher or theologian of his century. And so he insists in the present sermon that this ignorance should not come from ignorance; instead, from knowledge we must come to a state of ignorance. In other words, we need to have something to let go of, before we dare let go! The *via negativa* presumes an intellectual life, a thinking and vital consciousness that already relates deeply to creation. It presumes Path One. This is an extremely important point to make, as the entire history of spirituality since Eckhart's condemnation forgot it time and time again. All sentimental spiritualities are anti-intellectual, as are all sentimentalists, Anne Douglas points out.[10] Spiritualists are notorious for wanting to jump into the *via negativa* or into Eckhart's Path Two without having imbibed of creation itself or Path One. Eckhart roundly condemns such foolishness. He addresses anti-intellectualism head-on as a theological issue of faith, namely, that God has made us to know:

> You might say, "Sir, you are placing all our salvation in ignorance." This sounds wrong. God created human beings so that they could *have knowledge*. As the prophet says, "Lord, make them knowledgeable!" Where there is ignorance, there is a defect and emptiness. This is the way an animal-like person is, an ape or a fool!

And so Eckhart invents a term for the kind of knowledge he is talking about. He is talking about our coming to a *transformed knowledge*, and one does this by experiencing a transformed ignorance, that is, a willful ignorance that comes *after* knowledge and does not precede it. In *transformed knowledge we become knowledgeable with the divine knowledge and our ignorance becomes ennobled and adorned by supernatural knowledge.* In the previous sermon, Eckhart went out of his way to indicate that letting go did not mean putting down the body or the senses; so in this sermon he is being deliberately explicit about how this way of ignorance or letting go of intellect on no account is to be confused with putting down knowledge. Would that fundamentalist spiritualist theologians from the fifteenth century (I am thinking of Thomas à Kempis, for example) right up to today had heeded this important observation from Eckhart! Instead, what has often passed as spirituality since Eckhart's condemnation has been an enshrining of the *via negativa* and an "ascetic theology" (which is a term invented in the seventeenth century) that utterly ignores creation and Path One of Eckhart's spiritual journey.[11] After all, as we saw in the previous sermon and as Eckhart alludes to in this one, the purpose of any traveling down the *via negativa* at all is that we might see creatures as God sees them. This, he has said, is the ultimate test of whether we have traveled that route rightly or not. The purpose of developing the inner person in Eckhart's view is not that people will be introverted and withdrawn from outside activities—this will be very clear as we study Paths Three and Four—but that our outer activities might truly operate from our inner depths and be worthy of our divine origins. The *via negativa* is not meant to escape the world but to deepen our relationship to the world. It is meant to contribute to our transformation of the world, but to do this we need also to transform the very way we see the world. Thus Eckhart gives an analogy of a door and a hinge as standing for the outer and the inner person:

> However much our Lady lamented and whatever other things she said, she was always in her inmost heart in a state of immovable letting go. Let us take an analogy of this. A door opens and shuts on a hinge. Now if I compare the wood of the door to the outward person, I can compare the hinge to the inner person. When the door opens or closes, the outer boards move to and fro, but the hinge remains immovable in one place and it does not budge at all as a result. So it is also here, if you only know how to act rightly.[12]

"How to act rightly"—there is Eckhart's intention in taking us on this journey of blessed ignorance. He wants to get our hinge so well grounded in the foundation that is our soul and being that our swinging may be steady and sturdy and useful.

In inviting us to take the journey that is the *via negativa*, Eckhart urges us not to be afraid of the dark. After all, Paul's very conversion, as reported in Acts 9, was accompanied by his first going blind. While light is good and is a sign of life, and while birth needs light, still darkness can be a means to seeing the light more fully. By darkness our knowledge can be transformed. After all, in the very depths of the *soul's foundation* and in its *most spiritual place . . . no image has ever shed its light.* We need to make contact with that deep, dark ground. For what is at stake is the birth of *a new light* that will accompany a new creation. God brings this new light, with the result that even our body will become *full of brightness*. Transformed and translucent, enlightened through and through, from soul's ground to body's activities—there is the conversion or transformation that Eckhart envisions for us.

It is a characteristic of this birth always to take the lead with new light. It always brings a bright light into the soul, for it is a characteristic of goodness that it must be poured out wherever it is. In this birth God infuses himself into the soul with light in such a way that the light becomes so abounding in the soul's being and foundation that it pushes out and overflows into the powers as well as into the external person.

Our conversion or transformation of knowledge—like Paul's—will be accompanied by our being touched by God with a divine light. To bolster our courage in face of the darkness that precedes conversion and transformation, Eckhart distinguishes this kind of divine darkness from a darkness that *burdens and blocks* the light. Because *light and darkness cannot be together*, something must give when they encounter each other. One kind of darkness—that caused by evil and sin—blocks the light. The other kind, that of letting go, makes room for the light and allows transformation to take over. When God *enters* this kind of darkness, *the creature must at the same time go out.* Eckhart is suggesting that true evil prevents our letting go. It always seeks to control. Thus God cannot enter there. People driven in this way succumb to externals and superficialities and never come home again to their divine origin. *They end up so far outside that they never come home again or inside again. Thus they have not found the truth. For truth is inside in the foundation and not outside.* Eckhart's words to such people give no hint of moralizing or condemning but rather they glisten with a kind of sadness, for such people have simply *not found the truth.*

Those who have learned to let go and let be and have become more and more transformed to the way all is in God and God is in all are also people who have learned to receive. In the previous sermon Eckhart defined the new knowledge as a wonderful capacity for sensitivity and receptivity. He develops this theme further in this sermon where we are told that our receptivity or our *undergoing is our highest accomplishment.* We need to develop our capacity to receive and not only our capacity to give. And in receiving there are no limits. Every gift benefits our receptivity for a new gift and, indeed, for a greater gift. Every divine gift increases our receptivity and longing to receive what is higher and greater. Gift consciousness is the result of love of creation and of new creation. "Thank you" is the ultimate prayer, as we saw in Sermon Eight. We are divine in our capacity to receive gifts and ever new ones. *Just* as God is omnipotent in his deeds, the soul is just as profound in its capacity to receive. For this reason it is transformed, with and in God. It is our capacity to receive that ultimately allows us to be transformed. This capacity is what is learned in letting go and letting be. And what does this transformation consist of, what do we become by it? We actually begin to know with God's knowledge and love with God's love. Behold the rewards of letting go.

Sermon Nineteen: WISDOM AND FIERY LOVE—NOT REPRESSION—ARE THE RESULTS OF LETTING GO

"Child, get up." (Lk. 8:54)*

"Get up!"

Our Lord "placed his hand on the girl and said, 'Get up!'" The "hand" of God is the Holy Spirit. All deeds are accomplished in passion. If the fiery love of God grows cold in the soul, it dies; and if God is to have an effect on the soul, God must be united to the soul. If the soul is to be united or become one with God, it must be removed from all things and must be alone just as God is alone. For a deed that God accomplishes in an unencumbered soul is more valuable than heaven and earth. For this reason God has created the soul, that it might be united with him. A saint says: "The soul has been created from nothing, and he alone has created it with the help of no one. If anyone had created the soul with him, God would be quite anxious lest the soul be inclined to that other person. The soul therefore must be alone as God is alone."

Spiritual things and bodily things cannot be united. If divine perfection is to take action in the soul, the soul must be a spirit as God is a spirit. And if God were to endow the soul *within* the soul, he would have to do so with moderation. He therefore draws the soul into himself and to himself and in *this* way the soul is united with him. There is a comparison for this. Fire and a stone are united but still, because both are of a material nature, the stone, because of its materiality, inwardly remains cold. It is the same with air and light; everything you see in the air you see also in the sun. Because both air and light, however, are material, there is in a *whole* mile more light than in a *half mile*, and there is more in a half mile than in a house. However, the aptest com-

* "Puella, surge." (DW III, #85)

parison one can find is the one about the body and the soul. They are united in such a way that, just as the body cannot do anything without the soul, the soul cannot do anything without the body. As the soul is to the body, so is God to the soul, and if the soul is separated from the body, this means the death of the body. In a similar way, the soul dies if God departs from it.

Three obstacles cause the soul not to unite with God. The first is that the soul is too fragmented and, as a result, is not simple, for if the soul is inclined to creatures, it is not simple. The second is that the soul is mixed up with temporal things. The third obstacle is that the soul is inclined toward the body and thus cannot unite with God.

On the other hand, there are three *favorable factors* for the union of God and the soul. The first is that the soul is simple and unfragmented. The second is that it tarries above itself and above all temporary things and clings to God. The third is that it is separated from all bodily things and strives for the first purity [that is, for its divine origin]. Augustine says, concerning the free soul, "If you do not want *me*, I still want *you*. If I want *you*, you do not want *me*. If I hunt *you*, you fly from *me*. Pure spirits run back again along the same course toward the purity of God."

COMMENTARY: All Deeds Are Accomplished in Passion/The Soul
Needs to Be on Fire/Authentic Purity Means the Return
to Our Divine Origins Where Wisdom Dwells

In this brief sermon Eckhart applies the miracle of the resurrection from the dead that Jesus performed on the daughter of the synagogue official to ourselves. As we saw in Sermon Eight, he took this same biblical passage and applied it to the theme of spirituality as waking up, a theme that fit well into Path One. Now he applies this same theme of waking up to Path Two, for his emphasis here is on our being *removed from all things* and *being alone just as God is alone*. He is saying that just as the *via affirmativa* of Path One is a waking up, so too is the *via negativa* meant to be a waking up. A rising from sleep, from the dead, from spiritlessness. "Taking her by the hand he called to her, 'Child, get up.' And her spirit returned and she got up at once" (Lk. 8:54–55). The

Holy Spirit has roused her from sleepfulness, from unconsciousness, and has waked her.

The first thing we are waked up to is that God's love is a *fiery love* and a passionate love. Either we are on fire or we are cold, and a cold heart is a dead heart. God, whose love is a *fiery love, must be united to the soul.* Without this union with God's fiery love the soul dies. *The soul dies if God departs from it.* To be dead is to be cold; to be cold is to be dead. Rising from the death of unconsciousness is being warmed and made fiery once again. The Holy Spirit, the *hand of God* that touches cold hearts and bodies, came to the disciples in the form of tongues of fire. It too was a *fiery love.* Without being on fire and being like this flaming spirit, we can accomplish nothing. Our works will be as cold and as dead as we ourselves, for *all deeds are accomplished in passion.* Passion, for Eckhart, is not a bad word, as it is, for example, for Thomas à Kempis, who uses it exclusively in a pejorative sense in his *Imitation of Christ.* For Eckhart, a passionate person is a Godly person who does the works of the Father, works which are done out of a fiery love. *The soul must be a spirit as God is a Spirit.* We are to become as God is. Our spirit is to meet God's Spirit. And this is possible, because we are truly God's images and likenesses, provided we do not remain as cold as the stones are, provided we become heated as God is heated by fiery love. Fire can heat the stone only externally; the stone *inwardly remains cold.* Eckhart suggests that we too are often inwardly like stone—cold, apathetic, passionless, indifferent. God cannot work in such a person.

The result, then, of letting go and letting be is not more stony people, or more ice between people, or more hardness within people. It is fire and passion, a passion that leads to deeds that are born of deep, inward love that is the love of the Spirit. These deeds return life just as their source has received life in being raised from sleep and the land of death.

When God and the soul unite, the soul *strives for the first purity, that is, for its divine origin.* Eckhart cites Augustine, who says, *"Pure spirits run back again along the same course toward the purity of God."* What is this "purity of God" that is also our purity? It is, in its most basic form, a return to our origins, a recovery of our roots, a waking up from forgetfulness, a remembering of who we are and in whose image we all have been fashioned. It is a reminder of our divinity, as Eckhart put it at the conclusion of the previous sermon; it is the birth of our God-likeness.

Eckhart develops this theme of purity as return to our source on numerous occasions. It is significant that he does *not* define purity in terms of sexual abstinence or naïveté, as so many sentimental spiritualists since his time have done. His understanding of purity is a far more metaphysical and being-oriented one. When he does associate purity with children, it is not in terms of sexual innocence but in terms of their being nearer to their birth and therefore to their origins than are adults. We too need to be in touch with our youthfulness, and therefore our purity. Such purity is a transparency that carries us back to our divine origin. Eckhart says: "If Luke says a 'child,' this means something like a bit of pure air or something without flaws. And thus the soul should be pure and without stain, if the Holy Spirit is to have an effect on the soul."[1] Purity is that state of being that preceded original sin or the consciousness of dualisms and separations. It signifies our original freedom. Letting go means letting go even of the obstacles that have restricted us or our race from being in touch with this original freedom. As Schürmann puts it, a truly detached or letting-go person is one "who has retrieved his original liberty."[2]

Philosophers have a tendency to interpret Eckhart's search for origin and original purity as a Neoplatonic exercise. This is not the case, however, for he himself tells us that he got the idea from the prophetic and the wisdom literature in the Hebrew Bible (see Sermons One and Fifteen). If he uses Neoplatonism, it is to assist his language and imagination in this search, but it is not his starting point. In the Book of Ecclesiasticus we read:

> Before all other things wisdom was created,
> shrewd understanding is everlasting.
> For whom has the root of wisdom ever been uncovered?
> Her resourceful ways, who knows them?
> One only is wise, terrible indeed,
> seated on his throne, the Lord.
> He himself has created her, looked on her and assessed her,
> and poured her out on all his works
> to be with all mankind as his gift,
> and he conveyed her to those who love him. (Si. 1:4–10)

This same theme of the preexistence of wisdom is developed in Proverbs 8, and in Baruch, where the author laments the distance that separates people from wisdom:

. . . more recent generations have seen the day
and peopled the earth in their turn:
but the way of knowledge is something they have not known,
they have not recognized the paths she treads.
Nor have their sons had any grasp of her,
remaining far from her way . . .
the tale-spinners and the philosophers
have none of them found the way to wisdom,
or discovered the paths she treads. (Ba. 3:20–21, 23)

What are we to do to regain wisdom and to close the gap between
ourselves and wisdom? We must return to our source, says Meister
Eckhart, citing the Book of Ecclesiastes as he does so:

Solomon says that all waters, that is, all creatures flow and return to their source. Therefore, it is necessarily true, as I have
said, that similarity and fervent love draw up and lead and
bring the soul into the first source of the One, who is the Father of all in heaven and on earth.[3]

This is the culmination work of letting go and letting be: To return to the
fullness of Godhead where wisdom plays and has played from the beginning. The biblical reference Eckhart gives to support his search for
origin as a search for wisdom is as follows:

Into the sea all the rivers go, and yet the sea is never filled,
and still to their goal the rivers go. (Qo. 1:7)

The search for our origin, then, is a search for wisdom, according to the
biblical model of wisdom for Eckhart.
    Our origin is in the Creator, for we have flowed out of the Creator
but remained within. We, like wisdom, were somehow there in the beginning.

"In the beginning." This gives us to understand that the Father
has eternally begotten us out of the hidden darkness of eternal
mystery, remaining in the first beginning of the primal purity,
which is the fullness of all purity. Here I rested and slept eternally in the hidden knowledge of the eternal Father, indwelling
and unspoken.[4]

The "fullness of all purity" is the "primal purity" which is our primal origin. Our origin of origins is in God. We need to make contact with such a past as this. Indeed, this is possible because I could not have left home, Eckhart says, if I had not once dwelled there. "If someone were to ask me: 'Brother Eckhart, when did you leave home?' this would indicate that I must previously have been inside."[5] This origin that precedes all origins can be designated by the word nothingness. "All things have been drawn from nothingness; that is why their true origin is nothingness."[6] That is why letting go and letting be and sinking into nothingness are also sinking into our origin. "When this will turns for an instant away from itself, and returns to its first origin, then the will recovers its proper free fashion, and it is free."[7] In this way the return to our original liberty is accomplished.

In the sermon we are reflecting on, Eckhart says that *the hand of God that raised the girl from the dead is the Holy Spirit.* This is consistent with his teaching that it is the Holy Spirit who returns us to our origin. "If the soul were ready, the Holy Spirit would take it to the source from which it has flowed." A person who has learned to let go has

> a soul which has risen above all things and is lifted up by the Holy Spirit and raised to that source from which the Holy Spirit has flowed out. Yes, and the Holy Spirit brings the soul to that eternal image from which it has flowed out, that model in accord with which the Father has made everything, that picture in which all things are one, the breadth and the depth in which all things attain their end.[8]

Thus what is ultimately at stake in a return to our origins is a return to the Godhead in which all things are one. And this means a return to our own divinity that we share with the Godhead. And this in turn means a return to wholeness. And this return is what salvation is about: being whole again. "I have said frequently that the soul cannot be purged unless it returns to its original integrity and wholeness, as it was created by God."[9] Wholeness is holiness. This return constitutes our new creation. "God is the 'beginning,' and if we are united to him we become 'new' again."[10] The full return is the full waking up; indeed, it constitutes a resurrection from the dead. It is a return to our likeness and union with divinity. It is the *imago Dei* come back to life. Its sign is holistic instead of dualistic consciousness. We saw in discussing Sermon Twelve that purity there meant "separate from all twoness." That is what it means here also. The twoness of the human and the divine, the twoness of life and death, the twoness of I vs. you are all laid aside when we wake from our sleep, when we truly *"get up."*

Sermon Twenty: HOW LETTING GO AND LETTING
BE ARE TO BEAR FRUIT

"In the course of their journey he came to a castle, and a
woman named Martha welcomed him into her house." (Lk.
10:38)*

I have recited a little passage from the Gospel, first in Latin. It
runs as follows in the vernacular: "Jesus came to a certain castle,
and was welcomed by a virgin who was also a wife."

Now pay heed to what I have said. It had to be by a *virgin* that
Jesus was received. The word *virgin* means a person who is free of
all false images, and who is as detached as if he or she did not yet
exist. Lo, we might now ask how a person who has been born and
who has lived up to a state in life capable of reason could be so
free of all images, as if he or she had not yet existed. All the
same, he or she knows many things that are nothing but images.
How then can this person be free of them?

Pay attention now to the instruction that I wish to give you. If
I were possessed of such a comprehensive reason that all the images that all human beings have absorbed, as well as all the images within God himself, if all these images were within my
reason, and if this were true in such a way that I were just as free
of an ego attachment to those·images, as if I had not grasped one
of them as mine—either in action or inaction, in coming or going
—so that at this very moment I would be free and detached toward God's dearest wish and ready to fulfill it unceasingly, then I
would truly be a virgin without hindrance of all images. Certainly
this would be as if I did not yet exist.

I add also that the fact that a person is a virgin does not
remove him or her from all the deeds that that person has accomplished. All of this lets him or her be virginal and free with-

* "Intravit Jesus in quoddam castellum et mulier quaedam, Martha nomine, excepit illum in domum suam." (DWI, ※2)

out any hindrance toward the highest truth, just as Jesus is detached and free and virginal in himself. As the masters of the spiritual life state, two equals alone are the basis for a union. On that account, a person who is to receive the virginal Jesus has to be virginal and free.

Now pay attention and examine what I say carefully! If this person were always a virgin, no fruit would come from him or her. If this person is to become fruitful, then it is necessary for him or her to become a *wife*. The word *wife* is the noblest term that we can attribute to the soul; it is far nobler than *virgin*. It is good for a person to receive God into himself or herself, and in this receptivity he or she is a virgin. But it is better for God to become fruitful within the person. This is because becoming fruitful as a result of the gift is the only gratitude for the gift. The spirit is a wife through the continuously bearing gratitude in which it bears Jesus back into God's fatherly heart.

Many good gifts are received in virginity, but they are not born back into God in wifely fruitfulness with thankful praise. These gifts spoil and come to nothing, so that the person will never become more blissful or better as a result. Therefore, that person's virginity is of no use, for he or she does not become through it a wife in full fertility. The loss lies in this fact. Therefore, I have recited that "Jesus came to a certain castle, and was received by a virgin who was also a wife." It must of necessity be the way I have shown you.

Married people scarcely give rise to more than one fruit in a year. But I have in mind now another kind of "married people"— all those who egotistically cling to prayer, fasting, vigils, and all kinds of external practices and mortification. Every ego attachment to any kind of deed robs you of your freedom to be free and ready at this very moment to be at God's service and to follow him alone in the light through which he admonishes you to action and inaction, as if you had nothing else to do and wanted to do nothing else and could do nothing else. Every ego attachment and every intentional deed, which at all times rob you of this new freedom, are what I call now "a year." For your soul in this connection bears no fruit of any kind, unless your soul renounces the deed that you have egotistically taken up. Moreover, you will have no trust in either God or yourself until you have accomplished the deed you have taken up with egotistical attachment; otherwise you will have no peace. *This* is what I establish as "a year," and the fruit is small for all that, because it has emerged from the deed in ego attachment and not in freedom. I call such persons "married couples" because they are bound by ego attachment. Such persons bear little fruit, and what they bear is small, as I have already stated.

A virgin who is a wife, and who is free and liberated and without ego attachment, is always equally close to God and herself. She bears much fruit, and the fruit is of good size. It is no less nor more than God himself. This virgin who is a wife bears this fruit and this birth. Every day she bears fruit a hundred times or a thousand times or countless times, giving birth and becoming fruitful out of the most noble foundation of all. Let me put it in even a better way. Indeed, she bears out of the same foundation from which the Father begets his eternal Word and from which she becomes fruitfully pregnant. For Jesus, the light and reflection of the fatherly heart is united to her, and she to him, and she radiates and shines with him as a single unit and as a pure, clear light within the fatherly heart. (As Saint Paul says, Jesus is the glory and copy of the fatherly heart, and he radiates with power through the fatherly heart [cf. Heb. 1:3].)

I have often stated that there is a power in the soul that touches neither time nor flesh. It flows out of the spirit and remains in the spirit, and is totally and utterly spiritual. In this power God is as totally verdant and flourishing in all joy and in all honor as he is in himself. So cordial is the joy and so unimaginably great is the rapture that no one could announce it fully. For in this power the eternal Father unceasingly begets his eternal Son in such a way that this power engenders at the same time the Son of the Father and itself as the same Son in the inner power of the Father. If someone were to possess a whole kingdom or all the wealth of the earth, and were to give up all this purely for God's sake, and if the same person would become one of the poorest human beings living anywhere on earth, and if God were to give this person as much suffering as he has ever given anyone, and if this person were to endure all this up to his or her own death, and if God were to allow the person to see with one glance how God is in this power, then the joy of the

person would be so great that all the suffering and all the poverty
would be too little. Indeed, even if God afterward were to give
him or her the kingdom of heaven, this person would already
have received all too great a reward for everything that he or she
had suffered. For God is in this power as in the eternal now. If
the spirit were always united to God in this power, the person
could never grow old. For the now in which God created the first
human being and the now in which the last human being will
fade away, and the now in which I am speaking—all these nows
are alike in God and are only *one* now. Understand now that this
person dwells in *one* light with God. For this reason there is in
him or her neither suffering nor chronological order, but rather an
eternity of equal duration. In truth, all wonder is removed from
this person, and all things are essential in him or her. For this
reason, the person receives nothing new from future things nor
from any kind of chance, for he or she dwells in *one* now, which
is always new, and which is unceasing. Such is the divine loftiness
in this power.

There is another power that is also incorporeal. It flows out of
the spirit and remains in the spirit and is totally and utterly spiritual. In this power God is unceasingly glowing and burning with
all his wealth, with all his sweetness, and with all his bliss. Indeed, in this power there is such great joy and such great, immeasurable bliss that no one could express and reveal it fully. I
say again that if there were any person who looked with his or her
reason according to truth into the bliss and joy that is within this
power, then everything that he or she could suffer or that God
might wish to have this person suffer would be for him or her insignificant, or, indeed, a nothing. I say even that it would be totally a joy and a pleasure.

If you wish to know definitely whether your suffering is yours
or God's, you can judge the situation in the following way. If you
are suffering for your own sake, no matter what its form may be,
this suffering will hurt you and will be hard to carry. If you are
suffering for God and for his sake, the suffering will not hurt you
and will also not be hard for you because God will be carrying the
burden. In all truth, if a person were willing to suffer for God's
sake and purely for his sake, and if all the suffering that all
human beings had ever suffered and that the whole world had

ever borne at one time were to fall on him or her, all this would
not hurt the person, and it would also not be hard for him or her
because God would be carrying the burden. If anyone were to lay
a heavy burden on my neck, and if the person were then to place
another weight on my neck, I might just as soon laden myself
with a hundred such burdens as with only one. For the burden
would not be heavy for me, and would also not do me any harm.
To put the matter briefly, God will make whatever we suffer for
him and his sake alone easy and sweet. Thus at the beginning, at
the point where we began this sermon, I said that "Jesus came to
a certain castle, and was welcomed by a virgin who was a wife."
Why did this happen? It had to be that she was a virgin and in
addition a wife. Now I have told you how Jesus was welcomed,
but I have not yet told you what the "castle" was. I will now
speak about this matter.

I have occasionally said that there is a power in the spirit that
alone is free. Occasionally I've said that there is a shelter of the
spirit. Occasionally I've said that there is a light of the spirit.
Occasionally I've said that there is a little spark. Now, however, I
say that it is neither this nor that. All the same, it is a something,
which is more elevated above this and that than heaven is over
earth. For this reason I name it now in a more noble way than I
have ever named it in the past. Yet it mocks both such nobility as
well as my way of naming it, and is elevated above them. It is
free of all names and bare of all forms, totally free and void just
as God is void and free in himself. It is totally one and simple,
just as God is one and simple, so that we can in no manner gaze
into it. For that very power of which I have spoken in which God
is verdant and blooming with his whole Godhood as well as the
Spirit in God—it is in the same power that the Father begets his
only begotten Son as truly as in himself. For the Father really
lives in this power, and the Spirit gives rise along with the Father
to the same only begotten Son and to itself as the only begotten
Son, and the Spirit is the same Son in this light, and he is the
Truth. If you could have knowledge with my heart, you would
understand very well what I am saying. For it is true, and the
Truth itself says it.

Lo, now pay attention! So one and so simple in the soul is this
"castle" of which I am speaking and which I have in mind, and

so elevated is it above all ways, that the noble power of which I have spoken is not worthy to gaze even once into this castle. In addition, the other power of which I have spoken—the power in which God glows and burns with all his wealth and all his bliss—does not ever dare gaze into this castle. So totally one and simple is this castle, and so elevated above all modes and all powers is this unique way and power that a power or a way can never gaze into it—not even God himself. In all truth and as truly as God lives, even God himself will never gaze into it even for a moment. And he has never gazed into it insofar as he exists in the way and "attributes" of his person. This is easy to perceive, for this single way and power is without a way and without attributes. Therefore, if God should ever gaze into it, this would cost him all his divine names and his personal attributes. He must leave all this quite outside if he is ever to gaze into it. Rather, just as he is a simple One, without all ways and attributes, he is likewise neither Father nor Son nor Holy Spirit in this sense. Yet he is still something that is neither this nor that.

Lo, just as God is One and simple, he comes to this one thing, which I here call a castle in the soul. In no other way does he come to it. Only in this way, however, does he come to it and be in it. With this part of itself the soul is equal to God and nothing else. What I have told you is true. On this I pledge to you the Truth as well as my soul as witnesses.

May God help us to be such a "castle" to which Jesus will come and where he will be received and where he will remain eternally in the way I have said! Amen.

COMMENTARY: What a True Vine Really Does/How Bearing Fruit—Not Contemplation—Is the Fulfillment of Eckhart's Spirituality/How True Fruitfulness Takes Trust, Confidence, and Self-love/The Fruits of the Spirit That Come with Letting Go and Letting Be/How the Ultimate Letting Go Includes Letting Go of Letting Go

In this sermon Eckhart weaves together two biblical texts, borrowing from them images and issues that combine to form a powerful summation of his Second Path, the path of letting go and letting be. These are the story of Martha and Mary, as found in Luke's Gospel, and the parable of the vine that bears fruit, as found in John's Gospel. In Luke's Gospel we read:

> In the course of their journey Jesus came to a village, and a woman named Martha welcomed him into her house. She had a sister called Mary, who sat down at the Lord's feet and listened to him speaking. Now Martha who was distracted with all the serving said, "Lord, do you not care that my sister is leaving me to do the serving all by myself? Please tell her to help me." But the Lord answered: "Martha, Martha," he said, "you worry and fret about so many things, and yet few are needed, indeed only one. It is Mary who has chosen the better part . . ." (Lk. 10:38–42)

So taken was Eckhart by this story in Luke's Gospel that he builds another sermon around it—number Thirty-four, which we will consider in Path Four. In the present sermon Eckhart is particularly taken with the words "distracted with all the serving," as he addresses how one can be busy in the world while not being distracted overly much. The text he takes for this sermon is an altered text, one that is interpreted more in the allegorical tradition of mystical writers than is usually the case in Eckhart's use of Scripture. He offers us the following translation: *Jesus came to a certain castle and was welcomed by a virgin who was also a wife.* Following a long exegesis of this passage in Christian tradition, Eckhart has translated the name "Martha" as "wife" and also as "virgin."[1] It was not uncommon to attempt rather elaborate translations of proper names in allegorical exegesis.

The Martha/Mary story that inspires this sermon is the traditional text for spiritual writers to expound on the relationship between contemplation and action, between being in God and in the world. Eckhart resists the more traditional explanation both in this sermon and in Sermon Thirty-four—namely, that Mary is a contemplative and has chosen the "better part" and Martha is an activist who has chosen a lesser part. Instead of following this rather simplistic exegesis—which in fact exegetes no longer subscribe to today[2]—Eckhart uses the text to substantiate his spiritual way of letting go and letting be as a profound way of being in the world and in God all at once. To assist him in this effort, he borrows images and insights from the Gospel of John and the parable there of the true vine. The text reads as follows:

"I am the true vine,
and my Father is the vinedresser.
Every branch in me that bears no fruit
he cuts away,
and every branch that does bear fruit he prunes
to make it bear even more.
You are pruned already,
by means of the word that I have spoken to you.
Make your home in me, as I make mine in you.
As a branch cannot bear fruit all by itself,
but must remain part of the vine,
neither can you unless you remain in me.
I am the vine,
you are the branches.
Whoever remains in me, with me in him,
bears fruit in plenty;
for cut off from me you can do nothing.
Anyone who does not remain in me
is like a branch that has been thrown away
—he withers;
these branches are collected and thrown on the fire,
and they are burnt.
If you remain in me
and my words remain in you,
you may ask what you will
and you shall get it.
It is to the glory of my Father that you should bear much fruit,
and then you will be my disciples.
As the Father has loved me,
so I have loved you.
Remain in my love,
If you keep my commandments
you will remain in my love,
just as I have kept my Father's commandments
and remain in his love.
I have told you this
so that my own joy may be in you
and your joy be complete.

This is my commandment:
love one another,
as I have loved you.
A man can have no greater love
than to lay down his life for his friends . . .
You did not choose me,
no, I chose you;
and I commissioned you
to go out and to bear fruit,
fruit that will last . . ." (Jn. 15:1–13, 16)

It is evident from the themes that Eckhart treats in this sermon and from the very language and images he employs that he had this text from John in front of him as well as that from Luke's Gospel. His treatment of letting go may well parallel the references here to pruning and being pruned; his reflections on the *little castle of the soul* correspond to this text about making a home in one and about remaining in one. This theme is a development of Eckhart's panentheism, which is reflected in John's imagery of "remaining in me, with me in him," a mutual inness theology. In translating the word "home" as *castle*, Eckhart may well be picking up on the biblical tradition of the vine as a symbol of the kingdom of God (see Mt. 20:1–8; 21:28–31, 33–41). A castle is the home within the kingdom; it is the royal home. And so in this sermon Eckhart weaves in biblical themes from the tradition of the royal person that are so important to the theologian of creation spirituality (see Sermon Thirty-six) as well as themes of the kingdom of God that we have considered in Sermon Nine. The letting go motif is also present in the test of the truest love of all: the letting go of life for the sake of someone else. The reference in John to the person who withers parallels Eckhart's reference to *growing old*; the reference to the glory of the Father parallels those references in Eckhart to realized eschatology and to our deification; the reference to a full joy parallels Eckhart's to the same motif. And, above all, the imperative to bear fruit, "every branch in me that bears no fruit he cuts away," gives Eckhart the basic imagery for his entire sermon. Indeed, like John, he analyzes this fruit as *big, neither more nor less than God himself*. It must be a *total fruitfulness*, Eckhart warns. John has said that one will "bear much fruit" and that it will be a "fruit that lasts." Thus we can see that if we want to understand Eckhart's teaching on letting go and letting be in this sermon, it is wise to read it with John 15 in front of us. One might call this Eckhart's exegesis of what a true vine really is. And really does. A true vine *bears fruit.*

In applying this motif to our spiritual journeying, Eckhart insists that it is better to bear fruit than merely to receive God. *It is good for a person to receive God into himself or herself, and in this receptivity he or she is a virgin. But it is better for God to become fruitful within the person.* Schürmann points out that Eckhart is playing with a word in this passage: *empfagen* can mean both to receive and to conceive.[3] Thus for Eckhart, our receptivity must also be an experience of giving birth. We are not here merely to respond passively to a God experience but to respond fruitfully or creatively. To bear fruit. "In the supreme emptiness of detachment [our letting go], man and God are united in fertility; one sole determination joins them together: that of giving birth."[4] Eckhart, in insisting that bearing fruit or *being a wife* is better than being receptive or *being a virgin*, is making a very strong statement about the contemplative as distinct from the active vocation. As Schürmann insists, Eckhart's spirituality is not built around contemplation:

> The context of the expressions of union in Meister Eckhart differs considerably from a mystique of the vision, in which one "contemplates" the divine sovereignty and, "forgetting all things, entirely ignores oneself and penetrates even into God" [Richard of Saint Victor]. Meister Eckhart does not teach such a mysticism of contemplation. Detachment [letting go] is not oriented toward contemplation. It produces a new birth. It is on this point that he [Eckhart] most profoundly modifies the views of Proclus. From a philosophy of the intellect in the cosmos, he enunciates a call for a certain type of existence among things. Such is Eckhart's this-worldliness, which is opposed to the other-worldliness of the Neoplatonists . . . It is removed from the Platonic doctrines of the elevation of the soul by cosmic contemplation. The noetics of the cosmos itself has changed, "the world" has become "our world."[5]

To remain a virgin or a mere contemplative gazer *is of no use, for he or she does not become through it a wife in full fertility.* Eckhart discards the traditional argument that was so bogged down in his day—as in our own—between contemplation vs. action.[6] Instead, he prefers a new category to action, namely that of bearing fruit and of birthing. It is a refreshingly biblical category, as we have seen. It is a category of prayer as "thank you" for the blessings of creation, one of *wifely fruitfulness with thankful praise.* Indeed, it is the only prayer that qualifies as "thank you": *Becoming fruitful as a result of the gift is the only gratitude for the gift. The spirit is a wife when in gratitude it gives birth in return.* Here Eckhart reiterates his spirituality of gratitude and thankfulness that we saw in Sermon Eight. We see how thoroughly this thanks for the blessing of creation permeates Eckhart's theology. Eckhart advocates in language as strong as John's—a fruitless branch will be torn down and thrown in the fire—the imperative to journey from virginity (contemplation that does not bear fruit) to wifery (a spirituality that does bear fruit). *The word "wife" is the noblest term that we can attribute to the soul; it is far nobler than "virgin."* A virgin has received God—and that is good; *but it is better for God to become fruitful within the person.* Eckhart is saying that extrovert meditation is better than introvert meditation.

In summarizing his meaning of the word "virgin," Eckhart is summarizing the person who has learned Path Two, the path of letting go and letting be. We see in this definition many of the themes we have treated in previous sermons in this path. *The word "virgin" means a person who is free of all false images, and who is as detached as if he or she did not yet exist.*

Again, he cautions against interpreting this emptying of images in an anti-intellectual way or in a quietistic way. *All the same, he or she knows many things that are nothing but images.* The key is not that we bask in our ignorance—recall how in the previous sermon and commentary we were instructed in how knowledge must precede letting go. The key is our attitude toward what we know. If we are attached to it as to property (*Eigenschaft*), then we have not learned to let go and are not virginal. One could be the most intelligent person on earth and comprehend all human knowledge that ever was, and still be a person who lets go. If

> I were just as free of an ego attachment to those images, as if I had not grasped one of them as mine—either in action or inaction, in coming or going—so that at this very moment I would be free and detached toward God's dearest wish and ready to fulfill it unceasingly, then I would truly be a virgin without hindrance of all images. Certainly this would be as if I did not yet exist.

Thus, Eckhart's *via negativa*, unlike so many since his time, has nothing of anti-intellectualism to it whatsoever. You can know things—as much as there is to know—and still be free of your knowledge. That is true letting go. You can also do things, indeed we *ought* to do things, and as long as we do not relate to our work as to property, this too represents an authentic kind of letting go—indeed, it is the best kind, the "better part," for it is our fruitfulness. *The fact that a person is a virgin does not remove him or her from all the deeds that that person has accomplished. All of this lets him or her be virginal and free without any hindrance toward the highest truth.* So long as our work too is accompanied by this consciousness of letting go and being free, it is authentically spiritual and thus "virginal," as were the works of Jesus. *A person who is to receive the virginal Jesus has to be virginal or free.* Thus Caputo comments on Eckhart's understanding of the Mary/Martha story. The person who lets go is, "like Martha, at home in the world of things, has a new relationship to creatures, understands them for what they are, lets them be."[7] Such a person does not lead "a life of passivity and withdrawal but of active and robust commerce with things. For Eckhart the depth of mystical union is completely compatible with the bustle of virtue and good works."[8] This subject of spirituality and work will be developed much further in Sermon Twenty-nine and in Path Four.

In this sermon Eckhart reaches the most radical position possible on the subject of letting go. He is saying that a person must even be able to let go of letting go! This is clear from the vocabulary he has chosen. We need to pass from virginity to wifery, he is saying. The virgin has to let go of her or his virginity in order to bear fruit. In our sinking from something to nothing, we even have to sink deeper than letting go and must resist all temptations to cling even to letting go. As Schürmann puts it, "Detachment proves powerless to procure happiness, hence it too is to be left. In this final letting be, detachment is abandoned insofar as it is still a 'work' of man."[9] When such a radical letting go and letting be occur, then truly God is allowed to be God and thus *God is fully verdant and flowering. There the person who has passed from virginity to wifery becomes fruitful out of the most noble foundation of all. Let me put it in even a better way. Indeed, she bears out of the same foundation from which the Father begets his eternal Word.* Here the person has truly entered the Godhead, where the names of God and Trinity no longer hold sway. Here the kingdom of the Godhead is known and knows. We remain in it and it is us, but fruitfully, not passively. Here we meet all creation in its proper setting, namely, in God, and we know it perhaps for the first time. "The things that he has 'let be' in their singular being, he now recovers in their primordial being."[10] Here we are, at last, at our origins. But we do not stay there. In spiral fashion, we move on and out. As Saint John said: "I commissioned you to go out and to bear fruit." Things cannot be an obstacle; knowledge is no obstacle; works are no obstacle. Enemies and suffering are no obstacle. The world is no obstacle. Our freedom is too radical, too deeply rooted, too closely a part of the vine to be distracting to our spiritual journey. Martha was too easily "distracted" by her duties; we need not be. The only thing that can interfere with the spirit and can kill it is our attitude of *Eigenschaft* or ownership: our inability to let go and let be. It alone threatens our freedom.

Eckhart now introduces two subjects that are so important to a spirituality of giving birth but which ascetic spiritualists ignore almost completely. They are the subjects of self-confidence and self-love. He observes that what forces people to remain virgins and not move on to bearing fruit is that *you will have no trust in either God or yourself until you have accomplished the deed you have taken up with egotistical attachment*. In other words, what makes us compulsive grabbers who are unable to let go and let be is lack of trust and confidence. This confidence is not merely a matter of faith in God but also of faith in ourselves. *This is why you do not bear fruit.* Eckhart is touching on a very important theme that contemporary psychologist William Eckhardt also develops in his study on compassion. "Compassion is a function of faith in human nature (the belief that man is basically good), while compulsion is a function of lack of faith in human nature (the belief that man is basically evil)."[11] We can see how an exclusively *via negativa* spirituality that is constructed on an exclusively fall/redemption theology would have little or nothing to say about giving birth, whether to compassion or anything else. Only persons who trust themselves and the universe can give birth. That is why only a creation-centered spirituality such as Eckhart's includes a spirituality of compassion and of the artist (see Paths Three and Four).

The need for confidence in nature and in self and the need for self-love are developed by Eckhart on numerous occasions. They are the fruit of all letting be. "Love cannot distrust, it trustfully awaits only good."[12] The person who has learned to let be has learned to let himself or herself be himself or herself. Let self be self and then God shall flow. "Man is naturally inhabited by God," comments Schürmann, "under one condition only—that he let himself be."[13] Our confidence in the Creator is a supreme confidence and a basic attitude toward existence.

> No person could ever trust God too much. Nothing else that one can do is so fitting as great trust in God. With all those who ever obtained great confidence in him, he never failed to work great things. He has known in the case of all such people that his confidence comes from love, for love has not only confidence, but it has also true knowledge and unquestioning security.[14]

Our trust in God grows from God's trust in us. "People should not fear God, for those who fear him flee from him and fear is harmful . . . People should not fear him, but they should love him, for God loves people in the highest perfection."[15] Trust is the test of true love—"true and perfect love may be tested by asking whether one has great hope and confidence in God. For there is nothing by which one can better judge whether one has complete love than confidence."[16]

This confidence applies to oneself as well as to God. Indeed, for Eckhart a confidence in God that does not apply to confidence in self is a pseudoreligious attitude. For if you trust God, you trust God's creatures. And that means oneself. Indeed, it is lack of trust and confidence, Eckhart shrewdly observes, that drives people to too many tactical ecstasies in their spiritual lives. Concerning *those who egotistically cling to prayer, fasting, vigils, and all kinds of external practices and mortification:*

> Every ego attachment to any kind of deed robs you of your freedom to be free and ready at this very moment to be at God's service . . . For your soul in this connection bears no fruit of any kind, unless your soul renounces the deed that you have egotistically taken up. Moreover, you will have no trust in either God or yourself until you have accomplished the deed you have taken up with egotistical attachment; otherwise you will have no peace.

If we are truly God's children, we are trustworthy. We are also loved as children and need to trust as children, but also to love as parents, as birthers of the God-child in us. Eckhart develops the theme of self-love frequently.

> If you love yourself, you love everybody else as you do yourself. As long as you love another person less than you love yourself, you do not love yourself rightly—if you do not love all people as you love yourself. You will love all people in one person: and that person is God and human. Thus all is right for such a person, who loves himself or herself and all others as himself or herself. And this is as it should be.[17]

We are expected to love ourselves and all parts of ourselves, body included.

> Everyone loves himself to some degree. Those who imagine that they do not love their bodies, fool themselves. For if they hated themselves, they would cease to exist. We must love all things that lead us to God. That alone is love.[18]

Eckhart asks, "If you do not know how to love yourself, how is it possible that you will love God?"[19] There can be no love of neighbor without love of self.

> One should try to find out, therefore, if the person who is to be entrusted with the care of his neighbors loves himself, so that he may be in a position to love them as he does himself . . . Love your neighbor as you love yourself—not as you hate yourself.[20]

All creatures are to love themselves, for their existence is a blessing worthy of being loved.

> So dearly does a creature love its own being, which it has received from God. If someone were to pour forth on a soul all the tortures of hell, it would still not wish not to be, so dearly does a creature love its own being, which it has received directly from God.[21]

Eckhart cites Aristotle's observation in his *Ethics* that "friendly relations with another spring or come from friendly relations with oneself." Eckhart comments that there exists a "complete equality or parity, or rather identity . . . between love of self and love of one's neighbor . . . He who knows how to love himself loves God" (see Sermon Thirty-three). Such is the trust and confidence that is born of a true path of letting go and letting be. This path is not about putting down self or repressing anything that is in us or in nature. Indeed, integral to true letting go is letting go of lack of trust, lack of confidence, and lack of self-love. Only this kind of letting go will allow letting be to happen and ourselves to happen. Only this kind of letting go will allow God and God's love to happen. It alone *bears fruit.* There will be no fruit without it.

Eckhart plays with the concept of the fruits of the spirit in this sermon on bearing fruit. The fruits of the spirit he enunciates are joy, youthfulness or eternity, and simplicity. About joy, he promises what was promised in the scriptural text from John's Gospel: a divine joy. It comes to us from God, who flows forth *totally verdant and flourishing in all joy and in all honor as he is in himself.* The joy is ineffable: *So cordial is the joy and so unimaginably great is the rapture that no one could announce it fully.* This joy overcomes suffering—*the joy of the person would be so great that all the suffering and all the poverty would be too little.* For Eckhart, then, the *via negativa* culminates in joy. Schürmann calls Eckhart's path a path of "errant joy" or wandering joy. It is a joy of heaven begun on earth, a joy of realized eschatology, a joy of the Messianic times begun. Such a person "dwells in joy."[22]

Another fruit of the spirit to which the virginal and wifely person is now sensitive and open is youthfulness, or a new sense of time. As we saw in Sermon Six, eternity to Eckhart means to be "eternally young." And so youthfulness and timelessness are integral to the person who has allowed God to flow *ever verdant, ever flowering.* There happens an *eternal now* which, if a person were fully bathed in it, *such a person could never grow old.* When we live in God we begin to see things as God does. This is through the time of eternity or youthfulness. This person *dwells in one now, which is always new, and which is unceasing.*

Another fruit of this union and this release of the divine spark in us is freedom and the simplicity and spontaneity that freedom brings. We become as free and transparent as God is. We become *free of all names and bare of all forms, totally free and void, just as God is void and free in himself.* We make contact with our own—and with God's own—simplicity. *It is totally one and simple just as God is one and simple.* The

truth of the unity of God and creation, the full panentheistic truth, becomes ours to behold in a direct way. No intermediaries behold such a
truth. Not even God can steal a glance into this union. *So totally one
and simple is this castle, and so elevated above all modes and all
powers is this unique way and power that a power or a mode can never
gaze into it—not even God himself.*

In this castle or divine spark, which has now been allowed air and
space to burn, *God glows and burns with all his wealth and all his bliss.*
The experience of God is now so thoroughly God that it is, like God,
ineffable. *Indeed, in this power there is such great joy and such great,
immeasurable bliss that no one could express and reveal it fully.* Here
even suffering would become *totally a joy and a pleasure.* And we learn
to give our sufferings to God to bear for us. We can, finally, let go even
of our sufferings. Thus, Schürmann speaks of the realized eschatology
that is so typical of Eckhart's spirituality. Eckhart "transposes to the present life the unendingly growing union with God in which Thomas
Aquinas had recognized the dynamism of the eternal vision."[23] Here the
spark of the soul becomes a light for the world.

Here, in this *little castle,* the kingdom of God is encountered. It is simple and one as God is. *It is free of all names and bare of all forms, totally free and void, just as God is void and free in himself.* Here is the
space held in common by people and by God. Here lies our link with
the unnameable Godhead. God will have to *leave outside* the divine
names and Persons in order to enter. Here we realize our own divinity,
the fulfillment of our being God's image and likeness. *With this part of
itself the soul is equal to God and nothing else.* Our equality with God is
affirmed; our divinity is experienced. Eckhart calls upon Saint Paul to explain the origin of this teaching of how we are "the divine and deiform
being":

> In the nakedness of his essence, which is above every name,
> God penetrates and falls into the naked essence of the mind,
> which is elevated above the intellect and the will, as the es-
> sence is above its faculties. This is the castle into which Jesus
> enters, in his being rather than in his acting, giving graciously
> to the mind the divine and deiform being. This regards the es-
> sence of being according to the words: "By the grace of God
> I am what I am."[24]

The scriptural text Eckhart refers to speaks of the fruitfulness of this divine union:

> By God's grace that is what I am, and the grace that he gave me has not been fruitless. On the contrary, I, or rather the grace of God that is with me, have worked harder than any of the others. (1 Co. 15:10)

Equally on Eckhart's mind, no doubt, are Paul's words in Galatians: "I live now not with my own life but with the life of Christ who lives in me" (Ga. 2:20). We now live, we who have let go and let be, the life of God in us, which is also a life in God. It is a fruitful life, not an introverted one. It is a life *from the same foundation as the Father.* Schürmann rightly points out that this tradition of our deification, so lacking in Western theology's preoccupation with sin, law, and grace, was well developed long before Eckhart in Eastern theologians like Clement of Alexandria, Hippolytus, and Origen. This same tradition develops Eckhart's theme of the birth of God in us.[25]

In this sermon we have seen the inside of the person (the castle) and the outside (fruitful work as big as God) meet. We see the profoundly dialectical nature of Eckhart's theology, where *in* leads to *out* and *out* to *in.* We have seen, at a new depth, his theology of the word where the word flows out but remains within. We have seen how letting go even of letting go can lead to letting happen and letting be born. We have learned that birth is the logical outcome of those who follow the path of letting go and letting be. There remain to be discussed—in Path Three— what constitutes this birth and—in Path Four—what it is above all else that we humans who are divinized give birth to.

PATH THREE: BREAKTHROUGH AND GIVING BIRTH TO SELF AND GOD

Path Two led us on a journey of letting go and letting be. We are urged to be radical in our letting go so that we let go of fear, of death, of distrust, of everything. And ultimately even of letting go itself. When we learn to let go even of letting go, then we learn how birth comes about. As Path Two culminated in the scriptural passage of the vine that bears fruit, so Path Three explores the experience of how we bear fruit, of how we are to give birth, and of what this birthing entails. Eckhart envisions a threefold birth that takes place when we have journeyed the *via positiva* of creation and the *via negativa* of letting go. These births are the following: the birth of ourselves in a breakthrough in consciousness, the birth of God in us, and the birth of ourselves as sons and daughters of God. The theology of the divinization of humanity is overwhelmingly in evidence throughout all of the sermons in Path Three. For Eckhart is concerned with the breakthrough that divinity has made and can make in human history, human consciousness. Indeed, he will insist that "the essence of God is birthing" and that therefore those who give birth are participating in a divine activity.

We saw in Sermons Nine and Ten that fertility is a sign of blessing in ancient Israel. It is also a sign of blessing in the Celtic spiritual tradition. And it is prominent in Eckhart's theology, as we shall see. For with birth there is blessing, but without birth there can be no blessing. In the birth, Eckhart declares, "you will discover all blessing." But "neglect the birth and you neglect all blessing."[1] A creation or blessing spirituality, then, culminates in giving birth to still more blessing. The formula behind such a spirituality appears to be as follows:

$$\textit{via positiva} \text{ (creation)} + \textit{via negativa} \text{ (letting go)} \rightarrow$$
$$\textit{via creativa}$$

Eckhart's is a spirituality of the *via creativa*: how all are birthers and creators, as God is a birther and Creator. He admits a dialectic and a tension between the *via positiva* and the *via creativa*. Interestingly enough, this tension between living and creating is, according to psychiatrist and artist Otto Rank, *the* single most basic struggle in the soul of any artist.[2] Eckhart's therapy for healing such a struggle would appear to be Path Two: letting go and letting be. To create, the artist needs to let go radically of living; and to live, the artist needs to let go radically of creating. The *via negativa*, then, becomes a bridge that heals and links Paths One and Three and thereby encourages rather than discourages further birth and creativity. The first of the births that occur is that of the individual: an awakening, a rebirth, a birth of oneself. For this awakening Eckhart invented a word. He called it "breakthrough."[3]

Sermon Twenty-one: THREE BIRTHS: OURS, GOD'S, AND OURSELVES AS GOD'S CHILDREN

"When peaceful silence lay over all, and night had run the half of her swift course . . ." (Ws. 18:14)*

We celebrate here in temporality with a view to the *eternal* birth, which God the Father has accomplished and accomplishes unceasingly in eternity, so that this same birth has now been accomplished *in time* within human nature. What does it avail me if this birth takes place unceasingly and yet does not take place within myself? It is quite fitting, however, that it should take place within me.

Now we wish to talk about this birth, and how it takes place within *us* and is accomplished in the good soul whenever God the Father declares his eternal Word in the perfect soul. For what I here say should be understood with respect to the perfect person who has traveled God's ways and still travels them. It should not be understood with respect to a person who is quite far from and unaware of this birth.

The wise man says: "When all things were in the midst of silence, there came down to me from the royal throne on high a secret Word" (Ws. 18:14). This sermon will discuss this Word. We should note three things in this connection. First, *wherever* God the Father declares his Word within the soul, wherever the place of this birth may be, and wherever the soul may be receptive to this event, this must be in the purest and most noble and most tender place that the soul can offer. Truly, if God the Father in all his omnipotence had been able to give anything of a more noble nature to the soul, and if the soul had been able to receive anything more noble from him, God the Father would have had to delay the birth for that noble gift. For this reason, the soul

* "Dum medium silentium tenerent et nox in suo cursu medium iter haberet . . ." (Quint, ₦57)

in which the birth is to take place must remain very pure and must live in a way that is very noble and very collected and very spiritual. This soul must not flow out through the five senses into the multiplicity of creatures. It must rather remain quite inward and collected and in its purest state. This is its proper situation, and all less than it is in opposition.

The second part of this sermon takes up *how* people should behave with regard to this event or promise and generation. On the one hand, is it more useful for them to cooperate in the process so that they bring about and deserve to have this birth take place and be completed within them? This cooperation might mean that these people in themselves and in their reasoning and thinking form a concept and accustom themselves to it. The concept on which they reflect is that God is wise, all-powerful, and eternal. On the other hand, is it more helpful and advantageous for this generation through the Father that all thoughts, words, and deeds as well as all preconceived images be dismissed and removed from people's minds, and that the people simply undergo God, remain inactive, and allow God to take effect within them? By which of these two forms of behavior would people be of greater service in bringing this birth about?

The third point is the extent of the advantage inherent in this birth.

Understand first of all that I shall confirm this explanation with natural reasons so that you can see for yourselves that it is correct, even though I believe the Scripture more than I do myself. But my explanation will reach you more fully and better as a result of a thorough explanation.

Let us take up first the following passage: "In the midst of silence a secret Word was declared to me." Oh, Lord, *where* is the silence, and *where* is the *place* where this Word was spoken? We say, as I have already said, that it is in the purest place that the soul has to offer—in its most noble place, in the soul's foundation; yes, in the soul's being, that is, in its most hidden part. There the "means" is silent, for neither a creature nor an image can enter there. The soul knows *in that place* neither action nor knowledge. It is not aware *in that place* of any kind of image, either from itself or from any other creature.

All deeds accomplished by the soul are accomplished by means of powers. Whatever the soul knows is known through reason; whatever it remembers is recalled by memory; if the soul loves, it does so with the will, and thus it accomplishes deeds through powers and not through being. All its activity in the external world depends on some kind of mediation. The power to see takes effect through the eyes; without them the soul can neither use nor impart vision. And this is the way it is with all the other senses. The soul accomplishes all its external activities through a kind of mediation. In *being*, however, there is no activity, for the powers with which it acts flow indeed out of the foundation of being. In this very foundation, however, the "means" *is silent*. Here only peace and celebration for this birth and this activity are in command, while God the Father declares his Word there. For the Word is by its nature only receptive to the divine being, without any mediation at all. In this place, God enters the soul completely, not partially. God enters the *foundation* of the soul. No one touches the foundation of the soul except God. A creature cannot enter the soul's foundation, but must remain outside in the powers. There in the foundation the soul looks indeed at the image of the creature by means of which the creature has entered and received shelter. For when the powers of a soul come into contact with a creature, they remove and create an image and likeness of that creature, and bring them into themselves. This is the way in which they know the creature. The creature cannot come closer into the soul, and yet, the soul never approaches a creature unless it has previously received its image. And by means of this present image the soul approaches creatures. For the image is something the soul creates from objects with its powers. If it wishes to recognize a stone, a horse, a person, or something else, it draws out the image that it had previously incorporated, and in this way it can unite itself with that object by recognition.

When a person in this way receives an image, however, the image must of necessity come from outside through the senses. For this reason, the soul knows nothing so little as itself. Thus a master of the spiritual life says that the soul cannot create or draw an image of itself. Of nothing does it know so little as of itself because of the necessary intermediary.

For you must understand that the soul is inwardly free and

unencumbered of all mediations and of all images. This is, then, the reason that God can unite himself with the soul freely without an image or a likeness. Whatever capacity you acknowledge in any one of the masters of the spiritual life, you cannot help attributing the same capacity beyond all measure to God. Now the wiser and more powerful a master is, all the more directly does his accomplishment follow, and all the simpler will it be. People need many means in their external deeds. Before they can achieve the things they have in mind, there must be much preparatory work on the materials they will use. The sun, however, accomplishes its task of illumination very quickly as a result of its excellence. As soon as the sun sends out its rays, the whole world, far and wide, is filled with light at the same moment. Even higher is an angel, who needs even fewer means in his activity, and has also fewer images than the sun. The very highest, the seraphim, has only one image. Whatever is grasped in multiplicity by all who are beneath him is grasped by him as a single unit. God, however, does not need any kind of an image, and he *has* none. God is effective in the soul with no "means," image, or likeness. He is effective truly in the soul's foundation into which no image has reached except God himself with his own being. No creature can do this!

How does the Father generate his Son in the soul? The way creatures do in images and in likenesses? Surely not! Rather entirely in the same way he generates in eternity, neither less nor more. Now then, *how* does he generate the Son *there?* Pay attention! Behold, God the Father has a complete insight into himself and a distinct, complete perception of himself through himself, not through just any image. Thus the Father generates his Son in the true unity of the divine nature. Behold, in the *same* and no other way God the Father generates his Son in the foundation *of the soul* and in its being, and he thus unites himself with the soul. For if any image were there, it would not be a true union. Yet the whole happiness of the soul is situated in this true union.

Now you might say that there are nothing but *images* in the soul by reason of its nature. No, in no way is this true! For if it were, the soul would never be happy. In this case, God could create no creature from which you might receive perfect happiness. Otherwise *God* would not be the highest happiness and the last goal, although this is in accord with his nature and although he wishes *himself* to be a beginning and an end to all things. No creature *can* be your happiness. For this reason, it also cannot be your perfection here below because the perfection of *that* life (that is, the future life) follows the perfection of *this* (earthly) life, which consists of all the virtues combined. And for this reason you must of a necessity be and remain in being and in the *foundation*. *There* is where God has to touch you with *his* onefold being *without* the mediation of any image. No image aims at or points to itself. It rather aims at and points to the object of which it is the image. And since we only have an image of what is beyond ourselves and of what has been absorbed through the senses of creatures, and since an image always points to the object of which it is an image, it would not be possible for you ever to become happy through an image. For this reason, silence and quietness must reign there, and the Father must speak and generate his Son and accomplish his deeds there without any images.

What contribution can people properly make through their own actions so that they can achieve and merit the benefit of having this birth take place and be completed within them? Isn't it better for people to do something on their own, such as imagine what God is like or direct their thoughts toward him, rather than wait silently and peacefully for God to speak to them and have effect within them? I repeat what I've already said in the past: these statements and this conduct are concerned only with *good* and *perfect* people who have taken the essence of all the virtues to and within themselves in such a way that the virtues really flow from them and that the precious life and noble teaching of our Lord Jesus Christ are especially alive in them. Such people may understand that it is the best and most noble situation you can attain in life when you are silent and let God speak and be effective. Where all powers are deprived of all their deeds and images, this Word is spoken. Therefore he said: "In the midst of silence, the secret Word was spoken to me." On this account, the more you are able to bring all your powers to a unity and a forgetfulness of all the objects and images you have absorbed, and the more you depart from creatures and their images, the nearer and more receptive are you to the secret Word. If you were able to become completely unaware of all things, you could lose awareness of your own body, as Saint Paul added: "Whether I was in the body or not, I do not know!" (2 Co. 12:2). The spirit had so completely removed all powers into itself that Saint Paul had forgotten his body. Memory and reason had no longer any effect, nor could the senses and powers any longer exert their influences to lead and embellish the body. The fire of life and the warmth of the body were undone. For this reason his body did not lose weight in the three days that he neither ate nor drank. The same thing happened to Moses, who fasted for forty days on the mountain (cf. Ex. 24:18; 34:28) and still became no weaker. On the last day he was just as strong as on the first day. People should also escape from their senses and turn all their powers inwardly and attain a forgetfulness of all things and themselves. On this account a master of the spiritual life said to the soul: "Avoid the restlessness of external deeds! Flee and hide yourself before the storm of inner thoughts, for they create a lack of peace!" If God therefore is to speak his Word within the soul, the soul must be in peace and at rest. Then he declares his Word and himself within the soul—there is no image but God himself.

Dionysius says: "God has no image or likeness of himself, for he is essentially all goodness, truth, and being." God accomplishes all his deeds within and outside himself in a moment. Do not believe that when God made heaven and earth and all things, he made one thing one day and another thing the next day. Moses writes as if this were so, but he did it for the sake of people who could not have understood or grasped it otherwise. God did only this: he willed, he spoke—and all things were made! God is effective without means and without an image. The more *you* are without an image, the more receptive will you be to his influences; the more inwardly you are turned and the more forgetful you are of yourself, the nearer will you be to him.

At this point Dionysius admonished his disciple Timotheus in these words: "My dear son Timotheus, you are to swing with untroubled senses beyond yourself and all your powers, beyond your ability to perceive and beyond reason, beyond deed and mode and being into the hidden, silent darkness where you will come to a recognition of the unknown, transbegotten God. One must remove oneself from all things. God is opposed to working in images."

Now you might ask: "*What* is it that God works without images in the foundation and in being?" I cannot know that because the powers can grasp only in images, for they must grasp and perceive all objects in their *characteristic* images. They cannot perceive a horse in the image of a person. For this reason, since all images come from outside, the deed that God accomplishes in the foundation without an image remains hidden from them. But this is most useful for the soul. This ignorance impels the soul to something remarkable and causes the soul to pursue it. For the soul truly perceives *the fact* that something exists, but it does not know *how* and *what* it *is*. On the other hand, if people are aware of the circumstances surrounding things, they become quickly bored with these things and seek to learn something else and live henceforth in a troubled longing to know these new things, and still take no time to linger over these things to get to know them. For this reason, only an unknowing knowledge detains the soul long enough to linger over things and then impels it to further pursuit.

Therefore a wise man said: "In the middle of the night, when all things were in silence, a secret *Word* was spoken to me. It came as if it had been spoken in the manner of a thief" (Ws. 18:14, 15). How could he call it a "Word" since it was hidden? It is, after all, the nature of the Word to reveal what is hidden. It opened up and sparkled before me in order to reveal something to me, and it informed me about God. *For this reason*, it is called a *Word*. It was, however, not known to me *what* was hidden—such was its concealed arrival in whisperings and silence, in order to reveal itself. See how, since it is hidden, we must and should pursue it. It sparkled and yet was hidden; the purpose is for us to yearn and sigh after it. Saint Paul admonishes us to run after it until we perceive it, and never to cease until we seize it. When he was snatched up into the third heaven into God's gift of knowledge and looked at all things, he forgot nothing on his return. It lay, however, so deeply in his foundation that his reason could not reach it; it was concealed from him. Therefore, he had to run after it and reach it within himself, not outside himself. It is en-

tirely within, not outside—totally within. And since he knew this
well, he said: "I am certain of this: neither death nor any other
affliction can part me from what I feel within me" (Rm.
8:38–39).

In this matter, a pagan master made this beautiful statement to
another master: "I am becoming aware of something within myself that sparkles in my reason. I feel well *that* it is something,
but cannot grasp *what* it may be. Only I fancy one thing, that if I
could grasp it, I would know all truth." The other master replied:
"Fine! Go after it! For if you could grasp it, you would have the
essence of all goodness as well as eternal life." Saint Augustine
had the same thing in mind when he said: "I am becoming aware
of something within me that radiates and sparkles before my soul.
If it could be brought to completion and permanence within me,
it would have to be eternal life. It conceals itself and still makes
itself known. It comes, however, in the manner of a thief, and en-
deavors to remove and steal all things from the soul. Because it
still makes itself known and reveals itself, it would like to attract
the soul, cause it to follow it, and rob and divest the soul of itself." The prophet said of this: "Lord, take away their breath,
and give them in return your breath" (Ps. 104:29–30). This was
also the intent of the bride's statement when she said: "My soul
dissolved and melted away when my beloved spoke" (Sg. 5:6).
When the Word came in, I had to decrease. Christ also had this
in mind when he said: "Whoever gives up something for my sake
shall receive it back a hundredfold, and whoever wishes to possess
me, must divest himself and herself of all things, and whoever
wishes to serve me must follow *me*; he or she may not follow his
or her own interest" (cf. Mk. 10:29; Mt. 16:24; 19:29; Jn. 12:26).

Now you might say: "Alas, Lord, you wish the soul to turn
away from its natural course and to behave contrary to its nature!
Its nature is still to perceive *through the senses* and *in images*. Do
you wish to reverse this order of things?"

No, what do *you* know about the nobility God has placed in
nature that has not been fully described but remains still hidden?
For those who have written about the nobility of the soul have
not come further than their natural reason carried them. They
never reached its *foundation*. Therefore it must remain hidden
and unknown to them. On this account the prophet said: "I shall

be seated and be silent, and I shall hear what God declares within me" (Ps. 84:9). Because it is so hidden, this Word came in the darkness of the night. Saint John says: "The light shone in the darkness. He came to his own, and all who received him became sons of God by reason of power: power was given to them to become sons of God" (Jn. 1:5, 11, 12).

Now note here, finally, the *value* and *fruit* of this secret Word and of this darkness. Not only is the Son of the heavenly Father born in this darkness, but *you* also are born there as a child of the same heavenly Father and none other; and he also gives that power *to you*. Understand now how valuable this is! By all the truth that all the masters of the spiritual life have learned through their own reason and awareness, or will ever learn up to Judgment Day, they have never understood the least thing about *this* knowledge and *this* foundation. Even though it might be called ignorance and lack of awareness, it still contains more than all the knowledge and awareness outside this foundation. For this ignorance entices and draws you away from all knowledge about things, and beyond this it draws you away from yourself. This was what Christ meant when he said: "Anyone who does not deny himself or herself and leave his or her father and mother and everything that is external, is not worthy of me" (Mt. 10:37–38). It is as if he said: "Whoever does not leave all external aspects of creatures can neither be received into this divine birth nor be born." The fact that you rob yourself of yourself and of all that is external—*this* now is what truly gives this birth to you. And I truly believe and am certain that *those* people who are properly situated in this respect can never be separated from God in any way at all. I say that they can never fall into the slightest mortal sin, as even the saints did. I go so far as to say that they cannot even commit a venial sin of their own will nor can they allow others to do so if they can prevent it. They will be so strongly enticed to *him* and so drawn to and accustomed to him that they can never turn another way, for all their senses and powers are inclined in this direction.

May the God who was reborn today as a human being help us in this birth! May he eternally help us weak human beings so that we may be born in him in a divine way. Amen.

COMMENTARY: The Meaning of Breakthrough/Three Kinds of Birth or
                    Breakthrough/First, Our Birth into the Godhead/
                    Second, God's Birth in us/Third, Our Birth as Sons
                    and Daughters of God

Eckhart takes the occasion of the Christmas midnight liturgy to speak
about three births—that of ourselves in the Godhead, that of God in us,
and that of ourselves as Sons of God. As he puts it, *God was reborn
today as a human being* and we *human beings* are to *be born in him in
a divine way.* Eckhart asks about the first two of these births when he
puts these questions: "What is our name and what is our Father's name?
Our name is that we must be born and our Father's name is to bear
. . ."[1] "We must be born"—there lies the need for breakthrough and
the first birth treated in this sermon. But that "our Father's name is to
bear"—there lies the need for birth number two in this sermon. And birth
three will be the fruit of births one and two, for it will mean a birth of us
in relation to the Father, that is, our birth as Sons and Daughters of God.

Eckhart invented a word for our rebirth. He called it *breakthrough*
(*Durchbruch*). We have seen him invoke this term in Sermon Fifteen,
where he said:

> A great master says that his breakthrough is nobler than his
> flowing out, and this is true. When I flowed out from God, all
> things spoke: God is. But this cannot make me happy, for it
> makes me understand that I am a creature. In the break-
> through, on the other hand, where I stand free of my own
> will and of the will of God and of all his works and of God
> himself, there I am above all creatures and am neither God
> nor creature. Rather, I am what I was and what I shall remain
> now and forever. Then I receive an impulse which shall bring
> me above all the angels. In this impulse I receive wealth so
> vast that God cannot be enough for me in all that makes him
> God, and with all his divine works. For in this breakthrough I
> discover that I and God are one . . . Here God is one
> with the spirit, and that is the strictest poverty one can find.

In this passage we see how breakthrough entails our experience of the
Godhead and is thus even nobler than our experience of God in our
original creation; we see that breakthrough entails our being "poor" and

devoid of all will; and a happiness is experienced as we return to our origin in the Godhead, one in spirit with God: "In this breakthrough it is bestowed upon me that I and God are one." The breakthrough, then, is not God's breakthrough; God has been here all along and so too has the Godhead. The breakthrough is *our* breakthrough—a breakthrough in our consciousness, an awakening (Eckhart compares it to a lightning flash), an "eruption," an insight into the fact of our oneness with God. In Paths One and Two we saw that the spiritual process is a constant one of "waking up" and "getting up." Path Three or breakthrough is also one of awakening. The first awakening is a self-awakening, a birth of ourselves. As Schürmann puts it, "in the process of detachment, the fruit that man bears is man himself: he is delivered to himself, brought back from dispersion and constituted Son of God in the very being of his mind."[2] In our first birth, into creation, we understood that we are creatures—but this, Eckhart claims, is not enough. It does not satisfy our deepest longings. Until we have given birth to self, we have not even properly understood the rest of creation, for "those who know themselves know all creation" (Sermon Thirty-six). In this second birth or breakthrough we realize our nearness to divinity and the Godhead— here "it is bestowed upon me that I and God are one." For this reason, our second birth or second emanation is "even nobler" than our first.

Our breakthrough constitutes our being born again. It is a rebirth, as in the Nicodemus story in John's Gospel which Eckhart links to the subject of our birth in Sermon Seventeen. Elsewhere Eckhart says:

> In the soul that abides in a present now, God begets his only begotten Son, and in this birth the soul is born again in God. It is one birth: as often as the soul is born again in God, the Father begets his only begotten Son in the soul.[3]

The key statement here is that "it is one birth," for Eckhart's language is at times confusing when he is discussing our birth or breakthrough, God's birth in us, and the Son's birth in us. These are, from the point of view of analysis, split up into three different births. But from the point of view of the event itself, in one "present now," there is only one birth. Ours, God's, and God's Son's constitute one birth. Even though we undergo breakthrough often, it is still only one birth. "God does this: he begets his only begotten Son in the highest part of the soul. At the same time as he begets his only begotten Son in me, I beget him again in the Father."[4] Clearly, the three births are one birth.

The breakthrough is ours and not God's, because God is already there wanting to enter. Eckhart links this reality to that of the resurrected Christ appearing to the disciples through a locked door.

> I once spoke of how our Lord came to his disciples on Easter Day through a locked door. God does not first need to enter the person who is already free of all otherness and manmade things, because he is already there.[5]

Thus the breakthrough is the penetrating of the doors that oppose God's entry. But the penetration is not from the outside because "God is already there." It is more a penetration of consciousness, an awakening to how total the *permeation* of God's presence already is. Eckhart calls the breakthrough the fullest joy possible. "No other pleasure and joy can be compared with this union and this breakthrough and this joy." The breakthrough is a reception of "nothing less than God himself in the breadth and fullness of being."[6] Eckhart talks of the need to break into things as well as into God. "One must learn to break through (*durchbrechen*) things and to grasp one's God in them and to be able to picture him powerfully to oneself in an essential manner."[7] This suggests the image he uses on several occasions of breaking the kernel to get at the nut or core of things. "The shell must be cracked open if what is in it is to come out; for if you want the kernel, you must break (*zerbrechen*) the shell."[8]

Breakthrough is born of our desire for union with the Godhead, the God without a name.

> The intellect can never find rest. It aspires to God not as he is the Holy Spirit or as he is the Son: it flees from the Son. Nor does it want God inasmuch as he is God. Why? Because, as such, he still carries a name. And even if there were a thousand gods, it would still *break beyond*: it wants him where he has no name. It wants something more noble, something better than God as having a name. What then does the intellect want? It does not know; it wants him as he is the Father. This is why Saint Philip says: "Lord, show us the Father and it is enough for us." It wants him as he is the marrow out of which

goodness springs; it wants him as he is the nucleus from which goodness flows; it wants him as he is the root, the vein, from which goodness exudes. Only there is he the Father.[9]

The breakthrough is the intellect's breakthrough, thus a breakthrough in our consciousness, a breaking beyond boundaries of creating images. Eckhart substantiates this with scriptural arguments for our transformation of consciousness. Citing Saint Paul, Eckhart says: "The soul looks at God and God looks at it from face to face, as transformed into one image." The Pauline text Eckhart refers to goes as follows: "And we, with our un-veiled faces reflecting like mirrors the brightness of the Lord, all grow brighter and brighter as we are turned into the image that we reflect; this is the work of the Lord who is Spirit" (2 Co. 3:18). The breakthrough is the moment of our being transformed into another image, that of divin-ity. In it we break into the Godhead, having been invited from all eter-nity. In it we break into our most primal origins, having once been there from all eternity. In it we break into the silence that has preceded all birth from all eternity. In it we break beyond creation and even the Cre-ator to the God without a name who is the Godhead. In it we break into the "marrow," the "nucleus," "the root," "the vein" that is behind the goodness of creation and the goodness of the Creator. One might say that we touch the goodness behind goodness, the mystery behind mys-tery, the God behind God. The breakthrough becomes our own birth into the divinity, a discovery of our own divine origins. *We are to be born in him in a divine way.* It also becomes the ground for a new birth of God.

Time stops in the Godhead and in our breakthrough into the Godhead. So does all need for "means" and purposes, for there we learn what it is to seek and to live without a why. For ecstasy is its own reward, an end in itself.

Someone could ask a good person: "Why do you seek God?" "Because he is God." "Why do you seek the truth?" "Because it is the truth." "Why do you seek justice?" "Because it is jus-tice." Such people's attitude is the right one. All things that are in time have a why. Thus when someone asks a man: "Why are you eating?" "In order to gain strength." "Why are you sleeping?" "For the same reason." And so with everything that is in time.[10]

In the breakthrough we realize that life does not have only means but also ends and that these ends need no justifications. We learn that because our transformed intellect has learned that *there the "means" is silent. In this very foundation, the "means" is silent.* In the breakthrough we have learned how God acts: that is, without means. God is effective in the soul with no "means," image, or likeness.

What Eckhart calls the "breakthrough to the Godhead" constitutes our return to God just as our creation or flowing out ("emanation") constituted our entrance into the panentheistic circle of being. In our creation we are in God but in our breakthrough we know we are in God and in the Godhead. The union is total in the breakthrough. There "God and I are one." In such ecstasy all dualism dies, all separation ceases, union takes over. But this union is not enough for Eckhart, for as we saw in the previous sermon, fruitfulness is richer than union alone. Our union needs to bear fruit; it needs to give birth. And so a second kind of birth, that of God in us, needs to be considered.

The scriptural text that launches this sermon of Meister Eckhart's is that of the liturgy for Christmas. No doubt this sermon was a Christmas sermon and for this reason Eckhart begins it with the Incarnational question: *What does it avail me if this birth takes place?* In other words, what does Christmas—what does the Incarnation—mean? The fuller text from which Eckhart derived his sermon is as follows:

When peaceful silence lay over all,
and night had run the half of her swift course,
down from the heavens, from the royal throne, leapt your
    all-powerful Word;
into the heart of a doomed land the stern warrior leapt. (Ws. 18:14–15)

Eckhart tells us that his entire sermon *will discuss this Word.* If this sermon, then, represents his exegesis of the Word who leaps into human history, how does Eckhart interpret this word? It is a word of revelation, of uncovering what is hidden, of uncovering the Godhead. What, after all, does a word do? *It is the nature of the Word to reveal what is hidden,* declares Eckhart. The Word reveals what is hidden—namely the Godhead—but it does not reveal all hiddenness, says Eckhart. In other words, the leaping that the Word does is a leaping in the night—"when night had run the half of her swift course." *Because it is so hidden, this*

Word came in the darkness of the night, Eckhart comments, citing John's
Gospel, *"the light shone in the darkness"* (1:5). The darkness and the
hiddenness remain, but the revelation has broken through it all, *sparkling
and yet hidden,* says Eckhart. And this is how Paul describes this illumination also, an illumination within the darkness and coverup of daily tur-
moil. Eckhart cites from Paul's Letter to the Romans:

> For I am certain of this: neither death nor life, no angel, no
> prince, nothing that exists, nothing still to come, not any
> power, or height or depth, nor any created thing, can ever
> come between us and the love of God made visible in Christ
> Jesus our Lord. (Rm. 8:38–39)

The "making visible" is the work of the Word, the work of revelation.

In developing his theology of the Word, Eckhart appropriately makes
rich use of the role of the Word at creation. He insists that the Genesis
account of creation in six days ought not to be taken literally. *Do not
believe that when God made heaven and earth and all things, he made
one thing one day and another the next day.* Rather, the heart of the
story for Eckhart's purposes in this sermon is that *God did only this: he
willed, he spoke—and all things were made!* The divine Word is an all-
powerful word; once spoken, things are. That is the kind of Word that is
born anew on Christmas morning. And the Word that is creation is full
of mystery, full of divinity and of untold depths. *What do you know
about the nobility God has placed in nature that has not been fully described but remains still hidden?* Eckhart asks.

But Eckhart is not content to expound on a theological theory of the
Word and its birth at Christmas. He is a preacher trying to get persons
to practice and live their faith. Thus, as any spiritual theologian must, he
is intent on relating this theology of the Word to practice. What good is
it to us, he asks, if God was born at Bethlehem on Christmas morning?
The issue becomes: How does this Word affect us today? His answer is:
It is quite fitting that this birth should take place in me, and, indeed, *in all
persons. Now we wish to talk about this birth, and how it takes place
within us and is accomplished in the good soul whenever God the Father
declares his eternal Word in the perfect soul.* What the Incarnation
means, then, is that God is to be born in us. But where and how? The
where is in our depths. This is the reason, Eckhart declares, that the

Word had to come as revelation, in order to touch the very bottom of our deep, deep selves. As noble as the soul is, its true depth cannot be plummeted by reason alone.

> Those who have written about the nobility of the soul have not come further than their natural reason carried them. They never reached its *foundation* . . . Because it is so hidden, this Word came in the darkness of the night.

And so, it is in the very foundation and core of the soul that the birth of God will happen.

But how? By our remaining in this very depth and foundation. *You must of necessity be and remain in being and in the foundation. There is where God has to touch you.* What will characterize our remaining in the depths of our being and foundation so that God may be *reborn today as a human being?* Above all, silence will characterize our attitude toward giving birth. Elsewhere, Eckhart expands on the need for silence: "All voices and sounds must be put away and a pure stillness must be there, a still silence . . . In stillness and peace . . . there God speaks in the soul and expresses himself fully in the soul."[11] But Eckhart defines silence in a very special way. Silence means to be rid of all images and representations. To be silent is to have let go of all images. An image is a means, and the union with the Godhead is to be without means. *Silence and quietness must reign there, and the Father must speak and generate his Son and accomplish his deeds* there without any images. Eckhart's exegesis of the passage from Wisdom, "When peaceful silence lay over all," continues. *Be at peace and at rest,* he insists. Let go of all images, let yourself sink into that *unknowing knowledge* that was learned in Path Two. Even though our souls create images and these images of sound or color or conversation are good, still, there is a time for letting go of all images. For we create images for our own sakes, but God does not need them. The only image God wants in us at such a time is God with his own being. There is to be *no image but God himself* if our souls are to be the "birthplace" for God. *God is effective in the soul with no "means," image, or likeness—he is effective truly in the soul's foundation into which no image has reached except God himself with his own being.* Invoking the father of the *via negativa,* Pseudo-Dionysius, by name, Eckhart insists that we will birth God where we let the *silent dark-*

ness of the unknown God be. The unknown God or Godhead must be allowed to "let be"; we must not be afraid of the dark or of the silence or of being without images. Only then are we ready for the secret Word to enter. One reason why silence is so basic to the birth of God is that the birth takes place from the emptiness of our nothingness. It is such a pregnancy with nothingness that bears divine fruit. "A man had a dream, a daydream: it seemed to him that he was big with nothingness as a woman is with a child. In this nothingness God was born. He was the fruit of nothingness. God was born in nothingness."[12] Thus the via negativa is needed to give birth to God. Whoever does not leave all external aspects of creatures can neither be received into this divine birth nor be born. The fruit of letting go is birth.

The third event in breakthrough is our giving birth to God's Son, for "though we are God's sons, we do not realize it yet."[18] Breakthrough constitutes our realization of how the Word is a divine Word that leaps down from a royal throne.

> The more you are able to bring all your powers to a unity and a forgetfulness of all the objects and images you have absorbed, and the more you depart from creatures and their images, the nearer and more receptive are you to the secret Word.

The receptivity that has been learned in Path Two by letting go and letting be now finds a fruitful expression. That expression is the one image that makes us happy: the Son of God generated in us.

> The Father generates his Son in the foundation of the soul and in its being, and he thus unites himself with the soul. For if any image were there, it would not be a true union. Yet the whole happiness of the soul is situated in this true union.

The emptiness of the soul is filled by God. And in such a setting of emptiness the Word must be born. God is compelled to reveal him in such a person.

> Look solely for God and you will find together with God all that he is capable of offering . . . If God possessed still more, he could not hide it from you, he would have to reveal it to

you, and he gives it to you . . . and he does so by virtue of birth.

The Father bears his Son in eternity like to himself. "The Word was with God and the Word was God" . . . The Father bears his Son in the soul in the same way that he bears him in eternity, not in any other way. He must do it, whether he wishes to or not.[14]

But there is still another birth in this birth of self and of the Son of God and this is the fruit of the previous two births. The third birth, generated by the other two, is that not only do we give birth to the Son of God but that we, in fact, are reborn as sons of God. Our break-through has rendered us one with the Father—"God and I are one"—but to be one with the Godhead is to know the Godhead. However, "no one knows the Father except the Son." Thus Eckhart, not unfamiliar with Scholasticism's penchant for syllogisms, presents us with one:

No one knows the Godhead except the Son.
However, we know the Godhead (by the breakthrough experience).
Therefore, we are the Son.

Eckhart says: "This is what our Lord says: 'No one knows the Father ex-cept the Son, and no one knows the Son except the Father.' Perfectly to know the Father we must be the Son."[15] Thus our rebirth is not accom-plished until we become the Son. Eckhart develops this theme within a scriptural context. In the sermon we are considering, he repeats the words of John's Gospel, albeit a bit inaccurately. *All who received him became sons of God by reason of power: power was given to them to become sons of God.* Then he draws the following conclusion: *Not only is the Son of the heavenly Father born in this darkness, but you also are born there as a child of the same heavenly Father and none other; and he also gives that power to you.* And he insists that this revelation of our own divine sonship is not possible to philosophers alone. It required a birth of God in our midst to reveal it.

Understand how valuable this is! By all the truth that all the masters of the spiritual life have learned through their own reason and awareness, or will ever learn up to Judgment Day, they have never understood the least thing about *this* knowl-edge and *this* foundation.

The meaning of Christmas is our being born as the Son of God.

> It would mean little to me that the "Word was made flesh" for
> man in Christ, granting that the latter is distinct from me, unless
> he also was made flesh in me personally, so that I too would
> become the Son of God.[16]

We are the Son of God by grace; Christ is the Son of God by nature.[17]
We are, as the Scriptures say, truly God's children. "Think of the love
that the Father has lavished on us, by letting us be called God's children;
and that is what we are" (1 Jn. 3:1). Eckhart takes this passage very
seriously. Elsewhere, in commenting on John 1:12f., he explains that "I am
the son of everything which forms me and gives birth to me in its image
and likeness. A person so fashioned [is] God's Son."[18] Significantly, in
the scriptural text from Wisdom that forms the basis of our present sermon, there is a line that immediately precedes the text that Eckhart has
read in the Christmas liturgy. It is:

> They who, thanks to their sorceries, had been wholly incredulous,
> at the destruction of their firstborn now acknowledged
> this people to be son of God. (Ws. 18:13)

God's people as God's children—"this people the son of God"—there is
the biblical theme that Eckhart expands in his present sermon.

Thus we can begin to appreciate what Eckhart had in mind in Sermon
Eighteen when he declared that the "soul alone among creatures is
generative"—it is generative of the Son of God. And how it is that the
birth we undergo and that God undergoes in us is a blessing—with all
the biblical connotations of that rich concept—and that our birth is the
imago Dei that brings a new light. Indeed, a light that is like lightning
from which no creature turns and which no creature can ignore.[19] The
birth is a lightning bolt, a breakthrough, a blessing that brings all blessings with it.

> Tend only to the birth in you and you will find all goodness
> and all consolation, all delight, all being and all truth. Reject
> it and you reject all goodness and blessing. What comes to
> you in this birth brings with it pure being and blessing. But
> what you seek or love outside of this birth will come to noth-
> ing, no matter what you will or where you will it.[20]

But there is still one more piece of good news regarding the birthday of Christ, the birthday of ourselves, and the birthday of God. And that is that such breakthroughs do not occur only once a year. Nor even once a day. They are continuous—if we are prepared and receptive for them. God is birthed in the "spark of the soul."

> There is where the birth takes place; there is where the Son is born. This birth does not take place once a year or once a month or once a day but all the time, that is, beyond time in that space where there is neither here and now nor nature and thought.[21]

No wonder Eckhart calls on his listeners to *celebrate* this birth, for the birth itself is taking place "all the time," it is one constant celebration. We celebrate what is. We celebrate a celebration. *Here only peace and celebration for this birth and this activity are in command, while God the Father declares his Word there.*

Sermon Twenty-two: OUR DIVINITY AND GOD'S DIVINITY: TO BE GOD IS TO GIVE BIRTH

"This is my commandment, that you love one another as I have loved you." (Jn. 15:12)*

I have spoken three verses in Latin which stand written in the Gospel. The first verse that our Lord speaks is this: "This is my commandment that you love one another as I have loved you" (Jn. 15:12). The second verse Christ speaks is: "I have called you my friends because everything which I have heard from my Father I have revealed to you" (Jn. 15:15). The third verse he speaks is: "I have chosen you that you might go and bear fruit and that the fruit might remain with you" (15:16).

Now notice the first verse where Jesus says, "This is my commandment." I want to say something about this so that, as he has said, "the fruit might remain with you." "This is my commandment, that you love." What does Christ mean here when he says: "That you love"? He wants to say something that you should pay attention to: love is so pure, so simple, so detached in itself that the best teachers say that the love with which we love is the Holy Spirit. There were many who wanted to contradict this but this much remains true: every movement through which we are moved to love is a movement in which nothing other is moving us than the Holy Spirit. Love at its purest and most detached level is nothing else in itself than God. The teachers say: the goal of love, that toward which all the works of love are done, is goodness; and goodness is God. As little as my eyes can speak or my tongue recognize color, just as little can love tend toward anything else than goodness and God.

Now pay attention. What does he want to say that makes him

* "Hoc est praeceptum meum ut diligatis invicem sicut dilexi vos." (DW II, ※27)

so serious about this matter, that we love? He wants to say, the love with which we love should be so pure, so simple, so detached that it inclines neither to myself nor to my friend nor to anything else next to it. The teachers say that one can name no good work as a good work and no virtue as a virtue unless it has taken place in love. Virtue is so noble, so detached, so pure, so simple in itself that it recognizes nothing better than itself and God.

But now our Lord speaks: "This is my commandment." When someone offers me what is pleasant and useful and in which my happiness lies, that is very nice for me. When I'm thirsty, drink offers itself to me. When I'm hungry, food offers itself to me. And God does the same thing. He offers something so beneficial that the whole world can offer nothing like it. And the human being who once tastes this sweetness can truly no more turn in his love from this goodness and from God than God can turn from his divinity. It's much easier for such a person to let go of himself and his whole blessedness and then to remain with his love in the house of goodness and of God.

Now our Lord says: "Love one another." Oh, that would be a noble life, that would be a blessed life! Would that not be a noble life when everyone was inclined to his neighbor's peace as to his own and when his love was so pure and clear and simple in itself that it aimed at nothing but goodness and God? If you were to ask a good human being: Why do you love goodness? the answer would be: For the sake of goodness. Why, then, do you love God? For the sake of God. And if it is so that your love is so clear, so detached, so pure in itself that you love nothing else but goodness and God, then it is a sure truth that all the virtues which have ever been exercised by the whole human race belong to you as perfectly as if you had exercised them yourself—in fact, even clearer and better. For the fact that the Pope is Pope often causes him great sorrow, but you possess his virtue in a purer and more unconditional form and with greater peace and it belongs more to you than to him, insofar as your love is so clear, so pure in itself that you have nothing else in your mind nor love anything else than goodness and God.

Now our Lord speaks: ". . . as I have loved you." How has God loved us? He loved us when we did not yet exist and when we were his enemies. So great a need had God for our friendship that he could not wait until we asked him. He comes to us and asks us that we be his friends, for he desires from us that we should want it. He likes to forgive us. This is why our Lord quite rightfully says: "It is my will that you pray for those who do evil to you" (cf. Lk. 6:28). It should be an equally serious matter with us to pray for those who do us harm. Why? So that we might fulfill God's will, that we should not wait until someone asks us. We should rather say: "Friend, forgive me that I have betrayed you!" And just as serious should be our concern for virtue. The more the effort, so much the more should be our serious striving for virtue. So unitary should our love be, for love will never be anywhere else than there where equality and unity are. Between a master and his servant there is no peace because there is no real equality. A wife and a husband are not alike, but in love they are equal. This is why the Scripture is quite right in saying that God has taken the woman from the rib and side of the man (Gn. 2:22)—neither, therefore, from the head nor from the feet, for where there are two, there we find deficiency. Why? Because the one is not the other, for this "not" that makes the difference is nothing other than bitterness, precisely because there no peace is available. If I hold an apple in my hand, it arouses desire in my eye but it withholds its sweetness from my mouth. On the other hand, when I eat it, then I rob my eyes of the desire which I have for it. So therefore two cannot stand with each other, for one of them must lose its being.

It is for this reason that our Lord says: "Love one another"—in one another. The Scripture is quite clear on this. Saint John says: "God is love and whoever is in love is in God and God in him" (1 Jn. 4:16). He is speaking quite accurately here. For if God were in me but I was not in God or if I were in God and God was not in me, then everything would be divided. But when God is in me and I am in God, then I am not less and God is not higher. Now you can say: "Lord, you say I should love but I cannot love." Our Lord has expressed himself very aptly on this point in what he said to Saint Peter: "Peter, do you love me?" "Lord, you know very well that I love you" (Jn. 21:15). If you have given it to me, Lord, then I love you; if you have not given it to me, then I do not love you.

Now pay attention to another verse, where he says: "I have

called you my friends because I have revealed everything to you which I have heard from my Father" (Jn. 15:15). Notice that he says: "I have called you my friends." In that same primal source in which the Son originates, where the Father gives expression to his eternal Word, and from the same heart, there arises and flows the Holy Spirit. And were the Holy Spirit not an outflowing from the Son, then no one would have recognized a difference between the Son and the Holy Spirit. When I spoke on the feast of the Holy Trinity, I said a little verse in Latin, that the Father had given to his only begotten Son all that he wanted to ask—his whole divinity, his entire blessedness—and that he held nothing back for himself. Then a question arose: Did the Father give to the Son that which is proper to himself? And I answered yes, for the property of the Father to give birth is nothing else than his being God, and I have already said that he held nothing back. And I further say that it is the very root of divinity which he fully speaks into his Son. This is why Saint Philip says: "Lord, show us the Father and it is enough for us!" (Jn. 14:8). A tree that bears fruit drops its fruit down and out from itself. Whoever gives me the fruit does not give me the tree at the same time. But whoever gives me the tree and the root and the fruit, that person has given me more. Now our Lord says: "I have called you my friends." It is truly in the same birth where the Father bears his only begotten Son and gives him the root and his whole divinity and his entire blessedness and holds nothing back of himself, it is in this same birth that he calls us his friends. If you hear and understand nothing of this verse, still it gives a power in the soul—I spoke about this recently in one of my sermons—a power which is completely detached and entirely clear in itself and closely related to the divine nature, and it is in this power that the verse will be understood. And therefore he also says quite aptly: "Therefore I have revealed to you everything which I have heard from my Father" (Jn. 15:15).

Now Christ says: "What I have heard." The Father's speaking is his giving birth; the Son's listening is his being born. Now he says: "Everything which I have heard from my Father." Yes, everything which he has heard from his Father from eternity—that is what he has revealed to us and has hidden no part of it from us. I say that if he had heard a thousand times more, he would have revealed that to us too and not hidden any part of it from us. So we, too, should not hide anything from God; we should reveal everything to him which we would like to ask. For if you hold anything back for yourself, then you would be losing that much of your eternal blessedness, for God has hidden nothing of himself from us. This seems to be a heavy saying for many people. But no one should thereby doubt it. The more you give yourself to God, the more does God give you of himself in return. The more you empty yourself of yourself, so much the greater is your eternal blessedness. It recently occurred to me as I was praying the Lord's prayer that God himself has taught us: When we say, "Thy kingdom come, thy will be done" (Mt. 6:10), then we are constantly asking God thereby to strip us of ourselves.

About the third verse I will at this point say nothing more than note that Christ says: "I have chosen you, placed you, set you, put you so that you might go and bear fruit and the fruit might remain with you" (Jn. 15:16). But no one knows this fruit but God alone. And may the eternal truth, of which I have spoken, help us to come to this fruit. Amen.

COMMENTARY: How Love Is God/How Love Is Between Equals/How the Essence of God Is to Give Birth/How God Gives His Whole Divinity to His Son and to Us Who Are God's Children, Receptors of Divinity

The previous sermon ended with a prayer that "we might be born in God in a divine way." Eckhart pursues this theme of our divine birth in the present sermon, in which he considers what it would be like to be human and divine at once. One thing it would mean is a much more beautiful existence for us all, were we truly to believe in our own rebirth as children of God, our own divinity. *Oh, that would be a noble life, that would be a blessed life! Would that not be a noble life when everyone was inclined to his neighbor's peace as to his own?* Such an existence would stretch out to other places and other times. It would break through all such barriers and would celebrate the communion of saints and the mystical body, where beauty would feed on beauty and would be shared bountifully. *All the virtues which have ever been exercised by the whole human race belong to you as perfectly as if you had exer-*

cised them yourself—in fact, even clearer and better. In such an existence we ourselves would be giving birth to love and to the Holy Spirit as the Son does. *The love with which we love is the Holy Spirit.* In doing this, we are of course giving birth to God. For Eckhart does not only say that "God is love," but that *love is God. Love at its purest and most detached level is nothing else in itself than God.* He does not distinguish dualistically between a love for creatures and a love for Creator, as many spiritualist theologians do. Instead, the difference in loves is within ourselves. If our love is truly one of letting go and letting be, then every act of love, toward friends and creatures alike, partakes of the Holy Spirit. Every movement through which we are moved to love is a movement in which nothing other is moving us than the Holy Spirit. Every movement of love is God-inspired, he is saying.

Eckhart is probing what love means in the phrase from Jesus in John's Gospel, "that you love one another." He has two things to say about the experience of human love that he in turn applies to our experience of divine love. The first of these is that love is between equals. *Love will never be anything else than there where equality and unity are.* Where there is no equality—as between a master and his servant—there can be no love. But where there is equality—as between a husband and wife— there can indeed be love. True love, he is saying, is true union. When *one is not the other* there can be no love, for then *there are two and there we find deficiency.* Love is the end of separations and dualisms. This lesson applies to our need to love our enemies, as suggested in the Sermon on the Mount (Lk. 6:27ff.), and it also applies to God's love for us. If, as Eckhart says, *two cannot stand with each other,* because in such a situation *one of them* would be forced to surrender his or her *being,* then the same holds between God and people. We are not two in our relation of love with God but one. We are no longer human but divine. Thus he has used the analogy of married love to describe how our love—like that of the vine and the branches—is with God. If God is a divine vine and we are the branches, then we too are divinized.

The theme of divinization is a common one in Meister Eckhart's spiritual theology, repeated and amplified on many occasions. He writes elsewhere, for example, that

> the soul so much loves itself in God as divine and is so uninterruptedly united with him that it enjoys nothing but him and rejoices in him. What more could a human being want or

know when he or she is so blessed and united with God? It is
for this very union that God made human beings.[1]

He says:

> God gives the righteous person a divine existence and names
> him with that same name which belongs to himself. Therefore
> he can say: "My Father who art in heaven."[2]

Citing Saint Augustine's remark that a person becomes by love that
which he loves, Eckhart comments:

> Should we now say that, if a person loves God, that person
> becomes God? That sounds like heresy. In the love a person
> gives there are no two but one and union, and in love I am
> more God than I am in myself. The prophet says: "Ye are
> gods, and all of you sons of the Most High." This sounds sur-
> prising that a person should be able in such a way to become
> God in love; yet it is true in eternal Truth. Our Lord Jesus
> Christ proves it.[3]

The theme of the deification of humanity is a familiar one in creation-
centered theologians like Saint Irenaeus and in many Eastern thinkers,
such as Clement of Alexandria, who writes:

> The baptized, "in whom dwells the Word, possesses the beau-
> tiful form of the Word; such a person is assimilated to God as
> is beautiful himself or herself." It is then rightly that Heraclitus
> said: "Men are gods and gods are men." This mystery indeed
> is revealed in the Word: God in people and people in God.[4]

Eckhart develops at considerable length this important theme of the
deification of humanity, a theme so regrettably lost in Western spirituality, almost since his condemnation. But he is careful to make the proper
distinction, as, for example, in the following analogy:

> A prophet says that all things are as small compared with
> God as a drop in comparison with the stormy sea (cf. Ws.
> 11:23). When you pour a drop into the stormy sea, the drop
> changes into the sea and not the sea into the drop. This is also
> how it happens to the soul. When God draws the soul to him-

self, then the soul becomes divine, but not that God becomes
the soul. Then the soul loses its name and its power but not its
will and not its being. Then the soul remains in God as God
remains in himself.[5]

Thus we are reminded that the soul, like a drop in the divine sea, becomes the sea or God, but the sea does not become the drop. God
does not become the soul. At his trial Eckhart repeats this need to clarify
the meaning of our deification. "To say that the deified person is nothing
other than God is false and an error,"[6] he insists. So that, while becoming God, we also remain ourselves—with will and being intact, as he
said above. On many occasions Eckhart gives the reason for the Incarnation as our becoming divine and the child of the divine. In Sermon
Two, he declared: "The reason why God has become a person is that
he may beget you as his firstborn Son, and nothing less." No wonder
Schürmann can exclaim that for Eckhart "the glory of God is man
deified: a man such as this God 'must' love. His love for him 'cannot not
be' since he gives to this man the very love with which he loves his own
nature, that is, the Godhead."[7]
Eckhart points out that when Christ says, "I am in the Father and the
Father is in me" (Jn. 14:10), what is meant is that

not only is this in that, each in each, but this is that and each
is each: "I and my Father are one" (Jn. 10:10). For the Father
is what the Son is. Fatherhood is the same as sonship. The
power whereby the Father begets and the Son is begotten is
the same thing.[8]

It is evident, then, that the equality that Eckhart insists is necessary for
all love to happen has indeed happened between God and humans. For
humans are, by God's graciousness, deified and divinized. Thus love between the vine and the branches can happen. God and people are, in a
certain way, equal. There is not a case of the one not being the other
and of two not being able to stand with each other. One has become
one; we are equal to God and therefore able to love God.
A second analogy between human and divine love that sheds light on
both is that of panentheistic love. True love is a being in another. "Love
one another"—in one another, Eckhart says, quoting from John's
First Epistle. "Whoever is in love is in God and God in him." This inness

is a necessary part of equality and oneness—without it *everything would be divided.* Equality is once again the result, for *when God is in me and I am in God, then I am not less and God is not higher.* The scriptural text Eckhart employs at this juncture is a text recalling to mind our deification:

> We ourselves have known and put our faith in
> God's love toward ourselves.
> God is love
> and anyone who lives in love lives in God,
> and God lives in him.
> Love will come to its perfection in us
> when we can face the day of Judgment without fear;
> because even in this world
> we have become as he is. (1 Jn. 4:16–17)

"Even in this world we have become as he is"—a significant statement for understanding our own divinity and our own divine son/daughtership and our equality with God. "Undoubtedly no one loves God sufficiently and purely unless he is God's son. For love, the Holy Spirit, originates in and flows from the Son" to the Father.[9] This equality is stated another way when he cites Jesus' saying that *"I have called you my friends."* Only equals can be friends: the divine can only befriend the divine.

Where are we friends of God? We are friends in the birth and breakthrough, where we are also sons and daughters of God and where *the very root of divinity* is bestowed on us.

> Now our Lord says: "I have called you my friends." It is truly in the same birth where the Father bears his only begotten Son and gives him the root and his whole divinity and his entire blessedness and holds nothing back of himself, it is in this same birth that he calls us his friends.

God bestows *his whole divinity* on his Son—but we are God's sons and daughters! Eckhart has in mind the line from John's Epistle: "Think of the love that the Father has lavished on us, by letting us be called God's children; and that is what we are" (1 Jn. 3:1). "That is what we are"—here lies so much of Eckhart's inspiration for developing the theme of our divine son/daughtership in God.

But who is this God to whom we are related as sons and daughters and as friends in a common birth? Eckhart's God is a God who gives birth. The *very root of his divinity* is the *property to give birth*. It is also the meaning of *Dabhar*, the creative Word of God. God's speech is a birth in itself. For God to express God is for God to give birth.

> The property of the Father to give birth is nothing else than his being God, and I have already said that he held nothing back. And I further say that it is the very root of divinity which he fully speaks into his Son.

He repeats this understanding of God on another occasion: "God's supreme purpose is to beget. He is never content unless he begets his Son in us."[10] Just as God bears his Son by nature all the time, so we too are born as the adopted sons and daughters without ceasing. "The Father bears his Son incessantly, and I say still more: he bears me as his Son, and as the same Son."[11] Birthing and begetting are more intimate than mere similarity. That is why our union with the all-unitive Godhead is a union of birthing and not mere similarity. "Philip said: 'Lord, show us the Father and it suffices for us,' for 'Father' implies begetting and not similarity, and denotes the One in whom similarity is mute, and everything that has desire for being is silenced."[12] Birth is in silence; mere similarity takes images and is therefore noisy.

But what does it mean to say that we are children of God continually being born and reborn? It means that God is so generous with us that we are not received as only the tree or only the root or only the fruit of the divine vine. No, we are partakers of *the tree and the root and the fruit* of that divine vine whose essential property it is to give birth. If we are truly God's sons and daughters, then we too are truly birthers and creators, for it is *the property of the Father to give birth*. "A good person born of goodness and in God," Eckhart says, "enters into all the properties of the divine nature."[13] If this be the case, and if the essence of the divine nature is to give birth, and if God *held nothing back* in extending divinity to us, then our divinity too demands that we be creators. Like father, like son; like mother, like daughter. The Father gives birth; the Child is born. Our being born constitutes our very essence and our giving birth constitutes our adopted nature as sons and daughters of God. *The Father's speaking is his giving birth; the Son's listening is his being born.* Our response—our listening—to the Father's Word is our being born. Our being born in human and divine fullness has no limit—no one knows *this fruit but God alone.* Who can tell what fruit will emerge from a vine as divine as this one?

Eckhart explains our divine sonship, which is that of graced heirs and not of nature, on another occasion. He says:

> "Father" makes us think of sonship; the word "Father" signifies
> a pure generation and means the same as "a life of all
> things." The Father generates his Son in eternal knowledge.
> He generates his Son in the soul as in his own nature. He gen-
> erates him in the soul as his own, and his being is attached to
> the fact that he is generating his Son in the soul, whether for
> good or for woe. I was once asked what the Father did in
> heaven. And I said that he was generating his Son, and that
> this activity was so agreeable to him and pleased him so much
> that he does nothing other than generate his Son, and both of
> them flourish in the Holy Spirit. Where the Father generates his
> Son in me, I am that very same Son and no one else. "If we
> are sons, we are heirs as well" (Rm. 8:17). Whoever rightly
> knows the truth understands well that the word "Father"
> implies a pure generation and a production of sons. For this
> reason, we are here as a son, and are the same Son.[14]

In this passage Eckhart has identified the Father for us as "pure generation" and as the "life of all things." He also identifies the Father's constant activity as that of "generating his Son" and that this is all the Father does. But this generation of divine son/daughtership takes place all
the time in all of us, so that we too are children, "sons and heirs as
well," as Paul puts it. Eckhart is driven to these conclusions from the full
context of Paul's Epistle to the Romans, which he is trying to understand.
It reads as follows:

> Everyone moved by the Spirit is a son of God. The spirit you
> received is not the spirit of slaves bringing fear into your lives
> again; it is the spirit of sons, and it makes us cry out, "Abba,
> Father!" The Spirit himself and our spirit bear united witness
> that we are children of God. And if we are children we are
> heirs as well: heirs of God and coheirs with Christ, sharing his
> sufferings so as to share his glory. (Rm. 8:14–17)

We see from this text how Eckhart was involved in exegeting the sense of "Abba, Father" in his comments on the Father as pure generation and the "life of all things." Paul goes on to explain how our son/daughtership relates to the new creation and in doing so speaks of the "one great act of giving birth"—a topic that, as we have seen, constitutes so significant a theme in all of Eckhart's spiritual theology. One might say that these observations of Paul in Romans constitute the true starting point for Eckhart's Path Three or our breakthrough and giving birth to Self and God.

> I think that what we suffer in this life can never be compared to the glory as yet unrevealed, which is waiting for us. The whole creation is eagerly waiting for God to reveal his sons. It was not for any fault on the part of creation that it was made unable to attain its purpose, it was made so by God; but creation still retains the hope of being freed, like us, from its slavery to decadence, to enjoy the same freedom and glory as the children of God. From the beginning till now the entire creation, as we know, has been groaning in one great act of giving birth; and not only creation, but all of us who possess the first-fruits of the Spirit, we too groan inwardly as we wait for our bodies to be set free . . .
>
> We know that by turning everything to their good God cooperates with all those who love him, with all those that he has called according to this purpose. They are the ones he chose specially long ago and intended to become true images of his Son, so that his Son might be the eldest of many brothers. (Rm. 8:18–23, 28–29)

With this emphasis on all of creation being reborn into the glory of God that we share, it is little wonder that one criterion Eckhart offers for evidence of the authentic birth of the Son in us is that of a return to creation to find God there. "Grasp God in all things, for God is in all things." When you "grasp God in all things, that will be the sign for your new birth, by which you will have been begotten his firstborn Son, and not less."[15] Thus for Eckhart, the test for Path Three is a return to Path One, where we see creation anew. As great as our experience of breakthrough is, it is not meant to distract us from creation itself. Path Three is in no way isolated from Path One. In this way, we become what Paul says we are: "true images of his Son, so that this Son might be the eldest of many brothers [and sisters]."

Sermon Twenty-three: WE ARE CHILDREN OF GOD AND
MOTHERS OF GOD

"See what love the Father has lavished on us: we are called
God's children and we are." (1 Jn. 3:1)*

We must understand that knowing God and being known by him
as well as seeing God and being seen by him are essentially the
same thing. Inasmuch as we know and see God, we know and see
that it is he who causes us to see and know. Air that is illuminated consists of only one thing, the fact that it gives off light.
This is because air that gives off light is itself illuminated. In the
same way, we know because we are known and because God
causes us to know him. For this reason Christ said, "Again you
will see me." This means that because I cause you to see, you will
know me, and as a result, "your hearts will be full of joy" in seeing and knowing me, and "that joy no one shall take from you"
(Jn. 16:22).

Saint John says, "See what love God has given to us, so that
we shall be called and we are God's children" (1 Jn. 3:1). He
says not only that "we will be called" but also that "we are." In
the same way, I say that just as a person cannot be wise without
having knowledge, to the same extent he or she cannot be a child
without having the filial essence of God's child and without having the same essence as God's child. In the same way, one cannot
be wise without having knowledge. Therefore, if you are to be a
child of God, you cannot be one unless you have God's very
being, which a child of God has. This, however, is now hidden
from us, and as a result it is written, "My dear people, we are already the children of God" (1 Jn. 3:2). And what do we know
about this? We know what John adds: ". . . we shall be like
him" (1 Jn. 3:2). This means that we shall be the same as he is:

* "Videte, qualem caritatem dedit nobis pater, ut filii dei nominemur et
simus." (DW III, ⅋76)

the same being and perception and understanding and everything
that he is when "we see him as he really is" (1 Jn. 3:2). Therefore, I say that God could no more cause me to be a child of God
if I did not have the essence of a child of God than God could
cause me to be wise if I did not have the essence of what is wise.
But *how* then are we children of God? As yet we do not know.
"What we are to be in the future has not yet been revealed" (1
Jn. 3:2). We know only what he himself says about it: "we shall
be like him." Certain things exist that hide all this in our souls
and conceal this knowledge from us.

The soul has something within it, a tiny spark of the ability to
know, that is never extinguished. And onto this tiny spark, as
onto the most sublime part of our mind, is located the "image"
of the soul. Now there exists, however, in our souls also a form of
knowledge that is directed toward external things, namely, the
knowledge of the senses and of understanding. This is knowledge
in the form of images of ideas and concepts; it conceals from us
the other kind of knowledge.

How then are we "children of God"? We are so in this way,
that we have *one* essence with him; that we know somehow that
we are God's children. For this purpose we must know how to
distinguish between external and inner knowledge. Inner knowledge is knowledge that is found as something resembling reason
in the essence of our souls. Meanwhile, this *is* not the soul's essence but it is rather *rooted* in this essence, and it is something of
the soul's life. When we say that this knowledge is something
from the soul's life, this means the *rational* life. It is in *this* life
that a person is born as a child of God and to eternal life. And
this knowledge is without time and space and without here and
now. In *this* life all things are one, and all things are united with
one another, all in all and all in all.

I shall give a comparison. Within the body all parts of the
body are so united that the eye belongs to the foot, and the foot
to the eye. If the foot could speak, it would say that the eye in
the head is *more* the foot's than if it were in the foot; and the eye
would make the same comment. In the same way, I believe that
all the grace in Mary belongs more, and in a more characteristic
way, to an angel and is more in this angel—I am speaking now of
the grace in Mary—than if that grace were in the angel or in the

saints. For everything that Mary has, a saint has also, and it is more the saint's, and the grace within Mary pleases the saint more than if it were within himself or herself.

This interpretation is still too clumsy and materialistic because it depends on a comparison based on the senses. Therefore I shall give you another explanation that is even more transparent and spiritual. I say that in the kingdom of heaven everything is in everything else, and that everything is one, and that everything is ours. Whatever grace our Lady has is completely in me—when I am there—and in no way is it arising and flowing from Mary. Rather, it is something within me as my own, not something coming from outside myself. And so I say that whatever one person has there, another person has too. And the first person has it not as something coming from the other or as something within the other but rather as something within himself or herself. This takes place in such a fashion that the grace within the first person is also completely within the other, exactly as if it were one's own grace. This is also the way the spirit is within the Spirit. Therefore, I say that I cannot be a child of God unless I have the same essence as a child of God, even though by having the same essence, we become like him and we see how he is God. But it has not yet been revealed what *we* then become. Therefore, I say that in *this* misunderstood sense there is here nothing that is "like" and nothing that is different. Rather, without distinction we shall be the same essence and the same substance and nature that he himself is. But "that is not yet revealed"; for it will be revealed only when "we see how he is God."

God causes us to know him, and his essence is his knowledge. It is the same thing whether he causes me to know or whether I know. For this reason, his knowledge is mine, just as it is one and the same thing. It is the same in the teacher who is teaching, and in the disciple who is taught. Since his knowledge is mine, and since his substance, knowledge, nature, and essence are mine, it follows that his essence, substance, and nature are mine. And if his substance, essence, and nature are mine, I am a child of God. "See, brothers, what love God has given us so that we are called God's children, and we are!"

Pay attention now to *how* we are God's children. It is because we have the same essence as a child. *How*, however, are we God's children, or how *do we know* that we are, since God is still not like anyone? This last statement is, of course, true. Isaiah says, "To whom could you liken God? What kind of image could you contrive of him?" (Is. 40:10). Since it is God's nature that he is unlike anyone, we must of necessity reach the point that we are *nothing*, in that we can be removed into the same essence he himself is. When I come to the point when I no longer project myself into any image and fancy no images in myself, and toss away everything within me, then I can be transported into God's naked being, and this is the pure essence of the *Spirit*.* There every comparison must be driven out, so that I can be transported into God and can become one with him and *one* substance and *one* essence and *one* nature and in this way a child of God. And after this has happened, nothing more in God is hidden that will not be revealed or will not be mine. Then I shall be wise and powerful and all things, just as he is, and one and the same with him. Then Sion will be a true seer, a "true Israel," which means a "God-seeing man." For nothing in the Godhead is hidden from him. There a person will be guided to God. In order that nothing may remain hidden from me in God that has not been revealed, no likeness and no image may remain open in me, for an image does not open up to us either the Godhead or the essence of God. If any kind of image or likeness were to remain within you, you would never become one with God. Therefore, in order that you may become one with God, no image should be represented in you, either inwardly or outwardly. This means that nothing should be concealed in you that does not become unconcealed and tossed away.

Pay attention as to where our inadequacy lies! It comes from nothingness. Whatever of nothing remains in a person must be extinguished. For so long as anything inadequate is within you, you are not a child of God. The fact that a person complains and is full of sorrow always comes only from what is inadequate. Therefore, in order for a person to become a child of God, all this must be extinguished and driven out, so that there may be neither complaint nor suffering. A person is neither a stone nor a piece of wood, for all these things are what is inadequate and a

---

* The word *Sein* can be translated as "essence" or as "being" and in this passage it is translated in both senses. M.F.

nothing. We cannot become like "him" unless this nothing is driven out, so that we become everything in everything, just as God is "all in all" (1 Co. 15:28).

There are two kinds of births for a person. One is *into* the world, and the other is *out of* the world. This means out of the world and spiritually into God. Do you wish to know whether your child will be born and whether it will be destitute? In other words, whether you will become a child of God? So long as you have sorrow in your heart for anything, even for sin, your child will not be born. Do you have sorrow in your heart? Then you are not yet a "mother"; you are rather still in the act of bearing a child and *close* to the time of birth. On this account, however, do not rush into doubt if you are sorrowful about yourself or a friend of yours. If the child is still not yet born, it is *close* to the time of birth. But it is completely born when a person feels no sorrow in his or her heart. For that person has the essence and nature and substance and wisdom and joy and everything that God has. At that time, the same essence of a child of God will be ours and within us, and we shall come into the same essence of God.

Christ says, "Whoever wishes to follow me, let him deny himself and take up his cross and follow me!" (Mk. 8:34; Mt. 16:24). This means that you should drive all anxiety from your heart so that there will be only constant joy in your heart. Thus the child is born. If a child were born in me, and if I were to see my father and all my friends killed before my eyes, my heart would not be moved as a result. If my heart were to be moved, the child would not be born in me, even though it might perhaps be *near* the time of birth. I say that God and the angels have such great joy as a result of every kind of deed of a good person that no joy can match it. Therefore, I say that if it happens that the child is born in you, you will have such great joy as a result of each of those good deeds that take place in this world that your joy will attain the greatest constancy, so that it will never change. Therefore, he says, ". . . and that joy no one shall take from you" (Jn. 16:22). And if I am quite removed into the divine essence, God and all that he has will be mine. Therefore, he says, "I am Yahweh your God" (Ex. 21:2). *Then* I have true joy, and neither sorrow nor torment can take it from me. For then I am removed into the divine essence in which there is no place for sorrow. Let us see that there is in God neither anger nor affliction but only love and joy. If it seems that he grows angry now and then because of sinners, this is not anger. It is love, for it comes from the great, divine love. He punishes those he loves, of course, for "he is the love" (1 Jn. 4:16) that is the Holy Spirit. Thus God's anger comes from love, for he gives away without bitterness. When you reach the point where you cannot feel sorrow or anxiety over anything, and where sorrow is not sorrow for you, and where all things are a pure kind of peace for you, *then* a child is *really* born. Have concern so that a "child" will not only *be in the process of being* born but that it *be already* born, just as the Son *is* constantly born and *will* constantly be born in God.

May God help us so that this will happen to us! Amen.

COMMENTARY: Four Signs of Our Testing the Authenticity of Our Breakthrough and Rebirth/What Does It Mean to Be a Child of God?/Being in God and Being in the Son/ Eckhart's Mariology and Our Becoming Mothers of God

Eckhart summarizes his teaching on birth in this sermon. Our first experience of birth is our creation. The second is our breakthrough into God. *There are two kinds of births for a person: one is into the world, and the other . . . is spiritually into God.* The first corresponds to Path One and the second to Path Three in our spiritual journey. In this sermon he examines in greater depth still the implications of this rebirth or second birth into God, which is also, as we have seen, our being born as the Son or Daughter of God. One point he makes about this birth, a point alluded to in the previous commentary, is that this birth is a continuous process. *In God the Son is constantly born and will constantly be born.* The divine work of birthing is never completed but is eternally young, eternally in process. The same can be said of our breakthrough and birth: it takes place all the time, continually. "This birth does not take place once a year or once a month or once a day but all the time . . ."[1] Every time we undergo such births and rebirths, so does the Son of God. "As often as this birth takes place, the only begotten Son is born."[2] This is how Eckhart understands John's statement that the Word was in the beginning. "It is always 'in the beginning,'" and so, "if it is always 'in the beginning,' it is always in the process of being born, of being begotten . . . And so it comes about that the Son in the Godhead, the Word 'in the beginning,' is always being born, is always already born."[3] God calls forth the Son from us like an echo, and in this act we give birth to the Son.

> Out of the purity he eternally begat me as his only begotten Son in the same image of his eternal Fatherhood, that I might become a father and beget him by whom I was begotten. In the same way, if one were to stand at the foot of a high mountain and call out, "Are you there?" the echo would answer, "Are you there?" If one said, "Come out," the echo would also say, "Come out" . . . God does this: he begets his only begotten Son in the highest part of the soul. At the same time as he begets his only begotten Son in me, I beget him again in the Father.[4]

Eckhart is addressing two scriptural texts in the present sermon. The first is from John's First Epistle and reads as follows:

> Think of the love that the Father has lavished on us,
> by letting us be called God's children;
> and that is what we are.
> Because the world refused to acknowledge him,
> therefore it does not acknowledge us.
> My dear people, we are already the children of God
> but what we are to be in the future has not yet been revealed;
> all we know is, that when it is revealed
> we shall be like him
> because we shall see him as he really is. (1 Jn. 3:1–2)

This text urges Eckhart to put the questions he does on several occasions in this sermon, namely, When are we children of God? and What does it mean to be a child of God? He repeats John's words, the fact that we are dealing with a mystery, that *as yet we do not know* the full implications of this truth. Following the subsequent outline of chapters 3 and 4 of John's Epistle, he probes, as John does, what signs or signals or conditions might be present to indicate that we are indeed children of God. In this regard, he is following Jesus' advice, "by their fruits you will know them" (Mt. 7:16). It is important to Eckhart that he offer such criteria for testing the authenticity of our birthing and fruitfulness since, as he points out elsewhere, there are degrees to our being children of God.[5] In the previous sermon, one sign was given. In this sermon Eckhart offers four more.

The first of these signs is inness. We are in Christ as a wise person is in wisdom, Eckhart declares in a statement of Christological panentheism. We bathe in Christ as the light bathes in the air and the illuminated light becomes illumination itself. We are a child of God *by having that same essence that the Son has.* "To be in God is to be God," we saw in his sermon on panentheism; so to be in the Son is to be the Son or Daughter. *This means that we shall be the same as he is: the same being and perception and understanding and everything that he is when "we see him as he really is"* (1 Jn. 3:2). We are the child inside the Son because one cannot be the child outside of the Son of God's being and without having the identical being that the Son of God himself possesses. The Son of God permeates our existence as light does the air and as God does to panentheistic creation. There is no escaping such envelopment for the person who is reborn the child of God. We are in Christ, as Paul puts it.[6] Eckhart elaborates on why it is that when we are in Christ we are one with Christ.

> If you want to be blessed, you must be in the Son, not many sons but in one Son. Though you will be different in view of your physical birth, in view of eternal birth you must be one. For in God there is but oneness and that is why there can be only one natural emanation of the Son—not two, but one. Therefore, if you will be one Son in Christ, there may exist only one emanation with the eternal Word.[7]

Through our breakthrough we learn not only that we are in God the Creator and in God the Son but also that we are in God the Spirit. *In the same way the spirit is in the Spirit.* This inness is shared among others who are in Christ. When one is in, all are in. Thus Eckhart discusses the Mystical Body and the Communion of Saints as examples of shared inness by humans reborn as children of God. Just as the foot is related to the eye, so are all who are in Christ interrelated. *In the kingdom of heaven everything is in everything else, all is one and all is ours.* The beauty that others have received is not lost on the rest of us; in fact, *the grace within the first person is also completely within the other, exactly as if it were one's own grace.*

Still another example of inness is that of *the spirit in the Spirit.* This inness occurs to the extent that emptiness occurs. What Eckhart calls *that other way of knowing*—that way of unknowing and of divine ignorance that the *via negativa* brings with it—that is the emptying process that will *transport us into God's naked essence and this is the pure essence of the Spirit.* Having made contact with our nothingness, we are free to let go and let be and thus we are free to quit projecting any images at all. When that freedom is touched, God enters and we enter God and *become one with him.*

> When I come to the point when I no longer project myself into any image and fancy no images in myself, and toss away everything within me, then I can be transported into God's naked being.

Then we truly become God's children and like the panentheistic God. We can say with Meister Eckhart, we are *all in all, as God is all in all.* The in-Christ becomes an in-God and an in-Spirit, which in turn is an in-others, as in the Communion of Saints and the Mystical Body. We are *all in all, as God is all in all.*

The second text Eckhart is exegeting in this sermon is that from the Gospel of John. It reads as follows:

> "In a short time you will no longer see me,
>   and then a short time later you will see me again . . .
> I tell you most solemnly,
>   you will be weeping and wailing
>   while the world will rejoice;
> you will be sorrowful,
>   but your sorrow will turn to joy.
> A woman in childbirth suffers,
>   because her time has come;
>   but when she has given birth to the child she forgets the suffering
>   in her joy that a person has been born into the world.
> So it is with you: you are sad now,
>   but I shall see you again, and your hearts will be full of joy,
>   and that joy no one shall take from you." (Jn. 16:16, 20–22)

Using this text, Eckhart presents two more signs of our giving birth. The first of these is joy, *constant joy*. When one is in God there is a *joy that no one can take from you*. Realized eschatology is experienced and not only theorized about. Eternal life begins and with it a divine joy. *It is in this life that a person is born as a child of God and to eternal life.* Eckhart is so taken with this promise of eternal life before death that he dismisses speculation about life after death. *What we shall be hereafter is not yet revealed*, he rightly points out. So why waste one's energy getting to heaven when heaven has already arrived? *It will be revealed only when "we see how he is God."* The theme of joy as a fruit and sign of the spirit is a favorite one with Eckhart. The ecstasy of joy is near to death itself. "Just as one can die of anxiety *before* the blow, that is, before a murder is carried out, in the same way one can die of joy or of its anticipation. And so the soul dies within itself in joyful expectation of eternal bliss before it passes over to God."[8] When we are in God we share divine joy. "Now notice what a wonderful and happy life this person has on earth, as in heaven, in God himself! Discomfort serves as comfort to him, grief is the same as joy . . ."[9] In the joy that the breakthrough brings, a joy of realized eschatology, "the birth of the fire and the joy are beyond time and beyond distance. Pleasure and joy do not seem long or faraway to anyone."[10] For, "to rejoice always," as Saint Paul admonishes us, is to find joy "beyond time and outside of time."[11] It is to find our joy in the experience of realized eschatology, for in this experience there arrives a new sense of time. "This is the fullness of time, when the Son of God is begotten in you," Eckhart teaches.[12] "When the time was fulfilled, grace was born."[13] The end time, the Messianic time and the full time of realized eschatology, is as near as our rebirth in God or our breakthrough. At such a time, we undergo a new sense of time. "There it is God's day, in which the soul dwells in the day of eternity in an essential now, and there the Father begets his only begotten Son in a present now, and the soul is born again in God."[14] We have "immediate knowledge of the eternal life" in this life, Eckhart insists.[15] In this life a person "recovers the eternal being that he was, now is, and will eternally remain."[16] Schürmann comments on Eckhart's sense of realized eschatology:

> Eternal life means that man may live again, here and now, out
> of his ground, and that releasement may accomplish itself, so
> that God, man, and the world play their identity. In the beati-

tude promised for today, this interplay swallows up every difference or otherness. This blessed identity is already in me, not in germ, but in totality, exactly in the same way as God is in me: not according to his effigy, but in totality.[17]

Schürmann points out that this emphasis on eternal life now is what distinguishes Eckhart from so many other spiritual theologians before him and in his day. "In the present, and not only in eternal life, you possess the totality of the forms in the ground of your mind—not virtually but actually."[18] Lossky points out that it is this issue of realized eschatology more than any other that "puny" theological minds miss when trying to understand Eckhart.[19] Within the experience of realized eschatology and its new sense of time and of full joy, it is possible, Eckhart is saying, to *drive all anxiety from your heart, so that in your heart there will be only constant joy.* The joy that results fulfills Christ's promise that no one will take it from you, for it is an even joy that remains steadily in tribulation or in triumph. You will have such *great joy as a result of each of those good deeds that take place in this world that your joy will attain the greatest constancy so that it will never change.* This kind of joy, *neither sorrow nor torment can ravish.* For it is a joy in God, and therefore a divine joy. In God only joy reigns, there is *neither anger nor affliction but only love and joy.* In such a situation, *all things are a pure kind of peace for you.* Eckhart's thoughts on this kind of joy and on the sorrow of everyday living are triggered by the Gospel image of the woman who suffers in giving birth but who forgets the pain at the ecstasy of the newborn child. Citing this same passage elsewhere, he comments that this is the way in which "God says and exhorts us in the Gospel that we should ask our heavenly Father that our joy may be perfect."[20]

A third test of our being the children of God is our bearing the child of God. We must become mothers—mothers of God. We must be wifely and fruitful if we are true children of God. This same Gospel passage cited above on the mother who bears a child has no doubt triggered the theme of our motherhood in Eckhart's mind. This in turn suggests to him Mary, the mother of Jesus. Eckhart's Mariology is significant for how it avoids all sentimentalisms, all pedestal pieties, and all temptations to Mariolatry. He discusses her in the present sermon in the context of the Mystical Body and the Communion of Saints and of the joy that is ours and hers. *Whatever grace our Lady has is completely in me.* For Eckhart,

Mary is the human being who has shown all of us how to be mothers of God. She knew how to let go and let be.

> When the angel appeared to our Lady, all that she and he said to each other would never have made her the Mother of God. But as soon as she gave up her will, she became at once the true Mother of the Eternal Word and conceived God immediately. He became her Son by nature.[21]

We are to follow Mary's example. "As divinity completely gave itself reason in our Lady, she received—because she was pure and simple—God in himself. Then God broke the dam of his divinity and flowed over into the womb of our Lady. Now if she had not borne God in her reason, she would never have received Christ in her womb."[22] Mary gave birth in the fullness of time and we are told to do the same.

> Our Lady said: "How can it be that I should become the Mother of God?" Then the angel said: "The Holy Ghost shall come upon thee from above." David said: "This day have I begotten thee." What is today? Eternity . . .[23]

Today is eternity. Now is the hour and this is the place for birthing the Son as Mary once did. For Eckhart asks:

> What help is it to me that Mary is full of grace, if I am not also full of grace? And what help is it to me that the Father gives birth to his Son unless I too give birth to him? It is for this reason that God gives birth to his Son in a perfect soul and lies in the maternity bed so that he can give birth to him again in all his works.[24]

Eckhart even suggests that what drove God to becoming a child in Mary's womb was the "overflow" of the spiritual birth that she underwent. In other words, *her* breakthrough brought about God's breakthrough into human history.

> The teachers say that God was born spiritually in our Lady before he was born bodily in her. And from the overflow of the spiritual birth when the heavenly Father produced his only

born Son in her soul, the eternal Word received human nature
in her, and she became pregnant in a bodily way.[25]

By our imitation of Mary, we ourselves become mothers of God, birthers
of the child God in human history. When we are so fruitful, it is a sign of
our being children of God ourselves. *If you have sorrow in your heart,
you are not yet a "mother"; you are rather still in the act of bearing a
child and close to the time of birth. The child is born when divine joy is
born in you.* And this takes determination on our part. *Have concern so
that a "child" will not only be in the process of being born but that it be
already born. For as "the Scriptures say, 'the greatest of gifts is that we
should be God's children and that he should beget his Son in us.'"*[26]

Sermon Twenty-four: WE ARE OTHER CHRISTS

"Blessed is the womb that bore you and the breasts that
nursed you." (Lk. 11:27)*

We read in today's Gospel that a "woman," a "lady," said to our
Lord: "Blessed is the womb that bore you, and the breasts that
nursed you." "What you say is correct: Blessed is the womb
that bore me and the breasts that nursed me. But: 'Rather,
blessed are they who hear the word of God and keep it'" (Lk.
11:27–28).

Consider this phrase carefully. Christ said: "Rather, blessed are
they who hear the word of God and keep it." If *I* had said that a
person is more blessed who hears the word of God and keeps it,
more blessed than Mary inasmuch as she is the Mother of God—
I repeat, if *I* had said it—people would be perplexed. But Christ
himself said it, and we have to accept it as being true, because
Christ *is* the truth.

Consider what is being heard by the one who listens, the one
who "hears the word of God." Such a person hears Christ as
begotten of the Father, equal to the Father in spite of the hypostatic union. True God and true man, *one* Christ: *that* is the
word which is heard by him who listens perfectly to the word of
God and keeps it in its entirety.

Saint Gregory writes about four qualities which should distinguish a person who "hears the word of God and keeps it." The
first is control over all fleshly desires, rejection of all worldly
things, and death to all that is transitory in one's person. The second quality is this: that one gives oneself completely to the
knowledge and love of God and aspires with intimacy to God.
The third quality is that the person does not do to anyone what
he himself would not want others to do to him. The fourth is

* "Beatus venter, qui te portavit, et ubera, quae suxisti." (DW II, ※49)

that one gives freely of one's material and spiritual gifts. Some persons *seem* to give freely but in reality they give *nothing*. Such persons are those who give in order to receive something in return, for example, favors or honors. Such a gift does not deserve to be called a gift—it should be called a demand, because nothing is really given. Our Lord remained poor and free while he gave generously to others. In all that he gave he did not have his own advantage in mind but only the praise and honor of his Father and our blessedness. In true love he gave himself up to death. If, therefore, a person intends to give for the love of God, he must give without concern for his own gaining of some service or honor or praise; he must give out of concern for his brother. The same holds true in regard to spiritual gifts. They must be given because someone wants to receive them, because someone desires to improve the quality of his or her life for the sake of God. Such a giver should neither desire praise from the receiver nor any advantage from God. God's praise should be his sole desire. Their gift should leave them as free as Christ, who remained free and detached in everything that he has bestowed on us. A person who gives in such a manner truly gives. And anyone who gives in a manner that corresponds to the above-mentioned four principles of giving, such a person may be sure that he or she hears the word of God and keeps it.

All Christians honor and praise our Lady for having given birth to Christ, and that is fitting. Christians intercede to our Lady for special graces; she grants them, and that is fitting too. Though it is appropriate that Christians bestow high honors on Mary, they should bestow even greater honors on the one who hears the word of God and keeps it, for such a person is more blessed than our Lady, in view of her single privilege of being the Mother of God, as our Lord himself told us. Such great honor, and immeasurably more, is destined for the person who hears the word of God and keeps it. I intended this introduction for you so that you might become attentive.

I selected three passages from today's Gospel. The first is this: "Rather, blessed are they who hear the word of God and keep it" (Lk. 11:28). The second: "Amen, amen, I say to you, unless the grain of wheat falls into the ground and dies, it remains alone. But if it dies, it brings forth much fruit" (Jn. 12:24). The third is that which was spoken by Christ: "Amen, I say to you, among those born of women there had not risen a greater than John the Baptist" (Mt. 11:11).

Now I shall consider the first scriptural quotation. Christ said: "Rather, blessed are they who hear the word of God and keep it." Consider carefully! Our heavenly Father himself hears nothing but the Word, knows nothing but the same Word, speaks nothing but the Word, and he begets nothing but the Word. In this Word the heavenly Father hears himself, begets himself, knows himself in his essence and all that he is, and knows the Word as of the same nature in a distinct person. Reflect carefully on the manner of his speaking. The Father expresses knowingly the fruitfulness of his own nature in the eternal Word. This is not an act of his will, for it does not proceed from the will as do power and appetite which one can follow or ignore. The relationship between Father and eternal Word is not this kind of relationship. The Father must generate the Son as Word—he cannot but express himself in the Word—and generate it unceasingly, because the Word is with the Father by nature as a root. He is in the nature of the Father as the Father himself is in that root. That is why the Father speaks the Word without special intent. He speaks it naturally, but not as if proceeding from his nature. In this Word the Father speaks my spirit, your spirit, and the spirit of every person who resembles the Word. And in this utterance you and I are true sons of God, as the Word himself is Son of the Father. I have already mentioned the reason for this: The Father knows nothing but this same Word and himself and the entire nature of God and all things in the same Word. Everything that he recognizes in that Word is like the Word and is in truth and nature that same Word. When God the Father reveals himself to you and makes himself known to you he bestows upon you his own life and being and his Godhead in truth and entirety. A physical father transmits his nature but not his own existence or being because the child has his own existence—he is a being apart from the father. This can be explained as follows: The death of the father does not cause death in the child, nor does the child's death cause his father to die. If, however, they shared *one* life, *one* existence, it could not be otherwise: Both would have either to live or to die, because their being could not be divided. That is why we can say that they are "strangers," that they are separated as to their life and existence. If I were to take some fire from a flame, I would divide the flame, and though both parts would have the qualities of fire, one part would no longer influence the other. One could become extinct, the other could continue to burn. Thus fire is not eternal, nor does it have the quality of oneness in its nature. But, as I have mentioned before, our heavenly Father bestows on us his eternal Word, and in this Word he gives to us his own life, his own existence, his own divinity. Although Father and Son are *two* persons, they have but *one* life, *one* being. They are undivided. When God the Father assimilates you into that same light, so that you may recognize the light in his light, which is of one kind, he wants you to recognize him as he recognizes himself in the Word, in that light, in knowledge and truth. As I have said before, the Father knows of no separation between you and him and no preference as to Father and Word, because the Father and you and everything that is and the Word are one in the same light.

Now let us consider the second theme, the words of our Lord: "Amen, I say to you, unless a grain of wheat falls into the ground and dies, it remains alone; but if it dies, it bears much fruit, fruit a hundredfold." A "hundredfold" means immeasurably much fruit. But what is meant by the grain of wheat that falls into the ground? And what is meant by the soil into which it is supposed to fall? As I prefer to interpret it, the grain of wheat is the spirit, which is often called the human soul. And the soil into which it is to fall is the human nature of Jesus Christ, because there is no nobler soil which has ever been created or prepared for any type of fruitfulness. This soil was prepared by the Father, the Word, and the Holy Spirit themselves. But what was the *fruit* of this precious soil of the human nature of Jesus Christ? That was Christ's soul from that moment on, when through the will of God and the power of the Holy Spirit the noble nature and body became flesh in the womb of Mary and Christ's soul was created and united in a single moment to the eternal Word. This union came about so instantaneously and so truly that at the point of time when body and soul merged, Christ was its result. And in that same moment, he understood himself as true God and true man, as one Christ who is God.

Please consider the manner of his fruitfulness. His noble soul I shall call the grain of wheat which, like him, had to suffer, bear sorrow and death while buried in his human nature. For Christ himself was ordained to suffer and that prompted him to exclaim: "My soul is sorrowful unto death" (Mt. 26:38; Mk. 14:34). Christ, however, remained always united to the Highest Good, as a person of the Trinity. He never lost sight of his power; he enjoyed the same nearness and union with the Father and the Holy Spirit even during the height of his sufferings. No sorrow or pain or death could affect this union. Indeed, even when Christ's physical body died a painful death on the cross, his noble spirit lived in the contemplation of the Highest Good. In view of this sphere, however, in which his noble spirit was related to the senses and united with his holy body, inasmuch as our Lord called his created spirit a soul, insofar as it was the life principle of the body, and inasmuch as it was united to the senses and the mind, according to this manner and to that degree his soul was "sad unto death" for his body to die.

I claim that the grain of wheat, his noble soul, can be said to have died in two ways. As I distinguished above, his noble soul always contemplated the Highest Good inasmuch as it was united to the eternal Word. From that moment on, when the hypostatic union took place, Christ's soul, though the life principle of the body, had nothing to do with the death that had to be endured by his body. His soul's life was *with* the body, yet *above* it, united to God with an immediacy that knew no obstacle. In such manner, the soul of Christ died in the soil, to his body, and freed itself from it while remaining attached to it.

The other kind of death in the soil, in the body, as I have mentioned before, was when the soul gave life to the body and became united to the senses. At that moment, it shared with the body all toil, pain, and sorrow and "sadness unto death," and in this manner of speaking, while united to the body, the soul experienced no rest, peace, satisfaction, or immortality, as long as its body was mortal. And this is the other manner of dying: that the grain of wheat, the noble soul, Christ, dies in view of peace and quietness.

Now consider the fruit of the grain of wheat that is hundred-fold, immeasurable. The first fruit is this: the giving of honor and

praise to the Father and God's nature. Christ never divorced his
highest power for even a moment of time or point in space from
the contemplation of the Highest Good, no matter what occupied his mind or exhausted his body. He was always intent on giving praise to the Father. This is the one manner of fruitfulness of
the grain of wheat from the soil of his noble human nature. The
other manner is this: praise through the terrible suffering in his
nature as human being. All that he suffered in this life through
hunger, thirst, cold, heat, storm, rain, hail, snow, and all kinds of
evil and his bitter death, which he offered to the heavenly Father
to do him honor, this by itself gives praise to Christ himself and
raises the human nature to blessedness.

You have heard now how the soul of our Lord Jesus Christ became fruitful in his own sacred humanity. Now let us consider a
moment how we human beings can become fruitful. The person
who immerses the grain of wheat, his soul, into the soil of Jesus
Christ and lets itself be consumed by it becomes fruitful. This
kind of dying is also twofold: one is corporal, the other spiritual.
The physical death can be understood as follows: Whatever a
person suffers, be it hunger, thirst, cold, heat, rejection, un-
deserved pain—in whatever form God ordains it—he should accept it freely and joyfully without hope for reward in this or the
next world. Such persons should consider their sufferings small, as
a drop of water in the ocean, when compared to the sufferings of
Christ. Thus the grain of wheat, your soul, becomes fruitful in
the noble soil of Jesus Christ and in total surrender it will die
completely to itself. This is the first aspect of fruitfulness of the
grain of wheat that has fallen into the soil of Jesus Christ.

Now consider the second kind of fruitfulness of the spirit of
the grain of wheat. It consists in the following: All spiritual hunger and bitterness which God permits must be borne patiently.
And even if a person does all in his or her power inwardly and
outwardly, they must not seek any reward. Even if God should ordain one's condemnation so that one's existence would not be violated, even then the person should let God take over as if it did
not matter, as if one did not exist. God must be allowed to have
such power over all that you are, as if it were his own uncreated
nature. And another aspect is important. It consists in the following: If God removes all poverty from your life, if he bestows

upon you all his grace and the gift of himself to the degree that your soul is capable of embracing it, you must not cling to it and must take no credit for it. Possess the gifts freely, give God the honor, and be conscious that you were created out of nothing. This is the *second* type of fruitfulness which the grain of wheat, your soul, has received from the soil that is Jesus Christ: a soul that remains totally free in the enjoyment of the Highest Good. The soul must be able to identify with Christ's admonition to the Pharisees: "If I glorify myself, my glory is nothing. It is my Father who glorifies me . . . who sent me" (Jn. 8:54).

The third part of my sermon deals with the Scripture passage: "Amen, I say to you, among those born of women there has not risen a greater than John the Baptist, yet the least in the kingdom of heaven is greater than he" (Mt. 11:11). Think how wonderful and strange Christ's words are! He praises the greatness of John the Baptist, calls him the greatest born of women, but adds: "If a person were humbler than John, he would be the greatest in heaven." How are we to understand this? That I wish to show you.

Our Lord does not contradict himself when he claims that John the Baptist is the greatest. What he truly meant is that he was *lowly* and that he possessed true humility, and that that is his greatness. Christ says of himself: "Learn of me, for I am meek and humble of heart" (Mt. 11:29). All that we possess as virtues exist in God as pure essence. That is why Christ said: "Learn of me, for I am meek and humble of heart." However humble John the Baptist might have been, his virtue had limits and he, too, could not go beyond those limits. Our Lord said: "If someone would be lower than John the Baptist, such a one would be the greater in the kingdom of heaven." In other words, Christ was saying, if there is someone who transcends the humility of John the Baptist, even by an iota, the smallest measure, his humility would surpass that of John the Baptist and such a one would be the greater in the kingdom of heaven for all eternity.

Listen attentively! Neither John the Baptist nor anyone else has been placed before us as a limited goal which we are to follow. Christ, our Lord, *he* is the goal to which we must aspire. He is the model according to which we are to be fashioned, with whom we are to be united, equal in nature, as is fitting to such a union. No saint in heaven is so perfect, so holy, so that one could say his life on earth was without limit. No, a saint's virtues are measurable and he is ranked in the next life according to their degree. His perfection in heaven is determined by that measure. Indeed, if there were a man who would surpass the perfection of the greatest saint in heaven, whose virtues were greater, if such a person existed, he or she would be holier and more blessed still than any saint in heaven. I claim this and it is true, as true as the fact that God exists. No saint in heaven is so holy, so perfect that he or she could not be holier or more perfect than she is or you are. Therefore, I say: If someone were humbler and lower than John the Baptist, such a person would be eternally greater in heaven. That is true humility—when a person embraces complete abandonment while remaining in grace. Such a person faces serenely all that he or she is able or unable to do, and this is true humility. A second kind of humility is that of the spirit, when God is credited with every good and the self with nothing, as if the person did not exist.

May God assist us to become so humble. Amen.

COMMENTARY: What It Means to Hear the Word of God and Keep It/Who Is Jesus Christ?—Eckhart's Christology/Christ as the Word of God/Christ as the Model for Our Being Human and Divine/How Christ Was Fruitful and We Are Fruitful

Eckhart takes the occasion of the words in Luke's Gospel, "Rather, blessed are they who hear the word of God and keep it" (Lk. 11:27–28), to instruct persons not to exaggerate their devotion to Mary. This was an especially apropos criticism in his day, since the medieval Marian piety was known to get out of hand among devout but uncritical believers. He begins this sermon with a bit of humor—but humor with a message. Don't listen to me say this; listen to Jesus' words, he warns.

> If I had said that a person is more blessed who hears the word of God and keeps it, more blessed than Mary inasmuch as she is the Mother of God—I repeat, if I had said it—people would be perplexed. But Christ himself said it, and we have to accept it as being true, because Christ is the truth.

No doubt Eckhart is alluding to a rather well-known phenomenon among his hearers—namely, that he had the capacity to *perplex* his audience from time to time. But he is suggesting that Jesus' power for paradox and perplexing others far exceeds his own—and his *is the truth.* Eckhart simply takes the Gospel passage at face value when he declares that *honor and praise* for Mary *is fitting* and *bestowing honors* on her *is appropriate.*

But what is the word that we are to listen to and to keep? It is Christ. *One hears Christ . . . true God and true man, one Christ: that is the word which is heard by him who listens perfectly to the word of God and keeps it in its entirety.* The Christ we hear is the historical Christ of the Gospels, born of Mary, but also the Christ begotten in us. It is also ourselves who have been reborn as the sons of God. In other words, ourselves as other Christs. We too are the Word of God that must be listened to. *In this Word the Father speaks my spirit, your spirit, and the spirit of every person who resembles the Word. And in this utterance you and I are true sons of God as the Word himself is Son of the Father.* So thoroughly are we, by our breakthrough which is a new birth, made sons of God and divinized ourselves that it can be said that *God the Father actually bestows upon us his own life and being and his Godhead in truth and entirety.* We need to listen to our deepest selves to listen to the Word of God. We need to sink into this union that exists between us as sons of God and God as Father. In this listening process we learn the wonderful and good news that God has truly given *us his own life, his own existence, his own divinity.* We encounter divinity—our own—and how it is that God has shared it with us. So thorough is this filial relationship, this "Abba" or "Papa" relationship with God, that on God's side it cannot be lost. *The Father knows of no separation between us and him.* Only we can re-create a dualism, a distinction or a separation between us and God, us and our divinity. From God's point of view the union is total and lasts forever. For just as Christ has prayed in John 17 that people who follow him be "one as the Father and I and one," so, concludes Eckhart, this must be the case. We, the newly born sons of God, are one as Christ and God are one. *The Father and we and everything that is and the Word are one in the same light.* The panentheistic truth of our existence is illuminated.

But how do we develop this oneness? How do we nurture it? One way is by learning from the "firstborn of all creation" who was the first to undergo the profound breakthrough between God and humanity, namely, Jesus Christ. "He is the firstborn of all creation: 'the image of the invisible God, the firstborn of every creature'" (Col. 1:15).[1] Since he is the firstborn, he has led the way for us as model of what it means to be a son of God. And so one important dimension to Eckhart's Christology is Jesus as model for our divinity. Since we, like Mary, are to give birth to this Son of God, it behooves us to examine more closely what it is and who it is we are birthing. It is Christ who is *our goal to which we must aspire. He is our model according to which we are to be fashioned, with whom we are to be united, equal in nature as fitting to such a union.* For Christ is not only the image of God but also the image of humanity. "The nature assumed by God is common to all people without distinction of more or less. Therefore, it is given to every person to become the son of God, substantially indeed in Christ, but in himself or herself by adoption through grace."[2] Jesus has perfectly overcome the dualism between humanity and God. "Humanity and divinity are one personal being in the person of Christ," Eckhart says.[3]

Looking at Christ as model means that we forsake temptations to Christological narcissism or emoting or swooning over Christ and that we get down to the serious task of "doing his works"[4] and "behaving exactly like Jesus."[5] Eckhart resists absolutely all sentimentalizing of Jesus. His following of Christ is a following in the actions of Christ. "We must also be the same Christ, imitating him in his actions." For our "humanity and Christ's humanity are in one substance of the eternal being."[6] Some people, Eckhart observes, follow Christ "as a falcon follows a woman carrying tripe or sausages, as wolves follow a carcass or a fly a pot. It is against these that Christ says here, 'Follow me' . . . 'Follow' is a command to act."[7] Our following of Christ is a following of Christ's works so that divinity may become transparent through us.

> A person ought to have transformed himself or herself inwardly into our Lord Jesus Christ in all things, so that in that person one may find a reflection of all his works and divine appearance. And one should bear in himself or herself a perfect imitation, so far as one can, of all his works. You should work and he should receive it. Do your works with complete devotion and good intentions and may you mold yourself in all your works on his pattern.[8]

Christ is our model for our life and our work. "You often ask how you should live. Listen carefully to what I am going to say, and learn from it. What has been said of the image's way of being—exactly that should be your way of life."[9] Earlier in this particular sermon he identified the work of an image as "not of itself and not for itself." That is how Jesus lived and we are to live—as transparent images of the divine Godhead.

What are some of the works that Christ did and that we are to follow and to imitate? One fact of Jesus' life is that *he gave generously to others*—he knew what true gift-giving was about. In all that he gave, he did not have his own advantage in mind. And so Eckhart draws this conclusion from the model of Jesus as gift-giver: *If, therefore, a person intends to give for the love of God, he must give without concern for his own gaining of some service or honor or praise; he must give out of concern for his brother.* It is love for others, concern for one's brother, that makes all gift-giving fruitful and that truly improves the quality of one's life.

Another dimension to Jesus' example and his being a model for us is that he, of all people, knew how to let go and let be. He knew, for example, how to let go of life and to face death. It was not easy for him, there was much anguish involved, but he knew how to let the seed die. *The soul of Christ died in the soil, to his body, and freed itself from it while remaining attached to it.* In emphasizing this parable of the grain of wheat dying, Eckhart had the following scriptural passage in front of him:

"Now the hour has come
for the Son of Man to be glorified.
I tell you, most solemnly,
unless a wheat grain falls on the ground and dies,
it remains only a single grain;
but if it dies,
it yields a rich harvest.
Anyone who loves his life loses it;
anyone who hates his life in this world
will keep it for the eternal life.
If a person serves me, he must follow me,
wherever I am, my servant will be there too.
If anyone serves me, my Father will honor him.
Now my soul is troubled.

What shall I say:
Father, save me from this hour?
But it was for this very reason that I have come to this hour.
Father, glorify your name!" (Jn. 12:23–28)

Eckhart parallels this sadness at the letting go of life that Jesus underwent with the Garden of Gethsemane scene as described by Matthew:

> Sadness came over him, and great distress. Then he said to
> them, "My soul is sorrowful to the point of death. Wait here
> and keep awake with me." And going on a little farther he fell
> on his face and prayed. "My Father," he said, "if it is possible,
> let this cup pass me by. Nevertheless, let it be as you, not I,
> would have it." (Mt. 26:37–39)

Because Jesus was adept at letting go, he knew what true freedom was.
He "is free and unencumbered."[10] He knew external poverty, for "he
himself was poor on earth"[11] and this poverty became a poverty of consciousness, a way of seeing the world, a process of letting go. This is
why he *remained poor and free while he gave generously to others*.
Jesus, then, is the model of what true letting go is all about. For Jesus is
the "virginal" one (see Sermon Nineteen) who knows how to let go and
to let be. As Schürmann puts it:

> Jesus, "free and void and virginal in himself," who without any
> attachment has accomplished his work of salvation, is the ideal
> and the reality of a being who has retrieved his original lib-
> erty, who is eminently detached [that is, capable of letting
> go].
>   Jesus, both the model and the goal of this union, defines the
> condition for us to become one with the Word: freed from all
> possession of images and works, following him on the way of
> detachment, we shall be "virgin" in order to receive the vir-
> ginal Jesus. Exempt from all bonds of property to his own
> work, Christ has redeemed us.[12]

So full of letting go is Jesus that he was able to let go of life. So free of
letting go was the divine Word that it could become human. We, in turn,
are to be so full of letting go that we might let go of our humanness to
become divine. We even have to let go of Jesus—he had to die and as-

cend—in order for the Spirit to be sent. Eckhart warns that "the physical presence of Christ" can be an "obstacle to us in the reception of the Holy Spirit."[13] Jesus had warned his friends that if he did not leave them the Spirit would not come (Jn. 16:7). So too, our letting go must even touch our letting go of Christ in order to let the new Son of God be born in us. From this ever more radical meaning of letting go, it is clear that Eckhart's psychology of spirituality is a psychology that pits itself against all—absolutely all—compulsions, including—indeed especially— religious ones.

Of all Jesus' actions that we are to emulate and which flow most directly from his and our divinity, compassion is the fullest. And compassion, as we shall see in Path Four, means justice for Eckhart. Indeed, Jesus is the "Son of justice"[14] and he is the incarnation of the divine Compassion who actually became human because he "needed a back" on which burdens could be laid and suffering endured. Divinity, in a sense, needed to learn compassion from human suffering (see Sermon Thirty). Indeed, Christ is "unbegotten justice itself," the "offspring and Son of Justice," who is related to the Father as a just person is related to justice itself.[15] We are to emulate this Son of justice who is Compassion incarnate.

Another dimension to Christ as model is that he has given us an example of how to be both human and divine. "Humanity and divinity are one personal being in the person of Christ."[16] He is "Blessedness" itself with a "mouth of wisdom" who instructs us and goes before us in walking the way of wisdom.[17] He is also a "martyr" who knows the price that prophets pay. And he is a prophet, for he is the "Great Reminder" who calls us back to the law of Yahweh, a law of justice and compassion, and who calls us back to our divine origins and to the living out of the image of God that we truly are.[18] We are to go and do likewise—to become the reminders that all prophets must necessarily be. Christ is an "all-powerful Word" who has leaped from a "royal throne" (Ws. 18:18). The implications of Jesus' being a royal Word will be developed in Sermon Thirty-six. In a special way, Christ is a noble soul who has taken on our noble human nature and thereby praises and blesses our nature that we share with him, raising it to blessedness.

The culmination of Christ's freedom is his glory, and that is also the culmination of our own letting go and letting be. We are to possess the gifts freely—even the fullest of them, even God himself.

> If God removed all poverty from your life, if he bestowed
> upon you all his grace and the gift of himself to the degree
> that your soul is able to embrace, you must not cling to it, take
> no credit for it, possess the gifts freely, give God the honor
> and be conscious that you were created out of nothing.

Possession is not bad, but our attitude toward what we possess is, even if what we possess is God himself. All authentic possession must be free—*possess the gifts freely*. Only then are we imitating Christ. From this freedom born of letting go we learn what true humility is. It is *facing serenely all that one is able or unable to do*. Humility is not saying we cannot do or "I can't"—that, in fact, is psychologist Karen Horney's very definition of masochism. And there has been a lot of "I can't-ism" in the name of Christian humility since Eckhart's time. For Eckhart, humility is knowing what you *can* do as much as what you cannot do, and being equally serene before the truth of both aspects of self-knowledge. There is no masochism in Eckhart's spiritual psychology. He is too birth-oriented and action-oriented for that. Indeed, Eckhart discusses humility in this sermon in the context of the greatness that all people are capable of. He has a sense of the unlimits of human greatness so that *no saint in heaven is so perfect, so holy, so that one could say his life on earth was without limit*. Eckhart resists pedestal pieties and the corruption of hagiography that would project our vocations to greatness onto the saints. *If there were a person who would surpass the perfection of the greatest saint in heaven, . . . he or she would be holier and more blessed still than any saint in heaven*. This theme he develops in response to the biblical text in Matthew's Gospel that says that as great as John the Baptist is, "yet the least in the kingdom of heaven is greater than he" (Mt. 11:11). Eckhart senses that this passage, like that which refers to Mary and is the starting text for this sermon, suggests the unlimited greatness of those who can both listen to the word of God and keep it. Mary's calling as Mother of God and John the Baptist's as precursor of Christ both pale in comparison to the ultimate task of hearing the word of God and keeping it. (Taken from this perspective, both Mary and John are great themselves for having done exactly that, namely, hearing and keeping God's word.) What is at stake in the passage on John the Baptist is Eckhart's recognition that a new and magnanimous era has begun, with the kingdom of heaven being born so intimately in our midst, thanks to the birth of the Son of God in history and in us. Realized eschatology is now everywhere, and so is the fullness of human greatness and grace, for those who know.

Eckhart says that the word we hear is Christ. Christ is the word. What is behind Eckhart's theology of the Word of God? We have seen in Path One that a word is something that flows out but stays within. Thus Christ flows out of the Godhead but also remains within. A word is also an unveiler, a revealer. And Christ also reveals and reminds us of the nearness that humanity shares with God. In this sermon Eckhart emphasizes how the Word is the one preoccupation of God. The Word is God's self-expression, a kind of spontaneous word that is *not an act of his will* but which he *cannot but express and generate unceasingly.* The Word is a *root* and the Father is *in the same root.* The Word is generated from the root of the Godhead.

This same word is a seed generated in us who give birth to the Word of God. In us "God has showed his image and his likeness, and . . . he sows the good seed, the root of all wisdom, all knowledge, all virtue, and all goodness, the seed of divine nature. The seed of divine nature is the Son of God, the Word of God."[19] It is because this seed has been sown in us that we are bearers of the Son of God. One reason that the Father is so preoccupied with this one Word who is Christ is that God, like the perfect poet, is capable of saying it all in one word. "The 'Father' spoke a 'Word' that was his 'Son.' In this single 'Word' he expressed everything. Why did he say only one Word? Because all things are present to him."[20] Christ is the "innermost" Word of God.[21] "God speaks once (Jb. 33). He speaks in engendering his Son, for the Son is the Word. He also speaks in creating the creatures."[22]

If Christ is so intimate and singular a Word of God, then we, who are other Christs and bearers ourselves of the Son of God, need to be transformed into this God-like image. He cites Paul: "But we all, with unveiled face reflecting as a creature the glory of the Lord, are transformed into the same image from glory to glory" (2 Co. 3:18).[23] In this way, we are able to listen to the Word of God and to hear how the Spirit is talking to us. *In this Word the Father speaks my spirit, your spirit, and the spirit of every person who resembles the Word. And in this utterance you and I are true sons of God, as the Word himself is Son of the Father.* When we are "transformed into the image of God . . . to that extent the Son is born in us and we in the Son and we become one with the Son. Then we take on divinity and God's existence as the Son does: There exists but one Son, one existence, and that is God's exist-ence."[24] This transformation is a kind of resurrection from the dead, for Jesus is "the living Word, in whom all things live, and who upholds all things" and he raised people from the dead, as the son of the widow of Naim, simply by speaking to them. "Whenever the Word speaks into the soul and the soul answers in the living Word, the Son begins to live in the soul."[25] Thus for Eckhart the resurrection is very much this-worldly. It involves our learning to listen and keep the Word of God now. For Jesus is "eternal life itself."[26] The birth of God in us is an expression of the resurrection or the rebirth of Christ from the tomb. It is the vine that has grown from the seed that died.

Eckhart invents a word to describe how our being the Word of God is different from Christ's being the Word of God. He says that we are God's byword or adverb (Beiwort). We become an adverb for the Word itself.[27] The word spoken from God's spirit to my spirit is truly a fruitful word and a word of awakening and resurrection. It is a word that is barely a whisper, but it can be heard by those who listen and keep it. The divine whisper says to us: You are divine. I know no separa-tion between myself and you. Possess this gift freely. I give you my Word to remind you of this and to model yourself after. Spread the word.

Sermon Twenty-five: OUR DIVINITY: THE REASON GOD
BECAME A HUMAN BEING

"Eating with them, he instructed them not to leave Jerusalem." (Ac. 1:4)*

These words which I have spoken in Latin are read in today's liturgy. They are words our Lord spoke to his disciples when he
wanted to return to heaven: "Stay with one another in Jerusalem and do not depart. Cling to the promise of the Father that
after these days, which are neither many nor few, you will be
baptized" (Ac. 1:4).

No one can receive the Holy Spirit, for he dwells beyond time
in eternity. The Holy Spirit can be neither received nor given
in temporal things. When a person no longer centers on temporal
things and turns inward to his own heart, then he becomes aware
of a divine light which comes from heaven. It is under heaven
and yet breathes of heaven. It is in this light that such a person
finds something spiritual which is nonetheless so tangible that
one calls it material. It is like a piece of iron whose nature it is to
fall down which nevertheless lifts itself up against its nature and
hangs on to a magnet because of the power which the magnet has
received from heaven. Wherever the magnet turns, the iron
moves in the same direction. It is the same way with the divine
spirit in the human soul. This spirit does not allow itself to be
satisfied with that light. It storms the firmament and scales the
heavens until it reaches the Spirit that drives the heavens. As a result of heaven's movement, everything in the world flourishes and
bursts into leaf. The spirit, however, is never satisfied; it presses
on ever further into the vortex (whirlpool)† and primary source

* "Convescens praecepit eis, ab Jerosalymis ne discederent . . ." (DW II,
※29)
† I have taken Quint's in den Wirbel in preference to DW in den Gipfel
(Q, p. 290).

in which the spirit has its origin. This spirit—that is, the human spirit which we have been talking about—counts without numbers. It understands what it understands in numberless number—namely, in quantity-less, metaphysical number—and such a number (without number) is given not in the time of insufficiency (by this I mean in this earthly time of transiency and imperfection). In eternity, on the other hand, no one has any other root than precisely this numberless, quantity-less number. In heaven there is no one without number.

This spirit has to go beyond all quantity and break through all diversity. Then it will be broken through by God. Quite the same way, however, as God breaks through me, I shall break through him in return! God leads this spirit into the desert and solitude of himself where he is pure unity and gushes up only within himself. This spirit no longer has a why. If it were to have any kind of why, unity would also have to have its why. This spirit remains in unity and freedom.

The masters of the spiritual life say that the will is so free that no one can force it but God alone. God, however, does not *force* the will. He rather places it in freedom in such a way that it wishes nothing other than what God wishes. This, however, is not its lack of freedom; it is its innate freedom.

Certain people say: "If I have God and God's love, I can quite well do everything I wish." They do not understand this statement about freedom correctly. So long as you want something that is against God and his commandment, you do not have God's love. You might like indeed to deceive the world, just as if you possessed it. People who remain in God's will and in God's love take pleasure in doing everything that is pleasing to God and in giving up everything contrary to God. For such people it is just as impossible to give up something that God wants done as to do something that is contrary to God. Just as it would be impossible for someone whose legs were shackled to walk, it would likewise be impossible for a person who remains in God's will to do anything bad. The prophet says that if God himself had ordered me to do evil and to avoid virtue, I would still not be able to do evil! For no one loves virtue the way the one does who is virtue itself. People who have given up themselves and all things, who do not seek their own interests in any kinds of things, and who do all their deeds without a why and only out of love—such people are dead to the whole world, and they live in God and God in them.

Many people say: "You make fine speeches to us, but we don't understand anything." I have the very same complaint! This being is so noble and yet so common that you don't have to buy it, neither for a farthing nor for a halfpenny. If you only make a correct effort and have a free will, you'll *have* it. People who in this way have given up all things in their lowest being, and to the extent that things are temporary, will receive them again in God, where they are the truth. All that is dead here is life there, and all that is of a material nature here is in God's spirit there. If we were to pour pure water into a pure vessel—one that is completely pure and free of any stain—and if this vessel were held quite steadily while someone leaned his or her face over it, that person would see the vessel's bottom as it is in itself. It is the same way with all individuals who remain in freedom and unity within themselves. If they receive God in peace and quiet, they should also receive him in discord and restlessness. For it is completely fitting. If they cling to him less in discord and restlessness than in rest and peace, it is not fitting. Saint Augustine says: "Let those who are grieved by the day and bored by time turn to God in whom there is no boredom and in whom all things are at rest. Whoever loves justice will be seized by justice and will become justice itself."

Our Lord said: "I have not called you servants; I have called you friends, for a servant does not know what his master wishes" (Jn. 15:15). Even my *friend* might know something I did not know so long as he or she did not wish to make it known to me. But our Lord said: "I have made known to you everything I have heard from my Father" (Jn. 15:15). I am surprised at many priests who are very learned and would like to be important priests because they allow themselves to be so easily satisfied and made fools of. They receive the message our Lord proclaimed: "I have made known to you everything I have heard from my Father." They wish to understand this message in the following way, saying, "He has made known to us as much as is needed on the road to our eternal happiness." I do not agree that it is to be understood in this way, for this is not the truth. Why did God become a man? So that I might be born the same God. God has died so that I might die to the whole world and all created things. This is how we should understand the message our Lord declared: "I have made known to you everything I have heard from my Father." What does the Son hear from his Father? The Father can do nothing other than generate while the Son can do nothing other than be born. The Father generates in his only begotten Son whatever he has and whatever he is—the depth of divine being and divine nature. *This* is what the Son "hears" from the Father; *this* is what he has made known to us so that we may be the same only begotten Son. The Son has everything he has from his Father—being and nature—so that we may be the same only begotten Son. No one on the other hand possesses the Holy Spirit unless he be the only begotten Son. For in the place where the Holy Spirit becomes a spirit, the Father and the Son make him spiritual. For this is essential and spiritual. You may indeed receive the *gifts* of the Holy Spirit or *similarity* with the Holy Spirit. But it does not *remain* in you; it is inconstant. Just as if someone becomes red with shame and then pale again, this is something that happens to that person and then goes away. But a person whose nature is to be ruddy and handsome remains that way at all times. This is the same way with the human being who is the only begotten Son; the Holy Spirit remains in his same measure.

For this reason it is written in the book of wisdom: "I have borne you today in the reflection of my eternal light, in the fullness and brightness of all the saints" (Ps. 2:7; 110:3). He generates him *now* and *today*. Since the maternity bed is in the Godhead, they are "baptized in the Holy Spirit." This is the promise that the Father has made them. "After these days of which there were not many or few," this is the "fullness of the Godhead," in which there was neither day nor night. In it something that is a thousand miles away is as near me as the spot on which I am now standing. There is the fullness and bliss of the whole Godhead; there is the *unity*.

As long as the soul keeps any kind of differentiation, things are not well arranged with it. As long as any kind of thing looks into it, there is no unity as yet. Mary Magdalene sought our Lord in the grave; she sought a dead man and found two living angels. On this account she remained unconsoled. Then the angels said:

"Why are you disturbed? Whom are you seeking, woman?" (Jn. 20:11–12). It was just as if they wanted to say: "You are seeking a dead man and finding two living creatures." Thereupon, she might have said: "My complaint and my concern are precisely that I am finding *two* and was only seeking one!"

As long as any kind of differentiation of created things can still remain in the soul, this is a cause of concern to it. I say now, as I've often said in the past, that wherever the soul has only its natural, created being, there is no truth. I say that there is something *above* the created nature of the soul. Many priests, however, do not understand that there can be something that is so related to and one with God. It has nothing in common with anything else. Everything that is created is nothing. All creation and all that has been created, however, are distant and foreign to it. It is a unit in itself that absorbs nothing from outside itself.

Our Lord went to heaven, high above all light and above all understanding and all comprehension. People who are thus carried above all light dwell in unity. For this reason Saint Paul says: "God dwells in an inaccessible light" (1 Tm. 6:16), which is a pure unity in itself. On this account people must die; they must become completely dead, and nothing to themselves; they must be quite divested of all similarity and no longer resemble anyone. Then they are truly like God. For it is God's peculiarity and nature to be without any equal and to be similar to no one.

May God help us to be thus one in the unity that is God himself! Amen.

COMMENTARY: The Purpose of the Incarnation Explained/Baptism into the Holy Spirit Whose Origins Are a Whirlpool/In the Desert, God and We Become One Divine Person

Eckhart asks in this sermon the reason for the Incarnation. *Why did God become a man?* His answer is not the stock answer that a fall-oriented spiritual theology has dealt the West since Augustine. He does not even mention the erasure of original sin as the reason for the Incarnation. Rather, Eckhart answers the question this way: *So that I might be born the same God.* Christ, the great Reminder, has come to remind us of our divinity, and there lies salvation and healing—at one point he calls Christ a "doctor." Indeed, Eckhart dismisses the popular and superficial theological preaching that says that Christ came to tell us what *is needed on the road to eternal happiness.* Such preachers miss the point —*this is not the truth,* Eckhart declares. The point Eckhart is referring to is the promise in John 15:

> "I shall not call you servants any more,
> because a servant does not know
> his master's business;
> I call you friends,
> because I have made known to you
> everything I have learnt from my Father." (Jn. 15:15)

What is this "everything" that Christ learned from his Father? It is more than moral imperatives and the rules and ways of religion, says Eckhart. What does God wish that God's friends can know but which servants would not know? The fullest revelation is about this: our divinity. *That I might be born the same God.* This is why God bothered to enter human history as one of us: "The reason why he has become man is that he may beget you as his firstborn Son, and nothing less."[1] Eckhart frequently returns to this theme in his sermons. Christ "became the child of a human being in order that we might become the children of God," he declares.[2] "As true as it is that God became a human, so true is it that humans became God."[3]

What is it that Christ has "heard" from his Father and reveals to us? *The depth of divine being and divine nature.* At this depth, generation and birth take place all the time between Father and Son. *The Father can do nothing other than generate while the Son can do nothing other than be born.* The truth of this birthing is the revelation we have received by way of Christ from the Father. *This is what the Son "hears" from the Father; this is what he has made known to us.* What is the purpose of this hearing and this telling? Our divinity as adopted sons. This is why there is revelation through Christ—so that *we may be the same only begotten Son.* "And since this same nature, after which you strive, has become Son of the Eternal Father because he assumed the Eternal Word, you become Son of the Eternal Father with Christ by taking on the same nature which became God and was assumed by Christ."[4]

Being a Son of God means that we are filled with the Spirit in a constant way, irregardless of problems or difficulties. *No one possesses the Spirit unless he or she be the only begotten Son.*

Eckhart applies two psalms from the royal tradition of wisdom literature to those of us who, like Christ, are reborn as sons of God. It is important to remember that these psalms refer to a king who "obtains justice for the weak and the oppressed," as exegete Bernhard Anderson reminds us.[5] Eckhart does not limit the application of the royal personage to Christ alone but to all who are reborn as adopted sons of God. We all become royal persons with the full dignity and responsibility which that title entails.

> Let me proclaim Yahweh's decree;
> he has told me, "You are my son,
> today I have become your father." (Ps. 2:7)

God generates his Son, Eckhart comments, *now and today.* Wherever one is baptized in the Holy Spirit, there the maternity bed of the Godhead is ever active and God's Son is born in us and is being born. The Word is generated eternally and that means *now and today* as well as in the past. Another application is made to our royal lineage that we share with God's Son.

Yahweh's oracle to you, my Lord, "Sit at my right hand
and I will make your enemies a footstool for you" . . .

Royal dignity was yours from the day you were born, on the holy
    mountains,
royal from the womb, from the dawn of your earliest days. (Ps. 110:1, 3)

In Sermon Thirty-six we will examine the royal person tradition in greater depth.

The text for the present sermon which Eckhart has read at the liturgy is that of the opening of the Book of Acts. It is the story of what happened after Jesus' death and of how he had to leave the disciples—his friends —if the Spirit was to come.

> In my earlier work, Theophilus, I dealt with everything Jesus
> had done and taught from the beginning until the day he gave

his instructions to the apostles he had chosen through the Holy Spirit, and was taken up to heaven. He had shown himself alive to them after his Passion by many demonstrations: for forty days he had continued to appear to them and tell them about the kingdom of God. When he had been at table with them, he had told them not to leave Jerusalem, but to wait there for what the Father had promised. "It is," he had said, "what you have heard me speak about: John baptized with water but you, not many days from now, will be baptized with the Holy Spirit." (Ac. 1:1–5)

Who is this Spirit into whom we are to be baptized? This Spirit acts like a magnet, drawing people as a magnet does iron. More than that, the spirit is never satisfied. *It pushes constantly forward . . . it presses on ever further into the vortex or whirlpool which is the primary source in which the spirit has its origin.* Thus the spirit carries us ever and ever deeper into our center, which is a vortex of divine depths. When our spirit meets this Spirit a breakthrough occurs—a mutual piercing. *As he breaks through me, I shall break through him in return!* With this breakthrough a great unity occurs—a unity that can be compared to a desert where there is no room for two but only for one. *God leads this spirit into the desert and solitude of himself where he is pure unity and gushes up only within himself.* The desert is God. At this union in the desert called God the human spirit no longer has a why. Another sign of our being born the Son of God is our living without a why or wherefore. It is a part of the divinity to be without why or wherefore and therefore a part of our divinity and a sign of it.

> It is a property of God that God does all things for himself, that is to say, that he does not look for any "why" outside himself, but only for what is for his own sake. He loves and works all things for his own sake. Therefore, when a person loves him himself and all things and does all his works not for reward, for honor or happiness, but only for the sake of God and his glory, that is a sign that he is a son of God.[6]

We have met our end, and means no longer matter so much. There true *unity and freedom* occur, for the beginning becomes the end, the origin becomes the goal, and no whys need intervene. There too the will becomes like God's will. An *innate freedom* occurs. Eckhart cautions that this freedom is not license but is a freedom that love, which is without a why, brings to *all our deeds*. There, in this desert of unity and freedom and love, we *live in God and God in us*. There all the goodness of creation returns to us and we see all things through the transparency of their being in God. *All that is dead here is life there, and all that is of a material nature here is in God's Spirit there*. The peace of the desert, however, has nothing in common with a flight from the world into a narcissistic lap of tranquillity and quietude. Rather, *discord and restlessness* are themselves part of the desert and absorbed into it. Disturbances ought not to affect this deep unity and freedom. If

> all individuals who remain in freedom and unity within themselves . . . receive God in peace and quiet, they should also receive him in discord and restlessness. For it is completely fitting. If they cling to him less in discord and restlessness than in rest and peace, it is not fitting.

Thus Eckhart leaves us with the strong impression that this breakthrough and baptism in the Spirit is not the final birth we undergo but that there will be many additional labor pains and many more births that follow this one. But the source of it all is our deep, deep vortex or whirlpool where the spirit swims and into which we sink ever deeper as we let go and let birth happen.

The one obstacle that can prevent this sinking into the Spirit is a dualistic consciousness—Mary Magdalene was finding *two* but only *seeking one!* Such distinctions and divisions destroy the unity that the desert experience is all about. Ecstasy does not allow divisions. It is one or nothing. Because Christ came to teach us we are divine, it can rightly be said that "the most suitable good that God ever communicated to humans was to become a human himself."[7]

Sermon Twenty-six: THE HOLY SPIRIT, LIKE A RAPID RIVER, DIVINIZES US

"There is a river whose streams refresh the city of God, and it sanctifies the dwelling of the Most High." (Ps. 46:4)*

"The rapid or quick-flowing river has caused the city of God to rejoice" (Ps. 46:4). We should pay attention to three things in connection with these words. First, the "rapid river" of God; next, the city to which it flows; third, the advantage that comes from this.

Saint John says that from all of those who have a faith enlivened by divine love and who prove it by their good works "living waters will flow" (cf. Jn. 7:38). In this way, he wishes to point to the Holy Spirit. The prophet, however, does not know because of his astonishment what he should call the Holy Spirit because of the Spirit's quick and wonderful deeds. Therefore he calls him an "intoxication" because of his quick emanation, for the Spirit flows just as completely into the soul as the soul empties itself in humility and expands itself to receive him. I am certain of this: if my soul were as ready and if God should find as much space in it as in the soul of our Lord Jesus Christ, he would just as completely fill it with this "river." For the Holy Spirit cannot keep from flowing into every place where he finds *space* and he flows just as extensively as the space he finds there.

Next, we must pay attention to what this "city" is. In a spiritual meaning, it is the soul. A "city" means a *civium unitas* ("a unity of the citizens"). This means a city that is secure on the outside and united within as the "unity of its citizens." So also should the soul be into which God is to flow. On the outside the soul is preserved from encumbrances and on the inside it is united in all its powers. If I look a person in the eye, I see my

* "Fluminis impetus laetificat civitatem Dei: sanctificavit tabernaculum suum Altissimus." (DW III, №81)

image in it. And yet my image is rather in the air than in the eye. It would never be able to come to the eye unless it were previously in the air. Yet we do not see it in the air. Because the air is thin or diaphanous and not solid, no image can appear in it as we can perceive from the rainbow. If the air is solid, then the sun's image appears in manifold colors in the rainbow. If I look into a mirror, my countenance has its reflection there. This would not happen if a layer of lead had not been placed on the glass. So also must the soul be brought together and solidified to the noblest power found within it if the soul is to receive the divine "river" that fills it and causes it to rejoice. Saint John writes that the Apostles were gathered together and enclosed when they received the Holy Spirit.

On occasion I have already said that a beginner—one who is to begin a good life—should pay attention to the following comparison. Whoever wishes to draw a circle is like one who first sets down a foot. Then he or she remains standing while completing the circle with the other foot or with a string. Thus is a circle well made. This has the following meaning: let human beings first learn that their hearts must be constant. Then they will be constant in all their deeds. Whatever great accomplishments they may attain are of no avail if their hearts are inconstant.

There are two kinds of teachers. Some were of the opinion that a *good* person could not be "stirred." They based this idea on many a fine exposition. Others, however, did not agree. They were far more of the opinion that a good person might possibly be stirred, as the Holy Scriptures say. But that person will not be thrown off the track as a result. Our Lord Jesus Christ was often stirred, as were many of his saints. They were not thrown off the track into sin, however. This is what people who are accustomed to traveling by sea have learned. If they wish to sleep, they throw an anchor into the water so that the ship will come to a halt. Of course, they rock up and down on the water, but they do not move off. I have said that a perfect human being cannot easily be hindered. If, however, a person is annoyed about all kinds of things, then he or she is not perfect.

The third factor is the value that comes from the rapid river of the Holy Spirit. As the prophet says, "Our Lord dwells in the

midst of the soul, and therefore it is not altered." The soul wants
only what is purest. In order that God's purity may have effect
within the soul, it can endure no mixture that is crossed with
creatures. God our Lord accomplishes many deeds by himself and
without outside help, but he does many deeds also with outside
help. May the grace that is bound up in my words reach the soul
of my listener without outside intervention in such a way as if
God himself were speaking or working. Then the soul would be
converted at once, and would become holy and unable to withdraw from my words. If *I* speak God's word, then I am a co-
worker with God, and grace is mixed up with a creature, that is,
with myself. And therefore grace will not be *completely* taken up
into the soul. The grace, however, that the *Holy Spirit* brings to
the soul is received in a complete fashion insofar as the soul is
gathered into the simple power that recognizes God, that is, "the
highest reason" and the "spark of the soul." Grace arises from the
Father's heart and flows into the Son. In the union of them both
it flows from the wisdom of the Son into the goodness of the
Holy Spirit, and in this way it is sent with the Holy Spirit into
the soul. And grace is in this way a face of God, that is, of the
Holy Trinity, and it is infused in unmixed form into the soul
with the Holy Spirit and "shapes" the soul according to God.
God accomplishes *this* deed by *himself* without outside mediation. No angel is so noble that he could be of service in this action, nor could any human dignity be of help. Even if out of the
nobility of his nature an angel might want to help, God could
not permit any kind of creature to assist him in this action. For at
this moment he has raised the soul so high above its natural
home that no creature could reach it. And even if an angel might
indeed accomplish this deed and if God might let him be his servant, the soul itself would not allow it, for everything mixed up
with a creature is repugnant to the soul at this moment. Yes,
even the light of grace in which the soul is united to God would
be repugnant to the soul if the soul were not certain and did not
know that it receives *God* in this light. For God leads his bride,
that is, the soul, away from the dignity and nobility of all creatures to a solitary desert and into himself, and he himself speaks
into the soul's heart. This means that he makes the soul equal in

grace to himself. For this noble deed the soul has to gather and close itself up, just as we can recognize through this comparison: The soul gives life to the body in a proper sense without the mediation of the heart and all other members of the body, for, if the soul had to accept the help of the heart in this action, there would have to exist a second heart from which the soul would receive its life. In the same way God accomplishes directly the pure life of grace and goodness in the soul. Just as all the members of the body rejoice in the life of the soul, all the powers of the soul are fulfilled and rejoice as a result of the pure influence of our Lord's grace. For grace has the same relationship to God as light has to the sun and is one with him and brings the soul into the divine light and makes it God-like and causes the soul to "experience" the divine nobility.

Now the soul, which has received the flood of divine grace and has "experienced" the divine nobility, finds bitter and unbearable everything that is not God. On the other hand, the soul strives for the highest of all things so that it cannot endure anything above itself. Indeed, I say at least that it cannot endure even *God* above itself. If the soul has moved so far above all other things to the height of its freedom that it has touched God in his purely divine nature, the soul would never come to rest unless God brought himself into the soul and the soul into God. Even though God is far above the soul in his nobility and his nature, the soul can find no rest until it understands God, insofar as it is possible for a creature to understand God. And therefore the lord Solomon says that stolen water tastes far sweeter than other water. This means that the perfect soul would like to be bound to nothing. It needs to shake itself loose from all things and above all things to attain the divine freedom. For this procures for the soul great happiness.

The third factor that brings the flood of divine grace into the soul is that the soul longs for the greatest of all blessings that the divine nature can accomplish. This is that the divine nature should bring itself forward to the height of the soul and thus accomplish a comparison of the soul with itself, that is, with the divine nature. The greatest blessing in heaven and on earth is based on "equality." What the divine nature accomplishes at the height of the soul, that is, as the "spark of the soul," is "equality." No human beings can follow God completely without having an "equality" with God within themselves. Therefore we should take care whether all the graces human beings have received are divine, whether they "taste of" the divine nobility, and whether they are communicative and emanative, just as God is emanative with his goodness upon everything that in any way can accept him. Thus human beings should be communicative and emanative with all the gifts they have received from God. Saint Paul says, "What is there that we have not received from him?" (cf. 1 Co. 4:7). If human beings have something that they do not bestow on others, they are not good. People who do not bestow on others spiritual things and whatever bliss is in them have never been spiritual. People are not to receive and keep them for themselves alone, but they should share themselves and pour forth everything they possess in their bodies and souls as far as possible, and whatever others desire of them.

Saint Paul says, "It is the highest good that human beings should fortify their hearts through grace" (cf. Heb. 13:9). In these words we should pay attention to three things. First, where should we begin? With the heart. Second, with what should we begin? With grace. And third, why? So that we may remain good. Therefore we should begin with the heart, which is the noblest part of the body. It lies in the center of the body from which point it bestows life on the whole body. For the spring of life arises in the heart and has an effect like heaven. Heaven runs constantly in a circle; therefore it has to be round so that it can run more swiftly in a circle. For it bestows on all creatures their beings and their lives. And if it were to be still for only a second, people might take up fire in their hands and it would not burn them. If heaven were to be still, the waters would not flow, and all creatures would have no strength. Truly, without the soul and without heaven, all creatures would be lost completely, as if they had never been. Heaven does not have this power of itself but rather from an angel who causes it to revolve. As I have also often said, all the "images" and preliminary images or "ideas" of all the creatures were already created in the angels before they were created corporeally in creatures. Therefore an angel pours out his life and his power onto heaven and causes it to revolve constantly and thus accomplishes with heaven all the forms of life and all the strength in creatures. Consider how I pour out into a letter the intention I have in my heart through the work of my hand as I write the letter with my pen. Then I send the letter to another person and let her read it so that in this way the other person knows my intention. In a similar way, by causing heaven to revolve, the angel pours out all the first images of creation which he has received from God into creatures through the power of his will. Heaven is also in the middle of things. It is equally close to all the extremities. So also is the heart within a person quite close, and is active constantly in a circular manner. It beats and stirs itself without interruption. If the heart were to break up or be still for only a second, however, the person would be dead at once. Therefore it happens that if a person is in trouble, he or she grows pale. This comes about because the power of nature and the blood flow from all the members of the body and converge at the heart and wish to remain at the heart. For the spring of life is placed in the heart. On this account the heart is placed in the middle of the body so that if a difficulty should befall the body, it might not reach the heart right away. And if people are afraid that someone may cut or stab them, they place their hands in front of the heart and fear especially for it. It is the same way with grace, which God impresses directly upon the most secret part of the soul. Whatever happens to the body or the soul for the encumbrance of a person, grace is preserved so that we should not lose it. Therefore people should place themselves and everything that is not God in front of grace before they lose the grace on which the life of their eternal bliss depends. So long as people have the determination that nothing should ever be so dear or agreeable to them that they would not gladly do without it before they would be hindered with respect to grace, so long as this situation exists, these people are in perfection. For a *good determination* makes a good person, and a *perfect determination* makes a *perfect* person, and we love everything according to our own goodness. Let whoever wishes to be the best loved of all people be the best of all people. And the better he or she is, all the more will he or she be loved by God.

May God help us to this truth! Amen.

COMMENTARY: Who Is This Holy Spirit Who Divinizes Us?—Eckhart's
Theology of the Holy Spirit/How Grace Shapes the
Soul in God's Image/The Soul Should Stir and Be
Stirred

In the previous sermon Eckhart established that we are divinized and that
is why Christ came to earth. In this sermon he explores more deeply the
meaning of our divinization and the manner in which it comes about. For
*the divine nature . . . accomplishes a comparison of the soul with itself.
And this is the greatest of all blessings that the divine nature can accomplish.* Our divinization is the fullest of God's actions of creation.
What is necessarily implied in our divinization is an equality between us
and God.

> The greatest blessing in heaven and on earth is based on
> "equality." What the divine nature accomplishes at the height
> of the soul, that is, as the "spark of the soul," is "equality." No
> human beings can follow God completely without having an
> "equality" with God within themselves.

But we do have this equality with God—God does it—God *makes the
soul equal in grace to himself.* We become in a certain way equal to
God, though not identical with God, as Eckhart explains elsewhere. "The
soul is changed into God so that the soul becomes divine, but not that
God becomes the soul . . . Then the soul remains in God as God
remains in himself."[1]

How does God bring about such a divine transformation in the human
person? By the Holy Spirit, who is the "Transformer."[2] For "all holiness is
from the Holy Spirit."[3] The Holy Spirit is a *river* which cannot keep from
flowing into every place where he finds space—in other words this river
fills space like water fills an empty hole. The emptier the hole, the more
water is needed to fill it. So too with us, the more in touch with our
spacefulness we are, the fuller the Spirit can fill us. The soul, like a
balloon, can become "blown up beyond its limit."[4] Our divinity knows no
limits. Only the limits we put on it.

The imagery that Eckhart develops about the Spirit as a river is taken
from the scriptural texts he is preaching from. In Psalm 46 we read:

> There is a river whose streams refresh the city of God,
> and it sanctifies the dwelling of the Most High.

> God is inside the city, she can never fall,
> at crack of dawn God helps her;
> to the roaring of nations and tottering of kingdoms,
> when he shouts, the world disintegrates.

> Yahweh Sabaoth is on our side,
> our citadel, the God of Jacob! (Ps. 46:4–7)

First Eckhart discusses the "river" referred to in this passage and later the "city." The river, and water in general, is a symbol for the Spirit. Eckhart finds this same symbol utilized in Saint John's Gospel:

> On the last day and greatest day of the festival, Jesus stood there and cried out:
>> "If any man is thirsty, let him come to me!
>> Let the man come and drink who believes in me!"

> As scripture says: From his breast shall flow fountains of living water.
> He was speaking of the Spirit which those who believed in him were to receive; for there was no Spirit as yet because Jesus had not yet been glorified. (Jn. 7:37–39)

This connection between the flowing of water and the coming of the Spirit is common among the Israelites, who are a desert people. Thus the prophet Isaiah would announce:

> Oh, come to the water all you who are thirsty;
> though you have no money, come!
> Buy corn without money, and eat,
> and, at no cost, wine and milk . . .
> Pay attention, come to me;
> listen, and your soul will live. (Is. 55:1, 3)

The waters of the Spirit that quench the thirsty and especially the poor who are without money will characterize the fullness of time, the Messianic era. Wisdom literature also sings of the fountains of living water:

> Deep waters, such are the words of man:
> a swelling torrent, a fountain of life. (Pr. 18:4)

Living waters will flow, Eckhart comments, repeating the scriptural text, *from all who have faith.* And Eckhart goes on to point out that the waters stand for the Holy Spirit: *In this way he wishes to point to the Holy Spirit.* Just as Christ stood and shouted: "Come to me if you are thirsty," so too all of us who are reborn children of God in our break-through are to shout the same and to be fountains also of the Spirit that is *a rapid or quick-flowing river.*

For Eckhart, the Holy Spirit is the first gift that Christ sends us both by his earthly life and death and by the birth that we undergo as other Christs and Sons of God. "Just as the Son is called a Word, so the Holy Spirit is called a Gift—that's what the Bible calls the Holy Spirit."[5] In commenting on the Samaritan woman who drew water from the well and then was promised by Christ that she would never thirst again (Jn. 4:1–41), Eckhart says: "We read about a woman who received a gift from Christ. The first gift which God gives is the Holy Spirit; in that gift, God gives all of his gifts: That is 'the living water, whomever I give this to will never thirst again.' This water is grace and light and springs up in the soul and rises within and presses upward and leaps up into eter-nity."[6] Eckhart elaborates on how fountain-like this living water is that "springs," "rises," "presses," and "leaps."

The Holy Spirit is sent to us by the Son. That is why the Son had to leave earth before the Spirit would come and that is why we encounter the Spirit when we truly give birth to the Son. "The origin of the Holy Spirit is the Son. If there was no Son there would be no Holy Spirit." Without the Son's birth, there is no Spirit. "The Holy Spirit cannot have his outpouring and his blossoming anywhere else but in the Son. When the Father begets the Son, he gives him everything that he has essentially and by nature. In the act of giving, the Holy Spirit springs forth."[7] When we experience breakthrough and rebirth—our own and God's Son's—the Holy Spirit follows immediately.

> God begets his only begotten Son and in him all those who are God's children and born as sons. In him is the outflow and source of the Holy Spirit, from whom alone, since he is God's Spirit, and God himself is spirit, the Son comes into being in us.[8]

We too are fountains for this same Spirit as Christ was, for we too share his divine Sonship.

According as we are nearer to the One [Godhead], we are all more truly sons of God and the Son and also there flows from us God and the Holy Spirit. This is the meaning of the words spoken by our Lord, God's Son in the Deity: "Whosoever drinks of the water that I shall give, in him a well of water will arise, which springs up to eternal life" (Jn. 4:14) and Saint John (7:39) tells us that he said this of the Holy Spirit.[9]

God is the river behind the river that is the Holy Spirit, the fountain behind the fountain. Our breakthrough and rebirth constitute our being reborn into this fountain of fountains, this source of all sources of water and spirit. "The Son in the Deity gives nothing else than sonship, or being born as God, the fountain, origin, and source of the Holy Spirit." It is because we are God's sons that we can know the Holy Spirit who is love, "for undoubtedly no one loves God sufficiently and purely unless he is God's son. For love, the Holy Spirit, originates in and flows from the Son . . ."[10] The Spirit who is love is an *intoxication* because it can fill the soul that has expanded itself to the full. Like a river, this Spirit works *quick and wonderful deeds as it flows just as completely into the soul as the soul empties itself in humility and expands itself to receive him.* We could be as full of the Spirit as Christ was if we were emptied and expanded enough and therefore ready.

I am certain of this: if my soul were as ready and if God should find as much space in it as in the soul of our Lord Jesus Christ, he would just as completely fill it with this "river."

For the Holy Spirit fills and flows into *every place where he finds space and just as extensively as the space he finds there.* The Spirit, like water, displaces emptiness and looks not for *place* (institutions are places and people who have not let go of objects have only place or objects in them) but for *space.* Space is that experience that those who have let go and let be know so well. It is their own infinity and their own divinity, for God is in space and not in place. And we too, called to divinity, are to prefer space to place.

Eckhart develops his theology of the Holy Spirit as love. "The love by which the Father and the Son love one another is the Holy Spirit itself. They love with the Holy Spirit, as a tree flowers by flourishing and flowers with blossoms."[11]

> We will be loved in the Son by the Father with that love which
> is the Holy Spirit. For the Holy Spirit is the love which has
> sprung up from eternity and blossomed in an eternal birth; this
> is the Trinity's third Person, blossoming from the Son to the Fa-
> ther as their mutual love.[12]

His simile for the Holy Spirit as love is that of fire. "If it were not for this
love, in which God loves the soul, the Holy Spirit would not exist. It is in
the fire and the blossoming forth of the Holy Spirit that the soul loves
God."

As the wind blows, the fire increases in intensity. In this analogy the
Holy Spirit is the wind as well as the fire.

> We should understand love from the simile of the fire and we
> should understand the Holy Spirit from the simile of the wind
> with respect to the activity of the Holy Spirit in the soul. The
> greater love there is in the soul and the more strongly the Holy
> Spirit blows, all the more perfect is the fire.

But the Holy Spirit does not consume us with its loving fire; it works deli-
cately and gradually on us.

> This [fire of the Holy Spirit] occurs not just once but little by
> little for the purpose of the soul's growth. For if people were
> consumed by it, it would not be good. Therefore the Holy
> Spirit blows little by little so that people, even if they should
> live a thousand years, could still grow in love.[13]

The Spirit, then, is ever urging us to expansion and to the fuller heat that
fuller love brings. Once again, as in Sermon Seven, we see how
Eckhart's psychology of spirituality is a psychology of growth and not of
instantaneous conversion. William James indicates that such a spirituality
is one for adults, whereas a spirituality that overemphasizes instantaneous conversions is typically adolescent.[14]

This fire that is the Holy Spirit is the flame behind the "spark of the
soul" which, as we have seen in Sermon Six, constitutes the innermost
part of the person. In the "spark of the soul"

> is hidden something like the original outbreak of all goodness,
> something like a brilliant light which incessantly gleams, and

something like a burning fire which burns incessantly. This fire is nothing other than the Holy Spirit.[15]

In the present sermon Eckhart tells us that *the spark of the soul is the simple power that recognizes God.* Love recognizes love as fire recognizes fire and as spirit recognizes spirit. It is our likeness and equality with God that makes this fire which is the Holy Spirit burn.

> It is God's will that he should give himself completely to us. In the same way, when fire seeks to draw the wood into itself, and to draw itself into the wood again, it finds the wood unlike itself. But all this takes time. First of all, the fire heats the wood, then it smokes and crackles, being unlike the wood, and the hotter the wood becomes the more still and quiet it grows. The more the wood is like the fire, the more peaceful it is until it turns completely into the fire. If the fire is to press the wood into itself, all unlikeness must be at an end.[16]

Schürmann is correct in insisting that Eckhart's "spark of the soul" is *in* a human faculty and is not the faculty itself.[17] The Spirit is in us *firing* us up, *intoxicating* us, and *pressing* us more and more into the divine image that we are.

The Holy Spirit does still another thing for us. It takes us by the hand —"the hand of God is the Holy Spirit"[18]—and takes us on a journey. It is a journey into purity—*the soul wants only what is purest.* However, as we saw in Sermon Nineteen, purity means a return to our origins. And so the Holy Spirit takes us on the journey back to our primal roots and our most divine origins. There we meet the Father and the Son.

> The Holy Spirit receives the soul, the consecrated place, in its clearest and highest form, and carries it up to its origin, that is the Father, into the ground, the beginning, where the Son has his being.[19]

The Holy Spirit is eager to take us to the source of its own fountainhead.

> The Holy Spirit draws the soul up and lifts it up with itself and if the soul were ready, the Holy Spirit would take it to the source from which it has flowed . . . The Holy Spirit brings the soul to that eternal image from which it has flowed out,

that model in accord with which the Father has made everything, that picture in which all things are one, the breadth and
the depth in which all things attain their end.[20]

Thus the Holy Spirit leads us into the Godhead and into the depths of
the panentheistic origins of all creation. The Holy Spirit is our guide, one
might say, from Path Three—our birth—back to Path One—our origins.
This journey is itself a gift of the Spirit—"it is truly a great gift that the
soul is so led by the Holy Spirit."

> When the soul is secure in God, then it will be led by the Holy
> Spirit into that image and united with it. And with the image
> and with the Holy Spirit it will be led through and into the
> source. There where the Son is imaged the soul will be imaged
> too. The soul which is so led in and hidden and enclosed is in
> God and all creatures are subject to it.[21]

Thus, while Christ is the great reminder of our divinity and the *imago Dei*
deep within us, the Holy Spirit is the guide who takes us into that image
and accompanies us on our journey to our source. Once there, we see
all creatures in their oneness with the Godhead, where they swim in a
panentheistic sea of divine grace.
    The Holy Spirit is accomplished by grace. Grace "carries the Holy
Spirit on its back."

> Grace comes with the Holy Spirit. It carries the Holy Spirit on
> its back. Grace is not a stationary thing; it is always found in a
> becoming. It can flow out of God and then only immediately.
> The function of grace is to transform and reconvey the soul to
> God. Grace makes the soul God-like.[22]

The Holy Spirit is uncreated grace, it is essentially "the uncreated act" of
God. Grace, like the Holy Spirit, *flows* like a river. *Grace arises* from the
Father's heart and flows into the Son. In the union of them both it flows
from the wisdom of the Son into the goodness of the Holy Spirit, and in
this way it is sent with the Holy Spirit into the soul. Grace is what *God
impresses directly upon the most secret part of the soul.* It is to our soul
what the heart is to the body and ought to be protected as our life
source just as we cover the heart when attacked. It is this grace that
shapes the soul according to the image of God. Grace makes the soul

equal to God and therefore God is pleased to lead the soul *to a solitary desert and into himself* where *he speaks into the soul's heart.* Grace is the source of our joy—all the powers of the soul are fulfilled and rejoice as a result of the pure influence of our Lord's grace. What grace is to God, light is to the sun. An equation might look like this:

$$\frac{grace}{God} = \frac{light}{sun}$$

The soul is rendered *God-like* or divine by grace and thus *experiences the divine nobility.* Grace is not dispensed minimally or parsimoniously— the river that is the Holy Spirit is a bountiful and deep river—one that creates a *flood of divine grace.* This flood culminates in a freedom that is a *divine freedom* and an experience of *great happiness* and divine joy. For, having entered our divine origins and seen the inness from within, nothing can disturb such joy, indeed, grace *is* this very dwelling in God. "Grace is the indwelling of the soul in God" Eckhart remarks.[28] Notice that he has not said that grace is God in us but that it is us in God. He resists the overly introspective theology of grace that has often held hegemony in Western Christian theology. His doctrine on grace is as consistently panentheistic as his doctrine on God. Our graced existence is a graced inness.

The text for Eckhart's sermon says that the river refreshes the city of God. How does Eckhart understand the word "city" in this text? *In a spiritual meaning it is the soul,* he says. Such a city or soul ought to be *secure on the outside and united within* if God is to flow there. To receive the Holy Spirit an individual must imitate the Apostles, who *were gathered together and enclosed* when the Spirit came to them at Pentecost. How is this personal gathering together and enclosure accomplished? By developing a constant and steady attitude toward things. *Let human beings first learn that their hearts must be constant. Then they will be constant in all their deeds.* In other words, we must be capable of letting go and letting be, whether it be pleasure or pain that we are interacting with.

But does constancy of heart mean stoicism? Does it mean never feeling deeply, never being powerfully moved, never yielding to ecstasy? Some, says Eckhart, teach exactly that. But he, looking at the biblical examples, teaches just the opposite. *A good person* might possibly be stirred, for this is what *the Holy Scripture holds.* He gives Jesus and the saints as examples. *Our Lord Jesus Christ was often stirred, as were many of the saints. They were not thrown off the track into sin, however.* What is his advice on reconciling the dialectical tension between constancy and ecstasy, constancy and being stirred? *Anchor yourself,* he says. That is how one prevents being *annoyed about all kinds of things.*

> This is what people who are accustomed to traveling by sea have learned. If they wish to sleep, they throw an anchor into the water so that the ship will come to a halt. Of course, they rock up and down on the water, but they do not move off.

We may rock about a bit, but our steadfastness will not move far off. In this advice, Eckhart—and he sees this himself—is being Jewish and biblical rather than either Stoic or Neoplatonic. He is not advocating a flight from passion and being stirred but rather an anchoring. In a similar opinion Rabbi Heschel has written that the biblical person is a fiery person, one who is profoundly stirred, and one whose ideal is not in ascetic detachment or emotional coolness (cf. Sermon Nineteen).

Of all the blessings that the soul longs for, the greatest is our being divinized and thus made equal to God. *What the divine nature accomplishes at the height of the soul, that is, at the "spark of the soul," is "equality."* Since this grace is accomplished by God and the Holy Spirit, who is a *rapid river,* we should take the advice from the Letter to the Hebrews and not multiply our tactical ecstasies or ascetic practices.

> Remember your leaders, who preached the word of God to you, and as you reflect on the outcome of their lives, imitate their faith. Jesus Christ is the same today as he was yesterday and as he will be forever. Do not let yourselves be led astray by all sorts of strange doctrines: it is better to rely on grace for inner strength than on dietary laws which have done no good to those who kept them. (Heb. 13:7–9)

Our inner strength, Eckhart is counseling, itself comes from grace and not from a multiplication of religious practices. *Begin with the heart,* he advises, for that is where grace most touches us. *It bestows life on the whole body. For the spring of life arises in the heart and has an effect like heaven.*

One reason why Eckhart is in favor of our hearts and souls being stirred while they retain an inner constancy is that he believes that "all deeds are accomplished in passion" (see Sermon Nineteen). And Eckhart insists that all gifts and all graces are for others and that our deeds need to go out to others. Indeed, those graces that are not capable of flowing out to others are not truly divine graces. For to *"taste of" the divine nobility*, gifts need to be communicative and emanative, just as God is emanative with his goodness upon everything that in any way can accept him. Thus human beings should be communicative and emanative with all the gifts they have received from God. In this way we become *co-workers with God*. For Eckhart, such flowing out or such creativity and extrovert meditation is absolutely essential to the good person.

> Saint Paul says, "What is there that we have not received from him?" (cf. 1 Co. 4:7). If human beings have something that they do not bestow on others, they are not good. People who do not bestow on others spiritual things and whatever bliss is in them have never been spiritual. People are not to receive and keep them for themselves alone, but they should share themselves and put everything they possess in their bodies and souls as far as possible, and whatever others desire of them.

This is strong language, aimed at any temptations to spiritual narcissism. For Eckhart, divinity that does not imitate the Divinity and therefore *pour forth everything* good that one has received is a lie and a deception. Such overly introvert attitudes actually expose people who *have never been spiritual*. Thus the sharing and pouring forth and communicating of goodness is a criterion Eckhart employs to test the spirits of persons. When one *pours forth* all and *bestows* on others, then heaven begins to happen. Heaven is not apart from things or cut off from things. In fact, *heaven is in the middle of things. It is equally close to all the extremities.* This is a perfectly dialectical existence—to be in the middle of things, anchored there, and equally close (not equally distant) to all the extremities. This is being alive and being heavenly. It is living realized eschatology. It is living as if the last days did indeed already begin. It is loving everything that happens to us, since we are anchored in love, for *we love everything according to our own goodness.* Our very love of things and events becomes a mirror and a revelation of our own goodness. For there is only one Spirit and that Spirit, a rapidly running river, flows where it wills. And where it wills is everywhere. In our letting go and letting the river be the river, we then become the river that *pours forth itself* to others. We too, who wear grace which is *the face of God*, will carry on God's works, all of which are a rapidly flowing river of goodness made refreshing at their primal source.

Sermon Twenty-seven: HOW ALL CREATURES EXPERIENCE THE DIVINE REPOSE

"In all things I sought rest." (Si. 24:11)*

These words are written in the book of wisdom. We wish at this time to explain them as if the eternal wisdom were conducting a dialogue with the soul, saying: "I have sought repose in all things" (Si. 24:11). And the soul replies: "He who created me has rested in my tent" (Si. 24:12). Next the eternal wisdom says: "My repose is in the holy city" (Si. 24:15).

If I were asked to give valid information concerning what the Creator's aims were when he created all creatures, I would say: "Repose." If I were asked for the second time what the Holy Trinity was seeking in all its deeds, I would answer: "Repose." If I were asked for the third time what the soul was seeking in all its motions, I would answer: "Repose." If I were asked for the fourth time what all creatures were seeking in all their natural efforts and motions, I would answer: "Repose."

First, we should understand and know how the divine countenance, by its divine nature, maddens and drives all souls out of their senses with longing for it so as to draw them to itself. For God enjoys the divine nature, which is repose, so much, and repose is so pleasing to him that he has placed it outside himself in order to attract the longing of all creatures and to draw them to himself. Not only is the Creator seeking his own repose in that he has placed it outside himself and formed it for all creatures, but at the same time he is seeking to draw all creatures with him back again to their origin, which is repose. Moreover, God loves himself in all creatures. Just as he is seeking love for himself in all creatures, he is seeking also his own repose in them.

Second, the Holy Trinity is seeking repose. The Father seeks

* "In omnibus requiem quaesivi." (DW III, ※60)

repose in his Son in that he has poured out all creatures in him and "formed" them in him. Both seek repose in the Holy Spirit because he has proceeded from both of them as an eternal immeasurable love.

Third, the soul seeks repose in all its powers and motions, whether people know this or not. People never open or shut their eyes without seeking repose. Either they will cast something away from them that hinders them or they will draw something to themselves in which they will rest. People do all their deeds for the sake of these two things. I have also said that people can never feel joy or pleasure in any creature if God's likeness is not within it. I love the thing in which I most recognize God's likeness. But nothing resembles God in all creatures so much as repose.

Concerning this third point, we should know how the soul should be in which God wishes to rest. It should be pure. In what way does the soul become pure? By clinging to spiritual things. By being raised up. The higher it is raised up, the purer it will become in its devotion. The purer its devotion is, the more powerful its deeds will be. In consideration of this, an astronomer says: "The nearer the stars shine to the earth, the weaker are they in their effect because they are not in their proper situation. If, however, they reach their proper situation, they are at their highest point. Then, however, they cannot be seen on earth, and yet their effect on earth is most powerful." Saint Anselm says to the soul: "Withdraw a little from the commotion of external deeds. Second, flee, and conceal yourself before the storm of thoughts that also bring great unrest to the soul. Third, people can request nothing more precious than repose." God neither heeds nor needs vigils, fasting, prayer, and all forms of mortification in contrast to repose. God needs nothing more than for us to offer him a quiet heart. Then he accomplishes in the soul such secret and divine deeds that no creature can serve them or even add to them. Indeed, not even the soul of our Lord Jesus Christ can gaze into that place. The eternal wisdom is of such delicate tenderness and so shy that it cannot allow any kind of an admixture of any creature to be in the place where God alone has effect in the soul. For this reason the eternal wisdom cannot allow any creature to gaze into that place. On this account our Lord says:

"I shall lead my bride out into the desert and shall speak there into her heart" (Ho. 2:14). This means in the wilderness, away from all creatures.

Fourth, Anselm says that the soul should rest in God. God cannot accomplish divine deeds in the soul so long as "everything that enters the soul is surrounded by measure." But measure is what excludes or includes something in itself. This is not how it is with divine deeds, however. They are unlimited, and unreservedly determined in divine revelation. On this account David says: "God is enthroned above the cherubim" (Ps. 80:1). He does not say that he is enthroned above the seraphim. The word "cherubim" means wisdom, which is knowledge. This is what takes God into the soul and leads the soul to God. But it cannot bring the soul into God. For this reason God does not accomplish his divine deeds in knowledge because knowledge is surrounded by measure. He accomplishes them much more as God in a divine way. But then, after knowledge has conducted the soul to God, the highest power comes forward—this is love—and penetrates God and leads the soul with knowledge and with all its other powers into God, and is united with God. God has effect there above the powers of the soul, not in the soul—that is, not in the realm of the soul—but in a divine way as God. The soul is there submerged in God and baptized in the divine nature. It receives there a divine life and takes on the divine order so that it is ordered according to God.

We can learn from a comparison. The masters of the natural sciences write that as soon as a child is conceived in the womb, it has the formation and appearance of the limbs. When the soul is infused into the body, however, the form and sensation that the child had at first yield, and the child becomes something unique. Through the power of the soul it receives another form from the soul as well as a new appearance that is proportionate to the life of the soul. This also takes place with the soul. When it is completely united with God and baptized in the divine nature, it loses all its hindrances and weakness and inconstancy, and is completely renewed in the divine life. It is ordered in all its habits in the same way we can recognize from the light. The nearer a flame burns to the wick, the blacker and coarser it will be, while the higher a flame blows above the wick, the clearer it will be. The higher a soul is carried above itself, the purer and clearer it will be, and all the more completely can God accomplish his divine deed in it within his own likeness. If a mountain were to rise up two miles high above the earth, and if we were to write upon it letters in dust or sand, the letters would remain entirely, so that neither rain nor wind could destroy them. Similarly, truly spiritual people should be raised up—completely and unchangeably in the divine deeds—in the right kind of peace. Spiritual people can well feel ashamed because they are so easily subject to a change of behavior to grief, anger, and annoyance. Such people have not yet become spiritual to the proper degree.

Fourth, all creatures seek repose from their efforts, whether they know it or not. They prove this through their deeds. A stone will never be deprived of its drive to fall constantly to the earth so long as it is not right on the earth. Fire acts in the same way, it strives to rise, and every creature seeks its own place according to its nature. In this they reveal similarity with the divine repose that God has allotted to all creatures.

May God help us to seek the divine similarity of divine repose and to find it in God! Amen.

COMMENTARY: The Panentheistic Pleasure Called Repose/How the Creator Seeks Repose and the Trinity Seeks Repose/ How the Soul That Has Broken Through into God Experiences Repose/How Repose Is the Law of Pleasure for All Creatures

In the previous sermon Meister Eckhart spoke of grace as the "face of God." He said: Grace is "a face of God, that is, of the Holy Trinity, and it is infused in unmixed form into the soul with the Holy Spirit and 'shapes' the soul according to God." In the present sermon he elaborates on this shaping process that takes place before the face of God. What does the face of God do to the soul? It drives it and draws it to itself. *The divine countenance, by its divine nature, maddens and drives all souls out of their senses with longing for it so as to draw them to itself.* Coming face to face with God by grace, all souls are driven mad by the divine beauty and the taste of one's own divine nature. But what is this divine nature to which we are so madly driven? *The divine nature . . . is repose.*

Eckhart derives his appreciation of the divine love of repose from wisdom literature, where, in the Book of Ecclesiasticus, we read:

"I came forth from the mouth of the Most High,
    and I covered the earth like mist.
I had my tent in the heights,
    and my throne in a pillar of cloud . . .
Over the waves of the sea and over the whole earth,
    and over every people and nation I have held sway.
Among all these I searched for rest,
    and looked to see in whose territory I might pitch camp.
Then the creator of all things instructed me,
    and he who created me fixed a place for my tent.
He said, "Pitch your tent in Jacob,
    make Israel your inheritance."
From eternity, in the beginning, he created me,
    and for eternity I shall remain.
I ministered before him in the holy tabernacle,
    and thus was I established on Zion.
In the beloved city he has given me rest,
    and in Jerusalem I wield my authority.
I have taken root in a privileged people,
    in the Lord's property, in his inheritance . . .
I am like a vine putting out graceful shoots,
    my blossoms bear the fruit of glory and wealth." (Si. 24:3–4, 6–12, 17)

For Eckhart, *eternal wisdom* dialogues with the soul about repose and promises repose because eternal wisdom promises a return to our origins. But our origins are divine and *the divine nature is repose.* God the Creator is *seeking to draw all creatures with him back again to their origin, which is repose.* As we saw in Sermon Nineteen, purity is the search for one's origins and so a soul in search of repose is a pure soul. *We should know how the soul should be in which God wishes to rest. It should be pure.*

The creature is by no means alone in seeking repose. Repose is a divine activity and an activity of enjoyment: *God enjoys the divine nature,* which is repose. And God *the Creator*, one might say, depends on creatures to repose in, to "pitch his tent in." That is why he has *placed repose outside himself* as a kind of antechamber to beckon creatures in to what is ultimately the divine repose itself. Repose is the form and "shape" of the divine countenance, remade for creatures to share and delight in. In that divine tent God finds pleasure. *God loves himself in all creatures. Just as he is seeking love for himself in all creatures, he is seeking also his own repose in them.* There, in this tent of union between God and the soul, the "greatest of all blessings" (Sermon Twenty-six) is bestowed, the divine nature itself is shared. And there, too, the divine repose is also shared, for that is the divine nature.

The rest promised the soul is the rest of being in God and of God being in it. It is the rest, therefore, of panentheism—a panentheistic repose. "The soul would never come to rest unless God brought himself into the soul and the soul into God."[1] *The soul should rest in God*, we are told. But how is this done? It is not done by a multiplication of tactical ecstasies. *God neither needs nor needs vigils, fasting, prayer, and all forms of mortification.* What is it that God needs to accomplish the divine nature which is repose? *God needs nothing more than for us to offer him a quiet heart.* An existence of letting go and letting be, a place *in the wilderness away from all creatures* even if in the midst of them— that is the only preparation this *delicate, tender,* and *shy* eternal wisdom requires. Take the eye, for example. When the eye is shut it is for the sake of repose, but when it is open, it also reposes in the light and color that come to it. Therefore it can be said that *people never open or shut their eyes without seeking repose.* There is a dual dynamic to all living— open/shut, in/out—and *people do all their deeds for the sake of these two things.* Yet the goal of each, open-and-in or shut-and-out, is repose. *People will either cast something away from them that hinders them or they will draw something to themselves in which they will rest.* When we throw a hindrance off, it is for the sake of repose; when we draw something lovable near, it is for the sake of repose. This is the law of all creatures. It is the dialectical law of pleasure. Everything creatures do is for the sake of pleasure, which is repose. Even the law of gravity is a law of pleasure and repose.

> All creatures seek repose from their efforts, whether they know
> it or not. They prove this through their deeds. A stone will
> never be deprived of its drive to fall constantly to the earth so

long as it is not right on the earth. Fire acts in the same way, it
strives to rise, and every creature seeks its own place according to its nature.

This quest for repose, omnipresent in creation, is a divine likeness in
all things. Pleasure is a divine likeness in all things. *People can never feel
joy or pleasure in any creature if God's likeness is not within it.* The
greater repose and pleasure a creature extends to us, the more we love
it. *I love the thing in which I most recognize God's likeness.* But beyond
all the beauties of God found in creation, *nothing resembles God so
much as repose.* It is because the divine pleasure and the divine repose
are so intimate to all creatures that elaborate tactical ecstasies are a
distraction to true spiritual living. If we only let go and let be we shall
sink into the divine repose that is everywhere present.

Nor can we find true divine repose through knowledge and reason itself. For knowledge *takes God into the soul and leads the soul to God,
but it cannot bring the soul into God.* Knowledge does not bring about
the breakthrough that is our entrance *into* God. Therefore it does not
lead us *into* repose. Repose is a gift of panentheistic breakthrough and
rebirth. It is a gift that accompanies our divinization. The breakthrough is
a divine way of knowing. *God does not accomplish his divine deeds in
knowledge . . . he accomplishes them much as God in a divine way.* It
is accomplished in a new birth, a breakthrough and a baptism into God.
*When it is completely united with God and baptized in the divine nature,
it loses all its hindrances and weakness and inconstancy, and is completely renewed in the divine life.* Once again Eckhart links breakthrough
to baptism, but the baptism he speaks of is a baptism into the Holy
Spirit's river of divinization, a baptism of fire, a baptism of metanoia and
renewed life, a baptism that breaks through life as well as death. A baptism into God, into the panentheistic ocean. There God affects us *in a
divine way as God* and there we swim in the divine sea, *submerged in
God and baptized in the divine nature.* There we become divinized and
like the Creator who creates harmony from all watery chaos. The soul
receives there a divine life and takes on the divine order so that it is ordered according to God. Truly, a new creation emerges.

Like any birth, it takes place in water, our oceanic origin, in a womb.
And there is an evolution of growth in our constancy, our maturity, our
capacity to let go and let be in order to remain deeply in God and in
the repose and peace of God, even when confronted with *grief, anger,*

and annoyance. Indeed, until our repose can endure such troubles, and in the midst of activity, we have not yet developed, spiritually speaking. We are still fetuses clinging to the womb. For the repose that Eckhart speaks of is not a repose in competition with activity nor is it a flight from activity. It is rather a repose in the midst of activity (see Sermon Thirty-four) and, indeed, in the midst of the most strenuous activity. Such repose becomes a source of strength for the most God-like of activities —creativity. The more in touch with our origin we are, *the more powerful [our] deeds will be.* These *powerful deeds* of creativity imitate the divine deeds, and *divine deeds are unlimited.* If we are divinized, so must our works be divinized. We shall do the works of the Father. Our works, like the Son's works, will imitate those of the Father. They will be creative and they will be compassionate, as we will see in Sermon Thirty-one, for they will flow from that one womb, that ocean, that is the origin of divine repose and divine birthing. For that which is in God is God.

Sermon Twenty-eight: WHERE THE SOUL IS, THERE IS
GOD

"God is love, and anyone who lives in love lives in God, and
God in him." (1 Jn. 4:16)*

God lives in the soul with everything that he and all creatures
are. Therefore, where the soul is, there God is, for the soul is in
God. Therefore the soul is also where God is unless the Scripture
lies. Where my soul is, there is God, and where God is, there my
soul is also. And this is as true as God is God.

An angel is so noble in his nature that, if a tiny fragment or a
little spark were to fall from him, it would fill this whole world
with rapture and bliss. Now listen attentively to how noble an
angel is in his nature, and there are, God knows, so many of them
that they are countless. I say that everything is aristocratic in an
angel. If a human being had to serve until Judgment Day and the
end of the world in order to see an angel in all his purity, such a
service would have been well rewarded.

With all spiritual things we find that one of them can place itself as undivided inside another. Where the soul is in the purity
of its nature, separated from and freed of all creatures, the soul
has in its nature and through its nature all the perfection and all
the joy and all the rapture that all the angels have, in both quantity and number, through their nature. I have these qualities,
whole and entire, with all their perfection and all their joy and all
their bliss just as the angels have them. And I have distinguished
every angel in myself, just as I have distinguished myself in myself, without the encumbrance of any other creature. For no spirit
hinders another spirit. The angel remains unencumbered in his
soul. Therefore he surrenders himself to every soul completely,
unencumbered by another soul and by God himself. My soul re-

* "Gott ist die Liebe . . ." (DW III, ☀67)

joices not only through its nature but also beyond its nature in all the joy and all the bliss in which God himself rejoices through his divine nature, whether happily or unhappily. For only one thing is important there, and where this one thing is, I have everything. Where I have everything there is only one thing. This truth is certain. Where the soul is, God is, and where God is, the soul is also. And if I were to say that it is not so with God, I would be speaking incorrectly.

Truly now, pay attention to a little message I consider very much to the point. I am reflecting on how God is one with me as if he has forgotten all other creatures and as if nothing else existed besides myself. Now make entreaties for those who have been given into my charge! Those who ask for something other than God alone or for God's sake are asking wrongly. If I ask for nothing, I am asking for what is right, and such a prayer is appropriate and powerful. Whoever asks for anything else is praying to an idol, and we might say that this is pure heresy. I ask for nothing so rightly as when I ask for nothing and for no one—not for Tom, Dick, or Harry. The true men and women of prayer are those who pray to God in truth and in the Spirit, that is, in the Holy Spirit.

What God is in his power, we are also in the divine image that is in our soul. What the Father is in his power [*potestas*] and the Son in his wisdom [*sapientia*] and the Holy Spirit in his goodness [*bonitas*], this is what we are in the "image in our souls." "There we shall know, as we are known," and we shall love as we are loved. This knowing and being known, this loving and being loved in the "image" of the Trinity in our soul is, however, still not without action. For the soul is preserved in this way in the threefold "image" and functions in the divine power just like that power. The soul is taken up into the divine *Persons* and conducts itself in accord with the power of the Father, and the wisdom of the Son, and the goodness of the Holy Spirit. Above all this, no being is more efficacious. But *there*, in the threefold "image" of the soul, there is only being *and* action. Where the soul is, however, in the single, onefold *God* in contrast to the threefold Godhead—indeed, in accord with the complete absorption of the Persons into the pure, divine Being—there action and being are one. This is where God is. It is where the soul has taken hold of the Persons in the being that is in God. It is where the Persons have never emerged, and where a perfect image of the essence and the nature of God is found. This is the essential intelligence of God: the pure and unadulterated power of the intellect [*intellectus*] which the masters of the spiritual life call "receptivity."

Now listen to me! Only above what I have sought to characterize so far does the soul understand the pure "absoluteness" of a free being, which is without a place where it either receives or gives. It is rather a pure existence that is deprived of all being and all existence. There God grasps the soul strictly according to his divine existence where he is above all other being. If there still existed a soul in its being, this soul would receive its being in the absolute being. For there is nothing else there but *one* absolute existence. This is the highest perfection of the *spirit* to which we can attain in this earthly life in a *spiritual* way, that is, without the body. But this purely spiritual comprehension of God in our earthly life is *not* the highest perfection that we shall possess in the hereafter with our body and soul in such a way that our bodily person will be completely possessed by the personal being that is God. In the same way, humanity and divinity are *one* personal being in the person of Christ. In the same act of being possessed by God I am completely my own person by denying my personal understanding of self according to which in a *spiritual* way I am a unit according to the essence of my soul, just as the divine essence is *one* essence. And thus I remain the same person according to my bodily being, which is totally deprived of my *own* basis of support.

This personal union of God and humanity grows and hovers completely above the bodily individual, so that the latter can never reach it. Relying on himself or herself, the individual receives indeed from his or her person sweetness, consolation, and spiritual depth in various ways, which is a good experience. It is, however, not the highest experience. If the bodily individual were to remain thus within himself or herself, unsupported by God, the spiritual individual would have to turn aside from the essence in which he or she is one with the divine essence, even though he or she might receive consolation from grace and the cooperation of grace. But this is still not the highest experience. And the spiritual individual would have to conduct himself or herself according to the being full of grace by which he or she is bound. *On this account* the *spirit* can never become perfect unless body *and* soul are perfect. Just as the spiritual individual falls away from his or her *own* being in a *spiritual* way if he or she becomes *one* essence with the divine essence, in the same way the bodily individual would have to be deprived of his or her *own* substance in order to be completely of one substance with the eternal being—God—who is a person in himself.

Now there are in this connection two kinds of being. One being according to divinity is the pure essence of Christ. The other is the *personal* being of Christ. Yet both are one and the same *substance* or personality. Since the same substance of Christ's personality as the bearer of Christ's eternal humanity is also the substance of our soul, and since Christ is *one* in himself and in his personal substance, *we* must also be the same Christ, imitating him in his actions just as in his being he is one Christ in his humanity. For since I am the same type as Christ according to my humanity, I am so united to Christ's *personal* being that I am through grace one with Christ in his person and I remain also my own person. Since Christ is eternally present in the essence of the Father and since I am in him as *one* essence and as the same Christ who is a bearer of my own humanity, both my humanity and Christ's humanity *are* in *one* substance of the eternal being. Thus both beings—the being of the body *and* of the soul—are made perfect in the *one* Christ as *one* God and *one* Son.

May the Holy Trinity help us to experience all this! Amen.

COMMENTARY: Our Inness with God Is a Oneness with God/How All Saintly Beings Who Share This Inness Celebrate Together/Where Action and Being Become One/The Union of Humanity and Divinity That Christ Demonstrates to Us Who Are Other Christs

Eckhart explores more deeply what our inness with God is about in this sermon, which is based on the following passage from John's First Epistle:

We can know that we are living in him
and he is living in us

because he lets us share his Spirit.
We ourselves saw and we testify
that the Father sent his Son
as saviour of the world.
If anyone acknowledges that Jesus is the Son of God,
God lives in him, and he in God.
We ourselves have known and put our faith in
God's love toward ourselves.
God is love
and anyone who lives in love lives in God,
and God lives in him.
Love will come to its perfection in us
when we can face the day of Judgment without fear;
because even in this world
we have become as he is. (1 Jn. 4:13–17)

What does it mean to say that we "live in God" and that in this world
we "have become as he is"? These are questions that Eckhart pursues in
this sermon. The first thing it means, according to Eckhart, is what it says.
God is utterly transparent and because *no spirit hinders another spirit* we
can be in God and God in us at the same time. This union is so real
that, *unless the Scripture lies*, we must say that *where the soul is, there
God is. Where my soul is, there is God, and where God is, there my
soul is also.* So taken was Eckhart with this description that he repeats it
in this same sermon: *This truth is certain. Where the soul is, God is, and
where God is, the soul is also.* He repeats an almost identical saying in
another sermon when he says: "Where I am, God is; thus I am in God,
and where God is, I am there . . . Wherever I am, there is God. This is
the pure truth and is as truly true as God is God."[1] He repeats the same
formula on another occasion: "Wherever God is, the soul is, and wherever the soul is, God is."[2]

What is so clear in these statements and what is so significant to
Eckhart is their panentheistic implications. He destroys and insists on destroying all subject/object thinking about God and us. God is not out
there, above here, below here, or far from here. Very simply, where we
are, God is; where God is, we are. So transparent is our unity with God
that Eckhart says "the eye in which I see God is the same eye in which
God sees me. My eye and God's eye are one eye and one seeing and
one knowing and one loving."[3] Our oneness with God is very real and

very transparent, as in the seeing that eyes do. In this sense he can say that "our truest I is God."[4] He also suggests that our ears are God's ears and vice versa when he talks of our being the Word of God. We can

> dwell in eternity, and dwell in the spirit, and dwell in unity, and in the desert, and there [we] hear the eternal Word . . . In the eternal Word, that which hears is the same as that which is heard. All that the eternal Father teaches is his being and his nature and all his Godhead. He reveals this fully to us in his only begotten Son, and he teaches us that we are the same Son.[5]

Indeed, we have "become as he is" in this indescribable unity. Eckhart searches for metaphors for this unity—it is one that makes God forget all but us: *I am reflecting on how God is one with me as if he has forgotten all other creatures and as if nothing else existed besides myself. It is the highest spiritual experience to be one with God in this way*, though after death we will be completely possessed by the personal being that is God. In this unity we apprehend "God in his wilderness and in his own ground." Such a union is the greatest union there is, save for that of the Three Persons in God.[6] It is greater than that of body with soul. "The soul is much more closely united with God than body and soul, which form one person. This union is much closer than that of a drop of water poured into a barrel of wine. It would be water and wine, yet they would be so transformed into one that no creature could discover the difference."[7] Such a union is a divine touch received and given. The soul "receives a kiss from the Godhead" and

> is embraced by unity. In the first touch with which God touched the soul and still touches it as uncreated and uncreatable, the soul is as noble as God himself is, as a result of God's touch. God touches it as he does himself.[8]

Immersed in the divine inness, we are embraced and touched and kissed by unity itself. Indeed, "it is for this very union that God made human beings."[9]

One result of this union between God and us is a kind of divine joy and celebration. For where the Father begets the Son, joy reigns.

> God speaks into the soul and expresses himself completely in
> the soul. There the Father begets his Son and he has such
> great joy in the Word and has, moreover, such great bliss that
> he never ceases to speak eternally the Word that is beyond
> time.[10]

The Word spoken and begotten is a Word of joy, divine joy. We celebrate and share the divine joy that is ours too in our adopted divinity.
*My soul rejoices not only through its nature but also beyond its nature in
all the joy and all the bliss in which God himself rejoices through his divine nature, whether happily or unhappily. We rejoice because only one
thing is important, and we have that one thing. Where I have everything
there is only one thing . . . Where the soul is, God is, and where God
is, the soul is also.* Nor is our joy limited to the divine joy in God. It extends to the divine joy that embraces all creatures, angels included. *Just
a tiny spark from an angel's being could fill this whole world with rapture and bliss.* And yet we can participate with such beings not by tiny
sparks alone but by our shared inness in God and in one another. In
such a communion of saintly beings, *the soul has in its nature and
through its nature all the perfection and all the joy and all the rapture
that all the angels have, in both quantity and number, through their nature.* This communion of saints is a communion of shared perfection and
shared joy. *I have all these qualities, whole and entire, with all their perfection and all their joy and all their bliss just as the angels have them.*
   When we are in God and *the divine image that is in our soul* is allowed to become what it is, then we share the qualities of the Persons of
God. We share the power of the Father, the wisdom of the Son, and the
goodness of the Holy Spirit. Indeed, *this is what we are in the "image in
our souls."* We become the Trinity in action, ushering power, wisdom,
and goodness into human history. Indeed, it is absolutely essential to
Eckhart's theology that this Trinitarian union bear fruit in action. In this
instance Eckhart alludes to Paul's hymn of charity, where he insists that
without love all other gifts are void. Eckhart refers to the conclusion of
that hymn when he says, *"there we shall know, as we are known,"* and
we shall love as we are loved. Paul had written: "The knowledge that I
have now is imperfect; but then I shall know as fully as I am known" (1
Co. 13:12). Eckhart elaborates, much in the spirit of Paul's hymn to charity: *This knowing and being known, this loving and being loved in the
"image" of the Trinity in our soul is, however still, not without action.*

Why must action be so integral a part of our union with the Divinity? Because it is so integral a part of Divinity! Divinity is not just being, it is being diffusing itself, it is power, wisdom, and goodness pouring forth on the world. *There action and being are one.* And so, where the soul is, *there is only being and action. This is where God is*—where action and being are one. Eckhart is calling for a revitalized form of action, one that truly flows from our being; but he insists that being without action is not true divine being. If we are "to be as he is," our action and our being must become one. Action is the key to Eckhart's mysticism—so long as it is action that flows from our being. This distinguishes his mysticism from many species of quietistic spiritualities that have held sway in the West since his day. Indeed, Eckhart takes it for granted that action is part of being in God. "The soul dissolved into God and God into the soul. And whatever the soul *then* does it does in God."[11] The issue is not to stop acting, but to make sure that our actions, like our being, are in God. Our union with God means that we become God's tools—God is our overseer—as we do God's work.

> Human beings are the tools of God, and a tool accomplishes things according to the nobility of the overseer . . . The effect of grace is not enough for the soul because the soul is a creature. It must rather reach the point where God accomplishes things in his own nature, where the overseer accomplishes things according to the nobility of the tool . . . The soul is united with God and embraced by God, and grace escapes the soul so that it now no longer accomplishes things with grace but divinely in God. Thus the soul is in a wonderful way enchanted and loses itself.[12]

Union reaches its fullness when things are accomplished "divinely in God." The soul now *functions in the divine power just like that power.* The union and rest with the Trinity are not introverted or narcissistic but outward-oriented. The soul *conducts itself in accord with the power of the Father, and the wisdom of the Son, and the goodness of the Holy Spirit. Above all this no being is more efficacious.* And, in the intimacy of this union, we learn that there, *there is only being and action.* Pure being becomes pure action; pure action flows from pure being. This union of divine being and divine action will form the basis of Eckhart's theology of work, which we will see in greater detail in Path Four.

Eckhart points out in the present sermon that we have Christ as a model of our union with divine being and with divine works. Indeed, we are to do more than use Christ as a model; we are ourselves other Christs, sons and daughters of God, meant to imitate his union and his work. *We must also be the same Christ, imitating him in his actions just as in his being he is one Christ in his humanity.* For just like Christ, we bear both humanity and divinity in us. A resurrected person experiences that he or she *is completely possessed by the personal being that is God. In the same way, humanity and divinity are one personal being in the person of Christ.* It is by grace that we are other Christs in this life. *I am so united to Christ's personal being that I am through grace one with Christ in his person and I remain also my own person.* Eckhart does not find it necessary to destroy the individual personality of a person who becomes a child of God, another Christ. We share Christ's personal being as the *bearer of Christ's eternal humanity.* But because his personal and human being is related to his divine being because it is all one substance in God, and since we too are united in God, we share with Christ his divine origin in God.

This Trinitarian theology is not meant to be idle speculation for academic experts—it is experiential or it is nothing. *May the Holy Trinity help us to experience all this,* Eckhart prays at the conclusion of his sermon. For we are, as John said, "to know that we are living in him and he is living in us." This knowledge, which is a kind of tasting, is for all.

Sermon Twenty-nine: BE YOU CREATIVE AS GOD IS
CREATIVE

"It is all that is good, everything that is perfect, which is
given us from above." (Jm. 1:17)*

Saint James says in his Epistle: "The best gift and perfection
come from on high from the Father of lights" (Jm. 1:17).

Now pay attention! Concerning people who give themselves up
to God and in all industry seek only his will, whatever God gives
to such people is the best. Be as certain as you are of the fact that
God lives that this must be the best way of all, and that there is
no way that could be better. However, it may be that something
else seems better that would still not be so good for you. This is
because God wishes just this way and no other, and *this* way
must of necessity be the best way for you. No matter what
sickness or poverty or hunger or thirst God inflicts or does not
inflict upon you, and no matter what God gives or does not give,
all of this is best for you. It may be that you have neither devotion nor inwardness. Whatever you have or do not have, focus
carefully on the fact that you have God's honor in all things before your eyes, and whatever he then does to you is best.

Now you might ask: "How do I know whether or not it is
God's will?" If it were not God's will, it would not come to pass.
You have neither illness nor anything else unless God wishes it.
And since you know that it is God's will, you should have so
much satisfaction and gratification from this that you will regard
no suffering as suffering. Indeed, even if the most extreme suffering were to occur and you were to feel some pain or suffering, it
would still be completely turned around. For you would have to
accept it as the best thing from God, since it must of necessity be
the best way of all. This is because God's being requires him to

* "Omne datum optimum et omne donum desursum est." (DW I, ※4)

wish what is best. For this reason, I too must wish it, and nothing
else should suit me better. If I wished to please someone and
knew for certain that I would please that person by wearing gray
clothing more than any other color, there is no doubt that the
gray clothing would be more satisfactory and precious than any
other. If I wished to please someone, and if I knew that that person took pleasure in certain words and deeds, I would conduct
myself in that way, and in no other way. All right! Now examine
yourselves to see how your love is constituted. If you love your
God, nothing could give you more pleasure than whatever pleases
him best and the thought that his will should be carried out to
the greatest degree with respect to us. However heavy the suffering or hardship may seem, if you do not find an equal amount of
satisfaction in connection with it, something is not in order.

I am accustomed to use often an expression that is also true.
We call out every day and cry loudly in the Our Father: "Lord
your will be done" (Mt. 6:10). And then if his will is done, we
wish to get angry, and his will does not satisfy us. Meanwhile,
whatever he does should please us most. Those who accept it as
what is best remain in all circumstances in complete peace. Now
it seems not to be so to you from time to time, and you say: "Oh,
if it had been different, it would have been better," or "If it did
not happen in that way, it would perhaps have been better." So
long as it seems so to you, you will never attain peace. You should
accept it as the best of all things. This is the first meaning of this
expression.

There is also another meaning. Think about it carefully. Saint
James speaks of "every gift." Now the best of all and the highest
of all are really gifts in the most proper meaning of the term.
God gives away nothing so happily as big gifts. I stated once in
this place that God prefers to forgive big sins rather than small
ones. And the bigger they are, the more happily and quickly does
he forgive them. This is quite the way it is with grace and gifts
and virtues: the bigger they are, the more happily does he give
them. For it is his nature to give big gifts. And for this reason,
the more valuable the gifts are, the more does he give of them.
The most noble creatures are the angels, who are purely spiritual
and have nothing corporeal about them. There are a very great
many of them, and there are more of them than the sum total of

all corporeal things. Big things are called quite properly "gifts" and belong to God in the truest and most spiritual way.

I once said that whatever can be truly expressed in its proper meaning must emerge from inside a person and pass through the inner form. It cannot come from outside to inside of a person but must emerge from within. It lives truly in the most spiritual part of the soul. There all things are present, living and seeking within the soul what is spiritual, where they are in their best and highest meaning. Why don't you notice anything of this? Because you are not at home there. The more noble something is, the commoner it is. I have my senses in common with the animals, and my life in common with the trees. My being, which is more inward, is held in common with all creatures. Heaven is more encompassing than all that is under it, and for this reason it is more noble. Love is noble because it is all-encompassing.

What our Lord has commanded seems difficult—that we should love our fellow Christian like ourselves (Mk. 12:31; Mt. 22:39). Coarse people commonly say that the meaning of this is that we should love our fellow Christians with a view to the same benefit for the sake of which we love ourselves. No, this is not the case. We should love them just as much as ourselves, and that is not difficult. If you wish to think correctly on this matter, love is more of a reward than a command. A command sounds difficult but a reward is something to long for. All of us who love God as we should and must love him, whether willingly or not, and the way all creatures love him, must love our fellow human beings like ourselves. We must rejoice in their joys as much as in our own joys, we must long for their honor as much as for our own honor, and we must love a stranger as our own relatives. In this way, people are constantly in joy and honor, and a good situation, just as if they were in the kingdom of heaven. Thus they have more frequent joys than if they only had joy in their own benefits. And know for certain that, if your own honor causes more happiness than the honor of another, something is wrong.

Know that, whenever you are seeking your own interest, you will never find God, since you are not seeking God alone. You are looking for something along with God, and you are behaving exactly as if you were making of God a candle so that you could look for something. When we find the things we are looking for, we throw the candle away. Whatever you are seeking along with God is *nothing*. It does not matter what it is—be it an advantage or a reward or a kind of spirituality or whatever else—you are seeking a *nothingness*, and for this reason you find a *nothingness*. The reason that you find a *nothingness* is that you are seeking a *nothingness*. All creatures are a pure *nothingness*. I do not say that they are of little value or that they are something at all— they are a pure *nothingness*. Whatever has no being is nothing. All creatures lack being, for their being depends on the presence of God. If God were to turn away from all creatures only for a moment, they would come to nothing. I have from time to time made a statement that is also true: whoever added the whole world to God would have nothing more than if he had taken God by himself. All creatures have, without God, no more being than a gnat would possess without God—just exactly as much and not less or more.

All right, now listen to a true statement! If a person gave a thousand gold marks so that churches and monasteries could be built, this would be a fine thing. All the same, if another person who regarded a thousand marks as nothing gave much more, the second donor would have done more than the first one. When God created all the creatures, they were so unimportant and narrow that he could not move about in them. He made the soul, however, so like and similar in appearance to himself that he could give himself to the soul. For what he gave to the soul in addition is regarded by the soul as nothing. God must give himself to me just as much as he belongs to himself, or there will be no advantage to me at all, and nothing will agree with me. Any people who are to receive him so completely must give themselves up completely and be completely divested of themselves. Such people receive from God all God has and as much as our Lady and all those in heaven have. All of this belongs to these people in a similar and quite personal way. Those who have divested themselves of themselves to the same degree and have surrendered themselves will receive the same from God and no less.

And now let us consider the third part of our text from the Scripture: "from the Father of the light." The word "Father" makes us think of sonship or daughtership; the word "Father" signifies a pure generation and means the same as "a life of all things." The Father generates his Son in eternal knowledge. He generates his Son in the soul exactly as in his own nature. He generates him in the soul as his own, and his being is attached to the fact that he is generating his Son in the soul, whether for good or for woe. I was once asked what the Father did in heaven. And I said that he was generating his Son, and that this activity was so agreeable to him and pleased him so much that he does nothing other than generate his Son, and both of them flourished in the Holy Spirit. When the Father generates his Son in me, I am that very same Son and no one else. "If we are sons, we are heirs as well" (Rm. 8:17). Whoever rightly knows the truth understands well that the word "Father" implies a pure generation and a production of children. For this reason we are here as a child, and are the same Son.

Now note also the expression: "They come from above." I recently told you that whoever wishes to receive something from above must of necessity be below in proper humility. And know in the truth that whoever is not fully below will receive nothing, however insignificant it might ever be. If you have ever perceived this with respect to yourself or something else or someone else, then you are not down below and you will receive nothing. If you are really below, you will receive fully and completely. It is God's nature to make gifts, and his being depends on making gifts to us if we are down below. If we are not here, and if we receive nothing, we act violently toward him and we kill him. If we cannot do this to him, we are still doing it to ourselves and being violent as far as we are concerned. See to it that you give everything to him as his own, and that you humble yourself beneath God in proper humility, and that you raise up God in your heart and your perception. "God, our Lord, sent his Son into the world" (Ga. 4:4). I said once at this point that God sent his Son in the fullness of time—to our soul, if it has moved beyond all time. If the soul is unencumbered by time and space, the Father sends his Son into the soul. Now this is the meaning of the declaration: "The best gift and perfection come from on high from the Father of lights."

May the Father of lights help us to be ready to receive his best gift! Amen.

COMMENTARY: The Creator as Artist, the Son as Art/Eckhart's Theology of Creativity and the Artist/Because It Is God's Nature to Give Gifts, It Is Ours Also/Our Best Gifts or Works of Art Come from Within and Thus Praise God/ Our Divine Destiny and Glory Is to Receive Beauty and Birth Beauty—and This Is Salvation

It has been said that one can "extract an almost complete philosophy of art from Eckhart's writings,"[1] and that is true. This would seem to be demonstrated by the journey we have taken thus far. Through Path One we experienced the divine isness of all creation, so full of divine beauty planted there by an Artist. Through Path Two we learned to let go in order to let the beauty be. Through Path Three we learned that we are to be parents of the Beauty behind beauty and the Artist behind artists and that the Holy Spirit, spirit of gift-giving, inspires us to birth gifts. In the present sermon Eckhart, drawing on scriptural passages from James and Paul, summarizes the culmination of Path Three in the spiritual journey as an experience of birthing and creativity. Each of these epistles speaks of our vocation as children of God and "first-fruits" of the Creator's work. Thus the passage from James that forms the starting point for Eckhart's sermon reads:

> Make no mistake about this, my dear brothers: it is all that is good, everything that is perfect, which is given us from above; it comes down from the Father of all light; with him there is no such thing as alteration, no shadow of a change. By his own choice he made us his children by the message of the truth so that we should be a sort of first-fruits of all that he had created. (Jm. 1:16–18)

This reiteration of creation as a blessing and of the human race as the first-fruits of creation, a special blessing that makes us children of God, is a theme that Eckhart is pleased to treat once again. To explore more deeply the meaning of our son/daughtership to God, Eckhart invokes two passages from Paul's epistles. Each talks of not only the gift of being divine children but also the responsibility. We are heirs as well as God's sons and daughters, and we possess "the first-fruits of the spirit."

> Everyone moved by the Spirit is a son of God. The spirit you received is not the spirit of slaves bringing fear into your lives

again; it is the spirit of sons, and it makes us cry out, "Abba, Father!" The Spirit himself and our spirit bear united witness that we are children of God. And if we are children we are heirs as well: heirs of God and coheirs with Christ, sharing his sufferings so as to share his glory . . . From the beginning till now the entire creation, as we know, has been groaning in one great act of giving birth; and not only creation, but all of us who possess the first-fruits of the Spirit, we too groan inwardly as we wait for our bodies to be set free. (Rm. 8:14–17, 22, 23)

Eckhart comments on this passage: *When the Father generates his Son in me, I am that very same Son and no one else . . . We are here as a child, and are the same Son.* He turns to Galatians to reinforce his point, emphasizing our passage from being heirs to being sons:

An heir, even if he has actually inherited everything, is no different from a slave for as long as he remains a child. He is under the control of guardians and administrators until he reaches the age fixed by his father. Now before we came of age we were as good as slaves to the elemental principles of this world, but when the appointed time came, God sent his Son, born of a woman, born a subject of the Law, to redeem the subjects of the Law and to enable us to be adopted as sons. The proof that you are sons is that God has sent the Spirit of his Son into our hearts: the Spirit that cries, "Abba, Father," and it is this that makes you a son, you are not a slave anymore; and if God has made you son, then he has made you heir. (Ga. 4:1–7)

Eckhart interprets our coming of age as our receiving God in our souls. *God sent his Son in the fullness of time—to our soul, if it has moved beyond all time. If the soul is unencumbered by time and space, the Father sends his Son into the soul.* And this sending constitutes *"the best gift and perfection come from on high from the Father of lights."* It also constitutes our motherhood of God and our becoming Creators as God the Father is.

Nevertheless, it does not suffice for the noble, humble person to be the only begotten Son, whom the Father has eternally begotten, unless he or she also wants to be a father and to

enter this similitude of the eternal Fatherhood, and to beget
him by whom I am eternally begotten.[2]

Eckhart devotes considerable energy in this sermon to exploring what
"Abba, Father" might mean. Who is this God who is addressed as
"Abba, Father"? God is a being driven to generate or give birth. God is
pure generation and is the *life of all things.* The essence of God is to
give birth. *The word "Father" signifies a pure generation and means the
same as "a life of all things."* That which the Father most generates is his
Son, and this birthing is a constant birthing process.

> I was once asked what the Father did in heaven. And I said
> that he was generating his Son, and that this activity was so
> agreeable to him and pleased him so much that he does noth-
> ing other than generate his Son, and both of them flourished in
> the Holy Spirit.

Birthing the Son is God's constant activity. This is what is meant when we
call out, "Abba, Father." *The word "Father" implies a pure generation
and a production of children.* This generating is not restricted to a far-
off place called heaven. It actually takes place in ourselves. *He generates his Son in the soul exactly as in his own nature. He generates him in
the soul as his own, and his being is attached to the fact that he is generating his Son in the soul, whether for good or for woe.* But this generating that God does in us is also what the indwelling of God in us is
about. "His generating is at the same time his indwelling, and his indwelling is his generating."[3] Thus for Eckhart the indwelling of God is
meant to be fruitful and outward-oriented. It is not an inner symbol to
gaze at so much as an inner dynamism that is to generate our own
creativity and giving birth. Contemplation is not a rest in God but a
flowing out from God into birthing. What God generates and gives birth
to is ourselves as the Son of God. *Where the Father generates his Son in
me, I am that very same Son and no one else.*

We are sons and daughters of the Father! But to be children of the
Father who is *pure generation* means that we too are to generate, we
too are to be birthers who are divinely fruitful. This is our praise of God,
namely our creativity.

> What praises God? That which is like him. Thus, everything in
> the soul which is like God praises God. Whatever is at all

unlike God does not praise God. In the same way, a statue
praises the artist who has imprinted on it all the art that he has
in his mind, thus making it so very like his conception. The
similarity of the work of art to the artist's conception praises
the master without words.[4]

By discovering how we are artists as God is, we praise God, who in
fact intended that we be in his image and likeness and therefore creators also. Elsewhere Eckhart explains that the Father and the Son are related as is the artist to his or her art. Art stays with the artist like the
Word stays with the Father. It flows out but remains within. Eckhart links
in an explicit way his theology of creativity with his theology of the
Word.

From the start, once he has become an artist and as long as
he is an artist capable of creative work, art remains with the
artist. This is the meaning of "The Word was in the beginning
with God," that is, the art with the artist, coeval with him, as
the Son is with the Father in God.[5]

God's Word is God's work. It goes out but remains within. The same Is
true of us. "What is in me goes out from me; if I am only thinking it, then
my word reveals it and yet remains inside me. It is in this way that the
Father speaks the unspoken Son and yet the Son remains in the Father"
(Sermon One). Since we too are God's children, it follows that we too
are God's works of art. But also, being heirs of God come of age, we
too are artists as God is. To be a human being as well as to be a divine
being means that we are artists, for "humankind lives by art and reason,
that is to say, practically."[6] We are heirs of God, heirs of creativity. We
are heirs of the "fearful creative power" of God, as Eckhart puts it in
Sermon Thirty-two.

Psychologist Otto Rank has defined the artist as one who wants to
leave behind a gift.[7] Integral to an artist's consciousness is a gift-consciousness, a thank you for creation that is expressed in one's creativity.
We have seen in Sermons Eight and Ten how Eckhart's is a theology of
thanksgiving. We have also seen how his theology of the Spirit is a theology of gift-giving, for the Spirit is a gift (Sermons Eighteen, Twenty-
six). When God gives, God gives the best first, Eckhart explains in Sermon Thirty-six.

Nature begins its deeds on the smallest scale, but God begins his deeds on the most perfect scale. Nature produces an adult from a child and a hen from an egg. God, however, produces an adult before the child and a hen before the egg. Nature first causes wood to be warm and then hot; then it causes the essence of fire to be born. God, however, first gives to every creature its being, and afterward he gives every separate thing that belongs to this being in time and yet apart from time. God also gives the Holy Spirit before the gifts of the Holy Spirit.

In the present sermon Eckhart develops in a richer way how it is that God's consciousness is a gift-consciousness and therefore, using Rank's criterion, a consciousness of the artist. God needs to make gifts, Eckhart says. God is, as it were, compelled to be an artist. *It is God's nature to make gifts, and his being depends on making gifts to us if we are down below.* So important is this gift-giving to God's nature that if we refuse the gift, *we act violently toward him* and *we kill him.* In other words, a gift-giver requires a gift-receiver, as every artist requires an audience and a union with others. To refuse God that audience is to challenge the very core of God, for if it is his *nature* to give gifts, then truly *his being depends on it.* What kind of gifts does God like to give? The bigger, the better. *God gives away nothing so happily as big gifts . . . It is his nature to give big gifts.* Notice that this gift-giving is a *giving away.* It is not a giving for a return or a reward. It is a giving in order to give, it is gift for gift's sake, it is giving without a why. As Eckhart puts it, we even make God into a means as we do a candle. Then, *when we find the things we are looking for, we throw the candle away.* God must be an end and a mystery, not merely a means or a problem-solver in our lives. So too, all our gift-giving and thank-you's, all our art, are to be without a why like living and work. Art is without a why just like creation itself. In a previous sermon Eckhart had warned us that "those who give in order to receive something in return" are not giving gifts. "Such a gift does not deserve to be called a gift; it should be called a demand because nothing is really given" (Sermon Twenty-four). God is always ready with his gifts, but we often miss the opportunity. "As exalted as God is above human beings, to that same extent is God more prepared to give than human beings are to receive."[8] The most basic of the gifts we have received is of course being itself. This we have in common with all creatures and because of this gift *all creatures love God* (see Path One). So basic is being that even our art or gift-giving depends on it. "Each and every thing, whether produced by nature or by art, has its being or the fact that it is immediately from God alone."[9] The intimacy we share with God the giver of being is shared by all our art as well and all we give birth to. The greatest of the gifts we have received is the Son and we are driven to respond with what Schürmann calls a "supreme thankfulness":

> The reception of God . . . in us is a gift which must bear fruit: detachment is completed by fertility . . . one sole determination joins them [people and God] together: that of giving birth. United to God in begetting, man returns to God in an act of supreme thankfulness everything that he possesses.[10]

If it is God's nature to give gifts—and preferably big ones—then it is our nature as sons of God to do the same. Our divinization requires our creativity. One cannot be divine without being creative and fruitful.

What does it mean to be creative and to be an artist for Eckhart? It means to give birth from the very depths of our insides. It means being in touch with and being ready to express the inner and not the outer person.

> Whatever can be truly expressed in its proper meaning must emerge from inside a person and pass through the inner form. It cannot come from outside to inside of a person, but must emerge from within.

Introvert meditation—the taking in of a symbol given from the outside—is not enough for Eckhart. We need extrovert meditation as well—one that expresses our own deepest insides.[11] As we saw in the previous sermon, our deepest insides unite being and action. Thus our act of creativity must flow from our act of being. The culmination of the birth of God and us will be a creativity that is itself born of being and action, the way God's is. All creatures, Eckhart declares, "strive in their works toward what is like their own being."[12] We are urged to "bear fruit that remains" (Jn. 15:16), but it is what is deepest in us that remains. "What is inborn in me remains."[13] What is deep within the artist are images that are more than images—they are life itself—flowing out but remaining within, as does a word.

> The chest which issues or is produced externally into being nevertheless is and remains in the artist himself, just as it was from the beginning, before it became a chest . . . The chest in the mind and art of the artist is neither a chest nor is it made, but is art itself, is life, the living concept of the artist.[14]

Art, like life, is born from our deepest roots and centers. For art is life.

> What is life? That which is moved by itself from within. What is moved from without does not live. Hence, if we live with him, we must also cooperate with him from within, so that we do not operate from outside; we should rather be moved from whence we live, that is, through him. Now we can and must act from our own, from within. If, therefore, we shall live in him or by him, he must be our own and we must act from our own . . .[15]

Eckhart is hopeful—we "can operate from within"—that we can all be artists and creative people in some way. Indeed, we must be, for this is the only route in which authentic pleasure lies. *God's being requires him to wish what is best . . . If you love your God, nothing could give you more pleasure than whatever pleases him best.* Our greatest pleasure is in cooperating with the Creator, creator with Creator, artist with Artist. Every artist has experienced the ecstasy of "enchantment" that Eckhart speaks of for those who become instruments of the divine creativity. In the creative state, "the soul now no longer accomplishes things with grace but divinely in God. Thus the soul is in a wonderful way enchanted and loses itself."[16] To experience this ecstasy and pleasure that art brings, we need to trust our images as God does. The artist is driven to trusting his own images and concepts, to operating from within outward. True art is always from our depths to others' depths, a gift or a spirit that touches other spirits and flows from within to within. So committed must the artist be to trusting his or her images that the artist must actually become one being with the image and live for the image. "An image receives its being immediately from that of which it is an image. It has one being with it and it is the same being." Our life with our images —our artistic life—becomes a pattern for our spiritual lives. "You often ask how you should live. Note this carefully. See what has just been said of the image. In exactly the same way, you should live. You should be in

him and for him, and not in yourself and for yourself."[17] The trust and
spontaneity of the artist become models for our spiritual lives.

> Human beings should turn their will to God in all their activi-
> ties and keep their eyes on God alone, marching along with-
> out fear and without hesitancy about being right or not doing
> anything wrong. For if a painter wanted to consider every
> stroke of his brush when he made his first stroke, no picture
> would ever result . . . This is why we should follow the first
> suggestion and move forward.[18]

The reason the artist must plumb his or her inner life more than others
is that there is where the action takes place. All things are present there.
*There all things are present, living and seeking within the soul what is
spiritual, where they are in their best and highest meaning.* The reason
we do not grasp this is that we are strangers to our own capacity to
give birth and to imagine images. *Why don't you notice anything of this?
Because you are not at home there.*
The work of finding the transcendent within is the work that the Holy
Spirit accomplished in Mary's birth of Jesus, Eckhart says. Every artist
must make what is "above" be "within."

> The work that is "with," "outside," and "above" the artist must
> become the work that is "in" him, taking form within him, in
> other words, to the end that he may produce a work of art, in
> accordance with the verse "The Holy Spirit shall come upon
> thee" (Lk. 1:35), that is, so that the "above" may become
> "in."[19]

Once again Eckhart is relating his theology of creativity to his theology
of the Spirit and to his theology of birthing. The fruit of our birthing from
within, instead of merely from outside or even from above, will be God-
with-us, Emmanuel, still another birth of God in our midst. In this sense,
Mary was the first folk artist, the first one to birth God from within and
not merely from without or above. Mary had the imagination, the courage, and the discipline to make the most sublime the innermost. To bring
God *in* and to birth God outwardly. This is what is so noble and divine
about the "intellect," or what I prefer to call the imagination in us, the
imago Dei. But imagination does not come from wishing or fantasizing

alone. Eckhart distinguishes two kinds of willpower within us: that which is merely wishing and which is not born deeply from within, and that which is "determining and creative" and which is truly a will to create.[20] The latter is only tapped if we give birth from deep within us, as every true artist must. Art is not mere inspiration. It takes an act of the will and a willingness to discipline oneself. Thus it calls upon qualities of a person that mere wishing to be an artist does not; it calls upon inner discipline. "The artist does not find his nature sufficient for the practice of his art unless it is reinforced by the will to practice it, the capacity and the skill and so on, factors which are not, strictly speaking, the nature of the artist."[21] Clearly Eckhart prefers this kind of discipline to that of ascetic mortifications, for it is oriented toward bearing fruit and not just being a contemplative "virgin."

The journey that the artist makes in turning inward to listen to and trust his or her images is a communal journey. Jungians say that there is a collective unconscious. Eckhart puts it in the following manner. *My being, which is more inward, is held in common with all creatures*. The more outward we look at things, the more separately we see them. We have *senses in common with the animals, life in common with the trees*. But that which is in common with all other creatures, our being, is *more inward*. Thus the artist who is truly birthing from the depths of the inside is birthing from the depths of commonality. Such a person is giving birth to the "we" and not just the I. In fact, Eckhart wants to do away with the word "I":

> The word *ego*, which means "I", is appropriate only for God in his unity. The word *vos* means approximately "you." That fact that you are one in unity means that the words *ego* and *vos* ("I" and "you") point to unity. May God help us to be this unity and to remain this unity![22]

Eckhart addresses himself to the second part of the Epistle of James that he read for the day. It is a lesson of *doing* the word and not merely taking it in, of working to make the seed grow.

> Accept and submit to the word which has been planted in you and can save your souls. But you must do what the word tells you, and not just listen to it and deceive yourselves. To listen

to the word and not obey is like looking at your own features in a mirror and then, after a quick look, going off and immediately forgetting what you looked like. But the person who looks steadily at the perfect law of freedom and makes that his habit—not just listening and then forgetting, but actively putting it into practice—will be happy in all that he does.

Nobody must imagine that he is religious while he still goes on deceiving himself and not keeping control over his tongue; anyone who does this has the wrong idea of religion. Pure, unspoilt religion, in the eyes of God our Father is this: coming to the help of orphans and widows when they need it, and keeping oneself uncontaminated by the world. (Jm. 1:21–27)

James urges us to summon all our discipline in order to "listen to the word and obey it" and to "actively put it into practice." The artistic calling is a demanding one.

Eckhart invokes here the two commandments—love of God and of neighbor—that Jesus exhorts us to (Mk. 12:31; 22:39) and points out that what James is telling us we ought to have learned from our journey inward: *that love is all-encompassing.* To love oneself *is* to love one's neighbor if we love ourselves correctly. For we are all one with each other in the sea of God. *We should love them just as much as ourselves, and that is not difficult.* True love, for the person who has made the spiritual journey that Eckhart has outlined in three paths, is not a moral imperative. It is *more of a reward than a command,* because it is *something we long for.* It is a *pleasure* to do the acts of love out of a flow and an artistry and a creativity and an overflow that is the basis of all true art. For to love God is to love those in God and to celebrate with them. It is like living in *the kingdom of heaven* to be able to *rejoice in their joys as much as in our own joy* and to *long for their honor as much as for our own honor.* For the kingdom of heaven consists of such a celebrative banquet of blessings shared. All those who are blessed with birthing possibilities come to this banquet to celebrate. "Wait only for this birth within yourself, and you will discover all blessing and all consolation, all bliss, all being, and all truth. If you neglect this, you will neglect all blessing and all happiness."[23] We create from this blessedness: "In this same ground all of God's friends will receive their blessedness and create from it. That is the 'table in the kingdom of God.' "[24] At this table the gifts of the Spirit flow like a rapid river and we do not become ob-

stacles to such flowing, but ourselves drink of it and pass on its ever-
flowing energies.

This is the word that has been "planted in us and can save our souls,"
as James puts it—the word of our own creativity and rebirth as sons of
the Creator and heirs of divine creativity. Because our salvation lies in
our making contact with our divine origins, and it pertains to divinity to
create, therefore our salvation lies in creativity. For in the work of the
artist, subject/object distinctions are broken through and we experience
the unity of all creation once again, the unity of the circle of being that
resides in the Godhead. Healing now takes place. And this healing is
salvation, a unity in what Schürmann calls an "operative identity."[25] It is
a healing between us and the Creator and between us and creation and
between our deepest inner self and our outgoing self. From all these un-
ions a saving child is born. And its name is Beauty or the glory (doxa) of
the children of creation. The work of the artist is to carve out and unveil
the glory that is hidden in creation.

> If a skilled artist makes an image of wood or stone, he or she
> does not place that image within the wood but chisels away
> the pieces that have hidden and covered it up. The artist con-
> tributes nothing to the wood but rather takes away and
> removes the covering and takes away the blight; then what lay
> hidden underneath shines forth. This is the treasure that lay
> hidden in the soil, as our Lord says in the Gospel (Mt. 13:44).[26]

This unveiling of a shining treasure brings about healing and salvation.
"This, then, is salvation, when we marvel at the beauty of created things
and praise the beautiful providence of their Creator or when we
purchase heavenly goods by our compassion for the works of creation"
(see Sermon Thirty).

There is another way of looking at Eckhart's Three Paths of spiritual
consciousness that have culminated in creativity and birthing. That would
be to compare Eckhart's analysis of the spiritual life with the stages of
creativity as conceived by psychiatrist Silvano Arieti.[27] Dr. Arieti speaks
of the first stage as the Primary Process, wherein there are no denials, no
no's, but images are allowed to appear and interact freely. The second
stage is the Secondary Process, when images are consciously decided
upon, by rejecting some and choosing others. The third stage, or Tertiary
Process, constitutes the marriage of stages one and two and is greater

than the sum of its parts. Eckhart has led us on a first stage, called the *via positiva* (creation), a second stage, called the *via negativa* (letting go and letting be), and now a third stage, which can rightly be called the *via creativa* (breakthrough and giving birth). The biggest difference between his analysis of the spiritual journey and Arieti's analysis of the creative process would seem to be that stage two for Eckhart is more radical than it is for Arieti. Eckhart's is more a spirituality that undergirds the creative process than an entire psychology of such a process. Stage four for Eckhart will simply be an elaboration of what might be the fullest fruit and the finest birthing that creative people are capable of. Having made this journey to the point of giving birth, as all artists and creators do, we are now ready to move on to Path Four, which delineates for us what the greatest art and the finest birth would look like.

PATH FOUR: THE NEW CREATION: COMPASSION AND SOCIAL JUSTICE

For Eckhart, the spiritual journey does not culminate in contemplation but in compassion, and this preference for compassion reveals the biblical roots of Eckhart's spirituality. Contemplation is not a biblical category, but Compassion is the very name for *YHWH* and the presence of God among us.[1] In Path Four all the theological themes and experiences that Eckhart has developed in Paths One to Three come together and are put to work. For example, the theme of creation as a blessing. Indeed, compassion is the first of all blessings, for creation itself is bathed in compassion (see Sermons Thirty and Thirty-one), and compassion is the last blessing, the blessing that we, the new creators, are to give to others. Compassion thus constitutes the ultimate blessing we receive and give. Compassionate ones are "blessed" and compassion itself bestows "heavenly blessings" (Sermon Thirty). Compassion marks our return to the world to re-create society. This is possible because we have learned freedom from letting go (Path Two) and ecstasy from our breakthrough and birthing (Path Three): "People who have let go of themselves are so pure that the world cannot harm them . . . People who love justice will be admitted to justice. They will be seized by justice, and will be one with justice."[2] When we encounter God we encounter justice and compassion, as Moses learned on the mountaintop. "When the Lord descends, the soul is blessed by compassion, as happened in Exodus 3:8."[3] Compassion is the culmination of our rebirth and breakthrough and also of our birthing, for the ultimate act of grace and beauty is compassion. Compassion, then, is the fruit of our spiritual journey of faith. It is our response to the panentheistic and cosmic consciousness that reveals to us that all beings exist in the unity of a divine sea (see Sermon Thirty-one). In compassion the creative Word that launched creation continues to renew all things through our creative work (see Sermon Thirty-three). In compassion the truth about Jesus Christ is learned and the celebration at the arrival of the king/queendom of God is rejoiced in (see Sermons Thirty, Thirty-seven). The fullest artistic contributions to society are contributions of compassion, especially toward the poor and the outcast.[4] Since compassion means justice as well as cosmic awareness, in compassion, social justice and mysticism come together, and because compassion is a divine attribute, our meaning as sons and daughters of God, that is to say our divinity, is discovered (see Sermons Thirty, Thirty-two, Thirty-three). Compassion reveals our divinity to ourselves and to others, for, as Meister Eckhart puts it, the "land flowing with milk and honey" that is promised to Moses means a life flowing "with humanity and divinity."[5] In compassion we and our works become divine and God becomes a human once again. We return home to our divine—and compassionate—origin. All the beauty in heaven and on earth is united in compassion, for "compassion eventually leads to glory."

"Sermon" Thirty: BE COMPASSIONATE AS YOUR CREATOR IN HEAVEN IS COMPASSIONATE

"Be compassionate as your Father in heaven . . ." (Lk. 6:36–42)*

Three things are necessary for those wanting to prepare themselves for divine grace: humility of mind, firmness of heart, and the ability to give further whatever is received. The first characteristic—humility of mind—is evident in Mary, of whom it was said: "full of grace, the Lord is with you." In his Sermon on the Assumption, Augustine says: "Mary's humility became a heavenly ladder down which not merely grace but the God of every grace descended to earth." For it is proper to humility to be like the premise in a syllogism; a great part of its power lies in this. When the humility is true, then the conclusion of the syllogism is correct.

The second characteristic, firmness of heart, is manifest in the fact that sin and lack of firmness go together. As it is written in the first chapter of Lamentations: "Jerusalem sinned grievously and therefore she has become without firmness." And in Aristotle we read that "the opposites of those things follow as consequences." Therefore, we read in Hebrews 13:9, "it is best that the heart be made firm by grace." For it is good by means of grace to avoid sin; it is better by that same grace to make progress in the service of God; but it is best of all to make one's heart firm in God himself. The greatest help to this end is the love of eternal realities and the avoidance of what is merely terrestrial and transient. For in a teaching attributed to Anselm, we are told that the heart which is not fixed in eternity is more changeable than change itself.

The third characteristic, the ability to give further whatever is

* "Estote misericordes, sicut et pater vester . . ." (DW IV, ✳12)

received, is made clear toward the end of the fiftieth chapter of Augustine's work *On True Religion*, where he says: "The law of divine providence is such that people are not helped by those higher than themselves to the knowledge and experience of God's grace unless with a pure heart they help to the same end those who are lower than themselves."

All three of these characteristics are pointed to in this word *be*, which is a word having to do with what is substantive. For that prefix *sub* (under) indicates humility. As it is written in 1 Peter: "Humble yourself under the mighty hand of God." The other part of the word *substantive* comes from the Latin word for *stand* and indicates firmness. For about that land which Ecclesiastes says "stands into eternity," it is written in the Psalms: "You have founded the earth on your firmness." And the third characteristic, communicability, is indicated by *word*. For the word alone manifests the one speaking and communicates those things which are in his heart. There is an example in the uncreated word through which the Father communicates and pours out all things.

Be compassionate. In the first chapter of Acts it is written that "Jesus began to do and to teach." In last Sunday's Gospel we read that Jesus showed compassion and still shows compassion by receiving sinners, the lost which he joyfully puts on his shoulders, and by lighting the lamp to find the lost coin. We meet this example daily in the sacraments. We see another example in the Lord's passion when "the dominion was laid on his shoulders" (Is. 9). We see still another in the Incarnation. According to Gregory, "the lamp is the light in the earthen vessel, divinity in our flesh" and that is truly "the heart of compassion" through which and in which "the rising star has visited us" (Lk. 1). For although he eternally had all things in his nature—thus "rich in all things"—he in no way had a way of suffering nor a back which could be beaten. In this sense there is another legitimate explanation of what Paul is saying in 2 Corinthians 8: "for our sake he was made poor." For he did not have to beg for anything lacking to him, unless it be for the back which could receive blows. For the Psalms say, "Sinners hammer on my back." Thus in all these ways he showed compassion. And Luke says: "Go and do likewise." And this is what he teaches and taught, after he manifested it in deed.

He says: "Be compassionate, as your Father" and "a good measure." First Christ exhorts us to compassion: "Be compassionate." Then he gives us an example or model of this compassion: "as your Father." And finally, he promises glory, "a good measure."

Regarding the first point, we should know that there are four things for the sake of which we should understand ourselves as very much called to compassion. First, because it is this compassion which triumphs mightily over the enemy. There is where we should know about triumph over enemies, especially over such as those who themselves triumph over powerful people and frequently overcome great ones and who persecute with great vehemence and in every way are joyfully triumphant. This is the sort of thing we frequently read about in the biblical stories and in the canonical literature: Judith and Holofernes, Esther and Haman, the Maccabees; Isaiah 9:3, "They will rejoice in your sight as victors do when they take their spoils and divide their prizes." Our enemy, the hateful devil, brought to a fall even Adam, who was put into Paradise and endowed with every virtue and knowledge. And the case has been similar with many other such falls. For it is written: "If a woman brought Adam, Samson, David, and Solomon to a fall, who will in any way be secure?"

It ought then to be most laudable, joyful, and glorious to conquer such a foe as this who has waged war in so many ways, so frequently overcome such great people, and who is fighting not only for our life but also for the eternal death of our body and soul. Thus we find Cyprian saying in one of his exhortations: "If it is glorious for soldiers to return to the fatherland, then it is even more glorious to return as victors to that fatherland whence Adam was expelled, after conquering the enemy who caused Adam to fall and bringing back the victorious trophies, rejoicing with patriarchs, prophets, and apostles in possessing the kingdom of heaven, being equal to the angels, becoming a co-heir of Christ and standing at his side when he sits in judgment."

Compassion gives us this victory. The commentary on the phrase "my compassion and my refuge" is: "The devil is conquered by nothing so much as by compassion" and, further on, "for that person in whom is found a work of compassion, even if he have some ground for punishment, a wave of mercy like a flood of water will extinguish the fire of sin." And it is added that "compassion is shown in two ways: in giving and in forgiving." And this is what is meant in the Gospel statement: "Forgive and you will be forgiven; give and it will be given to you," and in Matthew 19: "Sell everything you have and give it to the poor and you will have treasure in heaven."

But this seems to be bad business: "Give what you have and you will have." Isaiah 61 states: "In your land you will possess twice as much." The lawyers say, "He who pays late, pays less; for by the extension of time, less is paid." "Give what you have and you will have." Someone says: "In the judgment of common folk *you have* is more valid than *you will have*. It is better to be related to *a* through *have* than to be related to *a* and *b* through *will have*." It should be noted that Scripture frequently puts the past tense instead of the present or the future because of the infallibility of the event and, on the other hand, puts the future instead of the present because of its eternity. Thus one is able to understand "You will have treasure in heaven" as referring to a double reward, essential and accidental, or according to the clothing of the body and of the soul.

Second, compassion divinely adorns the soul, clothing it in the robe which is proper to God. Both the theologians and the Scriptures teach that in every work which God works in a creature, compassion goes with it and ahead of it, especially in the inwardness of the creature itself. This is why Saint Gregory says that "it is proper to God to be compassionate." And the psalmist tells us that the compassion of God is over all his works. It does not say *in* all his works, as though it went *with*, but *over* all his works, because it goes ahead and overtops them. The Letter of James says that "compassion triumphs over justice" (allowing for other interpretations). For every work in a creature supposes the work of compassion and is grounded in it as in its root, the power of which preserves all things and works powerfully in them. For the psalmist says that "the earth is full of the compassion of the Lord" and, further, "his compassion is glorified to the heavens" and, further, "Lord, your compassion is in heaven" and "Your compassion is great above the heavens."

It is therefore evident that compassion clothes the soul with the robe of God and divinely adorns it. Isaiah 58 says, "When

you pour out your soul to the thirsty"—this pertains to corporal
compassion—"and when you fill the afflicted soul"—this pertains to spiritual compassion—"your light will rise in the darkness
and your darkness will be like the noontime; and God will grant
you rest forever and he will fill your soul with glories and liberate
your bones and you will be like a well-irrigated garden, and a
fountain of water which never fails." "The light will rise in
darkness"—a commentary on this text says: "Your light will rise
in the darkness means that even in the midst of evil men and
among adversities, the virtuous person will shine bright and
clear." And the text "your darkness will be like noontime" means
that the virtuous person will receive both of them—darkness and
noontime—without distinction. This is the fourth age of the new,
the inward, the heavenly human being.

Augustine in his treatise *On True Religion* (chapter 48) distinguishes seven ages or stages of the new human being, and he says
there that in the third age the carnal appetite is married to the rational power, when the soul has intercourse with the mind and is
shadowed in the veil of modesty, so that it will no longer allow
sin, even if everyone else were to allow it. The fourth age is what
Augustine calls the development of the perfect person, ready to
sustain and break the persecutions and all the storms and waves
of this world. The fifth age is when the soul lives totally at peace
in what it has and in the abundance of ineffable wisdom. The
sixth age means a transformation into the perfect form which is
perfect according to the image and likeness of God. This is the
new human being of whom it can truly be said: "You are
adorned in beauty and clothed in light as in a garment." The seventh age is eternal rest, a perpetual beatitude no longer able to be
divided into stages. And therefore blessed are the compassionate.
So much for this second point.

"Be compassionate." Third, compassion directs a person to relationships with his fellow human beings. Fourth, it wins for us
heavenly blessings and brings us to final salvation or beatitude.
Pertaining to these second, third, and fourth points we read in
Proverbs 21 that those who follow compassion find life and justice and glory. Life pertains to the second point in respect to oneself, justice pertains to the third point in respect to the neighbor,
and glory pertains to the third point in respect to God. And this

is what is promised to the compassionate in Isaiah 58: "Your healing will spring up speedily and justice will go before your face and the glory of the Lord will surround you." "Your healing"— that is your entire healthy life so that it can be called healed. For present life is a dying life or, according to Augustine, a living death. "For we who are born immediately cease to be" (Ws. 5:13). And "we all die and like water which does not return, we are poured out on the earth" (2 S. 14:14). It is not said of mortals that they *will* die but that they are dying.

But the life which the prophet calls healing is according to Isidore of Seville a living life. In his essay "On the Highest Good" in the next to last chapter, he argues that the present life does not merit the name life for this reason: "Our present condition does not deserve the name life because in order for us to be enlightened and be given life, eternal life came down and told us in John 10: 'I came that they might have life.' " Augustine makes the same point in a letter to Consentius, where he says: "This life is the act of the soul in the body, or its existence. But the soul in the present life does not have the power to give life to the body all the way to the taking away of corruption or death. But why would we call something hot which was not able to take away an object's coldness?"

It follows that "and your justice will go before your face" applies to the neighbor. For this is the nature of justice. This is explicitly said insofar as compassion is just to the extent that it gives each one what is his. This is why Isidore of Seville says in another chapter of the aforementioned treatise that "it is a great crime to give the wages of the poor to the rich and from the livelihood of the poor to increase the luxuries of the powerful, taking water from the needy earth and pouring it into the rivers."

There it is evident how compassion triumphs over the enemy, perfects a person in himself and adorns him, and is directed to the neighbor. It is because of this that the commentary on 1 Timothy 4:8 says: "The entire sum of Christian discipline consists of compassion and piety, and anyone following this discipline, if he experiences the deceits of the flesh, will without doubt be knocked about but will not perish." This is true if one is truly compassionate, as we read in Ecclesiasticus: "Having compassion toward your own soul, you are pleasing to God." Or, according to Aristotle, "Friendship toward others is rooted in the ability to be a friend to oneself." How then can anyone be compassionate toward me or toward you who is not compassionate toward himself? For, in the words of Ecclesiasticus 14:5: "If one is of no use to oneself, for whom can such a one be of any use?" It is for this reason that our Saviour says so explicitly, "Be compassionate!" For he wants us to be compassionate even to our own body and soul. Enough for this third point.

How does compassion merit heavenly rewards and finally save us and lead us to glory? In the treatise cited earlier, Isidore of Seville says that earthly things lead some people to perdition and others to salvation. This, then, is salvation, when we marvel at the beauty of created things and praise the beautiful providence of their Creator or when we purchase heavenly goods by our compassion for the works of creation. Notice which kinds of goods are purchased and you can see how compassion eventually leads to glory. And this is what I said above about the compassionate person *finding* glory (Pr. 21) and being *embraced* by the glory of the Lord (Is. 58). It is called finding because the glory far surpasses anything which could be merited. This is what we read in today's Epistle (Rm. 8:18) about the sufferings of this time not being worthy to be compared to the glory which is to come. The word "embrace" is used because in its abundance it exceeds any expectation of the soul. Thus it is written in Matthew 25: "You good and faithful servant, enter into the joy of the Lord."

We move now to a consideration of the text about the good and overflowing measure which is poured into our lap. We have already spoken of how Christ exhorts us to compassion: "Be compassionate, etc." It remains for us to see how he proposes a model or paradigm of this compassion—"as your Father is compassionate"—and finally how he promises a reward or crown—"a good and overflowing measure will be poured out in your lap."

As your Father is compassionate—first one must know that the heavenly Father is called compassionate and that he is compassionate in a twofold sense in providing the model which we are to imitate. He is compassionate without passion, and he is compassionate in a simple and essential act.

On the first point, we read in the first part of Augustine's book *On Patience:* "God is angry without perturbation, patient without passion, zealous without spite, showing compassion without sorrow." We therefore are compassionate like the Father when we are compassionate, not from passion, not from impulse, but from deliberate choice and reasonable decision. For Psalm 84 says: "Compassion and truth meet one another"—that is, passion and reason. And again in Psalm 32: "He loves compassion and judgment." Second Corinthians 9 says of compassion: "Each one as he decided in his heart, not as though out of sadness." A gloss on the phrase "as he decided" tells us that it means preordained, and "in his heart" means "in the deliberation of reason"; "not as though out of sadness" means that the passion does not take the lead but follows, does not rule but serves.

We find a sign of this in Genesis 21 and Galatians 4: "Throw out the maid and her son." The maid is that sensuality which should serve reason; her son refers to the force of passion. We should be very much on the alert lest the force of passion dominate our actions. This is why Jeremiah, in Lamentations, considers this to be a great scandal and says: "Consider, O Lord, what has happened to us and look at and view our scandal." And further in the text he says: "Servants have become our masters." Ecclesiastes 10 says: "It is an evil thing which I see under the sun —that a fool is placed in a high position and the rich sit beneath him." The fool here is sensuality or passion. It is called foolish, according to Boethius, both because it is not susceptible of discipline and because it clouds over the light of wisdom. "In a high position" means in leadership and power; the rich refers to the intellect and the will by which all of reality is ours; "sit beneath him" means being subject to passion. A following text says: "I saw servants on horses and princes walking on the ground like servants." Servants on horses shows how those whom passion dominates are very much like horses. It is against this that it is said in Psalm 32:9: "Don't be like the horse and mule . . ."

Another way in which we ought to be compassionate like our heavenly Father is with a sincere and simple intention. For just as God is compassionate without passion, so is he compassionate with nothing added, compassionate in a simple and essential act. Thus we are told in Wisdom 1: "Search for him in simplicity of heart." This simplicity of heart is a simplicity of intention.

Matthew 6:23 states that "if your eye is single, then is your whole
body bright." Augustine in his essay "On the Sermon on the
Mount" says: "We should understand *eye* here as intention."
And Augustine goes on to say: "What is to be considered is not
what anyone does but in what spirit he does it."

"If your eye is single." Jerome, in commenting on this text
from Matthew, says: "The bleary-eyed are accustomed to seeing
many lights, but the person whose eye is sound and healthy sees
reality clear and simple." Because, therefore, according to Augustine in his treatise *On True Religion*, chapter 16, "we seek the
one, than which nothing is more simple," we should seek that
one in simplicity of heart. This requires that from our part nothing else be added, and that we do not seek anything additional in
God, but only God himself. This is what Christ teaches us in
Matthew 6:3, where he speaks about the works of compassion:
"Do not let your left hand know what your right hand is doing."
The gloss on this text says: "What virtue does is something of
which either pride or vainglory or any other vice is ignorant, but
the light of a good deed flees the darkness of sin." For, as Max-
imus says in his Ash Wednesday sermon: "The master of heavenly teaching does not allow the work of those who call on him,
those for whom he prepares an eternal reward, to perish by the
vice of fruitless boasting."

"Let not your left hand know." For such as these belong to
those goats, standing at the left side, to whom those terrible
words are spoken: "Depart, cursed ones . . ." For a poet writes:
"The world and all its joys are only like a dream. Those who follow and love these things are given over to the depths of the
abyss."

The intention must be simple so that we seek nothing in addition to God and nothing except God. There is a gloss on the
phrase in Ephesians 3, "rooted in love": "If you love, love freely;
if you truly love, let your reward be the one you love." "See in
him the one who crowns you, your reward; and expect nothing
other than himself." Augustine says toward the end of the tenth
chapter of the *Confessions*: "Through my avarice I wanted to
possess the entire lie and so I lost you, because you could not be
possessed along with a lie." So the psalmist asks: "For what

reason do you love vanity and seek falsehood?" This is enough for
the point about God's being the example and paradigm of compassion: "like your Father . . ."

Sensuality as such cannot inherit the eternal kingdom because
it has nothing eternal in itself, whereas reason is eternal. Passion,
properly speaking, is a long distance from reason and intellect.
Nor is sensuality in the will or the senses, except at the periphery,
namely in the sense of touch, and that is only accidentally so.
Thereby we see that it is blameworthy to be led by passion, as the
blind person is led by a dog. Consider what great folly it is to sell
what merits eternal life for the wind of vanity! Thus it is that we
daily sing and pray: "May our inmost hearts be pure and may our
folly cease."

Now we move on to the third point, namely about the reward
or glory: "the good measure." Note this about the condition of
our true fatherland: it is the most excellent sublimity which belongs to those blessed ones who dwell in God, for "they will pour
the good measure into your lap." For the first and most simple
measure of all things is God, both in his existence and in general
in every perfection. But the good is the last thing, the goal and
the best: "No one is good but God alone" (Lk. 18:19; Mk.
10:18). God is good because he is simply the goal, and because he
pours himself out, which no one else can do. From this it is clear
how great is the happiness which is the inwardness of God. Who
as the first has in himself beforehand all those things in which
and through which and for which, as a goal, all beings love and
desire what is ultimate and best. Tobit 10:5 (Vulg.): "Having all
things in you, the One . . ." For the first is in himself rich and
is the greatest riches. For this reason the psalmist exclaims:
"Lord, how great is the multitude of your sweetness." Look at
the meaning of this. Not only are they in him but without him
they could not be and their life is in him. "For he is not the God
of the dead, for all things live in him" (Mt. 22:32).

We should note the perfect and unmixed purity of all those
over whom the saints rejoice, because the measure is called full.
Not: the pure and perfect integrity of joy in itself. First Corinthians 13:10 tells us that "when what is perfect comes, what is imperfect disappears." Taken literally, Paul is talking about the condition of our fatherland. Many know something and yet no one

on earth knows anything perfectly. This is true of this joy and its nature. For no one has this joy completely and this is the point Paul makes when he says in another place: "Now I know partially but then I will know as I am known." And 1 Peter 5: "The God of all grace will himself perfect, confirm, and make solid." Thus is fulfilled the text which says: "You will fill me with joy in your countenance; pleasures are in your right hand all the way to the end." For everything is full and pure in its source and precisely there, not outside. Thus it says "all the way to the end," for only at the goal will anything be fulfilled in what it is.

Consider also the variety and abundance of joys, for the measure is said to be "pressed down, shaken together." Boethius says that happiness is a state consisting of the gathering together of all good things. And "state" denotes a rest after a final end is reached. Isaiah 32:18 says: "My people will sit in the beauty of peace in the tents of faithfulness" and then follows the phrase "in a rich rest." What Isaiah calls rest, Boethius calls a state; and what Isaiah calls rich, Boethius calls a gathering of all good things (cf. Tobit 10:5: "Having all things in you, the One . . .").

Moreover, there is a fullness of the overflowing abundance of heavenly joy: *overflowing*. There are numerous ways in which this is explained: because this joy has no end; because it is beyond all merit; because it exceeds any hope; because it is beyond any desire; and because it is beyond all knowledge and apprehension. About the first, note Matthew 25: "The righteous will go into eternal life." Concerning the second, see Romans 8: "Our sufferings are not worthy . . ." Concerning the third, read Wisdom 5: "They marveled at the sudden arrival of an unhoped-for salvation." Concerning the fourth and fifth, see Ephesians 3: "superabundantly, beyond what we could ask for or understand." Also regarding the fifth, read Isaiah 64 and 1 Corinthians 2: "Eye has not seen nor ear heard nor has it entered into the heart of man what God has prepared for those who love him." "It has not arisen into the heart of a human being." The gloss on this reads that the eternal is not below but above the heart; "in the heart of man" means according to someone living in the human condition: "Are you not fleshly and do you not live like men?" "Not risen" means that "it is said that something rises in the heart which pleases the intellect." Or "not risen in the heart" can mean as material things which rise by abstraction. Or take "not risen" as in the example of a number rising through multiplication and always getting larger.

Concerning the final way we would better say: an overflowing measure. For happiness overflows so copiously from the higher powers to the lower that the senses seem to be transformed into the nature of reason and reason into something yet higher, as is written in the book *On Spirit and Soul*. For this joy overflows so powerfully into the very body that the body is totally submissive to the soul, like air to light, where there is no resistance, as is clear from the gifts of the risen body: clarity, inability to suffer, subtlety, and agility. Then life will be full indeed and the subjection of matter will be complete. For the psalmist says: "You will be inebriated from the fullness of your house . . ." Amen.

COMMENTARY: Four Reasons Why Giving Birth to Compassion Is the Finest Birthing We Can Do/Compassion Is a Divine Attribute and God Is Our Model for Compassion/Compassion Is About Works and Deeds of Justice, as Christ Teaches/Compassion Begins with Self—the Relationship of Passion and Compassion/Compassion Is About Celebration and Glory

In the previous sermon Eckhart established that all of us, like God the Creator, are called to give birth, to be artists and to leave gifts behind us. In the present sermon, and indeed in all of Path Four, Eckhart delineates what this most divine of gifts that we are to give birth to as children of God and as parents of God is all about. Its name is compassion. There are four reasons that *call us very much to compassion*, he says. They are as follows:

1. Compassion triumphs over enemies. Eckhart's biblical examples for this phenomenon are, interestingly enough, both women. Judith and Esther triumphed over their enemies by works of compassion.

2. Compassion renders us divine and clothed in our proper divinity, or, as Eckhart puts it, compassion *divinely adorns the soul, clothing it in the robe which is proper to God.*

3. Compassion *directs a person to relationship with his or her fellow*

human beings by way of justice and in this sense *compassion means justice.*

4. Compassion bestows *heavenly blessings* on us all and therefore begins the end time which is the time of our *final salvation* and healing and of *beatitude* or full happiness.

So much for a summary of Eckhart's four exhortations to compassion. In this commentary, based on Eckhart's own development of these themes, we will be developing his second, third, and fourth points. First, however, we should read the text that Eckhart was reading as he created this sermon on compassion:

> "But I say this to you who are listening: Love your enemies, do good to those who hate you, bless those who curse you, pray for those who treat you badly . . . Instead, love your enemies and do good, and lend without any hope of return. You will have a great reward, and you will be sons of the Most High, for he himself is kind to the ungrateful and the wicked.
>
> "Be compassionate as your Father is compassionate. Do not judge, and you will not be judged yourselves; do not condemn, and you will not be condemned yourselves; grant pardon, and you will be pardoned. Give, and there will be gifts for you: a full measure, pressed down, shaken together, and running over, will be poured into your lap; because the amount you measure out is the amount you will be given back." (Lk. 6:27, 35–38)

Commenting on this text, Eckhart points out that we are being told that God the Creator (whenever "Father" is used of God in the New Testament it means Creator, says scholar Thorleif Boman[1]) alone is the Compassionate One. Compassion was present at creation and indeed was the motivation for creation, Eckhart points out, following the tradition laid down in Jewish midrash. "The first of God's works is compassion," he says, and "the highest work of God is his compassion" (Sermon Thirty-one). All of creation is a continual process and in all this gift-giving of being by the Creator, compassion leads the way. *In every work which God works in a creature, compassion goes with it and ahead of it, especially in the inwardness of the creature itself . . . it goes ahead and overtops all his works.* Eckhart cites Saint Gregory, who teaches that *"it is proper to God to be compassionate."* Thus compassion is a uniquely divine attribute. Indeed, compassion forms the very core and

root of all creation and all creatures and that is why those in touch with
their true core or *inwardness* are in touch with and giving birth to compassion. *For every work in a creature supposes the work of compassion
and is grounded in it as in its root, the power of which preserves all
things and works powerfully in them.* And this is why the psalmist sings
that *"the earth is full of the compassion of the Lord"* and the Lord's compassion is glorified to the heavens. The heavens themselves are rich with
compassion, rich with divinity. Compassion is integral to a cosmic consciousness for Eckhart since a cosmos (from the word for *order*) implies a
plan, a providence. And the plan of Providence is compassion and the
continual birth of creatures from a matrix of compassion.

In the context of discussing compassion and creation Eckhart neatly
slides over the subject of original sin, which received so much treatment
in Augustine's theology but which can be an obstacle for trusting the
cosmos and trusting self and creation. This trust is a prerequisite for
compassion, as psychologist William Eckhardt points out.[2] Eckhart notes
that not only Adam fell, in the original Paradise, but there have been
many falls since, including Samson, David, Solomon, and others. Eckhart
refuses to allow an exaggerated doctrine of original sin to sidetrack
him from the basic message of the first chapters of Genesis, namely, that
God created things "very good" and very trustworthy and with compassion at the very heart of their origin. Indeed, a return to our origin *is*
a return to compassion. *Everything is full and pure in its source and precisely there, not outside.* Therefore, the true meaning of purity—since, as
we saw in Sermon Eighteen, purity means a return to our origin—is
compassion.

Because God is truly compassionate, people can learn lessons from
examining how God is compassionate. God is compassionate *with a sincere and simple intention, with nothing added.* God is wholly compassionate, compassionate *in a simple and essential act.* This is why letting
go and letting be properly lead to compassion. They lead to a *simplicity
of heart* and a *simplicity of intention.* We learn compassion from letting
go of all that is not compassion, that is, of all that is not God or is not in
God. *The intention must be simple so that we seek nothing in addition to
God and nothing except God.* Simplicity is the fruit of letting go and letting be. It is the root of all authentic compassion. In this respect we are
to imitate the simplicity of God. For compassion is not just one more virtue learned in the way one acquires virtues. It is a divine attribute, and
for this reason needs to be learned in our experience of the unity of all

things in God. It is the Creator alone who is our *example or model of this compassion*, warns Eckhart.

But if compassion is so divine, then it is also the breaking out of our own divinity. Compassion is the fullness of divine and human perfection, says Eckhart. It represents *the fourth age* of the new, inward, heavenly human being. It represents *the development of the perfect person, ready to sustain and break the persecutions and all the storms and waves of this world*. "The soul is made blessed by compassion," says Eckhart.[8] Compassion *divinely adorns the soul, clothing it in the robe which is proper to God*. Compassion *divinely adorns* the soul, he repeats in his sermon. Compassion is the true name for our breakthrough, the true art that we are to give birth to. We are to become—as God the Creator is —an artist of compassion.

What does it mean to give birth to compassion and to be artists of compassion? What is compassion besides being a divine attribute? Compassion is about *deeds*, Eckhart notes. Compassion is doing. Eckhart invokes on several occasions in this sermon chapter 58 of the prophet Isaiah. In that chapter the prophet, as we saw Eckhart do in Path Two, preaches against tactical ecstasies like fasting and other religious works in favor of active relief of the sufferings of others.

> Look, you do business on your fastdays,
> you oppress all your workmen;
> look, you quarrel and squabble when you fast
> and strike the poor man with your fist.
>
> Fasting like yours today
> will never make your voice heard on high.
> Is that the sort of fast that pleases me,
> a truly penitential day for men?
>
> Hanging your head like a reed,
> lying down on sackcloth and ashes?
> Is that what you call fasting,
> a day acceptable to Yahweh?
>
> Is not this the sort of fast that pleases me
> —it is the Lord Yahweh who speaks—
> to break unjust fetters
> and undo the thongs of the yoke,

to let the oppressed go free,
and break every yoke,
to share your bread with the hungry,
and shelter the homeless poor,

to clothe the man you see to be naked
and not turn away from your own kin?
Then will your light shine like the dawn
and your wound be quickly healed over

Your integrity will go before you
and the glory of Yahweh behind you.
Cry, and Yahweh will answer;
call, and he will say, "I am here."

If you do away with the yoke,
the clenched fist, the wicked word,
if you give your bread to the hungry,
and relief to the oppressed,

your light will rise in the darkness,
and your shadows become like noon.
Yahweh will always guide you,
giving you relief in desert places. (Is. 58:3–11)

All these deeds of relief and healing of the pain of others is what constitutes the works of compassion for Eckhart as well as for Isaiah. For it is
not enough that one listen to the Word, Eckhart declares. One must
develop *communicability or the ability to give further whatever is received.* In this way the word received becomes a creative word or work
as in the example given us *in the example given us in the uncreated Word through which the Father communicates and pours out all things.* We too are *to pour out all
things* as the Father does and as we saw in the previous sermon. Our
creativity culminates in creatively compassionate deeds. Eckhart speaks
of works of compassion that are *corporal* and of those that are *spiritual.*
Eckhart says that Jesus carried on this same tradition from the prophets in
his teaching and his living and even in his Incarnation itself. *In all these
ways he showed compassion.* Twice in this sermon Eckhart quotes from
the Last Judgment story in Matthew, which is a story about compassionate deeds. "I tell you solemnly, insofar as you did this to one of the
least of these brothers of mine, you did it to me" (Mt. 25:31–46). *Christ*

exhorts us to compassion and he *proposes a model or paradigm of this compassion* in the example of his *heavenly Father.* God the Creator is *the model* of compassion whom Christ followed and whom *we are to imitate.* For *it is proper to God to be compassionate.* Compassion, then, is the *imitatio Dei* for Eckhart as for Jewish theologians.[4]

First, regarding the Incarnation, Eckhart teaches that Jesus became one of us because he lacked the human condition that would allow God to suffer what people suffer and thus to know what true human compassion is about. *He begged from us the human flesh in which he could suffer and the back which could be beaten.* The meaning of Jesus' being made poor was that he was made vulnerable. He lacked nothing *unless it be a back which could receive the blows.* In compassion, Christ's humanity and his divinity come together to teach us by his parables as well as by his deeds what compassion is all about. Christ *our Saviour says explicitly,* "Be compassionate!" To be compassionate is the summary of his teaching that we are sons of God as he also is a Son of God. We are sons of the Compassionate One, like he is. Because Jesus taught us what compassion means, he also taught us what salvation means. It means to be compassionate, which means to enter into the fullness of the blessing that all creation is and to work to pass creation on as a blessing. Eckhart puts it this way: *This, then, is salvation, when we marvel at the beauty of created things and praise the beautiful providence of their Creator or when we purchase heavenly goods by our compassion for the works of creation. The works of creation* are the focus for our compassion—all of them, animals and earth, water and air, plants and music, children and adults. *Christ teaches us . . . about the works of compassion,* Eckhart observes. Our works are to be simple and sincere—like God's are—works that do not look for rewards. Works without a why. Compassion is about works, but it is not about reward for our works.

> "Be careful not to parade your good deeds before men to attract their notice; by doing this you will lose all reward from your Father in heaven. So when you give alms, do not have it trumpeted before you; this is what the hypocrites do in the synagogues and in the streets to win men's admiration. I tell you solemnly, they have had their reward. But when you give alms, your left hand must not know what your right is doing; your almsgiving must be secret, and your Father who sees all that is done in secret will reward you. (Mt. 6:1–4)

Compassion, then, is about relieving the misery of the poor, but not for philanthropy's sake or for the sake of one's reputation. Presumably we have learned to let go of such motivations and to act for God's sake and compassion's sake, that is, without a why.

Christ not only taught compassion, he did compassionate works of healing and relief of people's pain. *He manifested compassion in deed.* We too are to do the works that Jesus did. "Every believer becomes reddened and inflamed with the love of Christ and is wholly imbued with Christ, so that he or she is informed by Christ to do his works."[5] Our works, like Jesus', are to be works of compassion. The most basic work of compassion is justice, or, if you prefer, the relief of injustice. For without justice there can be no compassion, no love of neighbor that is also love of God, no love of God that is also love of neighbor. Eckhart invokes Proverbs, chapter 21, in this regard. It is a hymn to the royal person who is a just person.

> Like flowing water is the heart of the king in the hand of Yahweh,
>   who turns it where he pleases.
>
> A person's conduct may strike him as upright,
>   Yahweh, however, weighs the heart.
>
> To act virtuously and with justice
>   is more pleasing to Yahweh than sacrifice . . .
>
> For the virtuous person it is a joy to execute justice,
>   but it brings dismay to evil-doers . . .
>
> He who pursues virtue and compassion
>   shall find life, justice, and honor. (Pr. 21:1–3, 15, 21)

It is noteworthy that Eckhart's translation of the Bible in this case was evidently that from the Hebrew, which talks of compassion and justice, rather than that from the Greek, which talks of "life and honor."[6] For Eckhart comments on this text, *those who follow compassion find life and justice and glory.* And he invokes Isaiah's similar promise in chapter 58:8. The promise, Eckhart points out, is one of *healing. Your entire life will be called healed,* he suggests, when you have entered into compassion and its works of justice. For *a healing* life is a *living* life.

Eckhart is insistent on the identification of justice with compassion. It *is explicitly said* in Scriptures, he maintains, that *compassion is just to the extent that it gives each one what is his.* And Eckhart does not hesitate to invoke the criticism of unjust economic and political structures that Isidore of Seville railed against when he said: *"It is a great crime to give the wages of the poor to the rich and from the livelihood of the poor to increase the luxuries of the powerful, taking water from the needy earth and pouring it into the rivers."* Elsewhere too Eckhart defines compassion as justice. He says that in God "what is compassion is also justice"[7] If we are in God and acting out of this inness, then our compassion is also our justice and vice versa. Furthermore, Eckhart calls Jesus, the Son of God and the Son of Compassion, the "Son of Justice." God is called "Justissimus," the Most Just One, by Eckhart,[8] and Jesus is the Son of the Most Just One. So too, all who are reborn as the sons of God are the sons of Justice.

> The just man is the offspring and son of justice. He is called, and actually is, the son because he becomes different in person but not in nature. "I and my Father are one" (Jn. 10:30): we "are," that is to say . . . "one" in nature, because otherwise justice would not beget the just man, nor the Father the Son . . . Now if the Father and the Son, justice and the just man, are one and the same in nature, it follows that the just man is equal to, not less than, justice.[9]

Moreover, our being born into justice and into the son of justice is a process. "The just man is always in process of being born from justice itself." And Jesus is "unbegotten justice itself."[10] Eckhart explains this birthing to justice elsewhere:

> A person so fashioned, God's son, being good as the son of goodness, just as the son of justice, insofar as he or she is the son of justice alone, then justice is unborn and yet bearing, and the son to whom justice gives birth has the self-same being as justice has and is, and he enters into all the properties of justice and truth.[11]

It is important in Eckhart's theologizing on justice not to platonize him, for he himself has defined justice as *giving each person what is his.* He has also applied it to the subject of the rich over the poor, as we have seen. He also insists that justice is that dimension of compassion which *applies to your neighbor. For this is the nature of justice,* namely, to direct a person to relationships with his fellow human beings. Compassion as justice is this kind of compassion. It regulates the interactions of people and their institutions.

Since compassion also boasts a mystical side—that of our relation to all of the cosmos and its origins and goal in compassion—Eckhart invokes as a summary of his teaching on compassion the psalmist, who sings:

"Justice and peace have kissed." (Ps. 85:10)[12]

Eckhart insists that compassion begins at home, namely with oneself. We need to trust ourselves in order to trust the cosmos and to trust others, or, as Aristotle put it, *"friendship toward others is rooted in the ability to be a friend to oneself."* It is the love and compassion toward ourselves that we will project onto others, as Jesus warned us when he said: "Love your neighbor as you love yourself." Eckhart asks: *How then can anyone be compassionate toward me or toward you who is not compassionate toward himself?* And then Eckhart draws an explicit conclusion: Christ *wants us to be compassionate even to our own body and soul.* Both body and soul are part of the blessing that creation is: if we bless them, they will bless us in return. We are reminded of Eckhart's saying cited earlier, "the soul loves the body." We learn compassion even from the relationship of soul and body. We will never learn it if we fall into dualistic battles of body warring against soul. The dialectical relationship —instead of dualistic relationship—is to be the very manner in which we relate to all of life. Indeed, humility itself, Eckhart says in this sermon, is our capacity for strength and for gentleness at once. By it we *stand firm* and we stand *under,* as in the Latin word *substantia*—to stand under. A substance, that is, a whole person, is one who can stand firm and under at the same time. This is authentic humility.

In this context of compassion toward our whole self, Eckhart turns to the subject of passion and compassion. In saying that God is *compassionate without passion,* Eckhart is not denying the God who feels whom we met in Sermon Ten. After all, in another sermon he says that "the wrath of God comes from love, for he is wrathful without bitterness."[13] And in another place he warns that "love, which is charity, is a fire."[14] This is reminiscent of Thomas Aquinas' comment on Luke 6:36, when he writes that "compassion is the fire that Jesus came to set on the earth."[15] Eckhart also talks about our deeds of compassion as deeds of fire. He exegetes the flaming sword in the flight from Paradise story in Genesis in the following manner: "The flaming sword—this means that the soul should return to heaven through good and holy works which are done in a fiery love of God and fellow Christians. That we are thus brought home, God help us."[16] Thus Eckhart prays that we may become "fiery" in our love and passion for works of justice. Furthermore, he warns that without passion no compassionate deeds are accomplished: "All deeds are accomplished in passion. If the fiery love of God grows cold in the soul, it dies: and if God is to have an effect on the soul, God must be united to the soul."[17] What then is he getting at in talking of passionless compassion? He is emphasizing, as he points out, that compassion is not feeling or sentiment alone. It includes the intellect and decision-making; it includes justice. It involves the reason and the will as well as the feelings.

We therefore are compassionate like the Father when we are compassionate not from passion, not from impulse, but from deliberate choice and reasonable decision. For Psalm 84 says: "Compassion and truth meet one another," that is, passion and reason.

Indeed, Eckhart has just identified compassion and passion. Truth is reason, he says, and passion is compassion. Compassion, then, is a kind of passion, but it is not limited to emotions or rhetoric. Rather, it embraces reason and will as well as caring and feeling. And then it expresses itself in authentic deeds.

Eckhart nowhere calls for putting down passion, for that dualistic action would destroy the unitive starting point that all compassion presumes. Rather, he warns that passion by itself and without reason, judgment, and justice can get out of hand and mislead us. Thus he calls for our being *very much on the alert lest the force of passion dominate our actions.* "Being on the alert" is not the same as controlling, forgetting, or repressing. Otherwise we become *like the horse and mule.* Passion is present but not as our leader. It *does not take the lead but follows.* It is to be put to the service of our decision-making and commitments. It is important that we not leave it behind as the Stoics would want to do. To allow passion to lead, however, would be a mistake. Dogs lead blind people, but passion does not lead us where we most want to go. Justice is a rational as well as an emotional issue.

The true role of senses, sensuality, and passion is to be instruments in our transformation. They participate fully in the joy and celebration that all compassion is about. We and our senses are transformed by such ecstasy.

> The overflowing of happiness floods so copiously from the higher powers to the lower that the senses seem to be transformed into the nature of reason and reason into something higher, as is written in the book *On Spirit and Soul*.

Far from putting senses and passion down, compassion leads them into the origin and depth of ourselves where all transformation, and ultimately joyful celebration, dances. They are entrances to the depths of our selves. Our body becomes almost transparent when we become a risen body.

> This joy overflows so powerfully into the very body that the body is totally submissive to the soul, like air to light, where there is no resistance, as is clear from the gifts of the risen body: clarity, inability to suffer, subtlety, and agility.

Eckhart turns to the promise Jesus makes to those who are compassionate. *We move now to a consideration of the text about the good and overflowing measure which is poured into our lap.* The first good that is poured into our lap as a result of compassion is the Compassionate One, God. God comes to us as goal and as the source of compassion. *The first and most simple measure of all things is God . . . but the good is the last thing, the goal and the best: "No one is good but God alone."*

A second measure to our joy and celebration is that of the entire communion of saints. All saints swim in an ocean of compassion and rejoice where it is shared and lived out. All are *in God, who is not the God of the dead but the God for all things, which live in him. The measure is called full because of the perfect and unmixed purity, that is, origin, of all of those over whom they rejoice.* And so, the celebration is full and complete. It is a celebration, Eckhart points out, *of pure and perfect integrity of joy in itself.* It is a taste of heaven, of our fatherland. It is full because *everything is full and pure in its source and precisely there, not outside.* And compassion is our source. We have returned to celebrate at our origin, which is compassion. It is also a celebration of not yet, of our *goal*, for only with a taste of the goal is *anything fulfilled*. It is a rich rest where *all good things gather*. A reunion of goodness, Eckhart is saying! No wonder the celebration is so full. Furthermore, compassion is an *overflowing abundance of heavenly joy* that does not end, is not merited, exceeds our wildest hopes, expectations, and desires. Indeed, it is the origin of eternal life. This *overflowing of happiness floods* our whole selves—body and senses as well as spirit and mind—to the point of our being *inebriated from the fullness* of its energies. Eckhart describes this process elsewhere: "When the Lord descends the soul is fecundated and inebriated by compassion with an abundance of virtues and graces . . . 'there arises in his days justice and abundance of peace' (Ps. 72:7)." At such time we flow with "milk and honey, which means humanity and divinity."[18]

No wonder, given such human and divine celebration, Eckhart can say that compassion brings *glory and life* to the individual. Then life will be full *indeed*, he exclaims, and cites Paul: "Eye has not seen nor ear heard nor has it entered the heart of a person what God has prepared for those who love him" (1 Co. 2:9). Compassion indeed is the fullest of all divine births. It alone *eventually leads to glory*.

Sermon Thirty-one: COMPASSION IS AN OCEAN—THE MYSTICAL SIDE TO COMPASSION

"Have compassion on the people who are in you." (Ho. 14:4)*

The prophet says: "Lord, have compassion on the people who are in you" (Ho. 14:4). Our Lord answered: "All who are sick I will heal, and I will love them freely."

I will take for my text the words "The Pharisee asked the Lord to eat with him" and, further, "Our Lord said to the woman: V*ade in pace*, go in peace!" (Lk. 7:36, 50). It is good when someone goes from peace to peace. It is praiseworthy. However, it is not enough. One should *run* into peace, one should not begin in peace. God, our Lord, means: One should be grounded in peace and thrown into peace and should end up in peace. Our Lord says: "In me alone shall be your peace" (Jn. 16:33). Just so far as we are in God we are in peace. If any part of us is in God, it has peace; if any part of us is outside of God it has no peace. Saint John says: "Everything that is born of God overcomes the world" (1 Jn. 5:4). What is born of God seeks peace and runs into peace. Therefore he said: "V*ade in pace*, run into peace." The person who runs and runs, continually running into peace, is a heavenly person. The heavens are continually running and in their running they seek peace.

Now pay attention! "The Pharisee asked our Lord to eat with him." The food which I eat is united to my body as my body is united to my soul. My body and my soul are united in one being but not in one activity—as my soul is united in one work with the eye, that is to see; thus the food I eat is united in one being with my nature but not in one activity, and this signifies the great union that we will have with God in being but not in activity. Therefore the Pharisee asked our Lord to eat with him.

* "Populi ejus qui in te est, misereberis." (DW I, №7)

The word "Pharisee" means one who is set apart and does not know of any end. Everything belonging to the soul should be completely stripped off. The nobler the powers are, the more they strip off. Some powers are so high above the body and so detached that they peel away and separate off completely! A master says a beautiful word: "What has once touched corporal things never enters again." The second meaning of Pharisee is that one should be stripped off and detached and gathered inward. From this one can conclude that an unlearned person can learn knowledge and teach others through love and desire. The third meaning of Pharisee is that one should have no end and should not be closed off and should cling to nothing and should be so fully grounded in peace that he or she knows nothing more of strife, when such a person is grounded in God through the powers that are entirely stripped off. Therefore the prophet said: "Lord, have compassion on the people who are in you."

A master says: "The highest work that God has ever worked in all creatures is compassion." The most secret and forbidden work that he ever worked on the angels was carrying them up into compassion; this is the work of compassion as it is in itself and as it is in God. Whatever God does, the first outburst is always compassion, and I do not mean that he forgives a person his sins or that a person takes compassion on another. The master means much more. He means that the *highest* work that God works is compassion. A master says: "The work of compassion is so close to God that although truth and riches and goodness name God, one of them names him better than the other." The highest work of God is compassion and this means that God sets the soul in the highest and purest place which it can occupy: in space, in the sea, in a fathomless ocean; and there God works compassion. Therefore the prophet says: "Lord, have compassion on the people who are in you."

What people are in God? Saint John says: "God is love and whoever remains in love remains in God and God in him" (1 Jn. 4:16). Although Saint John says that love unites, love never establishes anything in God. Perhaps it connects something that is already united to him. Love does not unite, not in any way. What is already united it sticks together and binds. Love unites in works but not in being. The best masters say that reason peels entirely away and takes God unveiled, as he is, pure Being in himself. Knowledge breaks through truth and goodness and falls on pure Being and takes God naked, as he is without name. But I say: neither knowledge nor love unites. Love apprehends God himself insofar as he is good, and if God lost the name "Goodness" that would be the end of love. Love takes God under a skin, under a cloak. Reason does not do this. It takes God insofar as God is known to it. Reason can never comprehend him in the ocean of his unfathomableness. I say that beyond these two, beyond knowledge and love, there is compassion. In the highest and purest acts that God works, God works compassion.

A master says these beautiful words: "There is in the soul something very secret and hidden and far above it, from which the powers of reason and will break forth." Saint Augustine says: "Where the Son breaks out from the Father in the first outpouring is ineffable; so too there is something very secret about the first outbreak, where reason and the will break forth." A master who has spoken the best about the soul says that all human science can never fathom what the soul is in its ground. To know what the soul is, one needs supernatural knowledge. We do not know about what the powers of the soul do when they go out to do their work; we know a little about this, but not very much. What the soul is in its ground, no one knows. What one can know about it must be supernatural, it must be from grace. That is where God works compassion. Amen.

COMMENTARY: The Fullest of All God's Works Is Compassion/ Compassion Is an Unfathomable Ocean Greater than Knowledge and Love/We Are in Compassion When We Are in God/How This Inness of Panentheism Destroys All Otherness and Creates Interdependence/ The Need to Run into Peace

In the previous sermon Eckhart presented an overview of his theology of compassion. Beginning with this sermon and extending throughout the remaining sermons of Path Four we examine compassion in more specific detail. In the present sermon, for example, Eckhart examines the mystical side to compassion, the side of consciousness itself. In the sermons to follow he will deal with the economic side of compassion (numbers 32 and 35), the theology of work that compassion presumes (numbers 33 and 34), the political side (numbers 35 and 36), and the celebrative side (number 37). For Eckhart, compassion is not merely a moral norm. It is a consciousness, a way of seeing the world and responding to the world. It is a way of living out the truth of our inness with God and with one another as discovered in Path One. Compassion presumes a certain mystical consciousness or way of seeing the world. What is that way?

Eckhart repeats his conviction expressed in the previous sermon, namely that God is compassion. His sermon is based on the prophet Hosea, who, in Eckhart's translation of the Bible, said: *"Lord, have compassion on the people who are in you"* (Ho. 14:4), and who in a current translation says: "You are the one in whom orphans find compassion." In both translations the word *in* plays a prominent role and Eckhart, as we shall see shortly, develops his theology of compassion from his theology of inness or panentheism. But Eckhart says more about compassion and God in this sermon. Following Peter Lombard and Thomas Aquinas,[1] Eckhart declares that *compassion is the highest work that God has ever worked in all creatures.* Compassion, Eckhart says, is the origin of all God's creativity—God's motivation and God's goal. *Whatever God does, the first outburst is always compassion. Compassion is the highest work that God works. Compassion is fuller and deeper than either love or knowledge. Beyond these two, beyond knowledge and love, there is compassion.* Compassion is the best name there is for God. It alone comes close to naming the creative works of God, for *in the highest and purest acts that God works, God works compassion.* Compassion is therefore the one blessing and the one fruit that remains from creation through resurrection. It is the origin of all God's creativity and the fullness of all fruitful birthing. "For it is indeed a blessing when something bears fruit and the fruit remains. The fruit, however, remains to the one who remains there in love."[2] If we are to imitate God and to bear the fruit that God bears and to bear the Son of God and indeed to become the Son of God, then compassion is the ultimate way of our spiritual journeying. Where does this God-like way take us?

It takes us into God. The breakthrough that gave birth to the Son and the breakthrough that gives us a second birth both come from the same ground. We cannot name the ground for we cannot put our fingers on it —*what the soul is in its ground, no one knows.* It takes supernatural grace even to enter there. However, we can name the energy that goes on there, the fire that is burning by the blaze of the *scintilla animae* in the core of the soul. What goes on there is compassion—*that is where God works compassion.* In our very inner core, as innermost as we can get and as innermost as we are, God is busy working compassion. Eckhart hints that just as the best name for the unnameable God is Compassion, so too the finest name for the unnameable soul is Compassion. After all, the innermost part of the soul *is* the *imago Dei.* Where we create from our innermost being we are always creating compassion. In the text that Eckhart used for this sermon, Hosea announces:

> I will love them with all my heart,
> for my anger has turned from them.
> I will fall like dew on Israel.
> He shall bloom like the lily,
> and thrust out roots like the poplar,
> His shoots will spread far;
> he will have the beauty of the olive
> and the fragrance of Lebanon . . .
> I am like a cypress ever green,
> all your fruitfulness comes from me.
>
> Let the wise man understand these words.
> Let the intelligent man grasp their meaning.
> For the ways of Yahweh are straight,
> and virtuous men walk in them,
> but sinners stumble. (Ho. 14:5–7, 9–10)

All our fruitfulness comes from God who is the Compassionate one. Thus Compassion is the source of all creativity and birthing. And of all the fruits we give birth to, none is more Godly than the way of walking that is Yahweh's way, a way of walking in compassion.

Not only is compassion in us at our very core, where God energizes us and divinizes us into creators ourselves, but we are in compassion. For, as we learned in Path One, God is not only in us but we are in God. If God is Compassion, then our journeying into compassion is necessarily our journeying into God and vice versa. The deeper we go into God, the deeper we go into compassion. Eckhart calls on scriptural texts from John's theology to substantiate his position. Jesus talks about being in him:

"I have told you all this
so that you may find peace in me.
In the world you will have trouble,
but be brave:
I have conquered the world." (Jn. 16:33)

The peace we are to find is not apart from the world and the troubles
the world gives us but in the midst of the world because we are always
in God. Being in God we can also be in the world and sustain any
vicissitudes that the world extends to us. The victory over the world has
already happened for those who have broken through the consciousness
that would tell us that we are outside God:

> Anyone who has been begotten by God
> has already overcome the world;
> this is the victory over the world—
> our faith. (1 Jn. 5:4)

Eckhart comments that *if any part of us is in God, it has peace; if any
part of us is outside of God it has no peace.* For, as John has promised,
"everything that is born of God overcomes the world."

Eckhart gropes, searching and stretching his own imagination, for images of the panentheistic existence of being in God and in compassion
that he finds in John's Gospel and in the prophet Hosea. Already, in the
previous sermon, we saw Eckhart call compassion an ocean. But in this
sermon he develops that image more richly. Compassion is not only an
ocean, it is a *fathomless ocean,* it is not only a sea, it is *space* itself.
Eckhart is driven into cosmic language and driven to call on his cosmic
experience in an effort to picture compassion. A compassionate consciousness presumes a cosmic consciousness.

> Compassion means that God sets the soul in the highest and
> purest place which it can occupy: in space, in the sea, in a
> fathomless ocean; and there God works compassion. Therefore
> the prophet says: "Lord, have compassion on the people who
> are in you."

This picture of God setting the soul in an ocean of compassion conjures
up images of swimming and floating—yes, even skinny-dipping—in com-

passion. We are suspended, Eckhart is saying, in a sea of divine grace called compassion. We breathe compassion in and breathe compassion out daily if we are awake and aware. He turns to John's imagery of our panentheistic swimming in compassion:

> Anyone who lives in love lives in God,
> and God lives in him.
> Love will come to its perfection in us
> when we can face the day of Judgment without fear;
> because even in this world
> we have become as he is. (1 Jn. 4:16–17)

Clearly, for Eckhart, a consciousness of our inness in God is a consciousness of our inness in compassion. If Compassion is God's name and we have become as he is, then we have become compassion. A son or daughter of God is a son or daughter of compassion.

This sermon is an immensely maternal one. Eckhart's images of the divine sea of compassion conjure up images of the divine, maternal womb. Eckhart is saying that we are born in a sea of compassion, a compassionate fluid of divinely maternal grace. In painting these images Eckhart recalls the biblical roots for the word compassion. In Hebrew the word for compassion and the word for womb come from the same stem, *rehem* and *rahamim*. Compassion is a return to our origin.

What are some consequences of this breakthrough in consciousness by which we are awakened to the fact of our swimming in a space and a sea of compassion? One consequence is the breakdown of all dualistic thinking. For we are not alone in this divine sea. All creatures have been born in the same holy fluid; we do not swim alone but in a common sea of oneness with others. This means that all beings are interdependent. "God's peace prompts fraternal service, so that one creature sustains the other. One is enriching the other, that is why *all creatures are interdependent.*"[3] Creatures in this common sea serve one another and sustain one another. Eckhart's consciousness of interdependence is crucial to grasping what true compassion is about. Indeed, the late Thomas Merton defined compassion as a "keen awareness of the interdependence of all living beings which are all part of one another and all involved in one another."[4]

Another consequence of our swimming together in a common sea of compassion is that all otherness is broken down. We truly see the oneness that is ours. "In God there can be nothing alien, nothing other," warns Eckhart.[5] We recall Eckhart's explanation from Sermon Three about the threefold way we relate to creatures such as wine, bread, and meat: as creatures, as gifts, as "eternally not other." This third level of consciousness is the way of compassion, a way of knowing that all is one. For when we traffic in a consciousness of otherness, we destroy compassion and reduce it to philanthropy, pity, or moralizing. As Angelus Silesius observed, drawing on Eckhart's theology,

> there are no objects of compassion
> because there are no objects.

To know that there are no objects but only interdependencies and shared energies—this is the consciousness behind true compassion. This is the consciousness that heals, as Jesus promised in the scriptural text that began this sermon: *"All who are sick I will heal, and I will love them freely."* This healing and unitive consciousness is born of our letting go and letting be, as Kelley comments:

> Without detachment [letting go] love is "a going out to some other," humility is "an abasing of oneself before an other," and "mercy means nothing else but a man's going forth of self by reason of his fellow creature's lack." But in Principle there is no other.[6]

For we become as God is, that is, compassionate in our consciousness. "When a free intellect is really detached it takes God as its Self and were it to remain structureless and free from contingency it would take on the very knowledge that God is." We would become immovable in our rootedness. We are like a hinge, grounded in compassion and unitive consciousness. "When the door swings open or closes, the outer boards move to and fro, but the hinge remains immovable in one place and it is not changed at all as a result. So it is here, if you only knew how to act rightly." Bathing in one sea of compassion, "I become all things, as he is, and I am one and the same being with him." When all otherness is broken through, then we may "be all in all, as God is all in all."[7] Our oneness is a oneness in one another but also in God. This is why the two commandments that Jesus left us are really only one commandment—which is a reward, not an order. For the reward is the pleasure of swimming in a divine sea, and loving creature and Creator in one act of love. Eckhart says: "He who loves God more than his neighbor loves him well, it is true, but not perfectly." Why not? Ancelet comments:

> Eckhart takes literally and in all its rigor the Gospel precept: to love God is "the first and greatest commandment," but the second, to love one's neighbor as oneself is "quite like" unto it. He understands by this that for him who loves his neighbor as he should be loved, that is to say, in God, there can only be one sole love.[8]

Our love of self is the same way. When we are *grounded in God* we become *so fully grounded in peace that we know nothing more of strife.* When we are truly in God and in compassion we are *grounded in peace and thrown into peace and end up in peace.*

But Eckhart makes an important point: we ought not to exaggerate the experience of our inness with God and compassion to the detriment of our need to develop compassion and to seek it out in our work and activities. Indeed, we need to *run into peace.* We are not yet fully there, even though compassion is the starting point of our creation and the goal of it. It is *not enough to go from peace to peace* or to narcissistically meditate on our compassionate origins. We need to seek peace, to make peace, to *run into peace. What is born of God seeks peace and runs into peace.* Like the vast stars in the heavens, we must be on the move in this cosmic space that is peace. Indeed, a heavenly person will imitate the cosmos itself and will always be on the move toward peace. Such a person is a verb, not a noun, *running and running continually into peace.* Compassion too will be a verb and not a noun. After all, God's work is continually in process. God is always giving birth and desiring to give birth and his birth is always from compassion and toward compassion. Our work needs to be the same. Our union with God as Compassion is a union of being but not yet a union of activity. Compassion as being, then, has already begun. But compassion as work needs to be done. One activity of compassion is that of forgiving others, as Jesus does in Luke's Gospel (7:36–50) and which he links to compassion in his teaching in the previous chapter (Lk. 6:37). But that activity too must derive its full energy from the inness behind compassion before it is truly a compassionate work. For outside the sea of compassion, there is no compassion. Outside God there is nothing but nothing. But inside God there are all things so bathed in compassion that we can say with John: *"Everything that is born of God overcomes the world."* Compassion, which had the first word, will eventually have the last.

Sermon Thirty-two: DRIVING MERCHANT MENTALITIES
FROM OUR SOULS: ECONOMICS AND COMPASSION

"Jesus then went into the temple and drove out all those who
were selling and buying there." (Mt. 21:12)*

We read in the Gospel that our Lord went into the temple and
threw out those who were buying and selling there. To others
who were offering for sale pigeons and similar things he said:
"Take all this away . . . !" (Jn. 2:16). Why did Jesus throw out
those who were buying and selling, and why did he command
those who were offering pigeons for sale to get out? He meant by
this only that he wished the temple to be empty, just as if he had
wanted to say: "I am entitled to this temple, and wish to be
alone here, and to have mastery here."

What does this mean? This temple, which God wishes to rule
over powerfully according to his own will, is the soul of a person.
God has formed and created the soul very like himself, for we
read that our Lord said: "Let us make human beings in our own
image" (Gn. 1:26). And this is what he did. So like to himself
did he make the soul of a person that neither in the kingdom of
heaven nor on earth among all the splendid creatures that God
created in such a wonderful way is there any creature that resembles him as much as does the soul of a human being. For this
reason God wishes the temple to be empty so that nothing can be
in it but himself alone. This is because this temple pleases him so
and resembles him so closely, and because he is pleased whenever
he is alone in this temple.

Very well, now pay close attention! Who were the people who
were buying and selling in the temple, and who are they still?
Now listen to me closely! I shall preach now without exception
only about good people. Nevertheless, I shall at this time show

* "Intravit Jesus in templum et coepit eicere vedentes et ementes." (DW I,
✳1)

who the merchants were then and still are today—those who were buying and selling then, and are still doing so, the ones our Lord whipped and drove out of the temple. And he still is doing so to those who, despite everything, continue to buy and sell in the temple. He will not allow a single one of them to be there. Behold how all those people are merchants who shun great sins and would like to be good and do good deeds in God's honor, such as fasts, vigils, prayers, and similar good deeds of all kinds. They do these things so that our Lord may give them something, or so that God may do something dear to them. All these people are merchants. This is more or less to be understood since they wish to give one thing in return for another. In this way they wish to bargain with our Lord. They are cheated, however, in this transaction. For everything they possess, and everything they would like to do—if they were to give it all away for God's sake and if they were to be influenced entirely in accord with God's sake—God would still not be indebted to them or have to give them anything unless he wanted to do so of his own free will. For whatever they are, they owe to God, and whatever they have, they have from God and not from themselves. Therefore, God is not at all in debt to them for their deeds and gifts unless he should wish to do something of his own free will and favor, and not for the sake of their deeds or gifts. For they give not what is theirs; they achieve nothing by themselves. As Christ himself says: "Without me you can do nothing" (Jn. 15:5).

These people who wish to bargain in this way with our Lord are very silly. They have little wisdom or none at all. Therefore, our Lord threw them out of the temple and drove them away. Light and darkness cannot exist with one another. God is truth and light in himself. When God comes into this temple, he drives out of it uncertainty, which is darkness, and reveals himself with light and truth. The merchants therefore are driven away as soon as truth is known, for truth does not long for any kind of commercial deal. God does not seek his own interest. In all his deeds he is unencumbered and free, and accomplishes them out of genuine love. The person united with God behaves in the same way. This person is unencumbered and free in all his or her deeds, and accomplishes them for God's honor, seeking no personal interest. And God accomplishes them in this person.

I state further that so long as people by means of all their deeds are seeking anything at all from all that God may be pleased to give, such people resemble the merchants. If you wish to be completely free of this commercial viewpoint so that God may keep you in the temple, whatever deeds you may wish to do, you must accomplish only in praise of God. And you must remain as unfettered by all this as nothingness—which is neither here nor there—is unfettered. You must in no way long for such objects. If you accomplish your deeds in this way, your deeds are spiritual and divine. The merchants are at the same time driven out of the temple, and God is alone within it. For this person has only God in mind. Behold how in this way the temple is rid of the merchants. Behold how people who have neither themselves nor anything besides God alone and God's honor in mind are truly free and empty of any commercial spirit in all their deeds. Such people seek not their own interests, just as God is unencumbered and free in all his deeds and seeks not his own interests.

I have further stated that our Lord said to the people who were offering pigeons for sale: "Get rid of this, put it away!" He did not drive those people out nor did he scold them severely, but he spoke rather kindly to them: "Get rid of this," as if he might have wanted to say: "This is, of course, not bad, and yet it is an obstacle to the purer truth."

These are all *good* people who accomplish their deeds in relation to their own egos, to time and number, and to what comes before and what comes after. In their deeds they are prevented from attaining the best kind of truth. Such a truth would require them to be free and unencumbered, just as our Lord Jesus Christ is free and unencumbered. For our Lord, in a way that is constantly, unceasingly, and timelessly new, receives himself from his heavenly Father. At the same time our Lord gives rise to himself perfectly, in grateful praise to the Father's majesty, and with equal honor to himself. This is exactly the same way people should behave who are willing to receive the highest of all truth and live within it without beginning or end. Without hindrance from the deeds they accomplish or the concepts of which they become aware, such people newly receive God's gift in an unencumbered and free way, and give rise to it again in the same light with grateful praise in our Lord Jesus Christ. Thus if the doves were removed, this means the removal of the hindrance and ego connection caused by all the deeds that are otherwise good and in which people do not seek their own interests. Therefore, our Lord said in quite a kindly way: "Get rid of this, put it away!" Just as if he wished to say that it is, of course, good, but it brings a hindrance with it.

If this temple could thus become free of all hindrances, that is to say, from any ego connection and uncertainty, it would gleam so beautifully and shine so purely and clearly over and through everything created by God that no one could match its splendor except the uncreated God. And in all truth no one really resembles this temple except the uncreated God alone. Nothing beneath the angels resembles this temple at all. The highest angels themselves resemble the temple of the noble soul up to a certain degree, but still not completely. The fact that they resemble the soul to a certain degree is proven by knowledge and love. However, a limit has been set for the angels beyond which they cannot go. But the soul can indeed go beyond it. If a soul were to reach the same height as the highest angel—I am speaking of the soul of a person still living in the temporal dimension—such a person in his or her freedom might reach immeasurably higher than the angels in a new and timeless moment. This means without a mode and beyond the mode of the angels and all created understanding.

God alone is free and uncreated, and for this reason he alone is like the soul with respect to freedom, but not with respect to uncreatedness, since the *soul* has been created. If the soul comes into the unblended light, it throbs so far into its nothingness and so far away from its created something into nothingness that the soul of its own power cannot return to its created substance. And God places himself with his uncreatedness beneath the soul's nothingness and upholds the soul in his substance. The soul has dared to come to nothing, and cannot with its own power come back to itself again—so far has the soul left itself before God placed himself beneath the soul. That must of necessity be the case. For as I said earlier: "Jesus went into the temple and drove out all who were selling and buying there, and he said to them: 'Get rid of this!'" Yes, see how now I take the expression: "Jesus went in and began to say to them: 'Get rid of this!' and they got rid of it."

Behold how there was no one there except Jesus alone, and he began to speak in the temple. Behold, this you should truly know, that if anyone wishes to speak in the temple, that is, in the soul, except Jesus, our Lord will remain silent. For the soul has strange guests with whom it is conversing. If, however, Jesus is to speak within the soul, it must be alone and must itself be silent if it is to hear Jesus. In such circumstances he will go inside the soul and begin to speak. What does the Lord Jesus say? He declares what he is. What then is he? He is the Father's Word. And in this very Word the Father declares himself as well as the whole divine nature and all that God is, just as he knows it. He also knows how God is. And since God is perfect in his knowledge and in his capacity, he is therefore perfect also in his speech. While declaring the Word, he declares himself and all things in another Person, and he gives to the Word the same nature he himself has. And God declares all forms of spirit endowed with reason to be *similar* in essence to the Word according to the "image," to the extent that the Word remains within them. These forms of spirit, however, are not like the Word in the way in which the Word gives off light or in the degree to which every form of spirit has distinguished its own being. They—that is to say, the "images" that are given off—have kept, however, the possibility of attaining a grace-giving similarity to the Word. And the Father has declared completely the Word, as it is within itself, and all that is within the Word.

Since the Father has declared *this*, what does Jesus declare within the soul? As I have said, the Father declares the Word, and either speaks within the Word or not at all. Jesus, however, speaks in the *soul*. The manner of his speaking is as follows: he reveals himself and everything that the Father has declared in him in the way in which the Spirit is susceptible. He reveals the Father's ruling power to be an equally immeasurable force in the Spirit. When the Spirit receives this force in and through the Son, the Spirit himself becomes powerful in that progression so that the Spirit becomes equally powerful in all virtues and in perfect purity. As a result, neither love nor sorrow nor all that God has created in time can disturb a human being. Rather such a person remains full of power as if enveloped in a divine strength compared to which all others are small and powerless.

At another time Jesus reveals himself within the soul with the immeasurable wisdom that is himself—the same wisdom with which the Father in his totally paternal ruling power knows himself as well as the Word, which is also wisdom itself, and all the Word contains, since God is one. If this wisdom is joined to the soul, all doubt and all error and all darkness are totally removed, and the soul is brought into a pure, clear light, which is God himself, just as the prophet said: "Lord, in your light we shall know the light" (Ps. 36:9). For God becomes known to God in the soul. Then the soul knows itself and all things with this same wisdom. With the same wisdom the soul knows God himself, and his paternal majesty in its fearful creative power, and the essential original being in one unity without any kind of distinction.

Moreover, Jesus reveals himself with the immeasurable sweetness and fullness that gush out of the power of the Holy Spirit, overflowing and streaming into all sensitive hearts with an abundant fullness and sweetness. When Jesus reveals himself with this fullness and sweetness, and unites himself to the soul, the soul flows with fullness and sweetness into itself, and beyond itself, and beyond all things into its first origin through the action of grace with limitless power. For the external person is obedient to the inner person up to the point of death, and is then in constant peace in God's service.

May God help us so that Jesus can come into us and throw out and remove all obstacles and make us one being, just as he is one with the Father and the Holy Spirit. May we become one with him and eternally remain with him. Amen.

COMMENTARY: We Are the Temple, Image, and House of God/ Wonderful and Divine Events Happen in This Temple/ How a Merchant Mentality Destroys a Consciousness of Compassion and Ruins the Soul/How Dualism Is the Sin Behind All Sin

In this sermon Eckhart draws on two Gospel narratives, one from Matthew and one from John, that tell of driving moneylenders from the temple. Following John's narrative, Eckhart makes a connection between the temple and the person. In John's case, the sanctuary is that of Jesus and in Eckhart's application the sanctuary is every person reborn as a son of God. John writes:

> Just before the Jewish Passover Jesus went up to Jerusalem, and in the temple he found people selling cattle and sheep and pigeons, and the money changers sitting at their counters there. Making a whip out of some cord, he drove them all out of the temple, cattle and sheep as well, scattered the money changers' coins, knocked their tables over and said to the pigeon-sellers, "Take all this out of here and stop turning my Father's house into a market" . . . The Jews intervened and said, "What sign can you show us to justify what you have done?" Jesus answered, "Destroy this sanctuary, and in three days I will raise it up." The Jews replied, "It has taken forty-six years to build this sanctuary: are you going to raise it up in three days?" But he was speaking of the sanctuary that was his body . . . (Jn. 2:13–16, 18–21; see also Mt. 21:12–17)

This temple, comments Eckhart, *is the soul of a person. We who are the image of God, with a soul very like himself, are the new temple. How like God are we, this new temple? The soul's freedom is without limit— the soul can indeed go beyond the limit that has been set for the angels beyond which they cannot go. Indeed, so full is the soul's freedom that God alone is like the soul with respect to freedom. Only God is like this temple, only God's image mirrors it.*

> We read that our Lord said: "Let us make human beings in our own image" (Gn. 1:26). And this is what he did. So like to himself did he make the soul of a person that neither in the kingdom of heaven nor on earth among all the splendid creatures that God created in such a wonderful way is there any creature that resembles him as much as does the soul of a human being.

So divine is this temple that is us that in all truth no one really resembles this temple except the uncreated God alone. Nothing beneath the angels resembles this temple at all. So exquisite is the human temple that it would gleam so beautifully and shine so purely and clearly over and through everything created by God that no one could match its splendor except the uncreated God.

Not only is the soul a big and spacious temple, but wonderful and divine things happen in this temple. There, for example, Jesus speaks the full language of revelation. There we are told who God is.

> What does the Lord Jesus say? He declares what he is. What then is he? He is the Father's Word. And in this very Word the Father declares himself as well as the whole divine nature and all that God is, just as he knows it.

Thus the divine Word is uttered in the temple that is us. Nothing is held back. Revelation is full. In this soul Jesus *reveals himself and everything that the Father has declared in him in the way in which the Spirit is susceptible.* There, too, the power of the Holy Spirit *gushes out, overflowing and streaming into all sensitive hearts with an abundant fullness and sweetness.* There the soul meets wisdom—the wisdom that is Jesus himself and the wisdom that is the soul's. Revealed in this wisdom is the *fearful creative power* of God who creates all energy. So creativity, too, flows from this sacred temple. There the Spirit's power is revealed as being equal to that of the Creator—the new creation will not be less than the original creation in its beauty and its grace. What happens to a person in touch with this holy temple? Such a person is not easily disturbed and *remains full of power as if enveloped in a divine strength.* The envelopment of God and the person takes place, the person floats in a sea of divinity, full of God's creative power. In this temple God *becomes known to God*—God encounters God in our souls, God speaking to God face to face. This is how holy this temple is. And in this temple, *the soul knows itself and all things along with God himself;* it also knows the soul's own *essential original being in one unity without any distinction.*

What is necessary for these divine and marvelous happenings to occur in the temple that is ourselves? We need *to empty the temple,* says Eckhart. By our letting go and letting be, as discussed in Path Two, we are able to let God be God in us, to let God fill this temple and sanctify it. To let compassion in, we have to let other energies out. *God wishes the temple to be empty so that nothing can be in it but himself alone.* In this way we ourselves stay *in the temple.* One reason for staying *in the temple* is that God is there or, better, below there. God has *placed himself beneath the soul,* Eckhart insists, and for the soul who *has dared to come to nothing* God is present sustaining it. God *places himself with his uncreatedness beneath the soul's nothingness and upholds the soul in his substance*. We see here how consistently Eckhart carries on his images of sinking that we saw in Path Two. We sink into God who is under us, under our soul, under our nothingness sustaining us. We also see how thoroughly Eckhart rejects the motif of climbing Jacob's ladder—for God is not up for Eckhart but innermost and undermost. Those who have learned to let go and let be know this.

But what is it that is most cluttering up this temple and most interfering with God's plan to dwell there? What is preventing compassion from flowing? Eckhart calls it *the merchant mentality*. So poisonous is the merchant mentality, and so deep does the poison seep, that it creeps into good people's lives and very often into religious people's lives. A merchant is one who wants to trade—*they wish to give one thing in return for another*. Those who build their spirituality around ascetic practices are such religious merchants. *In this way they wish to bargain with our Lord*.

> Behold how all those people are merchants who shun great sins and would like to be good and do good deeds in God's honor, such as fasts, vigils, prayers, and similar good deeds of all kinds. They do these things so that our Lord may give them something, or so that God may do something dear to them. All these people are merchants.

There is an entire consciousness built up by too many tactical ecstasies or religious exercises—a consciousness of bargaining with God as Other that destroys true spirituality. For, in fact, God is free and need strike up no bargains. *Truth does not long for any kind of commercial deal. God does not seek his own interest*. Persons acting *out of their own egos* and with whys and wherefores are trafficking with God—good people included. *You must in no way long for such objects*, Eckhart warns. We need to rid ourselves of all objects to experience what already is. But a merchant mentality, based on dualisms of subject/object, seller/buyer, money/thing, is all about objects. Any work we ever do can be destroyed by this attitude of putting God in debt to us. God will not be bought. God does not have any price. For everything we do—even the bargaining—is already rooted in God, without whom we can do nothing. Eckhart sounds very much like Luther was to sound on the subject of "good works" two centuries hence.

What happens to merchants in our midst who are busy peddling things

that we may or may not need? And who, above all, peddle a thing consciousness that destroys a consciousness of interdependence and compassion? *Our Lord whipped them and drove them out of the temple.*
Eckhart makes it clear that he has his own contemporary culture on his
mind and the merchant-mentality persons of that culture, for he insists
that he is talking of the merchants who *were then and are still today.*
Apparently not much has changed since Jesus' time. These merchants
were buying and selling then, and are still doing so. And Jesus not only
drove them out with whips then but *he still is doing so to those who despite everything are still buying and selling in the temple.* There can be
no question that Eckhart has in mind the merchants of his day and place.
Cologne, where Eckhart gave this sermon, was the headquarters of
trade for western Europe and eastern Europe.[1] Eckhart's hearers understood his not-so-hidden references to the economics of his day and
Eckhart himself was not worldly unwise or naïve or divorced from the
economic turpitude of his time, as certain spiritual commentators of the
present time can be. Eckhart knew the repercussions on the imaginations
of his listeners from what he was saying and where he was saying it. His
attitude toward economics was repeated on several occasions (see, for
example, Sermon Thirty-five). He says in another place: "Certain people
are more afraid of losing a piece of money, or even a denarius, than
God. We condemn Judas because he sold Christ for thirty silver pieces,
and yet many persons sell God, truth, justice for a single quarter or even
for a penny."[2] Eckhart urges us to let go of money from deep inside ourselves. "To forsake money with all one's heart should not be difficult for
the heart; indeed, there is no one who would willingly have money in his
heart, for if the money were actually in it, the heart would assuredly
die."[3] Money in the heart kills a person. A monied soul is a dead soul.

Eckhart's criticism of merchant mentalities, or what we today would
call capitalism, cuts so deep because it cuts to the level of consciousness.
The very word he uses for "attachment" is the word for "ownership,"
Eigenschaft. It is the property mentality, the overattachment, indeed, the
anal relationship[4] that we must let go of in order to let God and things
be. Ownership or attachment "leaves the mind stupefied and forms an
obstacle to receptivity."[5] Our letting go ought to have rendered us
empty of any commercial deal. A clinging mentality kills the spirit and
prevents us from experiencing the ever new gifts that God is showering
on us. It also kills the spirit of gratitude and appreciation which, we saw
in Path One, is, in the long run, the only and ultimate prayer. Indeed, it

kills the gift spirit altogether, since in such a consciousness everything has its price. Only by driving out such mentalities can we *newly receive God's gift in an unencumbered and free way* and return it with *grateful praise.* A merchant mentality destroys all gift consciousness, all true art, therefore (see Sermon Twenty-nine) all celebration and all praise. This is why Jesus, as well as Eckhart, recommends anger and a righteous outrage at the spoilers of the beautiful and divine temple. For a profound sin lurks behind the merchant mentalities.

What is this sin? It is the ultimate sin, the sin behind all sin, the sin of a dualistic consciousness. This sin yanks us out of the sea of God in which we swim interdependently with all creatures. It sets us off from self, others, and God and therefore from interdependence and compassion, which is the law of creation and its goal. It cuts us off from our divine origin, rendering us impure, that is, unable to return to our origin. It thus stifles the energy of the soul that is a new temple that wants to *flow with fullness and sweetness into itself, and beyond itself, and beyond all things into its first origin through the action of grace with limitless power.* It alone prevents us from being *in constant peace in God's service.* For our destiny is that we be made *one being, just as he is one with the Father and the Holy Spirit.* But dualisms prevent this. They are sin, and the sin behind all sin.

In another sermon Eckhart declares that "a person should be at one with himself or herself."[6] When a person is at one with himself or herself, such a person is ready to be truthful to the oneness of creation and oneness with the Creator. But dualisms prevent this consciousness of unity and oneness from happening. As we saw in Sermon Twenty-five, Mary Magdalene complains to the angels at Jesus' empty tomb that "I find *two* and am only seeking *one.*" This experience of the extra other was also treated in the preceding sermon where, as Kelley put it, "there is no other." We are to live within compassion and truth and within unity and do our deeds from this grounding in unity, Eckhart says in the present sermon. We ought *to receive the highest of all truth and live within it without beginning or end.* For Eckhart, sin is a "deprivation or falling off from the good of created nature."[7] Sin is a sinful way of seeing the world, of seeing it devoid of its unity, its fullness, its divinity. While Eckhart would acknowledge that original sin "wounds" our way of knowing the world,[8] he refuses to blame Adam for all our troubles. It is we who are responsible for sin, for we are responsible for our dualistic consciousness. "Nothing more than we ourselves bear the responsibility for the fact that God is concealed from us. We are the cause of all our obstacles."[9] The principal obstacle is the way we relate to "objects" and "things," granting them existence as object which, in fact, they do not have. "You are yourself the very thing by which you are hindered, for you are related to things in an inverted way."[10] Caputo comments on this remark of Eckhart's that "the soul has an 'inverted' (verkehrt) relationship to things because it views them as things in themselves, independent of God, whereas they are nothing at all, not even something small, outside of God."[11] Here we see the metaphysical/moral implications of panentheism. If outside of God there is nothing but nothing, then sin is a nothing, a form of nonbeing. Eckhart says this. "Sin, however, and evil in general are not beings. For they were not made by him but without him."[12] In sin we fall out of the circle of being and out of the ocean of divine compassion that permeates all creation into nonbeing and nothingness. When we are outside God and the panentheistic circle of being, God cannot see us. "God does not know anything outside himself, but his eye is fixed only on himself. What he sees, he sees it all in himself. Therefore God does not see us if we are in sin. Hence God knows us as far as we are in him, that is as far as we are without sin."[13] When he comments on the creation story in Genesis, Eckhart points out that God called every act of creation "good" or "very good" except one. God never said, when God separated the earth and the sky, that the separation itself was good.[14]

The sin of a dualistic consciousness is a subtle, even demonic, evil that hides behind good works and good people. Eckhart says this sermon is directed exclusively at good people. The commercial and merchandising mentality is not always and evidently evil in itself. But behind it, because behind it there lies dualism, there is coiled a power and principality that must be driven entirely out of the temple.

Because the sin behind sin is a dualistic consciousness, it is also a superficial consciousness, a consciousness of an "outer" as distinct from an "inner" person. Evil and sin are outsiders. Evil "stands outside, draws and directs things outward, distracts from inner things, draws to what is other, smacks of otherness, of division, of withdrawal or falling away."[15] To fall into superficiality and outerness is falling into sin and vice versa. Sin, then, becomes a betrayal of the imago Dei that we are, a betrayal of the temple that is as deep as the fathomless ocean and as vast as space. If, as Eckhart says, the inward person is "spatiosissimus—most spacious" and is "great without magnitude," then it is this vastness that distinguishes the inner from the outer person. "Although the inward man and the outward person may be seen together at the same time and place, they are nevertheless further removed from one another than the highest heaven and the center of the earth."[16] Sin then becomes "a contraction of awareness"[17] that results in a contraction of our being, a contraction of the temple that we are, a contraction of God's oceanic energy called compassion. Sin is a drying up, a settling for puniness in the midst of potential divine vastness and oceanic invitations. Aquinas had taught that *accidie* was "a contraction of the mind"[18] and a flight from our divinity. Eckhart is, in effect, suggesting that *accidie* becomes a sinful consciousness that lurks behind all other acts of dualism and alienation. When he says that Jesus "has liberated us from our sins,"[19] he also points out that we are to become *free and unencumbered, just as our Lord Jesus Christ is free and unencumbered. We should behave in exactly the same way.* Free of dualisms, free of objects, free of thing consciousness:

> Our Lord in a way that is constantly, unceasingly, and timelessly new receives himself from his heavenly Father. At the same time, our Lord gives rise to himself perfectly, in grateful praise to the Father's majesty, and with equal honor to himself . . . Without hindrance from the deeds they accomplish or the concepts of which they become aware, such people [who behave as Jesus does] newly receive God's gift in an unencumbered and free way, and give rise to it again in the same light with grateful praise in our Lord Jesus Christ.

Thus we—the new temple and the receivers of a new creation—are, like Jesus, reborn, risen again, and ready to receive new power and light from divinity. Instead of fleeing creation and its goodness, we will look on it in a new way. Like the wisdom theology of the Bible that declares that "creation does not only exist, it also discharges truth,"[20] Eckhart wants us to see this truth. Caputo explains that

> in Eckhart's teaching, all the fault is to be laid at the feet of man himself, of the "ego." It is wholly and solely because man looks upon things in the wrong way that things present an obstacle to him. There is nothing wrong with things or people or places; it is the way we look upon them which is at fault. The

world which God "gives" us is resplendent with divine being and beauty.[21]

Eckhart has suggested in not overly subtle terms that our economic systems can be guilty of distorting this view of God's creation, bathed as it is in a sea of compassion. It is no small criticism and it is one that got him in a great deal of difficulty, from which now, six hundred years later, he is beginning to be extricated. For his radical critique of the merchant mentality was no small factor in his condemnation.[22] A change in consciousness implies a change in society and its institutions and a change in how we work, why we work, and what we work at. For Eckhart is not intent on merely driving merchant mentalities from our church vestibules; he insists that we drive them right out of our souls themselves. He is calling, from the very bosom of the trade capital of his day, for a holy economic exorcism.

Sermon Thirty-three: JUSTICE, THE WORK OF COMPASSION

"The just will live forever and their reward is with the Lord." (Ws. 5:16)*

These words are in the Epistle for today and are spoken by the wise person: "The just shall live forever" (Ws. 5:16). From time to time I have said what a just person is, but now I say it with a different meaning: A just person is one who is conformed and transformed into justice. The just person lives in God and God in him. Thus God will be born in this just person and the just person is born into God; and therefore God will be born through every virtue of the just person and will rejoice through every virtue of the just person. And not only at every virtue will God rejoice but especially at every *work* of the just person, however small it is. When this work is done through justice and results in justice, God will rejoice at it, indeed, God will rejoice through and through; for nothing remains in his ground which does not tickle him through and through out of joy. Ignorant people have to believe this, but enlightened ones should know it.

The just person does not seek anything with his work, for every single person who seeks anything or even something with his or her works is working for a why and is a servant and a mercenary. Therefore, if you wish to be conformed and transformed into justice, do not intend anything in your work and strive for no why, either in time or in eternity. Do not aim at reward or blessedness, neither this nor that. For such works are truly fully dead. Indeed, I say that even if you take God as your goal, all such works which you do with this intention are dead and you will spoil good works. And not only will you spoil good works but you will also

* "Justus in perpetuum vivet et apud dominum est merces ejus." (DW II, ※39)

sin, for you will be like a gardener who was supposed to plant a garden but instead uprooted the trees and then wanted to have a reward for it. In this way you will spoil good works. Therefore, if you want to live and if you want your works to live, you must be dead to all things and you must become in touch with nothingness. It is peculiar to the creature that it makes something from something; but it is peculiar to God to make something from nothing. Therefore, for God to make something in you or with you, you must first make contact with this nothingness. Therefore, enter into your own ground and work there and these works which you work there will all be living. And therefore the wise person says: "The just person lives." For because he is just, he works and his works live.

Now the wise person says: "His reward is with the Lord." Now take a minute to consider this. If he says "with," that means that the reward of the just person is there where God himself is; for the blessedness of the just person and the blessedness of God are *one* blessedness, because the just person is blessed where God is blessed. Saint John says this: "The Word was with God" (Jn. 1:1). He also says "with," and therefore the just person is like God, since God is justice. And therefore whoever is in justice is in God and is God.

Now we will speak further about the word "just." The Book of Wisdom does not say "the just person" or "the just angel" but, rather, only "the just." The Father gives birth to his Son as the Just One and the Just One as his Son; for all virtue of the just and every work of the just which are born from the virtue of the just person are nothing other than the event of the Son being born from the Father. Therefore the Father never rests; he always runs and hurries in order that the Son be born in me, as the Scriptures say: "For Zion's sake I will not hold my peace and for Jerusalem's sake I will not rest, until the just are revealed and shine forth like a flash of lightning" (Is. 62:1). "Zion" means the fullness of life and "Jerusalem" means the fullness of peace. Indeed, God rests neither for the fullness of life nor for the fullness of peace; he always runs and hurries for this purpose, that the just person may be made known. In the just nothing should work except God alone. For all works are surely dead if anything from the outside compels you to work. Even if God were to compel you to work from the outside, then such works would surely all be dead. If your works are to live, then God must move you inwardly, in the innermost part of the soul, if they are really to live. There is your life and there alone you live.

And I say that if one virtue seems greater than another and if you hold it in greater esteem than the other, then you do not live it as it is in justice and God does not work in you. For as long as a person values or loves one virtue more than another, he does not love and take the virtues as they are in justice; nor is such a person just. For the just person loves and works all virtues in justice as they are justice itself. Scripture says: "Before the creation of the world, I am" (Si. 24:9). This means "Before I am" which means that if a person is raised up beyond time into eternity, then the person works one work there with God. Some people ask how a person can work these works which God has worked a thousand years ago and which God will work a thousand years from now and they do not understand it. In eternity there is no before and no after. Therefore, what happened a thousand years ago and what will happen a thousand years from now and what is now happening is one in eternity. Therefore, what God did a thousand years ago and has done and what he will do in a thousand years and what he is now doing—all this is nothing but one work. Therefore a person who is risen beyond time into eternity works with God what God worked a thousand years ago and will work a thousand years hence. This too is for wise people a matter of knowledge and for ignorant people a matter for belief.

Saint Paul says: "We are eternally chosen in the Son" (Ep. 1:4). Therefore we should never rest until we become what we have eternally been in him (Rm. 8:29ff.). For the Father runs and hurries in order that we be born in the Son and become the same as what the Son is. The Father begets his Son and in this birthing the Father takes so great a rest and a pleasure that his entire nature is absorbed in it. For whatever is always in God moves him to beget; indeed, from his ground, from his essence, and from his being the Father is moved to beget.

Sometimes there is revealed in the soul a light and a person thinks he is the Son and yet it is only a light. For when the Son is revealed in the soul, the love of the Holy Spirit is also revealed there. Therefore I say that it is the essence of the Father to beget the Son and the essence of the Son that I be born in him and in his image. It is the essence of the Holy Spirit that I should be burned into him and should be completely consumed in him and become entirely love. Whoever is in love and, in this way, has become entirely love thinks that God loves no one but himself alone. And he knows of no one else who has loved anything else or has been loved by anyone else except by God alone.

Some professors maintain that the spirit receives its blessedness from love; others maintain that it receives it from the contemplation of God. But I say: It receives it neither from love nor from knowledge nor from contemplation. Now one might ask: Has the spirit no vision of God in eternal life? Yes and no. Insofar as it is born, it has no contemplation and no vision more of God. But insofar as it is being born, it has a vision of God. Therefore the blessedness of the spirit lies where it is born and not where it has been born, for it lives where the Father lives. This means in the simplicity and the nakedness of being. Therefore turn away from all things and take yourself naked into being. For what is outside of being is an accident and all accidents bring about a why.

That we "live forever," may God help us. Amen.

COMMENTARY: God Is Justice and to Be in God Is to Be in Justice/ Birth and Breakthrough Are Resurrections into Justice/ Toward a Spirituality of Work: Working Without a Why or Wherefore/Our Work, Giving Birth to the New Creation

Eckhart has an entire theology of work and it is based on his theology of creativity, justice, and compassion. We saw this theology of work as art and creativity in Sermon Twenty-nine. In the present sermon Eckhart explores the subject of work from the perspective of justice. Only work for justice and out of justice is *living work*. This kind of work makes God delighted—*God rejoices . . . especially at every work of the just person, however small it is.* Why is this? Because *God is justice.* Elsewhere Eckhart says that "God is the most just—*justissimus.*"[1] Again, "God is, as it were, justice itself."[2] Therefore to be in God is to be both in compassion and in justice. Indeed, as we saw in Sermon Thirty, "compassion means justice." Because "God and justice are completely one,"[3] Eckhart can say in the present sermon that *whoever is in justice is in God and is God.* So convinced is Eckhart that to be in justice is to be in God and to be in God is to be in justice that he can say elsewhere: "If God were not just, the just person could not consider God."[4] And again, "Since God is justice you must embrace justice as it is in itself, as it is in God."[5]

We are called to do justice in all our work, but first we need to be reborn into justice. For our true breakthrough and birth is a resurrection into justice and into God who is Justice. The birth of the divine Word is a birth of Justice. "For the just person, the 'word' of justice is justice itself, as we read later in the tenth chapter of John: 'I and the Father are one.' For the just person denotes justice alone."[6] Our birth is to be a *conformation and transformation into justice.* After all, if the Word of God by nature is the "Son of Justice,"[7] then we who are the adopted words—the bywords—and adopted sons of God must also be sons and daughters of justice.

> The just person is the "word" of justice, by means of which justice declares and manifests itself . . . The just person is the offspring and son of justice. He is called, and actually is, the son because he becomes different in person but not in nature . . . Now if the Father and the Son, justice and the just man, are one and the same in nature, it follows that the just man is equal to, not less than, justice.[8]

Since justice, like compassion, lies at the very core of the Godhead and at the center of the origin of our existence, our being born is a being born out of justice. "The just person is always in the process of being born from justice itself, just as he has been born from it from the beginning, ever since he has been just."[9] If the just person is the "word" of justice and if a word is that which flows out but remains within as we saw in Sermon Two, then the just person is rooted in justice at the same time that such a person is birthing justice. Eckhart links the birth into justice with the moment of breakthrough and of resurrection when he discusses the new experience of time—*in eternity there is no before and no after.* We are told to *rise beyond time,* to be resurrected from a time consciousness that thinks in terms of before and after, since that is the kind of time framework in which our own birthing takes place. To substantiate this point, Eckhart draws on wisdom literature and on Paul. In the Book of Ecclesiasticus we read:

From eternity, in the beginning, he created me,
and for eternity I shall remain . . .
I am like a vine putting out graceful shoots,
my blossoms bear the fruit of glory and wealth . . .
Approach me, you who desire me,
and take your fill of my fruits,
for memories of me are sweeter than honey,
inheriting me is sweeter than the honeycomb. (Si. 24:9, 17, 19–20)

And from Paul—not from Plato—there is a hint of this same preexistence in a time before time, a time beyond time:

Blessed be God the Father of our Lord Jesus Christ,
who has blessed us with all the spiritual blessings of heaven in Christ.
Before the world was made, he chose us, chose us in Christ,
to be holy and spotless, and to live through love in his presence,
determining that we should become his adopted sons, through Jesus
Christ . . . (Ep. 1:3–5)

And so, in Eckhart's as in Paul's theology, our rebirth as sons of God took place "before the world was made," that is to say in eternity. This link between our rebirth and the preexistence of Wisdom is made again in Romans, where Paul writes:

They are the ones he chose specially long ago and intended
to become true images of his Son, so that his Son might be
the eldest of many brothers. (Rm. 8:29)

Eckhart cautions that some people have already tasted of this eternity he speaks of—they *know* what he is talking about; others have still to believe in it. The *enlightened ones know*; the *ignorant believe* in these matters. It is evident that another scriptural text that Eckhart had in front of him for this sermon is from the prophet Isaiah, chapter 62. In that chapter the author discusses themes that have inspired Eckhart's treatise on justice and God—themes of the integrity of virtue that the just person maintains; themes of God's silence and of God's *running* and *hurrying* and of God's joy.

> About Zion I will not be silent,
> about Jerusalem I will not grow weary,
> until her integrity shines out like the dawn
> and her salvation flames like a torch.
>
> The nations then will see your integrity,
> all the kings your glory,
> and you will be called by a new name . . .
> but you shall be called "My Delight" . . .
>
> You who keep Yahweh mindful
> must take no rest.
> Nor let him take rest
> till he has restored Jerusalem,
> and made her
> the boast of the earth. (Is. 62:1–2, 4, 6–7)

Eckhart recognizes the similarity between Isaiah 62 and Wisdom 5 where both traditions, that of the prophets and that of wisdom literature, appeal to the royal throne as a symbol for justice. Isaiah says:

> You are to be a crown of splendor in the hand of Yahweh,
> a princely diadem in the hand of your God. (Is. 62:3)

Wisdom speaks:

> But the virtuous live for ever,
> their recompense lies with the Lord,
> the Most High takes care of them.
> So they shall receive the royal crown of splendor,
> the diadem of beauty from the hand of the Lord;
> for he will shelter them with his right hand
> and shield them with his arm . . .
>
> he will put on justice as a breastplate. (Ws. 5:15–17, 18)

We will discuss this theme of the royal person and justice in greater detail in Sermon Thirty-six. But the theme of a royal birth is very much in accord with Eckhart's treatment of our birth as the birth of a Godly Word, the birth of Justice. The fruit we are to bear is to be "neither more nor less than God himself," as we saw in the previous sermon. That would mean neither more nor less than Justice. When God's he becomes I, then "God and the soul are eternally doing one work very fruitfully."[10] This fruitful work is also a blessing. Eckhart's theology of blessing reaches a crescendo in the works of justice and compassion. (We saw in Sermon Thirty that "compassion means justice.") The blessedness of the just person and the blessedness of God is one blessedness because the just person is blessed where God is blessed. Justice is a name for the full blessing of God.

Here, then, lies the basis for Eckhart's theology of work: he envisions a trinity of word, birth, work. Our true work is from the creative Word itself. Eckhart's theology of work is based on his theology of the Word that flows out but remains within. You cannot separate word from work in Eckhart's thinking, for the truthful word is always fruitful and leads to the authentic work. They are related as fruit and vine. Indeed, the Word is the work when work is authentic. What is authentic work? Work that is without a why. Works that have an outside purpose to them are truly fully dead. Even if God is inserted as an outside purpose, such a work is spoiled. True work is ecstasy—an end in itself. It is the ecstasy that justice brings and the ecstasy that the work itself brings to self, others, or God. The just person does not seek anything with his work; for every single person who seeks anything or even something with their works is working for a why and is a servant and a mercenary. It is part of the merchant mentality to allow alienation and separation to come between us and our work. To work without a why is to touch one's origin. "The end is universally the same as the beginning. It has no 'why' or 'wherefore' but is itself the 'why' of and for all things: 'I am the beginning and the end'" (Rv. 1:8).[11] In this return to our origin we are also returning to the marriage of work and Word, for the Word is what "was in the beginning."[12] When our work is without a why, it is a work of love, for love

has no why. If I had a friend and loved him because good and all I wished came to me through him, I wouldn't love my friend but myself. I ought to love my friend for his own goodness and for his own virtue and for everything that he is in himself.[13]

Just as we are to love without a why and be just without a why, so are we to work without a why. Such work is a work of love, for "whoever is born of God as a son of God loves God for his sake, that is to say, he loves God for the sake of loving God and does all his work for the sake of working."[14] Our works that are done in God are to be works of justice.

> Where justice is at work, you are at work, because you could not but do the works of justice. Yes, even if hell were to interfere with the course of justice, you still would do the works of justice, and hell itself would not constitute any suffering; hell would be joy because you yourself would be justice, and that is why you could not but do the works of justice.[15]

Elsewhere Eckhart defines justice as "a certain rightness whereby every person receives his or her due."[16] We do the work of justice when we bring about this "certain rightness" among persons. Indeed, it is our just works that make us live. "For the just person as such to act justly is to live; indeed, justice is his life, his being alive, his being, insofar as he is just."[17] Like life itself, justice is its own reward. "The just person lives and works without reason of gain. As much as life has the reason for living in itself, in that same way the just person knows no other reason for being just."[18] Justice is the reason for justice. Just work is the reason for work.

To work without a why is to work from one's inner self. Therefore Eckhart advises the person interested in good work to *enter into your own ground and work there, and these works which you work there will all be living.* Living works come from where life is: from our inner core where no why or wherefore enters, where all is one.

> God's ground is my ground and my ground is God's ground. Here I live on my own as God lives on his own . . . You should work all your works out of this innermost ground without why. Indeed, I say, so long as you work for the kingdom of heaven, or for God, or for your internal happiness and thus for something outward, all is not well with you.[19]

Outside motivation is not worthy of the work we do. It separates us from our work and alienates us from our inner self. That way lies spiritual and personal death. When we work in that fashion our work is dead work.

Those deeds which do not flow from within your inner self are all dead before God. Those are the deeds which were engendered by causes outside of yourself, because they did not proceed from life. That is why they are dead, because only that is alive which has motion within itself. Consequently, for a person's deeds to be alive, they have to come from within, not from something alien and outside himself.[20]

One reason why outside-oriented works alienate us is that they are born of compulsion and not compassion or creativity, the way the creative Word gives birth. *All works are surely dead if anything from the outside compels you to work. Even if God did the compelling, they would be dead.* Psychologist William Eckhardt makes a similar observation when he insists that compulsion is the Number One psychological obstacle to compassion and works of compassion.[21] Meister Eckhart urges us to void all compulsion in our work. We should "become accustomed to work without compulsion," he insists. How do we do this? By working from within, from our own being and needs of being, and not from outside. Many people are "being worked rather than working." Such persons should learn to "cooperate with" God. This is learned from making contact with one's inner person.[22] It is from inside, as Jesus taught, that works are made holy.

People never need to think so much about what they ought to do, but they should remember what they are. Now if people and their ways are good, their works might shine forth brightly. If you are just, then your works are also just. One does not think of basing holiness on one action, one should base holiness on being. For works do not sanctify us, but we should sanctify the works . . . One should apply oneself with all diligence to being good, not so much to what one should do, of what nature the works are, but of what nature the ground of the works is.[23]

When we are truly grounded, it is God who is involved in our works.

Such a person carries God in all his works and at all places, and all this person's works are done purely by God, for if anyone is the cause of the work it is more properly and really

> his than that of the person who performs the work. If then we
> fix our minds on God purely and simply, then indeed he must
> perform our works and no one can hinder him in all his works,
> neither multitude nor place.[24]

Such work is an occasion for expression and even reception of our divinity since it is a share in God's work. We return God's creative work—his compassion—to him.

> The person whose aims and affections are thus fixed on God
> in all his works, to him God gives his divinity. All that this per-
> son works God works, for my humility gives God his di-
> vinity . . . God is not only the beginning of all our works and
> of our being, but he is also the end and rest of all beings.[25]

God is the beginning of our work of compassion and justice because God is "in the beginning," and when we are in God who is Compassion and Justice, and so firmly grounded there that our actions flow from this source, then God too flows from this source. The new creation is God's too—though we are the instruments for it. God is eager to flow into our work—"God wants to do your work himself," and will, "if you will only follow and resist him not at all."[26] One might even say that God depends on us for the divine work of compassion and justice to happen: "Just as little as I can do anything without him, he cannot really accomplish anything apart from me."[27]

What makes works live and makes them just and compassionate is the fact that they come from deep within. *If your works are to live, then God must move you inwardly, jn the innermost part of the soul, if they are really to live. There is your life and there alone you live.* Only this kind of work is pleasing to God and returns a blessing to God. "There, in the soul's innermost part, God works; there all works please God. No work will ever be acceptable to God unless it is accomplished there."[28] There is no conflict, no dualism between the "outside world" and the innermost self, for the innermost self, filled with a consciousness of interdependence and panentheism, is itself capable of unifying outside and inside. Here lies the cure for compulsion.

> One should not escape from the inward person, or flee from
> him or deny him, but in him, with him, and through him, one
> should learn to act in such a way that one breaks up the in-

wardness into reality and leads reality into inwardness, and that one should thus become accustomed to work without compulsion.[29]

The so-called outside world also is divine.

> You might say: "A person must turn outward if he or she has to do external things, for no work can be done except in its own form." That is quite true, but the external form of images is nothing external for experienced people, since all things have for an inward person an inward divine mode of being.[30]

Extrovert meditation, then, is not from the outside but from deep within, for even external forms of images come from that source in the experienced person. Work is not less divine because it is busy with external things; it is less divine if it does not flow from the innermost divine sources. It is from the inside that work is made vast and Godly.

> The inward work is God-like and Godly, and it suggests the divine attributes in this respect: this outward work, its quality and its size, its length and its breadth, does not in the least increase the goodness of the inward work; it has its goodness in itself.[31]

This is why all vocations are holy, all work is divine and is a divine vocation. "You should know and you should have considered to what vocation you are most strongly called by God. For all people are not called to God in one way, as Saint Paul says" in 1 Corinthians 12:4–11.[32] If the work is from inside, from our inness with God who is Justice and Compassion, it is God's work and of divine size.

> The outward work can never be small if the inward one is great, and the outward can never be great or good if the inward is small or of little worth. The inward work always includes in itself all size, all breadth and length. The inward work receives and draws all its being from nowhere else but from and in the heart of God.[33]

Drawing its energy from the divine energy, all work that proceeds from the inside of oneself and from the "heart of God" is abundant and divine. It is also free, like God's creative Word and work are free. God is free and untrammeled in all his works, and he works them out of genuine love. *That* person who is united with God does exactly the same thing. He or she also is free and untrammeled in all his or her works and works them solely for God's honor and does not seek his or her own; and God acts in that person.[34]

There is still another dimension—and a divine dimension it is—to our work when it is grounded from the inside of ourselves. In our acts of creation we are imitating the ground of all creation, the Creator or Father of all being and all works. But this Father is always giving birth. *From his ground, from his essence, and from his being the Father is moved to beget.* Indeed, it is the very *essence of the Father* to birth the Son. *It is the essence of the Father to beget the Son.* If this be the case, then, where my ground becomes the Father's ground, we give birth together and the Son is born at the time that the new creation is birthed. And the Father is eager and even busy to see this happen. Our work—so long as it originates in our center and inner core—is the birthing of God's Son. The new creation is even more splendid than the first creation. "Always bear in mind that the faithful and loving God brought humankind out of a sinful life into a divine life. He made out of his enemy a friend, which is more than to create a new world."[35] In the new creation we work one work there with God. There, in the bosom of Justice itself, all history is born anew. The Father gives birth to his *Son as the Just One and the Just One as his Son; for all virtue of the just and every work of the just . . . are nothing other than the event of the Son being born from the Father.* Thus our work becomes the Son, the new creation, the fruit of the "whole creation eagerly waiting for God to reveal his sons," a creation that "has been groaning in one great act of giving birth" (Rm. 8:19, 22). Our inward work

> receives the Son and is begotten as a son in the bosom of the heavenly Father . . . The outward work does not, but it receives its divine goodness by means of the inward work borne out and poured out in an emanation of the Deity.[36]

In this same act of new creation, the Son is birthed and the Spirit flows out upon human history, and we are reborn as a lover like the Spirit of God. *It is the essence of the Son that I be born in him and in his image.*

It is the essence of the Holy Spirit that I should be burned into him and should be completely consumed in him and become entirely love. In our work that is in God and therefore in Compassion and in Justice we become entirely Love. That is the goal of our work and of our being. But it is a goal without a goal, for love—like work—is without a why.

Sermon Thirty-four: WHEN OUR WORK BECOMES A SPIRITUAL WORK WORKING IN THE WORLD

"Jesus went into a certain city, and a certain woman named Martha received him." (Lk. 10:38)*

Saint Luke writes in the Gospel: "Our Lord Jesus Christ went into a small city. A woman named Martha received him. She had a sister named Mary, who sat at our Lord's feet and listened to his words. But Martha went about and served the dear Christ" (Lk. 10:38–40).

Three things caused Mary to sit at our Lord's feet. The first was that God's goodness had embraced her soul. The second was a great, unspeakable longing: she yearned without knowing what it was she yearned after, and she desired without knowing what she desired! The third was the sweet consolation and bliss that she derived from the eternal words that came from Christ's mouth.

Three things also caused Martha to run about and serve her dear Christ. The first was a maturity of age and a depth of her being, which was thoroughly trained to the most external matters. For this reason, she believed that no one was so well suited for activity as herself. The second was a wise prudence that knew how to achieve external acts to the highest degree that love demands. The third was the high dignity of her dear guest.

The masters of the spiritual life say that God is ready for every person's spiritual and physical satisfaction to the utmost degree that that person desires. We can clearly distinguish with respect to God's dear friends how God satisfies our spiritual nature while, on the other hand, he also provides satisfaction for our physical nature. Satisfying our physical nature means that God gives us

* "Intravit Jesus in quoddam castellum, et mulier quaedam, Martha nomine, excepit illum . . ." (DW III, ✳86)

consolation, bliss, and satisfaction. Being spoiled in this way causes God's good friends to go astray in the sphere of their inner senses. By way of contrast, spiritual satisfaction is satisfaction within the spirit. I speak of spiritual satisfaction when the highest peak of the soul is not so humbled that it drowns in a feeling of pleasure but rather stands in might above it. For people are in a state of spiritual satisfaction only when love and sorrow of creatures cannot humble the highest peak of their souls. I call a creature whatever we perceive and see beneath God.

Now Martha says: "Lord, tell her to help me." Martha did not say this out of anger. She spoke rather out of loving kindness because she was hard pressed. We must indeed call it a loving kindness or a lovable form of teasing. How was this? Pay attention! She saw that Mary was reveling in a feeling of pleasure to her soul's complete satisfaction. Martha knew Mary better than Mary knew Martha, for Martha had already lived quite a long time. Living offers the most noble kind of knowledge. Living causes pleasure and light to be better known than everything we can attain beneath God in this life. In a certain way pleasure and light are better known than what the light of eternity can bestow. For the light of eternity causes us always to know only ourselves *and* God but not ourselves without God; but life gives us to know ourselves without God (that is, by absenting ourselves from God). Only where life has looked at itself does it perceive more clearly the difference between like and unlike. Saint Paul on the one hand and the pagan scholars on the other attest to this. In his rapture Saint Paul saw God *as well as* himself in a spiritual way in God. And he still did not recognize intuitively in him each and every virtue in the most minute fashion. This was because he had not practiced each and every virtue in his actions. The pagan scholars, however, achieved through the practice of virtue such great knowledge that they clearly knew every virtue more accurately than Paul or any other saint in their first raptures.

This was how it was with Martha. Therefore she said: "Lord, tell her to help me." It was as if she meant: "My sister thinks that she *can* already do what she *wishes* so long as she is only seated beneath your consolation. Let her know now if this is so, and tell her to get up and go away from you!" Next, it was tender love although Martha said it after due reflection. Mary was so filled with longing that she yearned without knowing why and desired without knowing what she desired! We cherish the suspicion that our dear Mary somehow had sat there more out of a feeling of pleasure than for spiritual gain. Therefore Martha said: "Lord, tell her to get up!" For she feared that Mary would remain in this feeling of pleasure and make no further progress. Then Christ replied to her: "Martha, Martha, you are concerned, you are upset about many things. One thing is necessary! Mary has chosen the better part, which can never be taken from her."

Christ did not make this statement to Martha in a reproving way. He rather informed her and gave her the consolation that Mary would become the way she wished her to be.

But why did Christ say, "Martha, Martha," and call her *twice* by name? Isidore says: "There is no doubt that before God became man, he never called by name anyone who was then lost. Concerning those he did not call by name there is doubt." I characterize Christ's calling people by name as his eternal wisdom, recorded before the creation of all creation from eternity to the present in the living book of the "Father, Son, and Holy Spirit." None of those persons was lost who had been named by name or whose name was uttered by Christ. This is attested by Moses to whom God himself said, "I have known you by name" (Ex. 33:12), and by Nathaniel to whom Christ said, "I knew you under the fig tree" (Jn. 1:50). The fig tree signifies a disposition that does not deny itself to God and whose name from all eternity was written in God. Thus it is proven that no one has ever been lost or will be lost whose name has been named by our dear Christ with his human mouth out of the eternal Word—that is to say, out of the eternal book, out of himself.

But why did he call Martha *twice* by name? He indicated in this way that Martha had practically everything in the way of temporal and eternal goods that a creature could possess. By his first "Martha" he implied her perfection in temporal activities. When he said "Martha" a second time, he indicated that she lacked nothing of everything needed for eternal happiness. For this reason he said, "You are concerned." He meant by this that you are *among* things, but that things are not *in you.*

Those who are hindered in all their "pursuits," however, are full of cares. On the other hand, those who manage all their ac-

tivities in an orderly fashion after the model of the eternal Light
are without hindrance. We manage an "activity" externally, but
it is a "pursuit" if we devote ourselves to it internally and with
comprehensible prudence. Such people are *among* things and not
in things. They are quite close, and yet have no less than if they
were up at the circle of eternity. "Quite close," I say, for all creatures "serve as means." There are two kinds of "means." There is
one kind without which I could not reach God. This is activity
and "pursuits" in time that do not diminish our eternal happiness. The other "means" consists of giving up the first one. For
we are placed in time so that we come closer to God and become
more like him through "pursuits" that are enlightened by our
reason.

This is what Saint Paul meant when he said: "Overcome the
times; the days are evil" (Ep. 5:16). "To overcome the times"
means that we unceasingly ascend toward God through our
reason—not in the diversity of figurative ideas but in reasonable,
lively truth. You should understand "the days are evil" in the
following way. "Day" points to "night," for if there were no night
there would be no day, and we would also not speak of a day because then all would be just *one* light. This is what Paul was aim-
ing at. For a bright life is indeed too small for there to be in it
any darkness that veils or overshadows eternal happiness for an
exalted spirit. This was also what Christ meant when he said:
"Go forward as long as you have light" (Jn. 12:35). For all who
are active in the light are soaring toward God, free and unencumbered of all that is intermediary. Their light is their works and
their works are their light.

This was how things were with our dear Martha. Therefore he
said to her: "*One thing* is necessary, not *two things*. I and you,
embraced *once* by the eternal light—that is *one thing*." The "two
in one," however, is a burning spirit that is above all things and yet
is under God at the circle of eternity. This spirit is two things because it does not see God directly. Its knowledge and its being, or
rather its knowledge and form of knowledge, never become *one
thing*. We see God as quite formless where he is seen in the
spirit. There one thing becomes two; two *is* one thing; light and
spirit are *one thing* in the embrace of the eternal light.

Pay attention to what the "circle of eternity" is. The soul has three ways to God. One of them is to seek God in all creatures through multiple "pursuits" and through burning love. This is what King David meant when he said: "In all things I have sought rest" (Si. 24:11).

The second way is a wayless way that is free and yet bound. On it we are raised up and carried off without will and without form above ourselves and all things, although there is no essential permanency. This is what Christ meant when he said: "You are a happy man, Peter! Flesh and blood do not enlighten you but an elevation into reason when you say 'God' to me: my Father, rather, has revealed this to you" (Mt. 16:17). Even Saint Peter did not see God unveiled. Yet he indeed was swept up above all created power of comprehension through the power of the heavenly Father, up to the "circle of eternity." I say that he was seized fully unaware by the heavenly Father in a loving embrace with impetuous power and in a spirit that was gazing fixedly on high. This spirit was swept up above all power of comprehension into the might of the heavenly Father. Saint Peter was addressed from above in a tone sweetly creative but free of all physical joy, in the simple truth of the unity of the God-man and in the person of the heavenly Father and Son. I boldly state that, if Saint Peter had directly seen God in his nature at that time, as he later did, and as Saint Paul did when he was snatched up to the third heaven, the speech of even the most noble angel would have seemed coarse to him. But he spoke there many a sweet word of which our sweet Jesus had no need. For he who stands quite directly before God in the freedom of the true presence sees into the depth of the heart and the spirit. This is what Saint Paul meant when he said: "A man was caught up and heard such things that are unutterable for all humanity" (2 Co. 12:2-5). From this you can know that Saint Peter was just "at the circle of eternity" but still not seeing God's unity in his own being.

The third way is indeed called a "way," yet it means being "at home": seeing God directly in his own being. Our dear Christ says, "I am the Way, the Truth, and the Life" (Jn. 14:6): *one* Christ in the Person, *one* Christ in the Father, *one* Christ in the Spirit as *three*—Way, Truth, and Life—*one* as our dear Jesus in whom all this is. Outside this way all creatures form an encirclement and a separating "means." But *on* this way all creatures are led to God the Father by the light of his Word and are surrounded by the love of the Holy Spirit for them both. This goes beyond everything we can grasp in the Word.

Listen then to this wonder! How wonderful it is to be both outside and inside, to seize and to be seized, to see and at the same time to be what is seen, to hold and to be held—*that* is the goal where the spirit remains at rest, united with our dear eternity.

We now wish to return to our statement that our dear Martha and, with her, all God's friends are "*among* cares" but not "*within* cares." In this connection, activity in time is just as noble as any kind of linking of self and God. For it carries us just as close as possible to the highest thing, except for the vision of God in his pure nature. For this reason Christ says: "You are *among* things and *among* cares," and means that she was exposed indeed to the lower powers of sadness and sorrow, for she had not been spoiled by a tasting of the spirit. She was *among* things, not *in* things. She was separated from things and they from her.

In particular, three things are indispensable in our activity: that we act in an orderly, judicious, and prudent way. I call "orderly" whatever corresponds in all matters to what is highest. But I call "judicious" whatever we cannot do better at the time. And finally I call something "prudent" when we trace in good actions the lively truth with its beneficial presence. When these three points are present, they convey us just as close to God and they are just as beneficial as all the joys of Mary Magdalene in the desert.

Christ says: "You are concerned about many things, not about one thing." This means that, if a soul is purely, simply, and without all "pursuits" directed toward "the circle of eternity," it will be "concerned." If it is hindered by something like a separating "means" from its ability to remain up there in joy, then such a person will be concerned about this hindrance and will be among cares and affliction. But Martha possessed a mature, well-established virtue and an undisturbed disposition that was unhindered by all things. For this reason she wanted her sister to be placed in the same situation, for she saw that her sister was not yet essentially in it. Out of a mature depth of soul she wanted Mary to be in everything that has to do with eternal happiness. On this account Christ says: "*One thing* is necessary!"

What is this *one thing?* It is the One, and that is God. This one thing is necessary for all creatures. For if God were to attract to himself what is his, all creatures would become nothing. If God were to remove from Christ's soul what is his in the place where the spirit of the soul is united with the eternal Person, Christ would remain just a creature. Therefore we have indeed need of this one thing. Martha was afraid that her sister would remain in a feeling of pleasure. She wanted her to become like herself. On this account Christ meant: "Be reassured, Martha, she has chosen the better part, which will lose itself in her. The highest thing that can happen to a creature will happen to her. She will be as happy as you."

Let yourselves be instructed concerning the virtues! A virtuous life depends on three matters that have to do with our will. The first is to surrender our will to God, for it will be inevitable for us to carry out fully what we then know, whether it be in rejection or acceptance. There are three kinds of wills. The first is a "physical" will, the second a will "enlightened by reason," and the third an "eternal" will. The physical will yearns for instruction, and wants us to listen to truthful teachers.

The will enlightened by reason consists of our following all the actions of Jesus Christ and the saints. This means conducting our words, actions, and "pursuits" in a way uniformly directed toward what is highest. If all this is fulfilled, God will send down an additional depth within the soul. This is an eternal will along with the loving commandment of the Holy Spirit. Then the soul will say: "Lord, inspire me as to what your eternal will is!" If the soul satisfies in this way what we have demonstrated previously, and if the soul then is pleasing to God, our dear Father will proclaim his eternal Word in the soul.

Our upright people, however, say that we must become so perfect that no kind of joy can move us any longer, that we must be immovable to joy or sorrow. They are wrong in this matter. But I say that there was never a saint so great that he or she could not be moved. Moreover, I say in reply that it indeed happens, even in this life, that nothing can take the saints away from God. Do you think that, so long as words can move you to joy or sorrow, you are imperfect? It is not so! This was not the case even for Christ. He let us know this when he said: "My soul is grieved to the point of death" (Mt. 26:38). Christ was so grieved by words that even if all the woes of creation befell a single creature, it would not have been so bad as the woe Christ felt. This was because of the nobility of his nature and the holy union of the divine and human nature in him. Thus I say that there have never been saints whom sorrow did not grieve and love did not please, and there never will be such saints. Occasionally we might find saints so influenced by God's love, kindness, and mystery that we might reproach them for their belief or some other reason when they remain bathed in grace and indifferent to good times or bad times. On the other hand, saints may make so much progress that nothing can take them away from God. Even though the heart of such a saint may be grieved that people are not in the state of grace, his or her will remains quite uniformly in God and says: "Lord, I belong to you and you to me!" Whatever may happen to such a person does not hinder his or her eternal happiness so long as the very peak of the spirit is not affected in the place where the spirit is united with God's most precious will.

Christ says: "You are worried about many problems." Martha was so real that her works did not hinder her. Her activity and works brought her to eternal happiness. This happiness was indeed somewhat indirect, but a noble nature, constant industry, and virtue, as mentioned above, are very helpful in this connection. Mary also had to become such a Martha before she would become the mature Mary. For when she sat at our Lord's feet, she was still not the true Mary. Of course, she was so according to her name but not yet in her being. For she sat still in a feeling of pleasure and sweetness, was received into the school, and learned how to live. But Martha remained quite real there. Therefore she said: "Lord, tell her to get up!" as if to say: "Lord, I wish her not to sit there in pleasure. I would much prefer for her to learn how to live so that she will have life wholly as her own. Tell her to get up so that she can become complete." Her name was not Mary when she sat at Christ's feet. I rather call Mary a well-practiced body that is obedient to wise instruction. Also, I call it obedience when the will is sufficient for what our insight commands.

Our honest people believe that they can manage their affairs so that the presence of physical things no longer has any significance. But they cannot achieve this. I shall never reach the point where a painful buzzing is as beneficial to my ears as a

sweet piece of string music. In this connection we should add
that, if our insight perceives the painful buzzing, then a will
formed by knowledge suits the insight and instructs the physical
will not to be concerned about it. Then the will says: "I shall do
so gladly!" Behold, there would be a struggle against desire. For
what a person has to fight with great effort will become the joy of
that person's heart. Only then will it become fruitful.

Certain people, however, wish to manage things so extensively
that they become unencumbered of activities. But I said: "This
cannot happen!" Only after the disciples received the Holy Spirit
did they begin to carry out acts of virtue. For this reason, when
Mary was sitting at our Lord's feet, she was still learning. Then
she was admitted into the school and learned how to live. Later,
however, when Christ had gone up to heaven and she had received the Holy Spirit, she began to be of service. She traveled
across the sea, preached, taught, and became a helper of the disciples. When the saints become saints, they begin to carry out acts
of virtue. For only then do they gather a treasure for their eternal
happiness. Everything that formerly was accomplished atones
only for guilt and averts punishment. On this point we have a
proof in Christ. From the beginning, when God became a human
and humans God, he began to do things for our happiness until
the end when he died on the cross. There was no limb of his
body that had not practiced a special virtue.

May God help us to follow him sincerely in the practice of the
true virtues! Amen.

COMMENTARY: How Work Is as Noble and Spiritual as the Desert It-
self/How Spiritual Maturity Is the Basis for a Spirituality
of Work and Where This Maturity Is Learned/Work
Becomes Spiritual Work When We Are *Among* Things
But Not *In* Things/A Theology of Work Presumes an
Appreciation of Matter, the Senses, and Passion

It is evident from the previous sermon that Eckhart's spirituality is not in
opposition to complete involvement in the world. As deeply mystical as
he is, he in no way pits spirituality against activity or prayer against
work. In fact, as he insists in the present sermon, a person who is too in-

volved in religious feelings, who is "basking in religious feelings," as
Caputo puts it,[1] is an immature person living an immature spirituality. If
we have not yet integrated our activity and our mysticism, then we are
still dualists and part of the sinful condition that lies behind all sin and
lack of compassion. For Eckhart, work is an absolutely essential ingredi-
ent to the living and expression of spirituality. Our work is noble; it is
spiritual; it is divine. For it is the bringing about of the kingdom of God
and the new creation wherever we live and wherever we work. Far from
competing with spiritual activities, our work actually brings us closer to
God. *For we are placed in time so that we come closer to God and become more like him through "pursuits" that are enlightened by our
reason.* Our works that are done from within the Compassion and Justice
that God is convey us just as close to God and they are just as
beneficial as all the joys of Mary Magdalene in the desert. There is no
longer any conflict between contemplation and action for those who are
bathed in the true meaning and origin of work.

Indeed, our works "*overcome the evil times*" one often lives in insofar
as they bring about the new time, the end time, the new creation and
are immersed in realized eschatology. They bring about a time of light,
not darkness; joy, not sadness; peace, not discord. *For a bright life is indeed too small for there to be in it any darkness that veils or
overshadows eternal happiness for an exalted spirit.* For this exalted
spirit our works become the new light that accompanies the dawn of the
new creation—light was the first of God's acts of creation in Genesis,
chapter one—and the new light becomes our activities and work. For
those whose activities take place *in the light* of the new creation, *their
light is their works and their works are their light.* Called to become sons
of God, we are also called to become sons and daughters of light and
creation, who enlighten the world and whose reason and activity is itself
enlightened.

> "The light will be with you only a little longer now.
> Walk while you have the light,
> or the dark will overcome you;
> he who walks in the dark does not know where he is going.
> While you still have the light,
> believe in the light
> and you will become sons of light." (Jn. 12:35–36)

Eckhart combines this admonition to "walk in the light" with the warning from Paul that it is our lives and our activity that constitute this "walking" and this redeeming of our often evil times.

> You were darkness once, but now you are light in the Lord; be like children of light, for the effects of the light are seen in complete goodness and right living and truth. Try to discover what the Lord wants of you, having nothing to do with the futile works of darkness but exposing them by contrast . . . This may be a wicked age, but your lives should redeem it . . . be filled with the Spirit . . . so that always and everywhere you are giving thanks to God who is our Father in the name of our Lord Jesus Christ. (Ep. 5:8–11, 16, 18, 20)

If our gratitude to God the Creator is truly to be an "always and everywhere" gratitude, then surely for adults our work and activity is integral to this gratitude. In this sermon Eckhart continues to develop a theology of work as a spirituality. When does our work become a spirituality? A holy work? A work integral to building and maintaining spirituality?

First, when it arises from *the depth of our being*. In the previous sermon and Commentary we saw Eckhart develop at some length his theology of work as a theology of the creative Word—that all true work is born from the depths of one's creativity. Indeed, that only creative work is authentic human work (see also Sermon Twenty-nine). In the present sermon he lists three elements to what he calls the work of the *mature* person or three elements to what the economist E. F. Schumacher in our day calls "good work."[2] First is a *depth of being which was thoroughly trained to the most external matters*—in other words, Martha had the experience that practice brings in doing her work well. Indeed, she had such self-confidence in her own skills that *she believed that no one else was so well suited for activity as herself.* She had pride in her work and in her capacity to do her work well. Second, Martha, who is Eckhart's symbol of a mature person and a mature worker, possessed a *wise prudence that knew how to achieve external acts to the highest degree that love demands.* In other words, she could translate her goals of love and living without a why into her actions and her activity. She knew *how* to bring compassion about. And third, her work of *serving Christ* was born of the noble *dignity* of the person she was serving. The sign of Martha's maturity was the fact that her work did not hinder her relationship to

God and vice versa. She knew this ultimate truth about the interdependence of work and spirituality: *activity in time is just as noble as any kind of linking of self and God.* In other words, contrary to many traditional exegeses of the Martha/Mary story and the theology of action/contemplation that was behind these interpretations, Eckhart believes that contemplation is not better than, nor, in the mature person, even different from, work. For work too *carries us just as close as possible to the highest thing, except for the vision of God in his pure nature.* Compassion and the works born of compassion are themselves acts of contemplation. This is the fullness of spiritual maturity: to be in the world, active in the world, and yet not hindered by these actions from being always in God. It is our being *real: Martha was so real that her works did not hinder her. Her activity and works brought her to eternal happiness.* Caputo calls this interpretation of the Martha/Mary story by Eckhart a "startling reinterpretation" of the Gospel narrative and "one of Eckhart's most inventive sermons."[3]

Where does one learn this maturity of union between work and spirituality that Eckhart insists must be the sign of a spiritually advanced person or society? It is learned in the school of living. Martha was more mature than Mary because *Martha had already lived quite a long time.* Living is the finest school for spirituality and compassion: *living offers the most noble kind of knowledge.* Indeed, a life lived in depth and in appreciation and in awareness is the best spiritual training that exists. *Living causes pleasure and light to be better known than everything we can attain beneath God in this life.* And living includes working: it is far more than mere religious satisfactions or contemplative feelings. These latter goals are those of the immature spiritual seeker, whom we have in the example of Mary. *We cherish the suspicion that our dear Mary somehow had sat there more out of a feeling of pleasure than for spiritual gain.* Those who seek *feelings of pleasure* in their spirituality need to grow up to the level of living that includes integrating their work with their desire for compassion. For true spiritual breakthrough, as we saw in Path Three, is not at the level of emotion but at the full experience of birthing. In giving birth we are ourselves birthed. And our work is such an activity of giving birth. Mary was *learning how to live* while sitting at Jesus' feet, but Martha already knew how. Only later was Mary so full of the Holy Spirit that she knew what true service meant. She learned how to work and do works of compassion. *When the saints become saints, they begin to carry out acts of virtue.* The full expression of the Spirit, then, is in our work that brings about the Spirit's intentions. *Spiritual satisfaction is satisfaction within the spirit. Such a spirituality does not drown in a feeling of pleasure but, rather, stands in might above it* and does the works of the Spirit, unhindered by any temptations to dualism.

How do we learn to work in the world without being of the world and to work out of spiritual maturity instead of out of *feelings of pleasure* alone? How do we *learn how to live?* It is by learning to live *among things* but not in them. Jesus was saying to Martha, *you are among things, but things are not in you.* Work is deeply spiritual when we, like Martha and *all God's friends,* can exist "among cares" but not "within cares." What it means to be a person who is *among things but not in things* is that we do more than merely *manage* our affairs in an external manner; *we devote ourselves to them internally and with comprehensible prudence.* In other words, we are committed to works that are, in fact, of the highest order, of the new creation. There are two kinds of means or two ways we can treat the creaturely elements of our work: in one way, our activities lead us to God; in the other way they do not. In other words, for Eckhart there is no distinction between good works and bad works based on the being or nature of the work itself. The distinction is based on the end result of the work. For all work, like all being, insofar as it is being, is holy and good and divine. But its results may not be such, and if the work is not capable of drawing our commitment from deep within ourselves, it is most likely not a work that is worthy of our divine calling. When our work fulfills the following criteria, that is, when it *corresponds . . . to what is highest* and is therefore a striving for the best; when it is the best we can do *at the time;* and when we can *trace in good actions the lively truth of its beneficial presence,* in other words, when we see good fruits from it, then work becomes holy. So holy, in fact, that such work is at least as holy as contemplative experiences. *They convey us just as close to God and they are just as beneficial as all the joys of Mary Magdalene in the desert.*

How is it possible that we can work *among things but not in things?* It is possible to the very extent that we are already grounded and *at home* in God. If we are in God thoroughly, then we do not fall into being in things instead. Being concerned and being committed is a good thing. But the finest way to be concerned and caring is to remain outside of things, *without all works.* We are outside them because we are inside God. When we are well grounded in God, then we can be among

things and among our work without being *among cares and affliction.*
We can let go of our work. At some deep level we are beyond the hindrances that too much attachment can bring. *Martha possessed a ma-*
ture, well-established virtue and an undisturbed disposition that was
unhindered by all things. Because we are so intimately in God, the peak
of our spirit remains uninfluenced by the wearisome troubles that activity
brings with it. *Whatever may happen to such a person does not hinder*
his or her eternal happiness so long as the very peak of the spirit is not
affected in the place where the spirit is united with God's most precious
will. Thus Eckhart has recourse once again to his basic theology of
panentheism, a theology of inness, to explain his theology of work. The
third way to God is our *being at home* in all we do and wherever we
are. But being at home with God is being in God and having all of our
actions flow from this divine source. Such a way of being and of acting
is a dialectical way filled with wonder and beauty. *Listen to this wonder!*
How wonderful it is to be both outside and inside, to seize and to be
seized, to see and at the same time to be seen, to hold and to be held—
that is the goal where the spirit remains at rest, united with our dear
eternity. In this way and along its path we spin and flow out from the
circle of eternity like energy spiraling out of a falling star or springing
from a sprung and empty tomb. It is "eternal" energy because it is always new, always being born, always creative and giving birth. Such is
the work of those who work *among things* but in God and therefore not
in things. Such is the work of those mature persons who have learned to
let go and let be while still caring and committing themselves to the divine work that compassion is. Thus Caputo can comment how for Eckhart
true perfection "nourishes itself in the midst of activity" and deep spirituality that is adult takes place amid an "active and robust commerce with
things."[4]

The authentic grounding for our authentic work is God. There is one
thing necessary. *What is this one thing? It is God.* Yet our being bathed
in God as one thing, our swimming in the divine ocean of compassion, is
this very same one thing that erases all separations, all dualisms, all
two's. This union of us and God includes our work and God. Our work
is not two but one, and we and God and our work are not two or three
but one. When our consciousness toward work alters, then our work—
instead of being two things in relation to our spirituality—becomes
diaphanous and transparent. In it we can "apprehend all things." A per-

son "must always do one thing at a time; he cannot do everything at once. It must always be one thing, and in this one thing we must apprehend all things."[5]

When the one necessary thing, namely God, embraces us, then all becomes united and our work becomes our prayer and vice versa. For the God who embraces us is a God of Compassion and from this nearness to Compassion our compassionate works flow. It should be remembered in this respect that the Gospel text Eckhart is commenting on, Luke 10:38–42, follows immediately on two discourses by Jesus on compassion: that of the one great commandment and that on the Good Samaritan as an example of a compassionate person (see Sermon Thirty-seven). Eckhart was not unaware of how the Martha/Mary story properly belonged within this same instruction on how to become compassionate. As one contemporary exegete puts it, commenting on this same story of Martha and Mary: "Having illustrated the command to love one's neighbor [in the Good Samaritan story] Luke describes the meaning of the commandment to love God . . . In contrast to the Samaritans, who have rejected Jesus, Martha receives him as a guest in her house."[6]

True obedience, Eckhart suggests, is related to our work. It is *when the will is sufficient for what our insight commands*. True obedience to God's work carries out this word—which is always a creative work—in our work. It perseveres and is true to the insight it has received. Mere listening—which is what Mary did while sitting at Jesus' feet in hopes of learning the word of God—is not enough. We are called *to follow God truly in the practice of compassion*.

But true compassion presumes passion. It presumes a relationship—but a correct one—with things. There are *honest people who imagine that they can manage their affairs so that the presence of physical things no longer has any significance. But they cannot achieve this*. Physical things are important to the spiritual person and to the work of such a person and to deny it is to forsake compassion and to fall into dualisms. *I shall never reach the point where a painful buzzing is as beneficial to my ears as a sweet piece of string music*. In other words, love your senses! Let your ears be! Let them enjoy the difference between good music and painful noise and relish the former. From this spring of celebration and union, true compassion is learned. For Eckhart, as for the prophets of Israel,[7] the only proper basis for a prophetic or compassionate spirituality is a sensual one. Sensual spirituality forms a basis for his theology of work. For only a sensual spirituality is itself nondualistic and seeks out the harmonious living that all true compassion is about.[8] We cannot be compassionate toward others if we are dualistic and in a master-slave relationship with our own senses or our own passions. Eckhart resists all temptations to emotional stoicism. We are to *be moved,* not refrain from being moved!

> Our upright people, however, say that we must become so perfect that no kind of joy can move us any longer, that we must be immovable to joy or sorrow. They are wrong in this matter. But *I* say that there was never a saint so great that he or she could not be moved.

Being moved, being passionate, is integral to being perfect or compassionate. *Do you think that, so long as words can move you to joy or sorrow, you are imperfect? It is not so!* And Eckhart invokes the example of Christ, the firstborn of the compassionate sons of God. *Christ let us know* the importance of feeling and passion *when he said: "My soul is grieved to the point of death"* (Mt. 26:38). Indeed, the sensitivity Christ felt to pain and suffering stemmed from the very Godhead itself that suffers pain. His passion stemmed from the nobility of his nature and the holy union of the divine and human natures in him. We remain unmovable in God but vulnerable to the pain and suffering that is part of human existence. Indeed, there can be no authentic compassion without this sense of well-developed vulnerability.

A spirituality of work culminates in our becoming "fellow helpers with God."[9] Being fellow workers with the Creator, we are busy bringing about the new creation. By breaking into the depths of the Creator we emerge as co-creators "in everything we do."

> I have often said: "The shell must be cracked apart if what is in it is to come out; for if you want the kernel, you must break the shell" . . . When the soul finds the One who gathers all things into itself, there your soul must stay. Who "honors" God? He or she who intends to honor God in everything he or she does.[10]

Everything we do—all our work and activity—is an honor to God if it comes from within self and from within God, if it is born of our breakthrough and rebirth in God. Then the work and the Word become so closely united that the work is accomplished "divinely in God." For when the soul is united with God and embraced by God, and grace escapes the soul so that it now no longer accomplishes things with grace but divinely in God. Thus the soul is in a wonderful way enchanted and loses itself.[11]

Our work is more than work. It is an enchantment. A divine act of creation and re-creation which is also a recreation. It is compassion on the loose.

"Sermon" Thirty-five: BREAD IS GIVEN US FOR OTHERS,
ON ACCOUNT OF OTHERS, AND WITH
OTHERS—ESPECIALLY THE INDIGENT

"On the Lord's Prayer"*

"Our Father." There are some matters we should note before
considering the Lord's Prayer. First, that we tend to be lazy regarding the things of God and therefore we are first exhorted to
ask and to pray. Second, God commits us to his love, for when we
are still a long way off, he calls us back and attracts us. God's love
is so good that it is necessary that he give of himself. It should be
noted that nothing temporal is asked for from God in this prayer.
This is true, because the Lord's Prayer itself does not contain any·
thing of this sort. Besides, how could we ask him for the very
thing which he everywhere teaches us to hold in contempt? It is
not appropriate for God, who is eternal, to give things of such a
temporal nature. Temporal things are not asked for because, in
comparison with eternal things, they are nothing, and to pray for
nothing is not to pray.

"Father." We note first of all a point made by Chrysostom
that God wanted more to be loved than to be feared. This is why
the prayer begins "Our Father" and not "Our Lord." The word
"Father" is used that we might know that "he gave us the power
to be the sons of God." As a consequence, "if sons, then heirs,
too." "He who says 'Father,' through this one naming confesses
the remission of sins, the adoption and inheritance of sons,
fraternity with the only begotten Son, and the generosity of
the Spirit." We are to love the honor of God and grieve over ev-

* "Super Oratione Dominica" (Klibansky, ed , pp. 1–17) This "sermon" has been slightly edited. This editing consists exclusively of elimi-
nating some numbering phrases that Eckhart uses as an outline to himself. Strictly speaking, this was not written as a sermon but as a scriptural
commentary.

erything which opposes it, wherever it occurs, just as true sons act toward their fathers. The petitioners are to have confidence, for fathers are supposed to listen to their sons, and furthermore we have been told, "Ask and you will receive," and again, "Whatever you ask in prayer, believe that . . ."

"Our." Note first of all that the word is "our," not "my," because the prayer is very pleasing which is motivated by love and not by necessity. Jerome says: "The more a prayer communicates, the more efficacious it is." We are speaking here not of my or your or even everyone's father but of him from whom "all fatherhood in heaven and on earth is named." We say "our" in order that we might remember that all people are our brothers and co-heirs and thus we might love them and persevere to the end with them as brothers, keeping also in mind that other verse: "All of you are brothers."

"Who art in heaven." Note first of all what Chrysostom says: "We blush to fill our lives with earthly things when we realize that we have a Father in heaven." From the first sermon of Abbot Isaac we learn that we should avoid in total horror the present life which we live inasmuch as we are so far separated from our Father. And the psalm says: "Alas for me that my dwelling here is prolonged." We are reminded by these words that we should hasten with all the desire of our hearts to that place where we profess to have a Father. As the psalm says: "By the waters of Babylon we laid down our harps, for how could we sing to the Lord on foreign soil?" We are reminded that we should allow nothing to deprive us of a noble heritage of such great dignity. We recall the saying that we are heaven or, rather, the very heaven of heavens if we want our Father to be in us. Chrysostom says in his homily: "When one says 'in heaven' he does not merely point to God but he is taken from earth in prayer and placed in heaven above." We recall the words of Augustine in his commentary: "In heaven, that is among the saints and the righteous ones." "For there is as much spiritual difference between the righteous and sinners as there is physically between heaven and earth."

Augustine in the same commentary on the words "in heaven" says: "These words are said so that the soul is reminded to direct itself to its more excellent nature, namely to God. For there in heaven, its earthly body is transformed into a higher body, namely a spiritual one." "It is good that everyone, small and great alike, have some idea of God; therefore, since most people cannot think about God in a noncorporeal way, it is better that they believe God to be in heaven than on earth."

"Hallowed be thy name." "That is, may God's name be so known that everyone will understand that there is nothing more sacred." "Hallowed" has the further sense of "May thy name be glorified"—namely, that in everyone there may be this sentiment: "We expend our whole heart for the glory of our Father, our desire and our joy being the witness we give to his glory." The words of Jesus which we find in John's Gospel state: "That person is true who seeks the glory of him who sent him; there is no falsehood in such a person." Paul, too, declares that he could wish that he were cut off from Christ Jesus that the salvation of the whole people of Israel might be advanced to the glory of the Father. He could indeed be fearless in wishing to perish for Christ because he knew that no one could die for life itself.

Another meaning to the petition "Hallowed be thy name" is: "Father, make us such that we might merit either to understand the greatness of your holiness or to possess it." There is an additional sense of the text: "Make us live in such a way that through our conversation your name is glorified and made holy." Or, as we read in Matthew's Gospel: "Let them see your good works and glorify your Father." The text can also mean: "By a continuing growth in holiness may we be purged of our daily failings" in order that God's name is hallowed, that is, kept holy in us. We say "Hallowed be thy name" because what we know about God reflects a ray of his love and power. We pray that "knowing him we may fear his holy name and solicitously be on guard lest by chance we violate the holiness of his name through any evil deed of ours."

"Thy kingdom come." It is fitting that the petition "Hallowed be thy name" came earlier because, according to Saint Jerome, "It is a mark of great trust and a pure conscience not to fear the kingdom of God and his judgment." We pray "Thy kingdom come" first of all that with the devil driven out by the extinction of our vices, God might reign in us or rather in the whole world through the abundance of virtue. Second, the prayer refers to the future kingdom of which Jesus spoke: "Come, blessed of my Father, see the kingdom . . ." "For the saint knows by the testimony of his own conscience that when the kingdom of God shall appear, he will participate in it."

The text says "thy," for God is eternal spirit. Therefore, his kingdom is not corporeal, temporal, or anything of the sort but something much more sublime. It is called "thy" kingdom because it is in spirit, in eternity, and what the kingdom reveals is the power, wisdom, goodness, riches, and honor of God.

"Thy will be done on earth as it is in heaven." Concerning this petition, it is first to be noted that Chrysostom refers this phrase to the three preceding petitions. For these petitions do not say "sanctify" (in the imperative) or "may we sanctify" or "bring in your kingdom" or "may we receive your kingdom." Nor does it say "do your will" (in the imperative) or "may we do your will." Rather, these petitions are impersonally stated: "may it be hallowed" or "may it come" or "may it be done." What this teaches us is to pray for the whole world. It is important to notice the relationship of the third petition to the second, for it teaches us to receive celestial things, saying: "Thy kingdom come." And this before we ever arrive at heaven, bidding this very earth to become a heaven in saying: "May your will be done on earth as it is in heaven." "Let error be eliminated, let virtue grow, let evil be cast out, let goodness return, and then there will be altogether no difference between heaven and earth." And this is the first explanation of the third petition.

According to another exposition of this phrase, earthly things desire to be equal to those in heaven, for just as the will of God is fulfilled by the angels in heaven, so too it should be fulfilled by all people on earth. This is something we will readily pray for, if we believe that God is more solicitous for us than we are for ourselves. The will of God is our salvation, according to the text: "God wills all persons to be saved." We pray, therefore, to be saved or for salvation when we say: "Thy will be done on earth, as it is in heaven." For just as those who are in heaven are saved, so too those who are on earth are to be saved. Here is where we see more of the meaning of the earlier petition: "Thy kingdom come." For when this kingdom of God arrives, whether now through grace or in the future through glory, then the will of God will be done on earth as it is in heaven.

"As in heaven" also refers to the righteous and "on earth" refers to sinners. It is a prayer for the retribution of both good and evil which will occur in the final judgment, a future which is prayed for in the petition "Thy kingdom come." Heaven and earth can also refer to spirit and flesh. We are praying therefore that as the mind, which is spirit, is obedient to God, so may the flesh be obedient to the spirit. Moreover, "on earth as it is in heaven" implies "as in Christ, so in the whole church." We pray that as we already perceive the kingdom of God in our minds or spirits, while we are on earth, so may it be the will of God that we perceive it in our glorified body in the resurrection of the dead, thus attaining the salvation of both mind and body.

"Give us today our daily bread." In Matthew 6 we read: "Give us today our supersubstantial bread," but in Luke 11: "Give us today our daily bread." In his exposition of Matthew, Chrysostom employs the word "daily" and explains it in a fourfold way: first, "Grant us today to prepare and consume without sin our daily bread, that by which we are daily nurtured." For whatever is consumed or received without sin and in righteousness is certainly something given by God. For whatever is not given in this way is certainly not given by God but comes from concupiscence or the devil. Second, our bread, that which we already have, give us today; "daily" that is sanctified or whole or blessed. And this fits with the version of Matthew which speaks about "supersubstantial bread." Third, give us today our daily bread, that is, give us daily what we need for the day, namely for this one day, so that we do not spend today or in one day what suffices for us for one hundred days or for one hundred persons for one day—but give us today our daily bread or daily for today, that is, daily for one person or one day. Fourth, give us today our daily bread, that is, as much as is possible, for we do not want to have more than daily bread.

Regarding the word "our," Chrysostom in the exposition referred to above explains it in a twofold way: first, that we might understand that bread is given to us so that not only we might eat but that we recognize others in need, lest anyone say "my bread" is given to me instead of understanding that it is ours, given to me, to others through me and to me through others. For not only bread but all things which are necessary for sustaining this present life are given to us with others and because of others and given to others in us. Whoever does not give to another what belongs to the other, such a one does not eat his own bread but eats the bread of another along with his own. Thus when we justly eat the bread we have received, we certainly eat our bread; but when we eat evilly and with sin the bread we have received, then we are not eating our own bread but the bread of another. For everything which we have unjustly is not really ours.

"Our bread." This states that we pray to be given daily bread, that is, for today. This signifies that it would not be proper for us to be solicitous each separate day for all the things necessary for our support. There is an allusion to this in the Gospel According to the Hebrews which, according to Saint Jerome, has a gloss on this text from Matthew 6 which states: "Give us tomorrow's bread today."

"Give us today our daily bread" tells us that we are in need each day. Asking for bread today means in the present or during the time of our pilgrimage in this present age. For we are in need of material bread as long as we are mortal, fragile human beings. This same point is alluded to in the gloss from the sermons of the fathers quoted above. But it should be noted that part of the significance of the word "bread" is the sufficiency of this present life. One can read this in Augustine's letter to Probas about prayer to God: "It is not wrong to wish a sufficiency of life's goods, if one indeed wishes that and not more." It is in this same way that one can figuratively understand the Gospel reference to the tunic: "Nor should you have two tunics."

We can find significance in this word "bread" as heavenly teaching or inspiration or illustration, according to the text: "Not by bread alone does man live, etc." This is why Matthew uses the phrase "supersubstantial bread," insofar as God himself feeds every creature, always and everywhere. Or again, one can consider the text from John: "I am the living bread which came down from heaven." For insofar as Christ is divine, he too feeds all things.

In the sacrament of his Body, participation in which is our daily

thought, we say "our bread." There is no obstacle in our not receiving the sacrament daily, for we in no way less effectively participate if we are one body living in true love with those who receive the sacrament, wherever they might be. This agrees with
what is said about the apostles, "who because of their teaching
are always on the move," that thus they would keep nothing for
the next day.

It can also be noted here that we are not commanded to pray
for money or luxuries but for bread: "Give us today our daily
bread." "A disciple of Christ should ask for food for the day, lest
we seek to remain long in this present age, we who pray that his
kingdom may come quickly." For we say: "Thy kingdom come"
in the spirit of the text "Alas for me, Lord, that I am still dwelling, etc." and the other Pauline passage: "I desire to be dissolved,
etc."

Another understanding of this text is: "Give us the bread
which is today, in the sense of eternity which is always today."
Or, "Give us the supersubstantial bread today—that is, in eternity." This is the perspective we see in the text "Today I have
begotten you." Saint Augustine, toward the end of the sixth chapter of the *Confessions* says: "Your years are as one day and your
day is not daily but today, because your today does not lead to a
tomorrow any more than it succeeds a yesterday. Your today is
eternity. Therefore, you eternally begot him to whom you said:
'This day I have begotten you.'" He commands us to pray with
this temporal referent to show that not only spiritual things but
also temporal realities have their origin in God. This is first of all
in opposition to the Manichaean position. Also, you do not
choose a bread which is not flavored. Finally, this helps us to
know that the very least of the good things we have is from God.

"And forgive us our trespasses." Note how this gives us a way
of prayer, teaches us morals, takes away anger and sadness, the
root of all evil, and discloses the way in which we are able in our
prayer to ask for things we need and to temper the divine wrath
or judgment against us—all of this by saying, "Forgive us, etc."
We say "our trespasses" because, as Chrysostom points out, a certain amount of patience is praiseworthy in the case of personal injuries but to conceal in any way offenses against God is impious.
There are many people who are very prone to forgive the offenses

they themselves commit against their fellow creatures or even against God, but they are in no way so quick to forgive the injuries committed against themselves. Besides, if the one who is harmed prays fruitlessly unless he forgives his debtors, what do you think of the prayer of the one who is doing the harm?

There are some who simply pass over the phrase "as we forgive those who trespass against us," but those who do this are ignorant. Those who do not pray in the way Christ taught are neither Christians nor true disciples of Christ. Furthermore, the Father will not readily hear a prayer which the Son did not teach. The Father pays attention to and receives, not the words, but rather the meaning of the Son. "You can say anything you want in a prayer therefore, but you are not able to deceive God."

In regard to this fifth petition, "Forgive us, etc.," we should note several things. First of all, all those who call God "Father" are instructed to pray daily and to ask every day for forgiveness, saying, "Forgive us . . ." This commandment is given lest the innocent become self-satisfied and by praising themselves become more worthy of hell. Furthermore, in this petition, the paternal compassion of God is commended to us, "for he who teaches us to pray for the forgiveness of sins is the same who promised compassion." The prayer does not say "as we *will* forgive" but "as we forgive." For God does not want to forgive us unless we first forgive in the same way he forgives us. And he forgives us when we ask and pray for forgiveness. It is enough, therefore, if we forgive those asking and begging forgiveness. "For he who asks forgiveness of the one against whom he has sinned is no longer to be considered an enemy." Thus Augustine in the *Enchiridion* says that the love of our enemies "does not include that group of people whom we believe hear us when we say in prayer: 'Forgive us as we forgive.' "

It should also be noted that in the first three petitions, whenever the things of God are spoken of, they are spoken of in the singular—"your name," "your kingdom," "your will"—but in the other four petitions the plural form is used: "our bread," "our trespasses," "do not lead us," "deliver us."

"And lead us not into temptation." This is the sixth petition. Note first of all that we do not pray not to be tempted. For Job was tempted and so were Abraham and Joseph, so that their reward might be increased. But we pray not to be led, not to be

conquered—as though someone were to pray not that he not feel
the flame of the fire but that he not be consumed by it. What is
implied in this petition is that our enemy is not able to tempt us,
unless God permits it "so that all of our fear and all of our devotion be equally directed to God." What follows is: "but deliver
us from evil," which means, "do not permit us to be tempted beyond what we are able to handle and along with the temptation
give us the strength to resist it."

Another way of looking at this petition, "lead us not into temptation," is that we are praying for perseverance in holiness. But
we ask God not to lead us into temptation, even though Saint
James says that God does not tempt us to evil because, according
to Saint Augustine in *Concerning the Gift of Perseverance*,
"nothing happens unless God either does it himself or permits it
to happen."

"But deliver us from evil." This is the seventh petition. Note
first of all that we pray against evil, against sin, that we not be led
to it, an evil act which we have not yet committed. For we pray,
"lead us not, etc." But now we pray to be freed from evil, from a
sin already committed. The force of evil here is being in danger
of temptation. "From evil" also means "from the devil," because
he is the one who speaks evil or because of the relentless warfare
which he wages against us. "From evil" can mean from the vice
of asking for things which are carnal or temporal. "One might be
ashamed to ask for what one is not ashamed to desire." If one is
conquered by greed, then a good prayer is to be freed from that
very evil of greediness. "For you will ask and not receive what you
wrongly asked"—*wrongly* here means carnally or temporally.
Amen.

COMMENTARY: We Are Children and Heirs of God's Parental
Compassion/The Need for an *Our*—Not a *My*—Con-
sciousness/Our Works of Compassion Inaugurate
Heaven on Earth/How All Are Our Brothers and
Sisters—and Especially the Poor

In this sermon on the *Our Father*—the one prayer that Jesus left behind
—Eckhart draws out further implications of our relationship to God as a
child to a parent and of our power as children of God. To be a child in

relation to God means that we love God more than we fear God; it means trust and confidence between us and God, for *fathers are supposed to listen to their sons.* It means we share a *fraternity* with Christ, *the only begotten Son.* It also means that communication between us and God is open and necessary, as it is with a good parent and a loving child. But if we are children of God we are "heirs also." Heirs of what? Heirs of God's *Fatherhood* and solicitation for creation and creation's happiness. *God himself feeds every creature, always and everywhere.* Eckhart's concept of fatherhood includes the mothering or nurturing side of God as well.[1] God is a feeder, a nurturer, a mother. And so is Christ insofar as Christ is the Son of God. *Insofar as Christ is divine, he too feeds all things.* The implication is evident: We too, insofar as we are God's children, are to be nurturers, feeders, mothers of creation. In this way we inherit that unique divine attribute, compassion, and we deserve the title "sons and daughters of God." *The paternal compassion of God is commended to us.* In this manner we learn the lesson once again, to "be compassionate as your Father in heaven is compassionate."

If all creatures are offsprings of God—and they are, for *not only spiritual things but temporal realities too have their origin in God*—as we saw in Path One, then all creatures are interdependent. All are brothers and sisters with one, common, Parent. This Parent is our Creator and we swim together in the ocean that is being and that is God's love. *We are speaking here not of my or your or even everyone's father but of him from whom "all fatherhood in heaven and on earth is named."* But insofar as humans are uniquely born as images and sons of this Father, and uniquely reborn as children of God, to that extent all humans are brothers and sisters. *Remember that all people are our brothers and co-heirs and thus we might love them and persevere to the end with them as brothers, keeping also in mind that other verse: "All of you are brothers."* We share the same earth, the same origin, the same destiny, the same divine Parent. *Why then can we not love one another and persevere to the end with one another as brothers?*

One reason is that we do not think enough in these terms of shared brotherhood and sisterhood. We too often think *my* instead of *our.* And yet this prayer—the only one Jesus left behind—does not have a single *my* in it. It is all about, indeed it entirely presumes a *we*—not *me*—consciousness. *Note first of all that the word is "our," not "my," because the prayer is very pleasing which is motivated by love and not by necessity.* Prayers of necessity are often *my*-oriented prayers: Help me! Save me!

But prayers of an *our* consciousness demand love, a consciousness that goes beyond my own needs to others' needs. It requires compassion and a getting beyond the puny *I*. Even when we petition for human needs in the final four petitions, *the plural form is used of "our bread," "our trespasses," "do not lead us," "deliver us."*

When we learn to respond to life and to God and to our inner selves with an *our* instead of a *me* consciousness, we learn some powerful and significant lessons about sharing the goods of the earth. Drawing on Saint Chrysostom's criticism of the *me* mentality that riches so often spawn, Eckhart warns:

> Bread is given to us so that not only we might eat but that we recognize others in need, lest anyone say "my bread" is given to me instead of understanding that it is ours, given to me, to others through me and to me through others.

Here we have a beautiful summation of what the law of interdependence, the basis of what all compassion is about: an awareness of how energy flows *to others through me*—thus the divine importance of the work we do—and *to me through others*—thus the divine importance of a gift consciousness and a capacity to receive the gifts of others. Furthermore, the gifts themselves—the bread—are not *mine* but *ours*. The same holds for *all things which are necessary for sustaining this present life*— whether land or water, air or food, oil or rain, sunshine or laughter. *All things . . . are given to us with others and because of others and given to others in us.* Gifts exist for the sake of all of us, for we are all one and all in need. But our response is to be one of giving and of doing justice in order to see this sharing accomplished. It is not done by inheritance alone. We are not born into a world of justice and compassion, of *we*, not *I*. When we fail to act against injustice we are, in fact, busy stealing others' food, others' necessities. We are part of the problem of injustice instead of the healing that justice brings.

> Whoever does not give to another what belongs to the other, such a one does not eat his own bread but eats the bread of another along with his own. Thus when we justly eat the bread we have received, we certainly eat our bread; but when we eat evilly and with sin the bread we have received, then we are not eating our own bread but the bread of another. For everything which we have unjustly is not really ours.

We are praying to receive and to give *necessities, not luxuries. We are not commanded to pray for money or luxuries but for bread.* It is bread and the other necessities that unite people as brothers and sisters, and not the luxuries of living. Advertising and commercials notwithstanding, our common prayer will always be a prayer for necessities. For it is around our shared needs that our humanity and fraternity is learned and built up. Furthermore, we do not need luxurious quantities even of the necessities. *We do not want to have more than daily bread,* Eckhart claims, underlining his plea for a simple style of living. *We are in need each day,* and it is this common need that forms the basis of our common humanity and our common compassion. *Asking for bread today means in the present or during the time of our pilgrimage in this present age. For we are in need of material bread as long as we are mortal, fragile human beings.* Being all alike, mortal, fragile human beings, we ought to be busy about relieving one another of pain and indigency and deprivation of basic needs before we put any efforts into luxury needs.

The bread we pray for and work to receive and to give is a *material bread.* Is anything wrong with that? Of course not. Only the Manichaeans would object to this.

> He commands us to pray with this temporal referent [this day] to show that not only spiritual things but temporal realities too have their origin in God. This is first of all in opposition to the Manichaean position.

All good things are from God—we saw this in Path One—and being from God, we have a right to good things. *The very least of the good things we have is from God.* But the issue at hand is that they are *from God,* not from ourselves. They are gifts, not objects. That means that they have been lent us, not given to us. They are meant to be returned—to God, to creation, to others—as all loans are meant to be returned. They are not meant to be hoarded, grabbed, clung to, or worshipped. That is why the paths of letting go and letting be are presumed in this sermon on the sharing of the gifts of the earth. For the way discussed in Path Two is the antithesis of greed. And so, a *good prayer is to be freed from that very evil of greediness. "For you will ask and not receive what you wrongly asked."* And to live or ask greedily is to live or ask wrongly, with an *I* instead of an *our* consciousness.

Eckhart develops this theme of experiencing the gifts of life as a loan on several occasions, for it is so important a part of the letting go and letting be pathway. God never gave property to anyone—not even to his Mother, Eckhart notes.

> God does not wish in any way that we should have so much of our own as could be held in our eyes. For all the gifts that he ever gave us, both gifts of nature and gifts of grace, he gave to no other end than that he wishes us to have nothing of our own. And as personal property he never gave anything either to his Mother or to any person, or to any creature in any way.[2]

For Eckhart there is no such thing in the long run as personal—or corporate—ownership. If we are involved with important things—the necessities of living—then they are ours on loan. They are not our property to be possessed. God alone owns the graces and beauties of existence. From him they come; to him they are to return, via all God's other creatures who are invited to share in them.

> The ownership should not be ours, but his alone. On the contrary, we should have all things as if they were lent to us, without any ownership, whether they are body and soul, sense, strength, external goods or honors, friends, relations, house, hall, everything in fact.[3]

We see here Eckhart's continued criticism of the merchant mentality and how it can ruin our very consciousness of compassion if it drills in us a consciousness of possession. When we have let go of the ownership mentality, then God can take over. God "wishes himself to be only and absolutely our own . . . The more we have of our own, the less we have of him; the less we have of our own, the more we have of him, with everything that he can offer."[4] A property mentality has something dualistic and violent about it. It is a consciousness of passion over, instead of passion with. "For if I wish that the property I have should be given to me and not lent, I want to be the master."[5] Master-slave relationships do not hold in a life of compassion. Compassion is essentially nonsadistic, nonmasochistic. Instead of its being a power over or a power under, as in those energies, compassion is a passion with (cum patior). In this kind of dynamic, a loan mentality holds sway. "Everything that is good or consoling or temporal has been bestowed upon a person as a loan."[6] Our proper response to this is "Thank you," not "Give me."

God's loans are not loans to me but to us. That is why Eckhart urges us in this commentary on the Our Father to realize our interdependence and our shared fraternity with all creation and thus to pray for the whole world. For all are our brothers and not just those we are related to by family, nation, race, or religion. We all share divine origins, a noble heritage of such great dignity. He subscribes to the universalist doctrine of salvation, that God wills all persons to be saved. On our part there is a special need to consider those who are in need, lest anyone say "my bread" is given to me instead of understanding that it is ours. The poor have a special claim on our attention and on our work, which is to be a work of justice and compassion. Elsewhere Eckhart advises:

> What do poor people do who endure the same or more severe illness and suffering, and have no one even to give them water? They must seek their very bread in rain, cold, and snow from house to house. Therefore, if you would be comforted, forget those who are better placed and remember only those who are less fortunate.[7]

If God's gifts belong to all, then those who are left out because they are poor must be included in that "all" experience. Eckhart comments on how we are often accustomed to treating the poor.

> The poor are indeed left to God, for no one else takes an interest in them. If a person has a friend who is poor, he or she does not acknowledge the friend. If the friend, however, has possessions and is wise, this person says: "You are my relative," and quickly acknowledges the friend. But to a poor person he or she will say: "May God look after you!" and then feels ashamed. The poor are left to God.[8]

The human temptation is to let God take care of the poor and thus to piously brush them off while we go about our comfortable business and busyness. But Eckhart advises us to "forget those who are better placed and remember" the poor. And we remember the poor by acts of justice which are works of compassion.

How important are these works of compassion? They actually lead to the glorification of the Father here on earth. As we read in Matthew's Gospel: "Let them see your good works and glorify your Father." By them we glorify God's holy name, "we expend our whole heart for the glory of our Father." At the same time we turn earth into heaven, as it was meant to be. Before we ever arrive at heaven [we are] bidding this very earth to become a heaven in saying: "May your will be done on earth as it is in heaven." Indeed, we work and pray that the kingdom of God, a reign of justice and peace, begin now. This is the future kingdom of which Jesus spoke. When we seek God who is Justice and Compassion to be in us and us in him and that our work be one work, then one can say that we become heaven itself! We are heaven or rather the very heaven of heavens if we want our Father to be in us. This sense of realized eschatology permeates the Lord's Prayer and thus begins to permeate our own thinking. By it we can be sure that eternity is always today. However, this tasting of eternal life and realized eschatology contains still a hint of what is not yet and of something unrealized. For we now experience the kingdom in grace, but then in glory. For when this kingdom of God arrives, whether now through grace or in the future through glory, then the will of God will be done on earth as it is in heaven. And then our Father will be known as everyone's and every creature's Father. And all will know they are brothers and sisters bathing in a sea of compassion and peace. Then the lion will lie down with the lamb.

"Sermon" Thirty-six: EVERYONE AN ARISTOCRAT,
EVERYONE A ROYAL PERSON

"On the Aristocrat"*

Our Lord says in the Gospel: "A man of royal birth went to a distant country to be appointed king, and afterward he returned"
(Lk. 19:12). Our Lord teaches us in these words how royal people have been created in their nature, how divine is the state to
which they can rise through grace and, in addition, how people
are to reach that point. In addition, a large part of the Holy
Scripture touches upon these words.

We must first realize, as is also clearly apparent, that a person
has two natures: body and spirit. For this reason a passage of
Scripture says that those who know themselves know all creatures.
For all creatures are either body or spirit. For this reason the
Scripture says of human beings that there exists in us an exterior
person and another or inner person.

The exterior person possesses all that adheres to the soul but is
surrounded by and mixed up with the flesh. In each and every
member the person possesses bodily cooperation, as with the eye,
ear, tongue, hand, and so forth. The Scripture calls all this the
old person, the earthly person, the exterior person, the hostile person, and a menial person.

The other person, who is hidden within us, is the inner person.
Scripture calls this person a new person, a heavenly person, a
young person, a friend, and a royal person. This person is meant
when our Lord says that "a man of royal birth went to a distant
country to be appointed king, and afterward he returned."

In addition, we should know that Saint Jerome as well as the
masters of the spiritual life generally say that every person
possesses from the beginning of his or her human existence a

* "Vom edlen Menschen" (DW V). Strictly speaking, this was not a sermon but a treatise by Eckhart.

good spirit, which is an angel, as well as a bad spirit, which is a devil. The good angel counsels and constantly inspires toward what is good, what is divine, what is virtue, and toward what is heavenly and eternal. The bad spirit counsels and inspires the person at all times to what is temporal and fleeting, toward what is vice, and toward what is bad and devilish. The same evil spirit is in constant dialogue with the exterior person, and in this way constantly lays traps for the inner person, just as the serpent chatted with the woman Eve and through her with the man Adam (cf. Gn. 3:1ff.). The inner person is Adam. The *man* in the soul is the good tree that unceasingly bears good fruit and that our Lord speaks of (cf. Mt. 7:17). He is also the soil in which God has sown his likeness and image and in which he sows the good seed, the roots of all wisdom, all skills, all virtues, all goodness—the seed of the divine nature (2 P. 1:4). The seed of the divine nature is God's Son, the Word of God (Lk. 8:11).

The exterior person is the hostile and bad person who has sown and scattered weeds among the good seed (cf. Mt. 13:24ff.). Concerning this person Saint Paul says: "I find in myself something that hinders me and is against what God requests and what God counsels and what God has said and is still saying in the height and in the depth of my soul" (cf. Rm. 7:23). And elsewhere he speaks out and complains: "What a wretched man am I! Who will rescue me from this mortal flesh and body?" (Rm. 7:24). Elsewhere he says that a person's spirit and flesh constantly struggle against each other. The flesh is vice and evil; the spirit counsels love of God, joy, peace, and every virtue (cf. Ga. 5:17ff.). Whoever follows the spirit and lives according to it and its advice possesses eternal life (cf. Ga. 6:8). The inner person is the one of whom our Lord says that "a man of royal birth went to a distant country to be appointed king." This is the good tree of which our Lord says that it always bears good fruit and never evil fruit. For it desires goodness and is inclined to goodness—to the goodness that rises up within itself undisturbed by the things of this world. The exterior person is the evil tree that can never bear good fruit (cf. Mt. 7:18).

Concerning the royalty of the inner person and the spirit, and concerning the unworthiness of the exterior person and the flesh, the pagan authors Cicero (Tully) and Seneca also say that no soul gifted with reason is without God. The seed of God is in us. If the seed had a good, wise, and industrious cultivator, it would thrive all the more and grow up to God whose seed it is, and the fruit would be equal to the nature of God. Now the seed of a pear tree grows into a pear tree, a hazel seed into a hazel tree, the seed of God into God (cf. Jn. 3:9). If it happens, however, that the good seed has a foolish and evil soil, it grows to a weed, and it overshadows and crowds the good seed to such an extent that the good seed cannot grow up to the light. Origen, one of the great masters of the spiritual life, says, however, that God himself has sown this seed, and inserted it and borne it. Thus while this seed may be crowded, hidden away, and never cultivated, it will still never be obliterated. It glows and shines, gives off light, burns, and is unceasingly inclined toward God.

The first stage of the inner and new person, says Saint Augustine, is when the person lives according to the model of good and holy people, even though he or she still walks by leaning on chairs, depends on walls for support, and is still nourished by milk.

The second stage is reached when people not only look to external models, including good human beings, but also run in haste to the teaching and advice of God and the divine wisdom, turn their backs to humanity and their countenances to God, creep out of their mothers' wombs, and smile at the heavenly Father.

The third stage is reached when people more and more forsake their mothers and depart farther and farther from the womb, flee from care, and throw off fear so that, even though they might, without annoyance, do evil and wrong to all others, they have no desire to do so. For they are so devoutly connected by love to God that he places and leads them in joy and sweetness and happiness to where everything is repellent to them that is dissimilar or foreign to God.

The fourth stage is reached when people grow and become rooted in love and in God so that they are ready to take upon themselves every attack, temptation, vexation, and painful suffering willingly and gladly, eagerly and joyfully.

The fifth stage is reached when people everywhere live at peace within themselves, quietly resting in the richness and abundance of the highest inexpressible wisdom.

The sixth state is reached when people are formed from and beyond God's eternity and attain a completely perfect forgetfulness of this temporary and passing life, when they are drawn and changed into the divine image, that is, when they have become children of God. Beyond this point there is no higher stage. Eternal rest and bliss are there, for the final goal of the inner persons and new persons is eternal life.

Origen, the great master of the spiritual life, proposes a comparison for the inner, royal person in whom God's seed and God's image have been inserted and sown in such a way that this image of the divine nature and existence—God's Son—appears and becomes known, but is also occasionally hidden. God's image, which is the Son of God, is like a living fountain in the depth of the soul. If someone throws dirt, that is, earthly desire, upon the fountain, it will hinder and conceal it so that nothing is known or suspected of it. All the same, the fountain remains inwardly alive, and if the dirt that has been thrown upon it from outside be removed, it will reappear and be known again. He says that this truth is intimated in the Book of Genesis where it is written that Abraham had dug living fountains on his soil but that evildoers filled them with earth. When the earth was removed, however, the fountains quickly appeared to be living again (Gn. 26:14ff.).

Another comparison exists in this case. The sun shines unceasingly. Yet if cloud or fog should come between the sun and ourselves, we will not be aware of the sunshine. In the same way, if our eye is inwardly afflicted and damaged or becomes veiled, it cannot know the sunshine. In addition, I have occasionally proposed the following distinct comparison. If a skilled artist makes an image of wood or stone, he or she does not place that image within the wood but chisels away the pieces that have hidden and covered it up. The artist contributes nothing to the wood but rather takes away and removes the covering and takes away the blight; then what lay hidden underneath shines forth. This is the treasure that lay hidden in the soil, as our Lord says in the Gospel (Mt. 13:44).

Saint Augustine says that when the soul of a person turns completely to eternity and God alone, God's image shines and gives off light. If, however, the soul turns outwardly—even if it does so for the exterior practice of virtue—this image is completely covered over. This should be signified by the fact that women cover their heads while men go bareheaded, according to Saint Paul's teaching (cf. 1 Co. 11:4ff.). For this reason everything that is turned downward from the soul receives from the object to which it turns a covering or headpiece. By contrast, whatever is carried up from the soul is God's pure image, the birth of God, which is purely exposed in the exposed soul. King David speaks in the Psalms of the royal person and of how God's image—the Son of God, and the seed of the divine nature—is never destroyed in us even though it may be covered over. He says: "Although many kinds of destruction, sorrow, and pain may befall a person, he or she remains all the same in God's image and the image remains within the person" (cf. Ps. 4:2ff.). "The true light shines in the darkness even though we are not aware of it" (cf. Jn. 1:5).

"Take no notice," states the Book of Love, "that I am swarthy, for I am lovely and well formed. But the sun has burnt me" (Sg. 1:5). "The sun" is the light of this world and signifies that even the highest and best thing that has been *created* and *made* covers up and discolors the image of God within us. "Remove the blight from silver," says Solomon, "and the purest vessel shines forth and gleams" (Pr. 25:4), namely, God's image, or Son, in the soul. And this is what our Lord means when he says that "a man of royal birth went to a distant country." For people must emerge from all images and themselves and become far removed and unlike all that if they really wish to take on the Son and become the Son and remain within the bosom and heart of the Father.

Every kind of mediation is alien to God. God says, "I am the First and the Last" (Rv. 22:13). There is no division either in God's nature or in the Persons corresponding to the unity of this nature. The divine nature is one, and every Person is also one and the same thing as this nature. The difference between being and presence is grasped as one, and is one. Only where this one is no longer grasped within itself does it receive, possess, and show a difference. Therefore, we find God in one thing, and whoever is to find God must become one. Our Lord says: "A man went to a distant country." In dissimilarity we find neither the one thing nor being nor God nor rest nor happiness nor pleasure. Be one, so that you can find God! In truth, if you were really one, you would still remain one thing in what is different, and what is different would become one thing for you and could in no way hinder you. The one remains just as much one in thousands and thousands of stones as in four stones, and a thousand times a thousand is just as certainly a simple number as four is a number.

A pagan scholar states that the one was born of the highest God. It is characteristic of this God to be one with what is one. People who seek this one below God are deceiving themselves. The same scholar states on four occasions that this one has no more intimate relationships except with young women or maidens, just as Saint Paul says: "I arranged for you to be married as chaste virgins to one husband" (2 Co. 11:2). A person should be quite like this, for our Lord says: "A person went to a distant country."

"Person" in the correct meaning of the Latin word signifies one who humbles himself or herself with all that the person is and has before God, and accommodates all that he or she is and has to God. Such people look up to God and do not look at their own possessions, which they know to be behind, underneath, or beside them. This is complete and proper humility. They have this characteristic from the earth. I shall speak no more of this matter. When we say "person," this word also means something raised up above nature, above time, and above everything that is inclined to time or that tastes of time. I make the same statement about space and corporality. Beyond this a "person" has in a certain way nothing in common with nothing, so that he or she is neither formed like nor made similar to this one or that one. Such people know nothing of nothingness, nor do we become aware of nothingness in them. Nothingness has been so completely removed from them that we can only discover pure life, being, truth, and goodness. People who are so characterized are "royal persons" indeed, no less and no more.

There exists also another form of explanation and instruction for what our Lord calls a royal person. We should also know that those who know God without disguise at the same time know other creatures with him. For knowledge is a light of the soul, and by their nature all people long for knowledge. Even the

knowledge of evil things is good. The masters of the spiritual life
say that when we know a creature in its own essence, this is called
an evening knowledge. In this case, we see a creature in images of
multiple difference. If, however, we know a creature in God, this
is called, and is, a morning knowledge. In this way we see a creature without all differences, deprived of all images and stripped of
all similarity in the one who is God himself. This is the royal person of whom our Lord says that "a royal person went to a distant
land" because he or she is one, and recognizes God and a creature
in one.

I wish to speak and explore still another meaning of what a
royal person is. I say that when a person, a soul, a spirit sees
God, that person knows and recognizes himself or herself as
knowing. This means that the person sees God and knows him.
Some people have thought that the flower and seed of happiness
lie in that knowledge in which the spirit knows that it knows
God. For if I had all bliss and knew nothing of it, what use
would it be to me? What kind of bliss would that be for me? Yet
I state with certitude that this is not the case. If it is equally true
that the soul would not be truly blessed without it, blessedness
still is not in this. For the first characteristic of blessedness is that
the soul sees God without disguise. In this way the soul receives
its whole being and life, and creates all that it is out of the depth
of God. The soul knows nothing about knowledge or love or anything else. It wishes to be completely at rest and exclusively in
God's being. There it knows nothing but being and God. If the
soul knows and realizes that it is seeing, knowing, and loving
God, this means according to the natural order an interruption
from this situation and a reversion to the first stage. For no one
realizes that he or she is white except one who is really white.
Therefore, people who recognize themselves as white are building and relying on the quality of being white. Such people do not
take their realization indirectly and unwittingly directly from the
color. Instead, they derive this realization of the color and knowledge of it from what is really white. They do not create this realization exclusively from the color itself but rather from realizing
and knowing what is colored or white and realizes itself to be
white. What is white is much smaller and more exterior than the
quality of being white (or whiteness). For example, a wall is

something quite different from the foundation on which the wall is built.

The masters of the spiritual life say that there is one power that helps the eye to see and another power through which it realizes the fact that it sees. The first fact—that the eye sees—it derives exclusively from the color and not from the object that is colored. For this reason 't makes no difference if the colored object is a stone or a piece of wood, a person or an angel. Its essential quality lies in the fact that it has a color.

Thus, I say, a royal person derives and creates his or her whole being, life, and happiness only from God, through God, and in God—not from realizing God, seeing God, loving God, or similar actions. Therefore, our Lord says in noteworthy words that eternal life is knowing God alone as the one, true God (Jn. 17:3). He does not say that it is realizing that we know God. How can people who do not know *themselves* know themselves as knowing God? For surely people have no knowledge at all of themselves or of other things—not to speak of God alone—if they are happy in the root and depth of happiness. However, if the soul *knows* that it knows God, it gains at the same time a knowledge of God and of itself.

There is one power, as I indicated above, that enables people to see, and yet another power by means of which they know and realize the fact that they see. Of course, it is true that at present and here below the power within us through which we know and realize the fact that we see is more royal and higher than the power through which we see. For nature begins its deeds on the smallest scale, but God begins his deeds on the most perfect scale. Nature produces an adult from a child and a hen from an egg. God, however, produces an adult before the child and a hen before the egg. Nature first causes wood to be warm and then hot; then it causes the essence of fire to be born. God, however, first gives to every creature its being, and afterward he gives every separate thing that belongs to this being in time and yet apart from time. God also gives the Holy Spirit before the gifts of the Holy Spirit.

Thus I say to you that there is truly no blessedness unless people are aware and know well that they see and know God. But may God forbid that my blessedness should depend on this fact!

If this suffices for other persons, let them keep it for themselves, but let it be spared for me! The heat of fire and the essence of fire are quite unlike and surprisingly distant from one another in nature, even though they are quite close to each other in time and space. God's vision and our vision are completely unlike and distant from each other.

Therefore, our Lord says quite correctly that "a person of royal birth went to a distant country to be appointed king, and afterward, he returned." For a people must be one within themselves, and they must seek this in themselves, and in one thing, and they must receive it in one thing, namely, *seeing* God. "To return home" means to know and realize the fact that we know and realize God.

Everything explained here was announced in advance by the prophet Ezekiel when he said that "a large eagle, with huge wings and long wings covered with speckled feathers came to the purest mountain. It took hold of the core or heart of the highest tree, plucked off the top branch, and carried it off" (Ezk. 17:3–4). What our Lord calls a royal person is named by the prophet a large eagle. Who then is more royal than one who was born, on the one hand, from the highest and best that a creature possesses and, on the other hand, from the most intimate depths of the divine nature and its wilderness? Through the prophet Hosea our Lord says: "I am going to lure her and lead her out into the wilderness and speak to her heart" (Ho. 2:16). One with one, one from one, one in one, and eternally one in one. Amen.

COMMENTARY: The Nobility of Our Birth Makes Us All Kings/How All Are Called to Be Royal Persons/The Tradition of the Royal Person in Israel/Compassion: the Meaning of Being the Son or Daughter of God, a Royal Person/Eckhart's Democratic Political Philosophy

In the preceding sermon Eckhart has commented on the coming of the royal kingdom which is the divine kingdom. We have seen this theme that is so important in creation theology treated before by Meister Eckhart—for example, in Sermon Nine where Eckhart insists that we are kings but we must become conscious of this fact, and in Sermon Eighteen where he talks of experiencing the "newborn king." In the present sermon Eckhart elaborates on how it is we are of royal blood, on who is of royal blood—it is all of us—and of what it means to be of royal blood—in one word, compassion.

The first point he makes is that, by our divine origin as images of God and as creatures of the Creator, we ourselves are already noble: aristocrats and of royal blood. *Our Lord teaches us in these words how royal people have been created in their nature. In us God's image shines and gives off light.* Eckhart no doubt has the psalmist's hymn to creation as a royal creation in mind:

> You have made them little less than God,
> and crowned them with glory and honor,
> you have given them dominion over the works of your hands,
> putting all things under their feet. (Ps. 8:5–6)

The images of being crowned, of having dominion over works, of things being placed under one's feet, are images of kings. But this psalm refers to all humans. Thus, the psalmist—like Eckhart—sees all human beings as kings. All are created to be royal persons. Indeed, throughout the Hebrew Bible the Yahwist tradition "presents human beings as kings."[1] This is the tradition Eckhart knows so well and is drawing from in this treatise.

But there is a divine connection to our kingship according to the Scriptures. For in the last analysis only Yahweh is King. Only Yahweh performs perfectly the true functions of the perfect King: to lead and to order, that is, to liberate and to create.[2] It is God who is "King of all the earth" and who "reigns over the nations" (Ps. 47:8f.). People who are born into this lineage, however, who are born sons of God and therefore heirs of this divine King have inherited such a kingship whose responsibilities include liberating and creating. And that we are born of such a royal and divine lineage is what Eckhart continually insists on. Borrowing from scriptural sources, he establishes that *the seed of God is in us.* Who has sown this seed? God who is King of the earth. *God himself has sown this seed and inserted it and borne it.* For this reason, while the seed can be neglected or forgotten or covered over, *it will never be obliterated.* No one can take our royal blood—which is God-given—from us. This seed is more than our link to royal blood, it is also our link to divinity. Eckhart's conclusion from the fact of our possessing the divine seed in us is that we become divine. *Now the seed of a pear tree grows into a pear tree, a hazel seed into a hazel tree, the seed of God into God.* While Eckhart accredits the theologian Origen twice in this sermon with developing these themes, the source of both Origen's theology and Eckhart's is from biblical passages that Eckhart also refers to. For example:

> No one who has been begotten by God sins;
> because God's seed remains inside him,
> he cannot sin when he has been begotten by God. (1 Jn. 3:9)

The seed is a seed for our divinization.

> By his divine power, he has given us all the things that we need for life and for true devotion, bringing us to know God himself, who has called us by his own glory and goodness. In making these gifts, he has given us the guarantee of something very great and wonderful to come: through them you will be able to share the divine nature . . . (2 P. 1:3–4)

Eckhart invokes the parables of Jesus which center around stories of sowing seeds and growing from seeds. In the parable of the sower, for example, we are told that "the seed is the word of God." But the seed requires good soil, which in turn signifies those people "with a noble and generous heart who have heard the word and take it to themselves and yield a harvest through their perseverance" (Lk. 8:11, 15). And in Matthew's Gospel we read of the wheat being separated from the chaff, a parable in which "the kingdom of heaven may be compared to a man who sowed good seed in his field" (Mt. 13:24–30). In making the connection between the divine and ourselves, then, Eckhart is making the connection between the coming of the kingdom—the royal rule of God —and our own coming to birth.

For he insists, as Jesus does in his parables, that a noble seed requires a noble soil to grow in. Only in this way do we bear the fruit that is within us, the fruit that distinguishes the false prophet from the true prophet, as we are told in Matthew's Gospel:

> "Beware of false prophets who come to you disguised as sheep but underneath are ravenous wolves. You will be able

to tell them by their fruits. Can people pick grapes from thorns,
or figs from thistles? In the same way, a sound tree produces
good fruit but a rotten tree bad fruit. A sound tree cannot
bear bad fruit, nor a rotten tree bear good fruit." (Mt.
7:15–18)

Says Eckhart: *If the seed had a good, wise, and industrious tiller it would
thrive all the more and grow up to God whose seed it is, and the fruit
would be equal to the nature of God.* "Equal to the nature of God"—
there lies our fullness and our fruitfulness, that our works be worthy of
our royal and divine lineage. Eckhart is so taken with this theme of our
royalty and our divinity because, as he points out, the Scriptures are
filled with it. *A large part of the Holy Scripture touches upon these
words.*

Eckhart is in search of the royal person, the divine seed, among us. Is
it restricted to those whom society calls aristocrats and nobles? By no
means. Everyone is an aristocrat who lives a life from his or her inner
self and not a life of superficial outwardness. Our true royal and divine
personhood is *hidden within us* and is rightly called by Scripture a *new
person, a heavenly person, a young person, a friend, and a royal person.* This is the person born of the seed and tree that *unceasingly bears
good fruit* and that our Lord speaks of. Eckhart applies the Gospel text
for his sermon (Lk. 19:11–27) to this person. This Gospel text is a parable
on the kingdom of God and its appearance.

Jesus went on to tell a parable, because he was near
Jerusalem and they imagined that the kingdom of God was
going to show itself then and there. Accordingly he said, "A
man of noble birth went to a distant country to be appointed
king and afterward return . . ." (Lk. 19:11–12)

Who then is the royal person? Anyone who lives a life from the core of
his or her inner self, divine image or seed.

The inner person is the one of whom our Lord says that "a man
of royal birth went to a distant country to be appointed king."
This is the good tree of which our Lord says that it always
bears good fruit and never evil fruit. For it desires goodness
and is inclined to goodness.

Interestingly enough, Luke's parable that forms the basis for Eckhart's discourse is also mixed with that of developing one's talents. Eckhart picks up on this theme in his insistence on the preparation and nurturing that good soil demands for the growth of noble seedlings. Indeed, the inner person is *the soil in which God has sown his likeness and image and in which he sows the good seed, the roots of all wisdom, all skills, all virtues, all goodness—the seed of the divine nature.* Eckhart's images in this sermon for the aristocrat in all of us are earthy images. Seed, soil, ground, are the pictures in his mind. Moreover, he says that *humility is a characteristic we have from the earth.* Here he is following a medieval etymological derivation of the word *homo* or "human person" from *humus* or "earth" or "soil." The word *humilis* or "humble" comes from the same word, meaning "on the ground." For Eckhart, a true aristocrat has his or her roots planted deeply in the soil—this is humility.

Good soil requires good cultivation and good development in order that the best fruit may be born. And what is this best of fruits? It is nothing less than the Son of God. Here Eckhart links Path Three, the birth of God in us, to Path Four, so that the breakthrough and birth that are ours are also the breakthrough into history that is the birth of the Son of God who bears the kingdom of God in our midst. *The seed of the divine nature is God's Son, the Word of God.* For we are instructed by Christ not only in how noble we are by our creation as images of God, but also *how noble is the state to which we can rise through grace.* This resurrection has been accomplished at our rebirth and breakthrough, provided we are enlightened and not ignorant people. If we follow a consciousness of letting go and letting be, as discussed in Path Two, if we can let go of images in order that God be born, then an eternal birth will take place, a birth of a royal person in us.

As one would expect from his images of seed coming to fruition and from his Sermon Twenty-nine, Eckhart is very conscious of development and creativity in the present sermon. Indeed, he speaks of *creating* on several occasions in this talk. Thus Path Three finds a culmination in this sermon, since what it is we give birth to first in ourselves and then in society is the royal person. The royal seed in us is more than a seed, it is a *living fountain* that will not be turned off. The divine seed and the divine source cannot be extinguished or put out. The flame that ignites us, the spark of our soul, is an eternal flame.

When Eckhart insists that every person is an aristocrat to the extent that he or she is in touch with his or her noble creation and divine rebirth, he is making a political statement. Eckhart is a democrat in his political philosophy four hundred and fifty years before Thomas Jefferson. Eckhart says we need to "practice equality in human society."

> Since then Christ's whole nobility belongs equally to us all and is equally near to us, to him as much as to me, why do we not receive it equally? Well, you must understand that, if someone wants to come by this gift equally to receive this good and the common nature which is equally near to all people, you must needs practice the same equality in human society, being no nearer to yourself than to another, just as in human nature there is nothing alien, nothing farther or nearer.[3]

As we saw in the previous sermon, if we are all brothers and sisters in one God, then we are all equals. This is the insight of compassion. "You are to love, esteem, and consider all people like yourself; what happens to another, be it bad or good, should be for you as if it happened to you."[4] All love demands equality. "Love will never be anything else than there where equality and unity are. Between a master and his servant there is no peace because there is no real equality." Peace and tranquillity among peoples demand their equality. The same is true of marriage. "A wife and a husband are not alike, but in love they are equal."[5] Love only exists, and with it peace and pleasure, where persons are living equality or dedicated to creating it. "Now there can be no love where love does not find equality or does not create equality." This principle applies as well to our leadership roles in society.

> People cannot accomplish things with pleasure unless they find equality with themselves in what they are accomplishing. If I were to lead people, they would never follow me with pleasure if they did not receive equality with me. For a movement or a deed is never accomplished with pleasure in the absence of equality.[6]

If we are all sons and daughters of the divine King, all royal with the royal seed in us, then we indeed share the equality of which Eckhart speaks. We can say with him that the "common nature is equally near to all people" and that each of us is a large eagle. In employing this image, Eckhart is playing on the German words *Edler* (noble) and *Adler* (eagle). But to be an eagle means we soar where we want to and that no one is above us.

> Who then is more royal than one who was born, on the one
> hand, from the highest and best that a creature possesses and,
> on the other hand, from the most intimate depths of the divine
> nature and its wilderness?

If no one is *more royal* or *more noble*—which is what Eckhart is saying
—then no one has the right to be lord over us.

This message and its political implications were not lost on Eckhart's
listeners. Especially is this the case with those aristocrats who heard
Eckhart preach these egalitarian messages to the peasant classes. These
aristocrats could not fail to hear Eckhart's message that those whom society knighted "royal" or "aristocrat," to the extent that they were only
superficial people, were the furthest from nobility and royalty. Recall that
the Beguines with whom Eckhart associated closely were of the lower
and not the aristocratic classes.[7] The aristocrats who banded together to
get Eckhart condemned included the Archbishop of Cologne, who was
von Virneberg, an aristocrat and a Franciscan. Since Eckhart was a
Dominican who favored the Pope in his struggle with the Emperor and
since the Franciscans at the time favored the Emperor in that dispute, we
can see how Eckhart's preaching was not without its deep political fall-
out. It is significant, for example, that Eckhart's inquisitors raised the
issue, on several occasions at his trial and elsewhere, that he was
preaching to the peasant people in their vernacular, "confusing them" by
telling them that they were, among other things, aristocrats. If he would
only preach in Latin, he was told, the simple people would not be disturbed and neither would the guardians of the social order. Eckhart
replied, however: "If one is not to teach the unlearned, then no one will
ever be learned and no one will be able to teach or to write. For one
teaches the unlearned to the end that from unlearned persons they may
become learned ones. If there were nothing new, nothing would ever
become old."[8]

In pursuing the theme that all are royal persons, Eckhart is highlighting
a biblical tradition found among the patriarchs, for example, who are
types of the royal person. Jesus too is meant to be such a model for all
his followers. Thus Professor Kenik writes:

> In a very real sense every Christian is called to be a *royal
> person*. Like the kings, every person is created to have domin-
> ion in the world, that is, to be stewards of the world and
> builders of community within society.[9]

In this respect Eckhart's entire spirituality is a spirituality of the emergence of the royal person in us and among us. Such a person is responsible for the gift of creation and its preservation and such a person is meant to create order that is just and fair. The preservation of order is an issue of justice. Justice is the means by which life is preserved and passed on. It is the ultimate test of the goodness of the king.

> There is but one reason for the king's sovereignty—that the life of God's people may be preserved. The dominion of the king is meant to guarantee that each and every person receives justice, that the integrity of society is guarded because individuals gain an equal hearing.[10]

For in the royal tradition of the Bible, the royal household is responsible for justice. In the Book of Hosea, which is so important to Eckhart in the present sermon, we read:

> Listen to this, priests,
> attend, House of Israel,
> listen, royal household,
> you who are responsible for justice . . . (Ho. 5:1)

And in the prophet Micah we read:

> Listen now, you princes of the House of Jacob,
> rulers of the House of Israel.
> Are you not the ones who should know what is right,
> you, enemies of good and friends of evil?
> When they have devoured the flesh of my people
> and torn off their skin
> and crushed their bones . . .
> then they will cry out to Yahweh.
> But he will not answer them. (Mi. 3:1–4)

It is especially on behalf of the poor that justice needs to be done. "The primary motivation for judgment can be expressed as *justice*: God's concern is for the poor, the captives, the blind, the stranger—all those who become the objects of abuse."[11] These persons are Eckhart's main concern also. He preached to them *in their language* about how noble, how royal, how divine they were. No wonder Marxist philosopher Ernst Bloch could declare that Eckhart was a precursor of Karl Marx. Eckhart, Bloch contends, demystified economic and political facts of life for the "common people" whom he inspired

> in the revolutions of the next two centuries, along with its predecessor, the mysticism of Joachim of Floris, Abbot of Calabrese—among the Hussites, and with Thomas Munzer in the German Peasant War; events, indeed, not notable ideologically for the rule of clarity, but ones in which the mystic fog was at least not of service to the ruling class . . . One thing is certain: Eckhart's sermon does not intend to snuff man out for the sake of an Other-world beyond him: it does not intend religion to be an alienation of the self . . . A subject who thought himself to be in personal union with the Lord of Lords provided, when things got serious, a very poor example indeed of serfhood.[12]

No wonder, too, that Eckhart got himself in so much trouble. As prophets are wont to do. But he advises us in this sermon to expect that and to be able to let go even of that. *When people grow and become rooted in love and in God, they are ready to take upon themselves every attack, temptation, vexation, and painful suffering willingly and gladly, eagerly and joyfully.* Prophets arouse people's anger, as Eckhart knew well. "People should not be sorry because people are angry with them," he observed. "They should rather be sorry if they merited the anger."[18] Anger has its place in the work and life of the just person and such a person cannot be deterred by society's opposition. As Dr. Kenik indicates, the role of the prophet vis-à-vis the king is to "remind" the king of the law of justice, to call the king back to his royal roots which are divine roots. Eckhart too would say that believers need sometimes to be kings and sometimes to be prophets to the king to remind even oneself to return to our divine origin. Indeed, Eckhart calls Christ the "great Reminder" for this very reason. Jesus has reminded all of us of our divinity and royalty. He is a prophet *and* a king in this sense. And we, reborn sons of God, are to be the same.

The prophet must be willing to step out from the security of the womb and even to leave mysticism behind at times.

> Sometimes one must abandon ecstatic joy for the sake of something better out of love, and sometimes in order to do a

work of charity when it is necessary, in the spiritual or the physical sphere. As I have already said, if a person was in an ecstasy as Saint Paul was and he knew of a sick man who needed a bowl of soup from him, I should think it far better to desist out of love for the poor person and to serve God with greater love.[14]

To do this we need to leave the confines of maternal love and affection, as Gregory Baum has suggested:

The longing desire for the warm and understanding total community is the search for the good mother, which is bound to end in disappointment and heartbreak. There are no good mothers and fathers, there is only the divine mystery summoning and freeing us to grow up.[15]

Eckhart, like Baum, instructs us to *creep out of our mothers' wombs and smile at the heavenly Father.* This journey is a journey of courage and of trust. *It is reached when people more and more forsake their mothers and depart farther and farther from the womb, flee from care, and throw off fear.* The prophet within us and the prophet among us are to call the royal person back to the work of Justice, the work of Yahweh, the Creator and the Orderer. In other words, to call back—whatever the personal price—the royal person and the whole realm to Compassion, which is, as we have seen, both the origin and the goal of creation and the fullest expression of Justice.

What characterizes the royal person? Eckhart treats this important subject at considerable length in this sermon. Such a person possesses *morning knowledge,* which is not merely seeing creatures in their essences—that is *evening knowledge*—but is knowing creatures *in* God. In other words, the royal person possesses a consciousness of panentheism —of the whole world bathed in God—which is also a consciousness of the oneness of all things in God. The royal person sees everything insofar as it is in God and therefore interdependent. *Whoever is to find God must become one . . . Be one, so that you can find God!* To "be one" is to begin the journey of compassion, for differences and the emphasizing of differences is the origin of dualism, sin, and violence. *In dissimilarity we find neither the one thing nor being nor God nor rest nor happiness nor pleasure.* In short, we find *nothing.* But a true royal person will reject this nothingness that separatisms bring and will immerse himself or herself in the sea of compassionate wholeness where he or she *can only discover pure life, being, truth, and goodness.* The person who knows *nothing of nothingness* does know of oneness and compassion. So thorough and so intimate is this tasting of the salty sea of compassion that the royal person's most complete definition would be: *One with one, one from one, one in one, and externally one in one.* All is one—there lies the vision of the royal person.

From this divine sea and divine source in the ocean of compassion, all the royal person's consciousness, creativity, and work flow. *The soul receives its whole being and life, and creates all that it is out of the depth of God.* Grounded *exclusively in God's being . . . it knows nothing but being and God.* And this knowledge is the very meaning of "eternal life" as put forth, for example, in John's Gospel:

"And eternal life is this:
to know you,
the only true God . . .
May they all be one.
Father, may they be one in us,
as you are in me and I am in you,
so that the world may believe it was you who sent me.
I have given them the glory you gave to me,
that they may be one as we are one.
With me in them and you in me,
may they be so completely one
that the world will realize that it was you who sent me." (Jn. 17:3, 21–23).

Eckhart identifies eternal life and the moment of our breakthrough as children of God. At such a moment

people are formed from and beyond God's eternity . . . They are drawn and changed into the divine image, that is . . . they have become children of God. Beyond this point there is no higher stage. Eternal rest and bliss are there, for the final goal of the inner persons and new persons is eternal life.

Eckhart comments: *Thus, I say, a royal person derives and creates his or her whole being, life, and happiness only from God, through God, and in God.* This "knowledge," which is, in fact, a consciousness that is drunk in like the salty sea itself, is so immediate and so intimate that there is no

need or even possibility to reflect on it or to pause to name it. There is
no standing back from it, only the full immersion of swimming in it. John
does not say that it [eternal life] is realizing that we know God. This
knowing is a *return home.* "To return home" means to know and realize
the fact that we know and realize God. Our return home is a return to
the *wilderness* or *desert* where the Godhead dwells, a return to our origins. There we were birthed *from the most intimate depth of the divine
nature and its wilderness.*

Eckhart admits that he derives this image from the prophet Hosea: *"I am
going to lure her and lead her out into the wilderness and speak to her
heart"* (Ho. 2:16). But Eckhart's treatise on the royal person derives more
than just this sentence from Hosea's second chapter. That entire chapter
depicts a court scene of a legal procedure between husband (standing
for Yahweh) and wife (standing for the corporate people of Israel). The
issue in this royal court scene is not divorce but reconciliation. Israel is
accused of refusing to acknowledge where her blessings come from. Her
punishment will be the withdrawal of these blessings.

> She would not acknowledge, not she,
> that I was the one who was giving her
> the corn, the wine, the oil,
> and who freely gave her that silver and gold
> of which they have made Baals.
>
> That is why, when the time comes, I mean to withdraw my corn,
> and my wine, when the season for it comes . . .
> I will lay her vines and fig trees waste . . .
> I am going to make them into thickets
> for the wild beasts to ravage. (Ho. 2:10, 11, 14)

But hope is offered for the reconciliation between God and God's people in the form of fruitful agricultural gifts. One thinks of Eckhart's hazel
tree and pear tree image.

> That is why I am going to lure her
> and lead her out into the wilderness
> and speak to her heart.
> I am going to give her back her vineyards,
> and make the Valley of Achor a gateway of hope. (Ho. 2:16, 17)

When will that new courtship, that second honeymoon commence? What will be its sign? It will be a time of compassion. When all people—all royal people—learn to coexist responsibly with all the creatures of the earth with whom they are in fact interdependent. The time of compassion will be marked by a betrothal to justice.

> When that day comes I will make a treaty on her behalf
>   with the wild animals,
> with the birds of heaven and the creeping things of the earth;
> I will break bow, sword and battle in the country,
> and make her sleep secure.
> I will betroth you to myself for ever,
> betroth you with integrity and justice,
> with compassion and love;
> I will betroth you to myself with faithfulness,
> and you will come to know Yahweh. (Ho. 2:20–22)

It will be a day of cosmic celebration.

> When that day comes—it is Yahweh who speaks—
> the heavens will have their answer from me,
> the earth its answer from them,
> the grain, the wine, the oil, their answer from the earth,
> and Jezreel his answer from them.
> I will sow him in the country,
> I will love Unloved;
> I will say to No-People-of-Mine, "You are my people,"
> and he will answer, "You are my God." (Ho. 2:23–25)

It will be a day as glorious—as full of compassion, justice, and celebration—as was that first day of creation. For the Yahwist author of the original creation account "presents human beings as kings" responsible for ensuring God's order in the world. The court scene of Hosea that Eckhart invokes parallels creation accounts.[16] The new creation that all royal persons, meaning all awake persons, are called to is the one creation renewed.

Sermon Thirty-seven: COMPASSION AS CELEBRATION

"Love the Lord your God with your whole heart . . ." (Lk. 10:23–37)*

Note first of all that what is loved the most and loved first is the measure of all things that are lovable or loved. Hence, according to the philosopher, "friendliness toward another comes or flows from friendliness toward oneself." The person who loves God with his or her whole heart surely loves himself or herself on account of God or in God. Hence the Lord, in instructing us in the meaning of love or affection, most fittingly puts the love of God with the whole heart in first place; and when this is achieved there follows most appropriately the commandment: Love your neighbor as yourself. And so you are to love yourself as you do your neighbor on account of God and in God. Otherwise, God would not be the first thing loved or the measure of our love. "For what is first in anything whatsoever is the cause of those things which come after."

Again, God is not loved with one's whole heart if something is loved that is not in him and not on account of him. Jesus mentions the "neighbor" first and "yourself" second in order to point out the full equality or parity or even identity of love of self and love of neighbor. The love of self, therefore, is no measure of the love of neighbor, but love of God from the whole heart is the measure or the principle and cause of love of both self and neighbor.

The measure of all love and of every virtuous act in general is, in principle, virtue or the love of virtue. Indeed, every virtuous person loves virtue more than oneself and one's neighbor as oneself. For such a virtuous person, virtue stands for God and, in fact, virtue is like God and God is virtue for him or her. Conse-

* "Diliges dominum deum tuum ex toto corde tuo." (LW IV, ※30)

quently, the law of God and the commandment of God—virtue and truth—are loved by every virtuous or perfect and good person from the whole heart and "more than gold and topaz" (Ps. 119), and beyond oneself and "beyond thousands of gold and silver pieces" (Ps. 119:72).

Augustine writes in his *De Vero Religione* and in the *De Libero Arbitrio* that the law of God is the principle and root of all human laws and actions, and, further, that it is not right to judge the divine law, but that our laws ought to be judged according to it. Augustine especially says that the law of God is superior to us and therefore we ought not to pass judgment on it. When he says it is superior to us, he means that it is more loving toward us than we are toward ourselves and therefore it is the principle and measure of love by which we also love ourselves and our neighbor. For otherwise it would not be beyond us or superior to us, that is, more excellent or more gracious and more pleasing. Bernard says in his *Epistle on Charity*: "In this love the joys of eternity and all heavenly sweetness are stored. In this love are peace, patience, long-suffering, and joy in the Holy Spirit and whatever pleasure the mind can conceive and more."

"Your neighbor as yourself." Augustine, near the beginning of his *De Domo Disciplinae*, says: "Your neighbors are many. Every person is a neighbor to every other person. Father and son, father-in-law and son-in-law are neighbors to one another. Nothing is so much of a neighbor as a person and another person . . . One should seek to discover, therefore, whether the person who is committed to neighborly love loves himself so that he may love these others as himself. Truly 'he who loves iniquity hates his own soul' and therefore if you love iniquity you hate yourself. How could you want to be committed to your neighbor and love him as you do yourself if you are busy destroying yourself? For if you love yourself in this way, that is, as destroying yourself, I do not want to love anyone else as you do yourself. Either perish alone or change your way of loving and quit society."

Love "your neighbor as you love yourself"—not as you hate yourself. Augustine says in the fourteenth book of *De Trinitate*: "He who knows how to love himself loves God. But he who does not love God, does not even love himself, even if it is natural for him to do so. Hence it can be said that he hates himself since he acts to his own disadvantage and he persecutes himself as if he were his own enemy . . . But when the mind loves God it is right and proper to love one's neighbor as oneself. For then one is loving not perversely but rightly when he loves God whose image we participate in. Our participation is not only in the image as it is, but even more so as it is renewed from having been old and is reformed from its deformity and is restored from wretchedness to blessedness."

"Your neighbor as yourself." This is not only a commandment, but also a promise or reward. For if I love any neighbor at all, as I do myself, then I enjoy, I delight and rejoice at his or her reward, merit, and glory just as much as at my own. Moreover, in such a situation there is no *my* nor *your* nor do I love or have affection for what is mine or yours. For this reason I rejoice no less at this person's joy than at my own. One therefore will rejoice just as much at another's glory as at one's own. Take the example of a foot. It loves the eye in the head more than itself. And when the foot is stepped on, the tongue speaks out: "You are stepping on my foot." When it comes to things that are first, each is in each and "all are in all." In Corinthians (1 Co. 3:22) we read: "All things are yours." A person rejoices, therefore, at the good of another, both because he loves him equally and because they are one, although this does not mean that they make one single person.

Take the example of the whole person who sees with the eyes, hears with the ears, speaks with the mouth, and so forth. Or consider the example of the whole fiery sphere that fills space according to different parts which are natural and appropriate with each and every part. Taking and having through another what it does not take or have in itself, it shares its being with every other part. Its being in one thing is not different or superior to another, but it is immediate, being without a medium, and supreme without being superior. These analogues apply in moral matters as well and in the matter of gratuitous gifts: The blessed person takes divine gifts in himself or in others, and then his desire can rest, when all are one in God, in charity and in the Holy Spirit. That which he does not receive in himself he rejoices to see received in another, especially since he loves the other as he loves himself. For when a person with whom I am one receives anything at all,

I also receive it. Yes, I too. For all the saints are one in God but do not make one single person.

Consider this example: When part of a log is thrown in the fire and changes into a spark or a sort of fire, soon it deserts the log by which, through which, and in which it once had its whole being as an intimate part of itself and it flees backward and tends upward, as it were, forgetting itself, even though it will be extinguished on its way. Everyone, therefore, who loves God from one's whole heart necessarily loves his neighbor as himself. Otherwise he does not love "with all his heart."

"As yourself." The word "as" bespeaks equality; this is clear from Augustine's *De Disciplina Christiana*, where he says: "You will not find an equal to God, of whom it may be said: Love God as you love that person. A rule has been found for you concerning your neighbor because you have been found to be equal to your neighbor." Therefore, one who has God and who loves him loves his neighbor equally and on a par with himself. Whence Augustine in the passage referred to on several occasions above uses the text found in Mark 12: "Love your neighbor as much as (*tamquam*) yourself." "As much as" is what the word *tamquam* means. Thus we see in nature that the eye does not see for itself more than for another part of the body. It sees first of all for the whole and for itself, and on account of the whole it sees for other parts and for itself and insofar as they are in the whole and insofar as they are something of the whole in fact or in anticipation, that is to say, either because they already are or they may be.

But Luke in his tenth chapter seems to say the opposite. To the lawyer who asks: "Who is my neighbor?" the Lord replies that neither priest nor Levite is a neighbor but the one "who had compassion." Therefore, not every person should be loved or liked as much as one loves oneself. Therefore, not every person should be loved in the same way or as much as one loves oneself.

But my reply to this objection is that by the very word of the Lord what I am saying is true. For he says: "Go and do likewise." It is as if he were saying, like the Samaritan, who was neither a priest nor a Levite, and who cared for the wounded man, pouring wine and oil on his wounds, etc.: "So too should you act toward every person regardless of ties of affection, relationship, or reward.

Take nothing into account except the need and the necessity of this other person."

"With your whole heart." The creature is distinguished in its own way by the fact that it cannot be divided. It is divided from others but undivided in itself. Hence the more undivided or the less divided it is in itself, the more divided it is from others; and, conversely, the more it is distinguished from others, the less it is distinguished in itself. In the first example we have a cause; in the second, a sign. And so with a person or a soul whom God has told to love with all one's heart, it might be said as it was of certain others: "Their heart is divided, now they will die (Ho. 10:2). The first reason for such a death is that a person divided from God is thereby divided from being, which is from God alone. A second reason is that every division is a separation from the one, from the whole, from the perfect, and therefore from being. For one and being are interchangeable. A third reason why death results from division is that division of its very nature is a journey into nonbeing (*non esse*). If an object of two cubits is divided, none of its parts is two cubits. Moreover, a division is of its very nature a privation. But nothing—no thing, no being—exists as a result of privation. Furthermore, God is not in division; but since God is in all being, that in which God does not exist is nonbeing. Therefore, since God has ordered that he be loved with the whole heart, whatever in the heart does not love God is nothing. It is nothing both because it is divided and because all things love God. The psalmist sings: "All things serve Thee" (Ps. 119:91).

Again, a heart is said to be divided when it is dispersed in many directions and toward many objects. However, "every kingdom divided against itself shall be brought to ruin" (Lk. 11:17). Taken literally, we see that a virtue that is divided grows defective, is extinguished, and decays. Near the beginning of the first book in his *De Ordine*, Augustine says: "A soul which sets out toward many things is pursuing poverty greedily, completely oblivious to the fact that greed can be avoided only by keeping oneself apart." And then he adds: "The more the soul seeks to embrace many things, the more it suffers deprivation." He gives the following example: "Take any sized circle and there is a center where everything converges . . . This center dominates everything else by a certain law of equality so that if you wished to exit from it into any direction everything would be lost by your decision to journey into so much multiplicity. In the same way, a soul poured forth from itself is torn apart by too much universality and is wasted by true poverty or falsity because its very nature urges it to seek oneness everywhere; yet multiplicity prevents its finding this oneness."

Augustine alludes to this point in *De Vita Christiana*: "The great virtue of piety is peace and unity, because God is one." And therefore, "those who are cut off from unity do not possess this" —or God. The reason is that one and many are opposites. And yet without unity there would be no multiplicity. Hence Augustine says at the end of chapter twelve of the fourteenth book of his *De Trinitate*, "It is a great misery of the human person not to be with him without whom one could not exist. For there is no doubt that without him in whom we exist there is no being. And still if we do not remember him and if we do not understand him or do not love him, then we are not with him."

"You should love your Lord your God" because in him alone does the soul find rest. In the first book of the *Confessions*, Augustine says: "You have made us for yourself . . ." First, because nothing better than God can be imagined. Second, because he is the "Beginning and the End" (Rv. 22:13). Third, because "his flowers are fruits" (Si. 24:23). Fourth, because a person does not do well who could do better, as Augustine has said. And vice versa—if he cannot do better, he is doing well.

"Your God." Augustine says your God will be yours wholly. You will eat him up, lest you starve, you will drink him, lest you thirst, you will be illumined by him lest you go blind, you will be sustained by him, lest you grow weary. Whole and entire, he will possess you whole and entire, lest you become narrow there. With him, with whom you possess the whole, you will have the whole, because you and he will be one and he who will possess us will have one whole. The reason for this is that without him all things would be nothing for you.

Here it should be noted that those who love and savor God himself do not love him on account of his eternity nor do they love him more because he is eternal or because he is wise or good or any other such thing. On the contrary, they love, enjoy, and savor eternity, wisdom, and all such things solely because they are God and from God and in God. One does not love God for the sake of something else but one loves all other things, no matter what names they might boast of, on account of God. And they love God for his own sake.

COMMENTARY: The Meaning of Torah Is Compassion, Where Love of God and Love of Neighbor Are One Love/Holiness Means Wholeness/The Identity of Ourselves and Our Neighbor/The Mystical Body Rejoices Banquet-style Because All Things Love God/God Too Rejoices and Is Tickled Through and Through by Our Works of Compassion

The Gospel text that Eckhart has chosen for this sermon is a classic text on Jesus' teaching about the law of Yahweh. This *Torah* or way of walking through life is less a commandment than a *promise or reward.* It is less an ethic than it is a way of life, a *Torah,* a spirituality. It is a law of life and a way of life called compassion. Compassion realizes that all is one, all is in God and therefore to love self or others is to love God. And to relieve the pain of self or others is to relieve God's pain; and the converse is true also, to love God *is* to relieve the pain of self and others. This is why the story of compassion—the Good Samaritan story— follows from the quest about the one great commandment in Luke's Gospel. The following text, then, is Eckhart's starting point for this sermon:

> There was a lawyer who, to disconcert Jesus, stood up and said to him, "Master, what must I do to inherit eternal life?" He said to him, "What is written in the Law? What do you read there?" He replied, "You must love the Lord your God with all your heart, with all your soul, with all your strength, and with all your mind, and your neighbor as yourself." "You have answered right," said Jesus, "do this and life is yours."
>
> But the man was anxious to justify himself and said to Jesus, "And who is my neighbor?" Jesus replied, "A man was once on his way down from Jerusalem to Jericho and fell into the hands of brigands . . . But a Samaritan traveler who came upon him was moved with compassion when he saw him. He went up and bandaged his wounds, pouring oil and wine on them . . . (Lk. 10:25–30, 33–34)

The summary of the law or Torah is oneness: God-love and neighborly love are one. But compassion too is a law of oneness and wholeness. It too is a summation of Torah and the way to walk in the law of God. If our *heart is divided, we will die,* warns Eckhart—we were made for unity, for compassion. Or as Jesus puts it, "do this and life is yours." The doing of Torah, the doing of God's one great commandment, is the doing that Jesus is talking of. Compassion is not restricted to feeling—it is doing: a doing based on awareness of the pain of others. Jesus says: *"Go and do likewise." It is as if he were saying, like the Samaritan, who was neither a priest nor a Levite, and who cared for the wounded man, pouring wine and oil on his wounds, etc.: "So too should you act toward every person."* Eckhart invokes one of the Torah psalms, Psalm 119, on several occasions in this sermon and makes the connection between the law Jesus asks the lawyer to reflect on and the joy he promises from following this law—a law that is not a commandment but a *promise and reward.* In that psalm we read:

> I put the Law you have given
> before all the gold and silver in the world.
>
> Yahweh, my maker, my preserver,
> explain your commandments for me to learn.
> Seeing me, those who fear you will be glad,
> since I put my hope in your word . . .
> Treat me tenderly, and I shall live,
> since your Law is my delight. (Ps. 119:72–74, 77)

The theme of delight at God's law permeates Eckhart's sermon and, as we shall see, crescendos in a banquet of heavenly rejoicing. It also permeates Psalm 119, where numerous times God's law is called our "delight."

But the doing that God's law is about, and that is the doing of compassion, is not just any doing; it is not even an ethical doing of right over wrong. It is a doing born of a consciousness of wholeness and oneness. It is born of the common sea that we are all bathed in. It is born of the holiness that wholeness is. It is born of our experience of being altogether in God. *A person divided from God is thereby divided from being, which is from God alone.* To exist outside the circle of being that is God is not to exist at all. *For one and being are interchangeable.* To divide is to destroy. An object of two cubits cut in half is no longer and will never again be the object of two cubits. Separateness, the sin behind sin, is a *journey into nonbeing.* Thus it is as much a journey into death as the law Jesus pronounces from the Torah—a law of oneness, interdependence, and compassion—is a journey into life. Our experience of being in God is a holistic experience, the source of all our compassionate actions. *Whole and entire, he will possess you whole and entire.* Everything we love and take delight in comes from this same holistic source. We *love, enjoy, and savor eternity, wisdom, and all such things solely because they are God and from God and in God.* These ecstatic experiences become God for us because whatever is in God is God. But all things are in God, *all things serve God,* as the psalmist sings:

> Creation is maintained by your rulings,
> since all things are your servants. (Ps. 119:91)

But, as Eckhart comments, *all things love God.* All creation loves God, for all creation is in God. Only the human personality is capable of imagining and acting out a division between God and us, between others and us. Thus only it can become a house divided and bent on ruin and destruction. It alone can choose the separation which sin is. If we would let creation go and let creation be, all things would teach us their common love of God. There is no escaping our unity with God and all things. The only way out is nothingness itself, for outside God there is nothing but nothing. Thus *whatever in the heart does not love God is nothing.* After all, God is wholly ours, *your God will be yours wholly.* And that is why we are already holy, already perfect. To be *whole* means to be *perfect* and vice versa and that is why a departure from the whole that is panentheism is a death-dealing separation *from the one, from the whole, and therefore from being.*

The wholeness that holiness is applies to our relationship to ourselves as well as our relationship to God. Compassion and wholeness begin at home. So do division and separation. As Aristotle put it, *"friendliness toward another comes or flows from friendliness toward oneself."* We love ourselves *in* God and therefore in the wholeness of the sea that compassion and existence are about. Indeed, the compassion that pours forth from this divine sea *is more loving toward us than we are toward ourselves.* That is where we first learn self-love and all love of creation and Creator. It is the "fountain of being" that never stops flowing, never stops bathing us if we let it. Since we are instructed to love our neighbor as we love ourselves, there can be no holistic love of others without a holistic love of self. If we haven't learned to love ourselves well, we ought to *perish alone or change our way of loving or quit society*. For we are called to love our neighbor as we love ourselves—not as we hate ourselves. If ours is a self-destructive love, it is no love to project onto others; love of self must be learned first. As Augustine put it, *"he who knows how to love himself loves God."* Self-love that is authentic is a holistic love, a love of our roots in the divine sea of creation and blessedness. For, in fact, there exists a *full equality or parity or even identity of love of self and love of neighbor.* Here, then, lies the core reason for the Torah that Jesus calls us back to: that separate loves do not exist, for separations of others and self are a lie, a nothingness or falsehood. Our unity as one body, one mystical body—but *not one single person*—is so real and so great that *there is no "my" or "your" nor do I love or have affection for what is mine or yours.* The divisions of "my" and "your" are broken through in the breakthrough that ushers in the full compassionate consciousness and way of living. *God is one and those who are in God are one—all are one in God, in charity and in the Holy Spirit.* God is also Compassion and Compassion presumes the oneness that God and all creatures are. Eckhart gives as analogies the human body and the cosmic body. Our wholeness presumes a oneness, for it is *the whole person who sees with the eyes, hears with the ears, speaks with the mouth,* and even the parts of the body that do particularized work for us do it for the whole person. The mystical body of people reborn to wholeness is no different, nor is the communion of saints, for *all the saints are one in God but do not make one single person.* Uniqueness is preserved in Eckhart's view of our oneness, for our unity is a verb-oriented unity, a unity of the flowing process that all growth and all existence are. It is a unity of lovers, not of nouns. He takes an example from the stars. All beings are interdependent in their constant action of receiving and giving.

> The whole fiery sphere . . . fills space according to different parts which are natural and appropriate with each and every part. Taking and having through another what it does not take or have in itself, it shares its being with every other part. Its being in one thing is not different or superior to another, but it is immediate being without a medium and supreme without being superior.

Equality of being is returned to in this image of Eckhart's. If all beings are equal as being, then there are no superior and inferior beings, there are no intermediaries as we swim in this bath called compassion. The mystical body harbors no inequalities. *Everyone, therefore, who loves God from one's whole heart necessarily loves his neighbor as himself. Otherwise he does not love "with all his heart."* For to love with all one's heart is to love from a whole heart—a heart that knows the wholeness of all that is and has been.

It has been said that Eckhart's doctrine is "essentially that of the identification with Christ the mediator, the head of the body of which the Christians are the members, which modern theology has called the doctrine of the mystical body."[1] Ms. Ancelet is correct, for the mystical body is the body of compassion and panentheistic creation that has been renewed and born anew by the instruction and reminding of Jesus. We have seen Eckhart stress this same unity of the mystical body in previous sermons, for example, number Two and number Twenty-nine. The resurrection and breakthrough are the resurrection of all or none. "All are sent or no one is sent, into all or into nothing." "In the kingdom of heaven all is in all, all is one and all is ours."[2]

But the kingdom of heaven, as we saw in the previous sermon, has already arrived! Realized eschatology has happened, even if not fully and definitively yet. What does this imply? It implies celebration and rejoicing, a rejoicing at all the gifts and all the beauty and all the grace that are already everywhere. We are bathing in it already—not a grace or beauty of "yours and mine," but a glory that is ours. Not something divided, hoarded, used competitively or divisively, but something that flows in and out of all of us. Because all "my" consciousness and all envy have been washed away by the sea named compassion, we can say with Eckhart: *I rejoice no less at this person's joy than at my own. One therefore will rejoice just as much at another's glory as at one's own.* The celebration seems to have no end, no limit, no death built into it. Ecstasy shared is ecstasy unbounded. Joy shared at beauty—at all beauty—one's own and others' which is also one's own—is a sign of the kingdom of heaven begun. In such a kingdom, *each is in each and "all are in all."* As Paul has written, *"all things are yours"* (1 Co. 3:22). In such a reign, praise of one another will be valued more than rivalry. Indeed, "the mark of a good person is that a good person praises good people."[3] Instead of competing against one another, we are invited to drink in one another's beauty. Others' joy is ours, others' goodness is ours, others' wholeness is ours. Blessedness is shared. *That which he [the blessed person] does not receive in himself he rejoices to see received in another, especially since he loves the other as he loves himself.* If there is no separateness in being, there is no separateness or hoarding of gifts. *For when a person with whom I am one receives anything at all, I also receive it. Yes, I too.* Desire rests when one is open to goodness everywhere and where celebration breaks through competition. *The blessed person takes divine gifts in himself or in others, and then his desire can rest, when all are one in God.* This rest, a repose at the source of all creativity and all birthing, is not a passive sort of rest but a celebrative rest at the origins of the One who is the *"Beginning and the End."* Eckhart calls on wisdom literature to express the kind of nourishing and nurturing rest that is being spoken of.

> From eternity, in the beginning, he created me,
>   and for eternity I shall remain.
> I ministered before him in the holy tabernacle,
>   and thus was I established on Zion.
> In the beloved city he has given me rest,
>   and in Jerusalem I wield my authority . . .
> I am like a vine putting out graceful shoots,
>   my blossoms bear the fruit of glory and wealth.
> Approach me, you who desire me,
>   and take your fill of my fruits,
> for memories of me are sweeter than honey,
>   inheriting me is sweeter than the honeycomb.
> They who eat me will hunger for more,
>   they who drink me will thirst for more.
> Whoever listens to me will never have to blush,
>   whoever acts as I dictate will never sin. (Si. 24:9–11, 17–22)

All come to the celebration, for *all beings love God.*[4] There is joy all around, filling up is plentiful. Compassion rains down joy. There is joy at equality and since the sin of separation is let go of, equality reigns at this banquet. We saw in the previous sermon how people are equal. In this sermon Eckhart elaborates on this theme. *One who has God and who loves him loves his neighbor equally and on a par with himself.* Equality is an attitude we bring to all of life and its celebrations. In Sermon Twenty-nine we saw Eckhart insist on this same theme (see p. 399). To rejoice at another's joy, then, is like "being in heaven." Joy returns as the fruit of realized eschatology. Celebration is multiplied when we are "constantly in joy and honor." There is joy at justice. "Justice cannot harm them, for all joy, pleasure, and happiness are justice."[5] There is joy at works of justice. The just person "rejoices inexpressibly more in the work of justice than he—or even the highest angel—has joy and happiness in this natural being or life." The saints too come to this celebration. They are the ones who "for this reason gladly gave their lives for the sake of justice."[6] There is joy, not sorrow, wherever the works of compassion are being carried out. "The person who finds a good and godly work heavy and burdensome does not yet have God the Father working in him and has not yet tasted 'how sweet the Lord is'" (Ps. 34:8).[7] As we saw in Sermon Nine, the kingdom of heaven *is* a community of compassion and celebration and to "rejoice in all our neighbor's joys as if they were our own" is like finding "the kingdom of heaven itself."[8] The whole body of Christ is resurrected, unleashed, celebrating the divine breakthrough.

> All we faithful are one body with Christ, the firstborn (1 Co. 12:12ff. and 27). But of the whole and its parts, there is one being and one function. If one suffers, all suffer with it; if one rejoices, all rejoice.[9]

The relief of the suffering of one is the relief of the suffering of all. Therefore suffering and its relief also come to the celebration. There is no complaining at the celebrative gathering since "the gifts of all people are my own."[10] Sadness, which is the "root of all evil,"[11] has been driven out. Even God is caught rejoicing at this gathering. As we learned in Sermon Thirty-three, God will "rejoice especially at every *work* of the just person, however small it is. Indeed, God will rejoice at these works through and through. For nothing remains in his ground that is not thoroughly enlivened by joy."[12] Yes, God too is invited to this celebration of the compassionate ones.

What else goes on at such a grand and glorious party? Eating does. There is a banquet. Just as in the story of the first fall into dualism, as reported by the Yahwist author of Genesis where the word "eat" or "food" is used at least fifteen times,[13] so in the vision of the full times eating is reexperienced. But it is an eating of oneness—a banquet *together*—not an eating that separates and divides. We eat at "the table in the kingdom of God."

> Our Lord said to one of his disciples: "Those who follow me will sit at my table in my Father's kingdom and will eat my food and drink my drink—the table which my Father has prepared for me and which I have prepared for you" (Mt. 19:28; Lk. 20:29).[14]

All are invited. All beings can come to the feast. "Surely we have been invited to the greatest feast ever, where the king of heaven 'puts on a feast for his son's wedding' (Mt. 22:1-14)."[15] The host for this banquet is altogether unique. "He who has prepared the supper for God and man, the ineffable One, has no name . . . Who prepared this feast? A person. The person who is God."[16] And what is being served at this banquet? Union, still more union between God and creatures, creature and creature, God to God. Life to life. Christ said that he "was the bread giving life to the world . . . What is proper to heavenly bread is that it give life."[17] The bread eaten is body to body.

> Indeed, in the body of our Lord the soul is so closely joined to God that all the angels, both of the cherubim and of the seraphim, cannot know or find any difference between them. For, where they touch God they touch the soul, and where they touch the soul they touch God. There never was so close a union. For the soul is much more united with God than body and soul which form one person.[18]

The menu for the banquet is nothing less than the compassionate Creator of all. "In the Last Supper God gives himself with all he is as food for his dear friends."[19] With this eating, this total union, the breakthrough is achieved once again. We reenter God still another time. "The soul enters into God more than any food enters into us; in fact, it changes the soul into God . . . My soul is more closely united with God than food with my body."[20]

The banquet is a celebration of divinity in which transformation takes place. God with people; people with God. God into food; food into

God; God into people; people into God. Many are called to this great sacrament of eating. How many will respond to this invitation? How many are hungry enough to eat Compassion? And how many would dare to become what they eat?

NOTES

Following are abbreviations of primary source texts used in the notes:

DW *Meister Eckhart: Die deutschen Werke*, ed. by Josef Quint, vols. I, II, III, V (Stuttgart: 1958–76).

LW *Meister Eckhart: Die lateinischen Werke*, ed. by E. Benz, J. Koch, et al., vols. I–V (Stuttgart: 1938–75).

Q   *Meister Eckhart: Deutsche Predigten und Traktate*, ed. and tr. into modern German by Josef Quint (Munich: 1963).

Following are abbreviations of primary translations, other than my own, used in the notes:

ANC Jeanne Ancelet-Hustache, *Master Eckhart and the Rhineland Mystics* (New York: Harper Torchbooks, 1957).

CL   James M. Clark, *Meister Eckhart: An Introduction to the Study of His Works with an Anthology of His Sermons* (London: Thomas Nelson & Sons, Ltd., 1957).

M   Armand A. Maurer, *Master Eckhart: Parisian Questions and Prologues* (Toronto: Pontifical Institute of Medieval Studies, 1974).

SH   Reiner Schürmann, *Meister Eckhart: Mystic and Philosopher* (Bloomington: University of Indiana Press, 1978).

SK   James Clark and John V. Skinner, *Meister Eckhart: Selected Treatises and Sermons Translated from Latin and German with an Introduction and Notes* (London: Faber & Faber, Ltd., 1958).

Introduction
1. Bengt R. Hoffman, *Luther and the Mystics* (Minneapolis: Augsburg Press, 1976), pp. 124, 154, 41ff., and *passim*.
2. ANC, p. 171. The connection between the Rhineland mystics and the Spanish Carmelite school preoccupied my former professor, Louis Cognet, for years. See Louis Cognet, *Introduction aux Mystiques Rhéno-Flamands* (Paris: Desclée et Cie, 1968), p. 343. It has been said that "Ignatian spirituality has much in common with that of Meister Eckhart; it is impossible, indeed, to approve the one while rejecting the other" (Walter Nigg, *Warriors of God* [New York: Alfred A. Knopf, 1959], p. 338).
3. Ernst Bloch, *Atheism in Christianity* (New York: Herder & Herder, 1972), pp. 63ff.; Erich Fromm, *To Have or To Be?* (New York: Harper & Row, 1976), says: "Eckhart has described and analyzed the difference between the having and being modes of existence with a penetration and clarity not surpassed by any teacher" (p. 59). See also: Matthew Fox, "Meister Eckhart and Karl Marx: The Mystic as Political Theologian," *Listening* (Fall 1978), pp. 233–57.
4. D. T. Suzuki, *Mysticism: Christian and Buddhist* (New York: Harper,

1957), p. 3; Thomas Merton, *Zen and the Birds of Appetite* (New York: New Directions, 1968), p. 13; Thomas Merton, *Conjectures of a Guilty Bystander* (Garden City, N.Y.: Doubleday & Company, 1968), p. 53. On the Zen/Eckhart influence on Merton, see Sister Therese Lentfoehr, *Words and Silence* (New York: New Directions Publishing Corp., 1979), pp. 55–63, 106–8.

5. C. G. Jung, Commentary to Richard Wilhelm's translation and explanation of *The Secret of the Golden Flower* (New York: Harcourt Brace Jovanovich, 1962), p. 93. Jung's references to Eckhart are numerous, as one can learn from the *General Index to the Collected Works of C. G. Jung*, compiled by Barbara Forryan and Janet M. Glover (Princeton, N.J.: Princeton University Press, 1979), Bollingen Series XX, Vol. 20, p. 238.

6. ANC, p. 178.

7. *The Imitation of Christ*, Bk. III, ch. 42. The same kind of attitude of struggle *against* nature and creation prevails in our society today, for example, in big-business farming, as Berry points out. See Wendell Berry, *The Unsettling of America: Culture and Agriculture* (New York: Avon Books, 1977).

8. Matthew Fox, "Meister Eckhart on the Fourfold Path of a Creation-Centered Spiritual Journey," in Matthew Fox, ed., *Western Spirituality: Historical Roots, Ecumenical Routes* (Notre Dame, Ind.: Fides/Claretian, 1979), pp. 215–47.

9. Philippe Dollinger, "Strasbourg et Colmar Foyers de la Mystique Rhénane (xiiie–xive siècles)," in *La Mystique Rhénane* (Paris Presses Universitaires de France, 1963), pp. 4ff.

10. Barbara W. Tuchman, *A Distant Mirror: The Calamitous 14th Century* (New York: Alfred A. Knopf, 1978), p. 24.

11. See David M. Nicholas, "Town and Countryside: Social and Economic Tensions in Fourteenth-Century Flanders," *Comparative Studies in Society and History* (1968), pp. 458f., 471.

12. Tuchman, *op. cit.*, pp. 38, xvi.

13. Dollinger, *op. cit.*, p. 4.

14. Tuchman, *op. cit.*, pp. xix, 575.

15. *Ibid.*, pp. 26f.

16. See Richard K. Weber, "The Search for Identity and Community in the Fourteenth Century," *The Thomist* (April 1978), pp. 182–96.

17. Norman O. Brown, *Life Against Death* (Middletown, Conn.: Wesleyan University Press, 1972), pp. 318, 137.

18. Tuchman, *op. cit.*, pp. 40, 42.

19. *Ibid.*, p. 322.

20. *Ibid.*, p. 104.

21. SH, p. 89.

22. ANC, p. 27.

23. *Ibid.*, p. 132.

24. *Ibid.*, pp. 124f.

25. Merton, *Conjectures*, pp. 53f.

26. M. D. Knowles, "Denifle and Ehrle," *History* LIV (1969), 4. Cited by Armand A. Maurer, *Master Eckhart: Parisian Questions and Prologues* (Toronto: Pontifical Institute of Medieval Studies, 1974), p. 7.

27. Lossky's study is a fine one and one of the few theological studies on Eckhart, yet it is far weaker than Eckhart in biblical spirituality. See

Vladimir Lossky, *Théologie Négative et Connaissance de Dieu chez Maître Eckhart* (Paris: J. Vrin, 1973).

28. Q, p. 416.

29. Q, pp. 262f.

30. I am referring to C. F. Kelley commenting on LW IV, pp. 5ff. In C. F. Kelley, *Meister Eckhart on Divine Knowledge* (New Haven, Conn., and London: Yale University Press, 1977), p. 27.

31. See p. 143, comparing C. H. Dodd's theology to Eckhart's. See also Helen A. Kenik, "Toward a Biblical Basis for Creation Theology," in Fox, *Western Spirituality*, pp. 27–75.

32. See Philip David Bookstaber, *The Idea of Development of the Soul in Medieval Jewish Philosophy* (Philadelphia: Maurice Jacobs, 1950), pp. 21, 65.

33. Alwyn Rees and Brinley Rees, *Celtic Heritage* (London: Thames & Hudson, 1978), p. 99; John B. Noss, *Man's Religions* (New York: The Macmillan Company, 1969), p. 73.

34. Erwin Rohde, *Psyche: The Cult of Souls and Belief in Immortality Among the Greeks* (London: Routledge & Kegan Paul Ltd., 1950), p. 158.

35. Patrick's Creed is reproduced in Mary Aileen Schmiel, "The Finest Music in the World: Exploring Celtic Spiritual Legacies," in Fox, *Western Spirituality*, pp. 173f. I am indebted to Ms. Schmiel's work on Celtic spirituality.

36. *Ibid.*, p. 172. Robert F. Evans, *Four Letters of Pelagius* (New York: Seabury Press, 1968), comments on Pelagius' meaning of *justitia*. It is his "characteristic and all-embracing word for the complete obedience to all that God commands. It includes both 'not sinning' . . . and the doing of those good works enjoined upon all Christians" (p. 76). For Pelagius' relationship with women, see Robert F. Evans, *Pelagius: Inquiries and Reappraisals* (New York: Seabury Press, 1968), pp. 32ff.

37. William Blake, "The Laocoön," in *Complete Writings*, Geoffrey Keynes, ed. (London: Oxford University Press, 1969), p. 776.

38. Rees, *op. cit.*, p. 213.

39. See Krister Stendahl, "Judgment and Mercy," in *Paul Among Jews and Gentiles* (Philadelphia: Fortress Press, 1978), pp. 100f. It is peculiar to English and German to separate "justice" from "righteousness" but not so in Hebrew, Greek, and Latin. "Righteousness and justice . . . are the one and only *justitia*."

40. Rees, *op. cit.*, p. 17.

41. See Edward A. Armstrong, *Saint Francis: Nature Mystic* (Berkeley: University of California Press, 1976), pp. 40f.; and A. N. Tommasini, *Irish Saints in Italy* (London: Sands & Co., 1937).

42. Armstrong, *op. cit.*, p. 34. See pp. 34–41.

43. Jean A. Potter and Myra L. Uhlfelder, eds., *John the Scot: Periphyseon on the Division of Nature* (Indianapolis, Ind.: The Bobbs-Merrill Co., 1976), p. xx.

44. See Armstrong, *op. cit.*, pp. 127–31, 189, 231–35.

45. Christopher J. Kauffman, *Tamers of Death: The History of the Alexian Brothers* (New York: Seabury Press, 1976), p. 123. Kauffman demonstrates the connection between Eckhart and the Beghards and the Beghards and the Alexian Brothers.

46. See also Q, Sermon #31.

47. SK, p. 148.
48. ANC, p. 10.
49. Dayton Phillips, *Beguines in Medieval Strassburg* (Stanford University, Calif.: Stanford University Press, 1941), p. 27.
50. *Ibid.*, pp. 224, 228.
51. R. W. Southern, *The Making of the Middle Ages* (New Haven, Conn.: Yale University Press, 1978), p. 324.
52. Cited in Ernest W. McDonnell, *The Beguines and Beghards in Medieval Culture* (New Brunswick, N.J.: Rutgers University Press, 1954), p. 524. I am indebted for this section on the Beguines to the excellent study done by Anne Metzler, "The Beguines: An Alternative Life-style for Medieval Lay Women" (Chicago: Mundelein College Master Thesis, unpublished, 1979).
53. Martin Erbstosser and Ernst Werner, *Ideologische Probleme de Meittelalterlichen plebejertums* (Berlin: Akademie Verlag, 1960), p. 34.
54. Joan Evans, ed., *The Flowering of the Middle Ages* (New York: McGraw-Hill, 1966), p. 258.
55. Kelley, *op. cit.*, p. 82.
56. SH, pp. 230, n. 21, 38.
57. *Ibid.*, pp. 140f.
58. Thomas Franklin O'Meara, "Meister Eckhart's Destiny," *Spirituality Today* (December 1978), p. 357. This two-part article provides an excellent summary of Eckhart's influence through the ages. The same author has also put together a most useful and comprehensive bibliography on Meister Eckhart in *The Thomist*, April 1978, pp. 313–36.
59. Kenik, *op. cit.*, p. 63.
60. DW III, p. 582.
61. C. G. Jung, *Aion: Researches into the Phenomenology of the Self*, in *The Collected Works of C. G. Jung* (Princeton, N.J.: Princeton University Press, 1959), Bollingen Series XX, Vol. 9, Part II, p. 40.
62. Claude Tresmontant, *A Study of Hebrew Thought* (Paris: Desclée et Cie, 1960), p. 26.
63. SH, p. 13.
64. *Ibid.*, p. 69.

Path One
1. See Helen A. Kenik, "Toward a Biblical Basis for Creation Theology," in Matthew Fox, ed., *Western Spirituality: Historical Roots, Ecumenical Routes* (Notre Dame, Ind.: Fides/Claretian, 1979), pp. 62f.

Sermon One
1. Cited in C. F. Kelley, *Meister Eckhart on Divine Knowledge* (New Haven, Conn., and London: Yale University Press, 1977), p. 72.
2. DW III, p. 587.
3. SK, p. 134.
4. Q, p. 421.
5. SK, p. 134.
6. SK, p. 175.
7. SK, p. 219.
8. Q, p. 346.
9. CL, pp. 163f.

10. P. van Imschoot, "Word," *Encyclopedic Dictionary of the Bible*, Louis F. Hartman, tr. (New York: McGraw-Hill, 1963), col. 2598.

Sermon Two

1. CL, p. 248.
2. SK, p. 199.
3. Sigmund Freud, *New Introductory Lectures on Psychoanalysis*, W. J. H. Sprott, tr. (London: Hogarth Press, 1933), p. 99.
4. SK, p. 201.
5. CL, p. 212.
6. SK, p. 183.
7. LW I, pp. 161f.
8. SK, p. 129.
9. Q, p. 329. Translation in SH, p. 123.
10. SK, p. 78.
11. Q, p. 329. Translation in SH, p. 123.
12. Q, p. 332. Translation in SH, p. 126.
13. M, pp. 77f.
14. "That which is in God is God." *Compendium Theologiae*, 37, 41.
15. See Sermon Twenty-three.

Sermon Three

1. CL, p. 246.
2. See John D. Caputo, *The Mystical Element in Heidegger's Thought* (Athens, Ohio: University of Ohio Press, 1978), p. 106.
3. See Sermon Fourteen.
4. DW I, p. 156.
5. Q, p. 295. Translation by Caputo, *op. cit.*, p. 243.
6. CL, p. 163.
7. CL, p. 167.
8. CL, p. 241.
9. Q, p. 350.
10. M, p. 91.
11. Cf. Matthew Fox, *WHEE! We, wee All the Way Home: A Guide to the New Sensual Spirituality* (Wilmington, N.C.: Consortium Books, 1976).
12. SH, p. 91.

Sermon Four

1. SK, p. 175.
2. M, p. 88.
3. CL, p. 167.
4. LW III, p. 51.
5. SH, pp. 62f.
6. DW III, p. 587.
7. LW II, p. 282.
8. LW III, p. 77; LW I, p. 169.
9. See M, pp. 77–98.
10. DW I, pp. 106, 115. Translation by C. F. Kelley, *Meister Eckhart on Divine Knowledge* (New Haven, Conn., and London: Yale University Press, 1977), pp. 230–31.
11. LW II, p. 65.

Sermon Five
1. See LW I, p. 235. Cf. SH, p. 154, and also Jean A. Potter and Myra L. Uhlfelder, eds., *John the Scot: Periphyseon on the Division of Nature* (Indianapolis, Ind.: Bobbs-Merrill Co., 1976). See also Vladimir Lossky, *Théologie Négative et Connaissance de Dieu chez Maître Eckhart* (Paris: J. Vrin, 1973), pp. 182f.
2. Q, p. 167.
3. DW III, p. 582.
4. DW I, p. 646.
5. Q, p. 215.
6. DW I, p. 148.
7. DW III, p. 579.
8. Q, pp. 226f. Translation in SH, p. 102.
9. DW III, p. 570.
10. DW I, p. 376.
11. See Sermon Twenty-nine.
12. DW III, p. 587.
13. M, p. 70.
14. DW III, p. 510.
15. M, p. 72.
16. SH, p. 89.
17. LW III. p. 189.
18. See Sermon Twenty-three.

Sermon Six
1. DW III, p. 582.
2. Q, p. 171.
3. Q, p. 140.
4. SK, p. 129.
5. Q, p. 153.
6. DW III, p. 514.
7. Q, p. 226.
8. CL, p. 216.
9. Q, p. 344.
10. Q, p. 230.
11. Q, p. 229.
12. Q, p. 231.
13. Q, p. 197. Translation by John D. Caputo, *The Mystical Element in Heidegger's Thought* (Athens, Ohio: University of Ohio Press, 1978), p. 108.
14. Q, p. 180.
15. SH, pp. 144f.
16. DW II, p. 676.
17. SH, p. 145.
18. Caputo, *op. cit.*, p. 110.
19. Q, p. 210.
20. M, p. 60.
21. CL, p. 209.
22. Q, p. 340.
23. CL, p. 214.
24. CL, p. 198.

25. DW III, p. 584.
26. CL, p. 160.
27. LW IV, p. 145.
28. M, p. 78.
29. DW II, p. 595.
30. M, p. 90.
31. DW III, p. 589.
32. M, p. 92.
33. LW IV, p. 147.
34. LW IV, p. 149.
35. LW IV, pp. 351f.
36. Q, p. 341.
37. SK, p. 94.
38. Q, p. 249. Translation in ANC, p. 116.
39. Q, p. 162.

Sermon Seven
 1. Q, p. 153.
 2. Q, p. 141.
 3. Q, p. 142.
 4. *Ibid.*
 5. SK, p. 233.
 6. DW III, pp. 585f.
 7. DW III, p. 587.
 8. Q, p. 431.
 9. Q, pp. 166f.
10. SH, p. 147.
11. Q, p. 167.
12. Q, p. 291.
13. DW III, p. 582.
14. SK, p. 97.
15. SK, p. 101.
16. SK, p. 97.
17. SK, p. 103.
18. SK, p. 101.
19. DW II, p. 691.
20. St. Augustine, *Literal Commentary on Genesis*, XII, 7.16; *On Music*, VI, 5, 13. Translations in Vernon J. Bourke, *The Essential Augustine* (Indianapolis, Ind.: Hackett Publishing Co., 1978), pp. 94, 46f.
21. DW II, p. 747.
22. See M, pp. 26f. Cf. M. D. Chenu, "Body and Body Politic in the Creation Spirituality of Thomas Aquinas," in Matthew Fox, ed., *Western Spirituality: Historical Roots, Ecumenical Routes* (Notre Dame, Ind.: Fides/Claretian, 1979), pp. 193–214.
23. Q, p. 296.
24. DW III, p. 580.
25. Q, p. 295.
26. CL, p. 198.
27. See M. D. Chenu, "Spiritus: Le vocabulaire de l'âme au XIIᵉ siècle," *Revue des Sciences philosophiques et théologiques*, XLI (1957), pp. 227ff.
28. DW I, p. 523.
29. DW III, p. 585.

30. DW I, p. 490.
31. Q, pp. 290f.
32. Q, pp. 294f.
33. DW I, p. 490.
34. DW III, p. 586.
35. DW III, p. 587.
36. DW III, p. 511.

Sermon Eight
  1. CL, p. 199.
  2. Q, p. 265.
  3. DW III, p. 589.
  4. *Ibid.*
  5. DW II, p. 690.
  6. DW III, p. 521.
  7. DW III, p. 515.
  8. SK, p. 71.
  9. SK, p. 72.
 10. SK, p. 96.
 11. DW II, p. 666.

Sermon Nine
  1. Cf. C. H. Dodd, *The Parables of the Kingdom* (London: Fontana Books, 1967), pp. 28ff.; Joachim Jeremias, *The Parables of Jesus* (New York: Charles Scribner's Sons, 1971).
  2. Dodd, *op. cit.,* p. 35.
  3. *Ibid.,* p. 41.
  4. *Ibid.,* p. 144.
  5. Cf. Rosemary Ruether, *The Radical Kingdom* (New York: Harper & Row, 1970), pp. 15ff.
  6. See Matthew Fox, "Sexuality and Compassion: From Climbing Jacob's Ladder to Dancing Sarah's Circle," in Matthew Fox, *A Spirituality Named Compassion* (Minneapolis, Minn.: Winston Press, 1979), pp. 36ff.
  7. *The Jerusalem Bible,* Alexander Jones, Gen. Ed. (Garden City, N.Y.: Doubleday & Company, 1966), p. 1019, note j.
  8. SK, p. 86.
  9. SK, p. 97.
 10. See Dodd, *op. cit.,* pp. 34f.
 11. Claus Westermann, *Blessing in the Bible and the Life of the Church* (Philadelphia: Fortress Press, 1978), pp. 3f.
 12. Cited in *ibid.,* pp. 20f.
 13. DW II, p. 706.
 14. DW III, p. 575.
 15. DW II, p. 704.
 16. *Ibid.*

Sermon Ten
  1. Raymond Bernard Blakney, *Meister Eckhart: A Modern Translation* (New York: Harper Torchbooks, 1941), p. 245.
  2. Q, p. 267.
  3. Q, p. 214.

4. CL, p. 226.
5. See Sermon Nineteen.
6. See Sermon Twenty-three.
7. SK, p. 104.
8. Q, p. 169.
9. SK, p. 79.
10. SK, p. 140.
11. For the God who suffers and is passionate, see Abraham J. Heschel, *The Prophets* (New York: Harper & Row, 1962), pp. 92, 190, 232, 237f., 319–21, 435, 484–88, and *passim*.
12. Raymond E. Brown, *The Gospel According to John I–XII* (Garden City, N.Y.: Doubleday & Company, 1966), p. 536.
13. M, pp. 107f.
14. M, p. 108.
15. See Brown, *op. cit.*, pp. 342ff.
16. See M, p. 33, note 70.
17. CL, p. 230.
18. *Ibid.*
19. Claus Westermann, *Blessing in the Bible and the Life of the Church* (Philadelphia: Fortress Press, 1978), p. 18.
20. Cited in Westermann, p. 20.
21. Q, p. 255.
22. Westermann, *op. cit.*, p. 18.
23. *Ibid.*, pp. 18f.
24. CL, p. 232.
25. SK, p. 247.

Path Two
1. CL, p. 165.
2. DW III, p. 522.
3. DW III, p. 580.

Sermon Eleven
1. CL, p. 216.
2. Q, p. 55. Translation by John D. Caputo, *The Mystical Element in Heidegger's Thought* (Athens, Ohio: University of Ohio Press, 1978), p. 186.
3. C. H. Dodd, *The Parables of the Kingdom* (London: Fontana Books, 1967), pp. 108, 110.
4. DW III, p. 521.
5. DW II, p. 692.
6. DW II, p. 706.
7. Q, pp. 195f.
8. CL, p. 236.
9. Q, p. 193.
10. SK, pp. 100f. Cf. Thomas Aquinas, *Sum. theol.*, I, q. 1, art. 1, ad 2.
11. DW III, p. 514.
12. SK, p. 69.
13. Q, pp. 55f.
14. CL, p. 247.
15. CL, p. 248.

16. SK, p. 205.
17. CL, p. 248.
18. Cited in C. F. Kelley, *Meister Eckhart on Divine Knowledge* (New Haven, Conn., and London: Yale University Press, 1977), p. 139.
19. DW III, p. 574.
20. Pseudo-Dionysius, *De mystica Theologica*, 3:2. A contemporary study of this same theme is Eulalio R. Baltazar, *The Dark Center* (New York: Paulist Press, 1973).
21. CL, p. 217.
22. CL, pp. 158f.
23. DW I, pp. 95f.
24. Cf. M, pp. 40f.
25. CL, p. 159.

Sermon Twelve
1. CL, p. 158.
2. DW III, p. 574.
3. SK, p. 194.
4. SK, p. 93.
5. SK, pp. 181f.
6. See Mary Constance Barrett, *An Experimental Study of the Thomistic Concept of the Faculty of Imagination* (Washington, D.C.: Catholic University of America Press, 1941). Barrett describes the medieval term "imagination" as: "the mere conservation of the images of past experiences . . . very much the same thing as that which modern psychology deals with under the name of memory" (p. 45). See also Étienne Gilson, *Christian Philosophy of Aquinas* (New York: Random House, 1956). Imagination for the medievals is a "power to preserve," a "treasury in which the forms apprehended by the senses are stored" (pp. 205f.). Our contemporary use of the word "imagination" owes much to Coleridge for whom imagination is a source of art. It is in this sense that I apply the term to Eckhart's notion of "soul." For Coleridge, imagination "disciplines, diffuses, dissipates, in order to re-create . . . it struggles to idealize and to unify. It is essentially *vital*." (Cited in A. R. Manser, "Imagination," *Encyclopedia of Philosophy*, III [New York: The Macmillan Company, 1967], p. 137.)

Sermon Thirteen
1. Victor Paul Furnish, "The Letter of Paul to the Ephesians," *The Interpreter's One-Volume Commentary on the Bible*, Charles M. Laymon, ed. (Nashville, Tenn.: Abingdon Press, 1971), p. 841.
2. LW II, p. 77.
3. SK, p. 108.
4. DW III, p. 583.
5. Q, pp. 328, 331. Translation in SH 122, 125.
6. John D. Caputo, "The Nothingness of the Intellect in Meister Eckhart's 'Parisian Questions,'" *The Thomist*, XXXIX (January 1975), p. 91.
7. LW V, p. 44.
8. LW V, p. 50.
9. Caputo, *op. cit.*, p. 98.
10. *Ibid.*, p. 104.
11. *Ibid.*, p. 114.

12. DW II, p. 594.
13. SK, p. 103. See also the fine study by Maurice de Gandillac, "La 'dialectique' de Maître Eckhart," in *La Mystique Rhénane*, (Paris: Presses Universitaires de France, 1963), pp. 59–94.
14. CL, p. 205.
15. SK, p. 107.
16. SK, p. 89.
17. LW III, p. 70.
18. LW III, p. 69.
19. LW III, p. 202.
20. SK, p. 191.
21. DW III, pp. 579f.
22. DW III, p. 580.
23. SK, p. 124.
24. DW II, p. 326.

Sermon Fourteen

1. DW III, #82, p. 583.
2. LW III, p. 41.
3. Q, p. 384.
4. LW II, p. 22.
5. Q, p. 300.
6. SK, pp. 133f.
7. SK, p. 64.
8. SK, p. 97.
9. SK, p. 98.
10. Q, p. 299.
11. Q, p. 227. Translation in SH, p. 102.
12. Cf. my understanding of adult prayer as a "radical response to life" in Matthew Fox, *On Becoming a Musical, Mystical Bear: Spirituality American Style* (New York: Paulist Press, 1976).
13. Q, p. 171.
14. Q, p. 334. Translation in SH, p. 128.
15. SK, p. 68.
16. SK, p. 69.
17. SK, p. 70.
18. SK, p. 86. For an explanation of "tactical ecstacies," see Matthew Fox, *WHEE! We, wee All the Way Home: A Guide to the New Sensual Spirituality* (Wilmington, N.C.: Consortium Books, 1976).
19. DW III, p. 515.
20. CL, p. 236.
21. See Sermon Fifteen.
22. Q, p. 175. Translation in ANC, pp. 105f.
23. DW II, p. 751.
24. Q, p. 171.
25. DW III, p. 587.
26. DW II, p. 705.
27. SK, p. 240.
28. Q, pp. 328, 332.
29. DW III, p. 522.
30. Q, pp. 328, 332, 333.

31. Q, p. 332.
32. DW III, p. 523.

Sermon Fifteen
1. SH, p. 84.
2. DW V, p. 542.
3. DW V, p. 540.
4. John D. Caputo, *The Mystical Element in Heidegger's Thought* (Athens, Ohio: University of Ohio Press, 1978), p. 15.
5. DW V, p. 546.
6. DW V, p. 542.
7. Q, pp. 214f.
8. SK, p. 130.
9. SK, p. 70.
10. SH, p. 85.
11. Caputo, *op. cit.*, p. 119.
12. SK, p. 123.
13. SH, p. 16.
14. DW III, p. 514.
15. Caputo, *op. cit.*, p. 180.
16. SK, p. 70.

Sermon Sixteen
1. DW III, p. 513.
2. SK, p. 75.
3. DW II, p. 610.
4. SK, p. 66.
5. SK, p. 196.
6. SK, p. 114.
7. SK, p. 98.
8. SK, p. 135.
9. See Sermon Twenty.
10. SK, p. 114.
11. SK, p. 115.
12. John D. Caputo, *The Mystical Element in Heidegger's Thought* (Athens, Ohio: University of Ohio Press, 1978), p. 209.
13. SK, p. 78. Translation adapted.
14. See Sermon Twenty.
15. SK, p. 79.
16. SH, pp. 41–42.
17. Q, p. 386. Translation in SH, p. 58.
18. SK, p. 89.
19. SK, p. 135.
20. See Sermon Twenty-three.
21. *Ibid.*
22. See Sermon Two.
23. SK, p. 75.

Sermon Seventeen
1. SK, p. 122.
2. See Vladimir Lossky, *Théologie Négative et Connaissance de Dieu chez Maître Eckhart* (Paris: J. Vrin, 1973), p. 431.

Sermon Eighteen
1. SK, p. 161. Translation adapted.
2. SK, p. 167.
3. SK, p. 168. Translation adapted.
4. SK, p. 160.
5. SH, p. 91.
6. Cf. Thorleif Boman, *Hebrew Thought Compared with Greek*, tr. by Jules L. Moreau (Philadelphia: The Westminster Press, 1961), pp. 206ff., for a discussion of a hearing-oriented as distinct from a seeing-oriented culture.
7. CL, p. 162.
8. See Sermon Thirty-six.
9. *Ibid.*
10. For more on the relationship between anti-intellectualism and sentimental spiritualistic pieties, see Anne Douglas, *The Feminization of American Culture* (New York: Alfred A. Knopf, 1977).
11. My *WHEE! We, wee All the Way Home: A Guide to the New Sensual Spirituality* (Wilmington, N.C.: Consortium Books, 1976) is an attempt to mend the damage done by this dualism in spirituality and to put the *via affirmativa* and the *via negativa* back in their proper place of dialectical tension and harmony.
12. SK, p. 167. Translation adapted.

Sermon Nineteen
1. DW III, p. 581.
2. SH, p. 17.
3. SK, p. 124.
4. CL, p. 214. It is true, of course, that the philosophical tradition of Plato and Aristotle had developed doctrines of pre-creation of the soul and Eckhart was familiar with these traditions, especially through Albert the Great's influence. However, we must not ignore the biblical traditions on this subject, for Eckhart does not ignore them.
5. See Sermon Three.
6. DW I, p. 94.
7. *Ibid.*, p. 95.
8. DW I, p. 521.
9. DW II, p. 595.
10. *Ibid.*

Sermon Twenty
1. Albert the Great, for example, translated "Martha" in an allegorical sense. See SH, p. 228, note 2.
2. William Baird, for example, in his "The Gospel According to Luke," *The Interpreter's One-Volume Commentary on the Bible*, Charles M. Laymon, ed. (Nashville, Tenn.: Abingdon Press, 1971), p. 689, sees the story as an illustration of the command of compassion or loving one's neighbor.
3. SH, p. 11.
4. SH, p. 19.
5. SH, pp. 23; 230, note 21; 38, 47.
6. Cf. Jon Sobrino, "Prayer in the New Testament and Early Christian

Community," in Matthew Fox, ed., *Western Spirituality: Historical Roots, Ecumenical Routes* (Notre Dame, Ind.: Fides/Claretian, 1979), pp. 76–114, for a consideration of prayer that takes one beyond the contemplation/action dilemma. Also, Matthew Fox, *On Becoming a Musical, Mystical Bear: Spirituality American Style* (New York: Paulist Press, 1976).

7. John D. Caputo, *The Mystical Element in Heidegger's Thought* (Athens, Ohio: University of Ohio Press, 1978), p. 180.
8. *Ibid.*, p. 139.
9. SH, p. 32.
10. SH, p. 36.
11. William Eckhardt, *Compassion: Toward a Science of Value* (Oakville, Ontario, Canada: CPRI Press, 1973), pp. 4f.
12. Q, p. 75.
13. SH, p. 28.
14. SK, pp. 82f.
15. CL, p. 215.
16. SK, p. 82.
17. Q, p. 214.
18. DW II, p. 595.
19. LW IV, p. 408.
20. SK, p. 215.
21. DW III, p. 587.
22. SH, p. 210.
23. SH, p. 18.
24. Gabriel Théry, ed., *Rechtfertigungsschrift* (Eckhart's Defense), ※II, art. 51, Solution. Translation in SH 46.
25. See SH, pp. 24f., 43, 46f.

Path Three
1. Q, p. 425. See Sermon Eighteen.
2. See Otto Rank, *Art and Artist* (New York: Agathon Press, 1975), pp. 37–65.
3. The idea that the artist must himself or herself undergo a profound death and rebirth is also invoked by Rank, who says that a "new type of humanity" can be born from the artist who "will be able to put his creative impulse *directly* in the service of his own personality." (See Rank, *op. cit.*, pp. 430f.)

Sermon Twenty-one
1. Q, p. 220.
2. SH, p. 23.
3. CL, p. 203.
4. CL, p. 214.
5. Q, p. 203.
6. SK, p. 123.
7. Q, p. 61.
8. Q, p. 265.
9. Q, p. 385.
10. Q, p. 384.
11. Q, p. 237.
12. Q, p. 332. Translation in SH, p. 126.

13. DW III, p. 315.
14. Q, p. 185.
15. Q, p. 186.
16. LW III, pp. 101f.
17. See John D. Caputo, *The Mystical Element in Heidegger's Thought* (Athens, Ohio: University of Ohio Press, 1978), p. 115.
18. SK, p. 111.
19. See pp. 251, 252, 254.
20. Q, p. 425.
21. DW II, p. 677.

Sermon Twenty-two
  1. DW II, p. 752.
  2. DW II, p. 705.
  3. Q, p. 175.
  4. Clement of Alexandria, *The Pedagogue*, III, 1. Translation in SH, p. 24.
  5. DW III, p. 574.
  6. From Eckhart's *Defense*; translation in SH, p. 160.
  7. SH, p. 82.
  8. SK, p. 190.
  9. SK, p. 132.
 10. Q, p. 208.
 11. Q, p. 185. Translation in John D. Caputo, *The Mystical Element in Heidegger's Thought* (Athens, Ohio: University of Ohio Press, 1978), p. 114.
 12. SK, pp. 126f.
 13. SK, p. 133.
 14. Q, p. 172.
 15. See Sermon Two.

Sermon Twenty-three
  1. DW II, p. 677.
  2. CL, p. 201.
  3. SK, pp. 234f.
  4. CL, p. 214.
  5. SK, p. 132.
  6. See Adolf Deissmann, *Paul: A Study in Social and Religious History*, tr. by William E. Wilson (New York: Harper Torchbooks, 1957), pp. 295–99.
  7. DW II, p. 707.
  8. DW III, p. 588.
  9. SK, p. 119.
 10. SK, p. 126.
 11. Q, p. 208.
 12. CL, p. 219.
 13. CL, p. 222.
 14. CL, p. 201.
 15. Q, p. 332.
 16. See Sermon Fifteen.
 17. SH, p. 110.
 18. SH, p. 147.

19. Vladimir Lossky, *Théologie Négative et Connaissance de Dieu chez Maître Eckhart* (Paris: J. Vrin, 1973), p. 188.
20. SK, p. 126.
21. SK, p. 78.
22. DW I, p. 521.
23. CL, p. 248.
24. See Sermon Four.
25. DW III, p. 569.
26. CL, p. 218.

Sermon Twenty-four
 1. SK, p. 246.
 2. SK, pp. 221f.
 3. See Sermon Twenty-eight.
 4. SK, p. 221.
 5. See Sermon Twenty.
 6. DW III, p. 528.
 7. SK, p. 178.
 8. SK, p. 89.
 9. Q, p. 226.
10. See Sermon Thirty-two.
11. See Sermon Fifteen.
12. SH, p. 17.
13. SK, p. 170.
14. SK, p. 111.
15. SK, pp. 237ff.
16. DW II, p. 528.
17. See Sermon Fifteen.
18. LW IV, p. 429. Eckhart links redemption and reminding: "For this reason, therefore, has the wisdom of God wanted to show our redemption by himself assuming flesh—in order that our instruction in divine, natural, and moral matters would be remembered" (LW III, p. 156). C. F. Kelley writes: "Christ is before all else the 'Reminder.' He reminds us of the truth that has been 'forgotten' and hidden from our conscious and subconscious minds" (*Meister Eckhart on Divine Knowledge* [New Haven, Conn., and London: Yale University Press, 1977], p. 131).
19. SK, p. 150.
20. DW III, p. 587.
21. SK, p. 246.
22. *In Gen. II*, 1.1. Translation in ANC 57.
23. LW III, p. 13.
24. DW II, p. 690.
25. CL, p. 168.
26. Q, p 343.
27. Q, p. 200.

Sermon Twenty-five
 1. See Sermon Two.
 2. Q, p. 431.
 3. DW II, p. 707.
 4. *Ibid.*

5. Bernhard W. Anderson, *Out of the Depths: The Psalms Speak for Us Today* (Philadelphia: The Westminster Press, 1974), p. 131. Cf. Ps. 74.
6. SK, pp. 133f.
7. DW I, p. 377.

Sermon Twenty-six
1. DW III, p. 575.
2. LW III, p. 285.
3. Q, p. 233.
4. Cited in C. F. Kelley, *Meister Eckhart on Divine Knowledge* (New Haven, Conn., and London: Yale University Press, 1977), p. 223.
5. DW I, p. 522.
6. DW II, p. 676.
7. CL, p. 219.
8. SK, p. 131.
9. SK, p. 132.
10. *Ibid.*
11. SK, p. 189.
12. See Sermon Four.
13. Q, p. 201; DW III, p. 582.
14. See William James, *Varieties of Religious Experience* (New York: Mentor Books, 1958), p. 164.
15. Q, p. 385.
16. CL, p. 219.
17. SH, p. 146.
18. DW III, p. 590.
19. CL, p. 167.
20. DW I, p. 521.
21. *Ibid.*, p. 522.
22. Raymond Bernard Blakney, *Meister Eckhart: A Modern Translation* (New York: Harper Torchbooks, 1941), p. 237.
23. DW II, p. 326.

Sermon Twenty-seven
1. See Sermon Twenty-six, p. 366.

Sermon Twenty-eight
1. DW III, p. 522.
2. CL, p. 203.
3. Q, p. 216. Translation in John D. Caputo, *The Mystical Element in Heidegger's Thought* (Athens, Ohio: University of Ohio Press, 1978), p. 126.
4. Cited in C. F. Kelley, *Meister Eckhart on Divine Knowledge* (New Haven, Conn., and London: Yale University Press, 1977), p. 68.
5. CL, p. 223.
6. CL, p. 203.
7. SK, pp. 92f.
8. CL, p. 203.
9. DW II, p. 751.
10. CL, p. 164.
11. DW III, p. 589.
12. DW III, p. 582.

Sermon Twenty-nine

1. C. F. Kelley, *Meister Eckhart on Divine Knowledge* (New Haven, Conn., and London: Yale University Press, 1977), p. 29.
2. CL, p. 249.
3. Q, p. 302.
4. CL, p. 164.
5. SK, p. 249.
6. LW III, p. 10.
7. See Otto Rank, *Art and Artist* (New York: Agathon Press, 1975); Ernest Becker, *The Denial of Death* (New York: The Free Press, 1973); Matthew Fox, "Otto Rank on the Artistic Journey as a Spiritual Journey, the Spiritual Journey as an Artistic Journey," *Spirituality Today*, March 1979, pp. 73–83; Matthew Fox, *A Spirituality Named Compassion* (Minneapolis, Minn.: Winston Press, 1979), chapter 4: "Creativity and Compassion."
8. DW II, p. 515.
9. SK, p. 257.
10. SH, p. 19.
11. Cf. Matthew Fox, "The Case for Extrovert Meditation," *Spirituality Today*, June 1978, pp. 164–77. A classic work on extrovert meditation is Mary Richards, *Centering* (Middletown, Conn.: Wesleyan University Press, 1964).
12. Q, p. 301.
13. CL, p. 249.
14. SK, pp. 234f.
15. Q, p. 176.
16. DW III, p. 582.
17. DW I, pp. 269, 271. Translation in SH, p. 94.
18. DW III, p. 515.
19. SK, p. 251.
20. SK, p. 97.
21. SK, p. 229.
22. Q, p. 342.
23. Q, p. 425.
24. DW II, p. 706.
25. SH, p. 105.
26. See Sermon Thirty-six.
27. See Silvano Arieti, *Creativity: The Magic Synthesis* (New York: Basic Books, 1976).

Path Four

1. Samuel H. Dressner, *Prayer, Humility and Compassion* (Philadelphia: Jewish Publication Society of America, 1957), pp. 236f. See also Matthew Fox, *A Spirituality Named Compassion* (Minneapolis, Minn.: Winston Press, 1979), chapter 1.
2. Q, p. 300.
3. LW IV, p. 396.
4. This point was made in the previous sermon.
5. LW IV, p. 396.

Sermon Thirty

1. Thorleif Boman, *Hebrew Thought Compared with Greek*, tr. by Jules L. Moreau (Philadelphia: The Westminster Press, 1961), p. 173. Cf. 1 Co. 8:6; Mt. 11:25.
2. See William Eckhart, *Compassion: Toward a Science of Value* (Oakville, Ontario, Canada: CPRI Press, 1973), pp. 4f.
3. LW IV, p. 396.
4. *Sifra Deuteronomy* 49. Rabbi Heschel said: "God created a reminder, an image. Humanity is a reminder of God. As God is compassionate, let humanity be compassionate" ("Abraham Joshua Heschel, Last Words: An Interview by Carl Stern" in *Intellectual Digest*, June 1973, p. 78).
5. SK, p. 221.
6. *The Jerusalem Bible*, Alexander Jones, Gen. Ed. (Garden City, N.Y.: Doubleday & Company, 1966), p. 961, note f.
7. DW III, p. 588.
8. LW IV, p. 392.
9. SK, p. 238.
10. SK, p. 239.
11. SK, p. 111.
12. LW IV, p. 395.
13. See Sermon Twenty-three.
14. LW IV, p. 384.
15. Thomas Aquinas, *Super II Cor.*, ch. XI, 6.
16. DW II, p. 752.
17. DW III, p. 590.
18. LW IV, pp. 395, 396.

Sermon Thirty-one

1. See *Sum. theol.*, I, q. 21., a. 4.
2. Q, p. 299.
3. DW II, p. 746.
4. Thomas Merton, "Marxism and Monastic Perspectives," in John Moffitt, ed., *A New Charter for Monasticism* (Notre Dame, Ind.: University of Notre Dame Press, 1970), p. 80. I relate this mystical insight to that of contemporary science in Matthew Fox, *A Spirituality Named Compassion* (Minneapolis, Minn.: Winston Press, 1979), chapter 5.
5. DW I, p. 56.
6. C. F. Kelley, *Meister Eckhart on Divine Knowledge* (New Haven, Conn., and London: Yale University Press, 1977), p. 221. The citations within Kelley are from DW V, pp. 413–22.
7. See Sermon Twenty-three.
8. ANC, p. 135.

Sermon Thirty-two

1. See B. Kuske, *Quellen zur Geschichte*; Jacques Heers, *L'Occident aux XIVe et XVe Siècles: Aspects Économiques et sociaux* (Paris: 1970); David M. Nicholas, "Town and Countryside: Social and Economic Tensions in Fourteenth-Century Flanders," *Comparative Studies in Society and History* (1968), pp. 458–72.
2. LW IV, p. 389.
3. SK, p. 186

4. Norman O. Brown, *Life Against Death* (Middletown, Conn.: Wesleyan University Press, 1972), for his chapter on "Filthy Lucre," pp. 234–304, and "The Excremental Vision," pp. 179–201.

5. SH, p. 13.

6. CL, p. 199.

7. LW IV, p. 186.

8. C. F. Kelley, *Meister Eckhart on Divine Knowledge* (New Haven, Conn., and London: Yale University Press, 1977), p. 14.

9. Q, p. 177.

10. Q, p. 55. Translation by John D. Caputo in *The Mystical Element in Heidegger's Thought* (Athens, Ohio: University of Ohio Press, 1978), p. 136.

11. Caputo, *ibid.*

12. SK, p. 257.

13. Q, p. 174.

14. Cf. LW I, pp. 246–50.

15. SK, p. 196.

16. SK, p. 201.

17. Kelley, *op. cit.*, p. 72.

18. Thomas Aquinas, *De malo*, XI, a. 3, ad 4.

19. CL, p. 199.

20. Gerhard von Rad, *Wisdom in Israel* (Nashville, Tenn.: Abingdon Press, 1978), p. 165.

21. Caputo, *op. cit.*, p. 188.

22. See Matthew Fox, "Meister Eckhart and Karl Marx," in Richard Woods, ed., *Understanding Mysticism* (Garden City, N.Y.: Image Books, 1980), pp. 555–60 for the section on "Eckhart's Political Condemnation."

Sermon Thirty-three

1. LW IV, p. 392.

2. LW III, p. 210.

3. SK, p. 112.

4. DW II, p. 690.

5. DW II, p. 707.

6. SK, p. 255.

7. See SK, pp. 111, 237.

8. SK, p. 238.

9. SK, p. 239.

10. DW III, p. 586.

11. SK, p. 255.

12. SK, p. 245.

13. Q, p. 299.

14. SK, p. 134.

15. DW II, p. 707.

16. SK, p. 254. Elsewhere, Eckhart writes: "Who are the just? A writer says: 'One is just who gives to each person what is his or her due.' They are just who give to God what is his, and to the saints and the angels what is theirs, and to one's fellow human beings what is theirs" (Q, p. 182).

17. SK, p. 185.

18. DW II, p. 691.
19. Q, p. 180. Translation by John D. Caputo, *The Mystical Element in Heidegger's Thought* (Athens, Ohio: University of Ohio Press, 1978), p. 100.
20. DW II, p. 707.
21. William Eckhardt, *Compassion: Toward a Science of Value* (Oakville, Ontario, Canada: CPRI Press, 1973), pits compulsion against compassion throughout his study. See especially pp. 256–71.
22. SK, p. 102.
23. SK, p. 67.
24. SK, p. 68.
25. CL, p. 249.
26. Q, p. 342.
27. CL, p. 249.
28. CL, p. 162.
29. SK, p. 102.
30. SK, p. 95.
31. SK, p. 131.
32. SK, p. 86.
33. SK, p. 131.
34. Q, p. 154. Translation by Caputo, *op. cit.*, p. 189.
35. SK, p. 80. We who are responsible for the new creation are the adverbs to God's verb or holy work of creation (Q, p. 200). Cf. Abraham Heschel, *God in Search of Man* (New York: Harper Torchbooks, 1955): "We have no nouns by which to describe God's essence. We have only *adverbs* by which to indicate the ways in which he acts toward us" (p. 161).
36. SK, p. 131.

Sermon Thirty-four

1. John D. Caputo, *The Mystical Element in Heidegger's Thought* (Athens, Ohio: University of Ohio Press, 1978), p. 138.
2. See E. F. Schumacher, "Good Work," Address at the Thirty-second National Conference on Higher Education, Chicago, March 23, 1977.
3. Caputo, *op. cit.*, pp. 138, 137.
4. *Ibid.*, pp. 138f.
5. SK, p. 99.
6. William Baird, in his "The Gospel According to Luke," *The Interpreter's One-Volume Commentary on the Bible*, Charles M. Laymon, ed. (Nashville, Tenn.: Abingdon Press, 1971), p. 689.
7. See Matthew Fox, WHEE! *We, wee All the Way Home: A Guide to the New Sensual Spirituality* (Wilmington, N.C.: Consortium Books, 1976), especially Parts I and IV.
8. See Matthew Fox, *A Spirituality Named Compassion*, chapter 5; Wendell Berry, *The Unsettling of America: Culture & Agriculture* (New York, Avon Books, 1977), chapter 7, "The Body and the Earth."
9. SK, p. 221.
10. Q, p. 265.
11. DW III, p. 582.

Sermon Thirty-five
1. See Adrienne Rich, *Of Woman Born* (New York: W. W. Norton & Co., 1976).
2. SK, p. 103.
3. *Ibid.*
4. SK, p. 104.
5. SK, p. 128.
6. *Ibid.*
7. SK, p. 115.
8. See Sermon Ten.

Sermon Thirty-six
1. Helen A. Kenik, "Toward a Biblical Basis for Creation Theology," in Matthew Fox, ed., *Western Spirituality: Historical Roots, Ecumenical Routes* (Notre Dame, Ind.: Fides/Claretian, 1979), p. 48.
2. *Ibid.*, pp. 32f.
3. Q, p. 175.
4. *Ibid.*
5. DW II, p. 646.
6. DW III, p. 582.
7. Cf. Dayton Phillips, *Beguines in Medieval Strassburg* (Stanford University, Calif.: Stanford University Press, 1941), p. 27: "It is obvious, therefore, that the Beguine condition found its greatest following among the lower classes."
8. SK, p. 148.
9. Kenik, *op. cit.*, p. 47.
10. *Ibid.*, p. 42.
11. *Ibid.*, p. 37.
12. Ernst Bloch, *Atheism in Christianity* (New York: Herder & Herder, 1972), pp. 63–65.
13. DW II, p. 704.
14. SK, p. 76.
15. Gregory Baum, *New Horizons* (New York: Paulist Press, 1972), pp. 141f.
16. Kenik, *op. cit.*, pp. 48, 73, note 26. Cf. W. A. Brueggemann, "David and His Theologian," *Catholic Biblical Quarterly* 30 (1968), pp. 156–81.

Sermon Thirty-seven
1. ANC, p. 67.
2. LW III, p. 342; see also Sermon Twenty-three.
3. CL, p. 240.
4. Cf. José Cardenale: "All things love another," from "*hymn.*"
5. SK, p. 112.
6. SK, p. 113.
7. SK, p. 187.
8. Q, p. 170.
9. Raymond Bernard Blakney, *Meister Eckhart: A Modern Translation* (New York: Harper Torchbooks, 1941), p. 297.
10. SK, p. 106.
11. See Sermon Thirty-five, p. 501.

12. See Sermon Thirty-three, p. 464.
13. Helen A. Kenik, "Toward a Biblical Basis for Creation Theology," in Matthew Fox, ed., *Western Spirituality: Historical Roots, Ecumenical Routes* (Notre Dame, Ind.: Fides/Claretian, 1979), p. 55.
14. DW II, p. 706.
15. LW IV, p. 346.
16. CL, pp. 158f.
17. LW IV, p. 37.
18. SK, p. 92.
19. Q, p. 246.
20. CL, p. 159.

INDEX TO SCRIPTURAL REFERENCES

All italicized page numbers refer to biblical quotations by Meister Eckhart.

1. HEBREW BIBLE

Genesis

1–4 . . . 44
1–11 . . . 148
1:26 . . . 106, 117,
    450, 456
1:27 . . . 75
2:22 . . . 315
3:1ff. . . . 511
12–26 . . . 26
21 . . . 424
26:14ff. . . . 513
28:12–22 . . . 144,
    145
28:16 . . . 138
39:23 . . . 93

Exodus

3:8 . . . 415
3:14 . . . 158, 160,
    169, 172
21:2 . . . 329
24:18 . . . 298
32:1–35 . . . 232
32:10 . . . 226, 231
32:11 . . . 226
32:32 . . . 226, 228
33:12 . . . 480
34:28 . . . 298

Deuterononomy

32 . . . 80

2 Samuel

14:14 . . . 422

Tobit

10 . . . 427
10:5 . . . 72
13:4 . . . 256
19 . . . 426

Job

33 . . . 352

Psalms

2:7 . . . 357, 360
4:2ff. . . . 514
8:2ff. . . . 102
8:3–9 . . . 105
8:5, 6 . . . 519
16:2 . . . 115, 121,
    153
16:9–11 . . . 121
32 . . . 424
32:9 . . . 424
34:8 . . . 543
36:9 . . . 455
46:4 . . . 363
46:4–7 . . . 370
47:8f. . . . 519
55:6 . . . 240
55:6–9 . . . 246
62:11 . . . 66
68:4 . . . 58
72:7 . . . 439
80:1 . . . 382
84 . . . 424, 437
84:9 . . . 301
84:10 . . . 240
85:10 . . . 436

104:29–30 . . . 300
110:1–3 . . . 360
110:3 . . . 153, 357
119 . . . 241, 532,
    538
119:72 . . . 532
119:72–74 . . . 538
119:77 . . . 538
119:91 . . . 535, 539

Proverbs

1:16 . . . 253
8:22–25 . . . 220
8:30f. . . . 220
18:4 . . . 370
21 . . . 423, 434
21:1–3 . . . 434
21:15 . . . 434
21:21 . . . 434
25:4 . . . 514

Ecclesiastes

1:7 . . . 270
10 . . . 424

Song of Songs

1:5 . . . 514
5:2 . . . 67
5:6 . . . 300
8:6 . . . 244

Wisdom

1 . . . 424
1:7 . . . 114, 121

1:13–15 . . . 121
1:14 . . . 112
2:27 . . . 112
5 . . . 427
5:13 . . . 422
5:15–17 . . . 470
5:16 . . . 464
5:18 . . . 470
7:11 . . . 152
7:27 . . . 112
10:10 . . . 141
10:10f. . . . 145
11:23 . . . 319
18:13 . . . 311
18:14 . . . 293, 299
18:14f. . . . 306
18:15 . . . 299
18:18 . . . 350

Ecclesiasticus (Sirach)

1:4–10 . . . 269
11:27 . . . 233
14:5 . . . 423
24:3–16 . . . 384
24:9 . . . 466, 469
24:9–11 . . . 542
24:11 . . . 380, 482
24:12 . . . 380
24:15 . . . 380
24:16 . . . 153
24:17 . . . 469
24:17ff. . . . 536, 542
24:19 . . . 469
24:20 . . . 469
30 . . . 423
45:2 . . . 68, 236

Isaiah

9 . . . 418
9:3 . . . 419
32:18 . . . 427
40:10 . . . 328
42:14 . . . 101
44:6 . . . 112
45:15 . . . 153, 169,
    174
45:18–19 . . . 174
49:8 . . . 154
49:10 . . . 154, 156
49:13 . . . 151
49:13–15 . . . 154
55:1 . . . 370
55:3 . . . 370
58 . . . 420, 422, 423,
    431
58:3–11 . . . 432
58:8 . . . 434
61 . . . 420
62:1 . . . 465
62:1f. . . . 470
62:3 . . . 470
62:4 . . . 470
62:6f. . . . 470
64 . . . 427

Jeremiah

1:4–7 . . . 64
1:9 . . . 57
1:9f. . . . 64
5:14 . . . 64
23:29 . . . 64

Lamentations

1 . . . 417

Baruch

3:20f. . . . 270
3:23 . . . 270

Ezekiel

12:13 . . . 138, 146
17:3–4 . . . 518

Hosea

2:10 . . . 529
2:11 . . . 529
2:14 . . . 529
2:16 . . . 240, 246,
    382, 518, 529
2:17 . . . 529
2:20ff. . . . 530
2:23ff. . . . 530
5:1 . . . 525
7:12 . . . 138
10:2 . . . 535
14:4 . . . 440, 443
14:5–7 . . . 444
14:9f. . . . 444

Micah

3:1–4 . . . 525

Zechariah

2:8 . . . 229

2. NEW TESTAMENT

Matthew

2:1f. . . . 259
2:2 . . . 251
5:3 . . . 152, 157,
    161, 213
5:8 . . . 189, 195
5:11 . . . 82
5:11f. . . . 87
6 . . . 499, 500
6:1–4 . . . 433
6:3 . . . 425

6:10 . . . 227, 317,
    398
6:23 . . . 425
7:7–11 . . . 157
7:15–18 . . . 521
7:16 . . . 332
7:17 . . . 511
7:18 . . . 511
10:22 . . . 82, 87
10:28 . . . 75
10:28–31 . . . 80
10:34–36 . . . 255

10:37–39 . . . 261
10:37–38 . . . 301
11:11 . . . 340, 344,
    351
11:29 . . . 344
13:24ff. . . . 511
13:24–30 . . . 520
13:44 . . . 412, 513
16:17 . . . 482
16:24 . . . 300, 329
19 . . . 300, 420
19:28 . . . 148, 544

19:29 . . . 205, 300
20:1–8 . . . 281
21:12 . . . 450
21:12–17 . . . 456
21:28–31 . . . 281
21:33–41 . . . 281
22:1–14 . . . 544
22:32 . . . 426
22:39 . . . 399
25 . . . 423, 427
25:14–30 . . . 171
25:31–46 . . . 157, 432
26:37–39 . . . 349
26:38 . . . 342, 484, 493

Mark

8:34 . . . 329
9:43–47 . . . 142
10:15 . . . 147
10:17 . . . 142
10:18 . . . 426
10:24 . . . 142
10:25 . . . 142
10:29 . . . 300
12 . . . 534
12:31 . . . 399, 411
14:34 . . . 342
22:39 . . . 411

Luke

1 . . . 418
1:35 . . . 409
2:42 . . . 238
2:42–46 . . . 238
6:27 . . . 429
6:28 . . . 315
6:35–38 . . . 429
6:36 . . . 436
6:36–42 . . . 417
6:37 . . . 448
7:11–16 . . . 130
7:12ff. . . . 126
7:14 . . . 126
7:16 . . . 136
7:36, 50 . . . 440
7:36–50 . . . 448
7:50 . . . 440
8:11 . . . 511, 520
8:15 . . . 520

8:21 . . . 93
8:52–55 . . . 132
8:54 . . . 266
8:54f. . . . 267
8:56 . . . 136
10:23–37 . . . 531
10:25–30 . . . 537
10:27 . . . 67, 74
10:33ff. . . . 537
10:38 . . . 273, 478
10:38–40 . . . 478
10:38–42 . . . 279, 492
11:17 . . . 535
11:27 . . . 338
11:27f. . . . 338, 345
11:28 . . . 71, 339
12:36 . . . 136
14:7–11 . . . 192
14:10 . . . 188, 190
14:25–27 . . . 171
14:27 . . . 166
17:20f. . . . 142
18:19 . . . 426
19:11f. . . . 521
19:11–26 . . . 171
19:11–27 . . . 521
19:12 . . . 166, 510
20:29 . . . 148, 544
21:29–31 . . . 142
21:31 . . . 137

John

1:1 . . . 128, 465
1:5 . . . 169, 175, 252, 301, 307, 514
1:11 . . . 301
1:12 . . . 301
1:50 . . . 480
2:13–16, 18–21 . . . 456
2:16 . . . 450
3:1–21 . . . 248
3:8 . . . 242
3:9 . . . 512
3:13 . . . 202
4:1–41 . . . 371
4:1–42 . . . 248
4:4 . . . 66
4:5ff. . . . 239

4:14 . . . 372
4:42 . . . 239
7:16 . . . 228
7:16–19 . . . 230
7:18 . . . 237
7:37–39 . . . 370
7:38 . . . 363
7:39 . . . 372
8:12 . . . 151, 152, 153, 158
8:54 . . . 344
9 . . . 159
10 . . . 422
10:10 . . . 320
10:30 . . . 435
12:23–28 . . . 349
12:24 . . . 339
12:26 . . . 300
12:35 . . . 481
12:35f. . . . 487
13:33–35 . . . 98
13:34f. . . . 91
14:6 . . . 482
14:8 . . . 316
14:10 . . . 320
15 . . . 359
15:1–13 . . . 281
15:5 . . . 451
15:12 . . . 313
15:15 . . . 313, 316, 356, 359
15:16 . . . 281, 313, 317, 407
16:7 . . . 350
16:16 . . . 333
16:20–22 . . . 333
16:22 . . . 325, 329
16:33 . . . 440, 445
17 . . . 346
17:3 . . . 517, 528
17:21–23 . . . 528
20:11ff. . . . 358
21:15 . . . 315

Acts

1:1–5 . . . 361
1:4 . . . 354
9 . . . 263
9:3 . . . 252
9:8 . . . 194
17:28 . . . 72

Romans

6:23 . . . 112
7:23 . . . 511
7:24 . . . 511
8 . . . 427
8:8–18 . . . 324
8:14–17 . . . 323, 403
8:14–29 . . . 26
8:17 . . . 323, 401
8:18 . . . 423
8:18–23 . . . 324
8:19 . . . 476
8:22 . . . 403, 476
8:23 . . . 403
8:28f. . . . 324
8:29 . . . 469
8:29ff. . . . 466
8:38f. . . . 307
8:38–39 . . . 300, 307
9:1–4 . . . 222
11:36 . . . 72
13:11 . . . 110, 137,
     143
13:12 . . . 110
13:14 . . . 102, 110

1 Corinthians

2 . . . 427
2:9 . . . 439
3:22 . . . 533, 541
4:7 . . . 367, 378
11:4ff. . . . 514
12:4–11 . . . 475
12:12ff. . . . 543
12:27 . . . 543
13:10 . . . 426
13:12 . . . 394
15:10 . . . 217, 290
15:28 . . . 329

2 Corinthians

3:18 . . . 305, 352
5:17–19 . . . 186

8 . . . 418
9 . . . 424
11:2 . . . 515
12:2 . . . 298
12:2–5 . . . 482
13:11 . . . 25

Galatians

2:20 . . . 290
3:28 . . . 181
4 . . . 424
4:1–7 . . . 403
4:4 . . . 104, 401
4:4–7 . . . 111
5:17ff. . . . 511
6:8 . . . 511

Ephesians

1:3–5 . . . 469
1:4 . . . 466
2:15 . . . 181
3 . . . 425, 427
4:1–6 . . . 193
4:4–10 . . . 188
4:6 . . . 188
4:17–24 . . . 181
4:23 . . . 177
5:8–11 . . . 488
5:16 . . . 481, 488
5:18 . . . 488
5:20 . . . 488

Colossians

1:15 . . . 347
3:10f. . . . 71

1 Timothy

6:16 . . . 358

2 Timothy

4:2 . . . 65, 74
4:5 . . . 74

Hebrews

1:3 . . . 275
11:32f. . . . 88
11:34–38 . . . 88
11:37 . . . 83
12:1 . . . 88
12:4 . . . 88
13:7–9 . . . 377
13:9 . . . 367, 417

James

1:16–18 . . . 402
1:17 . . . 397
1:21–27 . . . 411

1 Peter

5 . . . 427

2 Peter

1:3f. . . . 520
1:4 . . . 511

1 John

3:1 . . . 311, 321,
     325
3:1f. . . . 26, 331
3:2 . . . 326, 332
3:9 . . . 520
4:7–10 . . . 203
4:9 . . . 199
4:16 . . . 315, 330,
     388, 441
4:16f. . . . 321, 446
5:4 . . . 440, 445

Revelation

1:8 . . . 471
21:5 . . . 112
22:13 . . . 514, 536

INDEX TO SPIRITUALITY THEMES

All italicized page numbers refer to the texts of Meister Eckhart's Sermons.

Abgeschiedenheit. See Letting go.
Artist, art, and spirituality, *4–7, 9, 15–16, 29–30, 31–32, 46–49,* 135–36, 206, *285–88, 291–92, 397, 402–13, 416, 513–14.* See also Beauty, Birthing, Creativity, Image of God.
Asceticism. See Methods of spiritual discipline.

Beauty, 40, *79–82, 95–101,* 117–25, 160, 165, *190–92,* 192, *195–98,* 317, 332–33, *383–86, 402–12, 415–16, 427–28, 428–39, 456–63, 541–45.* See also Artist.
Being, 18, *27–28, 30, 44–46, 76, 83–86, 86–90, 91–94, 96–101, 105–13,* 121–25, *140, 149–50, 152–53, 158–60,* 168, 170, *171–76, 177–79, 183–85, 194–98, 209–12, 214–18, 230–31, 234–37, 246–49, 251–54, 259–64, 269, 294–99, 304–12, 315, 318–22, 325–30, 330, 332–35, 340–41, 346–53, 355–58, 359–62, 389–91, 395–96, 399–401, 406–12, 442, 453–55, 460–63, 466–67, 472–77, 481–83, 488–91, 504–9, 516–18, 527–30, 533–37, 538–45.*
Birthing; of self, *10, 28, 32, 46–48, 66–67, 109–13, 172–73, 217–18, 219–25, 238–43, 247–48, 251–57, 258–61, 273–78, 281–90, 291–92, 293–301, 302–12, 316–17, 317–24, 329–30, 330–37, 346–53, 356–58, 358–62, 371–74, 401, 402–13, 415–16, 428–39, 443–49, 464–67, 467–77, 489–94, 511–18, 518–29.*
of God, *10, 32, 45–48, 66–67, 95–96, 101, 103, 106–7, 111–12, 114–16, 169, 238–43, 247–48, 251–57, 258–61, 273–78, 281–90, 291–92, 293–301, 302–12, 316–17, 317–24, 329–30, 330–37, 346–53, 356–58, 358–62, 371–74, 386–87, 401, 402–13, 415–16, 428–39, 443–49, 464–67, 467–77, 511–18, 518–29.* See also Artist, Creativity, Image of God.
Blessing, *4–7, 24, 32, 44–45, 48–49, 55–56, 98–99,* 141, *147–50, 151–53,* 154, *161–63,* 165, 191, 192, *195–98, 199–202, 220–21, 232–36,* 241, 245, *286–88, 291–92, 311–12, 313–17, 317–22, 366–68, 369–79, 402–13, 415–16, 421–28, 428–39,* 443, *464–67,* 471, *478–86, 516–18, 533–34, 541–45.* See also Soul.
Body and spirituality, *4–7, 26–28, 34, 40–41, 42–43, 75, 86,* 116–17, 117, 122–24, 126–28, *178, 185–86, 241–42, 243–45, 249–50, 254–55, 266–67, 287, 297–98, 326–27, 341–44, 348, 365–68, 378, 390–91, 393–94, 419–28, 436–39, 440–41, 496–501, 510–12, 533, 539–45.* See also Earthiness, Passion, Sensuality.

Breakthrough, 10, 28, 46–49, 88, 133–36, 218, 224–25, 291–92, 293–301,
302–12, 323–24, 329–30, 330–37, 346–53, 355–58, 361–62, 371–74,
383–84, 385–87, 395–96, 415–16, 431–39, 441–42, 443–49, 464–67,
467–77, 479–86, 489–94, 522–29, 541–45. See also New creation.

Celebration, 5–7, 32, 45, 47–49, 116, 121, 136, 148–50, 155–63, 254, 312,
390–91, 391–92, 393–94, 410–13, 416, 428, 437–39, 529–30, 533–37,
537–45. See also Joy.
Children of God, 26, 45–48, 66–67, 110–11, 188–89, 205, 220, 257,
286–88, 291–92, 301, 302–12, 317–24, 325–30, 330–37, 340–41,
356–43, 358–61, 371–72, 402–13, 416, 428–36, 443–46, 455–56,
468–76, 487–88, 495–503, 503–9, 512–18, 518–29.
Christ, Christology, 4, 6–7, 47–49, 92, 98, 102–5, 109–11, 128–29, 129–36,
137, 141–50, 158–59, 166–68, 181–82, 186–87, 199–200, 202, 213,
219–24, 227–29, 230, 236–37, 238–42, 255–56, 258, 267–68, 273–78,
278–90, 297–301, 303–12, 313–17, 320–24, 325–30, 331–35, 338–45,
345–53, 354–58, 358–62, 369–79, 381–82, 390–91, 391–96, 402–12,
416, 417–25, 428, 432–36, 440, 444–49, 450–55, 455–63, 469, 478–86,
493, 496–502, 503–9, 510–18, 520–27, 531, 537–45.
as Son of God, 47–48, 104–5, 227–29, 296–301, 302–12, 316–17,
317–24, 330, 330–37, 340–42, 346–53, 435–36, 465–67, 468–77,
495–96, 502, 503–4, 510–14, 522.
as Son of Justice, 350–51, 435, 436, 468–69.
as Reminder, 26, 47–48, 350–53, 358–62, 375–76, 522, 541.
as Word, 26, 43, 47, 104–5, 129–31, 293–301, 306–12, 330–37, 338–41,
345–53, 454–55, 457, 464–66, 468–71, 511, 520–22. See also God,
Word.
Compassion, 4–7, 10, 24–25, 30, 40, 42, 44–49, 130, 249–50, 350–51,
415–16, 417–28, 428–39, 440–42, 442–49, 457–63, 467–77, 486–94,
495, 501–3, 503–9, 522–30, 531–37, 537–45. See also Justice, Love.
Cosmic consciousness, 3, 28–30, 40, 44–49, 70–74, 81–82, 86–90, 94–101,
117, 124–25, 129–30, 145–50, 161–63, 191–92, 195–98, 228–30,
236–37, 259–60, 282–90, 325–30, 332–35, 358, 361–62, 375–79,
380–83, 385–87, 390–91, 392–96, 409–13, 416, 430–39, 442–49,
460–63, 474–75, 481–84, 488–94, 495–503, 504–9, 514–18, 527–30,
534–37, 537–45. See also Being, Creation.
Creation, 4–7, 10, 24–29, 30–35, 40–49, 55–56, 57–60, 60–64, 65–67,
70–74, 75–77, 78–82, 84–86, 88–90, 91–92, 94–101, 102–3, 105–13,
114–17, 138–40, 141–50, 151–53, 154–62, 165, 166–69, 170–76,
182–86, 188–92, 193–98, 201–2, 203–12, 214–18, 219–25, 239–43,
245, 246–49, 251–57, 258–65, 281–90, 291–92, 294–301, 302–12,
317–24, 329–30, 330–37, 346–53, 356–58, 361–62, 365–68, 369–79,
380–83, 383–86, 388–91, 392–94, 399–400, 402–13, 415–16, 420–28,
429–39, 440–42, 442–49, 450–55, 455–63, 466–67, 469–77, 478–85,
493–94, 495–501, 503–9, 510–18, 518–30, 534–37, 538–45. See also
New creation.
Creativity, 4–7, 28–30, 31–35, 40, 42, 43–49, 65–66, 71–74, 75–77, 105–13,
184–87, 292, 298, 378, 387, 397–401, 402–13, 432–34, 443–49,
456–63, 467–77, 488–94, 519–30, 541–44. See also Artist, Birthing,
Image of God.
Creator, 5, 45–47, 65–67, 69–74, 75–76, 78–81, 119, 136, 148–50,
155–63, 174–75, 232, 269–72, 305–12, 317–24, 380–83, 383–87,

397–401, 402–13, 417–28, 428–39, 444–49, 450–55, 455–61, 469–77, 493–94, 503–9, 518–30, 539–45. See also God, Panentheism.

Darkness, 126, 131–33, 153, 159–61, 165, 169, 170–76, 180–86, 197, 210–12, 239–41, 245–50, 252–54, 263–64, 270, 298–301, 306–11, 421, 451, 455, 480–82, 487–88.
Death, 6, 83–86, 86–90, 126–27, 129–36, 172–73, 244–45, 267–72, 334, 342–43, 348–53, 356–58, 360–62, 421–26, 464–67, 471–75, 534–36, 538–39. See also Letting go.
Detachment. See Letting be, Letting go.
Dialectical consciousness, 4–7, 15, 30, 40–43, 46–49, 61–64, 65–69, 69–74, 76–77, 78–82, 99–101, 102–4, 124–25, 162–63, 165, 166–69, 171–76, 183–86, 189–90, 192–98, 210–12, 220–25, 246–50, 261–64, 290, 292, 352–53, 377–79, 385–87, 404–13, 436–38, 468–77, 481–84, 490–94, 531–37, 537–45.
Divinization, 26, 30, 34, 40, 42, 45–49, 66–67, 69–71, 75, 81–82, 103–5, 105–13, 117–25, 167–69, 173–75, 179–80, 183–86, 203–12, 218, 219–25, 268–72, 281–90, 291–92, 293–301, 302–12, 313–17, 317–24, 325–30, 330–37, 340–45, 345–53, 354, 356–58, 358–62, 363, 367–68, 369–79, 380–83, 383–87, 388, 390–91, 391, 393–96, 401, 403–7, 416, 420–28, 428–39, 443–49, 450–55, 455–63, 464–67, 467–77, 510–18, 518–30, 543–45. See also Children of God, Image of God.
Dualism, 5–7, 8, 31, 34, 40–41, 44–45, 46–47, 71–74, 90, 122–24, 185–87, 195–98, 204, 249–50, 269, 271–72, 306, 315, 317–18, 346–47, 362, 436–38, 445–46, 455, 458–63, 474–75, 481–84, 486–93, 507–9, 527–28, 534–37, 538–45. See also Sin.

Earthiness, 6, 30–32, 40, 44–45, 77, 84–86, 88–89, 99–101, 114–17, 117–25, 131–32, 141–42, 143–44, 148, 201, 207–8, 242–44, 266–67, 281–83, 291–92, 304–5, 316–17, 322–23, 339–44, 348–53, 361–62, 363–68, 369–79, 381–83, 385–87, 405–6, 420–22, 440–42, 444–48, 464–65, 510–18, 519–30, 533–34, 540–41, 543–45. See also Body, Sensuality.
Ecstacy. See Breakthrough.
Eschatology. See Realized eschatology.
Evil, 28, 40, 42, 47, 197, 227, 232–37, 244–45, 249–50, 252, 264, 285, 343, 420–26, 434–36, 460–63, 480–82, 487–88, 497–503, 506–9, 510–16, 527–28, 543. See also Dualism, Sin.

Freedom, 82, 160, 166–67, 195–96, 202, 203–12, 215–17, 219–25, 232–37, 255, 261, 267, 268–72, 273–78, 283–90, 323–24, 333, 338–39, 349–51, 355–56, 361–62, 366–67, 376, 451–55, 455–63, 475–77, 481–83, 502–3.

Gelassenheit. See Letting be.
God, 6, 15, 42–48, 57–60, 60–64, 66–69, 69–74, 75–77, 78–82, 83–86, 88–90, 91–94, 94–101, 102–5, 105–13, 114–17, 117–25, 126–29, 129–36, 137–41, 141–50, 151–53, 154–63, 165, 166–69, 170–76, 177–80, 180–87, 188–92, 192–98, 199–202, 203–12, 213–18, 219–25, 226–30, 230–37, 238–45, 245–50, 251–57, 258–65, 266–67, 268–72, 273–78, 279–90, 291–92, 293–301, 302–12, 313–17, 317–24, 325–30, 330–37, 338–45, 345–53, 354–58, 358–62, 363–68, 369–79, 380–83, 383–87,

388–91, 391–96, 397–401, 402–13, 415–16, 417–28, 428–39, 440–42, 442–49, 450–55, 455–63, 464–67, 467–77, 478–86, 486–94, 495–503, 503–9, 510–18, 518–30, 531–37, 537–45.

as Father, 57–60, 66–67, 71–74, 92–94, 101, 114–15, 127–28, 133–36, 153, 155, 160–61, 169, 177–80, 184–87, 188–90, 199–202, 227–29, 252–54, 268–71, 273–78, 279–90, 293–301, 302–12, 313–17, 317–24, 325–30, 330–37, 338–44, 346–53, 354–57, 358–61, 365, 371–76, 381–82, 387, 389–91, 391–96, 397–401, 402–13, 417–28, 428–39, 452–55, 456–63, 465–67, 468–77, 482–85, 495–503, 503–9, 512–14, 526–30, 543–45.

as Son, 33, 57–60, 66–67, 92–94, 95, 104–5, 110–12, 114–15, 127–28, 155, 179–80, 199–202, 203, 227–29, 248, 277–78, 296–301, 302–12, 316–17, 317–24, 330, 330–37, 340–42, 346–53, 356–57, 358–61, 365, 370–76, 381, 387, 389–91, 391–96, 400–1, 402–13, 435–36, 454–55, 465–67, 468–77, 482–83, 495–96, 502, 503–4, 510–14, 522.

as Holy Spirit, 47, 59–60, 94, 103, 106–8, 110–11, 114–17, 121, 145, 155, 166–69, 170, 179–80, 202, 207, 228, 248, 266–67, 267–72, 277–78, 304–5, 313–17, 317–24, 327–30, 332–34, 341–42, 346–53, 354–58, 359–62, 363–65, 369–79, 381, 383–87, 389, 391–96, 401, 402–12, 454–55, 456–60, 466–67, 476–77, 482–86, 517, 531–34, 539–41.

as Trinity, 46, 75–76, 93–94, 104, 114–15, 155, 160–61, 177, 179–80, 277–78, 316–17, 320–23, 342, 352–53, 365, 372–76, 380–81, 383–84, 389–91, 392–96, 476–77, 482–83.

as Word, 26, 43–44, 47, 57–60, 60–64, 104–5, 127–28, 129–31, 169, 251–56, 259–61, 275–78, 284–90, 293–301, 306–12, 316–17, 319–23, 330–37, 338–41, 345–53, 359–60, 370, 392–94, 404–12, 416, 418–19, 432–33, 454–55, 457, 464–66, 468–71, 480–85, 492–94, 510–11, 520–22.

as non-God, 45–46, 159–62, 175–76, 178–80, 180–87, 194–98. See also Christ, Creator, Darkness, Godhead, Panentheism, Spirit.

Godhead, 36, 45, 76–77, 78–80, 153, 160–61, 169, 173–75, 189–92, 193–98, 219–25, 228, 236–37, 270–72, 284–90, 302–12, 320–23, 328, 330–33, 340–41, 346–53, 357–58, 359–62, 371–76, 392–96, 468–77.

Grace, 30–34, 40, 42, 43–45, 91–94, 94–101, 104, 156, 172–73, 190–92, 193–98, 217, 222–23, 241–42, 289–90, 311–12, 320, 326–27, 333–37, 344–45, 365–68, 369–79, 383, 390–91, 395–96, 398–99, 415–16, 417–22, 442, 443–44, 459–60, 484–85, 506–9, 541–45. See also Creation.

Humor, 23, 48–49, 82, 155–61, 345–46.

Image of God, 40, 45–48, 71–73, 75–77, 79, 91–94, 102–5, 105–13, 116–17, 117–25, 162–63, 177–80, 181–87, 194–96, 201–2, 219–25, 251–56, 259–63, 268–72, 273–78, 283–90, 293–301, 305–12, 324, 325–30, 331–33, 346–53, 367–68, 369, 374–79, 380–83, 383–87, 388–91, 391–96, 401, 404–13, 421–28, 432–37, 444–48, 450–55, 455–63, 466–67, 474–77, 504–9, 510–18, 518–30, 533. See also Artist, Children of God, Creation, Creativity.

Jesus Christ. See Christ.
Joy, 28, 44–45, 48–49, 50–52, 76, 81–82, 91–94, 95–96, 121, 124, 133,

140, 146–50, 151–53, 154–63, 165, 218, 219–25, 227–29, 232–36,
247–50, 251–57, 275–78, 281–90, 296–97, 303–12, 313–17, 318–19,
325–30, 333–37, 366–67, 375–76, 381, 383–86, 388–91, 393–94, 399,
408–12, 418–28, 437–39, 464–67, 467–71, 478–86, 487–94, 496–99,
512–17, 525–30, 531–37, 537–45. See also Celebration, Realized
eschatology.
Justice, 4–7, 10, 28, 31–32, 40, 47–49, 104–5, 155, 350–51, 356, 415–16,
420–26, 428–39, 464–67, 467–77, 486–87, 505–9, 524–30, 542–45.
See also Compassion.

Kingdom of God, 44–45, 137–40, 141–50, 259, 281–89, 410–12, 416,
486–87, 495–503, 503–9, 510–18, 518–30, 541–45. See also Royal
person.

Letting be, 2–3, 10, 45–48, 165, 199, 201–2, 207–12, 213, 219, 220–25,
245–48, 264–65, 267–72, 273–78, 278–90, 291–92, 308–10, 333, 336,
348–52, 376–79, 385–87, 430–31, 446–48, 457–60, 491–93, 506–8.
Letting go, 3, 10, 23, 29, 45–49, 51, 68, 94, 165, 180, 183–87, 197–98,
204–9, 213, 218–19, 220–25, 226–30, 230–37, 238–44, 245–48,
258–65, 266–67, 267–72, 273–78, 278–90, 291–92, 308–10, 313–17,
333, 336, 348–52, 376–79, 385–87, 415, 430–31, 446–48, 457–60,
490–93, 506–8.
Love, 67–68, 74, 76, 90, 91–94, 94–101, 107–8, 114, 133–34, 152–53,
155–58, 170, 179–80, 188–92, 197–98, 199, 203–12, 215–17, 226–30,
233–37, 244–45, 249–50, 255–57, 266–67, 267–69, 280–88, 311–12,
313–17, 317–24, 325–30, 331–32, 338–39, 355–56, 361, 372–79,
380–81, 386, 388–90, 391–95, 398, 406–12, 425–28, 429–39, 441–42,
443–48, 466–67, 471–77, 478–85, 488–89, 495–503, 503–9, 511–14,
522–30, 531–37, 537–45. See also Compassion, Justice.

Mary, Mariology, 68, 93, 101, 199, 227–28, 236, 263, 278–85, 326–27,
335–37, 338–41, 345–51, 400, 409, 417.
Methods in spiritual discipline, 5–7, 32, 42–43, 45–46, 170–71, 196–98,
201, 205–10, 214–17, 220–24, 240–41, 243–45, 245, 247–50, 274–75,
285–87, 297–98, 376–78, 381, 385, 410, 431, 450–51, 458–59.

Nature. See Body, Creation, Earthiness, Grace, Sensuality.
New creation, 61–64, 70–74, 110–13, 181–87, 224–25, 259–65, 271–72,
323–24, 386–87, 411–12, 415–16, 456–63, 467–68, 474–77, 486–88,
529–30. See also Compassion, Justice.
Nothingness, 18, 29, 30, 34, 36, 45, 139–40, 167, 178–80, 183–84, 188–90,
192–98, 200–2, 203–12, 213–17, 219–25, 231–32, 238–42, 245–50,
258–63, 270–71, 308–9, 328–30, 333, 358, 399–400, 453–54, 457–58,
464–65, 515, 527–28, 538–40. See also Darkness.
Now moment, 65–66, 71, 104–5, 105–6, 110–13, 133, 136, 211–12,
217–18, 241–44, 245–46, 255, 258–59, 275–78, 288–90, 298, 303–12,
334–37, 357–58, 360, 453, 466–67, 468–71, 501, 508–9.

Oneness. See Compassion, Cosmic consciousness, Dialectical consciousness.
Origins, 31–33, 61–64, 69–74, 77, 78–80, 85, 88–90, 99–101, 102–4,
105–13, 120–25, 140, 160–62, 166–69, 188–92, 195–98, 199–202,
203–12, 214–18, 219–25, 238–44, 245–49, 263–64, 266–67, 267–72,

284–90, 295–301, 302–12, 316–17, 330, 331–33, 350–53, 354–55, 358–59, 360–62, 364–68, 371–79, 380–83, 384–87, 388–91, 391–96, 411–13, 416, 426–28, 430–39, 440–42, 443–49, 450–55, 456–63, 471–77, 482–83, 490–94, 501, 504–9, 516–18, 527–30, 536–37, 541–43. See also Compassion, Repose.

Panentheism, 30, 44–48, 66–69, 69–74, 79–82, 89–90, 94–101, 134–36, 137–40, 141–50, 160–63, 183–87, 188–92, 192–98, 201–2, 206–12, 214–18, 219–25, 234–37, 241–43, 246–49, 251–57, 259–65, 280–90, 299–301, 303–12, 315–17, 319–24, 325–30, 330–37, 340–41, 346–53, 355–58, 358–62, 369–79, 380–83, 383–87, 388–91, 391–96, 399–401, 402–13, 416, 426–27, 430–39, 440–42, 442–49, 450–55, 460–63, 464–67, 467–77, 482–83, 490–94, 495–96, 504–9, 516–18, 527–30, 533–37, 537–45. See also God, Transparency.
Passion, 4–7, 159, 266–67, 267–69, 377–79, 423–28, 428, 436–39, 485–86, 486–87, 492–94, 507–8. See also Body, Compassion, Sensuality.
Poverty, 33, 151–52, 157, 199, 213–18, 219–22, 232, 302–4, 339–45, 349–51, 397, 433–34, 495–503, 503–4, 506–9.
Prayer, 34, 42, 205–9, 215–18, 219, 221–22, 229–30, 231, 241, 243–45, 247–50, 274–75, 283, 285–87, 314–15, 389, 459–60, 486–93, 495–503, 503–9. See also Methods in spiritual discipline.
Prophecy. See Justice.
Purity. See Origins.

Realized eschatology, 30, 40, 44–49, 88–90, 104–5, 110–13, 132–36, 138–40, 141–50, 203–12, 281–90, 308–10, 326–30, 330–37, 351–53, 379, 417–28, 438–39, 466–67, 468–71, 486–88, 501, 508–9, 512–18, 527–30, 541–45.
Redemption. See Salvation.
Remembering, 154, 267–72. See also Christ as Reminder, Salvation.
Repose, 191, 241, 380–83, 383–87, 541–44. See also Origins.
Resurrection. See Breakthrough, New creation.
Royal person, 26, 47–49, 106, 137–40, 141–50, 199, 230, 236–37, 281–90, 293–301, 350, 360, 365–67, 376, 434–36, 450–55, 469–71, 507–9, 510–18, 518–30. See also Divinization, Kingdom of God.

Salvation, 32–34, 110, 147–50, 170–71, 256, 271–72, 349–50, 358–62, 410–13, 421–28, 428–39, 497–503. See also Compassion, Remembering.
Sensuality, 76–77, 86, 95–96, 116–17, 122–26, 127, 162–63, 185–86, 238–39, 243–45, 245, 249–50, 254–55, 293–301, 326–27, 342–43, 380–83, 384, 424–28, 436–39, 485–86, 486–87, 492–94. See also Body, Earthiness, Passion.
Sin, 28, 34, 40, 42, 88–90, 147, 178–79, 182–83, 252–53, 264, 301, 417–27, 430–31, 460–63, 464–65, 495–503, 527–28, 538–40. See also Dualism, Evil.
Social justice. See Justice.
Son of God. See Children of God, Christ, God.
Soul, 15, 27–28, 34, 40, 42, 45, 59, 65–67, 70, 75–77, 79, 83–86, 91–94, 102–5, 105–13, 115–17, 117–25, 126–29, 132–36, 138–40, 153–54, 155–63, 169, 172–76, 178–80, 183–86, 188–92, 192, 194–98, 215–17, 225, 237, 238–45, 245–50, 251–57, 258–65, 266–67, 267–72, 273–78, 281–89, 293–301, 303–12, 318–23, 325–27, 334–37, 341–44, 348–53,

354–58, 363–68, 369–79, 380–83, 383–86, 388–91, 391–96, 399–401,
402 .2, 415–16, 419–28, 428–39, 440–42, 443–44, 450–55, 455–63,
465–67, 470–75, 478–85, 493–94, 496–97, 510–18, 528–29, 535–37,
544–45. See also Spark.
Space, 66, 71–74, 114–17, 127–28, 133, 137–40, 141–50, 216–18, 219–25,
258–60, 312, 357–58, 363–67, 368–72, 401, 402–4, 441–42, 445–46,
455–63, 515, 533–34, 540.
Spark, 26, 108–13, 162–63, 225, 277, 288–89, 312, 325–27, 365–67, 369–77,
534. See also Soul.
Spirit, 75, 80–81, 108–13, 116–17, 119–25, 162–63, 177–80, 183–86, 201,
207, 213–18, 219–25, 241–45, 247–49, 260, 266–67, 267–69, 273–78,
282–88, 297–98, 302–3, 323–24, 327–30, 332–34, 340–43, 346–53,
354–57, 360–62, 363–67, 370–79, 388–91, 391–96, 453–55, 466–67,
478–85, 487–91, 496–99, 510–17. See also Body and spirituality. For
Holy Spirit see God.

Time, 65–67, 71, 86, 88–90, 103–5, 110–13, 114–17, 127–28, 133, 136,
139–40, 143–50, 179–80, 217–18, 219–25, 258–59, 275–78, 288–90,
293–94, 296, 305–12, 326–27, 330–37, 354–58, 360, 401, 402–4,
452–55, 466–67, 468–71, 480–84, 501, 508–9, 515. See also Now
moment, Realized eschatology.
Transparency, 44–45, 194, 208–12, 220–21, 233–34, 269, 288–90, 347–53,
355–58, 361–62, 391–96, 491–92. See also Cosmic consciousness,
Panentheism.
Trinity. See God.

Via negativa, 34, 45, 78, 159–61, 165, 170–76, 178–80, 180–87, 189–90,
193–98, 223–25, 238–45, 245–50, 260–64, 267–68, 283–90, 292,
308–9, 327–30, 333, 412–13. See also Darkness, Nothingness.
Via positiva, 43–44, 45, 58–62, 165, 170–76, 182, 197–98, 267–68, 292,
412–13. See also Being, Creation.
Void. See Freedom, Nothingness.

Women, 16, 28, 31, 35–41, 42, 93, 96, 101, 132, 273–77, 278–85, 315,
318, 325, 330, 333–37, 338–44, 371, 419, 428, 446, 478–86,
488–93, 503–9, 512–15, 526–27.
Word, 26, 43–44, 47, 57–60, 60–64, 65–66, 70–74, 80, 88, 104–5, 109,
118, 127–28, 129–31, 169, 240–41, 251–56, 259–60, 275–78, 284–90,
293–301, 306–12, 316–17, 318–23, 330–37, 338–41, 345–53, 359–60,
371, 393–94, 404–13, 416, 417–18, 432–33, 454–55, 447, 464–66,
468–71, 480–85, 492–94, 511, 520–22. See also Christ, Creation, God,
Image of God.
Work, 46 47, 61–64, 205–9, 216–17, 222–23, 237, 240–41, 268, 283–90,
387, 394–96, 404–13, 416, 433–34, 443–49, 464–67, 467–77, 478–86,
486–94, 503, 537, 543–44. See also Birthing, Creativity.

CROSS REFERENCES TO SERMONS TRANSLATED IN THIS VOLUME
including German Works, Latin Works, and English translations

The full reference for each abbreviation is given on p. 546. Numbers refer to sermon numbers in the respective editions. Where such a number is lacking the page number [abbreviated "p."] of the opening of that sermon or treatise is given.

FOX	DW	LW	Q	BL	CL	SK	SH
1	II, 53	—	—	—	—	—	—
2	II, 30	—	43	—	—	p. 58	p.181
3	—	—	26	27	XII	—	—
4	I, 8	—	9	16	XV	—	—
5	III, 75	—	—	—	—	—	—
6	I, 24	—	—	—	—	—	—
7	II, 47	—	—	—	—	—	—
8	II, 42	—	39	7	—	—	—
9	III, 68	—	36	6	—	—	—
10	III, 79	—	41	10	—	—	—
11	I, 15	—	—	—	—	—	—
12	III, 63	—	42	—	—	—	—
13	I, 21	—	21	—	XXI	—	—
14	I, 56	—	6	5	XXII	—	—
15	II, 52	—	32	28	—	—	p. 214
16	II, 25	—	38	17	III	—	—

FOX	DW	LW	Q	BL	CL	SK	SH
17	—	—	59	4	—	—	—
18	—	—	58	2	—	—	—
19	III, 85	—	—	—	—	—	—
20	I, 2	—	2	24	II	—	p. 3
21	—	—	57	1	—	—	—
22	II, 27	—	50	—	—	—	—
23	III, 76	—	35	—	—	—	p. 131
24	II, 49	—	—	—	—	—	—
25	II, 29	—	29	21	—	—	—
26	III, 81	—	—	—	—	—	—
27	III, 60	—	45	—	—	—	—
28	III, 67	—	—	—	—	—	—
29	I, 4	—	4	19	X	—	—
30	—	IV, 12	—	—	—	—	—
31	I, 7	—	8	—	XIV	—	—
32	I, 1	—	1	13	I	—	—
33	II, 39	—	25	—	—	p. 53	—
34	III, 86	—	28	—	—	—	—
35	—	V,p.109	—	—	—	—	—
36	V,p.109	—	p. 140	p. 74	—	p. 149	—
37	—	IV, 30	—	—	—	p. 213	—

For further reading

A SPIRITUALITY NAMED COMPASSION
Uniting Mystical Awareness with Social Justice
MATTHEW FOX

"Forceful and compelling. . . . A work of marvelous construction."
Spirituality Today

In *A Spirituality Named Compassion*, Matthew Fox establishes a spirituality for the future that promises personal, social, and global healing. Using his own experiences with the pain and lifestyle changes that resulted from an accident, Fox has written an uplifting book on the issues of ecological justice, the suffering of Earth, and the rights of her nonhuman citizens.

Fox defines *compassion* as creativity put to the service of justice and argues that we can achieve compassion for both humanity and the environment as we recognize the interconnectedness of all things. Working toward the creation of a gentler, ecological, and feminist Christianity, Fox marries mysticism and social justice, emphasizing that as we enter a new millennium society needs to realize that spirituality's purpose is to guide us on a path that leads to a genuine love of all our relations and acceptance of our interdependence.

ISBN 0-89281-802-6
$14.95 pb
288 pages, 6 x 9

CRAFTING THE SOUL
Creating Your Life as a Work of Art
RABBI BYRON L. SHERWIN, Ph.D.

Just as a sculptor starts with raw material and crafts it into a singular work of beauty, so are we each responsible for taking our own life and shaping it into something unique, beautiful, and meaningful. *Crafting the Soul* presents all the ingredients necessary to turn your life into a work of art—a process the author calls *soulcrafting*. Infused with deep spirituality, this book is the ideal companion for anyone curious about the meaning of life.

ISBN 0-89281-704-6
$14.95 pb
240 pages, 6 x 9

LESS IS MORE

An Anthology

EDITED BY GOLDIAN VANDENBROECK

This engaging anthology offers words of wisdom from the world's greatest thinkers on the virtues of simplicity. Included are writings from Ovid, Patañjali, St. Matthew, Milarepa, Rumi, Eckhart, Basho, Rousseau, Tagore, Suzuki, Illich, and many others.

ISBN 0-89281-554-X
$14.95 pb
334 pages, 6 x 9

GREEN PSYCHOLOGY

Transforming Our Relationship to the Earth

RALPH METZNER, PH.D.

"At once visionary and down-to-earth, Green Psychology *is an often profound exploration of the deeply disturbed relationship between humanity and nature."* **Publishers Weekly**

*"*Green Psychology *accomplishes things that few environmental books have— it involves the reader on more than the intellectual level; it personalizes the global issues on a deep, inner level; it allows one to embrace the shadow side of our industrialized past; it brings myths to life in a renewed way; and it weaves poetry to stir the heart and imagination. Ralph Metzner brings the light of understanding, training, intuition, experiences, and compassion to his book."*
ForeWord

ISBN 0-89281-798-4
$14.95 pb
192 pages, 6 x 9

THE INVISIBLE PLAYER

Consciousness as the Soul of Economic, Social, and Political Life

MARIO KAMENETZKY

For every individual who has ever dreamed of running a successful business without having to sacrifice personal integrity, this book offers a blueprint for recovering our psychological and political health.

"Profound and important—and a joy to read!" **Hazel Henderson**

ISBN 0-89281-665-1
$16.95 pb
288 pages, 6 x 9

CREATING THE WORK YOU LOVE
Courage, Commitment, and Career

RICK JAROW, Ph.D.

A career counselor presents an alternative approach to finding meaningful work and creating a life filled with purpose.

"This wise and inspiring book can help you create a life that is a work of art."
Yoga Journal

ISBN 0-89281-542-6
$14.95 pb
216 pages, 6 x 9

MEDITATIONS ON THE SOUL
Selected Letters of Marsilio Ficino

Praised by Thomas More in *Care of the Soul* as one of the most profound thinkers in Western cuture, Marsilio Ficino has been a guiding light to spiritual seekers for centuries. Ficino (1433–99) was the leader of the Platonic Academy in Florence, a magnet for the most brilliant scholars of fifteenth-century Europe. This collection of letters between Ficino and some of the most influential figures in European history covers the widest range of topics, mixing philosophy and humor, compassion and advice.

"This book is a profound service both to the student of Renaissance culture and to those interested in spirituality."
Library Journal

"Ficino was at the very fountainhead of some of the most influential aspects of the Italian Renaissance."
Times Literary Supplement

ISBN 0-89281-567-1 • $24.95 hc
ISBN 0-89281-658-9 • $16.95 pb
304 pages, 6 x 9

CHRIST THE YOGI
A Hindu Reflection on the Gospel of John

RAVI RAVINDRA, Ph.D.

"Looking at Christ through Hindu eyes, Ravindra's 'external' view of Christ is in ways more faithful to Christian history than much Western Christology now manages to be. This makes Christ the Yogi *something of a landmark in interfaith dialogue."* **Huston Smith, author of *The World's Religions***

ISBN 0-89281-671-6
$14.95 pb
256 pages, 5³/₈ x 8¹/₂

THE DIVINE LIBRARY
A Comprehensive Reference Guide to the Sacred Texts and Spiritual Literature of the World

RUFUS C. CAMPHAUSEN

From the Angas to the Zend-Avesta, from Apocryphal writings to the Yogini Tantra, and from the Bible to the Zohar, Camphausen traces the divine impulse as it has been expressed through the world's great traditions from earliest times to the present. This book is the first to offer a concise and comprehensive guide to the full spectrum of spiritual literature; 140 sacred texts are described in relation to the cultures from which they emerged and in the context of other sacred works of the same time period. Extensive bibliographical references to available editions, translations, and commentaries are provided.

ISBN 0-89281-351-2
$12.95 pb
224 pages, 6 x 9

THE SPIRITUAL WISDOM OF HAFÉZ
Teachings of the Philosopher of Love

HALEH POURAFZAL and ROGER MONTGOMERY

For six hundred years the Persian poet Haféz has been read, recited, quoted, and loved by millions of people in his homeland and throughout the world. Like his predecessor Rumi, he is a spiritual guide in our search for life's essence. In this beautiful volume his wisdom speaks directly to the cutting edges of philosophy, psychology, social theory, and education, and his message of spiritual transcendence through rapture and service to others is especially important in today's troubled world.

ISBN 0-89281-667-8
$24.00 hc
288 pages, 6 x 9

These and other Inner Traditions titles are available at many fine bookstores, or, to order directly from the publisher, please send check or money order payable to Inner Traditions for the total amount, plus $3.50 shipping for the first book and $1.00 for each additional book to:

Inner Traditions, P.O. Box 388, Rochester, VT 05767
Fax (802) 767-3726 • Or call 1-800-246-8648
Visit our Web site: www.InnerTraditions.com